COMPARATIVE ANALYSIS OF INTERIM MEASURES — INTERIM REMEDIES (ENGLAND & WALES) V PRESERVATION MEASURES (CHINA)

CONTEMPORARY COMMERCIAL LAW

Maritime Law in China
Emerging Issues and Future Developments
Edited by Johanna Hjalmarsson and Jenny Jingbo Zhang

Illegality in Marine Insurance Law
Feng Wang

Insurance Law Implications of Delay in Maritime Transport
Ayşegül Buğra

Online Arbitration
Faye Fangfei Wang

Double Insurance and Contribution
Nisha Mohamed

The Law and Autonomous Vehicles
Matthew Channon, Lucy McCormick and Kyriaki Noussia

FIDIC Yellow Book
A Commentary
Ben Beaumont

The Contract of Carriage
Multimodal Transport and Unimodal Regulation
Paula Bäckdén

FIDIC Red Book
A Commentary
Ben Beaumont

Blockchain Technology and the Law
Opportunities and Risks
Muharem Kianieff

Third Party Protection in Shipping
Carlo Corcione

Multi-sided Music Platforms and the Law
Copyright, Law and Policy in Africa
Chijioke Ifeoma Okorie

Reinsurance and the Law of Aggregation
Event, Occurrence, Catastrophe, Cause
Oliver D. William

Comparative Analysis of Interim Measures
Interim Remedies (England& Wales) v Preservation Measures (China)
Vivek Jain, Thomas Macey-Dare QC and Shengnan Jia

For more information about this series, please visit:

www.routledge.com/Contemporary-Commercial-Law/book-series/CCL

COMPARATIVE ANALYSIS OF INTERIM MEASURES —

INTERIM REMEDIES (ENGLAND & WALES) V PRESERVATION MEASURES (CHINA)

VIVEK JAIN, THOMAS MACEY-DARE QC
AND SHENGNAN JIA

informa law
from Routledge

Cover image: whitemay, Getty Images

First published 2022
by Informa Law from Routledge
4 Park Square, Milton Park, Abingdon, Oxon OX14 4RN

and by Informa Law from Routledge
605 Third Avenue, New York, NY 10158

Informa Law from Routledge is an imprint of the Taylor & Francis Group, an informa business

British Library Cataloguing-in-Publication Data
A catalogue record for this book is available from the British Library

Library of Congress Cataloging-in-Publication Data
A catalog record has been requested for this book

ISBN: 978-0-367-42943-0 (hbk)
ISBN: 978-1-032-25788-4 (pbk)
ISBN: 978-1-003-00031-0 (ebk)

DOI: 10.4324/9781003000310

Typeset in Times New Roman
by Deanta Global Publishing Services, Chennai, India

CONTENTS

FIGURES

TABLES

PREFACE

Interim remedies and provisional measures are a critical component of civil/commercial litigation and arbitration. The objective of this book is to set out not just the law and practice in relation to the primary *interim remedies* and *preservation measures* available in England & Wales and China, but also to provide a comparative analysis between the two jurisdictions concerning these interim measures. Accordingly, the book examines these interim measures in both jurisdictions in great detail not only in the context of *civil litigation* but also *arbitration* in both jurisdictions.

In recent decades China has become the centre of ever greater levels of economic activity, and as a result many international stakeholders are particularly interested in understanding how legal dispute resolution systems operate in China, including the principles and practicalities of obtaining interim preservation measures there. Accordingly, we have chosen to compare the well-established jurisdiction of England & Wales with that of China. The system for interim remedies in England & Wales is well-established, but on the other hand, preservation measures in China are a work in progress due to their recent origins; as a result, there are hardly any books on the topic of preservation measures even within China.

In addition, in-house counsel, cross-border litigators and arbitration lawyers acting on behalf of clients engaged in international trade and investment are regularly required to formulate adequate commercial strategies not just based on the theoretical legal position in a particular jurisdiction or jurisdictions, but also based on the practical realities of engaging in legal dispute resolution processes in those jurisdictions. The feasibility of being able to take effective legal steps is determined by various factors such as the applicable law and practice; costs; the competence and experience of local lawyers; the quality of the administration of justice, including the efficiency of court and arbitration services, and the competence, experience and impartiality of judges; the social, political and cultural assumptions and values which underlie the systems; and various other *invisible factors and contexts*. A comparative analysis, such as the one we attempt here, can provide a measure of guidance to various stakeholders as to what factors they need to consider when contemplating engaging in legal dispute resolution in foreign jurisdictions.

When judges and arbitrators grant or refuse interim measures, they almost invariably do so by exercising their discretionary powers. The nature of this discretion, and how it is exercised, is a key topic for examination in this work. This book, therefore, is an attempt at an academic exploration of *law in action* concerning the granting and refusal of interim remedies/preservation measures in the English and Chinese courts and arbitration. In this book, the analysis is carried out primarily with reference to visible factors such as written laws, decided cases and official guidance and practice directions produced by local courts and other official bodies addressed to practitioners in the respective jurisdictions. In this respect, practitioners in the field of interim remedies/preservations measures in both jurisdictions may find this book useful as a work of reference.

However, long before a cross-border dispute reaches the stage where it is handed over to specialist local practitioners in the particular jurisdiction where the litigation or arbitration will take place, it will often be managed by other stakeholders such as the client's own commercial and risk management personnel, in-house lawyers and legal expense insurance professionals, sometimes with the advice and assistance of external lawyers based in the client's own local jurisdiction. These stakeholders will have a broader commercial framework to consider when devising appropriate strategies to deal with the case. In order to do so effectively, they will need a proper understanding of not only the technical legal position, but also the practical realities of legal dispute resolution, in the jurisdiction where the proceedings will take place. In cross-border litigation and arbitration, the outcome of cases also is often heavily dependent on such factors and contexts and many stakeholders are therefore very keen to recognise them. Legal practitioners are subtly aware of such invisible factors in their own jurisdiction but are inclined to ignore them as they regard them as natural and obvious, woven into the very fabric of the legal culture in which they are accustomed to operate. However, to stakeholders who are unfamiliar with that legal culture, these features may appear surprising and even incomprehensible. It is critical that they are aware of these invisible factors in order to form a realistic assessment of the risks of dispute resolution in a foreign jurisdiction, to devise appropriate legal strategies and to maintain proper control over the case.

Accordingly, this book may be of use to cross-border litigators and international arbitration practitioners, along with the scholars of comparative law, scholars of comparative civil procedure law, administrators pursuing legal reforms, law students and so forth.

Additionally, as previously mentioned, there are hardly any books on preservation measures under Chinese law, let alone ones written from the perspective of comparative law. There is certainly a need for books on these topics, particularly given that, since 2014, deep legal reforms have been underway in China, which have included the adoption of major changes in legal philosophy, and the development of jurisprudence through promulgation of judicial interpretations, all of which have started to impact legal practice. Hopefully, this book can help fill that void as well. This book has also tried to cover the underlying principles and the evolution of interim measures in England & Wales and China to enable to readers to comprehend the relevant law and practice more easily. China has recently adopted the *Chinese Civil Code 2020*, and the authors while writing this book have incorporated all the relevant elements from the new Civil Code 2020. There is no equivalent of *Practice Directions* in China, and this book aims to fill that gap, drawing together the law and guidance which are presently scattered across numerous local courts in the different provinces.

The issues of *interim measures in arbitration* are also fully addressed in both jurisdictions. This topic has been allocated a separate Part II within this book for the readers to appreciate this issue in the arbitration.

The journey crisscrossed in bringing together this book in its current form has been very stimulating. The book started its voyage with respect to part of its contents as an academic thesis in 2017 on the topic of a comparative analysis of the pre-judgment power of courts concerning interim measures in England & Wales and China. The thesis was pursued by one of the authors, who is working in a firm in Singapore as Director, and he is regularly involved in issues of cross-border litigation and arbitration in his daily work. The contents and ideas within that academic thesis have been broadened and extensively upgraded over the last one and half years to blossom into this practitioners' book with massive involvement and contributions from a further two authors. Both these two authors are practitioners in the field of commercial and maritime law; one practicing as a QC in a renowned Barristers' Chambers in London and the other author practicing as a partner in a well-known law firm in Beijing, a professional supervisor at the prestigious CUPL, Beijing, and an adjunct lecturer at other high-profile academic institutions.

The journey traversed in writing this book has been even more interesting for the fact that all three of us are practicing litigation and/or arbitration and are based in three different geographical areas – London, Beijing and Singapore. Collectively, all three of us have current experience of litigation and/or arbitration, where applications for interim measures are a regular feature.

Readers may additionally find it interesting that one of the authors was the trainee (or "pupil") of another author a few decades previously, while another author, while in the middle of writing this book, successfully completed the final stage of her PhD thesis in London in the domain of substantive commercial maritime law. Therefore, the journey with regard to the writing of this book has been extremely exciting, including fascinating group dynamics encompassing all three of us. We are pretty sure readers can relate to it. In the last few months, the voyage also had to weather the COVID-19 disruptions to our schedules.

Even though there is a separate acknowledgement section after the Preface, the book in its current form would not have been possible without the support of our publishers, in particular the patience of Mr. Guy Loft.

The law is as stated as on 31 May 2021.
Dr Capt. Vivek Jain
Thomas Macey-Dare QC
Dr Shengnan Jia
30 September 2021

ACKNOWLEDGEMENTS

Vivek Jain wishes to thank his better-half Lifei Yang for her steadfast support for the last few years from the time of writing of the thesis that has now blossomed into this book. He is also thankful to her for drawing and formatting various figures for the Chinese section of the book. He is indebted to his children, Abhinav and Venya, for displaying patience for the last few years that were devoted to research on interim measures in civil litigation/arbitration. He takes the opportunity to thank his various professors, scholars and Chinese lawyers for various candid philosophical discussions held at the renowned Chinese University of Political Science and Law, Beijing, that provoked his interest in intellectual discourse and also assisted him to complete his PhD thesis on a comparative analysis in the context of law and practice concerning courts' pre-judgement powers in England & Wales and China. In addition, he is grateful to his co-author and previously his pupil master, Mr. Thomas Macey-Dare QC, for agreeing to become a co-author on this project in spite of his busy practice. He is also grateful to his co-author, Dr Shengnan Jia, for her immense contributions to the book against all odds in the last few months. Additionally, he is grateful to both his co-authors for allowing him to become the co-ordinator for this project. He is indebted to numerous judges, barristers, solicitors, advocates and arbitrators from jurisdictions such as the US, England & Wales, Germany, China, Singapore, India, Hong Kong and Australia for various discussions held over the years on various cases concerning interim measures. Last but not least, he is thankful to the P&I Clubs' eco-system in London, where he first got the inspiration for this book, while working on a case, to pursue the comparative analysis of interim measures some years previously. Most importantly, he is indebted to his late father, who always inspired him to appreciate different philosophies from around the globe without prejudging them.

Thomas Macey-Dare wishes to thank his co-authors, Dr Vivek Jain, for his vision in creating this project, for the drive and enthusiasm with which he has brought it to fruition, and for his unique insights into English and Chinese law, drawn from his years of experience of studying and practicing in London, Singapore and Shanghai, which he has poured into this work; and

Dr Shengnan Jia, for her extraordinary feat of scholarship and dedication, in mastering and synthesising such a vast and fast-developing field of Chinese law, while simultaneously completing a PhD in English commercial law; and to both of them for the super-human patience they have shown towards him during the long gestation of this book. He also wishes to thank his wife, Karon, and his children for their patience and support, with special mention to William who provided invaluable assistance as unofficial sub-editor; and his parents, Barry who died recently, and Mitzi who survives him, for their constant love and support.

Shengnan Jia wishes to express deep gratitude to co-authors, Dr Vivek Jain, who proposed this book, and Thomas Macey-Dare QC for his brilliant input into the book. With Vivek's encouragement, it was an honour to work on the relatively uncharted water of preservation measures in China. Shengnan is also indebted to and wishes to specially thank Mrs Rong Pan, Mr Song Zhao and Mrs Yuan Xing, and to colleagues Mr Haiyang Yu (NL, CECCA), Mr Yunlong Teng, Mrs Juan Xu, Ms Shu Wen (Beijing, Tahota), Mrs Lina Wei (Chengdu, Tahota) and Mrs Xiaoping Zhao (Xi'an, Tahota). In particular, Shengnan would like to show sincere gratitude to Professor Jason Chuah at City, University of London, Professor Steven Truaxl at Leiden University, Professor Chris Husbands at LSE and Associate Professor Gang Chen at Wuhan University of Technology for their contribution. There are just too many people, who over the years have provided generous support during her legal career, and she wishes to take this opportunity to thank them. She reserves special thanks for her friend, Mrs Bin Yu, who has supported from the different ways in Beijing for her to focus on the book. Last but not the least, she is grateful to her devoted and beloved parents, Mr. Tingyang Jia and Mrs. Yuying Guo, without which the contribution to the book was impossible.

TABLE OF CHINESE CASES

- Cases by the Supreme People's Court
- Cases by the High People's Courts of Different Provinces
- Cases by the Intermediate People's Courts (including the Maritime Courts, the Intellectual Property Courts and the Financial Court)
- Cases by the Primary People's Courts (including the Internet Courts)

Cases by the SPC

Cases of the High People's Courts from Different Provinces

Cases of the Intermediate People's Courts from Different Provinces

Cases of the Primary Courts from Different Provinces

TABLE OF CHINESE LEGISLATIONS AND LOCAL COURTS' GUIDANCE DOCUMENTS

- Primary Legislations
- Other Legislations (including pre-PRC)
- Regulations and Departmental Orders
- Judicial Interpretations by the SPC
- Judicial Guidance by the SPC
- Regional Interpretations and Guidance (from different provinces from China)
    1. Beijing
    2. Chongqing
    3. Fujian
    4. Guangdong
    5. Hunan
    6. Jiangsu
    7. Sichuan
    8. Shandong
    9. Shanghai
    10. Tianjin
    11. Zhejiang
- Arbitration rules

Chinese Legislations

Other Legislations (including pre-PRC)

Regulations and Departmental Orders

Judicial Guidance by the SPC

Regional Interpretations and Guidance

1. Beijing

2.Chongqing

3. Fujian

4.Guangdong

TABLE OF CASES

European Union

United Kingdom

United States

TABLE OF LEGISLATION

Others

PART 1

INTRODUCTION TO THE CONCEPTS IN THE BOOK AND LEGAL SYSTEM AND PROCEDURAL LAW OF ENGLAND & WALES AND CHINA

CHAPTER 1

Introduction to Interim Measures in England & Wales and China

Introduction to Interim Measures

Role of Interim Measures within a Civil Procedure System

1.1 A legal system comprising of an appropriate framework encompassing civil procedural rules is essential to manage the expectations of stakeholders with commercial interests. This framework is also essential for ensuring that legal disputes are resolved satisfactorily. The satisfactory resolution of the legal disputes in courts in any jurisdiction will ensure that local and international economies are encouraged, while also ensuring enhanced cross border trading. Therefore, a reliable civil procedure system, in theory, supports the disposal of commercial disputes without full civil trials or without final determination by the courts. As a result, an efficient civil procedure system in any jurisdiction will promote the legislators' objective of ensuring that legal cases are disposed effectively in its civil/commercial courts.

Interim Measures in England & Wales

1.2 In most developed jurisdictions such as England & Wales, the role of interim remedies within the framework of civil litigation is vital to fulfil the objective of disposing of legal disputes without resorting to full trials. Needless to say, the availability of interim remedies to litigants in England & Wales has ensured that a substantial number of international commercial disputes are resolved in England & Wales. In many respects, over the decades, the jurisdiction of England & Wales has been a pioneering jurisdiction that has introduced novel solutions, such as practical interim remedies for commercial legal disputes. It would not be erroneous to suggest that the availability of the interim remedies in English courts has ensured that England & Wales remain a popular forum in which to resolve international commercial disputes pursuant to *Civil Procedural Rules 1998* as revised over the years (hereinafter "CPR").[1] This book has considered all the amendments to CPR up to December 2020.

1 See Civil Procedural Rules 1998 (SI 1998/3132); refer also to 1.46.

DOI: 10.4324/9781003000310-2

Interim Measures in China

1.3 Conversely, the concept of provisional remedies is relatively very new in China. This is not surprising, taking into account the fact that the civil procedure system in China has no ancient origins.[2] After the Chinese economic reforms commenced in 1978, the first Civil Procedure Law (for trial implementation) was promulgated in 1982 which included the preservation procedural system to seek provisional measures termed as *preservation measures* in China. Thereafter, the first actual civil procedure law that was applicable throughout China was promulgated only in 1991, namely, the *Civil Procedure Law 1991* (hereinafter referred to as "CPL 1991").[3] CPL 1991 also revised the preservation system for seeking preservation remedies from the Chinese courts.

1.4 However, for stakeholders, the CPL 1991 was still not a comprehensive civil procedures system in respect of the preservation system for obtaining the preservation measures. In 2012, for the first time, the CPL 1991 was extensively revised, and these revisions introduced new preservation measures into Chinese civil procedure law.[4] In the last few years, the revised CPL 1991 was amended marginally but without affecting the preservation system for obtaining preservation measures. These amendments before 2020 will be hereafter referred to as "CPL 1991 (as amended until 2020)". From the outset, it is important to highlight that the references to Chinese law and articles in this book are English translations of relevant laws that were originally drafted in Mandarin.

Different Terminologies Used for Interim Measures

1.5 Interim orders are known by different terminologies in different jurisdictions, for example *interim measures/interim remedies/provisional measures/preservation orders/conservatory measures /interlocutory measures*. In England & Wales, interim measures are popularly known as interim remedies, whilst in China, the interim measures are popularly known as preservation measures.

2 Refer to footnotes 3 and 126 and 1.76–1.105 with regards to the origins and development of civil procedure in China in respect of the provisional remedy in China that is known as preservation measures.

3 Civil Procedure Law, *Order 44* of President of PRC on 9 April 1991. The Civil Procedure Law 1991 was adopted on 9 April 1991 at the Fourth Session of the Seventh National People's Congress of People's Republic of China. It has been revised many times since 1991, and the major revision to the CPL 1991 was carried out on 31 August 2012. This latest revision with amendments introduced many preservation measures to the civil procedure system; refer to 1.85–1.105 for further details on the evolution of the CPL 1991.

4 Decision of the Standing Committee of the National People's Congress on Revising the "Civil Procedure Law of the People's Republic of China", *Order No 59* of the President of the People's Republic of China, promulgated on 31 August 2012, effective from 1 January 2013.

Interim Measures and Cause of Action

1.6 In most jurisdictions, such as England & Wales, these interim measures are not the cause of action in itself,[5] but are rather an interim fix as a procedural remedy to maintain the *status quo* in legal cases until a full civil trial can resolve the issues between the parties. These interim measures also intend to protect the parties from irreparable harms until the all issues including the quantum of damages are resolved between the parties to civil/commercial disputes.

1.7 The Chinese courts will also require a proper cause of action that is prescribed under Chinese law for any application in a civil/commercial dispute. However, pursuant to *Notice of the Supreme People's Court on Issuing the Revised Provisions on Causes of Action in Civil Cases* and the case *Shenzhen Shengkangda Investment Co Ltd and Others v Shenzhen Limingtai Share Investment Fund Co Ltd*, the Chinese courts are obligated to accept applications within their case-filing docket system even if these applications cannot highlight proper causes of action.[6] Although this legal guidance by the Supreme People's Courts ("SPC") and the SPC's case did not mention specifically that it would apply to applications seeking preservation measures, it can still be inferred that a lack of cause of action in such applications will not fundamentally impact on these applications seeking preservation measures.

Delays in Civil/Commercial Litigation and Interim Measures

1.8 In any jurisdiction, the time from the commencement of a civil action until a judgment rendered by a judge will take months and sometimes even more than a year. As a result, in most jurisdictions, the advent of interim measures has gained prominence to maintain the *status quo* between the

5 In England & Wales, interim measures are procedural remedies and are not considered as a cause of action. Lord Dilplock in *Owners of Cargo Lately Laden on Board the Siskina v Distos Compania Naviera SA* [1979] AC 210, 256, had said in the context of interim injunction that "The right to obtain an interlocutory injunction is merely ancillary and incidental to the pre-existing cause of action". The cause of action should be one that is recognised in the jurisdiction where the applicant is seeking the interim remedy. However, it should be noted that in the case of *Merck Sharp Dohme Corp and Bristol-Myers Squibb Pharmaceuticals Limited v Teva Pharma BV* [2013] EWHC 1958, even though there was no breach or infringements of any legal rights of the applicants, there was a fear that wrong would be done to the applicants, and the courts granted the applicants a procedural remedy called *injunction quia timet*.

6 *Notice of the Supreme People's Court on Issuing the Revised Provisions on Causes of Action in Civil Cases* (Fa [2011] No 42), the Chinese courts cannot refuse to accept applications on the ground that there is no proper cause of action that has been highlighted in the application; see also, *Shenzhen Shengkangda Investment Co Ltd and Others v Shenzhen Limingtai Share Investment Fund Co Ltd* (dispute over the infringement) (2018) SPC Civil Final No 281 (Supreme People's Court, second instance and binding judgment) that was an application of the *Notice of the Supreme People's Court on Issuing the Revised Provisions on Causes of Action in Civil Cases* (Fa [2011] No 42).

parties to civil/commercial disputes. In addition, increasingly during civil/commercial litigation,[7] sophisticated parties are employing measures to sabotage opponents' chances of success in civil/commercial litigation. For all purposes, in this book, while discussing interim measures, there is no distinction made between commercial and civil litigation for either jurisdiction. For example, some of the measures employed by the parties could include destroying evidence or even could include browbeating their opponents. At times, these strong-arm tactics exert immense commercial strain on the claimants' businesses and even can affect the relationship of these claimants with their other contractual parties. At times, defendants may also require similar protections through interim measures. Therefore, the importance of the provisional measures is critical for transnational commercial litigations, and needless to say these litigations are notorious for time delays and uncertainties.[8] Additionally, in China, during criminal proceedings, at times there are issues of compensation, and therefore in such incidental civil litigation proceedings and/or proceedings involving administrative cases, preservation measures can be applied by the Chinese courts. However, this sub-topic is not discussed as it is beyond the scope of this book.

---

7 In England & Wales, from the analysis of various case laws, it is suggested that all civil matters, including commercial matters, except criminal matters, could be resolved in civil proceedings. For example see the dicta of Lord Goff in *Re State of Norway's Application (Nos 1 and 2)* [1990] 1 AC 723, 806 (Lord Goff). However in China, for a long time there was a slight difference between civil litigation and commercial litigation. There was the all-encompassing General Principles of Civil Code 1986 along with other material civil statutes such as the Marriage Law enacted in 1980 and revised in 2001, the Succession Law in 1985, the Adoption Law in 1991 (revised in 1998), the Contract Law of 1999, the Property Law of 2007, the Tort Liability Law of 2009 and the Law on the Application of Laws to Civil Relations with Foreign Aspects of 2011. In addition, there is the new General Principles of the Civil Law of the People's Republic of China 2017 that supplements the General Principles of Civil Code 1986. All above-mentioned separate civil statutes and General Principles 2017 have been incorporated into the Civil Code of China 2020 which came into force on 1 January 2021 and by its Article 1260 have been repealed. There are seven parts of the Civil Code 2020 comprising of General Rules, Property Rights, Contracts, Personality Rights, Marriage and Family, Right of Inheritance and Tort Liability with a total of 1260 articles. Even though commercial statutes, such as corporate or insurance law or similar laws are separately enacted within the Chinese legal system, the Civil Code 2020, it seems, in effect combines general rules of civil and commercial laws into a unified code. It follows that in China, principles of civil law are common to commercial law and many principles of commercial law are absorbed by the civil law as well. However, most of the controversial principles of the old civil code applicable to commercial litigation such as that all parties are *equal, the concept of fairness, issues of public order and good morals, honesty and credibility* are in fact still there in the new Civil Code of China 2020 pursuant to its Articles 6–10 and are bound to impact commercial litigation to some extent as well. Any further discussion on this topic is beyond the scope of the book; see also, Xuelu Xu and Peng Liang, 'Research for the Principle of Honesty and Credibility in Commercial Law' (2002) No 3 Law Review (Published by Wuhan University) 3; refer also to Chapter 11, fn 218 for different models of civil and commercial codes and the model that China has adopted.

8 Stephen C McCaffrey and Thomas O Main, *Transnational Litigation in Comparative Perspective: Theory and Application* (1st edn, Oxford University Press 2009) 6.

Issues of Interim Measures in Arbitrations

Interim Remedies/Preservation Measures in Arbitration

1.9 In many instances, even when there is an arbitration agreement in commercial and civil contracts, the national courts can assist the arbitration process by providing interim measures to the parties during the arbitration proceedings. Over the years, it is generally accepted, in these arbitrations, that the tribunals also have power to grant such interim measures.[9] However, the authors have examined that in spite of tribunals having power to grant interim measures in arbitration, in practice, there are many limitations to that power. A few such limitations are observed when seeking without notice interim measures or emergency interim measures. The authors have observed this limitation with almost all institutional arbitrations in all jurisdictions. However, pursuant to the Arbitration Act 1996, even though the English courts will not intervene in arbitrations, the applicants will often request the English courts to exercise their power to grant interim remedies during arbitration or before the commencement of arbitration, in many instances such as:[10]

a) There could be issues of enforceability of interim orders that were granted by the tribunal.
b) Generally, the tribunals do not have power to grant interim remedies that could affect a third party.
c) Urgent relief is required by a party to the arbitration (pre-action or post-action) and the tribunal will not be able to grant such urgent remedies in a short time.

Issues as to the Enforceability of Interim Remedies/ Preservation Measures Granted by Tribunal

1.10 Arbitral awards are easy to enforce in the jurisdictions that are signatory to the United Nations Convention on the Recognition and Enforcement of Foreign Arbitral Awards (New York 1958) ("NY Convention"). The NY Convention has been ratified by around 168 countries, and so enforceability is relatively easy for arbitration awards.[11] Article III of the New York

9 Refer to Part 2, Chapter 4, Chapter 4, 4.14–4.26; refer to Part 2, Chapter 4a, 4.a.32–4.a.35, for China, where it is analysed, from the perspective of the Chinese legal system, the preservation orders issued by the tribunal are ineffective, while the same preservation orders are recognised by certain other jurisdictions that have bilateral arrangements with China.

10 Refer to Part 2, Chapter 4, 4.27–4.35; refer to Part 2, Chapter 4a, 4.a.32–4.a.35, for China, where it was described how, in the Chinese legal system, pursuant to the existing law, the tribunal has no power to grant preservation orders, but some institutional arbitration rules do provide for a system of appointing an emergency arbitrator.

11 Refer to <https://uncitral.un.org/en/texts/arbitration/conventions/foreign_arbitral_awards/status2>, accessed 21 July 2021. The United Nations Commission on International Trade Law ("UNICTRAL") has compiled such data for stakeholders.

Convention, to which the UK and China are parties along with almost every other major trading nation in the world, requires contracting states to recognise arbitral awards made in any other contracting state as binding, and to enforce them in the same way as domestic awards, subject to a limited number of narrow exceptions. In addition, there were attempts by the United Nations Commission on International Trade Law ("UNICTRAL") to harmonise the national laws through the UNICTRAL Model Law on International Commercial Arbitration 1985 and its amendments in 2006 ("UNICTRAL Model Law"). The Convention does not, however, clearly provide for the recognition and enforcement of interim orders/interim measures/provisional measures/provisional relief made by arbitrators which are not strictly speaking final arbitral awards.[12] This means that interim remedies granted by arbitrators will only be enforceable under the New York Convention if they are embodied in an arbitral award.

1.11 The reason for difficulty with interim awards can also be found in Article V (1) (e) of the NY Convention that provides:

> 1. Recognition and enforcement of the award may be refused, at the request of the party against whom it is invoked, only if that party furnishes to the

---

12 Article III of NY Convention provides: "*Each Contracting State shall recognize* arbitral awards [emphasis added] *as binding and enforce them in accordance with the rules of procedure of the territory where the award is relied upon, under the conditions laid down in the following articles*". It is not clear from the wordings of Article III of the NY Convention whether provisional/interim measures/interim orders that are awarded by the Tribunal can be considered as "final award". There exist an issue as to how the arbitral award would be construed when the issue of enforcement and recognition of arbitral award will arise. In practice, such issues will be decided by the local courts according to the jurisprudence of that domestic court or according to the application of any treaty as was highlighted in the UNCITRAL Secretariat Guide on the Convention on the Recognition and Enforcement of Foreign Arbitral Awards (New York, 1958). For further discussion on the meaning of arbitral awards, the authors direct readers to the UNICTRAL Secretariat Guide. It appears that most courts have considered two aspects: "finality as to resolving all or a few issues in dispute and binding on parties" when deciding as to what constitutes the arbitral award for the purposes of Article III of NY Convention. The interlocutory procedural orders have not been considered as "arbitral award". However, there are conflicting decisions as to the interim orders/relief from various national courts. However, a common thread that emerges is that there must be certain end to some or all issues at dispute in the interim order/award from the Tribunal. Any further discussion on this aspect is beyond the scope of the book and readers should refer to UNCITRAL Secretariat Guide on the Convention on the Recognition and Enforcement of Foreign Arbitral Awards (New York, 1958) in particular pages 11–19. Globally, in national laws there are lots of variations, but the UNICTRAL Model Law 1985 and later 2006 did try to bring uniformity so that such issues are not interpreted differently across jurisdictions. For the sake of completeness, the national legislations of countries that have adopted the UNICTRAL Model Law on International Commercial Arbitration 1985 with 2006 amendments, then the issue is relatively more clear-cut due to the application of its Article 17 (G) that provides "*(1) An interim measure issued by an arbitral tribunal shall be recognized as binding and, unless otherwise provided by the arbitral tribunal,* enforced upon [emphasis added] *application to the competent court, irrespective of the country in which it was issued, subject to the provisions of article 17* (I)". The Article 17 (I) provisions mirror the provisions for the enforcement of the final arbitral award and the basis on which the enforcement can be denied by the courts.

> competent authority where the recognition and enforcement is sought, proof that:
>
> (e) The award has not yet become *binding on the parties* [emphasis added], or has been set aside or suspended by a competent authority of the country in which, or under the law of which, that award was made.[13]

However, the interim measures/provisional relief/interim orders that are granted by the tribunals are not final awards on merits concerning substantive issues. Therefore, in many jurisdictions, these interim measures are considered procedural or jurisdictional in nature and are therefore not considered final.[14] As such interim relief is not considered the final award, accordingly in these jurisdictions, these interim relief awards are not considered binding. The additional reasons could be that such interim measures/relief are not considered final and binding due to the fact that these interim measures can also be varied or suspended before the final award, and these interim measures are not considered as materially representing the end of the disputes on merits. Certainly, these legal issues are not harmonised in various jurisdictions and are debatable.[15] Any further discussion on this topic is beyond the scope of this book. In addition, in the case of an arbitration which has its seat in England, an interim remedy embodied in an interim order may be enforceable through the English courts if it is in the form of a peremptory order under section 42 of the Arbitration Act 1996, i.e. an order requiring a party to comply with an earlier order which he has previously disobeyed, and which is necessary for the proper and expeditious conduct of the arbitration.

1.12 The courts in almost all jurisdictions with seat of arbitration have power to grant interim measures in support of arbitration. This aspect of courts assisting the tribunals in ordering interim relief too has been controversial as for some academics and judges it could mean the violation of agreements to arbitrate.[16] In Chapter 4, the authors discuss the powers of

---

13 ibid.

14 ibid.

15 Tijana Kojovic, 'Court Enforcement of Arbitral Decisions on Provisional Relief: How Final Is Provisional' (2001)18 (5), Journal of International Arbitration 511; see also, Ronald A Brand, 'Working Paper No. 2020-32: Provisional Measures in Aid of Arbitration' Social Science Research Network Electronic Paper Collection <https://papers.ssrn.com/sol3/papers.cfm?abstract_id=3708453> accessed 16 June 2021.

16 UNICTRAL Model Law 1985 as amended in 2006, Article 17 J provides, "A court shall have the same power of issuing an interim measure in relation to arbitration proceedings, irrespective of whether their place is in the territory of this State, as it has in relation to proceedings in courts. The court shall exercise such power in accordance with its own procedures in consideration of the specific features of international arbitration". Any academic debate in other jurisdictions that the court's assistance was in fact intervention was rejected categorically by the House of Lords in *Channel Tunnel Group Ltd v Balfour Beatty Construction Ltd and Others [1993]* AC 334. For the sake of completeness, this approach was followed by the English court pursuant to Arbitration Acts that were applicable before the Arbitration Act 1996 came into effect in England & Wales; see also, Ronald A Brand, 'Working Paper No. 2020-32: Provisional Measures in Aid of Arbitration' Social Science Research Network Electronic Paper Collection, at pages 21–22 and fn 64 <https://papers.ssrn.com/sol3/papers.cfm?abstract_id=3708453>

the English Court to grant interim remedies in aid of arbitration proceedings under section 44 of the UK Arbitration Act 1996 and CPR Part 62, and the limits of those powers. On the other hand, in China, the methodology of obtaining preservation measures and the procedure required to obtain them in courts must comply with the CPL 1991 (as amended until 2020) and the Arbitration Law 1995 (as amended until 2020), even if the substantive law is subject to the agreed foreign law in their contract. Furthermore, the Chinese government has made two reservations to the NY Convention 1958 when implementing this Convention in China.[17] Therefore, China will not recognise preservation orders that are rendered by other tribunals in other jurisdictions, and it is impossible to apply the NY Convention 1958 to seek recognition in such scenarios.[18]

1.13 The authors have discussed interim measures in the context of arbitration in both the jurisdictions of England & Wales and the PRC in Part 2 of the book – Chapter 4 and Chapter 4a respectively. In England & Wales, the tribunals have powers to grant interim remedies but there are practical issues when enforcing them.[19] In the context of China in Chapter 4a, it has been discussed that, based on the general rule, the applications for arbitral preservation

---

accessed 16 June 2021, where the author of the working paper provided numerous cases where the courts have provided provisional/interim measures in support of foreign arbitration. Any further discussion on the topic is beyond the scope of the book.

17 The Chinese government made two reservations before the NY Convention came into effect in China. The ratifying countries are allowed to make reservation. One reservation is about the so-called "commercial reservation statement" that "this Convention shall only apply to the disputes arising from contractual and non-contractual commercial legal relationship. 'Contractual and non-contractual commercial legal relationship' specifically refers to the economic rights and obligations resulted from contract, infringement or arising according to law, such as sale of goods, lease of property, project contracting, processing, technology assignment, joint adventure, joint business operation, exploration and development of natural resources, insurance, credit, labor service, surrogate, consultation service, marine/civil aviation/railway/road passenger and cargo transportation, product liability, environment pollution, marine accident, dispute over ownership, etc., and it does not include the dispute between foreign investors and the host government". See *Circular of Supreme People's Court on Implementing Convention on the Recognition and Enforcement of Foreign Arbitral Awards Entered by China* (Fa (Jing) Fa [1987] No 5), Article 2.

18 Refer to Part 2, Chapter 4a, 4.a.8–4.a.13 for examination of this issue in detail.

19 Article 17 of UNICTRAL Model Law on International Commercial Arbitration 1985 specifically provides for the power of the Tribunal to provide such: "Unless otherwise agreed by the parties, the arbitral tribunal may, at the request of a party, order any party to take such interim measure of protection as the arbitral tribunal may consider necessary in respect of the subject-matter of the dispute. The arbitral tribunal may require any party to provide appropriate security in connection with such measure". For the sake of completeness, the Tribunal has inherent power to grant interim measures as per Model Law 1985 /2006, but pursuant to section 39(4) of Arbitration Act 1996 in England & Wales, such power of the Tribunal to grant interim remedies must be provided by the parties to arbitration and until then the Tribunal has no power. See also, Ronald A Brand, 'Working Paper No. 2020-32: Provisional Measures in Aid of Arbitration' Social Science Research Network Electronic Paper Collection, 12 <https://papers.ssrn.com/sol3/papers.cfm?abstract_id=3708453> accessed 16 June 2021; refer to Part 2, Chapter 4, 4.14–4.26, in the context of a similar issue in England & Wales.

measures can only be dealt with by competent Chinese courts. Furthermore, in the absence of relevant law, to obtain preservation orders from the courts concerning arbitration, it is necessary to adopt various procedural tactics. In addition, where an overseas tribunal disposes of a dispute, apart from maritime disputes, applications seeking arbitral preservation measures in other disputes cannot be recognised by the Chinese courts. In light of the complex state of affairs in China concerning these issues, apart from the discussion on the general rule, the authors have also discussed a few recent developments and also discussed specific domains, such as maritime arbitral preservation. Additionally, the authors have discussed the recent developments regarding the new law between mainland China and Hong Kong in the context of arbitral preservation measures and have examined these in detail.[20] Lastly, the authors have also discussed the issue of emergency interim measures that are provided to parties on applications in both jurisdictions in Chapter 4 and Chapter 4a respectively.[21]

Relevant Ecosystem for Interim Measures

Need and Role for Interim Measures in the Current Business Environment

1.14 In a scenario from commercial litigation, it would not be surprising to observe that when defendants are sued, these defendants will try to position themselves in such a way that the recovery of any debt or sum pursuant to future judgments or arbitration awards would become an arduous task for claimants. Accordingly, claimants will find that any future judgments from courts or arbitration awards from the tribunal in their favour cannot be enforced against the defendants' assets. Therefore, these claimants will discover later that these favourable judgments or awards were tantamount to a pyrrhic victory. The claimants while enforcing the favourable judgments or arbitration awards will usually find that the defendants are left with no assets, or they have already reallocated their assets to some another jurisdiction(s).

20 Refer to Part 2, Chapter 4a for further detail on such issues.

21 Emergency interim measure are needed by parties in scenarios where a Tribunal is still not set up or one party does not want to alert another party before taking the interim measures. It is called a "preliminary order" according to the terminology of the UNICTRAL Model Law on International Commercial Arbitration 2006. Pursuant to its Article 17 B (2), it provides, "The arbitral tribunal may grant a preliminary order provided it considers that prior disclosure of the request for the interim measure to the party against whom it is directed risks frustrating the purpose of the measure". However, the preliminary order needs to be converted into a final interim measure within 20 days pursuant to its Article 17 C (4). Refer to Chapter 4, 4.16, 4.26. In China, the Arbitration Law (2017 amendment) does not include any provision for emergency preservation orders; however, many arbitral institutions in China do have provisions for emergency orders. However, in future revision, it is likely such powers would be stated in the revised Arbitration Act as seen from drafts in circulation.

In some cases, the parties to litigations or arbitrations will seek to conceal or destroy evidence, thereby increasing the problems for their opponents.

1.15 The claimants can thwart the defendants' move in commercial disputes by taking *in rem* orders against property or *in personam* orders against the owners of the property.[22] It is the authors' contention that it is important to examine the basic concept of interim measures before discussing the specific interim remedies/preservation measures in both England & Wales and China. The three distinct interim remedies/preservation measures for both jurisdictions are discussed in detail in later Chapters 5–10. In any commercial dispute, any claimant having a claim against a defendant may result in varying scenarios that may necessitate the application seeking interim measures. These scenarios could ensue even before the action is commenced in the court/arbitration tribunal by filing a case or could arise after the action has been commenced in the court/arbitration tribunal by the claimant. A few of the common scenarios that are possible *before the action* is commenced and *after the action* is commenced are as follows:

a) Possibility of eliminating/destroying/suppressing/cover-up/camouf laging evidence/interfering with witnesses to obstruct a future civil trial.
b) Possibility of any party trying to exert commercial pressure or otherwise on another party leading to abuse of process, interference with business, whereby there is a need to take immediate and effective measures to halt such negative behaviour.
c) Possibility of parties trying to dispose of assets/transfer assets to other jurisdictions/getting involved in sham transactions to conceal assets in order to frustrate the final judgment.
d) Possibility of actions of parties as a result of which the legal costs will escalate for the other party.
e) Perishable goods that are the subject matter of the dispute may perish thereby frustrating the enforcement of the final judgment.
f) Possibility of abuse of process whereby there is a need to take immediate and effective measures to prevent such abuse.
g) Possibility of engaging in behaviour to harm the commercial interests of the other party or possibility of continuing to engage in actions that are in dispute.

---

22 In England & Wales nearly all interim remedies operate purely *in personam. This is a feature of their equitable origins, which is also reflected in their discretionary nature.* The exception is that the non-discretionary interim remedy of ship arrest operates *in rem* to constitute the arrested ship as security for the applicant's claim. Refer to Chapter 5, 5.12–5.15. On the other hand, in China, generally speaking, it must be emphasised that only action *in personam* is approved by law in relation to preservation measures. The exception is in the domain of maritime law, where both action *in rem* and action *in personam* are recognised by law.

h) Possibility of engaging in lengthy vexatious litigation in order to exert commercial pressure and increase litigation costs.
i) Possibility of actions such as nuisance by one of the party or other illegal actions to thwart the other parties' motives.
j) Defendants in case of injury or their dependents in case of loss of life requiring urgent payment, until the issue of damages is resolved in a full civil trial.

1.16 In international commercial disputes, the probability of the above discussed scenarios will be greater due to the fact that in such disputes between organisations – (i) a companies are registered in different jurisdictions, (ii) while the companies execute operations in other jurisdictions, (iii) at the same time, companies have assets and bank accounts in many other jurisdictions, (iv) the workforce are located in many jurisdictions and (iv) technological innovations, such as rapid remittances, have created more avenues for such companies to transfer and dispose of assets easily in any jurisdiction. In fact, one of the primary purposes of the interim measures is to thwart the above possibilities as discussed in the preceding paragraph.

Current Business Environment

1.17 The way the trade and commerce operates in a business environment is key to understanding the interim measures, including their principles that will be discussed later in Parts 3, 4 and 5 of the book. Currently, in trade and commerce, a few of the following key features of the current business environment need to be highlighted:

a) Ease with which funds can be transferred from one jurisdiction to another jurisdiction.
b) E-mails with attachments can be distributed within seconds to multiple parties across the globe.
c) Technological disruptive innovations are happening every other day.
d) Beneficial ownership of companies is hidden behind the secrecy of corporate veils, and such companies are intentionally registered in tax havens.
e) All of the above is further fuelled by the rapid growth of capital markets and global travel which has become effortless. The world is more connected than ever due to the advent of better transportation, the internet, IOT, blockchain technology and so forth.

1.18 In order to prudently analyse the issues of the interim measures in the context of the pre-judgment power of judges and arbitrators, the business environment surrounding international trade and commerce cannot be disregarded.[23] These days, commercial fraud is relatively widespread as compared to a few decades earlier.[24] In addition, in the money trail, it is often difficult to find the real beneficial ownership because it is not easy to pierce the corporate veil pursuant to company law.

Additional Reasons for Granting Interim Measures

1.19 In most jurisdictions, the courts are geared up to stop/forestall/stave off/anticipate the above activities of parties to disputes through interim remedies. However, the same courts will not be able to expedite the resolution of substantive disputes between the claimants and defendants. The measures that courts are willing to grant the parties to disputes are therefore called provisional measures or interim measures. These interim measures are suitable for providing temporary relief until the final judgments are rendered by the courts. Needless to say such interim measures are not totally disengaged from the future final judgments, and judges, in practice, do ponder over these issues before granting interim measures.[25]

1.20 Additionally in China, pursuant to the CPL 1991 (as amended until 2020), preservation measures, as an indispensable part of civil procedure, have been considered in light of jurisprudence, legal philosophy, including that governing civil procedural law in the following scenarios:[26]

23 Nicolas Browne-Wilkinson, 'Territorial Jurisdiction and The New Technologies' (1991) 25 (3) Israel L Rev 145, where he highlighted growing internationalisation, in particular the international nature of disputes; see also, Stephen C McCaffrey and Thomas O Main, *Transnational Litigation in Comparative Perspective: Theory and Application* (1st edn, Oxford University Press 2009) 10–11 for further discussion on the article by Sir Nicholas Browne-Wilkinson; see also, the comments of Lord Donaldson of Lymington MR in the case of *Derby & Co v Weldon* (No 2) [1989] 1 All ER 1002, 1007F (CA), where he said:

> "We live in a time of rapidly growing commercial and financial sophistication and it behoves the courts to adapt their practices to meet the current wiles of those defendants who are prepared to devote as much energy to making themselves immune to the courts' orders as to resisting the making of such orders on the merits of their case."

24 ibid.

25 It is the authors' contention that most lawyers while preparing for interim applications do ponder over the merits of the case in great detail to pre-empt any surprise during interim hearings.

26 Article 2 of the CPL 1991 of the People's Republic of China (hereinafter "PRC") provides *inter alia* very similar objectives as the Civil Procedure Law 1998 ("CPR 1998") in England & Wales, but it additionally provides the following objectives in China:

> "[civil procedure law] apply the law correctly, try civil cases promptly; and the law, *maintain the social and economic order*; and
> to guarantee the smooth progress of the *socialist* construction [emphasis added]."

See also, Vivek Jain, *Insight into China through Comparative Analysis of Invisible Factors and Contexts – Common Law v. Chinese Law* (1st Edn, Notion Press 2019) 9.

- To prevent urgent and serious deterioration of the legal relationship between parties in China to bring out justice and fairness.[27]
- To accelerate the delivery of justice in China.[28]
- To save judicial costs and maintain the authority and legitimacy of the civil justice system in the Chinese courts.[29]
- To prevent damage or irreparable injury in China.[30]
- To maintain social and economic order in China.[31]
- To guarantee the smooth progress of socialist construction, and to enhance the judicial reform of Chinese courts.[32]

Utility of Interim Remedies/Preservation Measures

1.21 In England & Wales, these days, interim remedies are also employed as an instrument to encourage settlement by the parties or as a litigation tool to compel an opponent to obtain a favourable settlement. As civil litigation has matured in this jurisdiction over the years, clever lawyers

27 Wenliang Zhang, 'Third Parties in Interim Remedies: From Chinese Civil and Commercial Interim Remedies Perspective' (2016) 38 (1) Modern Law Science 164; see also, Yiqiang Fan, 'Civil Preservation Procedure' (PhD Thesis, Southwest University of Political & Science 2008) 53–54 and 57–58.

28 ibid.

29 Wenliang Zhang, 'Third Parties in Interim Remedies: From Chinese Civil and Commercial Interim Remedies Perspective' (2016) 38 (1) Modern Law Science 164; see also, Yiqiang Fan, 'Civil Preservation Procedure' (PhD Thesis, Southwest University of Political & Science 2008) 57–59.

30 See Articles 100 and 101 of CPL 1991 (as revised in 2012).

31 See Article 2 of CPL 1991 (as amended until 2020); see also, Vivek Jain, *Insight into China through Comparative Analysis of Invisible Factors and Contexts – Common Law v. Chinese Law* (1st Edn, Notion Press 2019) 9.

32 ibid; in 2014, The Decision of the Central Committee of the Communist Party of China on Major Issues Concerning Comprehensive Deepening of Reform promoting the construction of China based on the rule of law and deepening reform of the judicial system was adopted at the 3rd Plenary Session of the 18th National Congress of the Communist Party of China (CPC). Furthermore, this committee at the 4th Plenary Session of the 18th CPC Central Committee defined the construction of a system of the socialist rule of law with Chinese characteristics and accordingly put forward a series of major reforms pertaining to scientific legislation, strict enforcement of law, impartial justice, compliance with law by the whole nation, etc. The Supreme People's Court (SPC) is in charge of all affairs concerning the judicial reforms. Accordingly, every year since then, the SPC has started to utilise the mandate to issue the selection of important projects involving judicial reforms of Chinese courts to guide and instruct further reforms. These projects pertaining to the judicial reforms also involved facilitation of preservation measures within the legal system; see also, Opinion of the Supreme People's Court on Comprehensive Deepening of Reform of People's Courts—The 4th Five-Year Outline of the Program for Reform of People's Courts (2014–2018) (Fa Fa [2015] No 3); Notice of the Judicial Reform Leading Group of the SPC on the Selection of Important Judicial Reform Projects of Chinese Courts (XI) (Fa Gai Zu Fa [2021] No 1); Notice of the Judicial Reform Leading Group of the SPC on the Selection of Important Judicial Reform Projects of Chinese Courts (X) (Fa Gai Zu Fa [2020] No 4); Notice of the Judicial Reform Leading Group of the SPC on the Selection of Important Judicial Reform Projects of Chinese Courts (VI) (Fa Gai Zu Fa [2019] No 2).

usually employ interim remedies as a tool for fulfilling clients' objectives. Therefore, it has become a tactical step employed by lawyers during civil litigation. It is reasonable to say that these interim remedies are an important tool in the hands of lawyers that can be used to offset the slow civil litigation process.[33]

1.22 There seems to be a view in a few common law courts such as the US that the pre-judgment powers of courts to grant such interim relief is very essential for the operations of capital markets, otherwise the risks to investors would increase considerably and accordingly the rate of return that the capital market would seek would be considerable. As a result, a lack of procedural interim remedies can disrupt the growth of capital markets.[34] However, the courts must resist the tendency to grant such interim orders with extraterritorial effects, and the courts accordingly should restrain themselves due to the concept of comity of nations. In one of the US cases, the court clarified that courts must restrain themselves from granting interim remedies if a foreign law and priority creditors such as the issue of tax payment to a foreign sovereign nation are involved.[35]

Doctrines Governing Interim Measures

Fundamental Principles of Interim Measures

1.23 In England & Wales, the onus of seeking interim remedies is on the parties to litigation. In practice, lawyers acting for the parties will apply to the English courts pursuant to CPR. In China, the practice of seeking preservation measures is similar, but the Chinese courts can also remind the litigants about the risk of the litigation so as to make the litigants realise the importance of seeking preservation orders in accordance with the legal guidance document of the SPC.[36]

---

33 See A A S Zuckerman, 'Quality and Economy in Civil Procedure: The Case for Commuting Correct Judgments for Timely Judgments' (1994) 14 (3) OJLS 353.

34 See *Grupo Mexicano de Desarrollo, S A v Alliance Bond Fund Inc*, February 16, 1999 WL 73810 (US).

35 See *Grupo Mexicano de Desarrollo, S A v Alliance Bond Fund Inc*, January 14, 1999 WL 23655 (US).

36 Article 6 of *Some Opinions of the Supreme People's Court on Punishment of Evasion of Enforcement* (Fa [2011] No 195) puts the onus on the Chinese courts to highlight risks of litigation and these courts give further advice to litigants regarding need to obtain preservation measures from the courts:

> "Strengthen *risk prompt* for parties concerned. In the initiation of a case and the hearing process, the courts in all places *shall specify* the litigation and enforcement risks to the parties concerned through clarification of the applicable law to intensify the risk prevention awareness of the parties concerned, *guide creditors* to promptly apply for property preservation and effectively prevent debtors from transferring the property before the enforcement process starts [emphasis added]."

1.24 In practice, the need for the above legal guidance document is due to the fact that the enforcement of court judgments/arbitration awards without preservation measures in place during civil proceedings in China is not very efficient. As a result, it is an arduous task for a great number of winning parties to obtain the corresponding damages and compensation depending on the effective judgments/awards. Therefore, the Opinion of the Supreme People's Court ("SPC"),[37] the highest tier court in China, expects the competent courts to *remind creditors/claimants* to apply for property preservation measures in the course of the litigation proceedings. These preservation applications will effectively prevent debtors from transferring their property any time before the commencement of the process to enforce judgments against them. In legal practice, in so doing, the Chinese courts perform their obligations by issuing a reminder of litigation risk and accordingly elucidate the process of the application for seeking property preservation measures.[38]

1.25 In the authors' view, readers should appreciate that this is unique instance of courts providing guidance to litigants due to the fact that the Chinese courts are themselves under an obligation to recommend preservation measures to the parties as pursuant to the Supreme Court's Opinion.[39] This guidance from the Chinese courts is unprecedented, and one would not expect similar guidance from judges in common law jurisdictions. In common law jurisdictions, judges will be guided by facts and evidence presented by the parties' lawyers or their representatives.[40]

37 It must be emphasised that this *Some Opinions of the Supreme People's Court on Punishment of Evasion of Enforcement* (Fa [2011] No 195) does not belong to the class of judicial interpretation and therefore cannot be regarded as a source of law in China, but is highly persuasive. However, it can be referred to during proceedings by Chinese judges, and for more detailed discussion on the topic, please refer to Chapter 3, 3.18–3.19.

38 Before 2018, the different local courts in China used to take different measures to remind parties in relation to the applications seeking preservation measures because there was no unified law. These local courts used to simply post the notice of such risks on their own official webpage. In some cases, some courts, apart from posting it online, additionally, used to send the hard copy of the notice of risk to the claimants after courts had received the applications in relation to the dispute. However, observing such variations, on 28 May 2018, the SPC issued *Opinions of the Supreme People's Court on the Coordinate Operation of Case Docketing, Trial and Enforcement by People's Courts* (Fa Fa [2018] No 9). Article 1 "Case Docketing" provides that "*when collecting litigation materials, the case docketing department of the court shall issue the reminder of a litigation risk which explain the litigation risks, the necessary process of the application for property preservation, the way of guarantee for the application in order to guide parties to promptly apply for preservation*". In particular, due to the impact of COVID-19, together with the experience of online litigations in the past several years, the SPC further issued *The Rules on Online Litigation Rules of the People's Courts* (Fa Shi [2021] No 12) on 16 June 2021 which came into effect on 1 August 2021. In this latest judicial interpretation, the SPC clarifies that the Principle of Protection of Rights involves strengthening courts' obligation to guide, explain and inform litigants; see Article 2 (3). Accordingly, it is anticipated that Chinese people's courts, regardless of the tier, will now provide guidance to applicants seeking preservation measures.

39 Ibid.

40 Refer to Part 6, Chapter 11, 11.83–11.105, where discussion on comparative legal philosophies as one of the invisible factors and context is carried out to examine the impact on

Judges' Primary Focus before Rendering Interim Remedies/Preservation Remedies

1.26 All interim remedies/preservation measures are granted by judges in both jurisdictions pursuant to the exercise of their discretionary power. In order to understand the interim remedies/preservation measures, it is important to appreciate from the beginning the role of judges. The judges not only need to protect the applicants' interests, but also at the same time they need to shield the defendants from hardships they may face as a result of the interim remedies/preservation measures. A few of the hardships that these defendants may encounter as a result of such orders are an inability to use their company assets or even having to deposit the sum with the courts.[41] The interim orders will likely result in affecting the cash flow of the defendants'/respondents' businesses. This in turn will affect these defendants'/respondents' ability to administer their businesses as a going concern. In practice, however, such interim measures at times could also work as a tool for exerting pressure on the opponents to obtain quick settlement and as a result also bypass delays that are common in any civil procedure system.[42]

1.27 Ideally, the judges in any jurisdiction in the context of interim measures have to maintain a good balance between the interests of applicants and respondents.[43] In addition, the judges will have to take into account the interests of possible third parties that could be stakeholders in the disputes or in the applications seeking interim remedies. As a result, judges will find themselves carrying out a fine balancing act before they can exercise their discretionary power to grant interim remedies/preservation measures. Before the judges decide to grant interim remedies/preservation measures pursuant to the exercise of their discretionary power, they will ponder a few relevant questions that arise in almost every application seeking these interim measures. A few such questions that judges will consider are as follows:

- To ascertain the substance and size of disputes.
- To determine according to the circumstances of the disputes a need for granting interim measures as requested by the applicants.

---

the applications seeking interim remedies/preservation measures. Additionally, Chinese judges have the power to investigate the cases on their own; see also, Vivek Jain, 'Sufficiency of Court's Pre-Judgment Power in Commercial Litigation: A Comparative Study Assessing the Law and Practice in PRC and England & Wales' (PhD Thesis, China University of Political Science and Law 2017).

41 Stephen C McCaffrey and Thomas O Main, *Transnational Litigation in Comparative Perspective: Theory and Application* (1st edn, Oxford University Press); Peter Westberg, 'Interim Measures and Civil Litigation' (2007) 51 Scand Stud L 538.

42 Refer to 1.21 of this chapter.

43 Refer to Chapters 2, 2.38, 2.121; 7, 7.15, 7.25–7.34 for examination of issues from English law. On the other hand, in relation to Chinese law, refer to Chapter 6, 6.109–6.112 (protection of information), 6.130–6.149 (protection of respondent's interests) and 6.150 (protection of non-profit entity) and Chapter 8, 8.127–8.134 (balance of interests and protection of public policy).

- To ensure that any interim orders, if granted, will prevent the abuse of process.
- To some extent assess the merits of disputes by pondering over the possible scenarios in case the dispute were to go through a full civil trial.[44]
- To ensure coercive effects of their interim order are cushioned including any effects on stakeholders that are not party to the applications.
- To ensure that they take into account extra-territorial effects.
- To ensure that any interim measures, if granted, are accordingly specific to the facts of civil/commercial disputes, location of assets, any potential foreign arbitration or litigation also in play and so forth.
- To assess the effect of the interim orders on third parties.
- Any other similar questions.

1.28 The need to balance the interests of parties to applications before the granting of interim measures is common to both jurisdictions of England & Wales and China. Ideally a subtle equilibrium will be required between jurisdictions that are applicants-/claimants-friendly in the sense that interim remedies are readily granted and jurisdictions that are respondents-/defendants-friendly in that it is relatively difficult to obtain interim remedies/preservation measures. The jurisdiction of England & Wales falls into the first category of applicants-/claimants-friendly jurisdictions while China falls into the second category as a respondents-/defendants-friendly jurisdiction.[45] In the authors' view, either extreme in the context of obtaining interim remedies/preservation measures is not ideal for enhancing trade and commerce and resolving civil/commercial disputes. For the sake of completeness, in any jurisdiction, if the interim remedies/preservation measures granted by judges are nearly equal to the remedies that the applicants could have obtained after full civil trials, then it could be argued that the court is depriving the defendants of their right to ordinary civil trials.[46] Therefore the English judges for

44 In the English courts, this consideration is most important in ordinary interim injunctions 7, 7.13–7.14, 7.31–7.33, 7.51, 7.61. On the other hand, for discussion on similar issues in the Chinese preservation system, refer to Chapter 10, 10.35–10.36. In recent years, the SPC have appreciated that the courts ideally must consider preliminary evidence rather than the full merits of the case, see 10.26–10.34; see also, Part 6, Chapter 11, 11.97–11.107, wherein it is discussed that in China, the judges demand a very high standard of proof from applicants.

45 Refer to Part 6, Chapter 11, 11.4; see also, Vivek Jain, 'Sufficiency of Court's Pre-Judgment Power in Commercial Litigation: A Comparative Study Assessing the Law and Practice in PRC and England & Wales' (PhD Thesis, China University of Political Science and Law 2017) for one of the conclusions reached in the thesis.

46 See Article 6 of the European Convention of Human Rights 1950, effective from 1953, for application on such issues in jurisdiction of England & Wales through the Human Rights Act 1998. However, how the law will evolve in this respect after Brexit is yet to be seen. Any further discussion on this topic is beyond the scope of this book.

many decades had to take into account such legal issues before granting interim remedies to applicants.

1.29 In common law, judges have devised various tests that every party to the application has to consider before the interim remedy can be granted. These tests are customarily devised by judges by taking into account the various factors as discussed in 1.26–1.28 of this chapter. The individual tests that are specific to distinct interim remedies/preservation measures will be discussed later in Chapters 5–10. It is the authors' contention that judges, if they were to grant the interim measures, are expected to be astute in considering commerce and trade practices, in evaluating the business risks and in evaluating the circumstances surrounding the disputes and lastly should also be able to evaluate the potential effects of the interim orders, if granted, on the third parties. In practice, in many jurisdictions, it has been observed by the authors that many judges are not adequately prepared or trained for such tasks.[47]

Interim Measures in England & Wales

Introduction to Interim Remedies in England & Wales

1.30 The history of interim remedies goes back many centuries in England & Wales. The authors have systematically analysed the historical origins of interim remedies along with the current development, in particular from 1970 onwards, in England & Wales. Since the authors have discussed interim remedies from jurisdictions as diverse as England & Wales and China, it was considered necessary by them to discuss the historical origins of the interim remedies including injunctions to fully appreciate the issues pertaining to interim remedies.

Interim Remedies in England & Wales

Equity, Equitable Remedies and Injunction

1.31 Historically, the courts of equity gained considerable power because the Court of Chancery had begun to grant equitable remedies including preventative injunctive relief in order to do justice, wherever the common law

---

47 Refer to Part 6, Chapter 11, 11.52–11.114, where the impact of invisible factors and contexts is analysed on the granting of interim measures, for example, in China where many judges are happy to remain in an administrative role due to many existing factors; see also, Vivek Jain, *Insight into China through Comparative Analysis of Invisible Factors and Contexts – Common Law v. Chinese Law* (1st Edn, Notion Press 2019) for analysis of invisible factors and contexts in common law and Chinese law and its comparative study for examination in detail of judges' power including discretionary power and their willingness to exercise that power.

courts were unable to assist the parties.[48] Historically, if there was a disagreement between the common law courts and the courts of equity, the courts of equity were supposed to prevail over the common law courts.[49] Historically, in the context of injunctions, the intent of the law was considered as more important as compared to the formal procedures and equity would accordingly always follow the law. Historically, law of equity could not be seen to be depriving stakeholders of their rights in law.[50]

History of Injunctions

1.32 From the beginning, it is the authors' contention that to understand the development of injunctions in the modern era, an appreciation of the history of the evolution of injunctions is essential. In addition, the role of other Commonwealth jurisdictions, in particular the influence of the US jurisdiction on the development of law of equity and injunctions, should be understood clearly.[51] An understanding of the evolution of injunctions is particularly relevant to readers from non-common law jurisdictions. In the previous paragraph, it was discussed that the injunction is an equitable remedy, but the injunction itself has a long history. As far back as Roman times, there were *Praetor's interdicts* that were similar to prohibitory injunctions, and

48 See Samuel L Bray, 'The System of Equitable Remedies' (2016) 63 (3) UCLA L Rev 530, 535–537; see also, Kevin C Kennedy, 'Equitable Remedies and Principled Discretion: The Michigan Experience' (1997) 74 (4) U Det Mercy L Rev 609, 610–612; see also, W S Holdsworth, 'The Early History of Equity' (1915) 13 (4) Mich L Rev 293, in order to understand the history of law of equity in various stages from the 12th century to the 19th century and of that of the Chancery Court; see also, Andrew Burrow, 'We Do This at Common Law but That in Equity' 22 (1) (2002) OJLS 1, where the debate between common law and equity was discussed including needless difference in terminologies; see also, David W Raack, 'A History of Injunctions in England Before 1700' (1986) 61 (4) Ind L J 539 <www.repository.law.indiana.edu/ilj/vol61/iss4/1> accessed on 16 September 2016, where injunction was described as an equitable remedy; see also, Howard L Oleck, 'Historical Nature of Equity Jurisprudence' (1951) 20 (1) Fordham L Rev 23, 24 <http://ir.lawnet.fordham.edu/flr/vol20/iss1/2> accessed on 15 October 2019, where it was discussed that the original purpose of equity was to remedy the rigidity of the common law.

49 See W S Holdsworth, 'The Early History of Equity' (1915) 13 (4) Mich L Rev 293, 297, where he described that conflict between common law and equity and later how it was resolved in favour of the Chancery Court by James I; see Howard L Oleck, 'Historical Nature of Equity Jurisprudence' (1951) 20 (1) Fordham L Rev 23, 32 <http://ir.lawnet.fordham.edu/flr/vol20/iss1/2> accessed on 15 October 2019, where he discussed that the law of equity in Roman law was developed within the other areas of law, while a millennium later in English law, a body of law of equity developed separately from the development in the common law, which led to considerable resistance from then-existing stakeholders.

50 See Samuel L Bray, 'The System of Equitable Remedies' (2016) 63 (3) UCLA L Rev 530, 545; see also, Kevin C Kennedy, 'Equitable Remedies and Principled Discretion: The Michigan Experience' (1997) 74 (4) U Det Mercy L Rev 609, 622.

51 See Howard L Oleck, 'Historical Nature of Equity Jurisprudence' (1951) 20 (1) Fordham L Rev 23, 25 <http://ir.lawnet.fordham.edu/flr/vol20/iss1/2> accessed on 15 October 2019, where the influence of the English Chancery Court on the US Courts of Chancery and other Commonwealth jurisdictions is discussed.

were used in relation to the possession of property.[52] In the 13th century, there were *King's writs*, which were similar to orders and mandates and were based on a need to provide justice to the stakeholders. Therefore, these could be considered as the first nearest relative to modern-day injunctions in England & Wales.[53]

1.33 Such equitable remedies were not limited to the Chancery Court,[54] but were also granted by much older common law courts through the *writ of prohibition* to prevent a particular court from handling a particular dispute, or by providing very similar remedies, such as an injunction directed at defendants, or a *writ of estrepment* to prevent the waste of the property after the judgment but before execution of the judgment.[55] The courts of equity were also developing very similar remedies, and were also applying equitable writs, which in fact led to the decline of the common law writs around the late 14th century. Thereafter, from 1400 ACE, injunctions were becoming

52 See David W Raack, 'A History of Injunctions in England before 1700' (1986) 61 (4) Ind L J 539, 540–541 <www.repository.law.indiana.edu/ilj/vol61/iss4/1> accessed on 16 September 2016, where Raack suggested in his paper that there were distinct similarities between the Praetor's interdicts and modern-day injunctions. It was also argued in his paper that it was likely these interdicts had influenced the development of injunctions at the Chancery Court; see also, Howard L Oleck, 'Historical Nature of Equity Jurisprudence' (1951) 20 (1) Fordham L Rev 23, 31 <http://ir.lawnet.fordham.edu/flr/vol20/iss1/2> accessed on 15 October 2019, where Oleck discussed that the magistrates in Roman times carried the title of Praetor and their extraordinary jurisdiction was similar to modern-day equity jurisdiction and the procedures in their courts had the hallmarks of quite wide discretion that was inherent in nature.

53 See David W Raack, 'A History of Injunctions in England before 1700' (1986) 61 (4) Ind L J 539, 541–543 <www.repository.law.indiana.edu/ilj/vol61/iss4/1> accessed on 16 September 2016. In such writs, the litigants would plead with the King to provide relief after having exhausted all other avenues of justice; see also, M M Bigelow, *History of Procedure in England* (Reprint of Macmillan 1880, AMS Press 1983) 192, who was quoted by Raack, in the context of the Kings' writs, which were described as "the forerunners of modern writ of injunction".

54 ibid 550. The Chancery Court came into existence between 1380 and 1400 ACE. The Chancery existed before but not as an institution that could dispose of legal disputes.

55 See David W Raack, 'A History of Injunctions in England before 1700' (1986) 61 (4) Ind L J 539, 545–549 <www.repository.law.indiana.edu/ilj/vol61/iss4/1> accessed on 16 September 2016. Common law courts were an extension of the King's court, so they were well versed in providing writs that had similarities with the current-era writs emanating from the law of equity; see also, Bracton Hde, 'Bracton's Note Book' in Frederic William Maitland (ed), *Bracton's Note Book: A Collection of Cases Decided in the King's Courts during the Reign of Henry III*, vol 2 (Cambridge University Press 2010) and a few cases from the Note Book were discussed by David W Raack, 'A History of Injunctions in England before 1700' (1986) 61 (4) Ind L J 539, 540–541 <www.repository.law.indiana.edu/ilj/vol61/iss4/1> accessed on 16 September 2016 to highlight the similarities of writs with modern-day injunctions; see also, George Burton Adams, 'The Origin of English Equity' (1916) 16 (2) Colum L Rev 87, 91; see also, Howard L Oleck, 'Historical Nature of Equity Jurisprudence' (1951) 20 (1) Fordham L Rev 23, 35 <http://ir.lawnet.fordham.edu/flr/vol20/iss1/2> accessed on 15 October 2019, where he discussed the role of the Chancellor as a secretary of the King in the 11th century, and as a result the Chancellor was the source of most writs. In turn, these writs actually became the source for various rules of equity and also evince the fact that courts of equity had branched off from the common law courts and the remedies that they used to grant to stakeholders.

common in the courts of equity as the common law courts could not provide these injunctions.[56]

1.34 Injunctions were developed in the local courts, Court of Exchequer and Court of Requests (though abolished in 1641), and all these courts had equitable powers.[57] Injunctions in the 17th century were gradually developed in areas of property law, tort law such as tort of nuisance, and so forth. The Chancery Court kept the procedures informal and simple as compared to the procedures in the common law courts.[58] However, this development of informality led to hostility between the Chancery Court and the common law courts, in particular during instances when the Chancery Court had initiated a process whereby they granted injunctions against the judgments of the common law courts by applying principles of justice.[59]

---

56 Howard L Oleck, 'Historical Nature of Equity Jurisprudence' (1951) 20 (1) Fordham L Rev 23, 40 <http://ir.lawnet.fordham.edu/flr/vol20/iss1/2> accessed on 15 October 2019, where in his paper, he discussed the basic procedures of equity inside the Chancery Court that comprise a petition and a bill containing the cause, and thereafter the Chancellor would issue a "subpoena" to defendants to enter their plea. The process was kept very simple; see also, David W Raack, 'A History of Injunctions in England before 1700' (1986) 61 (4) Ind L J 539, 555–556 <www.repository.law.indiana.edu/ilj/vol61/iss4/1> accessed on 16 September 2016, where Raack discusses a few cases in which the common law remedies were not possible or where no adequate remedies were available at the common law courts. The claimants had to seek the remedy of injunctions from the Chancery Court; see also, F J Stimson, 'The Modern Use of Injunctions' (1895) 10 (2) Political Science Quarterly 189, 196 <www.jstor.org/stable/2139728> accessed on 2 October 2019, where Stimson analysed the discussion on the "preventative or protective jurisdiction" of the equity jurisprudence in the Chancery Court.

57 David W Raack, 'A History of Injunctions in England before 1700' (1986) 61 (4) Ind L J 539, 561 <www.repository.law.indiana.edu/ilj/vol61/iss4/1> accessed on 16 September 2016.

58 ibid, 563–564, where Raack analysed that the Chancellor denied the common law lawyers' attempt to introduce technical pleadings in the Chancery Court and retained simple procedures inside the Chancery Court. This also led to the growth of the Chancery Court along with cases involving injunctions; see also, F J Stimson, 'The Modern Use of Injunctions' (1895) 10 (2) Political Science Quarterly 189, 197 <www.jstor.org/stable/2139728> accessed on 2 October 2019, where the author discussed how the equity procedures in the court were kept very simple; see also, Stephen N Subrin, 'How Equity Conquered Common Law: The Federal Rules of Civil Procedure in Historical Perspective' (1987) 135 (4) U Pa L Rev 909, 914–918, where Subrin compared the technical use of single issue pleading with flexible bills pursuant to law of equity in the Chancery Court.

59 David W Raack, 'A History of Injunctions in England before 1700' (1986) 61 (4) Ind L J 539, 564–565, 568–569, 571, 573–574, 577–578, 582–586 <www.repository.law.indiana.edu/ilj/vol61/iss4/1> accessed on 16 September 2016. The grant of many kinds of injunctions such as temporary or interlocutory injunctions that were available in following instances – for a quite possession pending trial, to stop repeat of litigation for same issue, for restraining proceedings or judgments at law that could include counsels in a case in the common law courts. Reciprocity was not granted to other courts and as a result they in turn could not grant injunctions to restrain the proceedings in the Chancery Court. However, there were instances of this, for example Chancellor Cardinal Wolsey in 1529 was removed due to his frequent use of injunctions against the common law judgments. Gradually, a time came when a lawyer from the common law court took over the Chancellorship of Chancery Court, that is, Thomas More in the year 1529, and the numbers of such injunctions were accordingly reduced. The complaints against the Chancery Court also reduced once the procedures of the Chancery Court were compiled by Chancellor Nicholas Bacon. Edward Coke, Chief Justice in 1613–1616, argued that the Chancellor's power was not above the law and even King James I's power was subject to legal limits. Therefore, the

1.35 As a result, gradually, the discretionary power of the Chancery Court was moderated, and rules were developed in the matters of injunctions, especially the principles of equity between 1619 and 1620 ACE.[60] Lord Nottingham in 1673 ACE produced the *first unpublished manual on injunctive rules and procedures*.[61] The rules of full and frank disclosure in injunctions were gradually developed during this time along with the orders to seek information from the defendants.[62] This unpublished manual led the Chancery Court to have a good relationship with the common law courts and that led to a systematic development of law in the area of injunctive reliefs.

Injunctions as an Equitable Remedy

1.36 In the preceding paragraphs, the authors have discussed the evolution of law of equity. The equitable remedies pursuant to law of equity historically can be coercive or restitutionary, and injunctions are types of coercive

---

issue of independence of the judiciary was also in play beneath the surface. Conflict between the Chancery Court and common law courts was gradually picking up pace with the fact that the common law courts had also commenced granting similar remedies against orders of the Chancery Court. Clearly, the wind had started to blow in the direction of the Chancery Court no longer being able to grant injunctions against the judgments of the common law courts. Raack further discussed the case of *Heath v Rydley* 79 Eng. Rep at 286, where Chief Justice Coke clearly in the judgment argued for disregarding injunctions from the Chancery Court, when given against the execution of the judgements from the common law courts. However, the common law courts were also not willing to correct the judgments when pronounced in error or the conduct of one of the parties to the litigation was unconscionable. King James I appointed a Commission in 1616. This Commission agreed with the Chancery Court's view that in case of conflict between the common law courts and the Chancery Court, the Chancery Court will prevail over common law courts. In this way, it also ensured that the system maintained the supremacy of King above the law. However, Chancery Court started to develop rules in the 17th century to dilute the criticisms, and injunctions against the common law court judgments were accordingly moderated; see also, Howard L Oleck, 'Historical Nature of Equity Jurisprudence' (1951) 20 (1) Fordham L Rev 23, 39, about the history of rivalry between the common law jurist Coke and Francis Bacon, a Chancellor, and the general acceptance that law of equity existed as a separate body of law during that time of rivalry.

60 Howard L Oleck, 'Historical Nature of Equity Jurisprudence' (1951) 20 (1) Fordham L Rev 23, 40 <http://ir.lawnet.fordham.edu/flr/vol20/iss1/2> accessed on 15 October 2019, where he discussed the development of equity procedures and the contribution of various chancellors, who had taken the initiatives over the years to develop a body of equity procedures; see also, David W Raack, 'A History of Injunctions in England before 1700' (1986) 61 (4) Ind L J 539, 587–588, where he discussed Chancellor Francis Bacon and his initiatives in issuing 100 procedural orders between 1619 and 1620. As a result his contribution was crucial in diluting the acrimony between the Chancery Court and the common law courts. Injunctions were dealt with in Orders 20 to 28. This reduced the arguments on issues concerning the abuse by the Chancery Court. A discussion of all of Bacon's procedural orders on injunctions is beyond the scope of the book. In summary, these orders ensured that it would not be a cake walk for the applicants to just easily obtain injunctions and courts would be judicious and vigilant when granting them to applicants. It also evinces the fact that the development of principles of equity started in the Chancery Court.

61 David W Raack, 'A History of Injunctions in England before 1700' (1986) 61 (4) Ind L J 539, 589.

62 ibid 590.

equitable remedies that are available in common law courts.[63] In an old case in the US, which is a common law jurisdiction like England & Wales, injunctions were described as "the strong arm of equity".[64] Injunctions can be *prohibitory* injunctions or *mandatory* injunctions and both are types of equitable remedies that are available in the courts. These injunctions, a form of interim remedy, are usually granted before judgments are rendered on the cases after full civil trials. Injunctions given after the decisions that are in favour of the claimants in the common law court of the US are called *permanent injunctions.*[65] This area of law saw an incremental development in other common law jurisdictions, most notably in the US. Such equitable remedies were relatively "qualitative and adverbial" and were difficult to enforce.[66]

1.37 Additionally, these equitable remedies were managed by the courts using "equitable managerial devices" such as:[67]

- Injunctions could be revised by the courts based upon changed circumstances both in law and in facts.
- Injunctions could be enforced by the courts using contempt proceedings after which judges could order discretionary punishments possibly through new injunctions, monetary award to the claimants or fines or even imprisonment. The courts definitely used the threat of these punishments.
- The courts appointed officials could be appointed in respect of many of the equitable remedies that were granted.

1.38 Another hallmark of equitable remedies, and in particular, injunctions is that the courts have shown over the years a "degree of flexibility",[68]

63 See Kevin C Kennedy, 'Equitable Remedies and Principled Discretion: The Michigan Experience' (1997) 74 (4) U Det Mercy L Rev 609, 627. Injunctions can be prohibitory or mandatory.

64 ibid 647 where the author cited *Bonaparte v Camden*, 3 F Cas 821, 827 (C C D N J 1830) (No 1617) (the US case) and it is from this case the quote was taken. It was further stated that injunctions are an extraordinary remedy as they have the potential to cause damage to the defendant.

65 Samuel L Bray, 'The System of Equitable Remedies' (2016) 63 (3) UCLA L Rev 530, 553; it must be emphasised that these days, permanent injunctions are also called *final* or perpetual injunctions in England & Wales, and are given after the full civil trial on merits.

66 ibid 564. Bray discussed that some orders were drafted using words like "promptly" as an example creating difficulties in relation to compliance by the defendants.

67 ibid. Bray discussed various means by which judges can control equitable remedies such as injunctions. These means he has classed as "equitable managerial devices" such as *ex post* revision, contempt, equitable help, onus on the decisionmakers to draft the remedy precisely and so forth. A good example of equitable help that can be seen in modern-day injunctions is the appointment of supervising solicitors in the case of search orders, as discussed in Part 5, Chapter 9.

68 ibid 570. Bray discussed that judges will evaluate various potential scenarios before granting the injunctions as an equitable remedy. The final order from judges will ensure a fine balance is maintained and harmless activities of the defendant are not affected.

when granting them by customising them for the particular circumstances of disputes and parties. Judges also take into account the business environment within which those disputes have arisen. It is important to appreciate there are costs associated with compliance with injunctions. These injunctions are capable of affecting the harmless activities of defendants, and therefore these costs of compliance could include direct costs of compliance as well indirect costs of compliance.[69] The costs associated with obtaining interim remedies could be initial court-related costs, costs of managers appointed by the courts and costs of any modifications required due to the changed circumstances in the matters related to the injunctions, and there could even be costs associated with the contempt proceedings.

1.39 It has always been a requirement that injunctive orders are *precisely worded* to avoid the defendants being in contempt of court inadvertently or by mistake without another legal remedy readily available.[70] The courts before granting equitable interim remedies usually follow equitable principles among many others, and these principles in a way could be deemed as constraints on courts' discretionary power and its application to the equitable remedy of injunctions:[71]

- Applications for claims are not delayed (laches).
- Applicants have to come with clean.
- Any interim order will not result in undue hardship to the defendants.
- An interim order of injunction is not granted with too little information.
- Any future facts have to be given consideration by judges as there may be a need to modify or amend the injunctions.
- Any relief granted by the courts is *extraordinary and not ordinary*.[72]

1.40 The issue can also be looked at from the point of view that the pre-judgment power of courts in relation to interim remedies is largely based on doctrines borrowed from law of equity. It is important to appreciate that judges' exercise of discretionary power is further reduced in relation to their granting injunction orders as these orders are required to be *precise*.[73] It is

69 Samuel L Bray, 'The System of Equitable Remedies' (2016) 63 (3) UCLA L Rev 530, 573. Bray discussed this in respect of the direct and indirect costs of compliance associated with the equitable remedy. He highlighted that any order will need a readjustment in relation to defendants' behaviour so that defendants' harmless activities are not affected by such orders or any party not represented in the court is affected due to the orders.

70 ibid 580.

71 ibid 581.

72 See, Kevin C Kennedy, 'Equitable Remedies and Principled Discretion: The Michigan Experience' (1997) 74 (4) U Det Mercy L Rev 609, 613.

73 See Samuel L Bray, 'The System of Equitable Remedies' (2016) 63 (3) UCLA L Rev 530, 579 and 586.

important to note that even in equitable remedies the discretion is not unlimited.[74] However, the discretion available to judges has been criticised as far back as the eighteenth and the nineteenth centuries.[75]

1.41 The exercise of discretionary power by judges in relation to discretionary equitable remedies requires considerable discretion, but not just the personal discretion of judges.[76] However, such remedies these days are governed by statutes, such as the CPR 1998 in England & Wales and some scholars term it *principled discretion*.[77]

---

74 Kevin C Kennedy, 'Equitable Remedies and Principled Discretion: The Michigan Experience' (1997) 74 (4) U Det Mercy L Rev 609, 609–610. In this paper, the author has discussed equity jurisprudence in detail. In equity jurisprudence, the power of judges; in particular, their exercise of discretionary power is not limitless. Accordingly, judges exercise their discretionary power bearing in mind the circumstances and facts of cases. However, the author of the paper emphasised that this exercise of discretion by judges cannot be used to dispense subjective justice. The author highlighted that judges still need to consider the practices and precedents from previous cases in the Chancery Court or other American courts sitting in equity. From pages 613–615, Kennedy highlighted that equitable remedy was never a "matter of right" but depended on judges sitting in these courts exercising their judicial discretion. This limit on discretion ensures that judges are prevented from creating legislations. Judges also need to consider various equitable maxims, and discussion of all maxims is beyond the scope of this book; see also, Howard L Oleck, 'Historical Nature of Equity Jurisprudence' (1951) 20 (1) Fordham L Rev 23, 25 <http://ir.lawnet.fordham.edu/flr/vol20/iss1/2> accessed on 15 October 2019, where he discussed that the impression of law of equity could be dangerous and discretion to many may appear as limitless, but the rules of equity have developed to keep this impression of unlimited discretion in check. However the author emphasised that the core of nature of equity will not change, even though the concept of "rights and justice" or "conscience" or "bona fide" or "good morals" and so on appear to be vague.

75 See W S Holdsworth, 'The Early History of Equity' (1915) 13 (4) Mich L Rev 293, 295; see also, Kevin C Kennedy, 'Equitable Remedies and Principled Discretion: The Michigan Experience' (1997) 74 (4) U Det Mercy L Rev 609, 613, where Kennedy highlighted the criticisms made against equity courts for excessive flexibility shown by them during the days of the development of law of equity; see also, Doug Rendleman, 'The Triumph of Equity Revisited: The Stages of Equitable Discretion' Nevada L Journal 2015 15 (3) 1397, 1400, where he discussed John Seldon's critical comments in the late 17th century that changes in law of equity seemed to change with the size of the Chancellor's foot; in fact, he was alluding to the fact that the conscience of the Chancellor can vary and this brings with it great uncertainty. He further quoted Lord Camden's critical comments from the late 18th century that the personal discretion of the equity courts' judges was leading to corruption and arbitrariness in the whole system; see also, Peter Birks, 'Rights, Wrongs, and Remedies' (2000) 20 (1) OJLS 1, 16–17, where he also criticised the discretion in granting remedies.

76 See Kevin C Kennedy, 'Equitable Remedies and Principled Discretion: The Michigan Experience' (1997) 74 (4) U Det Mercy L Rev 609, 614. The author of the paper clearly highlighted the difference between judges' unlimited "personal discretion" and "principled discretion" whereby precedents are consulted and checked if any statute has provided a possibility of granting equitable relief. Accordingly, in the authors' view, CPR is a good example that currently guides the judges in England & Wales to exercise their "judicial discretion", whereby the precedents and statutes can be consulted by the judges according to the circumstances of the cases.

77 See Doug Rendleman, 'The Triumph of Equity Revisited: The Stages of Equitable Discretion' Nevada L Journal 2015 15 (3) 1397, 1450, where he cited the examples of statutes limiting the judges' equitable discretion; see also, Kevin C Kennedy, 'Equitable Remedies and Principled Discretion: The Michigan Experience' (1997) 74 (4) U Det Mercy L Rev 609, 614 for examination of similar issues.

1.42 Historically, the judges had to keep the principles of equity in mind while relying on the statutes to guide them before granting interim remedies in their courtrooms. The principles of equity will be relevant also in pondering over any constraints before such a remedy can be granted by them and to determine the management process after the remedies are granted to the applicants. The authors will discuss the detailed CPR rules later,[78] which have ensured that the judges' exercise of discretion in granting this remedy is within the legal framework, and these rules will enhance judicial legitimacy by improving the public perception.

1.43 Another way to look at this discretion of judges in such cases is through this quote: "equitable discretion is in fact equitable restraint".[79] Legal scholars have warned that injunctions as an equitable remedy developed during times when the democratic roots of the legal system were still evolving, and a stronger authority was needed.[80] This means that judges are currently operating in a time when their exercise of discretionary power to grant such equitable remedies needs predictability, and this expectation from the stakeholders is only going to increase further in the coming years. The authors will not discuss the evolution of judges' discretion in granting injunctions or the issue of public interest here as it's a big topic in itself.[81] Such issues will be discussed appropriately in Chapters 5, 7 and 9 respectively.

General Evolution of Interim Remedies in the Modern Era

1.44 Up to the latter part of the 19th century, interim remedies in England and Wales were developed by judges on a case-by-case basis, in the incremental manner which characterises common law systems. During this period, the rules of law and equity were administered by separate courts, each with its own practices and procedures. Many of the interim remedies which are currently available in the English courts, including all forms of interim injunction, were developed by the courts of Chancery as part of their general discretionary powers.[82] They have since been codified and confirmed by statute. Thus, the courts' power to grant all kinds of injunctions is currently embodied in section 37(1) of the Senior Courts Act 1981. A key feature

78 Refer to Chapters 5, 7 and 9 where the interim remedies of freezing injunctions, interim injunctions and search orders are discussed in detail.

79 See Kevin C Kennedy, 'Equitable Remedies and Principled Discretion: The Michigan Experience' (1997) 74 (4) U Det Mercy L Rev 609, 654.

80 See Kevin C Kennedy, 'Equitable Remedies and Principled Discretion: The Michigan Experience' (1997) 74 (4) U Det Mercy L Rev 609, 655–656.

81 See Michael Byran, 'Injunction and Damages – Taking Shelfer off the Shelf' (2016) 28 SAcLJ 921; see also, *Shelfer v City of London Electric Lighting Co* [1895] 1 Ch 287; see also, *Lawrence v Fen Tigers Ltd* [2014] UKSC 13.

82 Refer to 1.31–1.43.

of these powers is their discretionary nature:[83] even where all the formal requirements for granting a remedy are satisfied, the Court still has a choice over whether or not to grant it and, if so, on what terms. In exercising that choice, the Court relies partly on established principles,[84] and partly on its own assessment of what would be just and convenient in the particular circumstances of the case.

1.45 The courts of common law and equity were merged under the Judicature Acts 1873. Shortly afterwards, a new, unified set of procedural rules, the Rules of the Supreme Court 1883, was promulgated to govern practice and procedure in the merged courts. These rules were gradually added to and amended over the years, including a wholesale revision in 1965. The Rules of the Supreme Court applied to proceedings in the English High Court, where more important civil cases are heard. A parallel code, the County Court Rules, was created for the County Courts, which decides more minor civil cases. Both sets of rules contained detailed provisions governing not only case management, but also the granting of various forms of interim relief. While the rules set out the conditions for granting such relief, and the procedure for applying such relief, the source of the courts' power to grant such relief was to be found elsewhere, either in the courts' inherent jurisdiction or in specific primary Acts of Parliament.

1.46 In 1998 English civil procedure underwent another wholesale revision, with the Rules of the Supreme Court and the County Court Rules both being replaced by a new unified code, the Civil Procedure Rules 1998 ("CPR"). Since its inception, the CPR has been regularly updated and amended. The CPR is accompanied by a comprehensive set of practice directions, which supplement and elucidate the rules themselves, and a set of specialist court guides (see below).

1.47 Like the codes which it replaced, the CPR and its accompanying practice directions contain detailed provisions rules governing the granting of various forms of interim relief. The most important provisions are Rule 25.1, entitled "Interim remedies and security for costs" and accompanying Practice Direction 25A, entitled "Interim injunctions", which govern the granting of interim injunctions, interim declarations, interim orders relating to specific property (detention, custody, preservation, inspection, sampling, testing and sale), freezing injunctions and ancillary disclosure orders, search orders and various other interim remedies. The rules permit the Court to grant interim remedies in certain circumstances before proceedings have formally been commenced, and even without giving prior notice to the defendant. The rules governing the exercise of the Court's powers to enforce interim

83 An exception is ship arrest in England & Wales, which is available as of right: *The Varna* [1993] 2 Lloyd's Rep 253. This reflects the fact that the remedy is not equitable in origin, but based on much older civil law practices.

84 See the discussion in *Fourie v Le Roux* [2007] UKHL 1.

remedies and to punish breaches of its orders are contained in Rule 81 and the accompanying Practice Direction 81, both entitled "Applications and proceedings in relation to contempt of court".

1.48 The CPR introduced a number of changes designed to streamline English civil procedure and make it more rational and user-friendly. One of the most important innovations in the CPR is the overriding objective of enabling the court to deal with cases justly and at proportionate cost. The courts are required to seek to give effect to this objective whenever they exercise powers under the CPR.

1.49 Alongside these changes in the procedural rules, the first tier of English civil courts has undergone organisational changes in recent years, designed to ensure that different categories of cases are decided by courts possessing the appropriate level of specialist knowledge, experience and other resources.[85] The primary divide between the High Court and the County Court remains. The High Court comprises three divisions, as it has done for many decades: the Queen's Bench Division, the Chancery Division and the Family Division. It is still primarily based in London, with various district registries operating in major regional cities. The important change has been the creation, under the umbrella of the Queen's Bench and Chancery Divisions, of a group of specialist courts for deciding commercial cases, called the Business and Property Courts. The longest-established of these specialist courts is the Admiralty Court, which hears certain kinds of shipping case. The best-known and most important is the Commercial Court, which hears a wide variety of major commercial disputes. Other specialist Business and Property Courts include the Technology and Construction Court, the Insolvency and Companies List and the Business List.

1.50 The Business and Property Courts have been established in order to serve the domestic and international business community. They have specialist expert judges and their own individual practices and procedures, tailored to suit the particular needs of the users of the courts, and formulated in consultation with them. These specialist practices and procedures are set out in the CPR – e.g. CPR Part 58 and its accompanying practice direction, which governs practice and procedure the Commercial Court – and in specialist Court Guides, such as the Admiralty and Commercial Courts Guide. These guides contain detailed rules and guidance about how to apply for various forms of interim relief, including freezing injunctions and search orders.

1.51 In addition to these procedural and organisational changes, there have been important developments in recent decades affecting the fundamental power of the English courts to grant interim remedies.

---

85 The principal change to the appellate courts has been the abolition of the judicial committee of the House of Lords and its replacement by the UK Supreme Court.

1.52 The most important of these, for present purposes, has been the development of the court's power to grant freezing injunctions and search orders, two powerful interim remedies which are of huge significance to modern commercial litigation. In the same period, the English courts have clarified and refined the principles governing the granting of other types of interim injunctions. These developments are discussed further below and, in greater detail, in Chapters 5, 7 and 9.

1.53 Parliament has also partially repealed the fundamental rule in *The Siskina*,[86] which states that the court can only grant interim remedies in support of substantive legal proceedings (including proceedings which have yet to be commenced) in the English court. That rule prevented the courts from granting interim remedies such as freezing injunctions in support of claims which were to be determined in a foreign court, or in arbitration. Section 25 of the Civil Jurisdiction and Judgments Act 1982 now allows the court to grant most forms of interim relief in support of foreign court proceedings,[87] in appropriate cases. Section 44 of the Arbitration Act 1996 allows the Courts to grant interim relief in support of arbitrations, subject to strict limits designed to promote the autonomy and independence of arbitration.

1.54 The European Convention on Human Rights has been enacted into English domestic law by the Human Rights Act 1998. Section 6 of that Act makes it unlawful for a court to act in a way which is incompatible with a Convention right. As a result, the courts have had to address whether the granting of interim remedies, and enforcing those remedies, is compatible with various Convention rights, including the rights to liberty (Article 5), fair trial (Article 6), freedom from unlawful punishment (Article 7), respect for private and family life (Article 8), freedom of expression (Article 10)[88] and protection of property (First Protocol, Article 1).

1.55 The UK has also joined, and then left, the European Union.[89] While the UK was a member, EU law applied in the UK: indeed, EU law took precedence over domestic UK law. When the UK left, it unilaterally chose to retain substantial parts of existing EU law as domestic law,[90] to avoid a "cliff

---

86 [1979] AC 210.

87 That section originally only applied to foreign court proceedings under the Brussels and Lugano Conventions; that restriction was removed by the Civil Jurisdiction and Judgments Act 1982 (Interim Relief) Order 1997, SI 1997/302. The English Court's power to grant interim relief in support of court proceedings in other EU member states is currently contained in Article 35 of the EU Judgments Regulation Recast, No.1215/2012.

88 Specific guidance on applications for interim injunctions restraining the publication of materials and the Human Rights Act 1998 is contained in the Master of the Rolls' official *Practice Guidance: Interim Non-Disclosure Orders* [2012] 1 WLR 1003.

89 The UK joined the European Economic Community, as it then was, on 1 January 1973 and left the European Union on 31 January 2020. The formal transition period (or implementation period), in which EU law continued to apply to the UK as if it were still a member, ended on 31 December 2020.

90 European Union (Withdrawal) Act 2018 s 2–4, as amended by the European Union (Withdrawal Agreement) Act 2020. The UK has retained pre-existing domestic legislation

edge" where the law in the UK changed radically overnight. It is anticipated that much of this retained EU law may be amended or repealed by the UK parliament in the coming months and years.

1.56 Some parts of EU law could not be retained unilaterally, as they require co-operation from the EU. Most importantly for present purposes, the UK is – at least for the time being – no longer a part of the so-called Brussels regime contained in the EU Judgments Regulation Recast ("JRR"), EU 1215/2012 and the 2007 Lugano Convention ("Lugano"). These instruments govern jurisdiction and the enforcement of judgments in civil and commercial matters between member states of the EU and the European Free Trade Association (Iceland, Liechtenstein, Norway and Switzerland). They include rules on the jurisdiction to grant provisional and protective measures in support of substantive proceedings in the courts of other European states.[91] The UK has applied to rejoin Lugano as an independent state,[92] but the EU has yet to agree to that. In the meantime, the only international agreement between the UK and the EU governing jurisdiction and enforcement of judgments in civil and commercial matters is the 2005 Hague Convention, which is very limited in its coverage and effect.

1.57 One controversial effect of the Brussels regime had been to prevent the English courts from granting anti-suit injunctions to restrain a party from pursuing legal proceedings in another European state, where those proceedings are in breach of a jurisdiction or arbitration agreement.[93] Anti-suit injunctions are a highly specialised form of relief, available on either an interim or a final basis, a detailed consideration of which is beyond the scope of this book. Unless and until the UK rejoins Lugano, or reaches a separate agreement with the EU on jurisdiction and enforcement of judgments in civil and commercial matters, English courts will once again be able to grant anti-suit injunctions restraining proceedings in other EU/EFTA states.

1.58 The expression "interim remedy" is not a term of art with a precise, fixed, definition in English law. The concept is similar but not identical to that of "provisional and protective measures" under the Brussels regime,[94] i.e. remedies which, in one way or another, serve to preserve the factual, legal or evidential position, so as to safeguard rights pending their final adjudication,

derived from EU law (i.e. statutes and regulations implementing EU directives), and it has transposed direct EU legislation (EU regulations) which was operative prior to the end of 2020 into UK law by re-enacting it as domestic legislation. It also continues to recognise and enforce other rights and obligations deriving from EU law which existed prior to the end of 2020.

91 JRR Article 35; Lugano Article 31.

92 Until 31 December 2020 it was a party by virtue of its membership of the EU.

93 *Turner v Grovit*, Case C-159/02, [2004] ECR I-3565; see also, *West Tankers Inc v Allianz SpA*, Case C-185/07, [2009] ECR 1-663. The English court has jurisdiction to grant this form of injunctive relief where foreign proceedings infringe the applicant's legal or equitable right or are otherwise vexatious, abusive or contrary to the interests of justice.

94 JRR Article 35; Lugano Article 31.

whether by the court which grants the interim remedy or by another court or tribunal.[95] Part 25 of the CPR contains a long list of interim remedies which are available in the English court, but the list is by no means exhaustive. It includes remedies which are temporary or provisional versions of remedies which can be granted as the final, substantive, relief in a claim, such as an interim injunction restraining a party from committing an allegedly unlawful act pending trial of a claim for a permanent injunction restraining him from doing the same thing. It also includes exclusively interim remedies, i.e. remedies which could not be granted as the final, substantive, relief in a claim, such as a freezing injunction restraining a party from removing or dissipating assets pending final determination of a substantive claim against him. And it includes special versions of remedies which are normally regarded as part of the Court's case management powers, such as orders for the disclosure of documents before proceedings have been commenced.

Evolution of Freezing Injunctions

1.59 A freezing injunction is a special form of interim injunction. An injunction is a court order addressed to one or more persons, either restraining them from doing something (a negative injunction) or, less frequently, requiring them to do something positive (a mandatory injunction). A freezing injunction is a negative injunction restraining a person from dealing with his assets unjustifiably, so as to put those assets beyond the reach of a claimant. The purpose of a freezing injunction is to prevent a defendant from frustrating the judicial process by making it more difficult, expensive or time-consuming for a claimant to enforce a judgment against him. In other words, it is an interim remedy designed to secure the claimant against the risk of the defendant illegitimately dissipating his assets.[96] Freezing injunctions are an important feature of modern commercial litigation, as the availability of such an injunction may determine whether a claim is worth pursuing or not. The availability of freezing injunctions is one of the factors that makes English courts and English arbitration such a popular choice for international dispute resolution.

1.60 Until 1975, the English courts generally refused to grant freezing injunctions to restrain a defendant from placing his assets beyond the reach

95 *Van Uden Maritime B.V. v Kommanditgesellschaft in Firma Deco-Line* (Case C-391/95) [1999] QB 1225. Some of the remedies discussed in this work, such as ship arrest, were not available in England as provisional or protective remedies within JRR Article 35 and Lugano Article 31. Section 25(7) of the Civil Jurisdiction and Judgments Act 1981 expressly excludes ship arrest and provisions for obtaining evidence from the interim remedies which the English court can grant in support of foreign proceedings.

96 But not the risk of the defendant's insolvency – thus a freezing injunction gives the applicant no security interest in the respondent's assets and no priority ahead of the respondent's other unsecured creditors.

of a claimant prior to judgment.[97] The only exception was where the claimant had a proprietary claim (i.e. a claim in which he asserted ownership over property in the hands of the defendant, and sought to recover that property). In such a case, the courts were prepared to grant an injunction restraining the defendant from disposing of the property which was the subject matter of the claim (sometimes called an *asset preservation order*): *Lister v Stubbs*.[98]

1.61 In 1975, the Court of Appeal granted the first non-proprietary, pre-judgment freezing injunction, to restrain a defendant from removing assets from the jurisdiction so as to make it difficult for the claimant to enforce any judgment it might obtain against him in a dispute under a charterparty. In 1978, the Court of Appeal approved that decision and effectively overruled *Lister v Stubbs*[99] in the celebrated case of *Mareva Compania Naviera SA v International Bulk Carriers SA*.[100]

1.62 This so-called *Mareva* jurisdiction was initially restricted to cases where the claimant could show that a foreign defendant had identifiable assets within the jurisdiction of the English Court (i.e. in England and Wales). Section 37(3) of the Senior Courts Act 1981 abolished the requirement for the defendant to be foreign. The courts have also dispensed with the need for assets within the jurisdiction, and are now prepared to grant freezing injunctions over assets located anywhere in the world.[101] These so-called worldwide freezing injunctions are now the norm.

1.63 The courts have also expanded the *Mareva* jurisdiction to cases where the defendant's assets are the hands of a third party, T. In such cases they are prepared to grant an injunction directly against T, even though the claimant has no cause of action against T.[102] They have gone even further and accepted that, where the claimant has a cause of action against D but not against T, but D does have a claim against T, the court may in special circumstances grant a freezing injunction directly against T, to prevent him from disposing of his own assets, which he might otherwise use to pay D, and which would thereupon become available to satisfy any judgment which claimant obtained against D.[103]

---

97 A procedure called foreign attachment, similar to the civilian *saisie conservatoire*, was available by custom in London and certain other English cities, but its application was limited to foreign defendants who were individuals and not companies, and who were not within the jurisdiction of the English court: see *Rasu Maritima SA v Perusahaan Pertambangan v Minyak Dan Gas Bumi Negara* [1978] QB 644.

98 (1890) 45 Ch D 1.

99 The other important point decided in *Lister v Stubbs* – that an agent who takes a secret commission in breach of his fiduciary duty to his principal does not hold the commission or its proceeds on trust for his principal – was eventually overruled by the UK Supreme Court in *FHR European Ventures LLP v Cedar Capital Partners LLC* [2014] UKSC 45.

100 [1980] 1 All ER 213.

101 *Babanaft International Co. SA v Bassatne* [1990] Ch 13.

102 *TSB Private Bank International SA v Chabra* [1992] 1 WLR 231.

103 *HMRC v Eglinton* [2007] BCC 78.

1.64 The courts have developed detailed rules governing the practice and procedure on an application for a freezing injunction, and on the wording of freezing injunctions. These will be discussed in detail in Part 3, Chapter 5 of the book.

Evolution of Interim Injunctions

1.65 As indicated above, a freezing injunction is simply a special form of interim injunction. In theory, the power of the courts to grant interim injunctions is almost unlimited: the power as codified in section 37 of the Senior Courts Act 1981[104] extends to any case where it appears to the Court that it is "just and convenient" to grant it. In practice, however, the courts' exercise of that discretionary power is tightly circumscribed by a series of judge-made rules created over the last few hundred years. The most important of these are the rule that an interim injunction can only be granted in support of a substantive legal or equitable right; and the principle in *The Siskina*, described above, which has been partially eroded by statute in recent decades. These rules apply equally to freezing injunctions and other interim injunctions.

1.66 The English courts have developed other detailed principles governing the granting of interim injunctions, other than freezing injunctions. The key approach was established authoritatively in *American Cyanamid Co v Ethicon Ltd*.[105] In that case the House of Lords set out the well-known three-stage test: (i) is the underlying claim serious (i.e. not merely frivolous or vexatious)?, (ii) if so, would damages be an adequate remedy to the claimant if the injunction was refused, or to the defendant if the injunction was wrongly granted?, (iii) if damages would be an inadequate remedy for both parties, where is the balance of convenience (i.e. which is greater: the risk of doing an injustice to the defendant by granting an injunction which later turns out to be wrong, or the risk of injustice to the claimant by allowing the defendant to continue acting in a potentially wrongful manner)?

1.67 The courts have elucidated that three-stage test and how it is to be applied in a number of subsequent decisions. They have also identified several special classes of cases where the test is either inapplicable or requires special weight to be given to particular factors, including cases where the injunctive relief sought is mandatory (i.e. ordering the defendant to do something positive, rather than ordering him to refrain from doing something) and where the dispute is unlikely ever to reach trial, so that the outcome of the application for an interim injunction will, in practice, finally determine the

104 The 1981 Act does not create the jurisdiction to grant injunctions; it merely empowers the modern higher courts to exercise that jurisdiction. The source of the jurisdiction is the inherent powers of the courts of Chancery: *Fourie v Le Roux* [2007] UKHL 1.

105 [1975] AC 396.

case in favour of one or other party. The rules will be discussed in detail in Part 4, Chapter 7 of the book.

Evolution of Search Orders

1.68 A search order is another special type of interim injunction, in which the Court orders one party (the respondent) to admit another party (the applicant) to premises to search for the evidence or property, and to take it away and retain it. Search orders are designed to preserve evidence or property where there is a strong risk that the respondent will destroy or remove it and thereby frustrate the legal process. In order to preserve the element of surprise, search orders are invariably made without giving notice to the respondent, and they may be made before legal proceedings have been formally commenced. Because of their draconian nature, and the impingement on the basic rights and liberties of respondents which they entail (including Article 8 of the ECHR), search orders are only available in exceptional cases, where the applicant can demonstrate the necessity of such an order.

1.69 The jurisdiction to grant search orders was originally developed by the courts in a series of cases decided in the mid-1970s, including the well-known Court of Appeal decision in *Anton Piller KG v Manufacturing Processes Ltd*[106] (which led to search orders being known as *Anton Piller* orders). The jurisdiction was later codified by section 7 of the Civil Procedure Act 1997. The courts have developed a series of criteria for determining when a search order may be granted,[107] but as with other interim remedies, the Court still retains discretion to refuse the remedy even if all the necessary criteria are satisfied. The courts also developed strict rules governing the procedure for applying for a search order, the terms on which a search order may be granted and the manner in which it is to be executed. These rules are now codified in section 7 of the 1997 Act and in paragraph 7 of Practice Direction 25A accompanying CPR Part 25. The rules will be discussed in detail in Part 5, Chapter 9 of the book.

Evolution of Other Interim Remedies (Including Relevant to Maritime Disputes)

1.70 The English courts have developed and adopted a range of other interim remedies and case management powers, some of which have been referred to above.[108] Among the most important in commercial litigation are

106 [1976] 1 Ch 55.

107 See e.g. *Arcelormittal USA LLC v Essar Steel Ltd* [2019] EWHC 724 (Comm) [97–98].

108 CPR 25.1 contains a non-exhaustive list of interim remedies available in the English courts.

ship arrest, which enables a claimant with a maritime claim to obtain security for his claim over the defendant's ship by arresting it when it enters English territorial waters; the anti-suit injunction, which requires a party to refrain from pursuing proceedings in a foreign court or tribunal in breach of a jurisdiction agreement or in circumstances which make the foreign proceedings vexatious or oppressive (anti-suit injunctions are generally sought as a substantive remedy, but the court may also grant an anti-suit injunction on an interim basis to maintain the status quo until it determines whether to grant the substantive remedy); and the *Vasso* order[109] which requires a party (usually a shipowner) to permit a surveyor to access a ship or other premises in order to carry out an inspection for the purpose of preserving evidence. The authors have discussed relevant interim remedies for dealing with maritime disputes in Chapters 5, 7 and 9 respectively.

1.71 Two other interim remedies which deserve brief mention here are interim payment and security for costs. The former is of limited importance in commercial litigation, being most often applied in claims for personal injury. The latter is of great practical importance in commercial litigation, not least for tactical uses. Neither of these remedies falls within the rubric of "provisional and protective measures" under the Brussels regime.[110]

1.72 The Court has the power to order a defendant to make an interim payment on account to a claimant, before final judgment, on a money claim, in certain limited circumstances: where the defendant has admitted liability, or the Court has determined liability, but has not yet determined the amount of that liability; and also where liability is in dispute, if the Court is satisfied that the claimant would obtain judgment for a substantial amount of money at trial.[111] The purpose of this power is not to secure the claimant against the risk that the defendant will not pay the final judgment, but to minimise the injustice to the claimant of delay in receiving the money to which he is (probably) entitled. If the final judgment is less than the interim payment, the claimant is obliged to repay the difference.

1.73 The Court also has power, in certain limited circumstances, to order a claimant to provide security to the defendant to cover the defendant's costs of defending the claim (a defendant who makes a counterclaim can also be ordered to secure the claimant's costs of defending the counterclaim).[112] The purpose of this remedy is to protect a defendant from the risk that the

109 *The Vasso* [1983] 1 WLR 838; see also *Unicargo v Flotec Maritime S de RL (The Cienvik)* [1996] 2 Lloyd's Rep 395.

110 *Van Uden Maritime VB v Firma Deco-Line* (Case C-391/95) [1999] QB 1225, a case on a Dutch remedy analogous to interim payment under English law.

111 CPR 25.6–9, enacted pursuant to s. 32 of the Senior Courts Act 1981.

112 CPR 25.12–14.

claimant will be unable or unwilling to pay the defendant's defence costs, if ordered to do so, as will normally be the case if the claim fails.[113]

Interim Remedies and Arbitration in England & Wales

1.74 Many of the interim remedies which the English Court can grant in support of legal proceedings in England or in foreign courts can also be granted by the courts in support of arbitration, pursuant to section 44 of the Arbitration Act 1996. The 1996 Act was motivated in part by international criticism that English law had previously permitted too much interference in arbitrations by the English courts, and in part by the UNCITRAL Model Law on International Commercial Arbitration 1985,[114] Article 5 of which provides that no court should intervene in matters covered by the law save except where so provided in the law. In keeping with that principle of non-intervention,[115] subsection 44(5) of the Act permits the Courts to grant interim remedies only if and to the extent that the arbitral tribunal or relevant arbitral institution lacks the power to do so or cannot do so for the time being (for example, in the case of an arbitral tribunal, because has not yet been constituted).

1.75 Section 44 of the Arbitration Act 1996 allows the Court to grant interim relief in support of arbitrations, subject to strict limits designed to promote the autonomy and independence of arbitration. In Part 2, Chapter 4, the authors have discussed the powers of the English Court to grant interim remedies in aid of arbitration proceedings under section 44 of the UK Arbitration Act 1996 and CPR Part 62, and the limits of those powers. The authors have discussed the detailed rules of interim remedies in the context of arbitration in Part 2, Chapter 4.

Preservation Measures in China

Introduction to Preservation Measures in China

1.76 From the point of view of comparative law, the interim remedies pursuant to English law are known by another term, "preservation measures", in Chinese civil procedure law.[116] It must be emphasised at the outset that even many concepts, standards of proof and procedures pursuant to Chinese law are very different from English law. Therefore, readers are warned that they should not try to understand the preservation measures in China through the

113 CPR 44.2(2).

114 The model law was subsequently amended in 2006 to include more detailed provisions on interim measures. Neither the original nor the amended version has been adopted wholesale into UK law.

115 Arbitration Act 1996, section 1(c).

116 Wenliang Zhang, 'Third Parties in Interim Remedies: From Chinese Civil and Commercial Interim Remedies Perspective' (2016) 38 (1) Modern Law Science 164.

lens of English law and vice versa.[117] However the purposes of interim remedies and preservation measures are similar to a large extent.[118]

1.77 Furthermore, there are three types of preservation measures under existing Chinese law including property, behaviour and evidence preservation measures.[119] The fundamental common purpose of preservation measures is to prevent "irrecoverable damage" and "irreparable harm" to a party in dispute and to ensure the realisation of the objectives of the civil trial proceedings and the smooth enforcement of future court judgments and arbitration awards.[120]

1.78 However, the Chinese legal system, following the civil law tradition with socialist and Chinese characteristics, strictly follows a systematic and conceptual framework to interpret and address legal issues in civil/commercial disputes. The characteristics of preservation measures are a bit controversial in China. One point of view is that the preservation measures belong to a kind of procedure remedy that combines the preservation procedure during various stages of civil case with the preservation procedure available at the stage relevant to enforcement of the judgment.[121] Another point of view is that the preservation measures constitute a special legal procedural remedy.[122] However, regardless of the different viewpoints from scholars, seeking preservation measures using a preservation procedure system is a separate system within the ambit of the civil procedural law.[123]

1.79 Some legal scholars in China consider that the complexion of the interim remedies in the common law system is equivalent to that of the preservation measures available in the civil law system,[124] while there has been ongoing debate surrounding this issue. Some legal scholars oppose this view

117 Refer to Part 6, Chapter 11 on comparative analysis of visible and invisible factors and their impact on interim remedies/preservation measures; see also, Vivek Jain, 'Sufficiency of Court's Pre-Judgment Power in Commercial Litigation: A Comparative Study Assessing the Law and Practice in PRC and England & Wales' (PhD Thesis, China University of Political Science and Law 2017).

118 Refer to 1.14–1.22.

119 Articles 81, 100 and 101 of CPL 1991 (amended until 2020); in Chinese legal practice, the practitioners have generally accepted these three categories of preservation measures. Preservation of property measures, preservation of behaviour/conduct measures and preservation of evidence measures are discussed in detail in Part 3 (Chapter 6), Part 4 (Chapter 8) and Part 5 (Chapter 10) respectively.

120 Shichun Li, 'Research on General Issues of Civil Preservation Procedure' (2005) 17 (1) Peking University Law Journal 43, 49; refer also, Chapter 6, 6.2 (the concept of the property preservation measures) and 6.11 (the concept of the preservation of maritime claim), Chapter 8, 8.55–8.56 (concepts of the behaviour preservation measures and of maritime injunction) and Chapter 10, 10.13–10.14 (concepts of the evidence preservation measures).

121 Shichun Li, 'Studies on the Civil Securing Judgement Procedure' (PhD Thesis, China University of Political Science and Law 2002) 34.

122 Yiqiang Fan, 'Civil Preservation Procedure' (PhD Thesis, Southwest University of Political & Science 2008) 47–48.

123 Refer to Figure 3.1 in Chapter 3, 3.3–3.4 (main procedural steps including preservation measures) and Figure 3.3 in 3.45–3.46 (preservation procedural steps).

124 Yiqiang Fan, 'Civil Preservation Procedure' (PhD Thesis, Southwest University of Political & Science 2008) 32; see also, Vivek Jain, 'Sufficiency of Court's Pre-Judgment Power

on the basis that the interim remedies and preservation measures are not the same because the procedural remedy of preservation of evidence measures is kept separate from the other two preservation measures, that is, the property preservation measures and behaviour/conduct preservation measures.[125] These scholars with an opposing view argue that, unlike in China, the search orders of the common law system have in fact been incorporated into the scheme of interim remedies.

1.80 In terms of the interrelationship between the procedures for seeking preservation measures (hereinafter "preservation procedure") and preservation measures themselves, it is not wrong to say that the civil preservation procedure is a comprehensive legal framework for regulating all legal issues regarding the procedural remedy of preservation measures. Evidently, the procedural remedy of preservation measures can be considered as one of the rationales for the establishment and enforcement of civil preservation procedures within the Chinese legal system.

1.81 Against the above background, through the following paragraphs, the authors will examine the evolution of the civil preservation procedures and preservation remedies in China.

Evolution of Civil Preservation Procedure and Preservation Measures[126]

Evolution of Civil Procedure Law and Preservation Procedures

1.82 Unlike common law with a history of hundreds of years, the history of the Chinese legal system is relatively new.[127] Accordingly, the history of the

in Commercial Litigation: A Comparative Study Assessing the Law and Practice in PRC and England & Wales' (PhD Thesis, China University of Political Science and Law 2017).

125 Shichun Li, 'Research on General Issues of Civil Preservation Procedure' (2005) 17 (1) Peking University Law Journal 43, 45.

126 In this section, the evolution simply refers to the advent and development of the preservation system after the People's Republic of China was established in 1949. In Chinese history, the preservation system was for the first time provided in the Draft Civil Procedural Law in 1910. Part 4 of this Draft Code stipulated that property and behaviour preservation measures in the course of litigation proceedings would be available. Before it could be enacted and entered into force, the last imperial Qing Dynasty fell in 1911. After the Nanjing National Government was established in China, a new Civil Procedural Law by reference to the Draft of Civil Procedural Law 1910 was promulgated in 1932. Afterwards, by reference to then-existing German law and Japanese law, the Civil Procedure Law 1932 was revised in 1935. Like the Draft Civil Procedural Law 1910, the preservation measures were yet again limited to property and behaviour/conduct preservation measures. After the Communist Revolution, the People's Republic of China was established in 1949, and immediately thereafter the Central Government abolished the entire legal system built by the Nanjing National Government. Therefore, the context in which the evolution of preservation measures is discussed will simply be development in China after 1949; see also, Yong Zhu (ed), *The Chinese Legal History, Vol. IX* (Law Press China 1999) 302 and 312; see also, Yun Gu, 'Research on Preservation Procedure of Civil Litigation' (Master Thesis, Wuhan University 2005) 23–24.

127 The Chinese legal system here refers to the system established by the People's Republic China since 1949. However, the effect of the ancient system of governance and jurisprudence

preservation system/preservation procedure is relatively brief. Generally, the development of the preservation measures in China can be divided into three stages – (i) a slow pace of development from 1949 to 1982, (ii) a gradual pace of development from 1982 to 2012 and (iii) a rapid pace of modernisation in the existing system of preservation measures from 2012 to present.

Evolution of Property Preservation Measures – The First Stage (1949–1982)

1.83 Between 1949 and 1982, the Committee of Legal Affairs of Central Government and the Supreme People's Court (hereinafter referred to as the "SPC") issued the Draft of General Rules of Civil Procedure 1950, the Civil Trial Procedure (draft) 1957 and Provisions for People's Court Civil Trial Procedure 1979. These legal codes and provisions all touched upon the civil preservation procedures that would govern the procedural remedy of preservation measures in China. Especially, with respect to property preservation measures, the *Reply of the Supreme People's Court on Which Ruling Can Be Filed an Appeal 1956*,[128] the Civil Trial Procedure (draft) 1957 and the *Provisions for People's Court Civil Trial Procedure 1979* all have granted rights to the parties to file an appeal in a higher tier court from a lower court's order on preservation measures.[129] Furthermore, the local laws issued by the provisional governments of some provinces, such as Hunan Province and Fujian Province, have provided the local courts guidance that will also be in play along with the civil procedure rules and various enacted provisions in the matter concerning the detainment of property.[130]

1.84 The above gradual development in the context of preservation procedures, whether at the national level or at the provincial level, still could not provide a comprehensive and unified preservation system governing

and the developments in the early 20th century can still affect the current legal system. For further discussion refer to Part 6, Chapter 11; see also, Vivek Jain, *Insight into China through Comparative Analysis of Invisible Factors and Contexts – Common Law v. Chinese Law* (1st Edn, Notion Press 2019).

128 See *Reply of the Supreme People's Court on Which Ruling Can Be Filed an Appeal 1956* (Yan Zi No 10535); see also, Mingmin Pan, 'Study on Legislation Perfection of the Property Preservation: Comments on The Interpretation of The Supreme People's Court of the Civil Procedure Law of People's Republic of China' (Master Thesis, Southwest University of Political Science and Law 2015).

129 Civil Trial Procedure (draft) 1957 was issued by the SPC. Article 15 of the draft civil procedural rules had provided that "the party concerned may *appeal* [emphasis added] for the ruling of preservation on seal-up, detainment freezing of property and of requesting the security". However, from the CPL (Trial) 1982 onwards, the parties to disputes are no longer entitled to file an appeal from the order of preservation measure; refer to Chapter 3, 3.223–3.230.

130 See *Interim Provisions on Handling Civil and Criminal Cases in All Courts of Hunan Province 1950* (Fa Xing Zi No 2), Article 16; see also, *Interim Provisions on Handling Civil and Criminal Cases in All Courts of Fujian Province 1950*, Article 76.

preservation measures in China.[131] Furthermore, traditionally, the Chinese legal system has always devoted excessive consideration to substantive law as compared to procedure law. Accordingly, before the Chinese Economic Reform in 1978, the legislations on the preservation measure had remained underdeveloped.[132] In addition, insufficient research was pursued in academia on preservation measures and preservation procedures to seek those preservation measures during those years.

Evolution of Property Preservation Measures
– The Second Stage (1982–2012)

1.85 In the second stage, in 1982, the Civil Procedure Law (for Trial Implementation) (hereinafter referred to as the "CPL (Trial) 1982"), as the first-tier source of law, stipulated that the litigation preservation system, entitled "preservation measures", would include two other procedural remedies, namely, "litigation preservation" and "advance payment".[133]

1.86 The CPL 1991 revised the legal terminologies, and thereafter "litigation preservation" and "advance payment" were henceforth called "property preservation" and "advance enforcement" respectively. It was generally recognised that "litigation preservation" in the 1982 Trial version of CPL could be interpreted as a combination of "property preservation" and "behaviour preservation", while "advance payment" could be interpreted as the enforcement of property preservation when the claimant had already filed an application in a civil court, that is, during the course of civil proceedings.[134]

---

131 Shichun Li, 'Research on General Issues of Civil Preservation Procedure' (2005) 17 (1) Peking University Law Journal 43, 56; see also, Yiqiang Fan, 'Civil Preservation Procedure' (PhD Thesis, Southwest University of Political & Science 2008) 11; see also, Yun Gu, 'Research on Preservation Procedure of Civil Litigation' (Master Thesis, Wuhan University 2005) 24–25.

132 Chinese economic reforms started on 18 December 1978. In order to stimulate economic development under the legal framework, since 1979, more and more legislations have been issued. In particular, China legally transplanted ideas from other jurisdictions into the Chinese legal system and learned from other jurisdictions. In a short period of time, there was fast-paced development in all aspects of the Chinese legal system including the preservation procedural system.

133 Civil Procedural Law of the People's Republic of China (for Trial Implementation) 1982, Articles 92–96; Shichun Li, 'Research on General Issues of Civil Preservation Procedure' (2005) 17 (1) Peking University Law Journal 43, 46; see also, Yiqiang Fan, 'Civil Preservation Procedure' (PhD Thesis, Southwest University of Political & Science 2008) 11; in this context, the term "litigation" refers to both litigation and arbitration, namely, "litigation preservation" includes both "litigation" and "arbitration" preservations. In addition, Article 162 of *Opinion of the SPC on Questions Concerning the Implementation of the General Principles of Civil Law (for Trial Implementation) 1988* (Fa (Ban) Fa [1988] No 6) introduced for the first time a concept similar to present-day behaviour preservation measures, but it must be emphasised that this advent of the new type of preservation measure was not introduced by way of legislation. For further details, please refer to Chapter 8, 8.14.

134 Shichun Li, 'Research on General Issues of Civil Preservation Procedure' (2005) 17 (1) Peking University Law Journal 43, 48.

1.87 In the CPL 1991, the term "property preservation" narrowed the scope of preservation measures. It means that, unlike "litigation preservation" in 1982, "property preservation" in 1991 simply refers to the preservation measures of property belonging to the respondent. The concept of "advance enforcement" that replaced that of "advance payment", in accordance with the interpretation of the SPC, was regarded as the enforcement of both property preservation and behaviour preservation measures in advance,[135] even if "behaviour preservation" arising from "advance enforcement" was not really an equivalent concept as compared to the behaviour preservation measures, which were provided recently through the 2012 revisions to the CPL 1991.[136] There have been many other amendments after the 2012 revision to the CPL 1991, and this book considers all such amendments until 2020. However, not all such recent amendments have affected the codes that are relevant to preservation measures. The authors have discussed the detailed rules about preservation of property measures in Part 3, Chapter 6 of the book.

Evolution of Behaviour Preservation Measures

1.88 In 2007, the CPL was amended again, but the provisions regarding the civil preservation procedure were not revised. Accordingly, the CPL 1991, until 2007, retained specific provisions on the property preservation measures, apart from the provision of "advance enforcement" as implied behaviour preservation measures; yet there was no provision pertaining specifically to the behaviour preservation measures in the CPL (Trial) 1982 and the CPL 1991/2007. Nevertheless, special fields of law such as maritime law and intellectual property law did provide for behaviour preservation measures in their specific codes from the early 20th century.[137]

135 Article 162 of *Opinion of the SPC on Questions Concerning the Implementation of the General Principles of Civil Law (For Trial Implementation) 1988* provided that "In the course of a litigation proceeding, if there is a need to stop an infringement, eliminate and obstruction, or remove a danger, the People's Court may make an award before the conclusion of the litigation based on the application of a party or on its own initiative"; see also, Shichun Li, 'Research on General Issues of Civil Preservation Procedure' (2005) 17 (1) Peking University Law Journal 43, 48; see also, Yiqiang Fan, 'Civil Preservation Procedure' (PhD Thesis, Southwest University of Political & Science 2008) 13 and 91; see also, Fuhua Wang, 'Research on Civil Preservation System' (PhD Thesis, China University of Political Science and Law 2005) 57–59.

136 For discussion in detail on the topic of advance enforcement, please refer to Chapter 8, 8.9–8.41.

137 See Maritime Special Procedure Law 2000, Chapter 4 'Maritime Injunction'; *Several Provisions of the Supreme People's Court on Issues Concerning Application of Law to Pre-Litigation Cessation of Patent Right Infringement (Fa Shi [2001] No 20)*; Interpretation of the Supreme People's Court on the Application of Law for Stopping the Infringement upon the Right to the Exclusive Use of a Registered Trademark and Preserving Evidence before Filing a Lawsuit (Fa Shi [2002] No 2) (expired on 1 Jan 2021); *Reply of the Supreme People's Court on Property Preservation and Enforcement of and Other Issues Related to the Exclusive Right to Use a Registered Trademark* (Fa Shi [2001] No 24). The behaviour preservation measures will be examined in great detail in Part 4, Chapter 8 of the book.

1.89 The inclusion of behaviour preservation measures in these specialist laws such as intellectual property law was also as a result of mandatory requirements from international stakeholders, considering that China entered into the World Trade Organization (hereinafter "WTO") on 11 December 2001. Much legislation was amended to ensure that the requirements of the WTO were met as these requirements were conditions to China's entry into the WTO. With respect to intellectual property laws including patent law, trademark law and copyright law, the establishment of behaviour preservation measures was necessary to comply with the TRIPS Agreement because their inclusion was a condition for China to join the WTO.[138] The authors have discussed the detailed rules of preservation of behaviour measures and any special rules in Part 4, Chapter 8 of the book.

Maritime Injunctions

1.90 Distinctly, from the beginning, the Chinese Special Maritime Procedure Law 2000 (hereinafter referred to as the "SMPL 2000") routinely employed the term "maritime injunction" rather than the term "behaviour preservation measure". This was done to ensure that the concept of maritime injunction in China corresponds to a similar concept in English law.[139] This approach was preferred in China as, by adopting English terminology in the context of maritime injunctions, China took into consideration the fact that English law had played an influential role in global maritime law. From this point of view as well, the development of the behaviour preservation measures was very much influenced by external factors. In the end, CPL 2012 revisions conspicuously brought behaviour preservation measures and related preservation procedures into the Code to seek this procedural remedy.

Evolution of Evidence Preservation Measures

1.91 In terms of the evolution of evidence preservation measures, this procedural remedy was not incorporated into the section containing preservation procedure of the CPL (trial) 1982 or of the CPL 1991/2007. Seemingly, this procedural remedy was kept outside of the preservation procedural regime

138 See Trade-Related Aspects of Intellectual Property Rights, in force from 1995 ("TRIPS"). The TRIPS Agreement is contained in the Appendixes to World Trade Organization's Protocol on Accession of China. In order to join the WTO, China amended the Patent Law in 2000, and the Trademark Law of PRC and Copyright Law of PRC in 2001; see also, Xiaoming Song, Chuang Wang, Junli Xia and Guimei Lang, 'Understanding and Application of *Provisions of the Supreme People's Court on Several Issues Concerning the Application of Law in Cases Involving the Review of Behaviour Preservation in Intellectual Property Disputes*' [2019] 7 The People's Judicature 19, 19.

139 Refer to Part 4, Chapter 8, 8.56–8.57 and 8.157 for further discussion on the maritime injunctions.

of the CPL 1991 that governed property preservation measures and advance enforcement. However, both legislations indeed allowed litigants to apply for evidence preservation.[140]

1.92 Furthermore, resembling the application of behaviour preservation measures, the provisions of evidence preservation in the CPL 1991/2007 and special laws were different. Distinctly, the CPL 1991/2007 merely provided a procedural remedy for evidence preservation in the course of litigation proceedings, but did not stipulate the possibility of pre-action evidence preservation measures. In other words, before a case is accepted by a competent court, no party is entitled to file an application for evidence preservation measures. However, the SMPL 2000 and Intellectual Property Laws all expressly granted the right to apply for pre-litigation evidence preservation.[141] The authors have discussed the detailed rules of preservation of evidence measures in Part 5, Chapter 10 of the book.

Relevant Academic Debates on the Evolution of Preservation Measures

1.93 Against the above background, for most of the 20th century and the early 21th century, in the context of preservation measures, the CPL had focused only on property and behaviour preservation measures.[142] However, a unified approach for preservation measures was always absent in the Chinese civil procedural system. Apart from these two types of preservation measures, some scholars argued that in the preservation procedure regime, another procedural concept of "advance enforcement" should also be regarded as the third type of preservation measure. However, other academic scholars in China argued that the third type of preservation measure should be classed as a personal preservation measure that is capable of restricting the personal freedom of debtors. For example, such preservation measures can ensure that debtors cannot travel overseas until they have repaid their debts to their creditors.[143]

---

140 Article 65 of the CPL (Trial) 1982 provides that "under the circumstances, where there is a likelihood that evidence may be destroyed or lost, or difficult to obtain later, the participants in the litigation proceedings may apply to the People's court for preservation of such evidence. The people's court may also take the initiative to take preservative measures". In fact, Article 74 of the CPL 1991 and Article 65 of the CPL (Trial) 1982 were identical.

141 Article 63 of the SMPL 2000, Article 67 of Patent Law (2008 amendment), Article 58 of Trademark Law (2001 amendment) and Article 50 of Copyright Law (2001 amendment).

142 Yiqiang Fan, 'Civil Preservation Procedure' (PhD Thesis, Southwest University of Political & Science 2008) 19.

143 Shichun Li, 'Studies on the Civil Securing Judgement Procedure' (PhD Thesis, China University of Political Science and Law 2002) 62; see also, Rongxing Guo, *An Introduction to the Chinese Economy: The Driving Forces behind Modern Day China* (John Wiley & Sons (Asia) 2010) 119, where he discussed the rapid economic development in China in the last two decades and how this fast-paced development has led to rapid social changes in Chinese society. Therefore, demands from scholars have been that these requirements in a fast-changing

1.94 Even so, within the Chinese legal system, only the categories of property and behaviour preservation measures were considered as routine preservation measures in the Chinese legal system for many years.

1.95 Regardless of the categories of preservation measures, the evidence preservation measure was excluded from the discussions concerning preservation measures by Chinese scholars. The primary reason for this exclusion has always been scholars' insistence on maintaining the purity of the traditional civil law system, whereby the concept of civil preservation procedures can never comprise of evidence preservation measures. This exclusion was insisted upon by these scholars even though many procedures for civil preservation measures and evidence preservation measures were overlapping from time to time.[144] Accordingly, any research pursued by Chinese universities on civil preservation procedures that govern the applications seeking preservation measures was also limited to the study of property and behaviour preservation measures. As a result, the research hardly touched upon the procedural remedy of evidence preservation measures.[145]

1.96 However, as discussed above, without doubt that both the CPL (Trial) 1982 and the CPL 1991/2007 recognised that the evidence preservation measures exist as a type of of preservation measure. Therefore, some legal scholars considered that in a broader sense, the evidence preservation measures should be incorporated into the civil preservation procedure, while other scholars, in a strict sense, considered that the civil preservation procedure simply should comprise only of property and behaviour preservation measures.[146] An appreciation of the debate is essential for readers to grasp the concepts going forward before the three preservation remedies are examined in detail in Chapters 6, 8 and 10 along with the common Chapter 3, where the preservation procedural system and civil procedure system of China are examined.

1.97 In spite of the academic debate, the primary purpose of the civil preservation procedure system is consistent and focuses on ensuring the realisation of objectives arising from the litigation/arbitration proceedings along with the enforcement of future court judgments and arbitration awards. In any event, the three types of preservation measures have always been generally

---

commercial landscape in China can be fulfilled through a very different kind of preservation measure.

144 Shichun Li, 'Research on General Issues of Civil Preservation Procedure' (2005) 17 (1) Peking University Law Journal 43, 45; see also, Shichun Li, 'Studies on the Civil Securing Judgement Procedure' (PhD Thesis, China University of Political Science and Law 2002).

145 Yiqiang Fan, 'Civil Preservation Procedure' (PhD Thesis, Southwest University of Political & Science 2008) 19; see also, Shichun Li, 'Studies on the Civil Securing Judgement Procedure' (PhD Thesis, China University of Political Science and Law 2002); see also, Fuhua Wang, 'Research on Civil Preservation System' (PhD Thesis, China University of Political Science and Law 2005).

146 Yun Gu, 'Research on Preservation Procedure of Civil Litigation' (Master Thesis, Wuhan University 2005) 12.

recognised in legal practice for the last few years in China in spite of the academic debates concerning the preservation measures and the actual meaning of the preservation procedure that would govern preservation measures.

Evolution of Property Preservation Measures – The Rapid Pace Stage (2012–Present)

1.98 In the third and final stage, in 2012, major amendments/revision was made to the CPL 1991. These were the first major amendments/revisions made in a real sense after the CPL was promulgated in 1991. In this context, the civil preservation procedures governing the regime of preservation measures was also revised and enriched thoroughly. It is generally acknowledged that the revision of the preservation procedure regime through the 2012 amendments adopted the good features of other jurisdictions such as the system of injunctions available in England & Wales and the provisional measures system in Germany.[147]

1.99 The several significant improvements in the 2012 amendments to the CPL 1991 brought in for the first time relevant procedural code for behaviour preservation measures in China. These days, the parties can apply for behaviour preservation measures in all kinds of legal disputes.[148] Additionally, in these revisions and amendments, well-defined clarity was provided for preservation procedures that govern the applications seeking evidence preservation measures. In accordance with Article 81 of the CPL 2012, it was made crystal clear that the civil procedure regime governing preservation of evidence measures will be similar to that of other property and behaviour preservation measures.[149] Prior to 2012, the preservation of evidence measures in the CPL were simply a provision on its own.[150] Accordingly, the CPL 2012 ended the academic debate as discussed in the preceding paragraphs, and the unified preservation procedure regime was enacted to govern all preservation measures.

---

147 Xuan Li, 'The Revision of The Civil Procedure Law: From a Practitioner Perspective' (2011) 5 Journal of National Prosecutors College 51, 51; see also, Pengchao Ding, 'A Study on the System of Civil Pretrial Evidence Preservation' (2015) 6 Journal of Henan University of Economics and Law 113, 113.

148 The CPL 2012 amendment, Articles 100 provides that "*the people's court may*, upon the request of the other party, make an order to preserve the property or order the party to do or not to do something".

149 The CPL 2012 amendment, Article 81 provides that "With regard to other procedures for the preservation of evidence, the relevant provisions of *Chapter 9 entitled 'Preservation'* herein shall apply as a reference" [emphasis added].

150 The CPL 1991/2007, Article 74 provides that "Under circumstances where there is a likelihood that evidence may be destroyed or lost, or difficult to obtain later, the participants in the proceedings may apply to the people's court for preservation of the evidence. The people's court may also on its own initiative take measures to preserve such evidence".

1.100 Apart from the clarification of the meaning of behaviour and evidence preservations, the CPL 2012, as compared with the CPL 1991/2007, has also immensely expanded the relevance of the preservation measures in China. For example, the CPL 1991/2007, simply provided that the litigants are entitled to apply to the courts to seek evidence preservation measures. Since the term "litigant" was only employed during the litigation proceedings, it was generally accepted in legal practice in China that the parties to disputes were not entitled to apply to the courts for such preservation measures before their cases were accepted by the court docking system.[151] However, now, with the new 2012 amendments to the CPL 1991, the newly amended codes certainly grant the rights to parties to apply to courts for pre-action evidence preservation measures.

SPC's Interpretations and Local Courts' Guidance Documents

1.101 Along with the thorough amendment of the civil preservation procedure in the CPL 2012, the Supreme People's Court has also issued judicial interpretation to guide stakeholders in China. The SPC's judicial interpretation is also complemented by local interpretations and guidance issued by the local courts in different provinces of China.[152] For example, Provisions effective throughout China – *Provisions of the Supreme People's Court on Several Issues Concerning the Handling of Property Preservation Cases by the People's Courts 2016*.[153] In addition, the local courts in the various provinces of China can also issue local interpretations of the Code to address any gaps that still exist even after country-wide guidance and provisions from the SPC.[154]

1.102 However, these local courts' interpretations and guidance are applicable only in the lower courts of the provinces, where the guidance and

151 Pengchao Ding, "A Study on the System of Civil Pretrial Evidence Preservation" (2015) 6 Journal of Henan University of Economics and Law 113, 114; see also, Lingzhang Kong, 'Pretrial Evidence Preservation: By Reference of German Independent Evidence Collection Procedure' (2011) 33 (3) Modern Law Science 124, 125.

152 The legal effect and status of the judicial interpretation and the local legal guidance will be discussed in Chapter 3, 3.16–3.21 (judicial interpretations and other judicial documents).

153 *Provisions of the Supreme People's Court on Several Issues Concerning the Handling of Property Preservation Cases by the People's Courts 2016* (Fa Shi [2016] No 22); another recent example is *Provisions of the Supreme People's Court on Several Issues Concerning the Application of Law in Cases Involving the Review of Behaviour Preservation in Intellectual Property Disputes* (Fa Shi [2018] No 21).

154 For example, *Some Provisions of the Beijing High People's Court on Property Preservation During the Case-Filing Procedure* (Jing Gao Fa Fa [2012] No 405); see also, *Provisions of the Shanghai High People's Court on Property Preservation (2017 amendment)* (Hu Gao Fa (Shen) [2014] No 3); see also, *Opinions of Guangdong High People's Court on Protecting Legal Interests of Private Enterprises and Standardizing Property Preservation 2019*; in addition, it must be emphasised that other lower courts, such as the intermediate people's court and the basic people's court, will also issue their own local courts guidance or guidelines in the context of the preservation measures. For further discussion on the tiers of the Chinese court system, refer to Chapter 3, 3.26–3.31.

interpretations have in fact originated. As a result, there is a strong possibility of divergent procedural practices governing preservation measures in the courts of different provinces.[155] These divergent practices will hugely impact on lawyers' practice in China. There have been further attempts to improve the CPL 1991 through regular amendments. Therefore, the authors will refer to "CPL 1991 (as amended until 2020)".

1.103 Unlike the hundreds of years of history of common law, the history of the Chinese legal system is relatively new, but to its credit, it has incorporated many novel ideas from around the world into its legal system. It is important to note, particularly for readers from common law jurisdictions, that there is still no term "injunction" in the terminology of Chinese procedural law.

Preservation Measures and Arbitration in China

1.104 Even before the advent of the new amendment to CPL 1991 (as revised in 2012) introducing the unambiguous preservation measures in the civil procedure system of China, the Arbitration Law of the People's Republic of China 1995[156] had already introduced provisions for seeking interim measures. In addition, the Chinese arbitral institutions, such as *CEITAC*,[157] had also introduced provisions for seeking interim measures in their rules, for example, its Article 23 of its 2015 Rules published on 4 November 2014.[158] The *China (Shanghai) Pilot Free Trade Zone Arbitration Rules*, published on 1 May 2014, contains a separate chapter on the procedures required to seek interim measures. However, in China, the arbitrators still have to request the assistance of the courts to seek preservation measures rather than depending on the arbitrators' order to seek and enforce preservation measures.[159] The authors have discussed the detailed rules of preservation measures in the context of arbitration in Part 2, Chapter 4a of the book.

Closing Remark on the Introduction of Preservation Measures in China

1.105 The above developments in preservation measures have highlighted that there was an appreciation and to some extent there has been realisation in the legal sector of China that the role of preservation measures in assisting

155 The examination of divergent practice in the context of preservation measures can be found in the forthcoming Chapters 3, 6, 8 and 10.

156 The Arbitration Law came into effect in 1995, and the latest amendment to it was introduced in 2017. The authors have incorporated even any minor amendments to this Law up to September 2021.

157 CIETAC is a famous arbitral institution in China. The arbitration rules in the context of preservation measures are discussed in Part 2, Chapter 4a of the book.

158 ibid.

159 See generally, Part 2, Chapter 4a.

parties engaged in civil litigation or arbitration is very important. Slowly after mid-2013, there has been a noticeable steady increase in the number of applications seeking preservation measures in the area of intellectual property cases. This trend is assisted by the Chinese courts' willingness to grant preservation measures provided the claimants can prove the high likelihood of success in a future civil trial, irreparable harm, that they can furnish security, that the likelihood of harm or loss is high to the applicants due to the defendants' conduct and lastly that any grant of the preservation order will not prejudice the public interest.[160]

Other Issues with Interim Measures

Interim Remedies as Commercial Litigation Tactics

1.106 In most jurisdictions, particularly in England & Wales, over the years, interim orders have become an important litigation tool in the battery of civil litigators as they are used for different tactical purposes.[161] From the discussion on the evolution of interim measures in both jurisdictions, it is clear that these have developed considerably in England & Wales as compared to China. Due to the recent origins of preservation measures, China is quickly settling the issues related to preservation measures. Furthermore, due to China's massive economy, its enlarged role in international trade and the requirement of judicial reforms, the development of the preservation measures has gained considerable pace in China. As a result, it is the authors' contention that the jurisprudence for preservation measures will develop swiftly in the near future in China.

1.107 A few examples of tactics used by the lawyers are demonstrated by scenarios such as where the parties need information from the opponents or any third parties through search orders,[162] where parties seek freezing injunctions at an appropriate time to impose commercial stress on their opponents[163] and where parties try to control the acts/omissions of the opponents.[164] Preservation measures are also employed in China as a litigation tac-

---

160 The details for obtaining such preservation orders will be discussed in Part 3, Part 4 and Part 5 of the book in Chapters 6, 8 and 10 respectively.

161 See Susan Blake, *A Practical Approach to Effective Litigation* (8th edn, Oxford University Press 2015) 388.

162 Refer to Part 5 of the book – Interim measures for Evidence – Search orders and Preservation of Evidence in England & Wales and China respectively. These interim measures are discussed in Part 5, Chapters 9 and 10.

163 Refer to Part 3 of book – Interim measures for Property – Freezing Injunction and Preservation of Property in England & Wales and China respectively. These interim measures are discussed in Part 3, Chapters 5 and 6.

164 Refer to Part 4 of book – Interim measures for Conduct– Interim Injunction and Preservation of Behaviour/Conduct in England & Wales and China respectively. These interim measures are discussed in Part 4, Chapters 7 and 8.

tic, such as the preservation of property, preservation of conduct or behaviour and preservation of evidence.

1.108 For the sake of completeness, in England & Wales, there are many other interim remedies such as the procedural remedy of obtaining summary judgments to cut the civil action short or inspection orders, interim payments or other court orders that are available pursuant to the Civil Procedure Law 1998.[165] These other interim remedies that are available in England & Wales are not discussed in this book except where the examination of them is necessary in the context of freezing injunctions, interim injunctions and search orders in Chapters 5, 7 and 9 respectively. In comparison, in order to fully comprehend the Chinese preservation system, other procedural remedies, such as advance enforcement seeking payment in advance or stopping the infringement that is available in the CPL 2012 and Chinese courts will be discussed in the Chinese section.[166]

Dispute of Facts in Interim Measures and Interim Hearings

1.109 It is important to appreciate that in the interim applications seeking interim remedies in England & Wales, the lawyers for both the applicants and the respondents along with the judges are unable to examine/evaluate the full case, witnesses and all evidence. In addition, none of the judges will have the opportunity to examine all the evidence in detail. Conversely, in full civil trials, the judges will have an opportunity to satisfy themselves of the credibility of witnesses from their demeanour and following their answers during the cross-examination. In comparison, the judges in interim hearings will have no such opportunity to go through the evidence in detail or to satisfy themselves in the usual course of hearings through cross-examination in England & Wales.[167] In a few instances, the judges can even deal with interim applications on the phone, and telephone hearings are in fact allowed under the CPR 1998.[168]

1.110 In China, on the other hand, generally speaking, there is no provision on the interim hearing procedure for preservation applications. However, the Chinese judicial interpretation provides an inquiry procedure, a procedure similar to the interim hearings, for applications seeking intellectual property behaviour preservation measures.[169] In addition, in legal practice, maritime

165 Refer to 1.70, where other interim remedies were subtly introduced.

166 Refer to Chapter 8, 8.9–8.54.

167 See *Civil Procedural Rules 1998, SI 1998/3132),* CPR r. 32.7, where judges can order cross-examination if required in certain instances even during interim hearings, and CPR r. 25.3(2). In practice, this power is very rarely exercised on an application for an interim remedy, as the court does not need to come to a concluded view on issues of fact, and will not permit the hearing to turn into a mini-trial: refer to Chapter 7, 7.39.

168 Refer to Chapter 2, 2.96.

169 Refer to Chapter 8, 8.149–8.156.

courts may organise hearings to determine whether a maritime injunction can be approved.[170]

1.111 In most interim applications, as discussed above, there is no cross-examination and therefore, all the evidence that is in written form remains untested in the courts.[171] There could be instances where the evidence is not fully presented, or is contradictory to other evidence or evidence could be essentially improbable or inconsistent. Furthermore, on one hand there could be some issues that are common to both the full civil trials and interim hearings and on other hand some issues that might be relevant only to the interim hearings. The judges need to balance these contradictions in such short interim hearings. How this balancing act is carried out by the judges in each of the jurisdictions of England & Wales and China will be discussed in detail in various chapters.

Concluding Remarks

Reasons for Comparing Interim Measures – England & Wales v China

1.112 England & Wales have traditionally been the financial centre of the world for more than a century, and a lot of modern development in the area of interim remedies has originated from here.[172] The widely accepted development of modern-day interim remedies in England & Wales happened due to the willingness of judges to exercise their discretionary power. Through the exercise of discretionary power, judges have come up with clever and innovative solutions to provide appropriate interim orders in commercial disputes. As a result, the parties to civil and commercial disputes in England & Wales are from every part of the world.

1.113 From the beginning of the 21st century, China has emerged as an economic powerhouse, and these days many international projects are financed by China. As a result, many parties in these international projects, in future, will seek preservation measures. The applicants will have to seek such preservation remedies within a system governed or influenced by the Chinese legal system. However, it is too early to decisively comment on whether the China International Commercial Court[173] or arbitration conducted with Chinese characteristics in various locations throughout the world will emerge as a favourable and reliable jurisdiction as compared to the jurisdiction of England & Wales. England & Wales as a jurisdiction wields considerable soft power around the world and its judges are respected widely.

---

170 Refer to Chapter 8, 8.157–8.158.

171 See *Civil Procedural Rules 1998, SI 1998/313*, CPR r. 23.7(2) and CPR r. 25.3(2).

172 Refer to "Evolution of Modern Interim Remedies" in 1.44–1.70.

173 A discussion on the recently established China International Commercial Court can be found in Chapter 3, 3.27 and Chapter 4a, 4.a.40–4.a.44.

1.114 Therefore, in this first of its kind book, the authors have decided to compare the concept of interim remedies with preservation measures. In fact, there is hardly any book on preservation measures available in China. One reason for thc absence of books or materials is that the preservation measures are relatively new in China, and accordingly they have not matured like the procedural interim remedies in England & Wales.

1.115 Another reason for attempting the comparative study is that these days many economic activities originate from China. Therefore, cross border litigation and arbitration lawyers acting on behalf of clients are regularly required to devise proper commercial strategy not just based on the legal steps in various jurisdictions, but also the feasibility of taking particular legal steps in those jurisdictions. These strategies are devised long before consulting any expert in a particular jurisdiction. Accordingly, the jurisdiction of China happens to be a very important jurisdiction. Mainland China also has bilateral treaties with Hong Kong (another financial centre in Asia), Macau and Taiwan, and increasingly many jurisdictions such as Singapore are more than willing to attract disputes with Chinese connections for arbitration in their locations.[174]

Arrangement of Chapters in This Book

1.116 In Part 1, there are three chapters. Chapter 2 and Chapter 3 specifically deal with the English and Chinese legal and civil procedural systems, in particular with regards to interim remedies/preservation measures. In Part 2, Chapter 4 and Chapter 4a deal with issues of interim remedies/preservation measures in respect of the arbitration in England & Wales and China respectively. Chapters 2 and 3 will be referred to regularly when examining the following:

- Part 3, Chapters 5 and 6 on freezing injunctions (England & Wales) and preservation of property (China) respectively.
- Part 4, Chapters 7 and 8 on interim injunctions (England & Wales) and behaviour preservation measures (China) respectively.
- Part 5, Chapters 9 and 10 on search orders (England & Wales) and preservation of evidence (China) respectively.

174 Refer to Chapter 3, 3.93–3.97 for applications seeking litigation preservation measures between Macau and mainland China, 3.98–3.109 for applications seeking litigation preservation measures between Hong Kong and mainland China and 3.110–3.113 for applications seeking litigation preservation measures between Taiwan and mainland China; refer also, Chapter 4a, 4.a.73–4.a.77 for applications seeking arbitration preservation measures between Macau and mainland China, 4.a.82–4.a.87 for applications seeking arbitration preservation measures between Hong Kong and mainland China and 4.a.78–4.a.81 for applications seeking arbitration preservation measures between Taiwan and mainland China.

1.117 In Parts 3, 4 and 5, the issues concerning interim remedies/preservation measures relevant to maritime disputes are also examined, but due to the limited space, there is a very limited discussion on maritime disputes. Lastly, in the final Part 6, Chapter 11 of the book, the specific interim remedies and preservation orders for both jurisdictions that were discussed in Parts 3, 4 and 5 will be compared. This will lead the authors to analyse the reasons for similarities and differences in comparable remedies in both jurisdictions, in particular in the context of invisible factors and contexts. The last chapter will attempt to be a bridge between the practice of interim remedies/preservation measures in English and Chinese courts. It will also be an attempt at academic explorations of *law in action* concerning the interim remedies/preservation measures in the English and Chinese courts. This academic exploration will also assist litigators involved in multi-jurisdiction litigation and factors that need to be considered for success.

A Small Warning for Readers

1.118 It is an appropriate time to emphasise that readers must not try to analyse the interim remedies in one jurisdiction through the lens of another jurisdiction. This means that experts from one jurisdiction should not assume that another jurisdiction will work in the same way as theirs. This is the reason why the authors have included Chapter 11 in this book. Each jurisdiction has its own legal philosophy and civil procedural philosophy, gone through its own evolution of jurisprudence and legal philosophy and culture including legal culture, traditions, customs, political philosophy, religion, civilisational norms, nuances in languages, stage of economic development, traditional power and discretionary power of judges, willingness of judges to exercise discretionary power, courts' administrative set-up and so forth. In interim remedies/preservation measures, it's the judges' discretionary power that is the primary driver in the whole process. In their own jurisdiction, lawyers without blinking their eyes can make assumptions about issues or how things will pan out in certain scenarios. However, if the same lawyers transpose their own assumptions of law and the administration of courts while ruminating about the same issues in other jurisdictions, they must be ready to face grave errors and unhappy clients.[175]

175 Refer to Chapter 11, 11.52–11.114; see also, Vivek Jain, *Insight into China through Comparative Analysis of Invisible Factors and Contexts – Common Law v. Chinese Law* (1st Edn, Notion Press 2019); see also, Vivek Jain, 'Sufficiency of Court's Pre-Judgment Power in Commercial Litigation: A Comparative Study Assessing the Law and Practice in PRC and England & Wales' (PhD Thesis, China University of Political Science and Law 2017).

CHAPTER 2

Legal System and Procedural Law in England & Wales

Sources of English Law

2.1 This work is concerned with interim remedies in the civil courts of England and Wales, and in particular the High Court, under English law. England and Wales are two of the four constituent nations of the United Kingdom.[1] Together they form one of the three legal jurisdictions within the United Kingdom, the others being Scotland and Northern Ireland, each of which has its own separate legal system.

2.2 For those not familiar with common law systems such as England and Wales, there are two main sources of English law: statutory law and judge-made law.

Statutory Law

2.3 Statutory law means legislation which has been enacted by the UK Parliament, or by another person or body to whom Parliament has delegated its legislative powers; and rules made pursuant to powers created by legislation. According to United Kingdom constitutional law, Parliament is sovereign. It has the power to legislate on any matter, and it cannot bind itself for the future. Parliament can delegate its legislative powers to government ministers or other bodies, by passing an Act of Parliament to that effect. Laws passed by Parliament itself are known as Acts of Parliament, and are sometimes described as primary legislation. They are identified by their short title and the year in which they were passed into law, e.g. the Senior Courts Act 1981.[2] Laws made under delegated legislative powers are

1 The UK, whose full name is the United Kingdom of Great Britain and Northern Ireland. Great Britain is the largest island in the British Isles, and contains the nations of England, Scotland and Wales. Ireland is the large island to the west of Great Britain, and is divided into Northern Ireland, which is part of the UK, and the Republic of Ireland, which is an independent member state of the European Union.

2 The long title of that act is "An Act to consolidate with amendments the Supreme Court of Judicature (Consolidation) Act 1925 and other enactments relating to the Senior Courts in England and Wales and the administration of justice therein; to repeal certain obsolete or unnecessary enactments so relating; to amend Part VIII of the Mental Health Act 1959, the

DOI: 10.4324/9781003000310-3

known as statutory instruments, and are referred to as delegated, secondary or subordinate legislation. English courts have no power to strike down a UK Act of Parliament, or to refuse to enforce it.[3] The validity of delegated legislation can be effectively challenged in the English courts on a limited number of bases. Current statutory law is freely available online at www.legislation.gov.uk.

Judge-Made Law

2.4 Judge-made law is of three kinds: judicial interpretation of statutory law, rules of common law and rules of equity.[4] The first category is self-explanatory: as in civilian and other types of legal systems, an important function of the English courts is to interpret statutory provisions. Inevitably, this requires the judges to fill in gaps in the legislation, and in effect to make new law. This incidental or "interstitial" judge-made law is to be contrasted with the second and third categories, which may be described as original judge-made law, and which has been developed organically by the English courts over many centuries. For historical reasons, this original judge-made law developed along two parallel tracks: the common law, which was formulated and enforced by the old courts of the King's Bench, Common Pleas and Exchequer; and equity, which was developed by the old Court of Chancery as a way to moderate some of the strictness of the common law.[5]

2.5 The distinction between courts of common law and courts of equity was abolished almost a century and a half ago,[6] and the rules of common law and equity are now administered by a single civil court system.[7] But the distinctive identities and characteristics of these two bodies of law are still very much alive. As will be seen, most of the principal interim remedies available

Courts-Martial (Appeals) Act 1968, the Arbitration Act 1979 and the law relating to county courts; and for connected purposes". Acts of Parliament are also identified as chapters of the (notional) book of statutes passed in a given calendar year. Thus, the Senior Courts Act 1981 is 1981 Chapter 54. An Act of Parliament becomes law when, having passed all the necessary stages in both Houses of the UK Parliament, it receives Royal Assent from the Queen.

3 The courts have a limited power under section 4 of the Human Rights Act 1998 to declare that a provision of a UK Act of Parliament is incompatible with rights under the European Convention on Human Rights, to which the UK is a party; but such a declaration does not affect the validity, continuing operation or enforcement of the provision to which it refers.

4 A further category may be added to this: customary international law and general principles of international law, which is judge-made inasmuch as judges declare what it is, and in that it is treated as part of English common law: *Zoernsch v Waldock* [1964] 1 WLR 675 at page 691 per Diplock LJ; *Owners of Cargo lately laden on board the Playa Larga v I Congreso del Partido* [1983] 1 AC 244.

5 See generally John McGhee QC and Steven Elliott QC, *Snell's Equity* (34th Edn, Sweet & Maxwell, 2019) Chapter 1.

6 In the Judicature Acts of 1873 and 1875.

7 Senior Courts Act 1981 s 49. In the event of a conflict between the rules of the common law and of equity, the rules of equity prevail.

under English law are equitable in origin. This has important practical consequences. Most significantly, it means that these remedies are discretionary. In other words, a person is not entitled to the remedy as of right, simply by virtue of satisfying a mechanistic legal test. Rather, the court must perform a balancing exercise in every case before deciding whether the interests of justice require it to grant the remedy, and on what terms.

2.6 A common factor in the development and importance of all judge-made English law is the doctrine of precedent (sometimes referred to by the Latin[8] expression *stare decisis*). According to this doctrine, where an English court decides a legal issue in a case before it, that decision is binding on courts lower down the judicial hierarchy (and sometimes on courts at the same level) in subsequent cases.[9] The decision itself *is* the law, unless and until overruled by a higher court or by an Act of Parliament.[10] The doctrine of precedent promotes consistency in judicial decision-making, and makes it easier for prospective litigants to predict how an English court will decide a case, by ensuring that when a legal issue has been authoritatively determined by a higher court, lower courts are obliged to follow suit. It also means that the law is constantly developing, expanding and adapting in an organic way to meet novel situations, as the courts refine and synthesise existing rules, and fashion new rules by identifying the principles which underlie the existing rules and extrapolating from those principles.

2.7 These features have allowed English law to evolve a set of detailed, flexible rules, based not on a rigid theoretical framework but on practical experience of real cases. The process involves the courts taking a large number of small, incremental, steps over a very long period of time, subjecting each new step to testing in subsequent cases, and discarding those which prove not to be fit for purpose – rather like natural selection. The ability of Parliament to control, adjust and overrule judge-made legal developments by passing legislation ensures that the process retains democratic legitimacy. One practical downside of this system is that English law is not to be found in a single codex or restatement, and it may be necessary to consult a specialist lawyer in order to find out what the law says on a particular point.

2.8 The rules of the English doctrine of precedent can be summarised as follows:[11]

---

8 English law abounds with Latin expressions such as this. Officially these are all now either banned or at least discouraged (with a few exceptions such as Admiralty proceedings *in rem*), but they are proving remarkably resilient. To make matters even more complicated, a number of important concepts in English law have Norman French names (a language which no-one has spoken for hundreds of years, and few know how to pronounce correctly). Fortunately these do not feature much in this work.

9 The structure of the English civil court system is explained below: see 2.48–2.65.

10 For this reason, the doctrine of precedent is an essential component of the common law and equity, without which those bodies of judge-made law simply could not exist.

11 See *Willers v Joyce* [2016] UKSC 44 per Lord Neuberger at [7–9].

a. Decisions of the UK Supreme Court, which is the highest appeal court in England and Wales,[12] are binding on all other courts. They are not strictly binding on the UK Supreme Court itself, but that court will normally regard itself as bound by its own previous decisions (or those of its predecessor court, the judicial committee of the House of Lords) in the interests of certainty and consistency.
b. Decisions of the Court of Appeal, which is the primary appeal court in most civil cases, are binding on the Court of Appeal itself and all courts below it in the hierarchy, but not on the UK Supreme Court.
c. Decisions of Justices of the High Court, which is the court of first instance for most important civil cases, are binding on judges of the County Court (the first instance court for less important civil cases). They are not strictly binding on other High Court judges, but should be followed unless there is a powerful reason not to do so.
d. Where a court is faced with two previous decisions of its own, which conflict with each other, it must choose which one to follow. The normal rule is that it must follow the later of the two conflicting decisions, if that was reached after full consideration of the earlier decision; but it can decline to do so if it is convinced that the later decision was wrong in not following the earlier decision.[13]
e. A court can also decline to follow an earlier decision of its own if that decision was reached *per incuriam*, i.e. in ignorance or forgetfulness of some binding judicial decision or statutory provision.[14]

2.9 Judicial decisions are binding in this way only insofar as the decision forms part of the *ratio decidendi* of the case in which it was decided, i.e. a necessary stage of the reasoning which led to the decision in the case. Where a judge expresses a concluded view on a legal issue, but that does not form part of the *ratio decidendi* of the case, it is not binding. These non-binding

12 While the UK was a member of the European Court, the UK Supreme Court and all other UK courts were bound by rulings of the Court of Justice of the European Union (CJEU) on matters of EU law, which has primacy over conflicting rules of national law of EU member states (the CJEU does not hear appeals against decisions of national courts, but decides questions of EU law which are referred to it by national courts). Following the UK's departure from the EU and the end of the Brexit implementation period on 31 December 2020, CJEU decisions decided on or before that date, on the interpretation of EU law which has been retained as part of UK domestic law, are initially binding on UK courts of first instance, but the Court of Appeal and the UK Supreme Court can choose to depart from them: European Union (Withdrawal) Act 2018, as amended by the European Union (Withdrawal Agreement) Act 2020, s 6(4)–(5); European Union (Withdrawal) Act 2018 (Relevant Court) (Retained EU Case Law) Regulations 2020, regs 3–5. CJEU decisions decided after that date are merely persuasive in relation to the interpretation of retained EU law: European Union (Withdrawal) Act 2018 (as amended) s 6(1)–(2).

13 *Colchester Estates (Cardiff) Ltd v Carlton Industries Plc* [1986] Ch 80 per Nourse J at 84F–85H.

14 *Desnousse v Newham London Borough Council* [2006] EWCA Civ 547 per Lloyd LJ at [70–75].

expressions of opinion are known as *obiter dicta*. In practice it can often be difficult to determine whether a judge's conclusions on a particular issue form part of the *ratio decidendi* of the case or are merely *obiter*.

2.10 Where a court is considering a legal issue for which there is no binding authority which it is obliged to follow, it should nevertheless have regard to any non-binding decisions and any *obiter dicta* on that issue. These non-binding authorities are described as "persuasive" authorities; the higher the court and the more eminent and respected the judge who expressed the non-binding decision or *dictum*, the more persuasive that decision will be and the more likely that another court will choose to follow it. Similarly, English judges will have regard to authorities from other common law jurisdictions, such as Australia and Canada, which are regarded as persuasive but not binding.[15] Legal textbooks and journal articles may also be treated as persuasive authority.

2.11 The doctrine of precedent only applies to decisions on issues of law. It does not apply to decisions on issues of fact, or to questions about how the court should exercise its discretion in a given factual situation. The distinction between issues of fact, law and discretion is an important one in the context of interim remedies. Before a court grants an interim remedy, it will have to be satisfied that facts exist which give it the power to grant the remedy, and that it is appropriate to grant that remedy in all the circumstances. The question whether a particular set of facts exists is, naturally, an issue of fact, which depends on the evidence placed before the court. The question whether those facts satisfy the legal requirements for granting interim relief is an issue of law. The question whether it is appropriate to grant the interim remedy in all the circumstances is an issue of discretion, although the question of which principles govern the exercise of that discretion is an issue of law.

2.12 Judge-made law is to be found in the official judgments handed down by the courts when they decide cases. Judgments contain not only the substance of the decision, but also the reasoning that led the court to that decision. They often include a detailed discussion of the facts, and of the legal arguments raised by the parties to the dispute. As a result, they are often substantially longer than judgments given by courts in jurisdictions which do not follow the common law tradition. They are nevertheless often rather easier to comprehend, as English judges strive (not always successfully) to use ordinary, non-technical language which can be understood by non-lawyers.

2.13 Judgments are primarily identified by the names of the parties involved, in the following format: Claimant (or Applicant or, in the case of an

15 The most persuasive type judgments of all are decisions of the Judicial Committee of the Privy Council, which is the highest court of appeal for a number of independent Commonwealth nations, along with certain Crown Dependencies and British Overseas Territories. The majority of the judges are sitting Justices of the UK Supreme Court.

appeal, Appellant) v. Defendant (or Respondent).[16] A standardised system of citation of judgments has been in place since 2001,[17] consisting of the year the judgment was given, a code identifying the court which gave the judgment (including, where applicable, the relevant division of the court) and a case reference number. So, for example, the judgment of the High Court, Chancery Division in a claim by Paul Atkinson against Sanjiv Varma in July 2020 is cited as *Atkinson v Varma* [2020] EWHC 1868 (Ch), which means judgment number 1868 given by the High Court of Justice of England and Wales, Chancery Division, in 2020. The judgment of the Court of Appeal, Civil Division, in Mr Varma's appeal from that judgment, is cited as *Varma v Atkinson* [2020] EWCA Civ 1692, which means judgment number 1692 decided by the Court of Appeal of England and Wales, Civil Division, in 2020.

2.14 Modern judgments are written in numbered paragraphs. When cited, paragraph numbers are placed in square brackets: thus paragraph 57 of the judgment of Lady Justice Rose in the Court of Appeal in Mr Varma's appeal would be cited as *Varma v Atkinson* [2020] EWCA Civ 1692 at [57] per Rose LJ.[18]

2.15 Many judgments are now available online for free at www.bailii.org, an open-source website maintained by the Institute of Advanced Legal Studies, part of the University of London.[19] All decisions rendered by the UK Supreme Court since its establishment in 2009 are freely available at

---

16 See 2.29–2.31 below for an explanation of the terms Claimant, Defendant, Appellant and Respondent.

17 Practice Direction (Judgments: Form and Citation) [2001] 1 WLR 194; see also Practice Direction (Supreme Court: Judgments: Neutral Citations) [2002] 1 WLR 346.

18 The letters LJ after a judge's name mean Lord Justice or Lady Justice, denoting a judge of the Court of Appeal (plural LJJ). The letter J means Mr(s) Justice, a (senior) High Court judge who deals with more complex and difficult cases. The title Master before the name of a judge means that (s)he is a Master, a junior judge of the High Court who deals mainly with procedural matters (in the Admiralty Court the title Admiralty Registrar is used instead of Master). JSC means Justice of the Supreme Court. HHJ means His Honour Judge, denoting a Circuit Judge, a senior judge of the County Court (or a senior judge hearing criminal cases in the Crown Court). DJ means District Judge, a junior judge of the County Court (or a junior court hearing criminal cases in the Magistrates' Court). Circuit Judges and District Judges may also sit as judges in local branches of the High Court situated outside London, known as District Registries. Certain senior judges occupying specific posts in the judicial hierarchy have individual titles, denoted by specific letters after their names: the Lord Chief Justice, who is the head of the judiciary and president of the courts of England and Wales, is LCJ; the Master of the Rolls, who is the head of the Court of Appeal, is MR; the Chancellor of the High Court, who is president of the Chancery Division, is CHC (until recently he was known as the Vice-Chancellor (VC)); and the Presidents of the Queen's Bench Division and the Family Division of the High Court are PQBD and PFD respectively. Cases in the High Court are sometimes heard by part-time judges, known as deputy High Court Judges, who are invariably practicing lawyers (barristers or solicitors): in their judgments they appear simply by their names, followed by the letters QC if they have attained the rank of Queen's Counsel.

19 Similar online services exist covering judicial decisions in other parts of the common law world: AfricanLII, AsianLII, AustLII, CanLII, CommonLII, HKLII, NZLII, PacLII, SAFLII and WorldLII. The original version, focusing on US law, is Cornell Law School's Legal Information Institute.

www.supremecourt.uk. From April 2022, a new official online depository of English court and tribunal judgments will be available via the National Archives.

2.16 Most significant judgments are also published in one or more periodicals known as law reports, most of which are available online on subscription services. Prior to 2002, law reports were the primary resource for finding judge-made law. There are four "official" law reports, produced by a not-for-profit organisation called the Incorporated Council of Law Reporting for England and Wales: the Appeal Cases (abbreviated to as AC), the Queen's Bench Reports (QB), the Chancery Reports (Ch) and the Family Reports (Fam). Other well-known law reports include the Weekly Law Reports (WLR) and the All England Law Reports (All ER), which are generalist publications. There are also numerous specialist series such as Lloyd's Law Reports (Lloyd's Rep) which deals with shipping and commercial cases; the Building Law Reports (BLR); the Intellectual Property Law Reports (IPLR), etc.

2.17 Typically, the report of a judgment in these law reports follows the same basic format. First the report identifies the court, the judge(s), the parties and their roles in the proceedings (Claimant, Defendant, etc.), the lawyers who represented each party, the date of the hearing and the date of the judgment. Next it sets out a short summary of the key facts and of the decision. This summary is known as the Headnote. Then the report lists all the statutes and caselaw cited in the judgment (and sometimes any other caselaw which was referred to at the hearing). There is often an additional section explaining the procedural background to the hearing. Finally comes the text of the judgment itself. It is important to remember that the Headnote, while useful as an introduction and summary, is nothing more than a précis written by the editors of the law report. It may not be accurate. It is certainly not an authoritative source of law. Only the text of the judgment itself has that status.

International Conventions

2.18 International conventions and treaties to which the UK is a party do not automatically become part of English law. They must first be expressly incorporated into English law by means of an Act of Parliament or by valid delegated legislation.[20] Incorporation may be direct, by legislation which simply incorporates the international convention by reference; or indirect, by

20 In the language of international legal theory, the UK is a dualist jurisdiction. Note that the rules contained in some international treaties may also form part of English law without express incorporation, where they belong to the body of internationally accepted customary international law and hence part of English common law, e.g. certain provisions of the Vienna Convention on Diplomatic Relations 1961: *Al-Malki v Reyes* [2017] UKSC 61 per Lord Sumption JSC at [6].

legislation which gives effect to the substance of the international convention by reproducing its provisions, more or less faithfully.[21]

2.19 European Union law was until recently part of English law by direct incorporation, through the European Communities Act 1972 and subsequent UK statutes. These statutes not only incorporated existing EU law into domestic UK law, but also delegated to the EU law-making bodies the power to make new EU law, which would automatically become binding in the UK and take precedence over other domestic UK law.[22] During the UK's membership of the EU, two important instruments in the field of civil litigation – the Brussels Regulation Recast and the 2007 Lugano Convention[23] – were directly incorporated into English law by this mechanism.[24] These instruments deal with the allocation of jurisdiction between the courts of the EU and EFTA member states, and the enforcement of judgments given by those courts, in civil and commercial matters. They contain specific rules on the granting by the courts of one member state of certain interim remedies – "provisional and protective measures" – in support of civil proceedings in another member state.[25] Since the UK's departure from the EU and the end of the Brexit transition period on 31 December 2020 these instruments no longer form part of English law.[26] The UK has, however, applied to rejoin the 2007 Lugano Convention as an independent contracting state, and has enacted legislation giving the government the power to reincorporate that convention into UK law if and when that application is granted. It has also

21 The 1957 Convention on the Arrest of Ships, which governs the detention of a ship by judicial process to secure a maritime claim, is an example of an international convention whose terms have been incorporated into English law indirectly, in sections 20–24 of the Senior Courts Act 1981.

22 R (Factortame Ltd) v Secretary of State for Transport (No.2) [1991] AC 603.

23 The Brussels Regulation Recast was directly applicable in the UK as an EU regulation. The 2007 Lugano Convention was incorporated by reference into UK law by section 3A of the Civil Jurisdiction & Judgments Act 1982, as amended.

24 The UK also enacted domestic legislation to supplement these instruments and to ensure their effective operation: Civil Jurisdiction & Judgments Act 1982, as amended.

25 The UK is also a party to the Hague Convention on Choice of Court Agreements 2005 (and has incorporated it into domestic law by section 1 of the Private International Law (Implementation Agreements) Act 2020), to which the EU, Denmark, Mexico, Montenegro and Singapore are parties, but Article 7 of that convention expressly excludes interim measures of protection from its scope.

26 They were revoked by sections 2 and 3 of the Civil Jurisdiction and Judgments (Amendment) (EU Exit) Regulations 2019, SI 2019/479, made pursuant to section 8 of the European Union (Withdrawal) Act 2018. The UK has applied to rejoin the 2007 Lugano Convention as an independent state (the UK was a party to that convention by reason of its membership of the EU, pursuant to Article 216(2) of the Treaty on the Functioning of the European Union (TFEU), one of the two treaties which currently form the constitutional basis of the European Union (the other being the Treaty on European Union (TEU)), and has already enacted legislation giving the government the power to reincorporate that convention into UK law: the Private International Law (Implementation Agreements) Act 2020 section 2.

retained certain aspects of the "Brussels regime" in its domestic jurisdictional rules.[27]

Key Statutes on Interim Remedies

2.20 The key statutes in the field of interim remedies are the Senior Courts Act 1981,[28] the Civil Jurisdiction and Judgments Act 1982, the Civil Procedure Act 1997 and the Arbitration Act 1996.

2.21 The Senior Courts Act 1981 sets out the subject-matter jurisdiction[29] of the High Court[30] and the Court of Appeal in civil matters. The most important provision of the Act is section 37.

a. Section 37 states the power of the English Court[31] to grant injunctions, including interim injunctions, and to appoint receivers.[32] Interim injunctions are the most important, and most fundamental, type of interim remedy available under English law. An injunction is a court order prohibiting a person from doing something (a "negative" or "prohibitory" injunction) or requiring a person to do something (a "positive" or "mandatory" injunction).[33] An interim injunction is an injunction granted at a stage of the proceedings when the full facts are not yet known and when the merits of the substantive dispute between the parties have not yet been finally determined. Like all other interim remedies, it is essentially temporary and provisional in its nature and effect. Interim injunctions are often granted for a specified period of time, or until the happening of a specified event. A number of other interim remedies available in the English courts, which go by different names, are specialised forms of interim injunction, the most obvious example being the freezing injunction, which prohibits a person from dissipating assets

---

27 See 2.76–2.78 below.

28 As amended by the Constitutional Reform Act 2005. These amendments included changing the name of the act from the Supreme Court Act 1981 to the Senior Courts Act 1981.

29 I.e. what matters the court can decide, and what remedies it can grant: see generally Nigel Meeson and John A Kimbell, *Admiralty Jurisdiction and Practice* (5th Edn, Informa Law from Routledge, 2017) Chapter 2. The expression "subject-matter jurisdiction" is sometimes used in a different sense: see 2.70 below.

30 The County Court, which is the court of first instance for lower value civil claims, is covered by a separate statute, the County Courts Act 1984. A number of specialist statutory tribunals, dealing with certain very specific categories of case, exist outside the normal civil court structure – see paragraphs 2.48–2.49 below. They are governed by different statutes.

31 Section 37 confirms the High Court's power to grant injunctions, but it is not the source of that power, which derives from the historical powers of the old Chancery courts: *Fourie v Le Roux* [2007] UKHL 1 at [25].

32 See 2.45 below.

33 See the Glossary to the Civil Procedure Rules.

so as to frustrate the enforcement of a potential judgment against him.

b. Section 37 also gives the Court the power to make any ancillary orders it considers necessary, for the purpose of ensuring that any interim injunction it grants will be effective.[34] A common example is an order requiring a party to provide information about relevant property or assets which are or may become the subject of a freezing injunction.[35] Ancillary orders of this type are usually treated as a separate type of interim remedy; but where an ancillary order requires a person to do something (such as provide information about relevant property), as is invariably the case, it can also be viewed as an interim injunction in its own right.[36]

2.22 Other important provisions of the Senior Courts Act 1981 include:

a. Sections 20–24, which set out the Admiralty jurisdiction[37] of the English Court. This includes the power to entertain proceedings *in rem* – literally "against the thing" (i.e. the ship) – where in form, if not in substance,[38] the proceedings are brought against the ship itself rather than against her owners or other persons who may be legally liable on the claim. Proceeding *in rem* brings with it the power to arrest the ship or other property proceeded against within England and Wales and their territorial waters.

b. Sections 33–35 of the Act, which give the English Court the power to grant certain interim remedies before court proceedings have been formally commenced, and against persons who are not parties to the court proceedings.[39]

---

34 *A J Bekhor & Co Ltd v Bilton* [1981] QB 923; *Maclaine Watson & Co Ltd v International Tin Council* (No.2) [1987] 1 WLR 1171. The power to grant ancillary orders, although not expressed in section 37, is inherent in the express power to grant injunctions.

35 See CPR 25.1(1)(g).

36 *Gidrxslme Shipping Co Ltd v Tantomar-transportes Maritimos Lda* [1995] 1 WLR 299 at page 309 (Colman J).

37 I.e. the power of the English Court to hear and to determine cases involving particular types of claim arising in connection with ships and the sea, and the remedies the English Court may grant in such cases.

38 Nigel Meeson and John A Kimbell, *Admiralty Jurisdiction and Practice* (5th Edn, Informa Law from Routledge, 2017) make a compelling case at §§3.2–3.17 that there are in fact two categories of *in rem* claim under English law: true *in rem* claims, where the claim is to enforce a maritime lien (a special type of security interest over the ship which arises automatically by operation of Admiralty law); and *quasi in rem* claims, where the claimant merely has a statutory right to bring a claim against the ship, and where the commencement of *in rem* proceedings creates a security interest (a "statutory lien") over the ship to secure that claim. They argue that a true *in rem* claim is in substance a claim against the ship; whereas a *quasi in rem* claim is in substance a claim against the person who owns the ship at the time when the proceedings are commenced.

39 Sections 33–35; see also section 8 of the Civil Procedure Act 1997, as amended by the Constitutional Reform Act 2005. See further 2.29–2.30 and 2.89–2.93 below.

2.23 Section 25 of the Civil Jurisdiction and Judgments Act 1982 gives the English court jurisdiction to grant many types of interim relief (but excluding warrants for the arrest of property or provisions for obtaining evidence), in support of substantive proceedings which have been, or are to be, commenced in a foreign court.[40]

2.24 The Civil Procedure Act 1997 introduced important reforms to English civil procedure. It created a body known as the Civil Procedure Rules Committee, and delegated to it the general power to make and amend rules governing the procedure to be followed in English civil courts, and to issue official practice directions to supplement those rules. The rules of court made under the Civil Procedure Act 1997 are known as the Civil Procedure Rules (CPR).[41] The CPR are of central importance to the availability of interim remedies in the English courts and are examined in more detail below. In addition:

a. Section 7 of the Civil Procedure Act 1997 codifies the power of the English Court to grant search orders requiring a party to allow another party to enter premises for the purpose of preserving evidence and property.[42]
b. Section 8 of that Act enlarges the power of the court to order disclosure of documents before the commencement of proceedings.

2.25 Section 44 of the Arbitration Act 1996 sets out the powers of the English Court to grant interim remedies in support of arbitration proceedings.[43] Those powers are restricted to making orders about the taking of evidence of

---

40 The text of section 25(1) itself only gives the English Court a limited power to do so, restricted to proceedings in Scotland, Northern Ireland and contracting states to the 2005 Hague Convention on Choice of Court Agreements (the EU, Denmark, Mexico, Montenegro and Singapore), and to proceedings whose subject-matter is within the scope of the Hague Convention 2005 as defined by Articles 1 and 2 thereof. Section 25(3) empowers the UK government to remove those limitations and expand the scope of the power. It exercised that power by making the Civil Jurisdiction and Judgments Act 1982) Interim Relief Order, SI 1997/302. The jurisdiction conferred by section 25 is subject to a rule of principled discretion, in subsection 25(2), that the Court may refuse to grant interim relief if it considers it inexpedient to do so by reason of the fact that it would not otherwise have jurisdiction in relation to the subject-matter of the proceedings. The meaning of this provision has been elucidated in a number of judgments: see 2.72(a) below.

41 Most, but not all, of the rules in the CPR are made pursuant to the rule-making powers in the Civil Procedure Act 1997. Some of the rules are made under other statutes, including the Torts (Interference with Goods) Act 1977, the Limitation Act 1980, the Senior Courts Act 1981, the Civil Jurisdiction and Judgments Act 1982 and the Access to Justice Act 1999.

42 Formerly known as Anton Piller orders after the Court of Appeal decision which confirmed that the Court had jurisdiction to grant them: *Anton Piller KG v Manufacturing Processes Ltd* [1976] Ch 55.

43 See also section 9, which empowers the English court to stay proceedings before it brought in breach of an arbitration agreement (see 2.45 below). Section 44 of the Arbitration Act 1996 only applies where there are actual or intended arbitration proceedings: *AES Ust-Kamenogorsk Hydropower Plant LLP v Ust-Kamenogorsk Hydropower Plant JSC* [2013] UKSC 35 per Lord Mance JSC at [40].

witnesses, the preservation of evidence, orders relating to property to which the arbitral proceedings relate (inspection, photographing, preservation, custody or detention, sampling and experimentation), ordering the sale of goods which are the subject of the proceedings and granting of an interim injunction or the appointment of a receiver. The section also sets out the (strictly limited) circumstances in which the Court may exercise those powers.[44] These restrictions and limitations reflect the policies of party autonomy and judicial non-interference which underpin the Arbitration Act 1996.[45]

The Civil Procedure Rules (CPR)

2.26 The Civil Procedure Rules apply to all civil proceedings in the English High Court, County Court[46] and Court of Appeal,[47] with the exception of insolvency proceedings, family proceedings and a few other specialist types of proceedings, which have their own rules.[48]

2.27 The CPR are divided into some 90 Parts,[49] most of which are supplemented by one or more official Practice Directions (CPR PDs). The Rules and Practice Directions are regularly revised. A definitive up-to-date version of the CPR and CPR PDs, together with current versions of the official Court Guides which give a narrative account of the practice and procedures followed by specialist courts and lists (such as the Commercial Court Guide), and a wealth of other information about the English judicial system, can be accessed online at www.judiciary.uk/you-and-the-judiciary/going-to-court/high-court/.

2.28 Before considering the provisions of the CPR of most importance to interim remedies, it is worth stating some basics of English civil procedure in cases where the CPR apply,[50] including some important terminology of relevance to interim remedies.

---

44 See 2.72(b)–(c) below.

45 See section 1 of the Act, entitled "General principles".

46 The County Court is the court of first instance for lower value civil cases.

47 The UK Supreme Court has its own rules: the Supreme Court Rules 2009 (not to be confused with the Rules of the Supreme Court, which were the civil procedural rules for the High Court and Court of Appeal prior to 1999 when they were replaced by the CPR), available online at www.supremecourt.uk/docs/uksc_rules_2009.pdf. It also has its own Practice Directions, which can be found at www.supremecourt.uk/procedures/practice-directions.html.

48 CPR 2.1(2). A number of specialist statutory tribunals exist outside the main civil court structure. These include the Employment Tribunal, the Immigration and Appeals Tribunal, the General Regulatory Chamber, the Tax Chamber and the Upper Tribunal which hears first appeals from these first-tier tribunals (appeals from the Upper Tribunal are heard by the Court of Appeal). These statutory tribunals have exclusive jurisdiction to determine cases involving specific subject-matter (e.g., in the case of the Employment Tribunal, claims by employees for unfair dismissal from employment, unlawful discrimination in relation to employment, unfair deductions from pay, etc.). They have limited powers compared with the High Court and apply their own procedural rules.

49 The precise number changes from time to time as the CPR are amended.

50 I.e. all claims in the High Court and County Court excluding insolvency proceedings, family proceedings and the other types of proceedings set out in CPR 2.1.

Civil Procedure Basics

2.29 English civil proceedings are formally commenced when the court issues a formal document referred to as "originating process", at the request of the person commencing the proceedings. In most cases, the document which serves as originating process is a Claim Form,[51] which identifies the parties and contains a concise statement of the nature of the claim which is being made and specifies the remedy which is being sought in the proceedings. The person who brings the claim and issues the Claim Form is the Claimant,[52] and the person against whom the claim is brought is the Defendant.[53] Together, they are described as parties[54] to the proceedings.[55] There may be multiple Claimants and Defendants in a single set of proceedings. The Defendant may in turn bring a cross-claim against the Claimant, called a counterclaim; and in certain circumstances, the Claimant and the Defendant may also join in additional parties and make claims against them.[56]

2.30 A party may apply to the court for an order during the course of proceedings or, in certain circumstances, even before proceedings have been formally commenced. The party making the application is the Applicant, and the party against whom the order is sought is the Respondent.[57] Applications are generally made by filing a document called an Application Notice,[58] setting out the order sought and brief reasons why it is sought, and serving it on the Respondent;[59] but the court may permit an application to be made without

---

51 Prior to the introduction of the CPR, the equivalent documents were the Writ of Summons, the Originating Summons and the Originating Notice of Motion. There are a few exceptions to the general rule that proceedings are commenced by a Claim Form. The most important, in the context of interim remedies, are where the final relief sought in the English proceedings is an order under section 33 of the Senior Courts Act 1981 for disclosure or inspection before a substantive claim has been commenced: CPR 25.4(1)(b). CPR 25.4(1)(a) provides that a claim for an interim remedy in support of foreign proceedings under section 25 of the Civil Jurisdiction and Judgments Act 1982 must also be commenced by Application Notice; but this does not apply in the Commercial Court (Commercial Court Guide §F15.15). See also footnote 118 below.

52 Prior to the introduction of the CPR, the person bringing the claim was called the Plaintiff. Where a different type of document serves as the originating process, the person bringing the claim may be described by a different title: thus, were an Application Notice serves as the originating process, the person bringing the claim is the Applicant.

53 Where the originating process is not a Claim Form, the person against whom the claim is brought may be differently described: thus where the originating process is an Application Notice, he is described as the Respondent.

54 There may also be additional parties: see CPR Part 20.

55 Or "to the claim". The word "claim" may be used to mean either the claim which is made in the proceedings, or the proceedings themselves.

56 See CPR Part 20.

57 CPR 23.1.

58 Prior to the introduction of the CPR, the equivalent documents were the Summons and the Notice of Motion. In claims for certain specific types of interim remedy, the Application Notice serves as the originating process: see footnote 51 above.

59 CPR 23.6–7.

notice in certain circumstances, such as where there is a need for secrecy or urgency.

2.31 A party may be entitled to bring an appeal to a higher court against a decision made by a lower court. The party bringing the appeal is the Appellant, and the party resisting the appeal is the Respondent. An appeal is treated as a separate set of proceedings for most purposes.

2.32 Court fees are payable at certain key stages of proceedings, including upon issue of a Claim Form, filing an Application Notice and filing a notice of appeal. Details are set out in Schedule 1 to the Civil Proceedings Fees Order 2008.[60]

2.33 A typical set of civil proceedings in the English High Court will often, but by no means always, involve some or all of the following stages:

a. Issue of the Claim Form by the Claimant.
b. Service of the Claim Form on the Defendant.
c. Acknowledgement of service by the Defendant.
d. Sequential service of statements of case, starting with the Claimant's Particulars of Claim, followed by the Defendant's Defence (which may include a Counterclaim), followed by the Claimant's Reply (and Defence to Counterclaim).
e. A Costs and Case Management Conference (CCMC) is held, at which the Court gives directions for the further conduct of the case.
f. The parties give disclosure of relevant documents.
g. The parties exchange written statements written by the witnesses of fact on which they rely.
h. The parties exchange written reports prepared by expert witnesses which the Court has permitted them to rely upon.
i. Trial, at which the factual and expert witnesses give oral evidence and are cross-examined on their testimony, and the parties' lawyers present their submissions on the facts and the law.
j. The Court gives judgment and makes orders about who shall bear the costs of the proceedings.
k. One or more parties may seek permission to appeal the judgment to the Court of Appeal.

Terminology: Interim, Interlocutory and Final

2.34 In order to properly understand the role of interim remedies in English law, it is important to distinguish between the expressions interim and interlocutory, and between each of those terms and the word final. Correctly used, "interim" refers to the *nature and effect* of a remedy; "interlocutory" refers to

60 SI 2008/1053.

a *stage of the proceedings*; and "final" can refer to either the nature and effect of a remedy or a procedural stage (or indeed both things at once), depending on the context.

2.35 The word "interim" literally means "temporary" or "in the meantime". It is not a term of art in English law; nor is the expression "interim remedy".[61] Its essential meaning is nevertheless clear. An interim remedy is a remedy which is only *temporary and provisional* in its nature and effect. It is to be contrasted with one which is final, in the sense of binding and conclusive in its nature and effect. A judicial decision is said to be final in this sense, if it finally and conclusively determines a substantive dispute between the parties – i.e. a claim by one party to enforce a cause of action[62] arising out of an alleged invasion, actual or threatened, of his legal or equitable rights,[63] or for a declaration of those rights – in a way which leaves nothing to be judicially determined in order to render the resulting order effective and capable of enforcement.[64] A judgment which embodies a conclusive, binding decision, and an order which gives effect to it, are similarly described as final in this sense.

2.36 A decision which is final in this sense gives rise to an estoppel *per rem judicatam* under English law – a legal bar which prevents the same parties[65] from relitigating the dispute that was the subject of the decision, or from challenging the court's conclusions on any matters which were necessarily determined in reaching that decision.

2.37 An interim order, by contrast, only involves the court making, at most, a temporary and provisional determination of a dispute, and does not bar the parties from continuing to litigate that dispute thereafter. Thus, where the court grants an interim injunction restraining the Defendant from committing an allegedly tortious act, pending final determination of the Claimant's claim for a final injunction permanently restraining the Defendant from committing the same act, the court's decision to grant the interim injunction does not involve a binding and conclusive decision that the act complained of is tortious, and the Defendant may continue to dispute that issue right up to final judgment.

---

61 See e.g. Civil Procedure (2020) note 25.1.5: "The expression 'interim remedy' is not a term of art and doubts may arise as to whether or not a particular power of the court is properly described as such".

62 A cause of action means all the facts which the claimant would have to prove (assuming that the Defendant did not admit them) in order to establish his right to the judgment of the court: *Coburn v Colledge* [1897] 1 QB 702 at page 706 per Lord Esher MR.

63 *The Siskina* [1979] AC 210 at pages 255–256 per Lord Diplock.

64 Subject only to the possibility of an appeal to a higher court or, in the case of an order obtained by default, to the possibility of order being set aside or varied on the grounds that it was obtained by default. See generally Hodge M Malek QC, *Phipson on Evidence* (19th Edn, Sweet & Maxwell, 2017) §§43-23 to 43-33.

65 Or their "privies" – persons with a relevant connection to one of the parties – see Hodge M Malek QC, *Phipson on Evidence* (19th Edn, Sweet & Maxwell, 2017) §43-23. The parties and their privies are bound as between themselves, but not normally as against no third parties.

2.38 The temporary and provisional nature of interim remedies reflects the fact that these remedies are most often sought at a stage where the court is in no position to form any more than a preliminary and tentative view of the merits of the substantive dispute. They are not granted in order to determine and give effect to the parties' substantive rights and obligations: that is usually a task for a later stage, when all of the relevant evidence has been gathered, placed before the court and tested at trial by oral cross-examination. Rather, they are granted in order to improve the chances of the court being able to do justice after a subsequent determination of the merits at trial.[66] The primary consideration on an application for a discretionary interim remedy, therefore, is whether granting or withholding the remedy is more likely to produce a just result in the end. The court grants interim remedies in order to mitigate the risk of injustice to the Applicant arising from the fact that the merits of substantive dispute will not be finally determined until a later date; but there is equally a need to mitigate the risk of injustice to the Respondent from being on the receiving end of an interim remedy, in circumstances when he may later be held not to be liable on the merits; and to that end it is important not to prejudge the merits.[67] This calculus can be seen most clearly in relation to interim injunctions governed by the principles in the case of *American Cyanamid Co v Ethicon Ltd*,[68] where the key criterion for the granting or refusal of relief is where, based on the incomplete evidential picture available at the time, the so-called "balance of convenience" lies.[69]

2.39 "Interlocutory" literally means "between hearings".[70] It is a somewhat dated expression. It does not feature at all in the CPR or the CPR PD. It nevertheless remains important, as it appears in a number of current

---

66 *National Commercial Bank Jamaica Ltd v Olint Corp Ltd* [2009] UKPC 16, a case about interim injunctions, per Lord Hoffmann at [16].

67 Interim remedies which are granted post-judgment, in order to aid enforcement of the judgment, are in a different category, as the merits of the substantive dispute will have been finally and conclusively determined in favour of the Applicant.

68 [1975] AC 396. These principles apply to interim injunctions which are temporary or provisional versions of remedies which are or could be claimed as the final, substantive relief in the proceedings. They do not apply to freezing injunctions and other specialised forms of exclusively interim injunctions.

69 *American Cyanamid Co v Ethicon Ltd* [1975] AC 396 per Lord Diplock at page 406: "The object of the interlocutory injunction is to protect the plaintiff against injury by violation of his right for which he could not be adequately compensated in damages recoverable in the action if the uncertainty were resolved in his favour at the trial; but the plaintiff's need for such protection must be weighed against the corresponding need of the defendant to be protected against injury resulting from his having been prevented from exercising his own legal rights for which he could not be adequately compensated under the plaintiff's undertaking in damages if the uncertainty were resolved in the defendant's favour at the trial. The court must weigh one need against another and determine where 'the balance of convenience' lies".

70 Steven Gee QC, *Gee on Commercial Injunctions* (7th Edn, Sweet & Maxwell, 2020) §2-002.

statutes relating to interim remedies,[71] as well as several of the official Court Guides;[72] and it is frequently used in legal textbooks[73] and by judges.[74] It is sometimes treated as synonymous with "interim", and indeed the two words are often used interchangeably.[75] Strictly speaking, however, they have distinct meanings.[76]

2.40 Correctly used, the word "interlocutory" refers to the *stage of the proceedings* at which an application is made, a hearing is held or a remedy is granted.[77] An interlocutory remedy is to be contrasted with one which is "final", in the sense that it is what the Claimant hopes to obtain as the final outcome of the English proceedings. A remedy which is claimed in a Claim Form is described as final in this sense; and a hearing at which the court decides whether or not to grant a final remedy is similarly described as a final hearing. A remedy which is requested in an Application Notice is usually[78] described as interlocutory because, at least in theory,[79] it is not the end goal of the legal proceedings: it will usually be envisaged that the proceedings will continue beyond that stage, to the final stage where the court decides whether or not to grant the final relief claimed in the Claim Form.

2.41 The distinctions between "interim" and "interlocutory", and between the two senses of "final", are widely ignored. Indeed, the CPR uses the word "final" in both senses without expressly acknowledging any distinction between them.[80] The distinctions are important, however, as interim remedies

71 Including section 4 of the Torts (Interference with Goods) Act 1977 and, more significantly, section 37(1) of the Senior Courts Act 1981.

72 *Viz* the Commercial Court Guide §N1.3 and the TCC Guide §§4.1.2, 4.3.1, 14.2.2, 14.3.1 and 16.2.1.

73 See e.g. Steven Gee QC, *Gee on Commercial Injunctions* (7th Edn, Sweet & Maxwell, 2020) §2-002; John McGhee QC and Steven Elliott QC, *Snell's Equity* (34th Edn, Sweet & Maxwell, 2019) §18-002.

74 For a recent example from the Court of Appeal, see *Bhamani v Sattar* [2021] EWCA Civ 243 per Nugee LJ at [25] *ff.*

75 See e.g. *SmithKline Beecham plc v Apotex Europe Ltd* [2006] EWCA Civ 658 at [23] per Jacob LJ; Adrian Briggs, *Civil Jurisdiction and Judgments* (7th Edn, Sweet & Maxwell, 2021) 31.01, 31.05.

76 See e.g. Steven Gee QC, *Gee on Commercial Injunctions* (7th Edn, Sweet & Maxwell, 2020) §2-002: "An interlocutory injunction is a form of interim injunction".

77 That is not purely a matter of timing: interlocutory orders can be made before the commencement of proceedings and even after final judgment, in aid of enforcement: CPR 25.2(1).

78 But that is not always true. For example, an application for summary judgment under CPR Part 24 – i.e. an application to bypass the normal procedural stages and skip straight to final judgment in a clear case – is an interlocutory application seeking final relief. Furthermore, proceedings for certain specific types of interim remedy as final relief must be commenced by issuing an Application Notice, which serves as the originating process in those proceedings: see footnote 51 above.

79 In practice, an interlocutory order granting interim relief is often the real final goal of the proceedings.

80 See e.g. CPR Part 27 ("The Small Claims Track") which refers to a "final remedy" (in contrast with interim) in rule 27.3, and a final hearing (in contrast with interlocutory) in rule 27.4. The CPR and CPR PD contain many other examples.

are available from the English court, not only in relation to substantive disputes which will be determined by the English court itself; but also in relation to ones which will be determined in a foreign court or in arbitration; and ones which may never be determined at all.[81] Where the English court is to determine the substantive dispute, it will grant interim remedies as interlocutory relief in the English proceedings. Where the substantive dispute is to be determined by a foreign court or arbitration, the English court can also grant most[82] types of interim remedy as the final relief in the English proceedings. But in either situation, the nature and effect of an interim remedy are always temporary and provisional, regardless of the procedural stage at which it is granted.[83]

Terminology: Temporary, Permanent and Perpetual

2.42 Three further terms which are apt to confuse, particularly in relation to injunctive relief, are temporary, permanent and perpetual. Correctly used, these

---

81 *Viz.* orders for pre-action disclosure under section 33 of the Senior Courts Act 1981 and Norwich Pharmacal orders. In *AB Bank Ltd, Off-Shore Banking Unit (OBU) v Abu Dhabi Commercial Bank PJSC* [2016] EWHC 2082 (Comm), Teare J, while recognising that a Norwich Pharmacal order was in some respects interim in nature, concluded that it was final in both senses of the word: it was granted as the final relief sought by the Claimant in the proceedings he brought against the Defendant; and it was based upon a substantive duty owed by the Defendant, as a person mixed up in wrongdoing, to the wronged Claimant, to provide information to assist him in righting the wrong.

82 The exception is ship arrest, which can only be granted as interlocutory relief. Where a Claimant wishes to arrest a ship as security for a substantive claim which is to be determined by a foreign court or in arbitration, he must commence substantive proceedings in the English court by issuing an *in rem* Claim Form containing that substantive claim. Once the ship has been arrested, the English court will stay its proceedings pending final determination of the substantive claim by the foreign court or arbitral tribunal, and in the meantime it will maintain the ship under arrest, or retain any alternative security provided to the court in order to secure the release of the ship from arrest, as security for the substantive claim: see section 26 of the Civil Jurisdiction and Judgments Act 1982 (foreign court); and sections 9 and 11 of the Arbitration Act 1996 (arbitration). Once the substantive claim has been finally determined by the foreign court or arbitral tribunal, any of the parties to the English proceedings can apply to the English court to lift the stay and to enter judgment based on that result. Where the substantive claim has succeeded, the Claimant can apply to the English court to enforce that judgment against any security retained by the court. See generally Nigel Meeson and John A Kimbell, *Admiralty Jurisdiction and Practice* (5th Edn, Informa Law from Routledge, 2017) §§4.32–4.33. In practice, the owner of the ship will often adopt a pragmatic approach and provide security to the Claimant at an early stage in order to avoid arrest. This will usually take the form of a guarantee or letter of undertaking from a bank or other financial institution, which may be worded so that it will respond directly to outcome of the substantive proceedings a specified court or arbitral tribunal.

83 A good illustration of the distinction between "interim" and "interlocutory" in this context is to be found in Order 29 rule 8A of the old Rules of the Supreme Court 1965 (the rules of court governing civil proceedings in the English courts prior to the introduction of the CPR) which provided: "An application claiming interim relief under section 25(1) of the Civil Jurisdiction and Judgments Act 1982 … shall be made by originating summons [equivalent to a modern Part 8 Claim Form] and the foregoing provisions of this Order … shall apply, with the necessary modifications, to such applications as they apply to applications for interlocutory relief in an action or proceeding in the High Court".

expressions simply describe the duration of the injunction. The expressions "permanent" and "perpetual" are also sometimes used as synonyms for injunctions which are final and conclusive, as distinct from interim,[84] in their nature and effect. That usage reflects the fact that a final and conclusive remedy may be permanent and perpetual in duration, whereas interim remedies are always temporary. But that usage can also be misleading, as final and conclusive remedies may also be of temporary duration, without being in any sense interim or provisional in nature and effect: for example, a final injunction granted following a trial of a substantive claim for breach of contract, which restrains a party from engaging in certain conduct for a fixed period, in accordance with the terms of a restrictive covenant of defined duration to which she has agreed.[85]

CPR Part 25: "Interim Remedies and Security for Costs"

2.43 Applications for most kinds of interim remedies are governed by CPR Part 25. As previously mentioned, English law does not contain a neat and consistent definition of interim remedies. CPR 25.1(1) contains a long list of interim remedies which are available from the English Court, but the list is not exhaustive. The remedies listed include ones which are temporary or provisional versions of remedies which are or could be claimed as the final, substantive[86] relief in the proceedings (such as an interim injunction temporarily restraining a Defendant from committing an allegedly unlawful act while the court determines the claimant's substantive claim for a final injunction restraining the Defendant permanently in the same terms); ones which can only ever be granted on an exclusively interim basis, and never as substantive relief (such as a freezing injunction);[87] and ones which amount to particular versions of remedies which are ordinarily granted under the court's procedural or case management powers, which it exercises to deal with cases justly and at proportionate cost (such as an order for the disclosure of documents).[88]

---

84 See e.g. Steven Gee QC, *Gee on Commercial Injunctions* (7th Edn, Sweet & Maxwell, 2020) §2-002; David Bean, Isabel Parry, Andrew Burns, *Injunctions* (13th Edn, Sweet & Maxwell, 2018) §§1-01, 2-01; John McGhee QC and Steven Elliott QC, *Snell's Equity* (34th Edn, Sweet & Maxwell, 2019) §18-002.

85 See e.g. the celebrated case of *Warner Bros Pictures Inc v Nelson* [1937] 1 KB 209, where Warner Bros obtained a final injunction restraining the Hollywood star Bette Davis (under her married name of Mrs Nelson) from working for a rival film studio for a maximum period of three years, in breach of her contract with Warner Bros. For an example of this misleading usage, see *Moore v Ullcoats Mining Co Ltd* [1908] 1 Ch 575 at page 586, where Warrington J referred to a substantive claim for "a perpetual injunction, that is to say, an injunction to continue so long as the lease continued in the same terms."

86 Substantive relief is relief which enforces or declares the existence and extent of the legal and equitable rights and obligations of the parties, such as an award of damages for breach of contract or a final injunction permanently restraining a Defendant from committing a tort.

87 *The Siskina* [1979] AC 210 per Lord Diplock at page 256.

88 The distinction between interim remedies and procedural or case management orders sometimes becomes entirely blurred: see e.g. The Interim Applications Court of the Queen's

2.44 The full list of interim remedies in CPR 25.1(1) is as follows (sub-paragraphs a.–p. below correspond with sub-paragraphs (a)–(p) of rule 25.1(1)):

a. An interim injunction, i.e. an interim order prohibiting a person from doing something or requiring a person to do something for a limited time or until a specified event.
b. An interim declaration as to the parties' rights and obligations, or as to the existence of facts, or as to a principle of law.[89] This remedy is very rarely granted. It is only available on an exclusively interim basis;[90] it is never granted as a temporary or provisional version of a final, substantive remedy claimed in the proceedings.[91]
c. An order in relation to relevant property which is the subject of a claim or as to which any question may arise on a claim:[92]
    i. For the detention, custody or preservation of the property.
    ii. For inspection of the property. An important application of this wide-ranging provision is the Electronic Device Order for the inspection of an electronic database, computer, mobile phone or other electronic device, by a party, a party's lawyers, or an expert appointed in accordance with CPR Part 35.[93]
    iii. For taking of a sample of the property. This form of relief may be useful in disputes over the condition and quality of commodities, and in intellectual property disputes involving pharmaceuticals, etc.
    iv. For the carrying out of an experiment on or with the property.
    v. For the sale of property which is of a perishable nature or for which any other good reason it is desirable to sell quickly. This form of order is commonly granted in shipping and commodities disputes, and in other cases where it makes financial sense

---

Bench Division of the High Court: A Guide for Litigants in Person (2013) §4 and Appendix 1, where the "interim" applications listed include applications for disclosure, applications to extend time for carrying out procedural steps, applications for permission to amend statements of case and applications for permission to adduce expert evidence (and see the Queen's Bench Guide 2021, §2.14).

89 See *Financial Services Authority v Rourke* [2001] EWHC 704 (Ch). Section 19 of the Senior Courts Act 1981 preserves the Court's former power to grant declarations, including interim declarations.

90 For example, an interim declaration that a particular transaction would not constitute a breach of the terms of an existing freezing injunction: *ABC v CDE* [2010] EWCA Civ 533.

91 See *N v Royal Bank of Scotland plc* [2017] EWCA Civ 253 at [30] where Hamblen LJ explained that it was inappropriate for the Court to grant an interim declaration on a substantive question, such as whether one party is in breach of contract, as that type of question "only permits of a final rather than a temporary answer" which the court can only give by way of a final and conclusive decision on the substance of the dispute.

92 For these purposes, property includes land and intangible property: *UTB LLC v Sheffield United Ltd* [2018] EWHC 1663 (Ch) (Fancourt J).

93 For the applicable principles, see *McLennan Architects Ltd v Jones* [2018] EWHC 1882 (Ch).

to liquidate the relevant property quickly rather than allow it to depreciate in value either through physical deterioration or through the cost of storing and maintaining it pending the final determination of the case. Typically, the order will stipulate how and by whom the sale is to be conducted, and will provide for the net proceeds of sale to be paid into Court, where it will be placed in an interest-bearing account pending further order.[94]

vi. For the payment of income from relevant property until a claim is decided.

d. An order authorising a person to enter any land or building which is in possession of a party to the proceedings, for the purpose of carrying out an order in relation to relevant property.

e. An order to deliver up goods, under section 4 of the Torts (Interference with Goods) Act 1977. Section 4 of the 1977 Act is entitled "Interlocutory relief where goods are retained" and gives the Court the power to make an order for the delivery up of any goods which are or may become the subject-matter of proceedings in the Court for wrongful interference (a category of tort under English law[95]), or as to which any question may arise in such proceedings.

f. A freezing injunction, restraining a party from removing from England and Wales[96] assets located there (a domestic freezing

94 Payments into Court are made to the Court Funds Office, in accordance with the Court Fund Rules 1987, SI 1987/821. The procedure governing payments into Court, and payment out of money paid into Court, is set out in CPR Part 37 and the accompanying Practice Direction. Further practical guidance is to be found online at www.gov.uk/pay-court-funds-office.

95 A tort is a civil wrong consisting of a breach of a duty imposed on the Defendant by law, without the need for a contract, which gives rise to liability to compensate the claimant by paying damages: see Professor Andrew Tettenborn, *Clerk & Lindsell on Torts* (23rd Edn, Sweet & Maxwell, 2020) §1-01 *ff.* Wrongful interference with goods means any tort which results in damage to goods or to an interest in goods. It principally encompasses four common law torts: (i) Conversion, where the Defendant unlawfully appropriates the claimant's goods by taking, receiving, retaining, purchasing, selling, disposing of or consuming them; (ii) Trespass to Chattels, where the Defendant directly and wrongfully interferes with the claimant's possession of goods; (iii) Reversionary Injury, which is equivalent to conversion or trespass to chattels but applies where the claimant neither has possession nor an immediate right to possess the goods at the time of the wrongful act; and (iv) Negligence, so far as it results in damage to goods or to an interest in goods: see The Torts (Interference with Goods) Act 1978 section 1 and *Clerk & Lindsell on Torts, cit.*, §§16-152. Section 3 of the 1977 Act provides that, in proceedings for wrongful interference against a person who is in possession or control of the goods, the Court may, instead of awarding the claimant damages at common law, order the Defendant to deliver the goods up to the claimant and pay consequential damages in addition. Section 4 of the 1977 Act provides that the Court may make an order for delivery up of goods as an interim remedy. The Court may order the goods to be delivered up to the claimant or to a person appointed by the Court for the purpose.

96 The rule says "removing from the jurisdiction", i.e. from England and Wales and any part of the territorial waters of the United Kingdom adjoining England and Wales, over which the English court exercises territorial jurisdiction: see CPR 2.3(1).

injunction), or from dealing with any assets whether located within England and Wales or not (a worldwide freezing injunction).

g. An order directing a party to provide information about the location of relevant property or assets or to provide information about the relevant property or assets which are or may be the subject of a freezing injunction. This form of relief is commonly granted as an ancillary order to a freezing injunction, in order to make the freezing injunction more effective and to enable the Court to police compliance with it.
h. A search order, requiring a party to admit another party to premises for the purposes of preserving evidence which may be relevant to existing or proposed proceedings, or of preserving property which is or may be the subject-matter of the proceedings or as to which any question arises or may arise in the proceedings.[97]
i. An order for disclosure of documents or inspection of property before a claim has been made, under section 33 of the Senior Courts Act 1981.[98]
j. An order for disclosure of documents or inspection of property against a non-party, under section 34 of the Senior Courts Act 1981.[99]
k. An interim payment order under section 32 of the Senior Courts Act 1981,[100] requiring a Defendant to make a payment, to another party or into Court, on account of any damages, debt or other sum (except costs) which the Court may later hold the Defendant liable to pay. This is a good example of an interim remedy which is a temporary or provisional version of a final, substantive remedy: the Court can order the Defendant to make an interim payment at a time when his liability to pay, and the amount of that liability, have not yet finally been determined by a judgment on the merits. The applicable procedure is set out in CPR 25.6.
l. An order for a specified fund of money to be paid into court, or otherwise secured, where there is a dispute over a party's right to the fund.

---

97 When a search order incorporates a power to seize and remove documents or goods from the searched premises, it is referred to as a "search and seize" order or a Search and Seizure Order (SSO): *Universal Thermosensors Ltd v Hibben* [1992] 1 WLR 840; *A v B* [2019] EWHC 2089 (Ch).

98 In County Court proceedings, the relevant provision is section 52 of the County Courts Act 1984.

99 This power was originally only exercisable in proceedings for personal injuries and death. That limitation was removed by article 5(a) of the Civil Procedure (Modification of Enactments) Order, SI 1998/2940, made pursuant to section 4(2) of the Civil Procedure Act 1997. In County Court proceedings, the relevant provision is section 53 of the County Courts Act 1984.

100 In County Court proceedings the applicable provision is section 50 of the County Courts Act 1984.

m. An order permitting a party seeking to recover personal property to pay money into court pending the outcome of the proceedings and directing that, if he does so, the property shall be given up to him.
n. An order directing a party to prepare and file accounts relating to the dispute.
o. An order directing any account to be taken or inquiry to be made by the Court (or, rather, a person appointed for that purpose by the Court).
p. An order under Art 9 of Council Directive (EC) 2004/48 on the enforcement of intellectual property rights. This EU Directive forms part of retained European law, which has been transposed into domestic UK law post-Brexit.

2.45 The list in CPR 25.1(1) demonstrates the range of interim remedies which are available in English civil proceedings. As CPR 25.1(3) makes clear, however, this list is not exhaustive. The following remedies, which are not included in CPR 25.1(1), may also be regarded as interim remedies:

- An order for the disclosure and inspection of documents by a party in the course of proceedings. Disclosure (referred to in other common law jurisdictions as "discovery") means stating whether a document exists or has existed.[101] Disclosure and inspection of documents is an essential aspect of many cases in the English courts. The CPR contain detailed rules requiring the parties to search for, give disclosure of and permit inspection of documents, and for managing the disclosure process.[102] Disclosure of documents, or at any rate the court's power to control the disclosure process and the extent, manner and timing of disclosure, is normally treated as part of case management. English law does not, however, draw a particularly clear distinction between interim remedies and procedural/case management powers; and as CPR 25.1(1)(i) and (j) demonstrate, an order to give disclosure and inspection may also be seen as an interim remedy.
- A "Norwich Pharmacal" order, requiring a person who is innocently caught up in the wrongdoing of another to disclose the identity of the wrongdoer, or documents or other information relevant to the potential claim against the wrongdoer, so that legal proceedings can be brought or other legitimate forms of redress sought against that wrongdoer.[103] The innocent person must be more than a mere

101 CPR 31.2.

102 CPR Part 31, Practice Directions 31A, B and C, and the Practice Direction 51U, the disclosure pilot scheme for the Business and Property Courts.

103 *Norwich Pharmacal Co v Customs and Excise Commissioners* [1974] AC 133; Mitsui & Co Ltd v Nexen Petroleum UK Ltd [2005] EWHC 625 per Lightman J at [21].

witness, but must somehow be mixed up in the wrongdoing; and the order must be necessary for a claim to be brought or redress sought against the wrongdoer. The power to grant a Norwich Pharmacal order forms part of the court's inherent equitable jurisdiction to prevent a denial of justice.[104] It is perhaps best described as a *quasi*-interim remedy, as it shares some of the characteristics of discretionary interim remedies but is based upon a substantive duty owed by a person mixed up in wrongdoing, to assist the person wronged by giving him information which will assist him in righting that wrong.[105]

- A "Bankers Trust" order, requiring a person to provide information or documents concerning the location and legal ownership of assets, in order to assist another person who asserts a proprietary claim to those assets, to trace and recover them.[106] This is another *quasi*-interim remedy, which is granted under the court's inherent equitable jurisdiction to protect trust property.[107]
- An order under section 37(1) of the Senior Courts Act 1981 for the appointment of a receiver to take possession of property for the purpose of preserving it.[108] An order appointing a receiver over the Respondent's property operates as an interim injunction restraining the Respondent from dealing with the property except as permitted by the order. A receiver may be appointed instead of, or in addition

104 *Norwich Pharmacal Co v Customs and Excise Commissioners* [1974] AC 133 per Lord Morris of Borth-y-Gest at page 180. See also CPR 31.18.

105 See *AB Bank Ltd, Off-Shore Banking Unit (OBU) v Abu Dhabi Commercial Bank* PJSC [2016] EWHC 2082 (Comm) per Teare J at [6–16]. Recent authorities have cast doubt on the existence of this substantive "duty", and have described it as a purely notional rationale for the existence of the court's equitable jurisdiction to intervene where the interests of justice require it: *Singularis Holdings Ltd v PricewaterhouseCoopers* [2014] UKPC 36 per Lord Sumption JSC at [22]; *Cartier International AG v British Telecommunications plc* [2018] UKSC 28 per Lord Sumption JSC [11].

106 *Bankers Trust Co v Shapira* [1980] 1 WLR 1274; *Kyriakou v Chrstie Manson & Woods Ltd* [2017] EWHC 487 (QB) per Warby at [14].

107 A trust is the relationship which arises whenever a person (called the trustee) is compelled in equity to hold property for the benefit of some persons (of whom he may be one and who are termed beneficiaries) or for some object permitted by law (such as charity), in such a way that the real benefit of the property accrues, not to the trustees, but to the beneficiaries or other objects of the trust: L A Sheridan, *Keeton & Sheridan on The Law of Trusts* (12th Edn, Barry Rose, 1993) 3; Lynton Tucker, Nicholas Le Poidevin QC, James Brightwell, *Lewin on Trusts*, (20th Edn, Sweet & Maxwell, 2020) Section 1.

108 See generally John McGhee QC and Steven Elliott QC, *Snell's Equity* (34th Edn, Sweet & Maxwell, 2019) §§19-001, 003, 007-008, 016. As with injunctions, the appointment of a receiver is equitable remedy whose existence is confirmed by section 37(1). If the property includes a business, the Court may also authorise the receiver to act as manager, with power to continue trading in order to preserve its goodwill and its value as a going concern: *In re Newdigate Colliery Ltd* [1912] 1 Ch 468 at p 472 per Cozens-Hardy MR; *JSC BTA Bank v Ablyazov* [2012] EWHC 648 (Comm) at [14] per Hamblen J.

to, a freezing injunction,[109] for example where there is concern that a freezing injunction alone will not be effective to preserve the property. In such a case, the order will expressly require the Respondent to give up possession of the property to the receiver.[110] Applications for the appointment of a receiver are governed by CPR Part 69.

- A warrant for the arrest of a ship or other property in Admiralty proceedings *in rem*, in order to secure the claimant's claim and to found jurisdiction in England. Unlike most other interim remedies under English law, ship arrest is not discretionary: it is available as of right if the statutory requirements are satisfied.[111] The relevant procedure governing this remedy is set out in CPR 61.5.
- An order requiring a Claimant to provide security for the Defendant's costs of defending the claim against him. The procedure is set out in Section II of CPR Part 25. The power to order security for costs is an important adjunct to the power of the English court to order one party (usually but not always the losing party) to pay some or all of the legal costs of the other party.[112]
- An order staying proceedings before the English court – i.e. bringing the proceedings to a halt (but not necessarily to a complete end) either generally or until a specified time or event.[113] The court may order a stay of proceedings before it on the grounds that the parties have agreed to refer the dispute to arbitration,[114] or that another foreign court has jurisdiction and is a clearly more appropriate forum for determining the dispute in the interests of justice,[115] or because

109 *Derby & Co Ltd v Weldon* (Nos. 3 & 4) [1990] Ch 65 (CA). Similarly, the Court may appoint a receiver instead of, or in addition to, ordering the detention, custody or preservation of relevant property under CPR 25.1(1)(c)(i).

110 Steven Gee QC, *Gee on Commercial Injunctions* (7th Edn, Sweet & Maxwell, 2020) §§16-020, 021.

111 This is subject to a very limited exception in CPR 61.5(4), which provides that a warrant of arrest will not be issued as of right in the case of property in respect of which the beneficial ownership, as a result of a sale or disposal by any court in any jurisdiction exercising admiralty jurisdiction in rem, has changed since the claim form was issued. The other notable non-discretionary interim remedy is the mandatory stay of English court proceedings brought in breach of an arbitration agreement under section 9 of the Arbitration Act 1996: *Sabbagh v Khoury* [2017] EWCA Civ 1120 at [117].

112 The power of the English court to make orders in relation to costs is discretionary and derives from section 51 of the Senior Courts Act 1981, which gives the court full power to determine by whom and to what extent costs are to be paid. It also gives the court the power to order a non-party to pay costs, and to join him as a party for that purpose alone.

113 See CPR 3.1(2)(f).

114 Section 9 of the Arbitration Act 1996 requires the Court to stay proceedings brought in breach of an arbitration agreement, unless satisfied that the arbitration agreement is null and void, inoperative or incapable of being performed. Where these requirements are satisfied, the Court has no discretion to refuse a stay: *JSC Aeroflot Russian Airlines v Berezovsky* [2013] EWCA Civ 784 per Aikens LJ at [98].

115 The foreign court is said to be the *forum conveniens* (the convenient forum). In those circumstances, the English Court will, as a matter of principled discretion, stay the proceedings

there are related proceedings between the same parties in a foreign court involving the same or similar issues,[116] or because it is just and convenient to do so for some other reason.

2.46 One of the two practice directions accompanying CPR Part 25, CPD PD 25A entitled "Interim Injunctions", sets out which level of judge has the power to grant and to discharge particular types of interim relief; and contains directions for how an application for interim relief is to be made, the form in which evidence in support is to be presented and the form which the order of the Court should take.

2.47 A number of other Parts of the CPR are also important in the field of interim relief:

- Part 1. "Overriding Objective": this part sets out and explains the overriding objective of the CPR, which is to enable the court to deal with cases justly and at proportionate cost. This involves seeking to ensure that the parties are on an equal footing and able to participate fully in proceedings; saving expense; dealing with cases in ways which are proportionate to the sums involved, the importance of the case, the complexity of the issues and the financial position of each party; ensuring that the case is dealt with expeditiously and fairly; allotting a proportionate share of the Court's resources to the case; and enforcing compliance with the Court's rules, practice directions and orders. CPR 1.4 requires the Court to further the overriding objective by actively managing cases, by encouraging the parties to co-operate with each other in the conduct of the proceedings; identifying the issues at an early stage; deciding promptly which issues need full investigation and trial and disposing summarily of the other issues; deciding the order in which the issues are to be resolved; encouraging the parties to use alternative dispute resolution procedures; helping the parties to settle the whole or part of the case; fixing timetables and controlling the progress of the case; considering whether the likely benefits of any procedural step justify the cost of taking it; dealing with as many aspects of the case as it can on the same occasion; limiting the need for the parties to attend Court in person; utilising technology; and giving directions to ensure that the trial of the case proceeds quickly and efficiently. The Court is obliged to seek to give effect to the overriding objective

before it – i.e. decline to exercise the jurisdiction which it has to hear and determine the case – in favour of the *forum conveniens*. See *Spiliada Maritime Corp v Cansulex Ltd* [1987] AC 460.

116 The foreign proceedings are said to be a *lis alibi pendens* (a case pending elsewhere).

when it exercises any power given to it by the CPR or interprets any rule of the CPR.[117]

- Part 2. "Application and Interpretation of the Rules": this part contains definitions of some important terms used in the CPR and explains how to interpret provisions which impose procedural time limits. Practice Direction 2B, entitled "Allocation of Cases to Levels of Judiciary", sets out which level of judge can hear particular types of case and grant particular types of remedy.
- Part 3. "The Court's Case Management Powers": this part sets out the various case management powers of the court, including the power in CPR 3.1(1)(3) to make an order subject to conditions, including a condition to pay money into court, and to specify the consequences of failure to comply with the order or a condition. This power is frequently used in connection with interim injunctions and other interim remedies.[118] Thus, the court will typically make the granting of an interim injunction conditional on the Applicant giving certain undertakings to the court, including an undertaking to compensate the Respondent by paying damages if it later turns out that the order ought not to have been granted; and it will often require the Applicant to fortify that undertaking in damages by providing financial security.[119]
- Part 6. "Service of Documents": this part contains rules about when, where, how, by and upon whom court documents may effectively be served, including the Claim Form or other form of originating process,[120] Application Notices, witness statements and court orders. As explained below, service of originating process has a critical role in English procedural law: the English court can only exercise personal jurisdiction[121] over a Defendant if he can be served with originating process, either within the court's territorial jurisdiction, or out of the jurisdiction in accordance with the rules contained in the CPR. In many cases, service out of the jurisdiction requires the

117 A modified version of the overriding objective applies to a limited number of rules relating to proceedings under anti-terrorism and security legislation.

118 Subsection 37(2) of the Senior Courts Act 1981 also expressly provides that an interim injunction and an order for the appointment of a receiver may be granted "either unconditionally or on such terms and conditions as the court thinks just".

119 See 2.117–2.123 below.

120 The rules about service of a "claim form" in CPR Part 6 apply to all forms of originating process: see CPR 6.2(c). To avoid confusion, in this work, the expression "originating process" is used instead of this wider sense of "claim form", and "Claim Form" with capital letters is used to mean a Part 7 or Part 8 Claim Form on practice forms N1 or N208; the corresponding Commercial Court forms N1(CC) or N208(CC); Admiralty Court forms ADM1 (*in rem*), ADM1A (collision), ADM15 (limitation); or the Arbitration Claim Form at Appendix A to CPR PD 62: see CPR PD 7 §§3.1, 3.4.

121 For an explanation of the term "jurisdiction" see 2.66–2.67 below.

permission of the English court, which can only be granted if certain specified criteria are satisfied.[122]

- Part 8. "Alternative Procedure for Claims": this part contains basic procedural rules applicable to cases which are unlikely to involve a substantial dispute of fact. It applies to cases where the only remedy sought from the English court is a discretionary interim remedy in support of substantive proceedings in a foreign court or in arbitration. In such a case, the applicant is required to issue a Claim Form in the special format stipulated by Part 8, rather than the standard version in Part 7. Many of the procedural stages of a standard "Part 7" civil claim in the English court are dispensed with in a "Part 8" claim, including the trial stage when the court would normally hear oral witness evidence.[123]
- Part 11. "Disputing the Court's Jurisdiction": this part sets out the procedure for challenging the jurisdiction of the English court to hear and determine a claim, either on the basis that the court lacks jurisdiction, or that it should decline to exercise its jurisdiction, usually in favour of another court or tribunal.
- Part 23. "General Rules about Applications for Court Orders": this part contains the main procedural rules governing interlocutory applications in English court proceedings, including the rules governing applications made without giving prior notice to the Respondent. Where a party to existing proceedings, or proceedings which have not yet been commenced, in the English court wishes to apply for an interim remedy in those proceedings, she must follow the procedure set out in Part 23. She must also follow that procedure (along with the Part 8 procedure) where she wishes to apply urgently for a discretionary interim remedy in support of substantive proceedings in a foreign court or in arbitration.[124] The procedural rules in Part 23 are supplemented, in the case of interim remedies, by other provisions of the CPR, including CPR 25.2–4, CPR PD 25A, CPR 31.16–17 and the rules and guidance applicable to specialist courts.[125]

---

122 See paragraphs 2.66–2.88 below.

123 The court nevertheless retains a power to require witnesses who have given written evidence in Part 8 proceedings to attend court for cross-examination, as in a trial: CPR 8.6(3); and it can direct that the claim should proceed as an ordinary Part 7 claim where appropriate: CPR 8.1(3).

124 CPR 25.4(2). Where the Applicant makes an urgent application for this type of interim relief in accordance with Part 23, she must also, in due course, formally commence proceedings by issuing a Part 8 Claim Form which includes a claim for the same interim relief: see CPR 25.2(3); §F.15.15 of the Commercial Court Guide 2017; and *Ras Al Khaimah Investment Authority v Bestfort Development LLP* [2015] EWHC 1995 (Ch) per Richard Spearman QC at [7]–[10].

125 *Viz.* CPR Parts 58 (Commercial Court), 59 (Circuit Commercial Courts), 60 (Technology & Construction Court), 61 (Admiralty Claims), 62 (Arbitration Claims), 63

- Part 31. "Disclosure and Inspection of Documents": this part contains procedural rules about the disclosure and inspection of documents, including the scope and timing of disclosure, and by whom and to whom documents are to be disclosed. It also governs applications for two types of disclosure order which are normally treated, not as part of the court's case management powers, but as interim remedies: an order for disclosure before the start of proceedings under section 33 of the Senior Courts Act 1981 (CPR 31.16), and an order for disclosure against a non-party under section 34 of the Senior Courts Act 1981 (CPR 31.17).
- Part 32. "Evidence": this part contains procedural rules about adducing factual witness evidence[126] in civil proceedings, including on applications for interim relief. The general rule in applications for interim relief, and other interlocutory applications, is that any fact that needs to be proved by the evidence of witnesses is to be proved by their evidence in writing, and not by the witness giving oral evidence and being cross-examined on that testimony in a trial. Written witness evidence usually takes the form of a witness statement; but a party may also rely on facts set out in his statement of case[127] or his application notice, provided that these have been verified by a statement of truth in the required form.[128] On applications for freezing injunctions, search orders and other orders requiring an occupier to permit another person to enter his land,[129] written evidence must be given by affidavit – a solemn document in which the witness swears an oath or solemnly affirms the truth of his evidence.[130] The maker

(Intellectual Property Claims) 63A (Financial List), etc.; the practice directions which accompany those Parts; the Commercial Court Guide (which incorporates the Admiralty Court Guide, the Circuit Commercial Courts Guide and the Financial List Guide); the Technology and Construction Court (TCC) Guide; the Chancery Guide; the Queen's Bench Guide, etc. The up-to-date versions of these guides can all be accessed online via www.judiciary.uk/you-and-the-judiciary/going-to-court/high-court/.

126 Evidence of fact is to be distinguished from evidence of opinion. Generally, opinion evidence is inadmissible in English proceedings: see Hodge M Malek QC, *Phipson on Evidence* (19th Edn, Sweet & Maxwell, 2017) §§33-01, 02. The most important exception to that rule is expert opinion evidence.

127 An expression which covers the Claim Form itself and any pleadings which the party files in the case, formally setting out his case. In typical proceedings governed by CPR Part 7, the pleadings are the Particulars of Claim, Defence (and Counterclaim), Reply (and Defence to Counterclaim), Reply to Defence to Counterclaim and any further information and clarification provided in accordance with CPR Part 18 (see CPR 2.3(1)). The rules for what a statement of case can and cannot contain are set out in CPR Part 16.

128 CPR 32.2, 32.6 and 32.8. The form which a witness statement must take is set out in Practice Direction 32.

129 I.e. an order under CPR 25.1(1)(d).

130 CPR PD 25A §3.1; Practice Direction 32 para 1.4. The maker of an affidavit must solemnly swear (on the Bible, Koran or other religious book) or affirm, before a person authorised to administer oaths and affirmations, that the contents of the affidavit are true to the best of his

of the witness statement or affidavit must identify himself and his role, explain which parts of the statement are within his personal knowledge and which are not, identify the sources of his knowledge and verify that he believes that the contents of the statement are true.[131] Witness statements and affidavits in support of or in opposition to an application for interim relief are usually made by the party on whose behalf it is made, or a director or other officer of that party where it is a corporation, or the solicitor representing that party in the litigation.

- Part 35. "Experts and Assessors": this part contains rules about adducing expert evidence in civil proceedings, including on applications for interim relief. It covers the form and content of expert evidence; the duties of expert witnesses, who are required to be impartial and objective, to assist the court and to limit themselves to matters within their expertise; and the procedural rules governing the preparation and service of expert reports. The general rule is that expert evidence will only be permitted where the court agrees that it is reasonably required to resolve the application,[132] and this rule is equally applicable to applications for interim relief. Expert evidence may be required on interim applications where the factual basis of the application involves matters of expertise. For example, on an application for a freezing injunction, expert accounting evidence may be necessary to interpret financial information indicating that a party is likely to hide assets; or on application for an order for the sale of property which is of a perishable nature, expert evidence may be necessary to demonstrate that the property is likely to deteriorate. Many of the procedural rules in Part 35 and the accompanying practice direction are rather cumbersome. They are primarily directed at expert evidence which will be adduced at trial, where the experts will give oral evidence and be cross-examined, and where the court will determine issues of fact finally and conclusively based on its assessment of that evidence: see for example the rules requiring parties to obtain permission in advance to adduce expert evidence on specific issues, the rules governing the format and content of written expert reports and the rules governing the exchange of expert reports, meetings of experts, preparation of joint memoranda by the experts, etc. Applications for interim relief, by contrast, are temporary and provisional in nature, are often urgent and will generally

knowledge, information and belief. See CPR 32.15–16 and Practice Direction 32, which also sets out the form which an affidavit must take.

131 Written evidence must be verified by a statement of truth, in the form stipulated by CPR Part 22.

132 CPR 35.1.

not involve oral evidence or (as discussed further below)[133] call for the court to make final determinations on disputed factual issues. The procedural rules in Part 25 are nevertheless applicable to applications for interim remedies. Where the application is urgent, the court will usually permit expert evidence to be adduced by means of a (factual) witness statement (or, where required, an affidavit) made either by the expert himself, or by another witness who relates the substance of the expert's opinion and/or exhibits a report or letter from the expert containing that opinion; with permission to adduce the expert evidence being sought at the hearing of the application.[134] In the absence of urgency, however, or once any initial urgent application has been heard, the court will typically insist on full adherence to the requirements of Part 35.[135]

- Part 36. "Offers to Settle": this part contains a detailed code governing the making and acceptance of offers by one party to another to settle the whole or a part of a case, and the consequences which follow where such an offer is either accepted or rejected. The most important of these consequences is that, if the offer is not accepted and the party who made the offer goes on to achieve a result in the case which is as good or better than his offer, the party who rejected the offer will generally have to pay all the offeror's legal costs from 21 days after the offer was made, substantially in full, interest on those costs and interest on any debt or damages awarded, at an inflated interest rate.[136] When used correctly, this technique can produce a strong financial incentive for a party who is unsure of the strength of his case to settle it rather than fight it out to the end.
- Part 40. "Judgments, Orders, Sale of Land etc": this part contains general rules about the form and content of court orders, who is to draw them up and who is to serve them. Some of these provisions are modified for specialist courts such as the Admiralty and Commercial Courts:[137] there the general rule is that the party applying for an interim remedy must produce a draft of the order he seeks prior to the hearing of the application; and, following the hearing, he must draw up the order made by the court, get it approved by the judge and sealed by the court office, and serve it on the Respondent himself.[138]

---

133 See 2.34–2.41 below.

134 *Pipia v Bgeo Group Ltd* [2019] EWHC 325 (Comm) per Moulder J at [18–25].

135 *BB Energy (Gulf) DMCC v Al Moudi* [2018] EWHC 2595 per Andrew Baker J at [48–50].

136 CPR 36.17.

137 See 2.53 below.

138 CPR 58.15; Practice Direction 58 paras 9 and 14; Commercial Court Guide 2017 §§D19.1(c), F11.1(b)(ii).

- Part 44. "General Rules about Costs": this part contains general rules about how the court will exercise its broad discretionary power to order one party (or even a non-party) to pay some or all of the legal costs of another party.[139] The risk of having to bear, not only one's own legal costs, but also those of the other party or parties, creates a powerful incentive for litigants in English civil proceedings to settle their disputes rather than fight them out in court.
- Part 57A. "Business and Property Courts": this part and accompanying Practice Direction 57AA contain rules about specialist courts dealing with particular types of commercial proceedings.[140]
- Part 58. "Commercial Court": this part and its accompanying Practice Direction modify a number of rules and procedures in the CPR for use in two specialist courts, the Commercial Court and Admiralty[141] Court, including rules about who is to draw up and serve court orders and other documents, and about the timetable for filing evidence in applications for interim relief.[142] The special practices and procedures of the Commercial and Admiralty Courts are explained in further detail in the Commercial Court Guide.
- Part 59. "Circuit Commercial Court": this part applies to proceedings in the Circuit Commercial Court, which deals with lower value commercial disputes.[143]
- Part 61. "Admiralty Claims": this part and its accompanying Practice Direction contain rules applicable to claims within the Admiralty jurisdiction of the English High Court, including claims *in rem*, collision claims, maritime limitation claims, etc. CPR 61.5–8 and CPR PD 61 §§5–7 contain the procedural rules governing the arrest or ships and other property in order to secure a claim *in rem* and/or to found jurisdiction for that claim in the English courts.
- Part 62. "Arbitration Claims": this part and its accompanying Practice Direction govern applications to the English court under the Arbitration Act 1996, including applications for interim remedies in support of arbitration.[144] Such applications are made using a modified version of the procedure in CPR Part 8.[145]

---

139 The source of this power is section 51 of the Senior Courts Act 1981.

140 See 2.53 below.

141 See CPR 61.1(3).

142 Practice Direction 58 para 13.

143 See 2.53 below.

144 CPR PD 62 §8.1.

145 There is an exception for applications under section 9 of the Arbitration Act 1996 to stay existing English court proceedings which have been brought in breach of an arbitration agreement: CPR 62.8.

- Part 81. "Applications and Proceedings in Relation to Contempt of Court": this part contains rules governing proceedings for contempt of court, including disobedience of court judgments and orders. The English court has power to enforce compliance with its orders and to punish contempt of court by committing a contemnor to prison, fining him and, in the case of a corporate contemnor, sequestering its assets.[146]

English Civil Courts

2.48 The organisation of the English civil court system is complex and can appear somewhat confusing. The civil courts form part of the wider English system of courts and tribunals, whose structure can be illustrated by the simplified diagram shown in Figure 2.1.[147]

2.49 For most types of civil case there are two possible courts of first instance: the County Court, which sits in numerous locations around England and Wales and deals with lower value disputes; and the High Court, which hears the more serious and complex cases. A number of specific categories of dispute, such as certain types of employment claim, and appeals by members of the public against decisions of Government departments or agencies, are dealt with by specialist statutory tribunals – independent judicial bodies set up by Parliament to rule on disputes between individuals or private organisations and state agencies – outside the main civil court system.[148] Family cases are dealt with by separate courts applying separate procedures. These specialist tribunals and family courts are beyond the scope of this book.

2.50 This work focuses on the practice of the High Court.

Organisation of the High Court

2.51 The High Court is based in London. It also operates from a number of District Registries located around England and Wales. Nearly all types of

146 Corporations act through their officers, who are natural persons, so where a company disobeys an order of the English court, the company's officers may also be punished personally for contempt of court, by committal to prison and fine.

147 For a more detailed diagram see https://www.judiciary.uk/wp-content/uploads/2020/08/courts-structure-0715.pdf.

148 For a summary of the structure of the statutory tribunal system, see www.judiciary.uk/wp-content/uploads/2020/08/tribunals-chart-updated-May-2020.pdf (which also covers Scotland and Northern Ireland). The First Tier Tribunal hears cases at first instance, and the Upper Tribunal hears appeals and reviews of first instance decisions. The First Tier Tribunal is divided into seven Chambers, each with a separate field of work. The Upper Tribunal is divided into four Chambers. Employment disputes are dealt with in a separate tribunal structure consisting of the Employment Tribunal and the Employment Appeals Tribunal. Second appeals from the Upper Tribunal and Employment Appeals Tribunal, lie to the Court of Appeal, Civil Division.

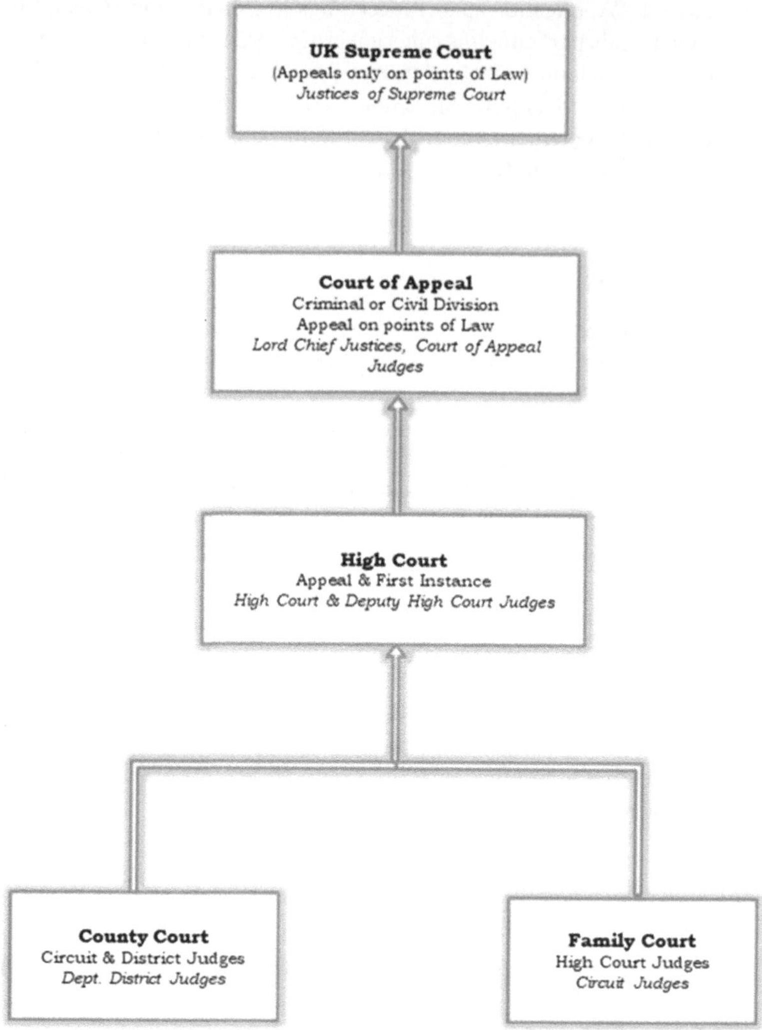

FIGURE 2.1 Basic structure of English civil courts.

civil case in the High Court are heard by a single judge sitting alone, without a jury.[149] This applies to interlocutory applications, including applications for interim relief, as well as trials and other final hearings.

149 Senior Courts Act 1981 section 19(3). There are a number of exceptions. Some judicial review cases are heard by a court comprising two or more judges (called a divisional court) in accordance with section 66(1) of the Senior Courts Act 1981 and CPR 3.1(2)(bb). In trials of cases involving claims of fraud, malicious prosecution, false imprisonment, a judge may, in

2.52 The High Court is officially organised into three divisions, whose names and main areas of work reflect the historical evolution of the English legal system: the Queen's Bench Division, which is the successor of the old courts of common law; the Chancery Division which is the successor of the old courts of equity;[150] and the Family Division which is self-explanatory. The Queen's Bench and Chancery Divisions both deal with commercial disputes, among other matters;[151] while the Family Division deals with the most difficult and sensitive cases involving families and is beyond the scope of this book.[152] Each division contains within it a number of specialist courts and lists, whose judges have particular expertise in certain types of dispute, and whose practices and procedures have been specially adapted to be suitable for determining those disputes.

2.53 Since 2017, a new organisational structure has been overlaid onto the existing divisions of the High Court, for work of a commercial nature. This new administrative grouping is called the Business and Property Courts. It covers the whole of the Chancery Division, and the specialist courts and lists of the Queen's Bench Division which deal with commercial matters. It is based at the Rolls Building, a modern court centre in the City of London. It also operates at District Registries in a number of other major English and Welsh cities: Birmingham, Bristol, Cardiff, Leeds, Liverpool, Manchester and Newcastle-upon-Tyne. It consists of the following entities:[153]

- The Commercial Court, which is the most important specialist civil court in the English court system. It handles complex domestic and international business disputes, including disputes over contracts and business documents, insurance and reinsurance, sale of commodities, carriage of goods, banking and financial services, agency and management agreements, shipbuilding and offshore construction and disputes relating to arbitration.[154]

---

accordance with section 69 of the Senior Courts Act 1981, sit with a jury of laypeople who will determine issues of fact, with the judge deciding issues of law, evidence and procedure. And in trials of collision claims and other cases involving issues of navigation and seamanship, the Admiralty judge will typically sit with one or more nautical assessors who will provide their expert opinion to the court, instead of the parties calling their own expert witnesses.

150 All civil courts administer the rules of both the common law and equity: Senior Courts Act 1981 section 49.

151 The matters assigned to each division of the High Court are set out in schedule 1 to the Senior Courts Act 1981.

152 The same goes for the Family Court, which hears ordinary family disputes, in much the same way that the County Court hears less serious civil disputes.

153 CPR Part 57A and Practice Direction 57AA paragraphs 1.1–1.4. The Commercial Court, Admiralty Court, Circuit Commercial Court and TCC are specialist courts of the Queen's Bench Division. The specialist lists all form part of the Chancery Division, with the exception of the Financial List which belongs to both the Queen's Bench and Chancery Divisions.

154 See section 62(3) of the Senior Courts Act 1981 and CPR 58.1(2).

- The Admiralty Court, which handles shipping and maritime disputes including disputes arising from collisions; carriage of goods by sea; salvage; ship finance, mortgages and securities; limitation claims; and claims by passengers and crew. The Admiralty Court exercises the Admiralty jurisdiction of the High Court,[155] including the right to entertain claims *in rem* brought against the ship itself, and the power to grant the interim remedy of ship arrest.
- The Technology and Construction Court (TCC), which handles disputes about construction, engineering and related professional negligence. The work of the TCC is often technically complex and high-value.
- The Circuit Commercial Court,[156] the Commercial Court's little brother, which deals with lower value commercial disputes.
- The Business List, which comprises three sub-lists. The Business sub-list deals with a range of business disputes including claims against company directors for breaching their fiduciary duties, disputes between investors, claims for conspiracy and fraud, professional negligence claims against professional service providers and contractual claims between businesses. The Financial Services and Regulatory sub-list deals with financial claims involving the Financial Conduct Authority and other government financial regulators. The Pensions sub-list deals with pensions disputes.
- The Financial List, which deals with high-value matters involving international banking and financial markets.
- The Insolvency and Companies List, which deals with personal bankruptcy, corporate insolvency, applications under the Cross-Border Insolvency Regulations, disqualification of company directors, winding up, striking off and restoring of companies, registration of company charges, etc.
- The Competition List, which deals with claims for conduct which prevents, restricts or distorts competition, unfair pricing, unfair trading and breaches of competition rules.
- The Intellectual Property List, which incorporates the Patents Court (disputes about patents, registered designs and plant varieties) and the Intellectual Property and Enterprise Court (lower value claims about patents and other intellectual property rights).
- The Property, Trusts and Probate List, which covers much of what would traditionally be regarded as Chancery work relating to real property,[157] trusts and inheritance.

155 See section 62(2) of the Senior Courts Act 1981 and CPR 61.1.
156 Formerly known as the Mercantile Court.
157 I.e. land, as distinct from personal property which includes goods.

- The Revenue List, which deals major points of principle involving central taxation.

2.54 Several other specialist courts and lists within the Queen's Bench Division of the High Court remain outside the aegis of the Business and Properties Courts. The most important of these is the Administrative Court, which has power to oversee the quality and legality of decision making in lower courts and tribunals and hears applications for judicial review of decisions of public bodies. The others are the Planning Court (technically a subdivision of the Administrative Court); the Media and Communications List, which deals with claims for defamation, misuse of data and private information and other claims relating to the media; and the Asbestos List, which deals with asbestos-related personal injury claims. Apart from this specialist work, the Queen's Bench Division deals with other claims for personal injury, professional negligence, breach of statutory duty, other tortious conduct, breach of contract, breaches of the Human Rights Act 1998 and non-payment of debts.

Allocation of Cases within the High Court

2.55 Civil proceedings in the High Court are (with a few important exceptions[158]) commenced by the issue of a Claim Form in accordance with CPR Part 7 or Part 8. Certain types of case are required to be commenced in a particular court or specialist list. Thus, for example, Admiralty claims *in rem*, collision claims, maritime limitation claims and salvage claims must be commenced in the Admiralty Court;[159] and most claims for remedies under the Arbitration Act 1996 must be commenced in the Commercial Court, Circuit Commercial Court or TCC.[160] Where there is no specific requirement to commence proceedings in a particular court or list, the Claimant can choose where to commence. The choice should, however, be based on the principal subject-matter of the dispute.[161] Once commenced, the claim may be transferred to a more suitable court, list or location, either on the application of one or more parties or on the courts' own initiative.[162]

2.56 In some circumstances, the court has the power to grant interim remedies before proceedings have formally been commenced by the issue of

158 See footnote 51 above.
159 CPR 61.2(1)(a).
160 CPR 62.3 and Practice Direction 62 para 2.3.
161 Practice Direction 57AA paras 2.2(1) 2.3(1).
162 See Senior Courts Act 1981 section 65; CPR 30.5; Practice Direction 57AA para 3.1. For the procedure for transferring cases to and from specialist courts see CPR 58.4 and Practice Direction 58 para 4 (Commercial Court); CPR 59.3 and Practice Direction 59 para 4 (Circuit Commercial Court); CPR 61.2(3) and Practice Direction 61 para 2.1 (Admiralty Court).

a claim form.[163] In such cases, the application for the interim remedy should be made to the court in which the proceedings will be commenced.

Power of Judges of the High Court to Grant Interim Remedies

2.57 There are several different levels of judge in the High Court:[164]

- Justices of the High Court, sometimes known as *puisne* judges or simply High Court Judges, deal with more complex and difficult cases. They hear trials and other final hearings, as well as interlocutory applications.[165] They can exercise the full range of powers of the High Court and are able to grant all the remedies which are available in that court. Part-time High Court Judges, known as deputy High Court Judges, have almost all the same powers as a full-time High Court Judge.[166]
- Masters are procedural judges who deal with case management and interlocutory applications, but do not normally hear trials. The Master assigned to the Admiralty Court is known as the Admiralty Registrar. In the Commercial Court there are no Masters, and all business in that court is dealt with by a High Court Judge.[167] Insolvency and Companies Court judges are the equivalent of Masters in the Insolvency and Companies list of the Business and Properties Court.
- Circuit judges perform the functions of High Court judges in District Registries of the High Court outside London. District judges similarly perform the functions of Masters in District Registries.

2.58 A number of interim remedies may only be granted by a High Court Judge.[168] This reflects the importance, sensitivity and potentially draconian effect of these remedies. The most important are:

- Freezing injunctions.
- Search orders.

---

163 See 2.89–2.93 above.

164 See footnote 18 above for the titles of different levels of judge.

165 High Court Judges also hear appeals from decisions of Masters, Registrars and District Judges sitting in the High Court, as well as some appeals from decisions of the County Court, including decisions granting or refusing interim relief: Practice Direction 52A Tables 1 and 2. Generally such appeals can only be made with the permission of the court: CPR 52.3(1).

166 Deputies do not have certain powers in relation to proceedings under the Human Rights Act 1998: Practice Direction 2B para 7A.

167 CPR PD 58 para 1.2.

168 Including a deputy High Court Judge.

- Ancillary orders under CPR 25.1(1)(g).
- Interim remedies relating to the liberty of the subject, criminal proceedings or judicial review.[169]

Court of Appeal and UK Supreme Court

2.59 The Court of Appeal, Civil Division, hears appeals from the High Court,[170] County Court[171] and statutory tribunals,[172] including appeals from decisions of the High Court and County Court to grant, or refuse, interim remedies.

2.60 The procedure governing appeals to the Court of Appeal[173] is set out in CPR Part 52 and the accompanying Practice Directions. Permission to appeal is required in almost all cases.[174] The application for permission to appeal and the appeal itself are separate procedural stages.

2.61 An application for permission to appeal may be made either to the court which made the decision appealed against (the "lower court"), at the hearing at which the decision was made,[175] or to the Court of Appeal, or indeed to both.[176] Permission to appeal is discretionary. The test for granting it is whether, in the view of the court, the appeal would have a real prospect of success, or there is some other compelling reason for the appeal to be heard.[177] This requires the court to form a provisional view on whether the appeal itself would succeed. The "real prospect of success" standard,

---

169 See CPR 2.4, Practice Direction 2B para 3.1 and Practice Direction 25A para 1.

170 From decisions of High Court Judges. Appeals from decisions of Masters, Registrars and District Judges in the High Court are heard by a High Court Judge: Practice Direction 52A Tables 1 and 2.

171 From decisions of Circuit Judges and from decisions of District Judges in insolvency matters: Practice Direction 52A Tables 1 and 2.

172 See footnote 99.

173 And also appeals from the County Court to the High Court; and appeals within the County Court and High Court, from a junior to a senior judge of the same court.

174 CPR 52.3(1).

175 In other words, the appellant may seek to persuade the judge to permit an appeal against the decision he has just made, which may call for a good deal of tact on the part of the appellant's advocate – judges do not like being told that they have got things wrong, any more than the rest of us.

176 CPR 52.3. An appeal from a decision under section 44 of the Arbitration Act 1996 to grant or refuse an interim remedy in support of arbitral proceedings may only be made with the permission of the judge who made the decision: see section 44(7); but the Court of Appeal may still give permission itself where the basis of the appeal is that the lower court lacked jurisdiction to make the order which it made, or where the lower court arrived at its decision as a result of some fundamentally unfair or improper process: *Cetelem SA v Roust Holdings Ltd* [2005] EWCA Civ 618 per Clarke LJ at [28] and [75]; and *c.f. Bunge SA v Kyla Shipping Co Ltd* [2013] EWCA Civ 734 per Longmore LJ at [10]–[15], a case on section 69 of the Arbitration Act 1996.

177 CPR 52.6. Where the appeal is from an order which was itself made on appeal (a "second appeal"), e.g. an appeal from an order of a High Court Judge hearing an appeal from an order made by a Master of the High Court, the test for permission to appeal to the Court of Appeal is more exacting: the appellant must show that the second appeal would have a real

which appears elsewhere in the CPR,[178] is a qualitative standard rather than a quantitative one. It does not mean that the appeal must, for example, stand a greater than 50% chance of success. It simply means that the prospect of success must be real rather than fanciful.[179]

2.62 Nevertheless, permission to appeal is only granted sparingly. That reflects a number of matters: the finite extent of the Court of Appeal's resources;[180] the financial burden on the parties of fighting an appeal; and a recognition that the Court of Appeal is often no better placed than the lower court to determine a particular question.[181] This last factor is of particular importance in relation to interim remedies, which invariably require the lower court to make evaluative judgments by weighing up competing factors, and to exercise its discretion about whether to grant the remedy or not. These are not hard-edged questions of fact or law, for which there is only one possible right answer. Rather, they are matters on which two different judges, applying the same set of principles, might legitimately come to two different answers. The Court of Appeal will generally only interfere with the decision of the lower court (whose judges will usually have far more day-to-day experience of determining applications for interim relief) on such matters where the judge has applied the wrong legal principles, taken irrelevant matters into account, ignored relevant matters or reached a decision which is so plainly wrong that it must be regarded as outside the generous margin entrusted to him.[182]

---

prospect of success and raise an important point of principle or practice, or that there is some other compelling reason for the Court of Appeal to hear it: CPR 52.7.

178 See CPR Part 24, which governs applications for summary judgment (final judgment without a trial) on claims or issues. A claimant may apply for summary judgment against the Defendant on the basis that the Defendant has no real prospect of successfully defending the claim; and the Defendant may likewise apply for summary judgment against the claimant on the basis that the claim has no reasonable prospect of succeeding. For a recent high-profile example of the former, see *HRH The Duchess of Sussex v Associated Newspapers Ltd* [2021] EWHC 273 (Ch).

179 *Tanfern Ltd v Cameron-MacDonald* (Practice Note) [2000] 1 WLR 1311 per Brooke LJ at [21].

180 The overriding objective in CPR Part 1 requires the court, when determining applications for permission to appeal, to take account of the need to allot an appropriate share of the court's resources to each case, while taking into account the need to allot resources to other cases: CPR 1.1(2)(e).

181 In some circumstances, the Court of Appeal is in a decidedly worse position: for example, in relation to facts found by the lower court, especially where those findings are made following a trial involving live oral witness evidence. An appeal court may only overturn a trial judge's findings of fact where it is satisfied that he fundamentally misunderstood the issue or the evidence, or that he plainly failed to take the evidence into account, or that he arrived at a conclusion which the evidence could not on any view support: *Volcafe Ltd v Cia Sud Americana de Vapores SA* [2018] UKSC 61 per Lord Sumption JSC at [41]. Of course, applications for interim relief do not usually involve oral evidence or final determinations of factual issues.

182 *Stuart v Goldberg Linde* [2008] EWCA Civ 2 per Clarke LJ at [81–2]; *Walbrook Trustees (Jersey) Ltd v Fattal* [2008] EWCA Civ 427 per Lawrence Collins LJ at [33]; *Lakatamia Shipping Company Ltd v Nobu SU Ltd* [2012] EWCA Civ 1195 at [27] per Longmore LJ.

2.63 Where permission to appeal is granted, the Court of Appeal has all the powers of the lower court in relation to the appeal, including the power to grant fresh interim remedies.[183] The Court of Appeal will generally not receive new evidence on appeal which was not before the lower court.[184] It will allow an appeal where the decision of the lower court was wrong, in fact, on the law or because it involved a plainly wrong exercise of discretion; or where the decision of the lower court was unjust because of a serious procedural or other irregularity.[185]

2.64 Importantly, a pending appeal (and *a fortiori* a pending application for permission to appeal) does not operate as a stay of the decision of the lower court which is being appealed against, unless either the lower court or the Court of Appeal specifically orders a stay.[186] That means that, pending the outcome of the application for permission to appeal and, if permission is granted, the appeal itself, the order being appealed against normally remains in full force and the Appellant is obliged to obey it. A stay will only be granted where, in all the circumstances, the risk of injustice to the Appellant if the stay is refused outweighs the risk of injustice to the respondent if the stay is granted.[187] That exercise of balancing the risks of injustice is characteristic of the English court's approach to discretionary interim remedies (of which a stay may be seen as an example[188]): it reflects the fact that the court has to decide whether to grant the remedy at a stage when the facts and the merits have not yet been finally determined.

2.65 Appeals from the Court of Appeal, Civil Division, lie to the UK Supreme Court.[189] Permission is required in every case, and can only be granted by the Supreme Court itself. Permission will only be granted where the application raises an arguable point of law of general public importance which ought to be considered by the Supreme Court at that time, bearing in

183 CPR 52.20.

184 It has power to do so under CPR 52.21(2), but will only exercise it where three criteria are satisfied: that the evidence could not have been obtained with reasonable diligence at the hearing before the lower court; that it would probably have had an important influence on the result, though it need not be decisive; and that it is apparently credible, albeit not necessarily incontrovertible: *Ladd v Marshall* [1954] 1 WLR 1489 per Denning LJ at p 1491; *Terluk v Berezovsky* [2011] EWCA Civ 1534 per Laws LJ at [32].

185 CPR 52.21(3).

186 CPR 52.16.

187 *Hammond Suddard Solicitors v Agrichem International Holdings Ltd* [2001] EWCA Civ 2065 per Clarke LJ at [22].

188 See 2.45 above.

189 Exceptionally, the Supreme Court also hears "leapfrog" appeals directly from the High Court in a few very limited categories of case, the most important being ones where the decision of the High Court involves a point of law of general public importance in respect of which the judge was bound by an earlier decision of the Court of Appeal or the Supreme Court, in previous proceedings, in which the point was fully considered: section 3(b) of the Administration of Justice Act 1969.

mind that the matter will already have been the subject of judicial decision and may have already been reviewed on appeal.[190]

Jurisdiction

2.66 Jurisdiction means the court's legal power to hear and determine a case.[191] It has a number of aspects, including personal jurisdiction (who can be brought before the court and made subject to its orders?), subject-matter jurisdiction (what matters can the court decide, and what remedies can it grant?) and territorial jurisdiction (where can the court exercise its powers and enforce its orders?).

2.67 The term "jurisdiction" is also often used in two other senses.

a. First, the expressions "jurisdiction" and "territorial jurisdiction" are often used as metonyms for the physical territory in which the English court is able to exercise its powers and enforce its orders: thus, the (territorial) jurisdiction of the English Court refers to the land and territorial waters of England and Wales. The word "jurisdiction" is used in this sense in a number of important provisions of the CPR,[192] including CPR Parts 6 and 62, and CPR PD 6B which contain rules about service of court documents "in" and "out of the jurisdiction". But in CPR Part 11, entitled "Disputing the Court's Jurisdiction", it bears its strict meaning of the court's legal power to hear and determine a case.
b. Secondly, the term "jurisdiction" is sometimes used to mean, not only the court's strict legal power to hear and determine a case or grant a particular remedy, but also any settled practice about the manner and the circumstances in which the court will or will not exercise that power.[193] This type of settled practice is particularly important in the field of interim remedies, almost all of which are discretionary; and in that context it is more correctly described as rules of "principled discretion".[194] It also includes the rules govern-

190 Supreme Court Practice Direction 3, para 3.3.3.

191 This is the "only really correct" meaning of the term, per Pickford LJ in *Guaranty Trust Co of New York v Hannay & Co* [1915] 2 KB 536 at page 563. As explained below, however, the term is often used in other senses, which has led to it being described as a "slippery" word: *Orexim Trading Ltd v Mahavir Port and Terminal Pte Ltd* [2018] EWCA Civ 1660 per Lewison LJ at [20].

192 CPR 2.3(1) provides that, unless the context otherwise requires, "jurisdiction" means England and Wales and any part of the territorial waters of the United Kingdom adjoining England and Wales.

193 *Société Eram Shipping Co Ltd v Cie Internationale de Navigation* [2003] UKHL 30 per Lord Millett at [78]; *Fourie v Le Roux* [2007] UKHL 1 per Lord Scott of Foscote at [25].

194 See e.g. *Masri v Consolidated Contractors Intl Co SAL* [2007] EWHC 3010 (Comm) per Gloster J at [65]. Lord Mustill in *Channel Tunnel Group Ltd v Balfour Beatty Construction Ltd* [1993] AC 334 at page 360 used the expression "judicial self-denial".

ing when the court will decline to exercise its jurisdiction to hear and determine a case altogether, either by refusing permission to serve originating process out of the jurisdiction (where such permission is required),[195] or by staying its proceedings, usually in favour of another court or tribunal.[196]

2.68 The English court has jurisdiction to grant an interim remedy against a person[197] if the following requirements are all satisfied:

a. The person is subject to the personal jurisdiction of the English court.
b. The remedy is within the subject-matter jurisdiction of the court.
c. Granting the remedy is permissible in accordance with any relevant rules of principled discretion.

2.69 Personal jurisdiction depends on whether the person against whom the interim remedy is sought is amenable to service of originating process – the formal court document by which proceedings are commenced, which in most cases means a Claim Form[198] – in accordance with the CPR.[199] If originating process cannot lawfully be served on the person in a given set of proceedings, the English court will only have personal jurisdiction over him if he has voluntarily entered an appearance and submitted to the jurisdiction of the court in those proceedings.[200] The rules governing service of originating process are discussed below.[201]

2.70 Subject-matter jurisdiction is a single expression which covers two slightly different requirements:

195 See 2.86(c) below.

196 See 2.45 above.

197 I.e. an individual or a corporation.

198 In a limited number of cases, discussed below, an Application Notice serves as the originating process: see footnote 51 above.

199 See generally Lord Collins of Mapesbury, Professor Jonathan Harris, *Dicey, Morris & Collins on the Conflict of Laws* (15th Edn, Sweet & Maxwell, 2018) §11-003; and *Cameron v Victoria Liverpool Insurance Co Ltd* [2019] UKSC 6 per Lord Sumption at [14]: "The court generally acts *in personam*. Although an action is completely constituted on the issue of the claim form, for example for the purpose of stopping the running of a limitation period, the general rule is that 'service of originating process is the act by which the defendant is subjected to the court's jurisdiction' ... The court may grant interim relief before the proceedings have been served or even issued, but that is an emergency jurisdiction which is both provisional and strictly conditional".

200 For example, by acknowledging service of originating process and then not disputing the jurisdiction of the English court in accordance with CPR Part 11; or by commencing the proceedings himself as Claimant, in which case the court has jurisdiction to grant an interim remedy against him on the application of the Defendant. See generally Lord Collins of Mapesbury, Professor Jonathan Harris, *Dicey, Morris & Collins on the Conflict of Laws* (15th Edn, Sweet & Maxwell, 2018) §§11-125 to 11-133.

201 See 2.74–2.88 below.

a. The first requirement is that court must have the power to determine the type of claim which is being brought, and to grant the type of remedy claimed, in the proceedings. The Admiralty jurisdiction of the High Court, as set out in section 20 of the Senior Courts Act 1981, is subject-matter jurisdiction in this sense.[202]
b. The second requirement is that the remedy sought must be consistent with principles of international comity, according to which the sovereignty of each state is territorial and should generally only be exercised in relation to persons and things within the state's territory or in respect of the state's own nationals. Comity requires that a court should not trespass on the authority of another state by attempting to seize property or assets within the territory of the foreign state, or by compelling the citizens of that state to do acts within its boundaries; nor should it require a third party abroad to choose between obeying an English court order and obeying his obligations under foreign law.[203] These principles are of particular importance for worldwide freezing injunctions and other interim remedies which may have significant extraterritorial effects.

2.71 The central rule of principled discretion applicable to discretionary interim remedies is that they cannot be granted in isolation, but generally are dependent upon the existence of a substantive claim or cause of action arising out of an actual or threatened invasion of the Applicant's legal or equitable rights or unconscionable behaviour.[204] Formerly, this rule required the substantive claim to be enforceable in the English court by final judgment, which in turn meant that the respondent had to be amenable to the personal jurisdiction of the English court for the purposes of determining the substantive claim.[205] As explained above, that requirement has since been largely removed by statute, and the English court can now grant discretionary

202 See Nigel Meeson and John A Kimbell, *Admiralty Jurisdiction and Practice* (5th Edn, Informa Law from Routledge, 2017) Chapter 2: "Subject-matter jurisdiction".

203 *Masri v Consolidated Contractors International (UK) Ltd* [2008] EWCA Civ 303 per Lawrence Collins LJ at [46–47]; Taurus Petroleum Ltd v State Oil Marketing Co of the Ministry of Oil, Iraq [2017] UKSC 64 at [48–51] per Lord Clarke JSC.

204 *The Siskina* [1979] AC 210 per Lord Diplock at page 256, a case on freezing injunctions; *South Carolina Insurance Co v Assurantie Maatschappij "De Zeven Provincien" NV* [1987] AC 24 per Lord Brandon of Oakbrook at pages 39–40, a case on anti-suit injunctions; *Channel Tunnel Group Ltd v Balfour Beatty Construction Ltd* [1993] AC 334 per Lord Mustill at page 362, a case on interim injunctions. This rule serves to limit the otherwise unfettered power of the court, in section 37(1) of the Senior Courts Act 1981, to grant an injunction or appoint a receiver "in all cases in which it appears to the court to be just and convenient to do so". See generally Steven Gee QC, *Gee on Commercial Injunctions* (7th Edn, Sweet & Maxwell, 2020) §§1-032 to 1-034, 12-001.

205 *The Siskina* [1979] AC 210 per Lord Diplock at page 256.

interim remedies in support of substantive proceedings in foreign courts,[206] or in arbitration;[207] but the core of the rule, that such remedies are intrinsically ancillary and incidental to a substantive claim, remains in place.[208]

2.72 The court's statutory powers to grant discretionary interim remedies in support of foreign proceedings or arbitration are, however, subject to additional limits:

a. The court's power to grant interim remedies in support of foreign proceedings in section 25 of the Civil Jurisdiction and Judgments Act 1982 is subject to a discretion not to grant the relief if, in the opinion of the court, the fact that the court has no jurisdiction apart from section 25 in relation to the subject-matter of the proceedings makes it "inexpedient" to grant the relief.[209] The court will invariably exercise this discretion against granting relief under this provision where the case has no significant connection with England and Wales, as to grant relief in such a case would be inconsistent with comity.[210] Where there is a sufficient connection with England and Wales, the court will have regard to five further criteria when determining whether it is inexpedient to grant relief, all of which similarly reflect the principle of comity: (i) whether the making

206 Civil Jurisdiction & Judgments Act 1982, section 25, as extended by the Civil Jurisdiction and Judgments Act 1982 (Interim Relief) Order 1997, SI 1997/392; *ETI Euro Telecom International NV v Republic of Bolivia* [2008] EWCA Civ 880 per Lawrence Collins LJ at [63]–[78].

207 Arbitration Act 1996 section 44. Indeed, the court has long had the power to grant interim remedies in support of arbitration: see the Arbitration Act 1934 section 9(1) and Schedule 1, paras 5, 6 and 8; and the Arbitration Act 1950 section 12(5)(e), (g) and (h). The 1934 and 1950 Acts have both been repealed. The scope of the court's power to grant interim remedies under section 44 of the Arbitration Act 1996 is considered in more detail in Chapter 4.

208 The scope of the rule in *The Siskina* was considered *obiter* by a somewhat sceptical House of Lords in *Channel Tunnel Group Ltd v Balfour Beatty Construction Ltd* [1993] AC 334. Lord Browne-Wilkinson indicated at pages 341–343 that the rule simply required the English court to have personal jurisdiction over the Defendant, and the Claimant to have a cause of action under English law: if those requirements were satisfied, he considered that the court could grant an interim injunction against the Defendant in support of substantive proceedings before any court or tribunal, in England or elsewhere, without the need for any further statutory powers such as those now contained in section 25 of the Civil Jurisdiction and Judgments Act 1982 and section 44 of the Arbitration Act 1996. Lord Mustill said at pages 361–363 that, at most, *The Siskina* established that the right to an interim injunction could not exist in isolation but was always incidental to and dependent on the enforcement of a substantive right, and that the English court should only grant interim relief where that underlying right was subject to the jurisdiction of the English court. He reasoned that, where proceedings to enforce such a right were brought in England in breach of an arbitration agreement, the English court could grant an interim injunction in support of the substantive arbitration proceedings at the same time as granting a stay of the English court proceedings, again without the need for any additional statutory powers.

209 Civil Jurisdiction and Judgments Act 1982, subsection 25(2).

210 *Mobil Cerro Negro v Petroleos de Venezuela* [2008] EWHC 532 (Comm) per Walker J at [119]; *Belletti v Morici* [2009] EWHC 2316 (Comm) per Flaux J at [54].

of the order will interfere with the management of the case in the foreign court; (ii) whether it is the policy in the foreign court not itself to grant the type of relief sought; (iii) whether there is a danger that the order will give rise to disharmony, confusion or a risk of conflicting or overlapping orders in other jurisdictions; (iv) whether there is likely to be a potential conflict as to jurisdiction rendering it inappropriate and expedient to grant the order; and (v) whether the English court is making an order which is likely to be disobeyed and which it cannot enforce.[211]

b. The court's power to grant interim remedies in support of arbitration proceedings in section 44 of the Arbitration Act 1996 is subject to strict limits which reflect the principles of autonomy and judicial non-interference which underpin that Act.[212] These are that, in non-urgent cases, the court can only act on the application of a party to the arbitral proceedings with the permission of the arbitral tribunal or the agreement of the other parties; in urgent cases, the court may act on the application of a party without such permission or agreement, but may only make such orders as it thinks necessary for the purpose of preserving evidence or assets; and in any case the court shall only act if, or to the extent that, the arbitral tribunal has no power or cannot act effectively.[213]

c. In addition, the court's power to grant interim remedies under section 44 of the Arbitration Act 1996 in support of arbitration *outside* England and Wales or Northern Ireland[214] is subject to a discretion not to grant the relief if, in the opinion of the court, the location of the seat of the arbitration makes it "inappropriate" to grant the relief.[215] Again, this rule reflects considerations of comity. In such a case there must, as a minimum, be a significantly strong connection with England and Wales to justify the court exercising its jurisdiction extraterritorially.[216] Where that threshold test is satisfied, the court is still likely to regard granting relief as inappropriate where a foreign court is seized or is likely to be seized of the matter; or where there is a more appropriate foreign court in which the application for

211 *Motorola Credit Corp v Uzan* [2003] EWCA Civ 752 per Potter LJ at [116].

212 Arbitration Act 1996 section 1; and see the Departmental Advisory Committee on Arbitration Law Final Report on the Arbitration Bill, February 1996, §§214–216.

213 Arbitration Act 1996, sub-sections 44(3)–(5).

214 And its power to make orders to secure the attendance of a witness who is in the UK, before an arbitral tribunal sitting in England and Wales or Northern Ireland (but not Scotland): section 43 of the Arbitration Act 1996.

215 Arbitration Act 1996 section 2(3).

216 Compare *Belletti v Morici* [2009] EWHC 2316 (Comm) per Flaux J at [54], equating the terms "appropriate" and "expedient" in the context of section 25 of the Civil Jurisdiction and Judgments Act 1981.

supportive measures may be made; or where the foreign court of the seat of the arbitration has corresponding powers; or where any order it makes is likely to be unenforceable in the country of the seat of the arbitration.[217]

2.73 The rule that discretionary interim remedies are dependent upon the existence of a substantive claim also forms the basis of the English court's so-called Chabra jurisdiction,[218] under which it has the power, in certain situations, to grant interim remedies against third parties against whom the Applicant asserts no substantive claim at all. The paradigm casc for the exercise of this power is where a third party, T, holds assets in his own name, but those assets belong in reality to another person, D, against whom the Applicant does assert a substantive claim. In such a case, the court may grant a freezing injunction directly against T, in support of the substantive claim against D, restraining T from disposing of the assets which he holds for D's benefit, so that they remain available to satisfy any judgment or arbitral award the Applicant obtains against D.[219]

Service of Originating Process

2.74 The general rule is that personal jurisdiction is territorial and restricted to persons upon whom originating process[220] can lawfully be served within the territorial limits of England and Wales ("within the jurisdiction").[221] This general rule is reflected by CPR 6.6(1) which provides that originating process[222] "must be served within the jurisdiction" unless otherwise provided

217 *U&M Mining Zambia Ltd v Konkola Copper Mines plc* [2014] EWHC 3250 (Comm) per Teare J at [53].

218 This jurisdiction takes its name from one of the foundational decisions on the topic, *TSB Private Bank International SA v Chabra* [1992] 1 WLR 231 (CA).

219 The scope of the English court's power to grant freezing injunctions and other interim remedies against third parties on this basis, and the limits of its personal and subject-matter jurisdiction to do so, are considered in more detail in Chapters 4, 5 and 9.

220 In the case of an application for an interim remedy against a third party under the English court's Chabra jurisdiction (see 2.73 above), in support of a substantive claim which is to be heard and determined by the English court itself, the general rule is that the court's personal jurisdiction is restricted to third parties upon whom an Application Notice issued in the substantive proceedings, seeking Chabra relief, can lawfully be served within the jurisdiction: *Mercedes-Benz AG v Leiduck* [1996] AC 284 (PC) per Lord Mustill at pages 298–299; *C Inc plc v L* [2001] 2 Lloyd's Rep 459 per Aikens J at [94(i)].

221 *The Siskina* [1979] AC 210 per Lord Diplock at page 254. CPR Part 6, Section II, permits a claim form to be served within the jurisdiction upon the Defendant himself or, in certain circumstances, upon his nominated solicitor or agent: CPR 6.8 and 6.11.

222 CPR 6.6(1) refers to the "claim form", which in this context also covers other forms of originating process: CPR 6.2(c). It also covers an Application Notice issued in substantive English proceedings, seeking an interim remedy against a third party under the Chabra jurisdiction (see 2.73 above), but only where the application for Chabra relief is made before the commencement of substantive proceedings: CPR 6.2(c).

elsewhere in the CPR. Section II of CPR Part 6 contains detailed rules about where, when, how and upon whom originating process[223] may be served within the jurisdiction.

2.75 There are, however, numerous statutory exceptions to the general rule,[224] which allow originating process to be served out of the jurisdiction in certain cases. It should be noted that these exceptions only apply to *in personam* Claim Forms: an *in rem* Claim Form against a ship can never be served out of the jurisdiction.[225] In many cases, service out of the jurisdiction requires the express permission of the English court. The current position can be summarised as follows:

(i) Permission not required: service within the UK[226]

2.76 Originating process may be served without permission in Scotland and Northern Ireland (constituent parts of the UK which are outside the territorial jurisdiction of the English courts) in a wide range of cases, depending on the subject-matter of the claim made in the English proceedings, the domicile of the parties or the existence of an agreement conferring jurisdiction on the English courts.

(ii) Permission not required: service outside the UK[227]

2.77 Originating process may be served without permission outside the UK, where the parties have concluded a choice of courts agreement in favour of the English courts in accordance with the Hague Convention 2005,[228] and the subject-matter of the proceedings is within the scope of that conven-

---

223 Those rules are contained in Section II of CPR Part 6. Section III of that Part contains detailed rules about service of other documents within the jurisdiction. The rules in Section III govern service within the jurisdiction of an Application Notice issued in substantive English proceedings, seeking an interim remedy against a third party under the court's Chabra jurisdiction (see 2.73 above), where the application for Chabra relief is made after the commencement of substantive proceedings.

224 The English court has no inherent jurisdiction to allow service of out the jurisdiction. Service out of the jurisdiction always requires express authorisation by statute or pursuant to the CPR: *Masri v Consolidated Contractors International Co SAL* [2009] UKHL 43 per Lord Mance at [32].

225 Nigel Meeson and John A Kimbell, *Admiralty Jurisdiction and Practice* (5th Edn, Informa Law from Routledge, 2017) §4.18. The person who would be liable on the claim if it were brought *in personam* may, however, acknowledge service of the *in rem* Claim Form, and thereby voluntarily submit to the personal jurisdiction of the English court for the purposes of defending the claim: CPR 61.3(6). Where he does so, the claim proceeds as an *in personam* claim against that Defendant as well as *in rem*: *The Gemma* [1899] P 285; *The Tatry* [1992] 2 Lloyd's Rep 552.

226 CPR 6.32.

227 CPR 6.33.

228 The Convention on Choice of Court Agreements concluded on 30 June 2005 at the Hague, the English text of which is set out in Schedule 3F to the Civil Jurisdiction and Judgments Act 1982, as amended by the Private International Law (Implementation of Agreements) Act 2020.

tion. The Hague Convention 2005 applies to international disputes in civil and commercial matters, but excludes a number of important topics from its scope, including carriage of goods, personal injury, "tort or delict claims for damage to tangible property that do not arise from a contractual relationship", intellectual property and arbitration.[229]

2.78 Originating process may also now be served without permission in any case where a contract contains a term to the effect that the court shall have jurisdiction to determine the claim.[230]

2.79 Permission to serve originating process outside the UK is also not required in a limited range of cases involving consumer contracts and contracts of employment,[231] and in a few other specific types of case where the English court has extraterritorial jurisdiction conferred by statute.[232]

2.80 Prior to 31 December 2020, originating process could be served without permission in other EU and EFTA states in a much wider range of civil and commercial cases, pursuant to the Judgments Regulation Recast and the Lugano Convention 2007. That position will be restored if and when the UK is permitted to rejoin the Lugano Convention 2007 as an independent contracting state.

(iii) Permission required[233]

2.81 In all other cases, service out of the jurisdiction requires the express permission of the English court.[234] Permission can only be granted if the proceedings fall within 1 or more of 24 jurisdictional gateways, which are set out in CPR PD 6B §3.1 and CPR 62.5. These gateways identify relevant connections with England and Wales which (together with the rules permitting service out of the jurisdiction without permission) serve to delineate the maximum extent of the jurisdiction which the English court is permitted to exercise over persons who are not within England and Wales.[235]

---

229 See Articles 1 and 2. The Hague Convention 2005 does not govern "interim measures of protection". It neither requires nor precludes the grant, refusal or termination of such measures and does not affect whether or not a party may request or a court should grant, refuse or terminate them: see Article 7.

230 CPR 6.33(2B)(b).

231 Civil Jurisdiction and Judgments Act 1982 sections 15A–15E.

232 See CPR 6.33(3). For the scope of this provision, see *Orexim Trading Ltd v Mahavir Port and Terminal Pte Ltd* [2018] EWCA Civ 1660 per Lewison LJ at [42]-[43]. An example of a claim within this provision is a claim under the Convention on the Contract for the International Carriage of Goods by Road 1956 (CMR), incorporated into UK law by the Carriage of Goods by Road Act 1965: *Royal & Sun Alliance v MK Digital FZE* [2005] EWHC 1408 (Comm) per Aikens J at [64].

233 CPR 6.36–37; and CPR 62.5

234 Again, this position will change if and when the UK is permitted to rejoin the Lugano Convention 2007 as an independent contracting state, whereupon it will become permissible to serve originating process in EU and EFTA states without permission in a wider range of cases, subject to the rules contained in that convention which govern the allocation of jurisdiction between the courts of contracting states.

235 *Brownlie v Four Seasons Holdings Inc* [2017] UKSC 80 per Lord Sumption JSC at [31].

2.82 Most of the jurisdictional gateways are only applicable where the Claim Form contains a substantive claim and seeks substantive relief from the English court. When one of these gateways applies, the relevant connection with England and Wales will be a feature of that substantive claim or that substantive relief. Where the court grants permission to serve out on a Defendant under one of these gateways, and service is effected in accordance with that permission, the court has jurisdiction to hear and determine the substantive claim against that Defendant. Its jurisdiction to grant interim remedies against the Defendant in those proceedings is dependent on, and ancillary to, that substantive jurisdiction. It grants interim remedies in those proceedings by way of interlocutory relief, on an application under CPR Part 23.[236]

2.83 The following jurisdictional gateways, which are particularly important in commercial disputes, fall into this "substantive connection" category:

- Where a claim is made for an injunction as final, substantive relief,[237] ordering the Defendant to do or refrain from doing an act within the jurisdiction (CPR PD 3.1 §2). For a claim to fall within this ground, it must itself be based on a substantive cause of action, such as breach of contract or tort, for which a final injunction[238] can be granted as a substantive remedy.
- Where a claim is made against Defendant B, who is a necessary or proper party to proceedings against Defendant A,[239] over whom the English court already has jurisdiction on some other basis (CPR PD 3.1 §§3 and 4).
- Where a claim is made in relation to a contract[240] which is made within the jurisdiction, or is governed by English law, or in relation to breach of contract committed within the jurisdiction (CPR PD 3.1 §§6–8).
- Where a claim is made in tort for damage sustained or acts committed within the jurisdiction (CPR PD 3.1 §9).
- Where a claim is made, whose subject-matter relates wholly or principally to property within the jurisdiction (CPR PD 3.1 §10).

236 *The Siskina* [1979] AC 210 at pages 255–256 per Lord Diplock.

237 As opposed to an interim injunction: *Rosler v Hilbery* [1925] Ch 250 at pages 261–262 per Warrington LJ and per 262–263 per Sargant LJ; *The Siskina* pages 255–256 per Lord Diplock.

238 As distinct from an interim injunction: see 2.42 above.

239 Defendant A is sometimes referred to as the anchor Defendant. For this gateway to apply, the claim against the anchor Defendant must itself be a substantive claim: *Belletti v Morici* [2009] EWHC 2316 (Comm) per Flaux J at [36]–[37]; *Cruz City 1 Mauritius Holdings v Unitech Ltd* [2014] EWHC 3704 (Comm) per Males J at [74]–[75].

240 Or a putative contract – see paragraph (8).

- Where a claim is made for breach of confidence or misuse of private information and detriment is suffered, or results from acts committed, within the jurisdiction (CPR PD 3.1 §21).

2.84 There are, however, three jurisdictional gateways which can apply – and in one case, can only apply – where the Claim Form contains no substantive claim and seeks no substantive relief from the English court. These are as follows:

a. Where a claim is made for an interim remedy in support of foreign court proceedings under section 25 of the Civil Jurisdiction and Judgments Act 1982 (CPR PD 3.1 §5). By definition, this gateway can only apply if the substantive dispute is to be determined by a foreign court rather than by the English court.
b. Where a claim is made or a remedy sought in relation to arbitration (CPR 62.5(1)(b)). This gateway can apply to substantive claims which are to be determined in the English court, including claims for a final antisuit injunction restraining a Defendant from pursuing foreign court proceedings in breach of an arbitration agreement.[241] But it also applies to claims for discretionary interim remedies in support of actual or proposed arbitration proceedings, under section 44 of the Arbitration Act 1996, in which the substantive dispute will be determined by the arbitral tribunal and not by the English court.
c. Where a claim is made under "an enactment which allows proceedings to be brought" but which is not covered by any other paragraph in CPR PD 3.1 (CPR PD 3.1 §20). The enactments within this gateway include any legislative provision which, properly construed, allows proceedings to be brought against persons who are not within England and Wales.[242] This includes both substantive proceedings,[243] and certain proceedings for free-standing interim remedies which may never result in substantive proceedings in

241 An antisuit injunction is available as a final remedy for an actual or threatened breach of contract, namely, breach of the implied negative covenant contained in an arbitration agreement, by which each party agrees not to bring proceedings which are within the scope of the agreement in any forum other than the contractually agreed arbitral tribunal: *AES Ust-Kamenogorsk Hydropower Plant LLP v Ust-Kamenogorsk Hydropower Plant JSC* [2013] UKSC 35 per Lord Mance JSC at [1] and [40]. The actual or threatened breach of contract is a substantive cause of action, and hence the claim for an antisuit injunction in such a case is a substantive claim for a final and conclusive, as opposed to interim, remedy.

242 *Orexim Trading Ltd v Mahavir Port and Terminal Pte Ltd* [2018] EWCA Civ 1660 per Lewison LJ at [35], [47] and [48].

243 For example, a claim to set aside a transaction defrauding creditors under section 423 of the Insolvency Act 1986: *Orexim Trading Ltd v Mahavir Port and Terminal Pte Ltd* [2018] EWCA Civ 1660 per Lewison LJ at [47].

England or elsewhere, such as an application for disclosure prior to the commencement of proceedings under section 33 of the Senior Courts Act 1981.[244]

2.85 Where the court grants permission to serve originating process which contains no substantive claim, and seeks no substantive relief from the English court, out of the jurisdiction on a Defendant under one of these gateways, and service is effected on the Defendant in accordance with that permission, the English court does not acquire jurisdiction to hear and determine the substance of the dispute. It acquires jurisdiction to grant interim remedies against the Defendant in those proceedings; but that jurisdiction is free-standing or, more correctly, ancillary to the substantive jurisdiction of whichever court or tribunal which will hear and determine the substantive claim.[245]

2.86 In such cases, the English court can grant interim remedies as the final relief in the English proceedings. Importantly, however, it can also grant interim remedies as interlocutory relief in those proceedings. Its jurisdiction to do so is ancillary to its jurisdiction to grant interim remedies as final relief. Take, for example, a case where the Claimant seeks an urgent freezing injunction from the English court in support of arbitration proceedings, under section 44 of the Arbitration Act 1996. He is required to commence court proceedings by issuing a Part 8 Claim Form, and to claim a freezing injunction as the final relief in those proceedings.[246] The court cannot grant that final relief before the Defendant has been notified of the proceedings and given a fair opportunity to be heard and adduce evidence in response,[247] as to do so would be a breach of the overriding objective of the CPR, of natural justice and of the Defendant's right to a fair trial under Article 6 of the European

244 *ED&F Man Capital Markets v Obex Securities LLC* [2017] EWHC 2965 (Ch). Note that section 37 of the Senior Courts Act 1981, which confirms the English court's power to grant injunctions, is not itself an "enactment which allows proceedings to be brought" for the purposes of CPR PD 3.1 §20: it simply provides for a particular remedy within proceedings whose legal basis has to be found elsewhere: *AES Ust-Kamenogorsk Hydropower Plant LLP v Ust-Kamenogorsk Hydropower Plant JSC* [2011] EWCA Civ 647 per Rix LJ at [126], Wilson LJ at [192] and Stanley Burnton LJ at [207].

245 I.e. ancillary to the substantive jurisdiction of the foreign court or the arbitral tribunal; or in the case of an application under section 33 of the Senior Courts Act 1981, ancillary to the English court's own substantive jurisdiction in the prospective proceedings, even though they may never materialise: one of the purposes of ordering pre-action disclosure under section 33 is to enable the parties to resolve their dispute without the need for substantive proceedings: see CPR 31.16(3)(d)(ii) and *ED&F Man Capital Markets v Obex Securities LLC* [2017] EWHC 2965 (Ch) per Catherine Newman QC at [20].

246 CPR 62.3(1) and 62.4(1).

247 See CPR PD 62 §6.1–6.6 which sets out the default procedural directions for exchange of written evidence, etc., in a claim under the Arbitration Act 1996, unless the court otherwise orders.

Convention on Human Rights.[248] In order to obtain urgent relief, the Claimant must therefore make an interlocutory application in those proceedings for a temporary freezing injunction,[249] pending determination of his claim for the same remedy as final relief in those proceedings.[250]

Obtaining Permission to Serve out of the Jurisdiction

2.87 Permission to serve out is itself a discretionary remedy. Applications for permission are governed by CPR Part 23 and by CPR 6.37.[251] In order for permission to be granted, the Applicant must satisfy three requirements:[252]

a. He must demonstrate that the claim for final relief which he makes in the proceedings raises a "serious question" for the court to determine. This is not a particularly demanding test: it simply means that the claim must have a real, rather than a fanciful, prospect of success.
b. He must establish a "good arguable case" that the claim for final relief in fact falls within one or more of the jurisdictional gateways in CPR PD 6B §3.1 or CPR 62.5.[253] The scope of the gateways is a question of law, but the question whether the claim falls within a gateway is a mixed question of fact and law.[254] The "good arguable case" test is somewhat imprecise and flexible. It is met where

248 See *Cameron v Liverpool Victoria Insurance Co Ltd* [2019] UKSC 9 per Lord Sumption at [17]: "Justice in legal proceedings must be available to both sides. It is a fundamental principle of justice that a person cannot be made subject to the jurisdiction of the court without having such notice of the proceedings as will enable him to be heard".

249 He may make that application without notice to the Defendant, and before proceedings are formally commenced by the issue of a Part 8 Claim Form: see 2.97–2.116 below.

250 In practice, where this occurs, the proceedings may never reach the final stage, because it may not be worthwhile for either party to progress the proceedings beyond the interlocutory stage; and if the proceedings do reach the final stage, that will often be because the court decides to adopt a rolled-up procedure whereby it determines the claim for final relief at the Return Date hearing of the application for interlocutory relief: see e.g. *Donohue v Armco Inc* [1999] 2 Lloyd's Rep 649 (Comm) per Aikens J at [69]; *Ulusoy Denizilik AS v Cofco Global Harvest (Zhangjiang) Trading Co Ltd (The Ulusoy-11)* [2020] EWHC 3645 (Comm) per Bryan J at [97]–[99].

251 Or, in the case of applications for permission to serve out a Part 8 Claim Form containing a claim for a remedy in support of arbitration proceedings, CPR 62.5.

252 *Seaconsar Far East Ltd v Bank Markazi Jomhouri Islami Iran* [1994] 1 AC 438; VTB Capital Plc v Nutritek International Corp [2013] UKSC 5 per Lord Clarke of Stone-cum-Ebony at [164].

253 CPR 6.37(1)(a). Where more than one claim is made in the same proceedings, every one of those claims must fall within a permissible ground.

254 I.e. do the alleged facts, which the Applicant contends bring the case within the jurisdictional gateway, exist; and if so, do those facts satisfy the legal requirements of that gateway? It is usually not enough for the Applicant to demonstrate a good arguable case on that legal question: he must generally satisfy the court that he really is right as a matter of law, or the court will not grant permission to serve out: *Altimo Holdings & Investments Ltd v Kyrgyz Mobil Tel Ltd* [2011] UKPC 7 per Lord Collins of Mapesbury at [81].

the court is satisfied that the Applicant has a better argument, on the material currently available, than the Respondent.[255] This is a higher standard than "serious question", but lower than the "balance of probabilities"[256] test which the court applies when making final determinations on questions of fact following a full trial. That is a reflection of the reality that the court has to decide whether or not to grant permission to serve out at a very early stage in the proceedings, when not all the evidence relevant to the issue of jurisdiction may be available, and before the evidence which is available on that issue has been fully tested by disclosure and cross-examination.[257] In this respect, applications for permission to serve out have much in common with applications for discretionary interim remedies; and the court applies the same "good arguable case" standard when deciding whether or not to grant many of those remedies.

c. He must demonstrate that the English court is clearly or distinctly the appropriate forum (the *forum conveniens*) for the determination of the claim for final relief, and that in all the circumstances the court ought to exercise its discretion to permit service of the proceedings out of the jurisdiction.[258] The appropriate forum is the one which has jurisdiction to hear and determine the dispute, and with which the dispute has the most real and substantial connection. The court determines this latter requirement by reference to connecting factors, which may relate to the convenience or expense of litigating in one court rather than another; or to the law governing the substantive dispute; or to where the parties reside and conduct business.[259]

2.88 Applications for permission to serve out are normally made without notice to the Respondent.[260] As with any without-notice application, the

---

255 *Brownlie v Four Seasons Holdings Inc* [2017] UKSC 80 per Lord Sumption JSC at [7].

256 Otherwise known as "more likely than not", i.e. a probability of over 50%.

257 *Canada Trust Co v Stolzenberg* (No.2) [1998] 1 WLR 547 at pages 555–558 per Waller LJ.

258 This is not an explicit requirement for applications under CPR 62.5 for permission to serve out a Claim Form containing a claim for an interim remedy in support of arbitration proceedings under section 44 of the Arbitration Act 1996. In such cases, the requirement will invariably be satisfied if the seat of the arbitration proceedings is or will be in England and Wales. The court can also grant such remedies in respect of arbitrations seated outside the jurisdiction: see sections 2(1) and 2(3)(a) of the Arbitration Act 1996, in which case the court will require the Applicant to demonstrate a substantial connection with England and Wales before it grants permission to serve out.

259 *Spiliada Maritime Corp v Cansulex Ltd* [1987] AC 460 at page 478 per Lord Goff of Chieveley. Similarly, where originating process is lawfully served either within the jurisdiction, or out of the jurisdiction without the need for permission, the person on whom it is served can apply to the court to stay the proceedings on *forum* non *conveniens* grounds, i.e. that another court has jurisdiction to hear and determine the claim and is clearly or distinctly more appropriate than England: see 2.45 above.

260 This is permissible under CPR 23.4(2). See further 2.97–2.116 below.

Applicant and his legal advisers have a duty to make full and frank disclosure to the court of all facts and matters which are material to the application and, in particular, to draw clearly to the court's attention any matter which might constitute a ground for not granting the application.[261] This duty arises from the fact that the court is being asked to make an order at a stage where the Respondent has had no opportunity to be heard or to adduce evidence.

2.89 Where permission to serve out is granted, the Respondent has an automatic right to apply to set that permission aside under CPR Part 11. If successful, that will deprive the court of the jurisdiction it acquired by the grant of permission and by service pursuant to that permission. On the application to set aside, the Respondent has the opportunity to adduce evidence and present arguments as to why permission could not or should not have been granted, whether on the facts, on the law or as a matter of discretion. Any failure by the Applicant to make full and frank disclosure at the original without-notice hearing is relevant to the court's discretion, and the court may set aside permission on that basis; but where the Applicant has not deliberately sought to mislead the court or been grossly negligent, the court may allow him to make a fresh application for permission, or simply allow the original permission to stand and deal with the failure of full and frank disclosure by an appropriate costs order.[262]

Procedural Stage at which Interim Remedies Can Be Granted

2.90 Most interim remedies in support of substantive English proceedings can be granted by way of interlocutory relief at any stage of the proceedings,[263] i.e.:

a. Before the proceedings are formally commenced by the issue of a Claim Form,[264] but only where the matter is urgent or it is otherwise desirable to do so in the interests of justice.[265]
b. After issue but before service of the Claim Form.
c. Between service of the Claim Form and final judgment on the merits.
d. After final judgment, in aid of enforcement of the judgment.[266]

261 *Masri v Consolidated Contractors International Co SAL* [2011] EWHC 1780 (Comm) per Burton J at [58]; *Tuguschev v Orlov* [2019] EWHC 2031 (Comm) per Carr J at [7]. See further 2.108–2.116 below.

262 *NML Capital Ltd v Republic of Argentina* [2011] UKSC 31 per Lord Collins at [136].

263 CPR 25.2(1).

264 CPR 25.2(1)(a).

265 CPR 25.2(2)(b). It is hard to see when the interests of justice might make it desirable to apply before the issue, as opposed to the service, of the Claim Form in a non-urgent case.

266 CPR 25.2(1)(b).

2.91 The principal exceptions to the above rules are that:

a. A warrant for the arrest of a ship can only be issued after the *in rem* Claim Form has been issued.[267]
b. An order for disclosure of documents or inspection of property before commencement of action, under section 33 of the Senior Courts Act 1981, can only be granted prior to the commencement of the "subsequent proceedings" to which the disclosure or inspection may be relevant.

2.92 The above rules apply where the Applicant for the interim remedy is the Claimant or intended Claimant in the English proceedings. A Defendant to those proceedings may also apply for an interim remedy at any stage,[268] but he will generally only be permitted to do so after he has accepted, or submitted to, the jurisdiction of the court to determine the substantive claim, by formally acknowledging service of the Claim Form or by filing a defence to the claim.[269]

2.93 Interim remedies in support of substantive proceedings in a foreign court under section 25 of the Civil Jurisdiction and Judgments Act 1982 can similarly be granted by way of interlocutory relief at any stage of the English proceedings, as well as by way of final relief in those proceedings.[270] The same is true of interim remedies in support of arbitral proceedings under section 44 of the Arbitration Act 1996; but the strict limits governing the granting of such remedies, contained in subsections 44(3)–(5) of the 1996 Act, apply to applications for interlocutory relief as much as to claims for final relief.

2.94 Regardless of the stage at which the application is made, the court can only grant the relief sought if it has jurisdiction to do so. Thus, where an interlocutory application for interim relief is made before English proceedings have been formally commenced, or before originating process has been validly served on the Defendant, the Applicant must satisfy the court that it has the necessary jurisdiction to hear and determine the claim for final relief claimed in the proceedings. If the Defendant is not in England and Wales and the permission of the court is required to serve originating process on him out of the jurisdiction, the Applicant must apply for that permission at the same time as making his interlocutory application for interim relief.[271]

---

267 CPR 61.5(1). This provision confirms that arrest also is available after judgment, on the application of a judgment creditor.

268 This does not apply to ship arrest. A Defendant who has acknowledged service of an *in rem* Claim Form may bring a counterclaim against the Claimant in those proceedings; but if he wishes to arrest the Claimant's vessel in order to secure or to found jurisdiction for that counterclaim, he must issue a fresh *in rem* Claim Form.

269 CPR 25.2(2)(c).

270 But see footnote 82 above in relation to ship arrest as security for a substantive claim which is to be determined by a foreign court or in arbitration, which is only available as interlocutory relief.

271 Note that, where the permission of the court is required to serve originating process out of the jurisdiction, it is also required to serve any other document in the proceedings out of

Procedure on an Interlocutory Application for an Interim Remedy

2.95 The appropriate procedure to be adopted on an interlocutory application for an interim remedy will depend on the nature and purpose of the remedy sought, the stage of proceedings at which it is sought, the urgency with which it is needed and any other relevant factors such as whether there is any need to keep the fact that the application is going to be made secret.

2.96 In an ordinary situation, where the Applicant seeks a discretionary interim remedy[272] during the course of existing English proceedings, and no special factors such as extreme urgency or the need for secrecy arise, the following standard procedure applies:

a. The general rule is that the application must be made by issuing an Application Notice and serving it on the Respondent, together with a signed witness statement, or sworn affidavit where required, containing evidence in support of the application.[273] It is good practice to attach a draft of the order sought to the Application Notice.
b. The Application Notice must be served on the Respondent at least three clear days in advance of the hearing at which the court is to deal with the application.[274] In many cases a considerably longer period will be appropriate, in order to give the Respondent a proper opportunity to obtain and serve evidence and to prepare submissions in response; and where the court considers that the period between service of the Application Notice and the hearing is inadequate, it is likely to adjourn that hearing to a later date in order to give the Respondent sufficient time to respond properly.
c. The Respondent is normally given a fixed period within which to serve evidence in response to the application, and the Appellant in turn has a fixed period for serving evidence in reply.[275] This procedural timetable can be varied by the Court,[276] and to a limited

---

the jurisdiction, including any Application Notice issued before the proceedings are formally commenced, and any interlocutory order made on such an application: CPR 6.2(c) and 6.38.

272 The same procedure, modified in accordance with CPR 62.8, applies to applications for a mandatory stay of English court proceedings under section 9 of the Arbitration Act 1996. Ship arrest is governed by a separate procedure: see CPR 61.5 and CPR PD 61 §5.

273 CPR 23.3(1), 23.4(1), 23.7(1) and (3), 25.3(2). Where the written evidence in support of the application is brief, it may be set out in the Application Notice itself, instead of in a separate witness statement: see e.g. the Commercial Court Guide 2017 §F1.5(b). Where an affidavit is required, that must be in a separate document: see CPR PD 32 §§3-16.

274 CPR 23.7(1)(b). The period is calculated in accordance with CPR 2.8. Service must be effected in accordance with CPR Part 6.

275 In the Commercial and Admiralty Courts, the standard default periods are 14 days for the evidence in response, and 7 days for the evidence in reply; but where the application is likely to require an oral hearing lasting more than half a day, these periods are each doubled: CPR PD 52 §§13.1-2.

276 CPR PD 23A §9.2.

extent by agreement between the parties, to suit the particular circumstances of the case.[277]

d. The parties will generally be required to exchange and file written submissions, known as skeleton arguments, by fixed deadlines in advance of the hearing.[278] These skeleton arguments will outline the relevant facts, state the applicable law by reference to relevant statutes and authorities and outline the parties' respective arguments on how the court should determine the application.

e. The court will then proceed to determine the application, either on an oral hearing at which the parties are represented by counsel,[279] or on documents alone if appropriate.[280] Oral hearings usually take place in public, reflecting the principle of open justice which is a fundamental aspect of English law.[281] The court must, however, conduct a hearing in private where it considers that to be necessary for one or more of a number of specific reasons, including where publicity would defeat the object of the proceedings, where the hearing involves confidential information and where the court otherwise considers it to be necessary to secure the proper administration of justice.[282] The court will also conduct the hearing in private in most cases where the application relates to arbitration.[283] Oral hearings have traditionally taken place in person; but they may also be conducted virtually, via videoconferencing platforms or by telephone, particularly where an in-person hearing is inappropriate due to urgency[284] or other reasons such as public health.[285]

---

277 CPR 2.11; but see CPR PD 58 §§7 and 13.4.

278 See e.g. the Commercial Court Guide §§F5.5-7, F6.5-7; F15.1(b).

279 "Counsel" means a barrister instructed to give legal advice and appear as an advocate on behalf of a party in proceedings. Barristers have full rights of audience in all English courts, including the higher courts: the High Court, Crown Court, Court of Appeal and Supreme Court. Solicitors have full rights of audience in the lower courts, and may also appear in the higher courts where (i) the hearing is being held in private or (ii) they have qualified as solicitor-advocate a with Higher Rights of Audience. There are currently around 5,000 solicitor-advocates with full rights of audience in the higher civil courts, compared with around 17,000 practicing barristers.

280 CPR 23.8. The court will generally direct an oral hearing where the application is contested: see e.g. the Commercial Court Guide §F4.1(a).

281 CPR 39.2(1), (3). Members of the general public and the press are free to attend hearings which are held in public, subject to the power of court security officers under section 53 of the Courts Act 2003 to restrain, remove and exclude individuals who disrupt or delay the conduct of the court business, cause disorder or threaten the safety of others.

282 CPR 39.2(3).

283 See CPR 62.10.

284 See CPR PD 25A §4.5.

285 See e.g. the Protocol Regarding Remote Hearings dated 26 March 2020, issued by the Judiciary of England and Wales in light of the COVID 19 pandemic: "1. The current pandemic necessitates the use of remote hearings wherever possible".

Detailed procedures and protocols have been established for managing remote hearings using these platforms.[286]

f. The court will give its decision on the application in the form of judgment, which may be delivered orally by the judge at the end of the oral hearing (an *ex tempore* judgment), or in writing thereafter (a reserved judgment). In either case, a written form of order will be drawn up, reflecting the outcome of the hearing and embodying the orders made, and sealed by the court.

2.97 The court has the power to dispense with many of the standard procedural requirements, in exercise of its case management powers, where it is necessary and appropriate to do so in accordance with the overriding objective of dealing with cases justly. This is often the case for interim remedies, particularly where they are sought before English proceedings have been formally commenced.

Without Notice Applications

2.98 The court may allow an Applicant to make an interlocutory application for an interim remedy without first serving the Application Notice on the Respondent, where there is a good reason for not doing so.[287] A hearing which takes place without the Application Notice having been formally served on the Respondent is described as "without notice".[288] A hearing which takes place after the Application Notice has been formally served is described as "on notice".

2.99 In the context of interim remedies, good reasons which would justify hearing an application without notice typically include urgency, i.e. where there is insufficient time to effect service of the Application Notice; or the need for secrecy, such as where giving the Respondent advance notice of the application would be liable to defeat the ends of justice by allowing him to take steps frustrate the purpose of the application before it can even be heard and determined by the court.[289] Certain types of application for interim

286 See CPR PD 23A §§6.1-1.11 and 7; CPR PD 51V ("the Video Hearings Pilot Scheme"); and the Protocol Regarding Remote Hearings dated 26 March 2020.

287 CPR 25.3. The application must be supported by evidence setting out why notice has not been given: CPR PD 25A §3.4.

288 The former Latin expression was "*ex parte*".

289 CPR 23.4(2); Commercial Court Guide §F15.1(b). The court will also dispense with prior service of the Application Notice as a matter of course where it is not possible to serve it lawfully in advance of the hearing, such as on an application without notice for permission to serve the Claim Form or other document out of the jurisdiction. Generally, however, the court will not dispense with prior service of the Application Notice merely on the basis that the identity or location of the Respondent is unknown, such as where the remedy sought is an interim injunction restraining unidentified protestors from committing allegedly unlawful acts of trespass, harassment, etc. Instead, it will use its powers under CPR 6.15 and 6.27 to direct service by an alternative method or at an alternative place, which is likely to bring the application to the

relief commonly involve urgency, or a need for secrecy, or both. The commonest example is the freezing injunction, where there may be a risk that the Respondent will imminently take steps to hide or remove his assets; and a risk that, if notified of the application in advance, he will use the period between notification and the hearing to accomplish that task while he can still do so without being in breach of a court order. Considerations of urgency and secrecy often also arise together in relation to search orders, where the material which the court-sanctioned search is intended to find and preserve may be at a particular location for only a short time; and where there is invariably a risk that the Respondent will quickly remove, hide or destroy that material upon learning of an impending application. There can, of course, be a need for secrecy where there is no urgency, such as where the Respondent is only expected to take steps to hide assets or dispose of material if he becomes aware of a proposed application for a freezing or search order. Similarly, there may be urgency but no need for secrecy, such as on an application under CPR 25.1(1)(c)(v) for an order for the sale of perishable property such as fresh foodstuffs.

2.100 Where there is "exceptional urgency" the court may permit an Applicant to make an interlocutory application for an interim remedy without having filed an Application Notice.[290] In such situations, the Applicant may not have had time formally to commence proceedings in the English court by issuing a Claim Form; and there may not even be sufficient time to draw up an Application Notice, or to draft and sign/swear a witness statement/affidavit in support of the application, before the hearing. If so, the court may be prepared to hear and determine the application on the basis of an unfiled draft Application Notice, and an unsigned or unsworn draft version of the witness statement or affidavit.[291] Where it does so, it will also require the Applicant to issue the Claim Form (if that has not been done), file the Application Notice and procure the signing/swearing of the witness statement/affidavit after the hearing.[292]

2.101 Indeed, in cases of extreme urgency, where there is not enough time even to prepare drafts prior to the hearing, the court may hear and determine the application solely on the basis of factual information provided to it orally by the Applicant's counsel at the hearing, based on the instructions which he

attention of the Respondents: for example, by publishing notices at appropriate physical locations, in newspapers and on websites: see generally *Cameron v Liverpool Victoria Insurance Co Ltd* [2019] UKSC 6 per Lord Sumption at [13] and [15]; and *Canada Goose UK Retail Ltd v Persons Unknown* [2020] EWCA Civ 303 per Sir Terence Etherton MR at [50] and [82].

290 CPR 23.3(2)(b); CPR PD 23A §§3(1) and 4.3(1)–(2).

291 See Commercial Court Guide §F15.3(a). Note that, if permission is required to serve originating process out of the jurisdiction on the Defendant, the Applicant must apply for that permission at the same time as the interlocutory application for interim relief.

292 See also CPR PD 25A §§4.3 and 4.4.

has received from the Applicant.[293] Where the court proceeds on this basis, it will require the Applicant to undertake by its counsel draw up and file an Application Notice, and to procure that a witness statement/affidavit is drawn up and signed/sworn setting out and verifying the substance of the information provided to the court in support of the application.[294]

2.102 Unless there is a need for secrecy, the court will only dispense with prior service of the Application Notice in cases of great urgency. In cases which are less critically urgent, the court will instead exercise its powers to shorten the period between service of the Application Notice and the hearing of the application;[295] or permit the Application Notice to be served by an alternative method or at an alternative place to those which are otherwise permitted by CPR Part 6;[296] and it may impose a compressed procedural timetable for the exchange of further evidence leading to an early hearing.

2.103 In any event, where there is no need for secrecy, the court will require the Applicant to take steps to give the Respondent as much advance notice and information about the application and the hearing as is practicable in the circumstances,[297] so that he has the best possible opportunity to prepare evidence and submissions in response to the application and to attend the hearing. Thus, even on an extremely urgent application, unless there is a need for secrecy, the Applicant's solicitors will be expected to use their best endeavours to notify the Respondent or his legal advisers in advance, by telephone and/or email,[298] of the application and of the time and place of the hearing; and, where practicable, to email or courier him copies of the Application Notice, witness statement or affidavit in support, and draft order, prior to the hearing. Failure to do so is likely to result in the court adjourning the hearing or even dismissing the application altogether.

2.104 Where the Respondent is notified informally of the hearing but is not formally served with the Application Notice in advance, the hearing is sometimes described as "without notice on notice"[299] (or, where the Respondent or his representatives actually attend the hearing, "opposed without notice"). Where the Application Notice is formally served on the

293 Steven Gee QC, *Gee on Commercial Injunctions* (7th Edn, Sweet & Maxwell, 2020) §8-008.

294 Steven Gee QC, *Gee on Commercial Injunctions* (7th Edn, Sweet & Maxwell, 2020) §8-008.

295 CPR 23.7(4)(a). Strictly speaking, the court cannot shorten the period; but it can declare that sufficient notice has been given in the circumstances and decide to hear the application notwithstanding the short notice.

296 CPR 6.15 and 6.27.

297 CPR PD 23A §4.2.

298 *National Commercial Bank Jamaica Ltd v Olint Corp Ltd* [2009] UKPC 16 per Lord Hoffmann at [13]; *Jeeg Global Ltd v Hare* [2012] EWHC 773 (QB) per Tugendhat J at [39].

299 An inelegant but serviceable expression, which does not appear in the CPR itself. It corresponds with the former mixed Latin and English expression "*ex parte* on notice".

Respondent in advance of the hearing, but not sufficiently far in advance to comply with the requirements of the CPR, the hearing is described as "on short notice". "Without notice on notice" and "opposed without notice" hearings are particular types of "without notice" hearing. A hearing "on short notice" is a particular type of hearing "on notice".

2.105 Counsel and solicitors representing the Applicant at a without notice hearing are under an obligation to take a full note of the hearing, and to ensure that the note is served on the Respondent, along with the evidence and skeleton argument relied upon at the hearing, as soon as possible thereafter.[300]

2.106 Where an application is heard without notice,[301] or on short notice, and the court grants the relief sought, it will invariably fix a date, usually one or two weeks in the future, known as the Return Date, on which it will rehear the same application, but this time on notice to the Respondent.[302] In addition, whenever the court makes an order on a without notice hearing, the Respondent has an automatic right to apply to set aside or vary the order, at any time within seven days after the date when the order is served on him.[303] Where the relief granted at the initial hearing is a freezing injunction or other form of interim injunction, the order will typically provide that the injunction shall only apply until the end of the Return Date hearing or further order.

2.107 All these practices reflect the basic principle of fairness, that the court always should hear sides before reaching a decision unless the ends of justice demand otherwise, and that it should only depart from that principle to the minimum extent necessary to ensure that the ends of justice are served. For the same reason, where the court grants an interim remedy at a without notice hearing, it will generally not exercise its jurisdiction to award the costs of the application to the Applicant at that hearing,[304] but will instead reserve the question of costs to the Return Date hearing when the Respondent will have a proper opportunity to be heard.[305]

2.108 If there is a need for secrecy which justifies hearing an application without notice, the court will hear the application in private, as publicising the hearing would defeat the object of the application.[306] Most applications

---

300 Commercial Court Guide §F2.5(b).

301 Without notice includes without notice on notice and opposed without notice.

302 Commercial Court Guide §F15.8(a). With the parties' agreement, the Return Date may be postponed in order to give them a proper opportunity to prepare their evidence and legal arguments: Commercial Court Guide §F15.8(c).

303 CPR 23.10. The court will sometimes require any such application to be made on a minimum amount of informal notice to the Respondent (i.e. the Applicant at the without notice hearing) or his legal representatives, which may be as little as an hour or less; but *c.f.* Commercial Court Guide §F15.9.

304 The general rule is that the unsuccessful party is ordered to pay the successful party's costs: CPR 44.2(2).

305 See e.g. the costs provision in the standard for of freezing injunction at Appendix 11 of the Commercial Court Guide.

306 Under CPR 39.2(3)(a) and/or (g).

for freezing injunctions, and almost all applications for search orders, are initially heard without notice[307] and in private for reasons of secrecy.[308] By the time of the Return Date, there will generally be no further need for secrecy, and so the Return Date hearing will normally be held in public unless there is another basis for holding it in private, such as where the application is in relation to arbitration.[309]

Full and Frank Disclosure

2.109 Whenever an application is heard without notice or on short notice,[310] the Applicant is under a duty to make full and frank disclosure at the hearing of all matters of fact, law and procedure that are material to the court's decision about whether to grant the relief sought, and on what terms to grant it.[311] The duty of full and frank disclosure is owed by the Applicant and by his legal advisers.[312] It is owed, not to the Respondent, but to the court itself.[313] It is distinct from, and additional to, the duty which all parties and their legal advisers owe to the court under all circumstances, not to mislead the court.

2.110 The duty of full and frank disclosure is of paramount importance in ensuring the integrity of the court's process. It is a necessary corollary of the court being prepared to depart from the basic principle of fairness, that it will hear both sides before reaching a decision – a principle which can only be derogated from in exceptional circumstances, such as where there is extreme urgency or the need for secrecy. The duty reflects the need of the court to be able to rely on the Applicant, who appears alone, to present the argument in a way which is not merely designed to promote its own interests; but in a fair and even-handed manner, drawing attention to evidence and arguments which it can reasonably anticipate the Respondent would wish to make.[314]

2.111 The duty requires the Applicant and his legal advisers to draw the court's attention to any significant factual, legal and procedural aspects of the

---

307 Steven Gee QC, *Gee on Commercial Injunctions* (7th Edn, Sweet & Maxwell, 2020) §8-001.

308 Commercial Court Guide §F1.7(c).

309 CPR 62.10(3); Commercial Court Guide §F1.7(b).

310 *CEF Holdings Ltd v Mundey* [2012] EWHC 1524 (QB) per Silber J at [179]–[183].

311 *Fitzgerald v Williams* [1996] QB 657 per Sir Thomas Bingham MR at page 667. The question of materiality is a matter for the court, rather than for the subjective judgment of the Applicant and his legal advisers: *Brink's Mat Ltd v Elcombe* [1988] 1 WLR 1350 per Ralph Gibson LJ at page 1356.

312 Commercial Court Guide §F2.5(a); *Fundo Soberano de Angola v Dos Santos* [2018] EWHC 2199 (Comm) per Popplewell J at [53].

313 *Memory Corp plc v Sidhu* (No.2) [2000] 1 WLR 1443 per Mummery LJ at pages 1459–1460.

314 *Tugushev v Orlov* [2019] EWHC 2031 (Comm) per Carr J at [7(ii)].

case.[315] It also requires them to identify and address any defences which the Respondent has already raised, or which he can be reasonably be expected to raise, and any other arguable defences that may be available to the Respondent in order to resist the application, whether or not he has intimated that he intends to raise them.[316]

2.112 The duty is not limited to matters which are actually known to the Applicant. It also covers matters which ought to have been known to him,[317] had he made all such inquiries as were reasonable and proper in the circumstances. Those circumstances may include the nature of the application, the likely effect of the remedy sought on the Respondent and on third parties and any considerations of urgency affecting the application (including whether the urgency is the result of delays on the part of the Applicant).[318]

2.113 The ultimate touchstone of the duty of full and frank disclosure is whether the Applicant has made a full and fair presentation of the application to the court in all material respects.[319] The Applicant must display utmost good faith in satisfying this requirement.[320] It is therefore not enough for the Applicant or his legal representatives to refer to material matters obliquely, or to include them within the body of written evidence (and certainly not within the exhibits) or the skeleton argument which is placed before the court, in the expectation that the judge hearing the application will unearth them for himself.[321] The Applicant and his counsel must draw all potentially adverse matters to the court's specific attention at the hearing, and explain them fully, so that the judge clearly understands what might be said on behalf of the Respondent in opposition to the application, were it to be made on proper notice.[322]

2.114 The duty also requires the Applicant to bring to the court's specific attention any unusual features of the remedy or the order sought. Thus, where the Applicant seeks an interim remedy for which there is an official recommended standard form of order, as is the case for freezing injunctions and

315 *Memory Corp plc v Sidhu* (No.2) [2000] 1 WLR 1443 per Mummery LJ at page 1460.

316 See e.g. *JSC Mezhdunarodniy Promyshlenniy Bank v Pugachev* [2014] EWHC 4336 (Ch) per Christopher Clarke J at [171]–[172]. The Applicant is not required to analyse every possible point in minute detail: *Tugushev v Orlov* [2019] EWHC 2031 (Comm) per Carr J at [7(vi)].

317 CPR PD 25A §3.3.

318 *Brink's Mat Ltd v Elcombe* [1988] 1 WLR 1350 per Ralph Gibson LJ at pages 1356–1357.

319 *Memory Corp plc v Sidhu* (No.2) [2000] 1 WLR 1443 per Robert Walker LJ at page 1444.

320 *Siporex Trade SA v Comdel Commodities Ltd* [1986] 2 Lloyd's Rep 428 per Bingham J at page 437.

321 *Siporex Trade SA v Comdel Commodities Ltd* [1986] 2 Lloyd's Rep 428 per Bingham J at page 437; *Rogachev v Foryainov* [2019] EWHC 1529 (QB) per Morris J at [78(2)].

322 *Fundo Soberano de Angola v Dos Santos* [2018] EWHC 2199 (Comm) per Popplewell J at [52].

search orders,[323] he must draw the court's specific attention to any differences between the order which he seeks and that standard form.[324]

2.115 The duty of full and frank disclosure applies regardless of whether the Respondent or his legal advisers are informed of the hearing in advance, and regardless of whether they actually attend the hearing. That is because, where the Respondent has not been formally served with proper, timely, notice, he cannot be expected to be properly prepared to meet the application or to be able to put all the relevant legal and factual information before the court at that hearing. Where, however, the Respondent or his legal advisers do attend the hearing and deal with all the factual and legal issues in the way in which the Applicant would have been obliged to do in order to satisfy his duty of full and frank disclosure, the Applicant is discharged from the obligation to give any further information.[325]

2.116 Where the duty of full and frank disclosure applies, it may continue beyond the initial hearing, until such time as the Respondent is in a proper position to apply to the court to vary or set aside the order made at the hearing and to put before it any information that he considers relevant. That will generally be when the order made at the hearing is served on the Respondent.[326] During this extended period, the Applicant is bound to return to court promptly in order to correct, update or add to any material information which was provided to the court at the initial hearing, so that the court can reconsider whether to discharge, amend or leave unchanged its original order.[327]

2.117 The duty of full and frank disclosure does not apply to the Return Date hearing, or to the hearing of any application brought by the Respondent prior to the Return Date to vary or set aside the order made at the initial hearing.

Undertakings

2.118 The English court has a power to impose conditions on the granting of discretionary interim remedies, including a condition that the Applicant must give certain undertakings to the court in return for the granting of the

323 Standard forms of freezing injunction and search order for general use are appended to CPR PD 25. A more refined standard form of freezing injunction for use in the Commercial Court is to be found at Appendix 11 to the Commercial Court Guide.

324 Commercial Court Guide §F15.7; *Frenkel v Lyampart* [2017] EWHC 312(Ch) per Amanda Tipples QC at [90–91].

325 *CEF Holdings Ltd v Mundey* [2012] EWHC 1524 (QB) per Silber J at [182].

326 *JSC BTA Bank v Ablyazov* [2018] EWHC 259 (Comm) at per Sir Andrew Smith at [13]. Where the Respondent and his legal advisers attend the original hearing, the duty of full and frank disclosure may only extend for a short time after the hearing, or not at all.

327 *JSC BTA Bank v Ablyazov* [2018] EWHC 259 (Comm) per Sir Andrew Smith at [12].

remedy.[328] An undertaking is a voluntary promise which is addressed to the court, rather than to another party. It is not a contractual promise, but it is nevertheless legally binding, inasmuch as breach of an undertaking is a contempt of court which is punishable in the same way as breach of a court order.[329]

2.119 The most important type of undertaking is the undertaking in damages. The court will invariably require an Applicant seeking an interim injunction of any kind, including a freezing injunction, or a search order,[330] to give an undertaking that he will compensate the Respondent in damages if the Respondent suffers loss as a result of the order sought, and the court decides that the Applicant should compensate him for that loss.[331] An undertaking of this type is generally regarded as part of the price which an Applicant has to pay, in order to obtain this type of discretionary interim remedy.

2.120 The court also has the power to require the Applicant, as a further condition of granting a discretionary interim remedy, to fortify his undertaking in damages by providing security in the form of cash or, more commonly, a guarantee or similar financial instrument from a first-class financial institution in England and Wales. The court will typically require fortification where the Applicant cannot show sufficient assets within the jurisdiction to satisfy the court that the undertaking in damages has real substance and that it can and will be honoured.[332]

2.121 The rationale behind the requirement for an undertaking in damages is fundamental to the English court's approach to discretionary interim remedies. It reflects the fact that interim remedies are never free standing but are always ancillary and incidental to a substantive claim; and that, at the time when the court is called upon to grant the interim remedy, the merits of that

---

328 See CPR 3.1(1)(3) and, in relation to injunctions, the Senior Courts Act 1981 s 37(2).

329 Steven Gee QC, *Gee on Commercial Injunctions* (7th Edn, Sweet & Maxwell, 2020)§11-001; see also 2.124–2.128 below.

330 The court may also require an Applicant to give an undertaking in damages where he seeks other forms of discretionary interim remedy. Ship arrest is not a discretionary remedy (but *c.f.* footnote 109 above) and so the court cannot require a Claimant in *in rem* proceedings to give an undertaking in damages as a condition for the issue of a warrant of arrest; but see 2.123 below.

331 The standard wording of the undertaking in damages for use in freezing injunctions in the Commercial Court is as follows (see to Appendix 11 to the Commercial Court Guide, Schedule B): "If the court later finds that this order has caused loss to the Respondent, and decides that the Respondent should be compensated for that loss, the Applicant will comply with any order the Court may make". The standard wording for use in search orders is somewhat wider (see the standard form annexed to CPR PD 25A, Schedule C: the wording not found in the standard form freezing injunction is underlined): "If the court later finds that this order *or carrying it out* has caused loss to the Respondent, and decides that the Respondent should be compensated for that loss, the Applicant will comply with any order the court may make. *Further if the carrying out of this order has been in breach of the terms of this order or otherwise in a manner inconsistent with the Applicant's solicitors' duties as officers of the court, the Applicant will comply with any order for damages the court may make*".

332 Commercial Court Guide §F15.4

substantive claim are yet to be determined. The object of granting an interim remedy is to avoid the risk of injustice to the Applicant, which arises from the fact that it will take some time before the substantive claim can be finally determined and final substantive relief granted in his favour. But granting an interim remedy at this early stage carries an inherent risk of injustice to the Respondent, in that the substantive claim may later turn out to be a bad one and determined against the Applicant, and in the meantime the Respondent may have suffered loss as a result of the interim remedy being granted. At the stage where the interim remedy is sought, the court does not and cannot know what the ultimate outcome will be, and therefore which of those risks of injustice will be eventually realised. It must therefore strike a balance which, so far as possible, protects both parties from the risks of injustice which they each face. The court seeks to strike this "balance of convenience" by ensuring that, where an interim remedy is granted to protect the Applicant against his risk of injustice, the Respondent will also be protected against risk of injustice to him (in the form of losses suffered as a result of an interim injunction which, in hindsight, should not have been granted to begin with), by ensuring that he will receive compensation for those losses.[333]

2.122 Thus, where the Applicant is unable to offer an undertaking in damages of any real substance (for example if he lacks the financial means to do so), or where the type of loss which the Respondent is likely to suffer as a result of the interim remedy being granted is not adequately compensable in damages (such as loss of his livelihood, permanent reputational damage, or financial loss which would be impossible to quantify with any kind of accuracy), this is often a powerful reason for the court to refuse an interim remedy.[334]

2.123 The court may require other types of undertaking from an Applicant/Claimant for an interim remedy, in certain circumstances. Thus:

a. Where an application is made before English proceedings have been formally commenced, the court will require the Applicant to undertake to issue and serve the Claim Form; where an application is made without notice, the court will require the Applicant to undertake to (issue and) serve the Application Notice, the order made, the evidence in support, the skeleton argument and the note of the hearing

333 See generally *American Cyanamid Co v Ethicon Ltd* [1975] AC 396 per Lord Diplock at page 406. The court can only achieve this by making the interim remedy conditional on the Applicant voluntarily offering an undertaking in damages. Without that undertaking, the Applicant is under no legal obligation to compensate the Respondent, as he generally commits no actionable wrong by successfully applying for an interim remedy in support of a substantive claim which ultimately fails, for which he could be liable in damages at law.

334 *American Cyanamid Co v Ethicon Ltd* [1975] AC 396 per Lord Diplock at pages 407–409.

on the Respondent.[335] And where the application/claim is made in support of prospective foreign proceedings under section 25 of the Civil Jurisdiction and Judgments Act 1982, or in support of prospective arbitration proceedings under section 44 of the Arbitration Act 1996,[336] the court will require the Applicant/Claimant to commence the foreign proceedings or arbitration proceedings.

b. Where the court grants a freezing injunction, it will require the Applicant to give additional undertakings to compensate third parties for costs which they incur as a result of the order; to inform certain third parties if the order ceases to have effect; not to use any information obtained as a result of the order for any other proceedings without the court's permission; and not to enforce the order outside the jurisdiction or seek a similar order elsewhere without the court's permission.[337]

c. Where the court grants a search order, it will require the Applicant personally to give additional undertakings not to use information or documents obtained as a result of the order for other any purposes or inform anyone else of the proceedings without the permission of the court; and to insure the items removed from the raided premises; and it will require the Applicant's solicitors to give separate undertakings to serve the Supervising Solicitor[338] with copies of the order, the Claim Form, the Application Notice, affidavits, skeleton argument and note of the hearing; to answer any question about whether a particular item is a "listed item" which must be removed from the raided premises; to retain all items obtained as a result of the order in their own safekeeping until the court otherwise directs; and to return all original documents obtained as a result of the order within two days of their removal. It will also require the Supervising Solicitor to give undertakings concerning the execution of his role in serving the order and other documents on the Respondent, explaining the order to the Respondent, the safekeeping of items retained by him, the maintenance of confidentiality and the provision of his report of the raid.[339]

---

335 See Schedule B to the standard form of freezing injunction at Appendix 11 to the Commercial Court Guide.

336 This does not apply where the interim remedy sought is an antisuit injunction to enforce the negative covenant in an arbitration or jurisdiction agreement: see footnote 241 above.

337 See Schedule B of the standard form of freezing injunction at Appendix 11 to the Commercial Court Guide.

338 An independent solicitor appointed by the court to supervise and participate in the execution of the search order: see Steven Gee QC, *Gee on Commercial Injunctions* (7th Edn, Sweet & Maxwell, 2020) §17-062.

339 See Schedules D–F to the standard form of search order appended to CPR PD 25A.

2.124 The court's power to attach conditions, such as the giving of undertakings, to the granting of discretionary interim remedies, is itself a discretionary power. Accordingly, it does not extend to the non-discretionary interim remedies of ship arrest,[340] and mandatory stay of proceedings under section 9 of the Arbitration Act 1996.[341] The CPR does, however, require the solicitor acting for an Applicant for a warrant of arrest to give a mandatory undertaking in every case, to pay the fees and expenses of the Admiralty Marshal[342] in relation to the arrest, care and custody and release of the ship.[343]

Court's Power to Enforce Interim Remedies and Undertakings

2.125 A party to English proceedings who disobeys a court order is in contempt of court.[344] So too is any person who knowingly aids and abets a breach of a court order by a party; or who knowingly sets out to subvert such an order; or who breaches an undertaking which he has given to the court; or who makes or causes a false statement to be made in a Claim Form, Application Notice, witness statement, affidavit or other document which is required by the CPR to be verified by a statement of truth, without an honest belief in the truth of the statement.[345]

2.126 Contempt of court of these kinds is called "civil contempt",[346] in order to distinguish it from other, more serious forms of conduct called "criminal contempt".[347] Civil contempt is not a criminal offence, whereas criminal contempt obviously is. Civil contempt is regarded as primarily a private matter, of legitimate concern to the parties to the litigation and to the court, but not to the wider public; whereas criminal contempt involves conduct which threatens the proper administration of justice to such an extent

340 *Willers v Joyce* [2016] UKSC 43 per Lord Clarke JSC at [68]; *The "Alkyon"* [2018] EWHC 2033 (Admlty) per Teare J at [16]–[17].

341 See 2.45 above, and David St John Sutton, Judith Gill, Matthew Gearing, *Russel on Arbitration* (24th Edn, Sweet & Maxwell, 2015) §7-036.

342 The government official responsible for ship arrest: CPR 61.5(8). In practice, arrests are usually performed on behalf of the Admiralty Marshal by Border Force (formerly the UK Border Agency), the government agency responsible for border control operations in UK territorial waters: see Nigel Meeson and John A Kimbell, *Admiralty Jurisdiction and Practice* (5th Edn, Informa Law from Routledge, 2017) §§4.60-4.63.

343 CPR 61.5(2) and CPR PD 61.5(1), which requires an application for a warrant of arrest to be made on form ADM4, which contains this mandatory undertaking.

344 Jonathan Fisher, QC, Andrew Herd, *Arlidge, Heady & Smith on Contempt* (5th Edn, Sweet & Maxwell, 2019) §3.73.

345 CPR 31.23(1), 32.14.

346 Or "contempt in procedure": *Hadkinson v Hadkinson* [1952] P 285 per Denning LJ at page 295; *R v O'Brien* [2014] UKSC 23 per Lord Toulson JSC at [42].

347 An example of criminal contempt would be bursting into a court room and disrupting a civil trial: *R v O'Brien* [2014] UKSC 23 per Lord Toulson JSC at [42]

that it merits criminal punishment from the public point of view.[348] The court has the power to impose sanctions on a person who commits a civil contempt, but those sanctions are (at least in theory) primarily intended to compel obedience or compliance with the court's order, or with his undertaking, rather than to punish him for his wrongdoing.[349] Proceedings for civil contempt are nevertheless regarded as criminal or quasi-criminal in nature. Accordingly the criminal standard of proof (proof beyond reasonable doubt) applies to them,[350] as does the right to remain silent.[351]

2.127 The principal sanctions available to the court for civil contempt are:[352]

a. Imprisonment (otherwise known as an order of committal) for a fixed term of not more than two years.[353]
b. A fine (i.e. an order to pay a fixed sum of money) in an unlimited amount.
c. Confiscation of assets (otherwise known as sequestration) by placing them in the hands of a court-appointed sequestrator to hold and manage until the court orders them to be returned or disposed of.

2.128 Proceedings for civil contempt are usually brought by a party to the proceedings in relation to which the contempt occurred, but they may also be brought by the Attorney General for England and Wales,[354] or by the court on its own initiative.[355] Proceedings for certain types of contempt require the permission of the court.[356] The procedure for bringing contempt proceedings is set out in CPR Part 81. Contempt proceedings are commenced by issuing an Application Notice in the main proceedings, in accordance with the procedure in CPR Part 23 as modified by CPR 81.4. The contempt proceedings are, however, treated for most purposes as separate from the main proceedings. Thus the party who brings contempt proceedings is referred to as the "Claimant" rather than the Applicant, and the person against whom they are

348 Jonathan Fisher, QC, Andrew Herd, *Arlidge, Heady & Smith on Contempt* (5th Edn, Sweet & Maxwell, 2019) §3.1.

349 In reality, sanctions for civil contempt often contain a distinctly punitive element, and sometimes they are exclusively punitive: see generally Jonathan Fisher, QC, Andrew Herd, *Arlidge, Heady & Smith on Contempt* (5th Edn, Sweet & Maxwell, 2019) §§3-13 to 3-25, 3-73 to 3-76.

350 *Re Bramblevale Ltd* [1970] Ch 128 per Lord Denning MR at page 137.

351 CPR 81.4(2)(n), 81.7(3).

352 CPR 81.9(1).

353 That limit is imposed by section 14(1) of the Contempt of Court Act 1981.

354 A government minister who acts as its chief legal adviser and who also has the power to bring court proceedings in the public interest.

355 CPR 81.6.

356 CPR 81.3(5).

brought is referred to as the "Defendant" rather than the Respondent, regardless of their titles in the main proceedings.[357]

2.129 Where the alleged contempt consists of disobeying a court order, the court will generally only entertain contempt proceedings if (i) the order contained a prominent notice on the front of the order known as a penal notice, warning that if the person against whom the order is made (and, in the case of a corporate body, a director or officer of that body) disobeys the order, the person (or director or officer) may be held in contempt of court and punished by a fine, imprisonment, confiscation of assets or other punishment under the law, and (ii) the order was served personally on the person alleged to be in contempt.[358] This general practice is reflected by the requirement in CPR 81.4(2)(c) that an Application Notice on a contempt application must include a statement confirming that the order allegedly breached or disobeyed was personally served, unless the court or the parties dispensed with personal service; and the requirement in CPR 81.4(2) that the Application Notice must confirm that the order included a penal notice, unless that is "wholly inapplicable".[359] The court nevertheless retains the power to waive the lack of a penal notice in the interests of justice.[360]

357 CPR 81.2(1). The Defendant to contempt proceedings may not be a party to the main proceedings at all.

358 This wording reflects the definition of a penal notice in CPR 81.2(1).

359 Former versions of CPR Part 81 expressly provided that an order to do or not to do an act could not be enforced unless a penal notice was prominently displayed on the front of the order (at CPR 81.9(1)). Notwithstanding the apparently clear terms of that provision, the court had the power to waive non-compliance as a technical error: *Shah v Patel* [2008] EWHC 1360 (Ch) per Morgan J at [10]; *Devere v Hither Green Developments Ltd* [2015] EWCA Civ 1365 per Sharpe LJ at [39]. The provision has now been repealed.

360 *Gill v Darroch* [2010] EWHC 2347 (Ch) per Vos J at [38]–[39]; *Serious Organised Crime Agency v Hymans* [2011] EWHC 3599 (QB) per Kenneth Parker J at [9]–[12]; *JSC Mezhdunarodniy Promyshlenniy Bank v Pugachev* [2016] EWHC 192 (Ch) per Rose J at [36]–[40].

CHAPTER 3

The Legal System and the General Rules for Preservation Measures in China

Introduction

3.1 This chapter will first provide an overview of the procedural steps in civil litigation followed by sources of law in China. This is then followed by a general overview of the court system in China. After that, all the steps relevant to preservation applications are discussed in detail – such as the relevant terminology for a preservation application, the preservation procedure system within the overall civil procedure code, the procedural steps that are taken in any application in order to obtain preservation measures, the issues of court jurisdiction, the format of a preservation application, the issues of security and countersecurity required in any preservation application and the types of securities that are acceptable to the courts. At the end, in the context of preservation applications, the issues of legal costs, the legal remedies for different parties, the sanctions for not obeying the preservation orders and compensation are discussed.

3.2 In conclusion, this chapter will provide the reader with general information about preservation applications in China and is a prelude to Chapters 6, 8 and 10 that deal with specific preservation measures.

The Civil Litigation Procedure System of China

3.3 In a narrow sense, the procedural steps of a civil litigation are subject to Civil Procedure Law of the People's Republic of China 1991, as amended and revised over the years (hereinafter referred to as "CPL 1991 (as amended until 2020)"). These civil procedural steps are discussed in Figure 3.1. In a broad sense, however, the civil procedural steps in the context of an application for preservation measures are governed by different sources of law, including not only the CPL 1991 (as amended until 2020) and its Interpretation, but also the preservation provisions in other laws. Some of these other laws include procedural civil law, such as the Special Maritime Procedure Law of the People's Republic of China 2000 (hereinafter referred

 DOI: 10.4324/9781003000310-4

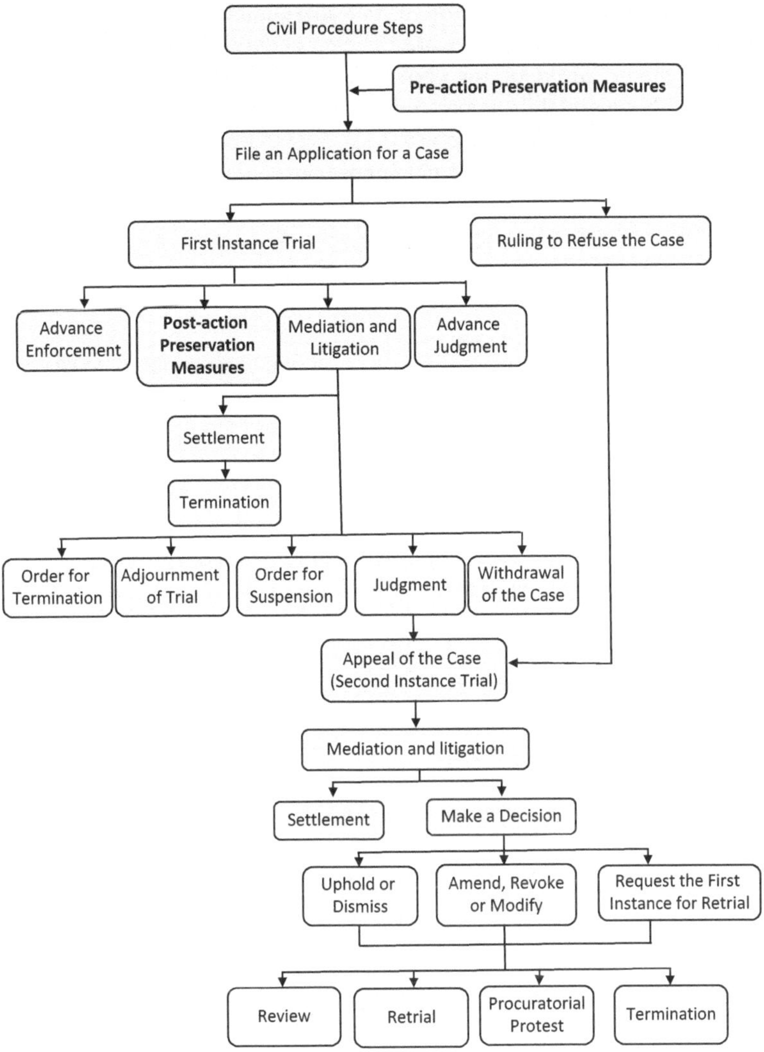

FIGURE 3.1 The civil procedural steps in China.

to as "SMPL 2000")[1] and also substantive civil law, such as the Civil Code of the People's Republic of China 2020 (hereinafter referred to as "Civil Code 2020").[2] This additional legislation will address not only the legal

1 The special Maritime Procedure Law of the People's Republic of China which was adopted by the 13th Session of the Standing Committee of the Ninth People's Congress on 25 December 1999 came into effect on 1 July 2000.

2 It must be emphasised that the Civil Code of the People's Republic of China was adopted by the National People's Congress on 28 May 2020 and came into effect on

issues arising from civil preservation, but also judicial interpretations and regulations relating to civil procedure.[3] The procedural steps included in this book cover the broad governing civil procedure that sets out the rules and standards with which Chinese people's courts expect the parties to comply when they bring a case before a court.

3.4 The major procedural steps in Chinese civil litigation proceedings are as follows:

(a) Prior to filing a case, a party may apply for a preservation measure if the matter is urgent (hereinafter referred to as "pre-action preservation application").[4]

(b) After a party has brought a case to a competent people's court, this court shall accept this case if the application and materials submitted with it satisfy the requirements of the CPL 1991 (as amended until 2020).[5] Alternatively, this court shall make a ruling to refuse the case if its requirements are not satisfied.[6]

(c) If the ruling is to refuse this case, the party is entitled to submit an appeal to the higher people's court within ten days of receiving the notification of the refusal, and in terms of the appeal, the ruling by the higher Chinese people's court is final and binding.[7]

(d) After the court has accepted the case, the claimant is entitled during the litigation proceedings to file an application for a preservation order (hereinafter referred to as "post-action preservation application") and/or for an advance enforcement.[8]

(e) If the case is *en route* for trial, the court may, prior to hearing the case, mediate between the claimant and the defendant unless the

1 January 2021. There are seven parts of the Civil Code 2020 including General Rules, Property Rights, Contracts, Personality Rights, Marriage and Family, Right of Inheritance and Tort Liability with a total of 1,260 articles. The relevant substantive provisions associated with the preservation measures are mainly covered by the Property Rights Part and the Tort Liability Part.

3 Yiwei Pu, Xuemian Wang and Xiaodong Guo, *Course of Civil Procedure Law* (Peking University Press 2016) Part I, Chapter I. In terms of the source of law, the Introduction and Applicable Law sections in Chapters 6, 8 and 10 will be introduced in detail.

4 CPL 1991 (as amended until 2020), Article 101; the exact meaning of "pre-action preservation application" can be found in 3.43; detail of the civil preservation can be found in Figure 3.3.

5 ibid Article 119.

6 ibid Article 123; it must be emphasised that in the Chinese legal system the court's decision merely contains "judgment" and "ruling" rather than "order". In order to match the international reader's taste, this book will use "preservation order" rather than "preservation ruling" but other types of rulings, such as a ruling to dismiss a case, still follow the original term.

7 ibid Articles 123 and 164.

8 ibid Articles 100 (a post-action preservation) and 153 (an advance enforcement); the exact meaning of "pre-action preservation application" can be found in 3.44.

nature of the dispute is not suited to mediation or the parties do not agree to mediation.[9]

(f) If the parties are able to agree and reach a settlement during or after hearing the case, this case can then be terminated; alternatively, in the light of the specific facts of the case, the court may make a ruling to dismiss it, or to suspend or terminate it, or to approve or disapprove its withdrawal.[10] If the case is ruled for dismissal, an appeal is allowed against this, to be made within ten days of receipt of the ruling. Other rulings, for cases to be suspended or terminated, or to approve or disapprove their withdrawal, may not be appealed against.[11]

(g) Apart from making a ruling according to the different facts of the case, the court will render a judgment; if the first instance is the final one,[12] the first instance court makes a definitive judgment; for other cases, any parties not satisfied with the judgment are entitled to submit an appeal within 15 days of receipt of the judgment.[13]

(h) During second instance proceedings, parties may reach a settlement;[14] alternatively, in terms of the original ruling, the second instance court may make a ruling to overrule the application for appeal, or to discharge or modify the original ruling, or to order the first instance court to retry the case, or make a new ruling directly; in terms of the original judgment, the second instance court may make a judgment to overrule the application for appeal, or to discharge or modify the original judgment, or to order the first instance court to retry the case, or make a new judgment directly.[15]

---

9 ibid Article 122.

10 ibid Articles 154 (3), (5) and (6); it should be noted that the claimant is generally entitled to withdraw the case after the court has accepted it. However, if the withdrawal of the case may impact on the interests of the state, the collective or the other person, the court will render a ruling to disallow the application seeking the withdrawal of this case; see also, Jiaxing Liu and Jianfeng Pan, *Civil Procedure Law* (5th Edn, Peking University Press 2017) Chapter 26, Part II.

11 CPL 1991 (as amended until 2020), Articles 154 and 164.

12 Article 162 of the CPL 1991 (as amended until 2020) provides that "when trying a simple civil case prescribed in Item 1 of Article 157 of the Law (CPL), the subject amount of which is below thirty per cent of the average annual salary of the employees of all provinces, autonomous regions, municipalities directly under the Central Government in the previous year, the primary people's court or the tribunal dispatched by it may apply the system under which the ruling in the first instance shall be final", and Item 1 of Article 157 provides that "Where a primary people's court and a tribunal dispatched by it try simple civil cases in which the facts are evident, the relationship of rights and obligations is definite and the disputes are minor"; this means that a small civil case based on the parties' agreement may apply the first and final instance trial. A case heard by the China International Commercial Court is also subject to the first and final instance trial, see 3.37.

13 CPL 1991 (as amended until 2020), Article 164.

14 ibid Article 172.

15 ibid Article 170.

(i) The second instance ruling or judgment is binding and final but, if the decision turns out to be erroneous, the people's court may decide to go for a retrial; alternatively, the aggrieved party is entitled to submit an application for retrial.[16]

(j) During the period of (e) and (i), an application seeking post-action preservation measures and/or advance enforcement is allowed, as long as the requirements of the application comply with the CPL 1991 (as amended until 2020) and the relevant laws.

Sources of Law Applicable for Preservation Measures

3.5 Sources of law mainly refer to the applicable law and other resources that are essential to study civil preservation measures. In accordance with the existing law and legal practice, sources of law in China can be categorised into four kinds – legislation, customary business practice, guiding cases and jurisprudence.[17] In addition to discussing applicable laws, a few principles of guidance provided by the regional courts and by judicial decisions give the reader a focus for appreciating the relevant reference points for the analysis of preservation measures in China. These sources will be briefly introduced in the following paragraphs.

Legislation

3.6 In terms of legislation, this can be further divided into

(a) Laws (including general law and special law).
(b) Regulations.
(c) Judicial interpretations and guidance issued by courts to guide judges and stakeholders.

Legislation (I): General Laws

3.7 Resembling other civil law jurisdictions, Chinese primary legislation can be divided into general laws and special laws. As far as preservation

16 ibid Articles 198 and 199.

17 General Rules of the Civil Law of the People's Republic of China was adopted by the 5th Session of the Standing Committee of the 12th National People's Congress of the People's Republic of China on 15 March 2017 and came into effect on 1 October 2017. In accordance with General Rules of the Civil Law of the People's Republic of China (2017), Article 10 provides that "Any civil dispute shall be resolved in accordance with the law, in the absence of relevant provisions set forth in law, usual practice may be followed, but the public order and good customs shall not be infringed upon". "Usual practice" in the business domain refers to customary business practice; see also, Huixing Liang, 'Understanding and Application of Certain Important Articles under General Rules of the Civil Law' (2017) 4 Journal of Sichuan University (Philosophy and Social Science Edition); after the Civil Code 2020 came into effect, Article 10 of the General Rules 2017 has been directly incorporated into Article 10 of the Civil Code 2020.

measures are concerned, the key primary legislation/relevant Code will be the CPL 1991 (as amended until 2020).[18] When the CPL 1991 was revised in 2007, there was no specific improvement in provisions that were relevant to preservation measures. The major development in preservation measures was largely carried out through CPL Amendment 2012. The CPL in its current form has also been amended in later years, most recently in 2017, but these revisions have not touched the codes relevant to preservation measures. In this context, this book will use the CPL 1991 (as amended until 2020) as the primary Code for analysing preservation remedies.

3.8 Apart from preservation measures in litigation proceedings, such measures are also needed in arbitral proceedings. Accordingly, the Arbitration Law of People's Republic of China 1995 (hereinafter referred to as "Arbitration Law 1995 (as amended until 2020)")[19] is the relevant applicable law in China for seeking preservation measures in connection with arbitration.[20]

3.9 In addition to procedural law, substantive laws relevant to this kind of dispute can be applied to dispose of matters of security and compensation that have arisen from erroneous or improper preservation measures. The relevant legal issues will therefore be mainly governed by the Civil Code 2020[21] and the State Compensation Law of the People's Republic of China 1995 (2012 Amendment) (hereinafter referred to as "State Compensation Law (2012 Amendment)"),[22] as well as other relevant substantive laws.

---

18 Refer to Chapter 1, 1.76–1.100.

19 The Arbitration Law was adopted by the Ninth Meeting of the Standing Committee of the Eighth National People's Congress on 31 August 1994 and promulgated by Decree No 31 of the president of the People's Republic of China on 31 August 1994, and the latest amendment was in 2017.

20 Preservation measures in connection with arbitration are discussed in detail in Part 1, Chapter 4 of this book.

21 In the Civil Code 2020, the applicable parts associated with the preservation measures mainly include Part II "Property Rights" and Part VII "Tort Liability". The main content of Part II "Property Rights" is derived from the Property Law of the People's Republic of China 2007, which was adopted at the fifth session of the Tenth National People's Congress on 16 March 2007, came into effect on 1 October 2007, although along with the development of property law, some provisions of the Property Law 2007 have also been replaced by the Civil Code 2020. Similarly, the main content of Part VII "Tort Liability" constitutes the Tort Law of the People's Republic of China, which was adopted at the 12th session of the Standing Committee of the 11th National People's Congress on 26 December 2009, came into effect on 1 July 2010.

22 State Compensation Law of the People's Republic of China 1995 (2012 Amendment) was adopted at the Seventh Session of the Standing Committee of the Eighth National People's Congress on 12 May 1994 and came into effect on 1 January 1995. The latest amendment was on 26 October 2012. Due to the limited space of this book, the detail of the State Compensation Law (2012 Amendment) will not be discussed. However, in terms of compensation arising from wrongful preservation applications, if the court is at fault, this law will be applied.

Legislation (II): Special Laws

3.10 Special laws/Codes relevant to preservation measures, as distinct from provisions available in the CPL 1991 (as amended until 2020), can be found mainly in the SMPL 2000 and in the intellectual property laws of the People's Republic of China. The intellectual property laws include the Patent Law of the People's Republic China 1985 (2020 Amendment),[23] the Copyright Law of the People's Republic China 1991 (2020 Amendment)[24] and the Trademark Law of the People's Republic of China 1983 (2019 Amendment).[25] The SMPL 2000, a maritime procedural code, will govern the procedural issues of maritime disputes in Chinese maritime courts. Unlike the SMPL 2000, which is a maritime procedural code, the three laws concerning intellectual property are substantive laws governing the issues within the sphere of civil law. The main steps of intellectual property preservation measures will also have to comply with the CPL 1991 (as amended until 2020) and the relevant judicial interpretations. To be precise, these three laws simply stipulate that parties are entitled to file an application for preservations;[26] they are silent on the detailed procedural steps but must apply the CPL 1991 (as amended until 2020) and the relevant interpretations.

3.11 In Chinese courts, in provisions for preservation measures in maritime disputes and intellectual property disputes, the first priority is accordingly given to the relevant provisions within special laws, if applicable and available, and only then to the general laws provided by the CPL 1991 (as amended until 2020). Relevant judicial interpretations are applied in order to fill the gaps where the relevant provisions within these special laws are inadequate.

3.12 For example, in the context of applications for maritime preservations, the provisions of the SMPL 2000 and the Interpretation of SMPL 2008[27] will

23 The Patent Law of the People's Republic of China was passed by the Fourth Session of the Standing Committee of the Sixth National People's Congress of the People's Republic of China on 12 March 1984 and came into effect on 1 April 1985. The latest amendment was adopted by the 22nd Session of the Standing Committee of the 13th National People's Congress of the People's Republic of China on 17 October 2020.

24 Copyright Law of the People's Republic of China was adopted by the 15th Session of the Standing Committee of the 7th National People's Congress of the People's Republic of China on 7 September 1990 and came into effect on 1 June 1991. The latest amendment was adopted by the 23rd Session of the Standing Committee of the 13th National People's Congress of the People's Republic of China on 11 November 2020.

25 Trademark Law of the People's Republic of China was passed by the 24th Session of the Standing Committee of the 15th National People's Congress of the People's Republic of China on 23 August 1982 and came into effect on 1 March 1983. The latest amendment was adopted by the 10th Session of the Standing Committee of the 13th National People's Congress of the People's Republic of China on 23 April 2019.

26 See Articles 72 and 73 of the Patent Law (2020 Amendment); see also, Articles 56, 57 and 61 of the Copyright Law (2020 Amendment); see also, Articles 65 and 66 of the Trademark Law (2019 Amendment).

27 *The Supreme People's Court Interpretations on the Application of the Special Maritime Procedure Law of the People's Republic of China (2008 Adjustment)* (Fa Shi [2003] No 3)

prevail over the CPL 1991 (as amended until 2020). Equally, as regards the intellectual property preservations, in the context of the absence of provisions of intellectual property laws and their judicial interpretations, only the provisions of the CPL 1991 (as amended until 2020) will be applied.

Regulations

3.13 In accordance with legislation and legal practice, regulations can be interpreted in a broad sense. The State Council, the People's Congresses of the different provinces, autonomous regions and municipalities, the State Council departments and committees, the People's Bank of China, the auditing offices and similar national authorities all have power to issue administrative regulations, decisions, orders or local decrees, autonomous decrees and special decrees within the scope of that department's authority.[28] These regulations can also be cited in any judicial decisions in a specific context.[29]

3.14 These regulations may be the applicable law in the context of applications for preservation measures. However, that will depend on whether the upper-tier law is silent on the specific legal issues that are included in an application for preservation measures. These regulations are at times utilised to fill the gaps in the main laws, as long as such regulations do not violate law.

3.15 For example, there are no stipulations in the CPL 1991 (as amended until 2020) or in the relevant interpretations to govern the issues concerning legal costs associated with preservation applications; as a result, by default, the *Measures on Payment of Litigation Costs 2006* promulgated by the State Council has become the applicable law.[30] Similarly, the CPL 1991 (as amended until 2020) does not stipulate in detail the scope of the property to be preserved. However, the Ministry of Labor and Social Security issued an order, entitled *Administrative Supervision Measure of the Social Security Fund*, to restrict the scope of the property to be preserved. This order is the

was adopted by the 1259th meeting of the Judicial Committee of the Supreme People's Court on 3 December 2002 and came into effect on 1 February. In accordance with the Decision of the Supreme People's Court on Adjusting the Sequential Number of the Articles of the Civil Procedure Law of the People's Republic of China Cited in Judicial Interpretations and Other Documents issued on 16 December 2008, it was adjusted. Hereinafter referred to as "Interpretation of SMPL 2008".

28 The Legislation Law of the People's Republic of China (2015 Amendment) was adopted by the Third Session of the Standing Committee of the Ninth National People's Congress of the People's Republic of China on 15 March 2000 and came into effect on 1 July 2000. The latest amendment was adopted by the 3rd Session of the Standing Committee of the 12th National People's Congress of the People's Republic of China on 15 March 2015; Legislation Law 2000 (2015 Amendment), Articles 65, 72 and 80.

29 *Provisions of the Supreme People's Court on Citation of Such Normative Legal Documents as Laws and Regulations in the Judgments* (Fa Shi [2009] No 14), Article 4.

30 *Measures on Payment of Litigation Costs 2006* (Order of the State Council No 481); it was adopted at the 159th Executive Meeting of the State Council on 8 December 2006 which became effective from 1 April 2007.

applicable law in this context for the property preservation measure that is discussed in Chapter 6.

Judicial Interpretations and Other Judicial Documents

3.16 China is a civil law jurisdiction, which is dependent on precisely drafted statute law or Codes.[31] However, in practice, this statute law cannot be revised or amended in time to keep pace with changes in circumstances and time. In addition, China is a country with a size equivalent of a continent and as a result, it will take time to revise or amend such statute law on a regular basis. Needless to say, the judicial interpretations by the highest tier body in the Chinese court system, the Supreme People's Court (hereinafter "SPC"), are essential and therefore an important source of law.[32]

3.17 For example, the SPC subsequently promulgated *Interpretations of Application of the Civil Procedure Law (2020 Amendment)* (hereinafter referred to as "Interpretation of CPL 2015 (2020 Amendment)"),[33] which is treated as the basic judicial interpretation providing the details pertaining to the application of the civil procedure law including preservation applications. In the context of specific preservation measures, there are four most important judicial interpretations handed down by the SPC, including *Provisions on Several Issues Concerning the Handling of Property Preservation Cases by the People's Courts (2020 Amendment)* (hereinafter referred to as "Interpretation of Property Preservation (2020 Amendment)"),[34] *Provisions on Several Issues Concerning the Application of Law in Cases Involving the Review of Behaviour Preservation in Intellectual Property Disputes 2018* (hereinafter referred to as "Interpretation of IP Behaviour Preservation 2018"),[35] *Some Provisions of the Supreme People's Court on Evidence in*

31 In this context, statute law refers to both laws and regulations discussed in 3.7–3.15.

32 Over the years, although many scholars have questioned the legality of such interpretations owing to the fact that the Legislation Law provides that the power to interpret a national law shall be vested in the Standing Committee of the National People's Congress and not the SPC. However, the prevalent view is that the Standing Committee of the National People's Congress has the authority to interpret vague and ambiguous provisions, whereas the SPC prescribed by the law has the power to interpret the application of these provisions in general. As a result, the judicial interpretation of the SPC is regarded as valid for its applications to issues before the courts; see also, Zhaoxiang Wu, 'Understanding and Application of *Provisions of the Supreme People's Court on Citation of Such Normative Legal Documents as Laws and Regulations in the Judgments*' (2009) 23 The People's Judicature (Applied) 29, 32.

33 *Interpretations of the Supreme People's Court on Application of the Civil Procedure Law of the People's Republic of China (2020 Amendment)* (Fa Shi [2015] No 5) (superseded by Fa Shi [2020] No 20).

34 *Provisions of the Supreme People's Court on Several Issues Concerning the Handling of Property Preservation Cases by the People's Courts (2020 Amendment)* (Fa Shi [2016] No 22) (superseded by Fa Shi [2020] No 21).

35 *Provisions of the Supreme People's Court on Several Issues Concerning the Application of Law in Cases Involving the Review of Behaviour Preservation in Intellectual Property Disputes* (Fa Shi [2018] No 21).

Civil Procedures (2019 Amendment) (hereinafter referred to as "Provisions on Evidence 2019")[36] and *Several Provisions of the Supreme People's Court on Evidence in Civil Procedures Involving Intellectual Property Rights* (hereinafter referred to as "Provisions on IP Evidence 2020").[37] Accordingly, all these judicial interpretations and other relevant interpretations, such as *Arrangement Concerning Mutual Assistance in Court-Ordered Interim Measures in Aid of Arbitral Proceedings by the Courts of the Mainland and of the Hong Kong Special Administrative Region*,[38] will be employed considerably, in particular, in Chapters 6, 8 and 10 of this book.

3.18 Judicial interpretations are of four basic forms – "interpretation", "provision", "reply" and "decision".[39] Generally speaking, if the legal guidance documents issued by the SPC are named by any of these four forms, they can be treated as the valid judicial interpretation and will be applicable to the legal disputes before the court in applications for preservation measures.

3.19 Regarding whether legal guidance documents can become the source of law, the other criterion is to look for the relevant Identification Number. A general rule was established in 1997 that stakeholders must look at the Identification Number of judicial documents.[40] As long as the Identification Number shows "Fa Shi (法释)", these guidance documents issued by the SPC constitute judicial interpretations, namely they are the source of law.[41] In the event that the Identification Number includes "Fa Fa (法发)" or other markings, these documents cannot be regarded as a source of law, but they can be cited in the *obiter dictum*.[42] In legal practice, these guidance documents

36 *Some Provisions of the Supreme People's Court on Evidence in Civil Procedures (2019 Amendment)* (Fa Shi [2019] No 19), the original number of this judicial interpretation was 'Fa Shi [2001] No 33' and it was revised and adopted by the SPC on 25 December 2019 and came into effect on 1 May 2020.

37 *Several Provisions of the Supreme People's Court on Evidence in Civil Procedures Involving Intellectual Property Rights* (Fa Shi [2020] No 12) was issued on 16 November 2020 and came into force on 18 November 2020. It should be noted that the general issues as to evidence preservation have been provided in Provisions on Evidence 2019 while some specific issues as to IP evidence preservation are governed by Provisions on IP Evidence 2020. The details will be discussed in Chapter 10.

38 *Arrangement Concerning Mutual Assistance in Court-Ordered Interim Measures in Aid of Arbitral Proceedings by the Courts of the Mainland and of the Hong Kong Special Administrative Region 2019* (Fa Shi [2019] No 14).

39 *Provisions of the Supreme People's Court on the Judicial Interpretation* (Fa Fa [2007] No 12), Article 6.

40 Zhaoxiang Wu, 'Understanding and Application of *Provisions of the Supreme People's Court on Citation of Such Normative Legal Documents as Laws and Regulations in the Judgments*' (2009) 23 The People's Judicature (Applied) 29, 32.

41 ibid.

42 ibid at 33; in China there is no specific concept of "*obiter dictum*" as there is in English law, but the official format of a judgment, a ruling or an order contains the legal reasoning part provided by the judge to analyse the facts and the law applicable to the case. It is the author's view that this part in the judgment, the ruling or the order is similar to what is cited as *obiter dictum* under English law.

constitute important references for the SPC and for all tiers of courts within the legal system.[43]

3.20 In addition, the High People's Court in different provinces, the Intermediate People's Courts or even the Primary People's Courts may issue regional interpretations and guidance that may be applied only in their territorial jurisdictions. Accordingly, as long as these regional interpretations and guidance issued by the lower courts are not in conflict with the general/special laws or with similar interpretations of the higher courts, these regional judicial guidances are also relevant to issues before the local courts in applications for preservation measures.

3.21 For example, *Some Provisions of Beijing High People's Court on Property Preservation During the Case-Filing Procedure 2012*, *Provisions of Shanghai High People's Court on Property Preservation (2017 Amendment)* (hereinafter referred to as "Provisions on Shanghai Property Preservation 2017") and *Opinions of Guangdong High People's Court on Protecting Legal Interests of Private Enterprises and Standardizing Property Preservation 2019* and so forth constitute the applicable law in their own territory.[44] Such regional judicial guidance, together with other relevant laws/regulations/interpretations, will be extensively employed, in particular in Chapters 6, 8 and 10 of this book.

Guiding Case and Reference Case

3.22 There is no tradition of adherence to the doctrine of case precedent in Chinese law that is comparable to common law doctrine of *stare decisis*. However, increasingly, the Chinese courts are these days providing explanatory guidance through judicial decisions. In particular, the SPC issued *Provisions of the Supreme People's Court Concerning Work on Case*

---

43 In practice, under certain circumstances, this criterion of "judicial interpretation" is not applied consistently. For example, pursuant to Article 6 of *Provisions of the Supreme People's Court on the Judicial Interpretation* (Fa Fa [2007] No 12), "Fa Fa" cannot be treated as a judicial interpretation. It means that this judicial guidance document itself and its Article 6 in relation to the category of four basic forms of judicial interpretations in 3.18 are not meaningful in defining the scope of the judicial interpretation. It is apparent that the SPC issued this judicial guidance to define the scope of the judicial interpretation. Therefore, this guidance plays a judicial interpretation rule. The highlighting of another inconsistency in context of identification numbers can be appreciated through another example, *the Notice of the SPC and Chinese Maritime Courts Seminar for Presidents 2001*. This legal guidance document has no Identification Number, but in legal practice it is always treated as a judicial interpretation. Such issues also highlight the need for stakeholders to retain a local lawyer to guide them on such issues.

44 Beijing, Shanghai and Guangdong are provinces, which are comparatively developed regions in China from the economic point of view. Accordingly, they dispose of more commercial cases in their courts, particularly, foreign-related cases. Apart from them, regional guidance by Jiangsu, Chongqing and Sichuan also plays an important role in dealing with commercial cases. This book will therefore mainly analyse the local provisions in these regions, even though other regions' local guidance may be discussed at times in Chapters 6, 8 and 10.

Guidance in 2010 for establishing a case guidance system.[45] Accordingly, the guiding cases issued by the SPC have officially become a source of law and all tiers of the court system within China respect that. These days, therefore, Chinese courts routinely refer to these published guiding cases when adjudicating a similar case.[46]

3.23 Apart from guiding cases, the SPC also publishes "gazette cases" in its official publications, namely since 1985 the *Gazette* of the SPC. These "gazette cases" can be made by any tier's courts. In 2018, the SPC emphasised that all tiers of courts shall regularly collate and organise leading judgments, rulings and orders as references for local courts.[47] Therefore, in recent years in legal practice, these "gazette cases" and other reference cases issued by the SPC or local courts have gained some authoritative weight.[48]

3.24 It should be noted that unlike guiding cases, reference cases were generally not considered the source of law for many years.[49] However, the SPC in 2020 issued *Guiding Opinions of the Supreme People's Court on Unifying the Application of Laws to Strengthen the Retrieval of Similar Cases (for Trial Implementation)* (hereinafter referred to as "Guiding Opinions 2020") which officially announces the establishment of similar cases retrieval system.[50] The scope of similar cases as compared with *Provisions of the Supreme People's Court Concerning Work on Case Guidance 2010* is broader, comprising:

a) Guiding cases released by the SPC.
b) Typical cases released by the SPC and cases decided by the SPC in which judgments have been effective.

---

45 *Provisions of the Supreme People's Court Concerning Work on Case Guidance 2010* (Fa Fa [2010] No 51).

46 See Article 7, *Provisions of the Supreme People's Court Concerning Work on Case Guidance 2010*. It is provided that "People's courts at all levels should refer to the guiding cases released by the Supreme People's Court when adjudicating similar cases"; all guiding cases can be found by the SPC's official link: <http://www.court.gov.cn/index.html>. Currently, there is no translation in English available for guiding cases.

47 *Notice of the Supreme People's Court on Issuing the Guiding Opinions on Strengthening and Standardizing the Analysis and Reasoning in Adjudicative Instruments 2018* (Fa Fa [2018] No10), Article 16.

48 See Mark Jia, 'Chinese Common Law? Guiding cases and Judicial Reform' (2016) 129 (8) Harv L Rev 2213, 2213–2234; see also Eric C Ip 'The Supreme People's Court and the Political Economy of Judicial Empowerment in Contemporary China' (2011) 24 (2) Colum J Asian L 367, 367–436.

49 In *Sichuang Xinshunda Financing Security Co Ltd and Others v Muxing Huang* (dispute over loan contract) [2014] Civil Shen Zi Di No 441 (The Supreme People's Court, retrial and binding judgment), the SPC held that gazette cases published by the SPC were not equivalent to guiding cases in accordance with *Provisions of the Supreme People's Court Concerning Work on Case Guidance 2010*. The SPC was accordingly of the view that the proposition that gazette cases should be treated as the reference for this dispute lacked legal foundation under the Chinese legal system.

50 Guiding Opinions of the Supreme People's Court on Unifying the Application of Laws to Strengthen the Retrieval of Similar Cases (for Trial Implementation) 2020 was issued and came into effect on 31 July 2020.

c) Reference cases issued by the high people's courts in which judgments have been effective.
d) Cases decided by the people's courts at the higher level and by the respective people's courts themselves in which judgments have been effective.[51]

3.25 The crucial provision in *Guiding Opinions 2020* is that if the retrieved similar case is a guiding case, the People's Court, regardless of the tier of this court, shall make a judicial decision by reference to that guiding case, unless such case is in conflict with newly issued laws, administrative regulations, judicial interpretations, or is replaced by new guiding cases. If the retrieved similar case belongs to any of the other three types, the People's Court may, but will not be obliged to make a judicial decision by reference to that retrieved similar case.[52] It follows that other similar reference cases may constitute a source of law depending on the judge's discretionary power. This book will therefore also utilise such similar reference cases of the SPC or other lower courts to shed light on the legal issues involved in the understanding and application of preservation measures.

3.26 In the end, although customary business practices[53] and jurisprudence constitute important sources of law, this topic is beyond the scope of the book.[54]

The Chinese Court System

Overview of the Court System

3.27 There is a four-tier court system in China including the SPC, the High People's Court, the Intermediate People's Court and the Primary people's

51 *Guiding Opinions 2020*, Article 4.

52 *Guiding Opinions 2020*, Article 9.

53 As regards "customary business practice", it has been clarified by t*he Interpretation II of the Supreme People's Court of Several Issues Concerning the Application of the Contract Law of the People's Republic of China* (Fa Shi [2009] No 5) (expired on 1 January 2021). Article 7 provided that: "1) the practice which is universally adopted at the place of transaction or in a certain field or sector and is known or should be known by the other party to the transaction when the contract is concluded; and 2) the customary practice often used by both parties". It should be noted that after the Civil Code 2020 came into effect on 1 January 2021, the interpretation II of contract law has expired. However, because the concept of "customary business practice" is absent in the Civil Code 2020, it is advised by the SPC that Article 7 of Interpretation II can still be referenced; see also, The Leading Group of the Implementation of the Civil Code of the Supreme People's Court (ed.), *Understanding and Application of Part 'Contract Law' of the Civil Code of the People's Republic of China (Volume II)* (People's Court Press 2020) 350.

54 However, in Chapters 6, 8 and10, a few aspects of customary business practices and differences in the impact of jurisprudence are briefly discussed in the context of interim remedies/preservation remedies. A few jurisprudential aspects are discussed in a comparative context to highlight invisible factors in the context of the preservation measures given in Chapter 11.

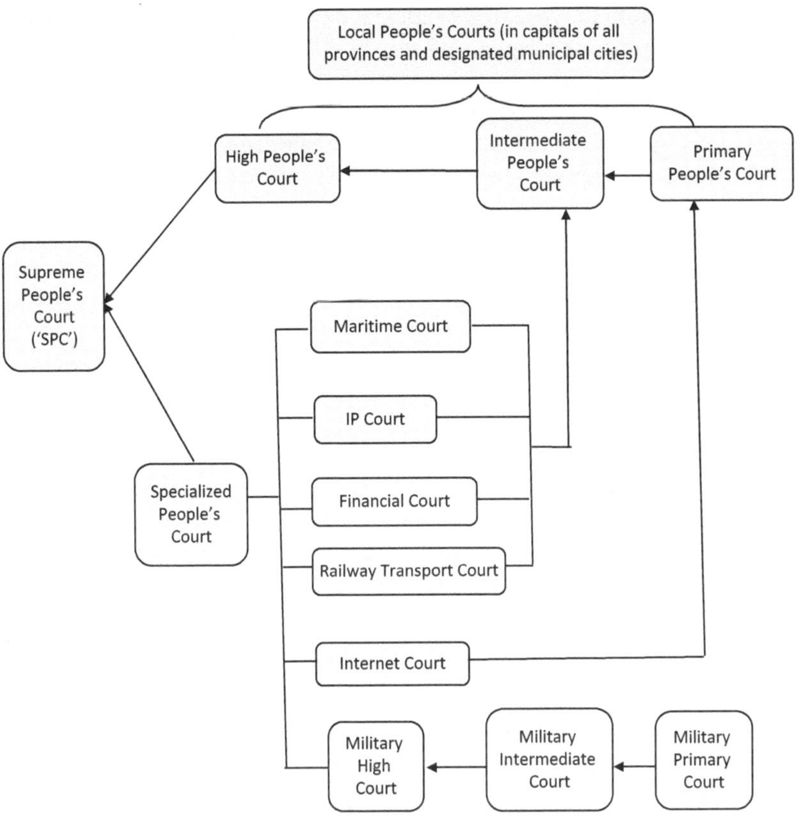

FIGURE 3.2 The Chinese court system.

court. Nonetheless, Hong Kong, Macau and Taiwan, as special administrative regions and province, have their own legal systems based separately on the English law and civil law traditions. The main content of this book will, however, be restricted to mainland China, unless otherwise stated.

3.28 The SPC lies at the highest level within the court system in China. Its headquarters is located in Beijing, the capital of China, and its branches comprise six circuit courts and the China International Commercial Court (hereinafter referred to as "CICC").[55]

55 The headquarters of the SPC – located in Beijing, the capital of China – hears cases in Beijing, Tianjin, Hebei Province, Shandong Province and Inner Mongolia. Since 2014, the headquarters of the SPC in Beijing has set up six circuit courts. The first circuit, located in Shenzhen, disposes of cases in Guangdong Province, Guangxi Province, Hainan Province and Hunan Province; the second circuit, located in Shenyang, hears cases in Liaoning Province, Jilin Province and Heilongjiang Province; the third circuit, located in Nanjing deals with cases

3.29 Apart from the SPC, the municipal cities (Beijing, Tianjin, Shanghai and Chongqing) and the capitals of provinces and autonomous regions have established the sole High People's Court;[56] all cities, including municipal ones, also set up one or more Intermediate People's Courts; city districts or counties set up Primary People's Courts and their dispatching tribunal.

3.30 Besides the above general court system, there are specialised courts, including the military court, the maritime court, the intellectual property court, the financial court, the railway transport court and the internet court, and these enjoy jurisdiction in these particular fields of law.[57] Owing to the fact that the military court has its own system, this is beyond the scope of this book.[58]

3.31 As to the other three types of specialised courts, the maritime court, the intellectual property court and the financial court are equivalent to the level of the local Intermediate People's Court.[59] The key difference among

---

in Jiangsu Province, Shanghai, Zhejiang Province, Fujian Province and Jiangxi Province; the fourth circuit in Zhengzhou hears cases from Henan Province, Shanxi Province, Hubei Province and Anhui Province; the fifth circuit in Chongqing disposes of cases in Chongqing, Sichuan Province, Guizhou Province, Yunnan Province and the Tibet Autonomous Region; and the sixth circuit in Xi'an deals with cases in Shaanxi Province, Gansu Province, Qinghai Province, the Ningxia Hui Autonomous Region and the Xinjiang Uygur Autonomous Region. The CICC simply disposes of international commercial cases and comprises the first and second international commercial courts located in Shenzhen, Guangdong Province and Xi'an in Shaanxi Province. These commercial courts are different from other courts established by the SPC; the CICC follows the concept of "first instance being final" rather than the general two instances' trial system; see also <http://english.court.gov.cn/organisation.html> and <http://cicc.court.gov.cn/html/1/219/193/195/index.html> accessed 15 July 2021 and see 3.37.

56 China comprises 23 provinces, 4 municipalities, 5 autonomous regions (Inner Mongolia, Xinjiang, Tibet, Ningxia and Guangxi), two Special Administrative Regions (Hong Kong and Mauro) and Taiwan Province.

57 The Law on Organisation of the People's Courts of the People's Republic of China 1980 (2018 Amendment), Article 15. The Law on Organisation was adopted at the Second Session of the Fifth National People's Congress on 1 July 1979 and came into effect 1 January 1980. The latest amendment was passed on 26 October 2018. It should be noted that traditionally the Railway Transportation Court has its own system. However, with the legal reform in China, some have been restructured into general courts. For example, the Railway Transportation Intermediate Court of Beijing Municipality and the Railway Transportation Intermediate Court of Shanghai Municipality have been restructured into the Fourth Intermediate Court of Beijing Municipality and the Third Intermediate Court of Shanghai Municipality respectively. In addition, the Railway Transportation Court of Hangzhou City has become the Internet Court. There are other two internet courts located in Guangzhou and Beijing. Even so, in some regions, the railway transportation courts still stand. For example, the Railway Transportation Intermediate Court of Lanzhou City of Gansu Province and the Tianjin Railway Transportation Court. As for the Internet Court, although it has not been incorporated into Article 15 of the Organisation Law, the SPC issued *Provisions of the Supreme People's Court on Several Issues Concerning the Trial of Cases by Internet Courts* (Fa Shi [2018] No 16) to clarify the status and jurisdiction of internet courts.

58 Military Courts are divided into a three-tier court system, including the High People's Court, the Intermediate People's Court and the Primary People's Court.

59 Not all provinces or regions have established specialised courts. First, a total of 11 maritime courts are located in Tianjin, Shanghai, Dalian, Qingdao, Wuhan, Xiamen, Guangzhou, Haikou, Beihai, Ningbo and Nanjing. Secondly, there are a total of four IP courts located in

these three specialised courts is that the maritime court has jurisdiction over the relevant disputes within its domain as the court of first instance, while the other two specialised courts may dispose of cases as a court of the first or second instance depending on the disputed amount of the case and the cause of action.[60] Nonetheless, depending on the complexity and the social influence of the cases, the high people's court or the SPC may have jurisdiction over the specialised cases as a court of first instance,[61] although it is unusual for such cases to be heard in the high people's court or the SPC as the first instance court.

3.32 The internet court is equivalent to the level of the primary people's court. The key feature of such internet courts is that they utilise advanced technology such as blockchain to deal with disputes over digital matters including internet trade disputes, copyright cases, online product sales and so forth.[62] Also, they conduct online trials with the help of an online video system. If the litigant were to file an appeal, then even the second instance court would also conduct an online trial. It should be noted that the development of court informatisation in accordance with the Outline of the Fifth Five-Year Reform Program of the People's Courts (2019–2023) has provided access to file cases online and to conduct trials in the same way in more Chinese courts.[63] Particularly, due to the COVID-19 pandemic in 2020, online trials have started to become the new normal in almost all courts. Furthermore, in order to regulate online trials, the SPC issued *Online Litigation Rules of the People's Courts* on 16 June 2021.[64] Therefore, online trials nowadays are not simply just applied by the internet courts. The process of these online trials is beyond the scope of this book; however, the authors will discuss the online preservation measures in 3.47.

Preservations in the Court System

3.33 In the context of the preservation procedure, except for maritime preservation, the general steps needed in an application to seek a preservation measure in different causes of action will have no fundamental divergences

---

Beijing, Shanghai, Guangzhou and Hainan Free Trade Port. Finally, there are two financial courts, located separately in Beijing and Shanghai.

60 *Provisions of the Supreme People's Court on the Jurisdiction of the Shanghai Financial Court* (Fa Shi [2018] No 14), Article 4; Provisions of the Supreme People's Court on the Jurisdiction over Cases by Intellectual Property Courts in Beijing, Shanghai and Guangzhou (Fa Shi [2014] No 12), Article 6.

61 CPL 1991 (as amended until 2020), Articles 19 and 20.

62 *Provisions of the Supreme People's Court on Several Issues Concerning the Trial of Cases by Internet Courts* (Fa Shi [2018] No 16), Articles 3 and 5.

63 See generally, Chen Su and Tian He (eds.), *Annual Report on Informatization of Chinese Courts No.4 (2020)* (Translator: Liu Ying, Social Sciences Academic Press, China 2020).

64 *Online Litigation Rules of the People's Courts* (Fa Shi [2021] No 12) was issued on 6 June 2021 and came into effect on 1 August 2021.

from other applications made to the courts. The only divergence that could be observed may relate to the difference in substantive law involved in such applications, and accordingly the evidentiary requirement may vary depending on the stage of the application, and the facts of a case. The details will be discussed in Chapters 6, 8 and 10.

Hierarchical Trial System

3.34 Generally speaking, there is a two-tier trial system for a civil case in China – the first instance court and the second instance court.[65] In accordance with the jurisdiction system of the CPL 1991 (as amended until 2020),[66] apart from the SPC, other tiers' courts, based on the disputed amount, complexity and social influence of a case, will determine jurisdiction over the first instance. If the parties refuse to accept the first instance judgment, ruling order, they can appeal to a higher court for a second instance trial.

3.35 For example, if the first instance court is an intermediate people's court, then in that scenario, the second instance court would be the local high people's court. The judgment, ruling or order of the second instance court will be the final and binding adjudication, and this judgment, ruling or order must be enforced by the parties.

3.36 Apart from the general trial system, pursuant to the procedure for trial supervision in the CPL 1991 (as amended until 2020), after a final and binding judgment, ruling or order is made, a case under special circumstances can be re-heard by the court that gave the judgement, ruling or order, the higher-tier court or the SPC.[67] Therefore, the competent courts that can hear or re-hear any cases are the first instance court, the second instance court and the retrial court.

3.37 Under the existing trial system, there are three exceptions as follows. The first exception relates to the rule of "first instance being final"; namely, no second instance proceedings are requested. First, in accordance with Article 162 of the CPL 1991 (as amended until 2020), if the disputed amount of a case is less than 30 per cent of the average annual salary in the previous year of the municipal cities, autonomous regions and provinces concerned, the case shall

---

65 Under the existing trial system, there are two exceptions, see 3.37.

66 CPL 1991 (as amended until 2020), Part I, Chapter 2 "Jurisdiction".

67 In accordance with the CPL 1991 (as amended until 2020), Part II "Trial Procedure", Chapter XVI "Procedure for Trial Supervision", there are four types of circumstances in which a case can be retried. Firstly, the people's court voluntarily decides to retry a case that is heard by itself. Secondly, the SPC or any higher tier court decides to retry a case that is heard by the lower court. Thirdly, in accordance with the party's application for a retrial, the higher tier court decides to rehear a case. Fourthly, further to the third circumstance, if the application for retrial is dismissed by the court, the parties may apply to the competent people's procuratorate (a supervisory body over judges within the legal system) for a procuratorial proposal or objection so that the court is requested to re-hear the case.

comply with the principle of the first instance being final without appeal.[68] Secondly, the CICC comprises the first and second international commercial courts located in Shenzhen, Guangdong Province, and Xi'an, Shaanxi Province, that simply dispose of international commercial cases. The CICC is different from other circuits established by the SPC to hear second instance cases.[69] It complies with the concept of "first instance being final" rather than the general two-instances trial system.[70]

3.38 The second exception is in relation to some intellectual property disputes. In accordance with *Decision of the Standing Committee of China National People's Congress on Several Issues Concerning Litigation Procedures of Patent and Other IP Cases*, from 1 January 2019 the second instance court of some intellectual property disputes is the Intellectual Property Division of the SPC rather than any high courts in any provinces, even though, pursuant to the hierarchical trial system, the direct higher court to hear as the second instance court should be the local high court.[71] The purpose of this unique procedure is to standardise the dispute resolution of

68 CPL 1991 (as amended until 2020), Article 162.

69 Depending on the complexity and the social influence of the cases, the circuits of the SPC can in theory have jurisdiction over the specialised cases as a court of first instance but in practice it's very rare.

70 In *Provisions of the Supreme People's Court on Several Issues Regarding the Establishment of the International Commercial Court* (Fa Shi [2018] No 11), Article 2 provides that "the international commercial courts shall accept the following cases (1) first-instance international commercial cases where the parties have, in accordance with Article 34 of the *Civil Procedure Law*, agreed to select the jurisdiction of the Supreme People's Court and where the subject amount is at least RMB 300 million; (2) first-instance international commercial cases where a high people's court has jurisdiction but believes that it is necessary for the Supreme People's Court to handle the case and obtains permission [to transfer the case]; (3) first-instance international commercial cases that have a significant impact on the country as a whole; (4) (cases) where preservation (of evidence, property, etc. before or during) arbitration is applied for in accordance with Article 14 of these Provisions, or where revocation or enforcement of an international commercial arbitral award is applied for [in accordance with the same provision]; and (5) other international commercial cases that the Supreme People's Court believes should be handled by an international commercial court". In addition, Article 15 provides that "the judgments and orders rendered by the international commercial courts are judgments and orders with legal effect"; see also China International Commercial Court, 'A Brief Introduction of China International Commercial Court' <http://cicc.court.gov.cn/html/1/219/193/195/index.html> accessed 10 July 2021.

71 *Decision of the Standing Committee of China National People's Congress on Several Issues Concerning Litigation Procedures of Patent and Other Intellectual Property Cases* was promulgated on 26 October 2018 and it became effective on 1 January 2019. It should be noted that Article 5 provides that "the Supreme People's Court shall report to the Standing Committee of the National People's Congress on the implementation upon three years' implementation of this Decision". It means that whether the SPC retains permanent jurisdiction as the second instance court for IP disputes will depend on the consequence of the implementation of this Decision between 2019 and 2021. There is a possibility that the jurisdiction of the SPC might be adjusted in the future in this context. The scope of intellectual property disputes heard by the SPC as the second instance is provided in Article 1 of this Decision.

complex intellectual property disputes and accordingly to strengthen the protection of the intellectual property regime in China.[72]

3.39 The third exception is about the right of appeal. Under the CPL 1991 (as amended until 2020), not all rulings or orders from the courts are appealable to, for example, *the orders for the preservation measures* [emphasis added], the ruling for suspension or termination of the cases.[73] However, as mentioned in 3.36, the retrial procedure can be applied if the preservation order was found to be wrong. It should be noted that only the court has authority to decide whether the preservation order which is binding should be revoked or not. The people's procuratorate has no power to request the court to retrial this preservation order.[74]

3.40 It must be emphasised that according to the exact translation, in the Chinese procedure system there should be a preservation "ruling (裁定)" rather than "order（令/命令）". In order to make it easy for common law readers, in this book the authors have used the terminology of the preservation order instead of the preservation ruling. However, in the context of other legal issues, the terminology of "ruling" has still been used. Other chapters relating to Chinese preservation issues will follow this rule.

Tier System in the Context of Preservation Measures

3.41 As mentioned in 3.39, a preservation order cannot be appealed. As for the tier system relating to the preservation measure, in accordance with Article 100 of the CPL 1991 (as amended until 2020) and its Interpretation, an applicant is entitled to apply for a preservation during the course of any trial

---

72 'Press Conference on Intellectual Property Division of the Supreme Court' (China.com, 29 December 2018) <www.gov.cn/xinwen/2018-12/29/content_5353373.htm#allContent> accessed 15 July 2021.

73 Article 154 of the CPL 1991 (as amended until 2020) provides that the scope of the available appeal does not include the following ruling/order: "4. preservation and preliminary execution; 5. approval or disapproval of withdrawal of an action; 6. suspension or termination of an action; 7. correction of clerical errors in a written judgment; 8. suspension or termination of execution; 9. cancellation of or refusal to enforce an arbitration award; 10. refusal to enforce a document on creditor's rights that has been rendered enforceable by a notary agency; and 11. other matters to be settled by a ruling or order".

74 In *Reply of the Supreme People's Court to a Wrong Pre-Action Preservation Order and a Wrong Ruling in the Enforcement Procedures Made by the People's Court, and to a Handling Opinion on the People's Procuratorate's Protest against a Pre-Action Preservation Order Made by the Court* (Fa Shi [1998] No 17), it is provided that "The President of the people's court should submit a pre-action preservation order to the adjudication committee to decide whether this preservation order should be revoked if he/she finds that such preservation order is at fault so that it is necessary to revoke it … There is no legal foundation to uphold the procuratorate's protest against a pre-action preservation order. Therefore, the people's court should notify the procuratorate that its protest is dismissed (if the procuratorate submits a protest against the pre-action preservation order)". Although this judicial interpretation simply refers to a pre-action preservation order, in the authors' opinion, it can also govern a post-action preservation order as well unless otherwise specified.

or retrial proceedings.[75] For example, after the final judgment of a case has been made, an order for a preservation in the course of the first and/or second instance will be discharged. If, however, the higher court decides to re-hear this case, the applicant during the retrial proceedings will be entitled to seek preservation measures again.

Preservation Procedural Steps in China

3.42 In the light of the different stages of the civil procedure, this book will consider the applications made to courts for Chinese civil preservation measures in two stages – *pre-action* and *post-action* preservation applications.[76]

Meaning of Pre-Action Preservation Application

3.43 A pre-action preservation application means that an applicant files an application for a preservation in the following scenarios:

(a) Before a court or an arbitration institution receives the application to commence an action.

---

75 Article 100 of the CPL 1991 (as amended until 2020) provides that "In the event that, due to the conduct of one party to proceedings or other reasons, it becomes impossible to enforce judgments by, or damage may occur to, the other party to the same proceedings, the people's court may, upon the request of the other party, make an order to preserve the property of the party against whom the request is filed or order the party to do or not to do something; in the absence of such requests, the people's court may, where necessary, also order the adoption of property preservation measures"; see also, Article 162 of the Interpretation of CPL 2015 (2020 Amendment), which provides that "where *the people's court of second instance* renders an order to renew the preservation measures taken by the people's court of first instance or to take new preservation measures, *the people's court of second instance may take measures on its own*, or entrust the people's court of first instance to take the measures. Where *the people's court that re-hears a case* renders an order to renew the original preservation measures or to *take new preservation measures*, the said people's court may take the measures on its own or entrust the people's court that originally hears the case or the court of enforcement to take the measures [emphasis added]". Renewing the original preservation measures refers to the renewal of the property preservation measure, because the law provides a time limit of an order for the property preservation measure; refer also to Chapter 6, 6.151–6.155. Also, note that taking the "new preservation measure" means that the second instance court, based on the fact of a case during the second instance proceedings, may, in certain circumstances, alter the preservation measure order, such as from sealing up the property to detaining the property.

76 It should be noted that the CPL 1991 and the relevant interpretations regarding preservation measures have generally employed the term "litigation" preservation. However, in accordance with Article 28 of Arbitration Law 1995 (as amended until 2020) and Article 101 of the CPL 1991 (as amended until 2020), an applicant seeking preservation measures before arbitration has commenced or during arbitration proceedings shall submit an application for a preservation to an arbitral institution and then only that institution will submit the application to the competent court. This book is inclined to use the term "action" to replace "litigation" to make it easy for the common law reader. The authors therefore have used the terminology, for instance, "pre-action" application instead of "pre-litigation" application.

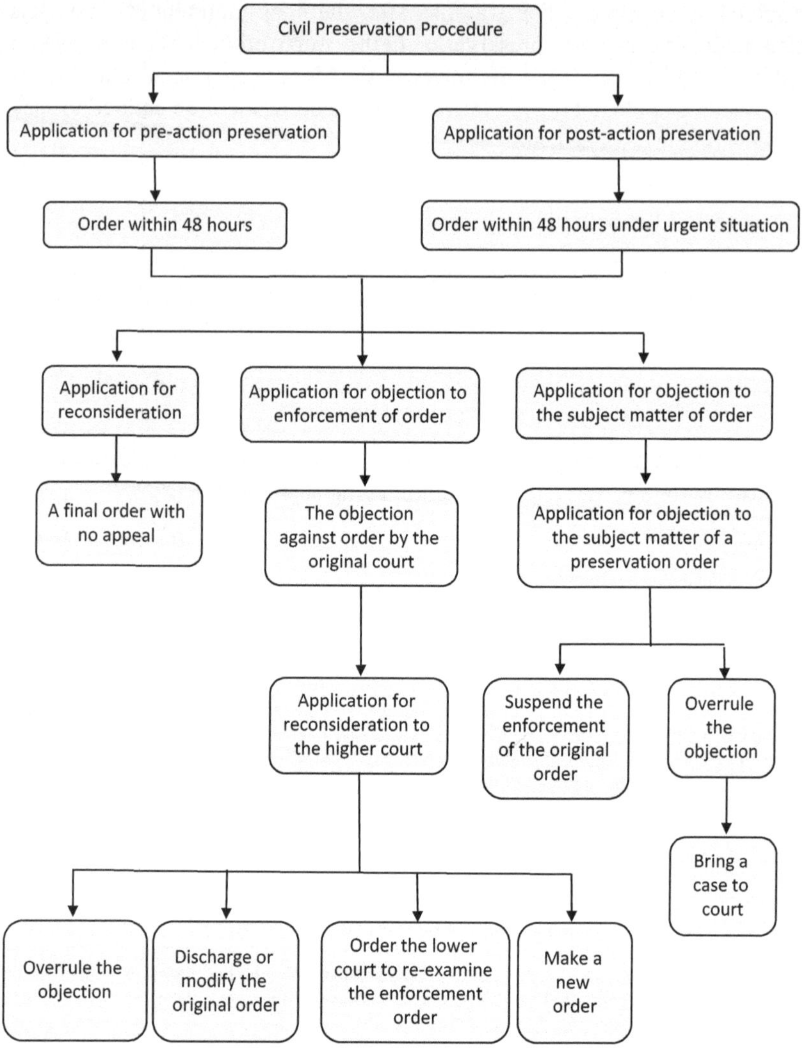

FIGURE 3.3 Preservation procedural steps.

(b) When a court or an arbitration institution receives the application to commence an action, but has not yet issued a notice of official acceptance to the applicant.

Meaning of Post-Action Preservation Application

3.44 Post-action preservation means that an applicant files an application seeking preservation measures after the court or the arbitration institution has already accepted the case and the notice of official acceptance has been issued to the applicant. However, in any event, it is before the start of enforcement of an effective judgment or arbitral award.

3.45 It should be noted that during the enforcement procedure,[77] the court on its own initiative can take compulsory measures to ensure the enforcement of judgments or awards. This kind of preservation measure is based on the public right, and any further discussion on this topic is beyond the scope of the book.

General Procedural Steps for Preservation Measures

3.46 Regardless of whether it is a pre-action or post-action preservation, the general procedural steps that are relevant for applications seeking preservation measures are similar. They are as follows:

(a) To decide a competent people's court, depending on the provisions on the tier's jurisdiction, the specialised jurisdiction and the territorial jurisdiction.
(b) To submit an application for a preservation measure and the necessary evidence to the competent people's court.
(c) To provide security in light of the legal requirement or the request of the court.
(d) To pay the application fee.

Online Preservation System of the People's Court

3.47 Traditionally, the preservation procedures mentioned in 3.46 (b)–(d) should be achieved in person, apart from the disputes in the internet people's courts. It follows that an applicant must go to the place where the competent court is located to submit the application and the security. However, in the context of the "Digital Rule of Law and Smart Justice" project operated by the Ministry of Justice of the People's Republic of China since 2018 and the development of court informatisation, some people's courts are gradually creating online preservation systems.[78] In January 2020, an online preservation system of the people's court (www.baoquan.court.gov.cn) was officially opened by the SPC. An applicant wherever he is located may submit an application seeking a preservation measure and the corresponding evidence, and

77 In the English versions some legislations or judicial interpretations use the term "execution procedure". There is no divergence between an execution procedure and an enforcement procedure.

78 See generally, Chen Su and Tian He (eds.), *Annual Report on Informatization of Chinese Courts No.4 (2020)* (Translator: Liu Ying, Social Sciences Academic Press, China 2020); see also <www.moj.gov.cn/subject/content/2018-10/31/491_42013.html> accessed on 15 July 2021.

meanwhile provide the security for this application on this uniform platform,[79] as long as he or his lawyer registers his real full name and chooses the competent court in light of the jurisdiction of the application. The applicant may follow the process of the online application by himself and will be notified of the result of such an application by a Short Message Service. In light of the online information posted, the court, after receiving the online application, will normally finish the verification within two days.[80] If the application is approved, the applicant will pay the preservation fee online.[81]

3.48 However, it must be noted that not all Chinese people's courts currently handle online preservation through this uniform platform. One reason is that this is a new system launched in January 2020 and cannot finish the integration of all Chinese courts in such a short time. It is supposed that the perfection of the operative uniform system will take at least several years. The other reason might be that more and more Chinese courts are opening their own online trial platforms to accept online filings, preservation applications and other applications. In this context, the competent court normally requests the applicant to submit the online application to its own online system. For this reason, if the applicant cannot find the competent court for the preservation application by the uniform online preservation system, it is inevitable that the applicant will submit the application by the corresponding court's own platform and guidance. Nonetheless, regardless of whether the uniform platform or an individual system court by court is used, there is an opportunity for international readers to scan the basic information online.

Various Types of Scenarios in the Context of Preservation Measures

3.49 After the applications seeking preservation measures are accepted by courts, these courts may encounter different issues and different scenarios that may vary from case to case. Correspondingly, the courts and the relevant

79 The discussion on online security is carried out in 3.177–3.179.

80 See <baoquan.court.gov.cn/#/home/particulars?id=11156690624436&form=issue> accessed 15 July 2021. However, it is not clear whether the two days might be sufficient in practice.

81 See Online Preservation System of the People's Courts <www.baoquan.court.gov.cn> accessed 15 July 2021. From the practical point of view, the online preservation system significantly enhances the efficiency of an application seeking a preservation measure and reduces the costs for the applicants. However, as compared to the submission of the application on the spot, the negative side of the online system is that both the format of the preservation application and the necessary evidence uploaded by the applicant must be succinct and there must be no doubt whatsoever as the applicant has no opportunity to clarify the unclear wording of the application in front of a judge. For this reason, any questions as to the format of the application and evidence may lead the judge to request supplementary explanation or evidence. Alternatively, the application will not be approved. In terms of the format of the preservation application, see 3.117–3.120. The evidence is relevant to the requirements for the different types of preservation measures which will be discussed in Chapters 6, 8 and 10 separately.

parties may take different paths to address these issues, a few of which are as follows:

(a) The court issues a preservation order or refuses to do so.
(b) A party, including the applicant, the respondent, the interested party and/or an outside third party not involved in the case, files an application for reconsideration of an order, which will be discussed in 3.232–3.246.[82]
(c) A party, including the applicant, the respondent, the interested party and/or an outside third party not involved in the case, submits an objection against the court's improper preservation order during the enforcement of this order, which will be discussed in 3.247–3.257.
(d) An outside third party submits an objection if he considers that he has a substantive right over the subject matter of a preservation order, which will be discussed in 3.258–3.265.
(e) The court gives sanction against the party, the interested party or an outside third party, for not obeying an order in the context of preservation measures, as discussed in 3.266–3.286.
(f) The issuing court or its superior court discharges the preservation order of the lower-tier court, as discussed in 3.287–3.291.
(g) The respondent or other parties claim compensation, as discussed in 3.292–3.306.

3.50 Based on the above different paths, the forthcoming paragraphs will provide some general rules one by one for all kinds of preservation measures. However, in the context of a particular preservation measure, these specific rules will be discussed in detail in Chapters 6, 8 and 10.

Jurisdiction of Courts for Civil Preservation Applications

3.51 An application for a preservation measure shall be made to the court that has jurisdiction over the case. Before an applicant brings a case to court or applies for an arbitration, it is important to identify the competent court that may have jurisdiction over the application. However, the jurisdiction issues under Chinese law are complex, and this section will simply provide the general rules relevant to preservation applications.

Court Tier Jurisdiction for Preservation Applications

3.52 In accordance with Articles 17 to 20 of the CPL 1991 (as amended until 2020), the principle of the Chinese courts' tier jurisdiction is as follows:

82 CPL 1991 (as amended until 2020), Article 108 and the Interpretation of CPL 2015 (2020 Amendment), Article 172. In addition, there is no legislation or interpretation to define "the interested party" and "outside party", and their different meanings are discussed in 3.226–3.231.

(a) The primary people's courts have jurisdiction as courts of the first instance over all civil and commercial cases, unless otherwise stipulated by the law.
(b) The intermediate people's courts have jurisdiction as courts of the first instance over the following types of civil cases:
  I. Significant cases involving foreign parties.
  II. Cases with significant impact in the areas over which the courts exercise jurisdiction.
  III. Cases determined by the SPC to come under the jurisdiction of the intermediate people's courts.
(c) The higher people's courts have jurisdiction as courts of first instance over civil cases with significant impact in the areas over which they exercise jurisdiction.
(d) The SPC has jurisdiction as the court of first instance over the following types of civil cases:
  I. Cases with significant impact on the whole country.
  II. Cases that the SPC deems that it should try itself.[83]

3.53 Even so, on the ground that China has a two-tier trial system and in order to ensure that any cases will be heard by at least two levels of courts within the hierarchy, the SPC does not in practice dispose of the first instance case. The only exception is in the scenario when the case has been accepted by the CICC. In that case, the CICC has authority to accept the first instance case and to make a final and binding decision.[84]

3.54 In the light of this concept of tier jurisdiction, if an applicant is planning to file an application for a pre-action preservation measure, he first needs to consider which court may have jurisdiction over the case or on the application seeking preservation measures. As far as a pre-action preservation is concerned, the court with jurisdiction over an application for preservation measures is not always the same court with jurisdiction over the overall case, where possibly the full civil trial will take place.

3.55 With regard to the meanings of "significant cases involving foreign parties" and "significant impact", those depend mainly on the disputed amount and the category of a case, that is whether a foreign-related element is involved.

Tier Jurisdiction of Domestic Cases

3.56 In terms of domestic cases, the high people's courts as the first instance simply dispose of cases where the disputed amount is more than

83 CPL 1991 (as amended until 2020), Articles 17, 18, 19 and 20.
84 Refer to 3.37.

RMB 5 billion.[85] In contrast, the criterion for the acceptance of a case in the intermediate people's courts is not uniform in all provinces. It is affected by the economic situation of the different provinces.

3.57 For instance, the intermediate courts located in Beijing, Shanghai, Guangdong, Jiangsu and Zhejiang can dispose of cases where the disputed amount is between RMB 5 billion and RMB 100 million, while other intermediate courts merely hear cases involving a disputed amount between RMB 5 billion and RMB 10 or 30 million.[86]

Tier Jurisdiction of Foreign-Related Cases

3.58 In terms of foreign-related civil and commercial cases of the first instance, unlike domestic cases, there is no uniform guidance that is available for both the high people's courts and intermediate people's courts.

3.59 For instance, the high people's courts, which are located in Beijing, Shanghai, Guangdong, Jiangsu and Zhejiang, can dispose of cases where the disputed amount is more than RMB 200 million, while other high people's courts in other provincial capitals can deal with cases involving a maximum amount of RMB 80 million, 40 million or 20 million.[87] Accordingly, the criteria for the acceptance of cases at the intermediate courts and the primary people's courts are again a complex subject because the concept of disputed amount is flexible and may vary according to the local economic environment.

3.60 Because the criteria for the acceptance of cases in foreign-related civil and commercial disputes are a complex subject and beyond the scope of this book, it is always advisable to check the regional criteria.

Tier Jurisdiction of Specialised Courts: Exclusive Jurisdiction

3.61 The specialised courts, including the financial court, the intellectual property court, the railway transport court and the internet court, generally

85 *Notice by the Supreme People's Court of Adjusting the Standards for Civil Cases under Original Jurisdiction of the Higher People's Courts and the Intermediate People's Courts* (Fa Fa [2019] No 14).

86 *Notice of the Supreme People's Court on Adjusting the Standards for the Jurisdiction of the Higher People's Courts and Intermediate People's Courts Over Civil and Commercial Cases of the First Instance* (Fa Fa [2015] No 7); see also, *Notice of the Supreme People's Court on Adjusting the Standards for the Jurisdiction of Part of the Higher People's Courts and Intermediate People's Courts Over Civil and Commercial Cases of the First Instance* (Fa Fa [2018] No 13).

87 *Notice of the Supreme People's Court on Clarifying Relevant Matters Concerning the Standards for Hierarchical Jurisdiction over and Centralized Handling of Foreign-Related Civil and Commercial Cases of First Instance* (Fa [2017] No 359).

follow the rule that the disputed amount will decide the issue of which tier of court will have jurisdiction.[88]

3.62 For example, if the value of a claim in a case involving issues of finance in Shanghai comes within the criterion of acceptance for the intermediate court, then that financial court as the first instance court will have jurisdiction over that case and will also consider applications for preservation measures. Conversely, if the value of a claim is within the authority of the primary people's court, then the preservation application in the first instance proceedings will be decided by the primary people's court; thereafter, the financial court would hear the second instance if the parties concerned were to appeal.[89]

3.63 However, in respect to the jurisdiction of maritime courts, there are no criteria dependent on the value of the claim in such cases. Different maritime courts as first instance courts can deal with all cases in their own territory, although, in theory, the local high courts where these maritime courts are located are also entitled to dispose of significant cases including preservation applications regarding these cases.

Territorial Jurisdiction to Consider for Preservation Applications

3.64 After addressing the issue of which tier jurisdiction should be approached with an application for a preservation measure, the applicant must also consider the appropriate territorial jurisdiction. This means that the applicant must also consider the location of the court that will have the requisite jurisdiction with regard to an application for a preservation measure.

3.65 With regard to the civil and commercial cases against Chinese domiciled parties, including a natural person/individual residing in China and organisations or legal entities/companies registered in China, the Chinese courts have lawful jurisdiction, unless the parties have an exclusive jurisdiction clause or have agreed upon a jurisdiction agreement to exclude the Chinese court's jurisdiction, provided this jurisdiction agreement does not

88 In terms of the jurisdiction over intellectual property disputes, the disputed amount is governed by *Notice of the Supreme People's Court on Adjusting the Standards for the Jurisdiction of Local People's Courts at Different Levels over Intellectual Property Rights Civil Cases of the First Instance 2010* (Fa Fa [2010] No 5). However, owing to the special requirements in relation to courts having to have sufficient knowledge of patent disputes, the jurisdiction over patents is governed by *Interpretation of the Supreme People's Court on Some Issues Concerning the Trial of Cases on New Plant Varieties* (Fa Shi [2001] No 5), *Circular of the Supreme People's Court on Starting the Trial of Cases of Integrated Circuit Layout Designs* (Fa Fa [2001] No 24) and *Several Provisions of the Supreme People's Court on Issues Concerning the Application of Law in the Trial of Cases on Patent Disputes (2015 Amendment)* (Fa Shi [2015] No 4).

89 *Provisions of the Supreme People's Court on the Jurisdiction of the Shanghai Financial Court* (Fa Shi [2018] No 14), Articles 1 and 4.

violate Chinese law. More detailed rules are provided by the CPL1991 (as amended until 2020), by the SMPL 2000 and by other judicial interpretations.[90] Further discussion is beyond the scope of this book.

3.66 In the event of the respondent[91] not being domiciled in China, the Chinese court will consider various aspects of a dispute, such as the contract between the parties or the rights of parties under the contract or otherwise, and interests in property. These factors may then become reasons for the Chinese courts to assert jurisdiction. Chinese courts will take into account the following conditions, as stated below:

(a) The place where the contract was executed or performed.
(b) The place where the subject matter of cause of action is located.
(c) The respondent has property available for distrainment.
(d) The place where the tort is committed.[92]
(e) The respondent maintains a representative office within the territory of China.[93]

3.67 In the event that the Chinese court has jurisdiction over a case, correspondingly, this competent court will also have jurisdiction over the pre-action preservation application. The specific provisions on territorial jurisdiction are based on Chapter 2, Section 2 "Territorial Jurisdiction" of the CPL 1991 (as amended until 2020).[94]

3.68 Apart from the court which has jurisdiction over the full case having jurisdiction over the pre-action preservation applications, preservation applications may also be made to the courts located in the following places:

(a) Where the property to which the dispute relates is located, when the applicant files an application seeking a property preservation measure.

---

90 CPL 1991 (as amended until 2020) from Article 21 to Article 32; see also, SMPL 2000, Article 6.

91 It should be noted that the respondent in this context refers to the respondent in both pre-action proceedings and post-action proceedings.

92 For example, in *Qualcomm Incorporated v Apple Computer Trading (Shanghai) Co Ltd and Other*, although both Qualcomm Incorporated and Apple Inc. were located in USA, the place where the alleged offence took place was located in China, the subsidiaries of Apple Inc. were also located in China, and the allegedly tortious conduct happened in China. The Intermediate People's Court of Fuzhou City of Fujian Province made a behaviour preservation order based on Qualcomm Incorporated's application; see also, *Qualcomm Incorporated v Apple Computer Trading (Shanghai) Co Ltd and Other* [2018] Min 01 Civil Chu No1208-1 (The Intermediate People's Court of Fuzhou City of Fujian Province, first instance and final order).

93 CPL 1991 (as amended until 2020), Article 265.

94 The territorial jurisdictions for Chinese courts vary according to the category of cases, such as contractual disputes, disputes involving tort, maritime disputes or others. The detailed rules have been provided by Section 2 of Chapter 2 of the CPL 1991 (as amended until 2020); see also, *Provisions of the Supreme People's Court on the Scope of Cases to Be Accepted by Maritime Courts* (Fa Shi [2016] No 4) and other interpretations. Any further discussion on this topic is beyond the scope of the book.

(b) Where the evidence is located when the applicant files an application for preservation of evidence.
(c) Where the respondent is domiciled.[95]

3.69 The above provisions do not clarify the tier of the court that will have the jurisdiction. In legal practice, a court normally examines whether the said court satisfies the requirement of the tier jurisdiction over an application for a preservation. After the issue of tier jurisdiction has been decided, only then will the issue of territorial jurisdiction over the preservation application be considered. In other words, it is important to appreciate that the tier jurisdiction rules will prevail over other rules concerning jurisdiction.

3.70 For example, if, according to the rules of the tier jurisdiction, the case needs to be heard in the first instance in the intermediate people's court, then in that scenario, the applicant can choose the local intermediate court that will have jurisdiction over the dispute. Alternatively, the applicant can choose the intermediate court where the property or the evidence is located, or where the respondent is domiciled.

Agreed Jurisdiction Clauses in Relation to Preservation Applications

3.71 In legal practice and in the authors' experience, no parties merely reach a jurisdiction clause or agreement for preservation applications. However, in accordance with Article 34 of the CPL 1991 (as amended until 2020), it is commonplace that the parties to a contractual dispute or other property dispute reach jurisdiction clauses. These jurisdictions can provide for a particular competent court to dispose of their disputes, provided such clauses do not fall foul of the provisions of the tier jurisdiction and the exclusive jurisdiction provided in the CPL 1991 (as amended until 2020).[96]

3.72 For example, a Chinese court will have exclusive jurisdiction over a dispute arising from the performance of a Sino-foreign equity joint venture contract, a Sino-foreign cooperative joint venture contract or a contract for Sino-foreign cooperative exploration and development of natural resources.[97] In such cases, the parties cannot exclude Chinese jurisdiction by written express jurisdiction clauses.[98]

95 CPL 1991 (as amended until 2020), Article 101. In addition, the issue of jurisdiction in the context of arbitration will be discussed in Chapter 4.

96 ibid Article 34.

97 ibid Article 266.

98 It must be emphasised that if the parties were to agree upon an arbitration clause to dispose of their dispute, then this agreed arbitration clause does not affect the exclusive jurisdiction of a Chinese court. To be precise, the chosen tribunal is entitled to hear the disputes for which the Chinese court should have had the exclusive jurisdiction.

3.73 Apart from the exclusive jurisdiction, pursuant to Article 34 of the CPL 1991 (as amended until 2020), the competent court chosen by parties may be located in the area where:

(a) The applicant/claimant or respondent is domiciled.
(b) The contract is signed or performed.
(c) The disputed subject matter is located.[99]

3.74 Accordingly, based on the above discussion of the territorial jurisdiction and the exclusive jurisdiction clauses, the applicant can choose a jurisdiction court for filing a preservation application based on guidance available in 3.65–3.68. Alternatively, parties can choose an agreed court based on guidance in 3.73. In case of applications for pre-action preservation measures, the strategy for selecting the right competent court is very important. Nonetheless, for the purpose of devising appropriate strategy, again prior to considering territorial jurisdiction, it must be emphasised that the rules for the tier jurisdiction will prevail.

Overseas Cases – Chinese Courts' Jurisdiction over Preservation Applications

3.75 A competent Chinese court that has jurisdiction over an application for a preservation measure is dealing only with the procedural rights of the parties. The court is not really deciding the matter on its merits, and as a result the court is not disposing of the issue of the substantive rights of the parties. Accordingly, in theory, even if there is no competent Chinese court that has jurisdiction over the substantive rights of the parties, it can be argued that a Chinese court can still have jurisdiction over applications for preservation measures required for a case being litigated or likely to be litigated in a foreign jurisdiction.

3.76 However, there are no express provisions available in various sources of the relevant laws that could provide any Chinese courts with the competent jurisdiction over applications connected with an overseas case that seek preservation measures in China. In addition, in accordance with the scope of the application of CPL 1991 (as amended until 2020), only civil actions within China's territory shall abide by the CPL.[100] If, therefore, a civil action is heard by a foreign court, the Chinese court does not have competent jurisdiction over any application for preservation measures that is associated with a case being litigated or likely to be litigated in a foreign court.[101]

99 CPL 1991 (as amended until 2020), Article 34.

100 CPL 1991 (as amended until 2020), Article 4.

101 In legal practice, this kind of a legal issue ordinarily is dependent on the judicial assistance in different jurisdictions. In addition, Chinese law is not resistant to parallel litigations. Even if a case has been brought in a foreign jurisdiction, a competent Chinese court that has

Maritime Courts' Jurisdiction over Preservation Applications for Overseas Cases

3.77 There is an express provision in relation to Chinese maritime courts' jurisdiction over maritime preservation measures required in such disputes where a foreign court has jurisdiction. Articles 14, 53 and 64 of the SMPL 2000 provide respectively:

> Preservation of a maritime claim shall not be bound by the jurisdiction agreement or arbitration agreement reached between the parties to an action in respect of that claim.[102]
>
> A maritime injunction shall not be bound by the jurisdiction agreement or arbitration agreement reached between the parties in respect of that claim.[103]
>
> Preservation of maritime evidence shall not be bound by the jurisdiction agreement or arbitration agreement reached between the parties in respect of that claim.[104]

3.78 Furthermore, the Interpretation of SMPL 2008 provides detailed rules for three types of maritime preservation application. Articles 21, 41 and 47 of the Interpretation of SMPL 2008 have stipulated that, where a foreign court has already accepted a related maritime case, or the relevant dispute has already been submitted for arbitration, then in the following cases the application can be accepted:

(a) The involved property being within Chinese territory, if a party applies for a maritime claim preservation with the maritime court of the place where the property is located.
(b) If a party applies for a maritime injunction[105] with a Chinese maritime court and furnishes to the court the relevant evidence for enforcement of the injunction.
(c) If a party applies for preservation of maritime evidence with a Chinese maritime court and furnishes relevant evidence proving the evidence has been preserved within China.[106]

3.79 For example, in *Eclipse Property Co Ltd (Marshall Islands) v Fujian Shenglong Shipbuilding Co Ltd and Wenzhou Runyang Import and Export Co*

---

jurisdiction over the same case based on the CPL 1991 (as amended until 2020) can still exercise its own jurisdiction. In this context, if the applicant files an application for the same dispute in the Chinese court, and meanwhile files a preservation application, the preservation application will certainly be accepted by that Chinese court. Nonetheless, the applicant will have to give thought to the legal costs, but it may be a commercial decision of the applicant to proceed in this way for tactical reasons; see also, Interpretation of the CPL 1991 (as amended until 2020), Article 533.

102 SMPL 2000, Article 14.

103 ibid Article 53.

104 ibid Article 64.

105 A maritime injunction is the same as a behaviour preservation measure; see also, Chapter 8, 8.1.

106 Interpretation of SMPL 2008, Articles 21, 41 and 47.

Ltd,[107] Fujian Shenglong and Wenzhou Runyang (two respondents) instituted an arbitration in the London Maritime Arbitrators Association (LMAA) against an applicant (Eclipse Property) in 2006. The applicant filed a counterclaim in the LMAA and thereafter applied in the Xiamen Maritime Court for the arrest of the ship, even though the Xiamen Maritime Court had no jurisdiction over the merits of the maritime dispute.

3.80 The Xiamen Maritime Court held in the case of *Eclipse Property* that, pursuant to Article 14 of the SMPL 2000 and Article 21 of the Interpretation of SMPL 2008, since the property to be preserved was located in China, the Chinese court would have jurisdiction, even if a foreign arbitration tribunal was hearing the merits of the full dispute. The court therefore accepted the application to arrest the ship.[108] This case became number ten of ten typical sample cases regarding the arrest and auction of vessels of Chinese maritime courts reported by the SPC.

Choice of Venue if There Are Two Competent Courts

3.81 In the event that more than one court may have jurisdiction over an application for a preservation measure, an applicant is entitled to institute a pre-action preservation application in any one of the competent courts of his choice.

3.82 If the applicant files the same application in two or more competent courts, the court that first receives the application is deemed to have jurisdiction over the preservation application. In a scenario where the applicant filed an application for a property preservation in a court with jurisdiction on the basis of where the respondent is domiciled before he had filed a similar application in another court on the basis of the location of the property, then the first court will have jurisdiction for dealing with the application seeking a preservation measure. In legal practice, it is possible and tactical for an applicant to file an application in different courts, because the applicant will lack knowledge of the uncertainty he may face while dealing with either of the courts, such as promptness, formality in terms of evidence and so forth.[109]

107 *Eclipse Property Co Ltd (Marshall Islands) v Fujian Shenglong Shipbuilding Co Ltd and Wenzhou Runyang Import and Export Co Ltd* (an application for the arrest ship) [2010] Xia Hai Fa Bao Zi No 52 (Xiamen Maritime Court, first instance and binding order) – number ten of ten typical sample cases regarding the arrest and auction of vessels of Chinese maritime courts reported by the SPC.

108 ibid; see also, *Dampskibsselskabet NORDENA / S v Grand China Logistic Holding Co Ltd* (an application for a property preservation) [2014] Jin Hai Fa Bao Zi No 7-1 (Tianjin Maritime Court, first instance and binding order); *Fengrun Shipping Co Ltd v Zhejiang Haibo Food Co Ltd* (an application for a maritime evidence preservation) [2014] Yong Hai Fa Zhou Zheng Zi No 1 (Ningbo Maritime Court, first instance and binding order).

109 In practice, even if an applicant chooses two or more courts to file a preservation measure, it is not necessary to pay the application fee twice. Once the first court accepts the application, the other application will be terminated.

3.83 However, if the applicant decides to lodge a case with a competent court other than the court that has given a pre-action preservation order, then all the materials in relation to the preservation application will be transferred to this new court. Accordingly, the court that has dealt with the application seeking preservation measures will transfer the formalities associated with the preservation measures to the other competent court that has accepted the case.[110]

Jurisdiction for Preservation Applications after Completion of the First Instance

3.84 On occasion, no party has asked for any preservation measures during the first instance proceedings and, as a result, there is no preservation order from the court of the first instance. In a scenario where, after the first instance judgment has been made but before the second instance court has received all the papers and formalities from the court of the first instance, then the first instance court still has jurisdiction over applications for preservation measures. Such applications can be made by the party concerned or *ex officio* under certain circumstances, such as the activities of one of the parties involving transfer, concealment or disposal of property, or damage to it.[111]

3.85 Nonetheless, the preservation order rendered by the court of the first instance shall be submitted in a timely manner to the second instance court.[112] This means that, if now the party concerned in the second instance proceedings applies for a renewal of the preservation measure, the second instance court will have the requisite jurisdiction.[113] In addition, the second instance court will have jurisdiction over the renewal of all preservation measures ordered by the court of the first instance.

3.86 Apart from the above scenario, the second instance court will have jurisdiction to deal with new applications seeking preservation measures. With respect to the issue of the enforcement of the renewed preservation or the fresh preservation order, the second instance court may entrust the obligation to deal with issues in relation to the enforcement of these preservation orders to the first instance court.[114]

3.87 If a case were to be reheard pursuant to the law, then the court that rehears the case has jurisdiction over the applications for renewal of the preservation measures or over the new application seeking fresh preservation

110 Interpretation of CPL 2015 (2020 Amendment), Article 160.

111 ibid Article 161.

112 ibid.

113 A preservation order is not always effective, especially for a property preservation order, and prior to the time deadline, the applicant must apply for the renewal of the original preservation order. See also, Chapter 6, 6.151–6.155.

114 Interpretation of CPL 2015 (2020 Amendment), Article 162.

measures. In terms of the enforcement of the preservation order, this retrial court may take this obligation upon itself, or entrust it to the court that originally heard the case or entrust it to the court of the enforcement of the previous effective judgment.[115]

Jurisdiction after Making an Effective Judgment or Award

3.88 After a judgment made by the first instance or the second instance court has become effective,[116] or an arbitral award is effective, a preservation order that is not cancelled or discharged by the relevant Chinese court *ex officio* and its legal effect will last from the stage of the trial to the stage of enforcement of a final judgement, then, in that scenario, such preservation orders will be converted automatically under enforcement procedures. Accordingly, once enforcement procedures have started, these measures may include sealing, distrainment or freezing of the relevant property.[117]

3.89 It should be noted that, after the enforcement procedure has started, regardless of the conversion of a preservation order, the nature of such actions of the court is different from that of the preservation measures arising from the party's application. The reason for this is that actions equivalent to the preservation measures during the enforcement proceedings are based fundamentally on the exercise of a court's legal obligation. Any further discussion on the topic is beyond the scope of this book.

3.90 However, if there is no effective order for the preservation measure before the commencement of the enforcement of a judgment or an arbitral award, a winning party is entitled to apply for preservation measures to the Chinese court that is going to enforce a court judgment or an arbitral award, provided that the applicant can prove that a failure to apply in a timely manner to seek preservation measures will lead to the binding legal instrument being unenforceable or difficult to enforce due to emergencies, such as the transfer of property by the counterpart.[118]

3.91 Accordingly, even if some courts were to have jurisdiction for dealing with such an application seeking preservation measures, that court, which is entitled to accept the application, would still refer such preservation applications to the court of enforcement of the effective judgment or award. Pursuant to Article 224 of the CPL 1991 (as amended until 2020), the court

115 ibid.

116 After the court of the first instance makes a judgment, if the parties concerned do not submit an appeal within 15 days, the judgment will come into effect automatically and becomes final and binding; if the parties submit an appeal, the judgment by the court of the first instance is not effective. Conversely, after the court of the second instance makes a judgment, such judgment is immediately final and binding; see also, CPL 1991 (as amended until 2020), Articles 164 and 175.

117 Interpretation of CPL 2015 (2020 Amendment), Article 168.

118 ibid Article 163.

of enforcement will normally refer these preservation applications to the first instance court. In some instances, according to the specific circumstances of the case, the court may even refer the preservation applications to a court at the same level as the first instance court – one where the property subject to enforcement is located.[119]

Application and Enforcement of Court Orders of Macau, Hong Kong and Taiwan

3.92 Macau, Hong Kong and Taiwan, as three special regions in China, have their own respective legal systems. The distinctiveness of Hong Kong lies in its legal system, which continued to follow common law practices after sovereignty over Hong Kong was handed back to China on 1 July 1997. Both Macau and Taiwan,[120] like mainland China, belong to the civil law tradition, and the concept of "civil preservation procedure" is similar in these two locations. As for these three jurisdictions, the mainland reached a bilateral agreement for the recognition and enforcement of civil and commercial judgments with Hong Kong and Macau respectively, and the SPC issued a judicial interpretation to cope with the recognition and enforcement of civil and commercial judgments made by a Taiwan court. However, the scope of application of these three judicial documents differs significantly.

3.93 Prior to further discussion, it should be clarified that the court orders in this context can be divided into two types. The first type of court order means that jurisdiction during the litigation proceedings renders a preservation order in the same jurisdiction. On the other hand, the second type of court order means that, where one jurisdiction during the litigation proceedings does not render a preservation order, an applicant should apply for a preservation order in another jurisdiction that is a party to the bilateral agreement. In such a scenario, the second jurisdiction renders a preservation order pursuant to its territorial law.

Macau and the Mainland

3.94 In 2006, the mainland and the Macau Special Administrative Region signed an *Arrangement between them for Mutual Recognition*

119 Article 224 of the CPL 1991 (as amended until 2020) provides that "a legally effective civil judgment or ruling (order), or that portion of a legally effective criminal judgment or ruling (order) that pertains to property, shall be enforced by the people's court of first instance or the people's court at the same level as the people's court where the property subject to execution is located".

120 The characteristic of Macau lies in its legal system following civil law after sovereignty over Macau was handed back to China by Portugal on 20 December 1999.

and Enforcement of Civil and Commercial Judgments 2006 (hereinafter referred to as "Mainland and Macau Judgment Arrangement 2006").[121] This Arrangement, in the context of mutual recognition and enforcement of judgments of civil and commercial cases in the mainland and Macau (including labour dispute cases in the mainland and civil labour cases in the Macao Special Administrative Region), governs various procedural aspects that are needed by stakeholders.[122] In this context, apart from the commercial disputes, the scope of disputes that may be governed by this Arrangement includes the distribution of marital property, wills and inheritances and insolvency cases.[123]

3.95 In addition to the scope of disputes, Article 2 of this Arrangement also clarifies the scope of the mutual recognition and enforcement of judgments that includes:

> the judgments, verdicts, decisions, mediation agreements and orders to pay in the Mainland; and include the judgments, verdicts, orders of confirming reconcilement, decisions or instructions of judges in Macau.[124]

3.96 Based on this, a preservation order made by a mainland court or a Macau court may be recognised and enforced by its counterpart, pursuant to the bilateral arrangement.

3.97 As for the second type of court order mentioned in 3.93, Article 15 of this Arrangement provides that:

> Before or after the court accepts an application for recognition and enforcement of the judgment, it may take preservation measures for the *property* of the party against whom the application is filed, according to the provisions in the laws of the requested party on property preservation and upon the strength of the application of the applicant [emphasis added].[125]

3.98 It follows that, even if the dispute is heard by a Macau court, a mainland court has the authority and jurisdiction to accept a preservation application and accordingly can render preservation measures, as long as the application abides by Chinese law.

3.99 However, when Article 15 of this Arrangement is applied, there are two rules. First, the type of the preservation measure in an application simply refers to an application for a property preservation; secondly, the application

121 *Arrangement of Mainland and Macau Special Administrative Region on Mutual Recognition and Execution of Civil and Commercial Judgments* (Fa Shi [2006] No 2) was promulgated by the SPC on 21 March 2006 and came into effect on 1 April 2006.

122 ibid Article 1.

123 Xixiang Song, 'Mutual Recognition and Execution of Civil and Commercial Judgment between Mainland and Macau' (2012) 4 (14) Academic Journal of One Country Two Systems 88, 89.

124 Mainland and Macau Judgment Arrangement 2006, Article 2.

125 ibid Article 15.

can be accepted in the mainland court only after the final decision has been rendered by the Macau court.[126]

Hong Kong and the Mainland

3.100 Similarly, in 2008, an *Arrangement of the SPC between the Mainland and the HKSAR on Reciprocal Recognition and Enforcement of the Decisions of Civil and Commercial Cases under Consensual Jurisdiction* (hereinafter referred to as "Mainland and HK Decision Arrangement 2008") was jointly issued by the SPC and the HKSAR.[127]

3.101 Article 2 of this Arrangement is similar to Article 2 of Mainland and Macau Judgment Arrangement 2006, providing for reciprocal recognition and enforcement of judgments, including decisions, orders, mediation awards and payment orders in the mainland, as well as decisions, orders and legal fee appraisal certificates in Hong Kong.[128] Based on this, a preservation order rendered by a mainland court or a Hong Kong court can be recognised and enforced by its counterpart in the bilateral arrangement.

3.102 However, compared with the Mainland and Macau Judgment Arrangement 2006, the scope of the application of the Mainland and HK Decision Arrangement 2008 is narrower.

3.103 First, the scope of the disputes refers only to a civil or commercial contract between the parties concerned, and it effectively excludes disputes concerning contracts of employment or contracts to which a natural person is involved as a party for purposes of personal consumption, family affairs, insolvency or other non-commercial purposes.[129]

---

126 Songyou Huang, 'Answers of Vice-President of the Supreme People's Court to Questions on *Arrangement of Mainland and Macau Special Administrative Region on Mutual Recognition and Execution of Civil and Commercial Judgments*' in The First Civil Division of the Supreme People's Court (eds.), *Reference and Guide to Civil Trial Vol. 25* (Law Press of China, 2006).

127 *Arrangement of the Supreme People's Court between the Mainland and the HKSAR on Reciprocal Recognition and Enforcement of the Decisions of Civil and Commercial Cases under Consensual Jurisdiction* (Fa Shi [2008] No 9).

128 ibid Article 2.

129 Songyou Huang, 'Answers of Vice-President of the Supreme People's Court to Questions on *Arrangement of the Supreme People's Court between the Mainland and the HKSAR on Reciprocal Recognition and Enforcement of the Decisions of Civil and Commercial Cases under Consensual Jurisdiction*' *People's Court Daily* (Beijing, 7 July 2008); see also, in the case of *Norstar Automobile Industrial Holding Limited*, an applicant applied to the First Intermediate People's Court of Beijing Municipality for recognition and enforcement of a provisional liquidation order made by a Hong Kong court. However, the SPC held that, pursuant to Article 1 of the Mainland and HK Decision Arrangement 2008, this order was not covered by this arrangement (an application for a HK provisional liquidator order) [2010] Yi Zhong Civil Te Zi No 8080 (the First Intermediate People's Court of Beijing Municipality); see also, an application to seek Reply from the Supreme People's Court to Request for *Beitai Automobile Industry Holdings Co Ltd*'s application for Recognition of the Court Order of the Hong Kong Special Administrative Region ([2011] Civil Si Ta Zi No 19, 28 September 2011).

3.104 Secondly, Article 1 provides that this Arrangement applies only to monetary judgments, which must be final, and does not apply to specific performances or confirmation of rights and interests.[130]

3.105 Thirdly, the condition precedent for application of the Mainland and HK Decision Arrangement 2008 is a written jurisdiction agreement between the parties. After the Arrangement comes into force, in accordance with Articles 1 and 3, the written jurisdiction agreement refers to the concluded agreement, which expressly stipulates in writing that a mainland court or a Hong Kong court will have exclusive jurisdiction over any dispute between the parties.[131]

3.106 Accordingly, if a written exclusive jurisdiction agreement is absent, the mainland court will not accept an application for property preservation under the bilateral arrangement. As the authors could not locate any reported case on this matter, it is not clear that how the mainland court will apply this rule to deal with applications seeking preservation measures.

3.107 It should be noted that, pursuant to Article 4 of *Arrangement on Mutual Recognition and Enforcement of Judgments in Civil and Commercial Cases by the Courts of the Mainland and the Hong Kong Special Administrative Region 2019* signed by the mainland and Hong Kong on 18 January 2019 (hereinafter referred to as "New Arrangement 2019"), orders on preservation measures are expressly excluded from this Arrangement.[132] Hong Kong and the mainland will therefore no longer recognise and enforce preservation measures rendered by each other's courts, pursuant to the New Arrangement 2019.

3.108 Although this New Arrangement 2019 has not yet come into effect, once it is effective, the Mainland and HK Decision Arrangement 2008 will be abolished.[133] As for the recognition of each other's preservation measures, there is a suggestion in the New Arrangement 2019 that the SPC and the HKSAR Government should consider drafting supplementary documents regarding assistance in preservation measures and interim relief that have been excluded from Article 4 of this New Arrangement.[134]

---

130 Mainland and HK Decision Arrangement 2008, Article 1

131 ibid Articles 1 and 3.

132 Article 4 of *Arrangement on Mutual Recognition and Enforcement of Judgments in Civil and Commercial Cases by the Courts of the Mainland and the Hong Kong Special Administrative Region 2019* (not yet in effect) provides that "for the purpose of this Arrangement, a 'judgment', in the case of the Mainland, includes any judgment, ruling, conciliation statement and order of payment *excluding order of preservation*; in the case of the HKSAR, includes any judgment, order, decree, and cost-assessment certificates for litigation, excluding any injunction and interim relief [emphasis added]".

133 ibid Article 30 provides that "on the effective date of this arrangement, Arrangement of the Supreme People's Court between the Mainland and the HKSAR on Reciprocal Recognition and Enforcement of the Decisions of Civil and Commercial Cases under Consensual Jurisdiction will be abolished on the same day".

134 ibid Article 28.

3.109 As for the second type of court order mentioned in 3.93, Article 14 of the Mainland and HK Decision Arrangement 2008 is also similar to Article 15 of the Mainland and Macau Judgment Arrangement 2006.[135] However, in the New Arrangement 2019, the express provision is a little different. The new provision provides:

> A court of the requested place may, before or after accepting any application for recognition and enforcement of a judgment, impose preservation or mandatory measures in accordance with the law of that place.[136]

3.110 Firstly, the type of preservation order that Chinese courts can grant is not limited. In other words, a Chinese court, pursuant to the CPL 1991 (as amended until 2020), may grant all three types of preservation order – property, behaviour and evidence.

3.111 Secondly, according to the understanding and application of this New Arrangement 2019 issued by the SPC, it must be emphasised that the condition precedent for a Chinese court to accept an application seeking a preservation measure is that a judgment rendered by the other court is effective. In other words, before the other court makes an effective judgment, the Chinese court will not accept such an application seeking the preservation measure.[137]

Taiwan and the Mainland

3.112 The SPC in 2015 promulgated the *Provisions of the SPC on the Recognition and Enforcement of the Civil Judgments Rendered by Courts in Taiwan Region* (hereinafter referred to "Provisions of Enforcement of Taiwan Judgment 2015").[138] Unlike the above two effective Arrangements, the Provisions of Enforcement of Taiwan Judgment 2015 are not a bilateral arrangement. These Provisions provide only how Chinese courts will recognise and enforce the judgments made by a Taiwan court.[139]

---

135 Article 14 of the Mainland and HK Decision Arrangement 2008 provides that "a court can make *a property preservation order* or take other compulsory measures against the party's property against whom the application is filed before or after accepting a petition for the recognition and enforcement of a judgment under the Arrangement [emphasis added]".

136 New Arrangement 2019, Article 24.

137 Qibo Jiang, Jiahai Zhou, Yanli Si and Kun Liu, 'Understanding and Application of *Provisions of the Supreme People's Court on Arrangement on Mutual Recognition and Enforcement of Judgments in Civil and Commercial Cases by the Courts of the Mainland and the Hong Kong Special Administrative Region 2019*' (2019) 7 The People's Judicature 30.

138 *Provisions of the Supreme People's Court on the Recognition and Enforcement of the Civil Judgments Rendered by Courts in Taiwan Region* (Fa Shi [2015] No 13) was promulgated on 29 June 2015 and came into effect on 1 July 2015.

139 In terms of a judgment made by a mainland court, pursuant to Article 74 of Act Governing Relations between the People of the Taiwan Area and the Mainland Area (amended on 24 July 2019), it is provided that "To the extent that an irrevocable civil ruling (order) or judgment, or arbitral award rendered in the Mainland Area is not contrary to the public order

3.113 The scope of "judgments" includes the effective civil judgments, orders, settlement transcripts, mediation transcripts and payment orders and other matters issued by courts of the Taiwan Region.[140] The Chinese courts therefore recognise and enforce preservation orders made by Taiwan courts.

3.114 In addition, even after a court in Taiwan renders an effective decision, an applicant can still apply for preservation measures in mainland China, in accordance with Article 10 that provides:

> Before or after the [mainland] people's court accepts an application for recognition and enforcement of the Taiwan Region court's judgment, in the light of an applicant's application, it may take preservation measures in accordance with the CPL and the relevant interpretations.141

3.115 It can be seen that, compared with the first two effective Arrangements (the Mainland and HK Decision Arrangement 2008 and the Mainland and Macau Judgment Arrangement 2006), the type of application for preservation measures in the Provisions of Enforcement of Taiwan Judgment 2015 is not restricted to property or property-related preservation. According to the effective time when the first two arrangements came into existence, the existing CPL 1991 (as amended until 2020) was not revised to include preservation measures such as behaviour preservation measures. Behaviour preservation was added in the CPL 1991 recently through revisions and amendments made to the CPL 1991 in 2012. Therefore, as compared to the other two Arrangements, the applicant may also apply for behaviour and evidence preservation measures in the Chinese court, pursuant to Article 15 of Provisions of Enforcement of Taiwan Judgment 2015.

Format of the Preservation Applications

3.116 From the outset, there are no standard precedent forms/form in China that an applicant can use for his preservation applications. However, there is customary practice about the contents that need to go into any kind of pleading and application to be submitted to the Chinese courts. The format of the application will vary according to the different types of preservation measures that are available in China. For the sake of completeness, the specific content of an application format seeking preservation measures and the substantial requirements of the evidence associated with such applications

---

or good morals of the Taiwan Area, an application may be filed with a court for an order to recognise it. Where any ruling (order) or judgment, or award recognised by a court's ruling (order) as referred to in the preceding paragraph requires performance, it may serve as a writ of execution". It follows that a preservation order made by a mainland court can be recognised by a Taiwan court. Further discussion on the issue is beyond the scope of this book.

140 Provisions of Enforcement of Taiwan Judgment 2015, Article 2.

141 ibid Article 10.

will be discussed in detail in Chapters 6, 8 and 10 respectively. Forthcoming paragraphs will simply introduce, in general terms, the formal requirements for the format of the application and evidence.

Written Format or Others

3.117 In accordance with Article 1 of the Interpretation of Property Preservation (2020 Amendment) and Article 4 of the Interpretation of IP Behaviour Preservation 2018, an application for property and IP behaviour preservations must take written form.[142] Although the Interpretation of IP Behaviour Preservation 2018 simply applies to intellectual property disputes, it is the authors' contention that applicants should adopt a written format for their applications in the context of applications seeking behaviour preservation measures, as well as for other kinds of application involving different causes of action.

3.118 There is no requirement for a specific format for the applications seeking the preservation of evidence, but, in the light of Article 81 of the CPL 1991 (as amended until 2020), the requirements that are relevant to applications for property and behaviour preservations are also applicable to other preservation applications. The requirement in relation to the format of applications seeking evidence preservation is therefore usually applied *mutatis mutandis* to the requirements in relation to the format of applications seeking other preservation remedies.[143] Accordingly, the applicant should make use of a written format for their applications seeking preservation of evidence measures.

3.119 In Chinese legal practice, written format generally refers to an original written application rather than to a specific precedent form or a copy version. If an applicant is a natural person, he must sign his name on the formal written application; if an applicant is a legal entity or other organisation, the official seal and/or the signature of the legal representative or the principal must be affixed to the form.

3.120 However, a few maritime courts may accept an application by other means, such as by fax or e-mail, especially under urgent circumstances.[144] In the case pertaining to the arrest of the *MV NERISSA*, an applicant applied for arrest of the ship by e-mail to the Qingdao Maritime Court, and this was

142 Interpretation of Property Preservation (2020 Amendment), Article 1 and Interpretation of IP Behaviour Preservation 2018, Article 4.

143 Article 81 of the CPL 1991 (as amended until 2020) provides that "The provisions in Chapter IX (Preservation and Advance Enforcement) of the Law concerning evidence preservation shall apply *mutatis mutandis* to other procedures concerning evidence preservation".

144 Liang Zhao and Lianjun Li, *Maritime Law and Practice in China* (1st Edn, Informa Law from Routledge 2017) Para 20.8; see also Lixin Han, Shaochun Yuan and Weimin Yin, *Maritime Litigation and Arbitration* (1st Edn, Dalian Maritime University Press 2007).

accepted.[145] In such a scenario, the maritime court requires the applicant immediately to provide the original application in a written format, after the court accepts the application by fax or other means.146

Requirements as to Translation

3.121 Simplified Mandarin (Chinese) is an official language in Chinese courts.147 Both the written application and the relevant documents must use the Chinese version. If an original application format or evidence uses a foreign language, a Chinese translation must be submitted along with the application.148

3.122 In accordance with Article 527 of the Interpretation of CPL 2015 (2020 Amendment), it is provided that:

> In the case that the parties concerned disagree on a Chinese translation, they shall jointly entrust a translation institution to provide a translated version. The people's court may determine such translation institution at its discretion, if the parties concerned fail to reach an agreement on the selection of a translation institution.149

3.123 It follows that there are no specific provisions on the qualifications of the translator or the translation company. In legal practice, Chinese courts normally accept the translation provided by a qualified translation company that is registered in China, but it will not accept a translation by any natural person. In order to avoid the submission of non-quality materials, it is therefore prudent for the applicant to submit all materials for a preservation application along with translations of these documents that have been done by a translation company acceptable by the court.

3.124 It is worth noting that the CICC may accept a written application and relevant materials in English, although the existing interpretation of the CPL 1991 (as amended until 2020) does not clarify this point. The reason is that *Provisions of the SPC on Several Issues Regarding the Establishment of*

145 Wenshan Xue, 'Salute to Chinese Judge and Chinese Legal System: port on Arrest of M/V NERISSA' *People's Court Daily* (Beijing, 19 September 2019).

146 Under certain circumstances, other courts can also accept an application by other means, as seen in the authors' experience.

147 Article 262 of the CPL 1991 (as amended until 2020) provides that "In hearing foreign-related civil cases, a people's court shall use the written and spoken language commonly used in the People's Republic of China".

148 Article 70 of the CPL 1991 (as amended until 2020) provides that "When documentary evidence in a foreign language is to be submitted, it must be accompanied by a Chinese translation"; see also, Article 527 of the Interpretation of CPL 2015 (2020 Amendment) which provides that "In the case the party concerned submitted any written document made in foreign language to the *people's court, it shall submit Chinese translation of such document at the same time*"*;* see also, *Article 17 of* Provisions on Evidence 2019 which provides that "a written documentary evidence or other information made in foreign language provided by parties concerned should be enclosed in Chinese language".

149 Interpretation of CPL 2015 (2020 Amendment), Article 527.

the International Commercial Court stipulate that the selected judges in the CICC must be proficient in English and at the same time must be bilingual. That means that the judges must be proficient in both Chinese and English, as both are working languages of the CICC. If the evidence that is submitted by a party is in English and the other party has consented to its submission, in that scenario that first party is exempted from submitting Chinese translations.[150] It is therefore the authors' view that applications submitted in English may be seen as officially acceptable by the CICC.

Requirements as to Notarisation and Legalisation

3.125 In accordance with the CPL 1991 (as amended until 2020) and Provisions on Evidence 2019, a few documents in relation to applications seeking preservation measures must be notarised by a notary public of the issuing country and thereafter must be legalised by the Chinese embassy located in that issuing country. Alternatively, these documents may be certified under the relevant procedure based on the treaty between China and the issuing country. A few such documents that must be notarised and legalised are as follows:

(a) Identity certificates, such as the business licence of a foreign enterprise or certificates of the organisation that is filing an application.[151]
(b) In case the applicant is to appoint a Chinese lawyer or other person as the agent *ad litem*, a power of attorney needs to be submitted by any applicant who is a foreigner, a stateless person, a foreign enterprise or a foreign organisation without a domicile within Chinese territory.[152]
(c) Evidence for a preservation application that has been collated outside Chinese territory.[153]

3.126 It should be noted that applicants from Hong Kong, Macau and Taiwan, as these are special regions in China, also need go through the procedure of notarisation, but there is no further need of any legalisation.

Flexible Requirements as to Notarisation and Legalisation in IP Disputes

3.127 Compared with the general requirements, in the new Provisions on IP Evidence 2020, the SPC proffers flexible requirements as to evidence from outside China. It is provided in Article 8 that:

150 *Provisions of the Supreme People's Court on Several Issues Regarding the Establishment of the International Commercial Court* (Fa Shi [2018] No 11), Articles 4 and 9.

151 Interpretation of the CPL 2015 (as amended until 2020), Article 523.

152 CPL 1991 (as amended until 2020), Article 264. It should be noted that an applicant is entitled to appoint a Chinese lawyer or other person as the agent *ad litem*. A power of attorney may therefore be provided to a Chinese lawyer or other person located in China.

153 Provisions on Evidence (2019 Amendment), Article 16.

> where the parties raise an objection only on the grounds that the evidence has not gone through the certification procedures such as notarisation and legalisation, the people's court shall not support the objection to the following evidence formed outside China:
>
> (a) It has been confirmed by a legally effective people's court;
> (b) It has been confirmed by the effective award of an arbitration institution;
> (c) Public publications, patent documents, etc. that can be obtained from official or public channels;
> (d) There is other evidence to prove the authenticity.[154]

3.128 In addition, Article 9 of Provisions on IP Evidence 2020 stipulates that:

> a People's Court will not accept an objection to non-legalisation for foreign-originated evidence if
>
> (a) The party who raised the objection clearly recognises the authenticity of the evidence;
> (b) The opposing party provides witness testimony to confirm the authenticity of the evidence, and the witness clearly indicates that he is willing to accept punishment if he commits perjury.[155]

3.129 It follows that as far as an IP dispute is concerned, it is more convenient for an applicant to provide the necessary evidence, without notarisation and legalisation, when seeking a preservation measure. In the authors' opinion, although these provisions temporarily apply to IP disputes, it is anticipated that the scope of their application may extend to other disputes.

Security for Applications for Preservations

Overview of Security for Applications for Preservations

3.130 All applicants seeking preservation measures have to comply with the mandatory requirements of furnishing details of security with a written letter of application. It is an important element of the preservation application, particularly for a pre-action application seeking preservation measures. The forthcoming paragraphs will therefore discuss various legal issues concerning applicants' obligation to furnish security for preservation applications. All rules and guidance in this section may apply all types of preservation measures.

3.131 In accordance with Article 101 of the CPL 1991 (as amended until 2020), an applicant seeking pre-action property or behaviour preservation

154 Provisions on IP Evidence 2020, Article 8.
155 ibid Article 9.

measures must provide security, even if under special circumstances, the judge's discretionary power may decide the application of mandatory security and the exact amount of security.[156] Although, pursuant to Article 81 of the CPL 1991 (as amended until 2020), an application seeking pre-action evidence preservation measures may apply the rule provided by Article 101, Article 26 of Provisions on Evidence 2019 does not provide that an applicant seeking pre-action evidence preservation measures must provide security except under the certain circumstances.[157] It follows that the judge's discretionary power may decide whether it is necessary for the applicant to provide security for a pre-action evidence preservation order.

3.132 On the contrary, in the light of Article 100 of the CPL 1991 (as amended until 2020), in the context of applications seeking post-action property or behaviour preservation measures, the law does not stipulate that the applicant must furnish security. However, the courts may exercise their discretionary power to seek security from the applicants even in post-action applications.[158] If the applicant fails to provide security with the post-action property or behaviour preservation application, then the court will reject that application.[159] In terms of applications seeking post-action evidence preservation measures, like the pre-action evidence preservation measures, Article 26 of Provisions on Evidence 2019 outlines certain circumstances in which security must be provided.[160]

3.133 If the court, in exercising its discretionary power, requires the applicant to furnish security, a written notice will be sent to him. This rule on the need to furnish security with preservation applications is applicable for all three types of preservation measures that will be discussed in detail in Chapters 6, 8 and 10.

Security for Maritime Preservation Measure Applications

3.134 In relation to applications for maritime preservation measures, regardless of whether such applications are pre-action or post-action, the issue concerning the applicant's obligation to furnish security will be dependent on the exercise of the discretionary power of the court.[161] If, there-

156 Interpretation of Property Preservation (2020 Amendment), Article 5.

157 Provisions on Evidence 2019, Article 26; see also, Chapter 10, 10.122–10.130.

158 CPL 1991 (as amended until 2020), Articles 81, 100 and 101.

159 For example, in *Xixi Hou v Zongkui Hou* (an application for a behaviour preservation measure) [2018] Shan 0322 Xing Bao No 1 (The Primary People's Court of Fengxiang of Baoji City of Shaanxi Province, first instance and binding order), an applicant, Xixi Hou, could not provide a cash security within the time limit requested by the court. This cash security was to be furnished with his application seeking pre-action behaviour preservation measures. Accordingly, the court refused his preservation application.

160 Refer to Chapter 10, 10.122–10.130.

161 Article 16 of the SMPL 2000 provides that "the maritime court, having entertained an application for preservation of a maritime claim, may enjoin the maritime claimant to provide

fore, the maritime court does not require the applicant to provide security, then in that case the applicant has no obligation whatsoever voluntarily to furnish the security.

3.135 Nonetheless, it is rare for maritime courts in China to waive the requirement of security to be furnished by the applicant. Conversely, the courts tend to require the applicant to furnish sufficient and reasonable security in order to avoid the underlying risks associated with a wrong preservation order being granted based on the facts presented by the applicant.[162] The reasons for courts' conduct in this manner are due to the application of the State Compensation Law (2012 Amendment), whereby, if the preservation measure order obtained from the court turns out to be wrongly granted, then the respondent is entitled to claim against the state for compensation.[163]

Countersecurity of the Respondent

3.136 The countersecurity system applies to property or behaviour preservation measures rather than evidence preservation measures.[164] It follows that the respondent must provide countersecurity in order to discharge the preservation order rendered against them. However, the legal issues that may arise in relation to the respondent's countersecurity vary in the context of different types of preservation measure.

security. If the maritime claimant fails to do so, the court shall reject the application"; Article 55 of the SMPL 2000 stipulates that "the maritime court, having entertained an application for a maritime injunction, may enjoin the maritime claimant to provide security. Where the maritime claimant fails to do so, the court shall reject the application"; and Article 66 of the SMPL 2000 provides that "the maritime court, having entertained an application for preservation of maritime evidence, may enjoin the maritime claimant to provide security. When the maritime claimant fails to do so, the court shall reject the application". It is generally recognised that all three Articles mean that the claimant has no compulsory obligation to furnish security with his application seeking the preservation of maritime claim, maritime injunctions and preservation of maritime evidence.

162 Xin Cheng and Lina Chen, 'The Trend, Reflection and Prospects of Liability Insurance of Preservation in Maritime Litigation' (2016) 27 (3), Chinese Journal of Maritime Law 83, 86.

163 Article 28 of the State Compensation Law 1980 (2012 Amendment) provides that "infringement of property right of a citizen, a legal person, or other organisations, resulting in damage being caused, shall be dealt with in accordance with the following provisions: ... (2) If properties have been sealed up, detained or frozen, the restraints shall be discharged; for properties thus damaged or missing, compensation shall be paid in accordance with the provisions of Items 3 and 4 of this Article; (3) If the property to be returned is damaged, it shall be restored to its original condition if such restoration can be done; if not, corresponding compensation shall be paid in accordance with the extent of damage; (4) If the property to be returned is missing, corresponding compensation shall be paid"; see also, Article 3 of *Interpretation of the Supreme People's Court on Several Issues Concerning the Application of Law in the Trial of Judicial Compensation Cases in Civil and Administrative Lawsuits* (Fa Shi [2016] No 20) which provides the circumstances in which preservation measures so granted can be considered as being illegal preservation measures.

164 The First Civil Division of the Supreme People's Court (ed), *Understanding and Application of New Provisions of the Supreme People's Court on Evidence in Civil Procedures, Volume I* (People's Court Press 2020) 278.

3.137 For example, in property preservation cases, where the main disputes in general are monetary or property-related, it is easier for judges to discharge the preservation order on the receipt of countersecurity from the respondent. To be precise, the court should then allow the discharge of the property preservation measure.[165] An exception occurs when the preserved property is the disputed property, and prior to the discharge of the order, the applicant must agree to it.[166] However, in the context of behaviour preservation orders, the discharge of the preservation order in an intellectual property dispute must seek the applicant's consent if the respondent expects to discharge the order by way of countersecurity.[167] There is no provision on discharging the behaviour preservation order in other types of dispute. Detailed discussion will be found at 8.143–8.148 in Chapter 8.

3.138 All in all, in Chinese courts it is essential for the parties to work out the types of security and countersecurity that are customarily acceptable to these courts.

Types of Security or Countersecurity

3.139 There are no comprehensive provisions in the CPL 1991 (as amended until 2020) and the relevant interpretations on the issue of types of security that are acceptable to Chinese courts. The main reason for lack of guidance on this issue in sources where they might be expected is that the rules and standards of security are in fact regulated by the Civil Code 2020 and its judicial interpretation.[168] There is no distinction made in these laws between the general rules of security and those of countersecurity.

3.140 It can be argued that the scope of the application of the Civil Code 2020 cannot govern preservation security because the Civil Code 2020 merely adjusts the civil relation involving the loan, sale, carriage of goods and so forth.[169] In contrast, preservation security cannot be treated as a pure civil and commercial relation between the parties.[170] The authors are of the view that the type of security provided in the Civil Code 2020 is irrelevant to the issue of the nature of preservation security. Therefore, the Civil Code

165 Interpretation of Property Preservation (2020 Amendment), Article 22.

166 ibid.

167 Interpretation of IP Behaviour Preservation 2018, Article 12.

168 The types and applicable scope of security relating to the preservation application in the Civil Code 2020 are the same as were available in the Property Law 2007 and the Security Law of the People's Republic of China 1995. Nowadays, these two laws have been abolished since the Civil Code 2020 came into effect. But in order to facilitate the readers to refer to the previous provisions in the Property Law 2007 and the Security Law 1995, where the provisions of the Civil Code 2020 available are provided, the corresponding provisions in the other two laws will be pointed out as well.

169 Civil Code 2020, Article 387; see also, Security Law 1995 (expired on 1 January 2021), Article 2 and Property Law 2007 (expired on 1 January 2021), Article 171.

170 Refer to 3.145.

2020 provides guidance as to the types of security that may be acceptable to Chinese courts in the context of applications for preservation measures. The types of security that can be provided are property security, cash security and a letter of guarantee.[171]

3.141 In most situations, the applicant in relation to security or the respondent in relation to countersecurity may choose a type of security from various options. However, some regional guidance from local courts mandates that a cash security is still mandatory for local courts, along with other types of security.[172] The most important thing is that along with the development of the court informatisation as discussed in 3.47, both a uniform online preservation system (www.baoquan.court.gov.cn) and an independent online filing system established by different people's courts endeavour to provide an integration platform/webpage for applications seeking preservation measures and preservation security. It follows that the applicant may choose the insurance company listed in the uniform or independent platform while submitting a preservation application. In this scenario, all cash security, property security and letters of guarantee might be out of date in the near future. Certainly, it is always necessary to check the detailed guidance from local courts prior to arranging and furnishing security with preservation applications.

---

171 It is worth noting that the Civil Code 2020 does not expressly provide the types of security in any provision after the security system under the Civil Code framework is more flexible, as compared with those of security law and property law, but in accordance with Article 586 of the Civil Code 2020 as to the cash security provision and Article 1 of the *Interpretation of the Supreme People's Court on the Application of the Relevant Security System of the Civil Code of the People's Republic of China* (Fa Shi [2020] No 28) (hereinafter referred to as "Interpretation on the Application of the Security of Civil Code 2020") issued on 31 December 2020 and in effect from 1 January 2021, the basic types of security are compatible with Article 2 of the Security Law 1995 providing five types of security, including guarantee, deposits, mortgage, pledge or lien. Firstly, the exercise of the guarantee is dependent on a letter of guarantee provided by the guarantor. Secondly, deposits in effect refer to cash. Thirdly, according to the category of secured property, security by way of a mortgage or pledge can also be submitted. Fourthly, the nature of a lien does not satisfy the application of a preservation security, because the lien is a type of a statutory secured right rather than a contractual/agreed secured right like other types stated above; see also Xiao Cheng, *Research on Secured Property Rights* (2nd Edn, Renmin University of China Publishing House 2019) 15–16; see also, Article 73 of the SMPL 2000, which provides for similar types of security that are acceptable to Chinese courts. Regional interpretations and legal guidance also expressly abide by the Security Law 1995 and Property Law 2007. Due to the delayed revision, most of regional interpretations and legal guidance have not changed the Security Law 1995 and the Property Law 2007 into the Civil Code 2020, but those old versions do not impact on the legal effect of these guidance. For example, *Procedure of the Hunan High People's Court on Property Preservation* (Xiang Gao Fa Ban Fa [2015] No 3), Article 9; Provisions on Shanghai Property Preservation 2017, Article 30. Apart from the five basic types of security, the Civil Code 2020 and Article 2 of its judicial interpretation also clarify that the other non-typical security such as retention of title, financial leasing and factoring. But all those non-typical securities from the perspective of their inherent nature cannot be applied as preservation security.

172 For example, in the territory of Beijing and Shanghai jurisdictions, refer to 3.168–3.169.

Property Security(I): Scope of Security

3.142 The secured property may belong either to the provider or to a third party who is willing to provide security on behalf of the applicant/respondent in Chinese courts in the context of an application seeking preservation measures. According to this category, this secured property as security may be submitted to the courts by way of a mortgage or a pledge.

3.143 In terms of security by way of mortgage, the security may comprise secured property that may include real estate, machines, means of transport and other properties provided in Article 395 of the Civil Code 2020, unless otherwise provided.[173]

3.144 In terms of security by way of pledge, the types of property include movables and some kinds of property rights. As for the movables, the law does not expressly restrict the scope of movables, unless otherwise provided.[174] As for property rights, the scope contains bills of exchange, cheques, promissory notes, bonds, certificates of deposit, warehouse receipts, bills of lading, shares of stocks, receivables that are existing and seem to be existing, the rights to exclusive use of trademarks, patent rights, copyrights or other property rights that can be pledged as prescribed by any law or administrative regulation.[175]

Property Security (II): Nature and Steps of Property Security

3.145 Even though the scope of security abides by the Civil Code 2020, the nature of the security in the context of applications seeking preservation measures is different from that of general civil security prescribed by the Civil Code 2020. The reasons for differences are primarily due to the fact that security in the context of preservation applications needs to be examined by Chinese courts. In other words, the Chinese courts have rights to

173 Article 395 of the Civil Code 2020 provides that "A mortgage may be established on the following properties of which the obligor or third party has the right of disposal: I) Buildings and other objects attached to the land; II) Right to use construction land; III) right to use sea areas; IV) Manufacturing facilities, raw materials, semi-manufactured goods and finished products; V) Buildings, vessels and aircraft under construction; VI) Means of transport; and VII) Other properties not prohibited from being mortgaged by any law or administrative regulation". This provision is based on the revision of Article 34 of the Security Law 1995 (expired on 1 January 2021) and Article 180 of the Property Law 2007(expired on 1 January 2021). The updated provision under the Civil Code 2020 has expanded the scope of mortgage available.

174 Article 426 of the Civil Code 2020 provides that "movable property which is prohibited by laws and administrative regulations from being pledged may not be pledged"; see also, Property Law 2007, Article 209; see also The Leading Group of the Implementation of the Civil Code of the Supreme People's Court (ed.), *Understanding and Application of Part 'Property Right' of the Civil Code of the People's Republic of China (Volume II)* (People's Court Press 2020) 1172–1174.

175 Civil Code 2020, Article 440; it is based on the revision of Article 223 of the Property Law 2007(expired on 1 January 2021).

intervene to seek answers in relation to the security or countersecurity that needs to be furnished by the applicant or respondent respectively. In contrast, general civil security is furnished on the basis of an agreement signed by the litigants which are assumed to have equal bargaining power. For this reason, the execution of preservation security involves the mortgagor/pledgor and the court handling the preservation application.

3.146 The exact steps in the practice of property security relating to the preservation measure are as follows:

(a) The parties, including the applicant or the respondent, who want to furnish security/countersecurity should provide the court with the certificate of the secured property;[176] the certificate refers to the endorsement of a right over the secured property issued by the authorities. For example, if the secured property is a house belonging to the applicant, he should submit the house registration certificate issued by the housing registration department; if the applicant or the respondent wants to use intellectual property rights as the secured property, he needs to submit to the court the certificate of the intellectual property right issued by the intellectual property bureau.
(b) The court holds this certificate until the discharge of the preservation order.
(c) The court issues a notice on execution assistance to the relevant departments, such as the housing registration department, and requires them to refuse to accept applications for the transfer or change of the secured property.[177] This means that the competent people's courts shall, subject to the law, take measures to seal up, detain or freeze the secured property provided by preservation applicants or others.[178]

3.147 It should be noted that, pursuant to Article 75 of the SMPL 2000, it is provided that:

> The type and amount of the security provided by a maritime claimant shall be determined by the maritime court. The type and amount of the security provided by a person against whom the claim is made shall be determined through consultation by the maritime claimant and the person against whom the claim is made; if consultation fails, the matter shall be determined by the maritime court.[179]

---

176 *Judicial Interpretation of the Supreme People's Court on Some Issues Regarding the Application of the Security Law of the People's Republic of China* (Fa Shi [2000] No 44) (expired on 1 January 2021), Article 132; it should be noted that this judicial interpretation has expired due to the advent of the recent Civil Code 2020. However, it is important to note that the Civil Code 2020 and the Interpretation on the Application of the Security of Civil Code 2020 do not prescribe a similar provision as Article 132. From the practical perspective, the authors have considered that the steps in aid of the preservation security are still workable.

177 ibid.

178 Interpretation of CPL 2015 (2020 Amendment), Article 164.

179 SMPL 2000, Article 75.

3.148 This means that when the respondent wants to provide countersecurity for an application to discharge a maritime preservation order, the applicant and the respondent may sign a written agreement that includes basic provisions, such as the particulars of the property, secured maximum amount and the time limit of security. This agreement becomes effective upon the conclusion of this agreement, which is binding on the parties to the agreement. However, in practice, this provision does not seem to work well because the bargaining power of two parties usually becomes uneven after the maritime preservation application has been accepted by the maritime court.[180]

Property Security (III): Legal Effect of Property Security

3.149 The next question that arises is whether the parties to the preservation application enjoy priority over the property put forward as security for obtaining preservation measures. In order to understand this, the authors will first analyse the issue of general civil security. In any general civil security, the preferred right is derived from the legislation.[181] The legal effect of the preferred right is dependent on the performance of the legal requirements. It follows that further to the security agreement between the parties, the mortgagee or the pledgee will have the preferred right over the secured property in the following two scenarios:

(a) If this security agreement is registered by the relevant authorities.
(b) If the secured property is delivered to the mortgagee or the pledgee.

3.150 In both scenarios, a right of mortgage or of pledge belonging to the mortgagee or the pledgee can challenge any *bona fide* third parties.[182]

---

180 Weiwei Yang, 'On Legitimacy of the Rule of Maritime Claim Security' (2013) 4 Journal of Henan University of Economics and Law 183, 190.

181 Article 386 of the Civil Code 2020 provides that "where an obligor fails to pay its due debts or any circumstance for realizing the Security Right as stipulated by the parties concerned occurs, the holder of the Security Right shall have the priority to seek payments from the secured property, unless otherwise provided by law"; in terms of the mortgage right, Article 394 of the Civil Code 2020 provides that "Where an obligor or a third party mortgages his properties to the obligee without transferring the possession of such properties in order to ensure the payment of debts, if the obligor fails to pay due debts or any circumstance as stipulated by the parties concerned for realizing the mortgagee right occurs, the obligee has the right to seek preferred payments from such properties"; in terms of the pledge rights, Article 425 of the Civil Code 2020 provides that "where an obligor or a third party pledges his/its movable property to an obligee for securing the payment of debts, if the obligor fails to pay due debts or any circumstance for realizing the pledge right as stipulated by the parties concerned occurs, the obligee has the right to seek preferred payments from the movable property"; see also, Property Law 2007 (expired on 1 January 2021), Articles 170, 179 and 208.

182 Article 402 of the Civil Code 2020 provides that "where any of the property stipulated in item (1) to item (3) of the first paragraph of Article 395 or a building under construction as stipulated in item (5) is mortgaged, mortgage registration formalities shall be completed. The mortgage rights shall be created at the time of registration"; Article 403 of the Civil Code 2020 provides that "for a mortgage on movable property, the mortgage right shall be established as

3.151 In order to further understand the issue of general security, it is supposed that if the mortgagor provides a vehicle as secured property, after the completion of the registration in the vehicle administration department, the mortgagee will have the preferred right over the secured property. Once the mortgagor becomes insolvent, the mortgagee is entitled to obtain payment by disposing of the secured vehicle before other creditors of the mortgagor could obtain payment against their debt.[183]

3.152 However, the existing law does not clarify whether the security put forward in the preservation applications should have the same features as a general security. Therefore, in scenarios where security has been provided in the context of preservation applications, the legal issue as to whether the mortgagee or the pledgee also has preferred rights over the secured property is not clear from the existing law. Nonetheless, Article 508 of the Interpretation of CPL 2015 (2020 Amendment) provides:

> Creditors enjoying priority of or holding security interest on the property sealed up, seized or frozen by the people's court may directly apply for participating in the distribution and claim the priority right to receive repayment.[184]

3.153 From analysis of the provisions, the majority opinion of legal scholars considers that the term "creditors" in the above provisions simply points towards the party who acquired the right of security over the property, on the ground that this party had reached a security agreement with the stakeholder. Accordingly, the applicants or the respondents have no right of priority over the preserved property that has been put forward as a security or countersecurity in the context of preservation applications.[185]

---

of the date the mortgage contract comes into effect. If the mortgage is not registered, the parties concerned may not challenge any bona fide third party"; Article 443 of the Civil Code provides that "as regards the pledge of fund units or stock rights, the pledge right shall be established as of the date the pledge registration is handled"; Article 444 of the Civil Code provides that "pledge of property rights in intellectual property such as exclusive rights to use registered trademarks, patent rights, copyrights, etc, shall be created at the time of registration of the pledge"; Article 445 of the Civil Code provides that "as regards the pledge of accounts receivable, the pledge right shall be established as of the date the pledge registration is handled"; see also, Property Law 2007 (expired on 1 January 2021), Articles 187, 188, 226, 227 and 228.

183 From the perspective of the insolvency law, the mortgagee/pledgee enjoys an exemption right. It follows that a creditor, as a mortgagee/pledgee enjoys an important priority over the secured property in the insolvency procedure and such secured property will not be incorporated into the other insolvent property; see also Xiao Cheng, *Research on Secured Property Rights* (2nd Edn, Renmin University of China Publishing House 2019) 216–218.

184 Article 508 of the Interpretation of CPL 2015 (2020 Amendment).

185 Chaojin Shi, 'Whether the Applicant of Property Preservation Enjoys the Right of Priority' (2015) 15 The People's Judicature (Applied) 103, 106; see also, Shichun Li, *Research on the Civil Preservation Procedure* (China Legal Publishing House 2005) 240–241; see also, Qunpei Xia and Enwei Lin, 'Deposits for Discharging a Preservation not Belonging to Security in Security Law' (2014) 8 The People's Judicature (Case) 71, 73. It should be noted that this topic is controversial in China. Any further discussion on this topic is beyond the scope of the book.

Cash Security (I): Introduction

3.154 Cash security, compared with property security, is more convenient and is considered relatively more reliable by the Chinese courts. Also, there are no issues such as fluctuation of the value of the mortgaged or pledged property in case of cash security, and the risk of loss in value is therefore not in existence. However, there are still two legal issues in relation to cash security that need to be analysed.[186]

Cash Security (II): Payment Method

3.155 The first issue is about the foreign currency put forward as a security in the context of the preservation application. In legal practice, there are two approaches that are followed by the courts in accepting cash as a security. The first approach is that a competent court issues an order to freeze the secured cash available in the bank account that belongs to the applicant/respondent.[187] The second approach followed by the court is to demand that the cash security be deposited in the court's designated account or in an agreed escrow account in China.[188]

3.156 As for the second approach followed by the court, there is no express provision on the exchange rate that the court should consider for accepting foreign currency as cash security. In accordance with *Notice of the SPC on Forwarding the Letter of the State Administration of Foreign Exchange on Issues Concerning the Opening of Foreign Exchange Accounts and Handling of Foreign Exchange Receipts and Payments by the People's Courts in Foreign-Related Judicial Activities*, Chinese Intermediate/Higher/Supreme People's Courts can open a foreign exchange account to deal with foreign exchange receipts and payments in foreign-related judicial activities in a bank.[189] In this context, if the foreign currency is provided by the foreign party to the court's foreign exchange account in the bank, it will

186 Actually, the cash security simply applies to an applicant who has great economic strength. The onus of providing cash security is however difficult for the applicant who is claiming for compensation against the respondent and such compensation is required for the extra cash flow to secure the preservation application. However, in legal practice, some courts can still request the applicant to provide a certain amount of cash security under certain circumstances; see 3.169 for further details.

187 *Provisions of the Shandong High People's Court on Some Issues Concerning Preservation Security (trial) 2015* (Lu Gao Fa [2015] No 6) (hereinafter referred to as "Provisions of Shandong on Preservation Security 2015"), Article 17.

188 ibid; see also, Liang Zhao and Lianjun Li, *Maritime Law and Practice in China* (1st Edn, Informa Law from Routledge 2017), para 23.11.

189 Notice of the Supreme People's Court on Forwarding the Letter of the State Administration of Foreign Exchange on Issues Concerning the Opening of Foreign Exchange Accounts and Handling of Foreign Exchange Receipts and Payments by the People's Courts in Foreign-Related Judicial Activities (Fa [2003] No 73).

automatically be converted to local Chinese currency (RMB) according to the bank's exchange rate.

3.157 The time period prescribed for a foreign-related case in the action proceedings is normally half a year at the first instance stage. After the second instance, the time period may well be more than one year from the time the security was provided. As a result, for a foreign litigant, the exchange rate loss may be substantial, as the cash security has been automatically converted to local Chinese currency.

Cash Security (III): Nature of Cash Security

3.158 The second issue relates to the nature of the cash security. As discussed in 3.140, although the preservation security refers to the type of security provided in the Civil Code 2020, this law adjusts the pure civil legal relation, but the preservation security cannot be deemed to be a pure civil relation. Accordingly, its nature is different from general civil security. This viewpoint has been confirmed in a case. In *COSCO (Nantong) Clavon Ship Enginerring Co v Zhejiang Jingang Shipping Co Ltd and Others*,[190] in order to apply for discharging the order of property preservation measures, Zhejiang Jingang (respondent) provided a cash countersecurity. After Zhejiang Jingang became insolvent, COSCO claimed the right of priority over the cash deposited as a cash security.

3.159 Both the Ningbo Maritime Court and the Zhejiang High Court held that the cash countersecurity provided by Zhejiang Jingang was furnished to secure the enforcement of a future judgment rather than to secure COSCO's claim itself. It followed that the cash provided by Zhejiang Jingang for discharging the order should not be treated as security as prescribed by the Security Law 1995.[191] COSCO's right over the money was therefore simply an ordinary claim and accordingly gave no priority over other creditors. Thus, COSCO did not enjoy a right of priority over the other creditors during Zhejiang Jingang's bankruptcy procedure.[192]

A Letter of Guarantee (Credit Guarantee) (I): Introduction

3.160 Generally, the guarantors through letters of guarantee are outside parties not related to disputes. In terms of who may constitute the outside

190 *COSCO (Nantong) Clavon Ship Enginerring Co v Zhejiang Jingang Shipping Co, Ltd, and Others* (dispute over a shipbuilding contract) [2012] Tai Wen Shang Chu Zi No 2037 (Ningbo Maritime Court, first instance and judgment); [2013] Zhe Tai Shang Zhong Zi No 340 (The High People's Court of Zhejiang Province, second instance and binding judgment).

191 Security Law 1995 was replaced by the Civil Code 2020 on 1 January 2021.

192 *COSCO (Nantong) Clavon Ship Enginerring Co v Zhejiang Jingang Shipping Co, Ltd, and Others* (dispute over a shipbuilding contract) [2012] Tai Wen Shang Chu Zi No 2037 (Ningbo Maritime Court, first instance and judgment); [2013] Zhe Tai Shang Zhong Zi No 340 (The High People's Court of Zhejiang Province, second instance and binding judgment).

parties (the scope of the outside parties), according to the First Civil Division of the SPC's opinion, there are no restrictions as to who can provide such a guarantee on behalf of the parties in a preservation application. As long as the outside parties, as guarantors, can convince the court as to their reliability and reputation, the Chinese courts will allow those outside parties to provide such letters of guarantee.[193]

A Letter of Guarantee (II): Lack of Unified Rule

3.161 By reference to the Interpretation of Property Preservation (2020 Amendment) and several regional judicial interpretations, the qualification of a guarantor and the amount of the guarantee required are very restrictive in nature. Also, the concept of qualification of a guarantor and amount of guarantee required may vary from court to court in China.

3.162 For example, Article 8 of the Interpretation of Property Preservation (2020 Amendment) provides:

> Where a qualified financial institution approved by the financial regulatory department provides the guarantee for the applicant's property preservation in the format of an independent guarantee letter, the court shall allow such guarantee.[194]

3.163 The qualified financial institutions providing a letter of guarantee are often banks, insurance companies, security companies, financial guarantee companies and their branches.[195] In addition, this provision simply clarifies the role of the qualified financial institution in the context of preservation security; in contrast, no provision is to express that the letter of guarantee can be furnished by other individuals or legal entities. Since the provision is silent, it may therefore be assumed that a letter of guarantee provided by individuals or other legal entities may not be acceptable to the courts.

3.164 In addition, lack of uniformity on the issue of the qualification of guarantors has led to stakeholders not being sure which companies are considered competent enough to be qualified as guarantors.

---

193 The First Civil Division of the Supreme People's Court (ed.), *Reference and Guide to Civil Trial* (Law Press of China 2008) 180.

194 Interpretation of Property Preservation (2020 Amendment), Article 8.

195 It should be noted that there are no specific codes or regulations to delineate the meaning of "qualified financial institution". However, pursuant to Article 5 of *Notice by the People's Bank of China, the China Banking Regulatory Commission, the China Securities Regulatory Commission, and Other Departments of Issuing the Provisions on the Size Classification Standards for Financial Enterprises* (Yin Fa [2015] No 309), the qualified financial institutions comprise generally recognised banks, financial holding companies, insurance companies, trust companies, securities companies and others. Similar provisions can be found in Guidance of the Shenzhen Intermediate People's Court on Pre-Action Property Preservation (6 December 2018), Article 19 and *Some Provisions of the Beijing High People's Court on Property Preservation During the Case-Filing Procedure* (Jing Gao Fa Fa [2012] No 405), Article 17.

3.165 For example, Shanghai, as one of the most developed economic regions in China, takes a comparatively relaxed attitude towards this issue. The local court guidance has provided that, if an applicant or a guarantor is a very large, well-known company, then the applicant's or guarantor's letter of guarantee can be accepted after thorough examination.[196] The Sichuan High People's Court in *Opinions on Corporation Property Preservation for Serving New Normal for Economic Development* (hereinafter referred to as "Opinions on Sichuan Property Preservation 2015") provides that four state-owned asset management companies and provincial asset management companies constitute the qualified guarantors.[197]

3.166 In contrast, according to the report of the High People's Court of Ningxia Hui Autonomous Region, many Chinese courts in this region do not accept letters of guarantee issued by any financial guarantee companies. When an applicant intends to provide a letter of guarantee issued by an insurance company, certain courts can simply recognise the designated insurance company as a competent guarantor to provide the letter of guarantee.[198]

3.167 Apart from the unclear scope of the competent financial institutions, the amount of the guarantee required with the preservation application and the evaluation of the credit worthiness of the guarantor are also not clearly defined in any provisions. These requirements can also vary from province to province in China, depending on the guidance from the local courts, if available at all.

3.168 For example, the Beijing High People's Court provides that, when an applicant is unable to provide security in the form of property that is equivalent to the value of the preserved property, provided the issues in the dispute are relatively clear, then in that case:

(a) The people's court may request the applicant to provide cash security, but such cash security may not be less than 20 per cent of the value of the preserved property.

---

196 Provisions on Shanghai Property Preservation 2017, Article 33, but there is no standard as to what will constitute a very large company pursuant to these Provisions. In this context, in accordance with *Notice of the National Bureau of Statistics on Issuing the Measures for Classification of Large, Medium, Small and Miniature Enterprises for the Purpose of Statistics* (2017), on the basis of different industry standards, the operating revenue, the total working capital and the number of the staff provide the grounds to classify companies into three types: large, medium and small. In this context it is safe to say that the application of Article 33 depends on the exercise of discretionary power of the judge.

197 *Opinions of the Sichuan High People's Court on Corporation Property Preservation for Serving New Normal for Economic Development* (Chuan Gao Fa [2015] No 391), Article 16; see also, Article 7 of *Procedure of the Hunan High People's Court on Property Preservation* (Xiang Gao Fa Ban Fa [2015] No 3), where it affirms the qualification of asset management companies.

198 Research Group of the First Civil Division of the Ningxia High People's Court, 'Research on Examination of Pre-action Property Preservation and Credit Guarantee' (17 August 2018) <www.nxfxh.com.cn/njfh/njfhdej/881.htm> accessed 15 July 2021.

(b) The remaining 80 per cent of the value of property may be covered by the letter of guarantee provided.[199]

3.169 The letter of guarantee cannot become the only type of security that is provided with the preservation application. Security by means of a letter of guarantee must therefore be accompanied by other types of security. In addition, and in any event, the maximum amount that can be covered by such letter of guarantee cannot exceed 80 per cent of the value of the preserved property and further should not exceed 30 per cent of the value of the registration capital of the company that is providing the letter of guarantee.[200]

3.170 In addition, some high people's courts, such as those of Beijing, Shanghai, Guangdong Province and Anhui Province, provide guidelines that include a series of strict standards to evaluate whether a financial guarantee company can be regarded as a qualified guarantor.[201]

3.171 For example, the guidelines pertaining to specific standards include requirements to evaluate the history of credit worthiness of such financial guarantee companies in the past five years,[202] to evaluate the Loss/Profit Statements of the last three years to ensure that it was profitable for these years, and lastly, to evaluate any criminal antecedents of such companies.[203]

3.172 Some people's courts do not stipulate the evaluation standards in local interpretations for the guidance of stakeholders. Instead, these courts will supply simply a list of companies that the applicants can choose from. Those companies that can provide the requisite letter of guarantee are acceptable to the courts. If, for some reason, the applicant does not agree with the names of the guarantee companies in a supplied list, a letter of guarantee

199 *Some Provisions of the Beijing High People's Court on Property Preservation During the Case-Filing Procedure* (Jing Gao Fa Fa [2012] No 405), Article 17.

200 Similarly, there are other examples, such as Article 34 of *Provisions on Shanghai Property Preservation 2017*, that do not require the party to provide cash security and a letter of guarantee together in lieu of property as a security. This means that just a letter of guarantee would be enough to provide security against 100 per cent of the value of the preserved property. However, when the letter of guarantee is provided, the amount is restricted to 30 per cent of the registered capital of the company that is providing the guarantee; see also, Article 3 of *Opinion of the Guangdong High People's Court and the Guangdong Government Financial Working Office on the Security Provided by the Financial Guarantee Company to the Litigant's Preservation Application* (Yue Gao Fa [2013] No 377), which provides that the amount cannot be more than 40 per cent of the registration capital of the company that is issuing the letter of guarantee. In the event that this amount of guarantee was to exceed the prescribed rate of 40 per cent, two guarantee companies must become co-guarantors.

201 Guangliang Luo, 'Study on Litigation Preservation Security Provided by Financial Guarantee Company Registered in Huizhou Province' (*Guizhou People's Government Legal Information Platform*, 15 February 2015) <sft.guizhou.gov.cn/ywgz_97/zfflgw/201905/t20190516_2548698.html> accessed 15 July 2021.

202 *Provisions on Shanghai Property Preservation 2017*, Article 34.

203 *Some Provisions of the Beijing High People's Court on Property Preservation During the Case-Filing Procedure* (Jing Gao Fa Fa [2012] No 405), Article 18.

provided by another company that is not included in the supplied list will probably not be recognised by the court.

3.173 For example, the Intermediate People's Court of Huizhou City of Guangdong Province requests all people's courts in its territory to accept only the financial guarantee companies from a supplied list of acceptable companies that can put up guarantee letters on behalf of applicants. These lists are usually drafted after the courts' review committee has evaluated these companies. After the list of companies is drafted by the review committee, only then is this list published for the guidance of stakeholders.[204]

3.174 It can be seen that, in the absence of uniform rules in relation to security and guarantee providers, local regulations in relation to it can vary between provinces in China; it is therefore imperative that stakeholders should do considerable research on this issue before embarking upon applications for preservation measures in these courts.

A Letter of Guarantee (III): Development of Credit Guarantee

3.175 Commercial banks are routinely willing to provide a letter of guarantee to applicants that are large, well-known, companies, and at times it is difficult for small companies and natural persons to obtain a similar letter of guarantee from banks for their own preservation applications. Although the financial guarantee companies are willing to provide guarantee letters on behalf of small companies, the former's qualifications are strictly evaluated by the Chinese courts as discussed from 3.170 to 3.173

3.176 Since 2015, many high people's courts, such as the Guangxi High People's Court,[205] the Sichuan High People's Court[206] and the Hunan High People's Court,[207] have accepted the concept of property preservation liability insurance. Furthermore, they issued the relevant interpretations to guide all people's courts in their territory in evaluating insurance guarantees.[208]

3.177 After an applicant has bought liability insurance by paying a premium to an insurance company, that insurance company will provide a letter

---

204 See Interim Measure of the Huizhou Intermediate People's Court of Guangdong Province on Regulate the Guarantee Institution to Apply the Judicial Preservation Security (Hui Zhong Fa Fa [2016] No 8).

205 Lei Zhang, 'Memorandum of the Guangxi High Court and Guangxi Bureau of China Insurance Regulatory Commission to Recognition on a Letter of Guarantee for Litigation Property Preservation by Insurance Company' *People's Court Daily* (Beijing, 14 November 2015).

206 Opinions on Sichuan Property Preservation 2015, Article 15.

207 Procedure of the Hunan High People's Court on Property Preservation (Xiang Gao Fa Ban Fa [2015] No 3), Article 7.

208 Several intermediate people's courts issue their own interpretations of the property preservation liability insurance, such as *Provisions of the Fourth Intermediate People's Court of Beijing Municipality on the Application of Liability Insurance Guarantee during the Civil and Commercial Proceedings* (25 February 2016).

of guarantee based on the insurance policy. The insurance company, through the letter of guarantee, promises the recipient (the court) that it will indemnify financial loss if suffered by the respondent as a result of the preservation application. The indemnity so provided is within the limits of loss as expressly stated within the scope of this insurance policy.

3.178 In legal practice, the SPC also accepts and recognises a letter of guarantee issued by the insurance company pursuant to the property preservation liability insurance.

3.179 In *Gansu Sanzhou Industrial Group Co Ltd and Others v Beijing Jinzhong Guolian Fuying Investment and Development Centre (Limited Partnership) (Jinzhong Guolian),*[209] Gansu Sanzhou Industrial Group Co Ltd submitted an appeal against a judgment made by the Beijing High People's Court to the SPC. During the second instance proceedings, Jinzhong Guolian filed an application seeking property preservation measures. The scope of property that was to be preserved involved cash, real estate, the right of equity, interests and other property. Jinzhong Guolian also provided a liability insurance guarantee issued by the Shandong branch of the China Continent Property & Casualty Insurance Company.

3.180 The SPC considered that the applicant seeking the property preservation measures had complied with the provisions of the law and held that the applicant had fulfilled the relevant conditions of applications. Accordingly, in this case, pursuant to Article 100 of the CPL the SPC issued an order to seal up, detain and freeze RMB3,099,167,31.03 or any other property equivalent to that amount.[210]

A Letter of Guarantee (IV): Maritime Law Domain

3.181 In the maritime domain, a P&I Club can be treated as a qualified guarantor to provide a letter of guarantee in that type of court. Furthermore, a letter of undertaking,[211] which is provided by a P&I Club/fixed premium insurer with good credit ratings (and also recognised in China), is always accepted by Chinese maritime courts.[212]

---

209 *Gansu Sanzhou Industrial Group Co Ltd and Others v Beijing Jinzhong Guolian Fuying Investment and Development Centre (Limited Partnership)* (dispute over a Share Transfer Agreement) [2016]SPC Civil Final No 205-1 (The Supreme People's Court, second instance and binding order).

210 ibid.

211 Letter of undertaking is a term defined by a P&I Club. It refers to "a document whereby the provider promises the receiver of it to reimburse his financial loss for carrying out certain actions. In addition, a letter of undertaking is a document whereby the provider promises the recipient of it to reimburse financial loss incurred as a result of a shipping incident"; see also, Gard, 'LOI, LOU and BLG—Confused?' (Gard yourship, Loss Prevention Circular No 01-10) <www.gard.no/Content/503153/No%2001-10%20LOI%20LOU%20and%20BLG%20-%20Confused.pdf> accessed 15 July 2021.

212 In *Rui Tai International Shipping Ltd and others* v *Yangwei Yu, The West of England Ship Owners Mutual Insurance Association (Luxembourg)* provided a letter of undertaking that

3.182 It should be noted that in 2008 the Fourth Civil Division of the SPC, which is responsible for disposing of foreign-related and maritime disputes, argued that, if an applicant were to provide security from an overseas body, the maritime court could request that applicant to provide additional security from one of the Chinese financial institutions. Furthermore, they argued that the maritime court should try to avoid accepting a letter of guarantee as the security.[213]

3.183 Nonetheless, in Chinese legal practice a letter of undertaking issued by a foreign P&I Club is still operative,[214] but over the last few years a local guarantee from a local Chinese insurer has been increasingly requested from applicants in most provinces.

A Letter of Guarantee (V): Online Guarantee

3.184 As discussed in 3.47–3.48, in the context of the "Digital Rule of Law and Smart Justice" project operated by the Ministry of Justice of the People's Republic of China since 2018 and the development of court informatisation, the SPC and some Chinese courts in the past several years have started to use online platforms to improve legal services. In the context of preservation measures, in order to guide stakeholders to rely on the liability insurance policy or information related to a qualified insurance company, the online preservation system (www.baoquan.court.gov.cn) has cooperated with some insurance companies.[215] As long as an applicant chooses online security in this system, he may choose an insurance company listed online according to the premium and the reputation of the insurance company. In

---

was accepted by the Beihai Maritime Court and the High People's Court of Guangxi Zhuang Autonomous Region. It should be noted that, in this case, there were two companies that provided letters of guarantee. Apart from the West of England P&I, the PICC (Dalian) Property and Casualty Company Limited also provided an insurance guarantee as a local guarantor based in China; see, *Rui Tai International Shipping Ltd and others v Yangwei Yu, The West of England Ship Owners Mutual Insurance Association (Luxembourg)* (dispute over damages arising out of collision) [2006] Hai Shi Chu Zi No 022 (Beihai Maritime Court, first instance and judgment); [2007] Gui Min Si Zhong Zi No 32 (The High People's Court of Guangxi Zhuang Autonomous Region, second instance, final and binding judgment).

213 Answers of the Fourth Civil Division of the Supreme People's Court to Questions in Foreign-Related Commercial and Maritime Trial 2008 (December 2008), Item 106.

214 In *PICC (Zhangzhou) Property and Casualty Co Ltd v Aevanguard Sdn Bhd, Gard (HK) Limited and Others* [2012] Xia Hai Fa Shang Chu Zi No 76, Assuranceforeningen Gard (Gjensidig) provided a letter of undertaking that was accepted by the Xiamen Maritime Court; see also, *Guangdong Green Oil Industrial Co Ltd v Golden Eagle Lines Ltd and Others* [2012] Guang Hai Fa Chu Zi No 69 (Guangzhou Maritime Court, first instance and binding order) London P&I Club provided a letter of undertaking to the Guangzhou Maritime Court that was accepted. In both cases, the courts accepted a foreign P&I club as the sole guarantor.

215 In light of the public information posted by the online preservation system, any insurance company may submit a proposal to become the insurance candidate. Whether the proposal is cleared will entirely depend on the decision of the SPC.

addition, a few Chinese courts, for example the First Intermediate People's Court of Beijing Municipality[216] and the Second Intermediate People's Court of Shanghai Municipality[217] and the Online Service Centre of the Fujian People's Courts,[218] have actively employed websites as a means to convey guidance.[219]

3.185 In recent years, the SPC has encouraged different regional courts to set up smart courts that incorporate advanced technology. It is expected that the online system will gain further popularity with stakeholders and that it can be used to apply for an online letter of guarantee/online policy. With the reforms in technology, the online procedures are becoming a more convenient and effective way for applicants to provide security to the courts in the context of preservation applications.[220]

3.186 Apart from the online applications seeking liability insurance, even if the parties have obtained a letter of guarantee offline, they can still upload their letters of guarantee onto the court's webpage. The recipient court will review the uploaded documents and, if all seems right after this review, it will accept these letters of guarantee as an adequate security.[221]

Exemptions from Providing Security[222]

3.187 Under the existing law, with regard to behaviour and evidence preservation measures, there are no specific provisions to govern the criteria for deciding whether the applicants can be exempted from providing security with their applications seeking preservation measures. However, by reference to the Interpretation of Property Preservation (2020 Amendment), it is

216 The First Intermediate People's Court of Beijing Municipality, 'Online Application for a Letter of Guarantee' <http://bjbq.86court.com> accessed 15 July 2021.

217 Tianming Lan, 'Blockchain to Facilitate Property Preservation in the Second Intermediate People's Court of Shanghai Municipality' (*Xinhua News*, 18 December 2019) <www.xinhuanet.com/2019-12/18/c_1125359869.htm> accessed 15 July 2021.

218 Online Service Centre of Fujian People's Courts <http://ssfw.fjcourt.gov.cn> accessed 15 July 2021.

219 Due to COVID-19, more and more Chinese courts are opening their own online platforms. In those platforms, preservation security, together with online preservation applications, is operative.

220 It is anticipated that the COVID-19 pandemic has stimulated the development of online trials, and accordingly online applications seeking liability insurance may swiftly become commonplace.

221 For example, Smart Preservation Platform by the Second Intermediate People's Court of Shanghai Municipality. Tianming Lan, 'Blockchain to Facilitate Property Preservation in Shanghai' (*Xinhua News*, 18 December 2019) <www.xinhuanet.com/2019-12/18/c_1125359869.htm> accessed 15 July 2021.

222 Because providing security during the pre-action preservation proceedings is mandatory, the judicial interpretation and the local guidance simply provide the exemption of providing security during the post-action preservation proceedings. However, it is the author's contention that under special circumstances these exemptions can be applied during the pre-action preservation proceedings.

the authors' contention that the provisions of exemptions may be applied even to applications seeking behaviour and evidence preservation measures, even though these provisions were meant to apply only for applications concerning the preservation of property.

3.188 Article 9 of the Interpretation of Property Preservation (2020 Amendment) provides that, where a party concerned in a lawsuit applies for post-action property preservation, the Chinese court may not require the security under any of the following circumstances:

(a) A party is claiming alimony, maintenance expenses, upbringing expenses, pension, medical expenses, labour remuneration, workers' compensation for injured workers, or damages arising from a traffic accident.
(b) A party is suffering from domestic violence or financial difficulty in a marital or family dispute.
(c) A public interest case is submitted by a procuratorship, which involves compensation.
(d) The damages have been caused by a contributing action.
(e) The case shows a clear and plain fact and legal relationship that may rarely cause a wrong preservation order to arise.
(f) An applicant belongs to a financial institution or its branch approved by the financial regulatory department, such as a commercial bank or an insurance company.[223]

3.189 Moreover, a few regional interpretations provide additional circumstances, whereby applicants can seek an exemption from providing security or a reduction in the security that needs to be provided. For example, the Provisions of Shandong on Preservation Security 2015 applies the relevant provisions in *Measures on Payment of Litigation Costs 2006*. In the Provision of Shandong 2015, it is provided that, if an applicant were to provide evidence to prove that he comes within the category of exemption, reduction or suspension of payment of litigation costs, pursuant to *Measures on Payment of Litigation Costs 2006*,[224] the court may then relieve or exempt the applicant from furnishing security with the preservation application.[225]

3.190 With regard to preservation security during post-action preservation applications, the *Procedure of the Hunan High People's Court on Property Preservation 2015* provides that, when the facts of the case and the legal relationship are clear, or the case may be subject to summary procedure, the applicant may be exempted from furnishing security, or the amount of

223 Interpretation of Property Preservation (2020 Amendment), Article 9.
224 *Measures on Payment of Litigation Costs 2006*, Articles 45, 46 and 47.
225 Provisions of Shandong on Preservation Security 2015, Article 14(2).

security that needs to be furnished may simply be reduced.[226] The Sichuan High People's Court also stipulates similar guidance.[227]

3.191 With regard to preservation after the effective judgment is made and before the commencement of its enforcement, the Interpretation of Property Preservation (2020 Amendment) exempts the winning party from the obligation to provide preservation security, if that party were to file a preservation application.[228] Most regional guidance also emphasises this kind of exemption for the winning party.[229]

3.192 It is the authors' submission that any applicant must carry out thorough legal research of the regional guidance in the context of seeking an exemption or reduction of the security. This local guidance will be available, in addition to guidance available on this area in the Provisions of Interpretation of Property Preservation (2020 Amendment).

The Scope of Application of Preservation Security Guidance

3.193 In practice, the property preservation measure is a widely discussed topic and results in most guidance from the local courts and cases. In this section there are a number of provisions discussed in the context of property preservation. Furthermore, most existing cases concentrate on the issue of security in applications that are seeking property preservation measures. Nonetheless, when the law is silent on similar issues affecting applications seeking behaviour and evidence preservation, it is the authors' contention that the above provisions and guidance on property preservation may also be consulted to find answers in such applications.

3.194 A few additional specific rules for three types of preservations pertaining to security and countersecurity will be further discussed in Chapters 6, 8 and 10.

Legal Costs in Preservation Applications

3.195 This section will introduce legal costs that the parties concerned should pay the court, to relevant authorities and to organisations for seeking preservation measures through applications to the courts. Under the existing law, these costs comprise the application fee and the underlying other fees.

226 *Procedure of the Hunan High People's Court on Property Preservation* (Xiang Gao Fa Ban Fa [2015] No 3), Article 6 (1) and (4).

227 Opinions on Sichuan Property Preservation 2015, Article 7 (1).

228 Interpretation of Property Preservation (2020 Amendment), Article 9.

229 For example, Opinions on Sichuan Property Preservation 2015, Article 7(3); see also, *Procedure of the Hunan High People's Court on Property Preservation 2015,* Article 7; see also, Provisions on Shanghai Property Preservation 2017, Article 42.

3.196 The main source of law on this issue is *Measures on Payment of Litigation Costs 2006*. In order to avoid misunderstanding, the term "litigation costs" is not used in this section. It will not be appropriate in a strict sense to use the term "litigation fees" for an applicant seeking preservation measures from the court during arbitration proceedings. The term "legal costs" rather than "litigation costs" is therefore more appropriate as it covers both scenarios.

General Legal Costs

3.197 In accordance with *Measures on Payment of Litigation Costs 2006*, the courts' costs in relation to legal proceedings that need to be paid by the parties are as follows:

(a) Acceptance fees for the first instance, the second instance and the retrial arising from new evidence submitted by the party.
(b) Application fees including, but not limited to, the application for preservations, for maritime injunctions or for the recognition and enforcement of a foreign court's judgment and/or arbitration award.
(c) Travel and accommodation expenses, the forgone wages of witnesses, expert remuneration and service fees of translators, inspectors and surveyors.[230]

3.198 Apart from the court's costs, other legal costs may also be applicable, such as the storage fee, the custodian fee, the appraisal fee and the transport fee, along with the application fee for seeking preservation measures from the court. The parties must pay these costs directly to authorities or organisations rather than to the courts.[231]

3.199 The amount of an application fee is dependent on the type of preservation measure that is requested from the courts. This aspect will be dealt with in the forthcoming chapters on different preservation measures. In the next paragraphs, fees that are common to all three preservation measures are introduced and described.

Insurance Fee for Security of Preservation

3.200 In certain circumstances an applicant must furnish security with their applications seeking preservation measures. As discussed in 3.175–3.180, along with the application of the Interpretation of Property Preservation (2020 Amendment), property preservation liability insurance constitutes an important mode for providing security during applications seeking preservation

230 *Measures on Payment of Litigation Costs 2006*, Articles 6, 10 and 11.
231 ibid Article 6.

measures. The relevant provisions do not specify whether the insurance premium may be considered as part of the overall legal costs and accordingly be made to be borne by the losing party. Furthermore, it may be argued that the decision of the applicant to purchase a liability insurance policy is a subjective one. In this context, many judgments highlight that courts do not consider such premiums as part of the legal costs and, accordingly, they cannot be recovered from the losing party.[232]

3.201 However, two judicial decisions made by the SPC in 2017 support the view that the insurance premium paid by the applicant is a component of the legal (litigation) cost. Accordingly, this insurance premium should be borne by the losing party.

3.202 In *Sanya Resort Investment Company v Qi Yan*,[233] the Share Transfer Agreement provided that the transferee shall bear the loss suffered by the transferor. The loss suffered by the transferor arises from the fact that the transferee did not pay the agreed share transfer fee. The loss suffered included litigation costs and the lawyer's fee.

3.203 The SPC held that the costs of obtaining an insurance policy should also be regarded within the overall loss suffered in light of the agreement. It was therefore decided that the insurance fee was the component of the litigation fee that was to be borne by the transferee.[234]

3.204 In *Harbin Corporate Limited of China National Real Estate Development Group v Jiangsu Suzhong Construction Group Co Ltd*,[235] unlike in the *Sanya Resort* case, the parties did not reach any agreement on the issue of which party should bear the burden of the loss arising from any dispute.

232 For example, in *Xinsheng Factoring Co Ltd v Shanghai Zhouxian Real Estate Development Co Ltd and Others* (dispute over a contract) [2016] Hu Civil Final No 478 (the High People's Court of Shanghai Municipality, second instance and final judgment), the court held that the litigation preservation was not essential for each case. Also, the applicant was entitled to choose different ways of providing the preservation security including cash security, real estate security, movables security and a third party's guarantee. Where Xinsheng Company, after considering the maximum interests to itself, chose the third party's guarantee on its own initiative rather than using its own property to secure the preservation, it was difficult to say that the cost for the third party's guarantee was reasonable and necessary. Therefore, it was held that Xinsheng Company should undertake this cost by itself; see also *China Railway Materials Group Co Ltd v Zhu Zhou* (dispute over a purchase contract) [2016] Xin 01 Civil Chu No 578 (the Intermediate People's Court of Xinjiang Uygur Autonomous Region, first instance and binding judgment); see also *Shaoxing Xiangkun Textile Co Ltd v Changsha Dongli Cotton and Hemp Technology Co Ltd and Others* (dispute over a purchase contract) [2017] Xiang 01 Civil Final No 3292 (the Intermediate People's Court of Changsha City of Hunan Province, second instance and binding judgment).

233 *Sanya Resort Investment Company v Qi Yan* (dispute over share transfer) [2017] SPC Civil Final No 414 (the Supreme People's Court, second instance and binding judgment).

234 ibid.

235 *Harbin Corporate Limited of China National Real Estate Development Group v Jiangsu Suzhong Construction Group Co Ltd* (dispute over a construction contract) [2017] SPC Civil Final No 437 (the Supreme People's Court, second instance and binding judgment).

3.205 Even so, the SPC held that the insurance premium was a reasonable expense that could be regarded as a loss suffered by Jiangsu Suzhong (the winning party). Harbin Corporate (the losing party) should therefore undertake to compensate the winning party for the insurance premium.[236]

3.206 It is the authors' contention that although property preservation liability insurance is not applicable to other types of preservation measures, it is advisable to apply the same principles for similar issues in behaviour and evidence preservations only after applicants have obtained liability insurance from a competent provider. In addition, in *Sanya Resort Investment Company v Qi Yan*,[237] it is safe to say that the SPC was based on the principle of the freedom of contract to uphold the allocation of the agreed cost. It follows that as far as a dispute over a contract is concerned, the best solution for parties to a contract to avoid a dispute over the security expense is to reach a deal during the negotiation of the contract.

Lawyer's Fee

3.207 In China, the lawyer's fee is not included in the legal costs in accordance with *Measures on Payment of Litigation Costs 2006*, except the three intellectual property laws expressly provide that the losing party shall bear the reasonable fee associated with the winning party's lawyer's fee for investigation and collating evidence.[238]

3.208 Unless there are exceptions in intellectual property disputes, it is a general rule that the lawyer's fee shall be "borne by the parties on their own accounts, and neither party can seek reimbursements from the counterpart".[239] There are many reasons for the existence of the general rule. A few of the reasons are:

a) Legal representation is not mandatory in China.
b) There is a policy in China to curtail legal costs and thereby ensure that access to justice is enhanced in Chinese society.
c) Ensuring that the people are not scared to access the courts because they might be worried about having to pay the winning side's lawyer's costs.

236 ibid.

237 *Sanya Resort Investment Company v Qi Yan* (dispute over share transfer) [2017] SPC Civil Final No 414 (the Supreme People's Court, second instance and binding judgment).

238 Since 2001, in the field of the intellectual property laws, China has established the rule regarding "the compensation system for the lawyer's fee". In light of this rule, regardless of whether the parties have reached an agreement, the winning party is entitled to claim the reasonable lawyer's fee. This issue is not discussed in detail as it is beyond the scope of the book; see also, Geng Zhang and Shujun Wang, 'The Limited Payment of Lawyer's Fee in the IP Dispute' (2014) 9 The People's Judicature (Applied) 97, 98.

239 Jianguo Xiao and Xin Tang, 'Cost and Fee Allocation in Civil Procedure' (2011) 4 (1) Tsinghua China 43, 45–46.

d) There is a difficulty encountered by the judges in assessing lawyers' costs.[240]

3.209 However, the parties are not prevented from reaching agreements on the allocation of legal costs and fees, as long as such contracts are valid. For example, in *Sanya Resort Investment Company v Qi Yan*,[241] the SPC held that the transferor provided the original receipts for the lawyer's fee and these costs were reasonable. The SPC therefore allowed the claim for the lawyer's fee, and accordingly the losing party was responsible for reimbursing these costs to the winning one.[242]

3.210 What is the test for "reasonable legal fees"? In accordance with the *Notice of the National Development and Reform Commission on Opinions for Decontrolling the Prices of Some Services 2014*, the lawyer's fee may be provided based on the market price. Further, this Notice clarifies that there is no need to take into account the unified rate provided by the government.[243] Different regions, in light of the different rate of economic development, provide for different rules and recommended rates.

3.211 For example, the *Measures on Payment of Beijing Lawyer's Fees 2016* suggest the market rate of the lawyer's fee for a case with a disputed amount of between RMB 1 million and RMB 10 million should be 4 per cent of the disputed amount,[244] while the *Measures on Payment of Shanghai Lawyer's Fees 2017* suggest that the lawyer's fee for a case having a similar amount in dispute should be between 3 and 5 per cent of the disputed amount.[245] However, the *Measures on Payment of Chongqing Lawyer's Fees 2018* simply provide general rules, requesting the lawyer's fee to be applied according to the Lawyers' Law (2017 Amendment) and the Price Law 1998.[246]

3.212 Generally, judges exercise their discretionary power to evaluate the lawyer's fees, either on the basis of the local market price or the suggested price. In addition, in the event of the absence of receipts for the lawyer's fees, no matter whether the lawyer's fee is reasonable or not, the court will never allow such fees.[247]

---

240 ibid.

241 *Sanya Resort Investment Company v Qi Yan* (dispute over share transfer) [2017] SPC Civil Final No 414 (the Supreme People's Court, second instance and binding judgment).

242 ibid.

243 *Notice of the National Development and Reform Commission on Opinions for Decontrolling the Prices of Some Services 2014* (No 2755 [2014] of the National Development and Reform Commission), Article 1. This legal document is equivalent to the level of regulation.

244 *Measures on Payment of Beijing Lawyer's Fees* (No 10 [2016] of Beijing Development and Reform Commission).

245 *Measures on Payment of Shanghai Lawyer's Fees* (No 3 [2017] of Shanghai Development and Reform Commission).

246 *Measures on Payment of Chongqing Lawyer's Fees* (No 1 [2018] of Chongqing Price Regulation).

247 *Ansai Jinjunhang Small Loan Co Ltd v Chunsheng Wang and Dongguan Village Committee of Qiaogou Zhen of Baota District* (dispute over a Guarantee Contract) [2016]

3.213 It is worth noting that the above discussion of the lawyer's fee has been considered in the context of full litigation proceedings until a judgment has been made. However, these provisions have not clarified the issue of costs in preservation applications.

3.214 In legal practice, Chinese lawyers do not normally request a separate fee for just the preservation applications from their clients, as this element of the fees will be part of the overall legal fees for the full civil case. Nonetheless, if the lawyer's fee for the preservation application is separate, in light of the prevailing legal reasoning, such a fee is considered as acceptable and the ground is discussed in the forthcoming paragraphs.

3.215 In the context of applications seeking preservation measures, the application fee comprises the court fee and other underlying fees that are associated with the applications. Although the scope of underlying fees is not clear under the existing law, the SPC has allowed reasonable fees arising from applications seeking preservation measures, and these fees shall be borne by the losing party, provided the original receipts are available from the winning party.[248] Under these circumstances, the lawyer's fee for preservation applications can be regarded as underlying fees.

The Burden of Legal Costs and Application Fees

3.216 The legal costs must be borne by the losing party in the final proceedings in accordance with the rule "loser pays all", unless the winning party volunteers to pay all the costs. If the final and binding judgment is not totally in favour of one party, then the allocation of costs depends on the exercise of the discretionary power of the judge.[249]

3.217 The allocation of the application fee shall be in accordance with the allocation of costs made by the judge. There are no specific provisions in the law to deal with the allocation of the application fee. In certain Chinese courts, the allocation of costs is calculated proportionally following the judgment – that is, a percentage of the disputed amount is recovered after the judgment.

3.218 For example, in *Xinyuan County Fengze Branch of Yili Jinxin Construction Engineering Co Ltd and Other v Xinyuan County Real Estate Development Co Ltd*,[250] the High People's Court of Xinjiang Uygur

Shan No 06 Civil Chu No 00083 (the Intermediate People's Court of Yan'an City of Shaanxi Province, first instance and binding judgment). In this case, the court had allowed the application fee and the relevant insurance premium that could be claimed from the respondent.

248 Refer to 3.201–3.206.

249 *Measures on Payment of Litigation Costs 2006*, Article 29.

250 *Xinyuan County Fengze Branch of Yili Jinxin Construction Engineering Co Ltd and Other v Xinyuan County Real Estate Development Co Ltd* (dispute over a construction contract) [2017] Xin Civil Final No 425 (the High People's Court of Xinjiang Uygur Autonomous Region, second instance and final judgment).

Autonomous Region held that there was no express legislation to provide for the allocation of costs including the preservation security expenses, the preservation fee and the relevant appraisal cost. Accordingly, it was held to be not improper for the first instance court to decide the allocation of costs in light of the allocation of the litigants' wins and losses.[251]

3.219 If it is supposed that the applicant/claimant may have claims for RMB 100 million against the respondent/defendant but, after the judgment, the court allows only RMB 60 million out of the disputed RMB 100 million, the applicant will then end up bearing 40 per cent of the court's costs and the application fee.

3.220 The above general rule has various exceptions and modifications pursuant to the *Measures on Payment of Litigation Costs 2006*.[252] Any further discussion is beyond the scope of the book.

3.221 In maritime disputes, the pre-action application fees for preservation of maritime claims and maritime injunctions should be borne by the applicant in advance and then the applicant may claim it in the bill of complaint. However, the pre-action evidence preservation must be borne by the applicant in accordance with the *Measures on Payment of Litigation Costs 2006*.[253]

The Time Limit for Rendering Orders

3.222 After accepting an application for the pre-action preservation, a competent court must issue an order within 48 hours, regardless of which type of preservation measure has been requested. On the other hand, in relation to applications seeking post-action preservation measures, only if the circumstances are "urgent" are the courts obligated to issue an order within 48 hours of accepting the preservation applications. The meaning of "urgent circumstances" in the context of preservation applications and other rules will be discussed specifically in Chapters 6, 8 and 10 for each individual preservation measure.

3.223 If an applicant files an application seeking post-action preservation measures and there are no urgent circumstances, the time limit for rendering three types of orders is different. The discussion in detail can be found in Chapter 6, 6.125 for post-action property preservation measures, Chapter 8, 8.158 for post-action behaviour preservation measures and Chapter 10, 10.135 for post-action evidence preservation measures.

3.224 With regard to applications seeking maritime preservation measures, the timeline is tighter compared with other disputes. A maritime court

251 ibid.
252 For example, Articles 9 and 26 of *Measures on Payment of Litigation Costs 2006*.
253 ibid Articles 39(1) and (2).

must issue an order within 48 hours of accepting the application without differentiating between the applications for a pre-action preservation measure or those for a post-action one.[254]

3.225 It is worth noting that according to the information posted by the online preservation system (www.baoquan.court.gov.uk), a court, after receiving the online preservation application, should normally verify the application within two working days.[255] However, the meaning of "verification" is ambiguous. Whether it follows that the result of both the pre-action and post-action application should be made within two working days is not clear. Accordingly, the information posted online is not very helpful for the applicant to get the result within a shorter time.

Legal Remedies against an Order (I): The Subject of Remedies

Concept of Interested Party and Outside Party

3.226 In any civil disputes, even though applicants and respondents are the parties who are affected by preservation orders, such orders can also have an impact on the interests of other parties. In China, those other parties will include interested parties having a stake in ongoing civil disputes and also outside parties. The subject of legal remedies must therefore include remedies for all stakeholders.

3.227 The existing laws are silent on the exact meanings of "interested parties" and "outside parties". Nonetheless, in light of the legal framework of the civil procedure law, it can be observed that interested parties and outside parties are actually different concepts within the regimes mandating various remedies. Sometimes the scopes of interested parties and of outside parties overlap within the procedural regime.

3.228 An interested party refers to the party who submits an objection to the procedural order made by the court.[256] The outside party may be regarded as a party who claims that their substantive rights are affected due to particular subject matter(s) included in the procedural order.[257] The outside party may claim that he is affected, even before the enforcement of the procedural order.

254 SMPL 2000, Articles 17, 57 and 68.

255 See <baoquan.court.gov.cn/#/home/particulars?id=11156690624436&form=issue> accessed 15 July 2021.

256 Guixiang Liu and Xiangyang Fan, 'Understanding and Application of *Provisions of the Supreme People's Court on Several Issues Concerning the Handling of Enforcement Objection and Reconsideration Cases by People's Courts 2015*' (2015) 11 The People's Judicature (Applied) 23, 28; it should be noted that *Provisions of the Supreme People's Court on Several Issues Concerning the Handling of Enforcement Objection and Reconsideration Cases by People's Courts* was amended in 2020, but the substantive content has not been changed; see also, CPL 1991 (as amended until 2020), Article 225.

257 By reference to the CPL 1991 (as amended until 2020), Articles 225 and 227.

3.229 By reference to *Provisions of the Supreme People's Court on Several Issues Concerning the Handling of Enforcement Objection and Reconsideration Cases by People's Courts (2020 Amendment)* (hereinafter referred to as "Provisions on Objection and Reconsideration (2020 Amendment)"),[258] under any of the following circumstances, any citizen, legal entity or other organisation other than a party to the case may be regarded as an interested party to a preservation order:

(a) Claiming that the matter for which the court is requested for assistance has exceeded its scope of assistance services or has violated the law.
(b) Claiming that during the enforcement of the preservation measures, such as sealing up, detainment or freezing property, the court's executive conduct infringes his lawful rights and interests.
(c) Claiming that any other lawful rights and interests have been infringed upon by the court's unlawful executive conduct during the enforcement of a preservation order or by the court's other improper conduct.[259]

3.230 Apart from the above circumstances, if an interested party considers that he enjoys substantive rights over the subject matter of a preservation order, and the legal arguments supporting his substantive right may overrule the legality of the preservation order, he, as an outside party, can also claim against this preservation order.

3.231 The issues can be explained using an example. Let say that a court requested a warehouse company to assist them to exercise a preservation order and, accordingly, the warehouse company was expected to stop the delivery of cargo from its warehouse to the respondent. However, this warehouse company argued that they actually had a proprietary interest in the cargo and this proprietary interest was not vested in the respondent. In this context, the warehouse company, as the interested party to the preservation order, may claim that the court's request for assistance had exceeded the scope in their preservation order and accordingly may raise an objection. Alternatively, as the outside party, the warehouse company may also directly contend its substantive right over the cargo was affected by the preservation

258 In *Provisions of the Supreme People's Court on Several Issues Concerning the Handling of Enforcement Objection and Reconsideration Cases by People's Courts* (2020 Amendment) (Fa Shi [2015] No 10) (superseded by Fa Shi [2020] No 21), Article 5 provides that under certain circumstances a party concerned or an interested party during the enforcement of a preservation order is entitled to apply for an objection against the order. This provision may therefore be regarded as clarifying the meaning of "interested party", even if this Article does not directly provide its meaning.

259 By reference to Articles 5 and 7 of Provisions on Objection and Reconsideration (2020 Amendment), the authors have summarised the circumstances for any party to be considered within the category of "interested party".

order, as it is affecting their proprietary interest. In this example, the warehouse company has two procedural remedies, one as the interested party and alternatively as the outside party.

Legal Remedies against an Order (II): Reconsideration

Reconsideration[260]

3.232 After a court renders an order on an application seeking a preservation measure, the court expects that this order will be immediately enforced. If an applicant, a respondent or an interested party is dissatisfied with the order, then within five days of receiving the notice of the preservation order, any one of these is entitled to apply for reconsideration of the order to the court that has rendered this order in granting the preservation measure.[261]

3.233 Where the court decides that the original order was correctly rendered, it will then dismiss the application requesting reconsideration. However, if, after reviewing the application for reconsideration, the court held that the preservation order was improper, it would then modify or discharge the original order. These decisions must be made within ten days of having received the application for reconsideration.[262]

3.234 It is important to note that the enforcement of the preservation measure will not be affected during the period of reconsideration by the court.[263] This means that an order becomes effective and should be enforced immediately once the order has been rendered and, during the reconsideration, the enforcement procedure will not be suspended.

3.235 Any party must apply for reconsideration within five days of the pronouncement of a preservation order. If any concerned party does not apply for reconsideration within five days, it means that he has waived the right to a reconsideration.

3.236 In maritime courts, the obligations on the courts in relation to the time limit are stricter as compared to other civil/commercial claims. Compared with the time limit of ten days, maritime courts must pronounce their decision within five days of receiving an application for reconsideration.[264]

Appellate Remedy

3.237 Article 154 of the CPL 1991 (as amended until 2020) excludes the right of an appeal if the party concerned is still not satisfied with the court's

---

260 Format of Application for Reconsideration, see Annex 1.

261 CPL 1991 (as amended until 2020), Article 108 and Interpretation of CPL 2015 (2020 Amendment), Articles 171 and 172.

262 Interpretation of CPL 2015 (2020 Amendment), Article 171.

263 CPL 1991 (as amended until 2020), Article 108.

264 SMPL 2000, Articles 17, 58 and 69.

decision on the application seeking reconsideration.[265] It means that there is no appellate remedy available for any stakeholder who wants to appeal a preservation order. Furthermore, a competent court during the preservation procedure and the reconsideration remedy procedure will simply refer to the court that has rendered the preservation order, no matter whether this court is the first, second or retrial instance court. In other words, because there is no appeal procedure, the court that has rendered the order is the only competent court for the reconsideration procedure.

Claims of the Interested Party

3.238 In legal practice, there seems to be a tendency that a court will allow an application seeking preservation measures as long as an applicant can provide security as prescribed by law or as requested by the court. Generally, the applicant does not therefore submit an application for reconsideration, and it is only the respondent or an interested party who will apply for reconsideration of a preservation order.

3.239 Since the court that had rendered the preservation order will also review the reconsideration application against that order, it is unusual that it will overrule the preservation order or even modify it.[266] In legal practice, the success rate for applications seeking the procedural remedy of reconsideration is not high.

3.240 As the success rate for applications seeking the procedural remedy of reconsideration is low, the respondents are motivated to try their luck during a civil trial to claim against applicants. The interested parties may also apply during the civil action to join the ongoing civil litigation.

3.241 By reference to Article 56 (2) of the CPL 1991 (as amended until 2020), under the following conditions an interested party shall have the right to institute a lawsuit in order to join in the civil litigation process:

(a) The subject matter of the preservation order is just the disputed subject matter of the case.
(b) The subject matter of the preservation order has a direct connection to the interested party.[267]

3.242 In such a scenario, the third party (the interested party) may enjoy an independent claim against both the applicants and the respondents.

265 CPL 1991 (as amended until 2020), Article 154.

266 Junbo Liu, 'Interpretation and Restructure of Legal Remedy for Property Preservation' (2018) 12 (5) Tsinghua University Law Journal 178, 182–183.

267 Article 56 (1) of the CPL 1991 (as amended until 2020) provides that "if a third party considers that he has an independent claim against the object of an action of two parties, the third party shall have the right to institute an action".

3.243 Instead of commencing the reconsideration procedure, the interested party will find that joining in the ongoing litigation proceedings may be relatively advantageous to him. In particular, when the interested party claims substantive rights over the subject matter of the preservation order (that is the preserved property), the reconsideration procedure cannot resolve the dispute over the property rights. However, if the interested party participates in the case, his claim on the property may then be determined by the court.

3.244 If the interested party fails to participate in the ongoing legal proceedings and the reasons for such failure do not arise due to his acts or omissions, there is still one route available to seek justice. This is only possible if the interested party has evidence to prove that an original effective judgment, order or mediation statement is partially or wholly incorrect in its contents and has damaged his civil rights and interests. Such interested party, within six months of having known or being reasonably assumed to have known of such damage to his civil rights and interests, may institute legal proceedings at the court that had issued the judgment, order or mediation statement.[268]

3.245 It should be noted that, even if an interested party has no independent claim, he would still be able to apply to the court to allow him to join the ongoing legal proceedings, provided that he may prove the future decision/order on the ongoing case would impact on his rights.[269]

3.246 For example, when the subject matter of a preservation order is not the disputed subject matter of the case, the interested party may argue that he has a proprietary interest over that subject matter. Such interested party still has no independent claim in the ongoing litigation, but the final decision of the case may affect his rights. However, it is submitted that this is not the best way to preserve rights. The best route available for such interested party would be to submit an objection to the subject matter of the preservation order, a strategy that will be discussed in 3.258–3.265.

Legal Remedies against a Preservation Order (III): Raising Objection

3.247 An objection against a preservation order is another important procedural remedy in China. The parties concerned, the interested party and the outside party, may all use this remedy to raise an objection against the order. However, the grounds on which this objection remedy is available to the original parties to the dispute, to the interested parties and to outside parties are different.

268 CPL 1991 (as amended until 2020), Article 56 (3).

269 Article 56 (2) of the CPL 1991 (as amended until 2020) provides that "if a third party has no independent claim against the object of an action of two parties but the outcome of the case will affect his legal interests, he may apply to join in the action".

3.248 The objections on which the application may be filed are:

(a) An objection to the enforcement of the preservation measures that has been granted available to the original parties to the dispute and to the third parties.
(b) An objection to the subject matter of the preservation order available to the third parties.

3.249 As discussed in 3.228, as for the first situation, the third party may be called the "interested party"; as for the second situation, the third party may be named as the "outside party".

Procedural Remedy of Objection to Enforcement of a Preservation Order

3.250 The difference between a reconsideration of a preservation order and an objection against the enforcement of a preservation order is that the former argues that there is no reasonable ground for a court to have rendered such a preservation order, while the latter is to assert that the measures taken to enforce the preservation orders are unlawful, or the enforcement measures undertaken are improper. The nature of an objection to the enforcement of a preservation order is to question the legality and legitimacy of the court's conduct during the enforcement of any preservation order.

3.251 In accordance with Article 225 of the CPL 1991 (as amended until 2020) providing any party or interested party may submit an objection to the court responsible for enforcing a judgment,[270] even though this provision merely governs the mechanism for raising an objection to the enforcement of a final judgment in the civil case, the SPC has extended the scope of the application of the objection. This means that the SPC has recognised that the enforcement of a preservation order also comes within the ambit of this provision.[271]

3.252 Furthermore, Provisions on Objection and Reconsideration (2020 Amendment) provide the exact guidance to apply the objection. They state:

> Where a party or an interested party holds that any of the following acts taken in the enforcement process or in the process of order for preservation or advance enforcement is illegal and raises an objection regarding that, the people's court shall conduct an examination under *Article 225 of the Civil Procedure Law:*

270 Article 225 of CPL 1991 (as amended until 2020) provides that "Any party or interested party may submit a written objection to the court responsible for enforcing a judgment if he considers enforcement of the judgment to be contrary to the provisions of the law".

271 *Notice of the Supreme People's Court on Issuing the Several Opinions on the Reasonable Allocation and Scientific Exercise of Enforcement Power* (Fa Fa [2011] No 15), Article 17. It should be noted that Article 17 provides that an objection to the enforcement of a property preservation order is subject to Article 202 of the CPL 2007. Here Article 202 of the CPL 2007 refers to Article 225 of CPL 1991 (as amended until 2020) after the CPL was revised.

(a) Such enforcement measures as sealing up, detainment, freezing, auction, disposal, expiation of debts in kind, suspension of enforcement, discontinuation of enforcement, and termination of enforcement;
(b) The statutory procedures that should be followed regarding the enforcement period and sequence; and
(c) Any other act taken by the people's court that has infringed upon the lawful rights and interests of the party or interested party.[272]

3.253 The above provision does not stipulate the exact time limit of submitting an objection. It is merely provided that the party concerned or the interested party is entitled to apply for an objection before the termination of the enforcement of the order.[273] The court with jurisdiction to hear the objection raised against the preservation order is the court that first rendered it. After receiving the written objection, this court will evaluate the objection and accordingly will pronounce its decision within 15 days.[274]

3.254 In the event that the parties concerned, or the interested party, are not satisfied with the decision made on the objection raised, they may still apply for reconsideration to the higher people's court within ten days of receiving the decision on their application asserting objection against the enforcement of the preservation order.[275]

3.255 After evaluating the application seeking the reconsideration, the higher court may render a decision to overrule the objection, to revoke or modify the original order, to request the lower court to re-examine the case or to make a new order directly in light of the fact of the case.[276]

3.256 For example, in *Lanzhou General Machine Manufacturing Co Ltd v Lanzhou Xinqu Huiyin Small Loan Company*,[277] Lanzhou General Machine applied for an objection to the enforcement of a property preservation order, because Lanzhou General Machine claimed that the property preservation measure taken by the High People's Court of Gansu Province exceeded the order's reasonable scope. They cited evidence in relation to the fact that these enforcement measures undertaken by the court had involved excessive seal-up of their real estate. After the High People's Court of Gansu Province rendered an order to overrule their objection, Lanzhou General Machine again filed an application seeking the reconsideration of this order. This time the application seeking reconsideration was made to the SPC.

3.257 After examination, in accordance with Article 225 of the CPL 1991 (as amended until 2020), Article 156 of the Interpretation of CPL 2015 (2020

272 Provisions on Objection and Reconsideration (2020 Amendment), Article 7.
273 Ibid Article 6.
274 CPL 1991 (as amended until 2020), Article 225.
275 ibid.
276 Provisions on Objection and Reconsideration (2020 Amendment), Article 23.
277 *Lanzhou General Machine Manufacturing Co Ltd v Lanzhou Xinqu Huiyin Small Loan Company* (dispute over an objection application) [2014] Zhi Fu Zi Di No 25 (the Supreme People's Court, second instance and final order).

Amendment) and Articles 7(1) and 23(1)(i) of Provisions on Objection and Reconsideration (2020 Amendment), the SPC held that on the facts there was no excessive enforcement and accordingly made a final order disallowing the application seeking the procedural remedy of reconsideration.[278]

Procedural Remedy of Objection to Subject Matter of a Preservation Order

3.258 The procedural remedy of objection to the preservation order on the basis of the subject matter included is different from the procedural remedy of objection to the enforcement of the order, because the nature of this application seeking the objection is to question the validity and legality of the rights over the subject matter of the order. To be precise, the outside party argues that they by themselves enjoy the lawful rights over the subject matter of the preservation order and the original parties to the dispute have no right on it.

3.259 The mandatory condition for this procedural remedy of objection is that the subject matter of the preservation order must not be the same subject matter as that of the main civil dispute. If the subject matter of the preservation order and of the main civil dispute are the same, then the outside party, as an independent party, must seek to join the ongoing civil litigation, as discussed in 3.241–3.244.

3.260 A controversial and debatable issue for a while has been whether an outside party, in the face of a preservation order, is entitled to apply for this procedural remedy, in addition to the procedural remedy of reconsideration.

3.261 In an authoritative book, titled *Understanding and Application of the Interpretation of the CPL*, after deliberating upon the opinions of the Legislative Affairs Commission of the Standing Committee of the National People's Congress and legal experts, the senior judge of the SPC asserted that the reconsideration procedure available to the outside party, pursuant to Article 172 of the Interpretation of CPL 2015 (2020 Amendment),[279] seemed in his view sufficient to achieve procedural justice and the procedural remedy of objection was therefore not applicable to such outside and/or interested parties.[280]

3.262 In legal practice, many Chinese courts follow this opinion and hold that the outside party has no legal right to apply for an objection because the

278 ibid.

279 Article 172 of the Interpretation of CPL 2015 (2020 Amendment) provides that "here an interested party applies for reconsideration on the ground of objections to the preservation order or advance enforcement, the people's court that had rendered the relevant order will evaluate the application in accordance with Article 108 of the Civil Procedure Law".

280 Deyong Shen (ed.), *Understanding and Application of the Interpretation of the CPL* (People's Court Press 2015) 491.

enforcement of a preservation order is different from the enforcement of an effective judicial decision. These courts are of the view that the preservation order does not fundamentally impact upon the substantive rights of the outside party as compared to the enforcement of a final decision.[281]

3.263 However, Interpretation of Property Preservation (2020 Amendment) grants rights to the outside party whereby he may apply to seek the procedural remedy of objection, provided that the subject matter of the preservation order is not related to the subject matter of the case.[282]

3.264 Interpretation of Property Preservation (2020 Amendment) does not provide the exact time limit of filing an objection. By reference to Pursuant to Article 6 of Provisions on Objection and Reconsideration (2020 Amendment), the outside party should submit an objection prior to the end of the enforcement of the disputed subject matter in the preservation order; if the party concerned acquires the disputed subject matter based on the binding judgment, the objection should be submitted prior to the termination of the enforcement of the binding judgment.[283] Following the objection, the court must review the application seeking procedural remedy of objection within 15 days of receiving the written application.[284] If the outside party is not satisfied with the court's decision on the application seeking the objection, then the outside party or the party concerned must file a case. The cause of action under this case would be based on the substantive right over the subject matter of the preservation order. In other words, the court that has accepted the case must now decide whether the outside party enjoys the substantive right over the subject matter of the preservation order.

3.265 In legal practice, it has been observed that certain local courts and judges still hold the opinion that the outside party has no right to lodge such application seeking procedural remedy of objection,[285] even though the

281 Xiling Chen, 'No Right for Outside Party to Apply for the Litigation of Objection During the Post-Action Property Preservation: (2017) Chuan No 15 Civil Chu No 63' (2018) 20 The People's Judicature (Case) 71, 72; see also, Junbo Liu, 'Interpretation and Restructure of Legal Remedy for Property Preservation' (2018) 12 (5) Tsinghua University Law Journal 178, 180.

282 Interpretation of Property Preservation (2020 Amendment), Article 27.

283 Provisions on Objection and Reconsideration (2020 Amendment), Article 6.

284 CPL 1991 (as amended until 2020), Article 227. Article 227 provides that "where the person who is not a party to the case or any party to the case is not satisfied with the order and considers the original judgment or order to be erroneous, the case shall be handled in accordance with the procedure for trial supervision; where the original judgment or order is considered to be irrelevant, the relevant party may lodge a case with the people's court within fifteen days after receiving the order".

285 For example, *Tongliao Xinda Automobile Commerce Co Ltd v Alashankou Branch of China Construction Bank Corporation and Other* (dispute over a litigation of an outside party's objection) [2017] Xin Min Chu No 39 (the High People's Court of Xinjiang Uygur Autonomous Region, first instance and binding ruling), in this case, the High People's Court of Xinjiang Uygur Autonomous Region held that apart from the reconsideration of a preservation order, the law did not grant the outside party other legal remedy and meanwhile, the order did not damage the outside party's substantive right. Therefore, the High People's Court of Xinjiang Uygur

Interpretation of Property Preservation (2020 Amendment) now grants the outside party the right to apply to seek procedural remedy of objection. The positive tendency is that, these days, most Chinese courts, particularly the SPC in its judgments, have expressly granted the right to the outside party to seek procedural remedy of objection pursuant to Article 227 of the CPL 1991 (as amended until 2020).[286]

Sanctions for Not Obeying Preservation Orders

Sanctioned Behaviours and Parties

3.266 In England and Wales the concept of contempt of court governs the issue of disobeying the preservation orders granted by the English courts. In China, there is no such concept that can be considered as equivalent to that of "contempt of court". However, as early as 1991, the first version of the CPL provided certain sanctions, such as detention or a fine that can be levied against the parties based on their conduct. The sanctioned behaviours concerned are as follows:

(a) Forging or destroying important evidence, thereby obstructing the trial of the case by the people's court.
(b) Concealing, removing, selling off or destroying property that has been sealed up or detained, or that has been inventoried and placed in his custody by order, or moving assets that have been frozen.
(c) Using violence, threats or other methods to obstruct judicial personnel from performing their duties.
(d) Refusing to perform a legally effective judgment or order made by the people's court,[287] for example:

Autonomous Region denied the outside party's objection; see also, Xiling Chen 'No Right for Outside Party to Apply for the Litigation of Objection during the Post-Action Property Preservation: (2017) Chuan No 15 Civil Chu No 63' (2018) 20 The People's Judicature (Case) 71. In this article, Judge Xiling Chen shed light on two conflicting opinions in the Sichuan Yibin Intermediate People's Court on the legal issue of whether an outside party was entitled to apply for an objection. Her opinion was that the outside party was not entitled to seek procedural remedy of objection.

286 *Quanzhou Branch of Bank of Communications v Guobei Jiang and Other* (dispute over a litigation of an outside party's objection) [2018] SPC Civil Final No 560 (Supreme People's Court, second instance and binding judgment); see also, *Guangzhi Wang v Chuqiao Branch of Chengdu Rural Commercial Bank and Other* (dispute over a litigation of an outside party's objection) [2019] SPC Civil Final No 370 (the Supreme People's Court, second instance and binding judgment).

287 The CPL 1991, Article 102(1)(3)(5)(6); see also, Article 111(1)(3)(5)(6) of the CPL 1991 (as amended until 2020), which has not made any changes. This Article does not discuss in particular disobeying the preservation order granted by the Chinese courts. However, it is seen in legal practice that this Article is used to address this issue. Furthermore, only the first, third, fifth and sixth types of conduct are chosen in this book, as they are most compatible with the expression of violating evidence, property and behaviour preservation orders.

I) Where the person conceals, transfers, sells or destroys property or transfers property gratis, transacts property at obviously unreasonable prices, waives matured creditors' rights, provides security for others free of charge, etc., after the order came into effect, and thereby leaving the court unable to enforce this order.

II) Where the person conceals, transfers, destroys or disposes of property that has been provided as security to the court without the latter's permission.

III) Where the person is a natural person who is under obligations to provide assistance during enforcement but refuses to assist upon receipt of the notice issued by the court for providing assistance during enforcement.[288]

3.267 Where a legal entity commits any of the behaviours listed in the preceding paragraph, the people's court may impose a fine or period of detention on the principal of the legal entity or the person who is directly responsible. If the behaviour constitutes a criminal offence, such person will be prosecuted accordingly, as prescribed by law.[289]

3.268 This provision grants rights to Chinese courts to exercise their legal obligation to ensure their preservation orders are obeyed.

3.269 In addition, the CPL 1991 (as amended until 2020) provides that the relevant legal entity or organisation must assist the enforcement authorities to guarantee the enforcement of preservation orders. Under the following circumstances, the relevant entities, organisations and directly responsible persons may be fined, detained or prosecuted:

(a) The relevant legal entity or organisation refuses to cooperate with or obstructs the investigation and collating of evidence by the court.

(b) The legal entity or organisation concerned refuses to provide assistance in connection with the inquiry, sealing-up, freezing, transfer or appraisal of property after receiving the notice of the court requiring such assistance.

(c) The relevant legal entity or organisation, after receiving a notice from the people's court to assist in execution, refuses to assist by withholding the revenue of the person subject to enforcement, or in transferring the relevant title deeds, or in passing on the relevant negotiable instruments, certificates or other property.

(d) It refuses to provide other assistance during the enforcement of an order.[290]

288 Interpretation of CPL 2015 (2020 Amendment), Article 188.
289 CPL 1991 (as amended until 2020), Article 111.
290 ibid Article 114.

Fine and Detention Penalty

3.270 In relation to a natural person who does not obey a preservation order, the fine imposed should be less than RMB 100,000. As regards a legal entity or organisation, the fine imposed shall be between RMB 50,000 and RMB 1 million.[291]

3.271 In terms of orders in the field of maritime law, there is no specific fine for violating property and evidence preservation orders, but in the case of maritime injunctions, a fine for disobeying the injunction against a natural person shall be between RMB 1,000 and RMB 30,000. Similarly, a fine against a legal entity or organisation shall be between RMB 30,000 and RMB 100,000.[292]

3.272 In terms of detention penalties, regardless of the field of maritime law and other fields, a period of detention should not be longer than 15 days.[293] The court shall deliver detainees to the custody of the public security authority. If a detainee admits and corrects his wrongdoings during the period of detention, the court may then decide to release him before the end of his detention term.[294]

3.273 In legal practice, the sanctioned cases reported are rare so that the cases in one of the authoritative law webpages, namely Lawinfochina Webpage (北大法宝www.lawinfochina.com),[295] are simply published dozens of.[296] Nonetheless, in the past two years, the judicial sanction was officially highlighted. For example, in a recent case reported by the People's Court Daily, an employee in a bank was fined RMB 5,000 in accordance with Articles 111 (5), 114, 115 and 116 of CPL 1991 (as amended until 2020), because he obstructed the court in freezing the bank account. The comment on this case was to remind every citizen/organisation to perform or assist in performing the binding legal instrument properly on the ground that this is a legal duty.[297]

---

291 ibid Article 115.

292 SMPL 2000, Article 59.

293 ibid; see also, CPL 1991 (as amended until 2020), Article 115.

294 CPL 1991 (as amended until 2020), Article 115.

295 The Lawinfochina webpage was produced by the Law School of Peking University in 1985 and then in 2003 this webpage cooperated with the SPC to report judicial decisions, law and relevant judicial interpretations.

296 For example, in *Long Jiang and Zhiyong yang v Haitao Feng* (dispute over a sale contract) [2016] Ji Zhi Jian No 70 (the High People's Court of Hebei Province, retrial and binding ruling), a house belonging to Haitao Feng was sealed up due to a dispute over a sale contract. However, during the period of sealing, the Real Estate Management Office, Zhenglan Banner of Inner Mongolia Autonomous Region, as an executor assist, put into practice the mortgage registration to the sealed house based on the Haitao Feng's application. On the fact of this case, the High People's Court of Hebei Province held that the Real Estate Management Office unlawfully registered for mortgage to the sealed house. Nonetheless, there was no material loss arising from this unlawful conduct. Therefore, in accordance with Articles 114 and 115 of CPL 1991 (as amended until 2020), Real Estate Management Office was fined RMB 50,000.

297 Jun Wang, 'A Case over Obstructing the Enforcement of a Judicial Document' *People's Court Daily* (Beijing, 1 December 2020).

3.274 If the party is not satisfied with the decision with regard to a fine or detention, the natural person or the legal entity or organisation is entitled to apply to the higher court to seek the procedural remedy of reconsideration. However, the enforcement of the fine or detention will continue during the period of evaluation of the application seeking this procedural remedy.[298]

Criminal Penalty

3.275 Apart from the penalty in light of the civil procedural law discussed above, two circumstances may lead a liable person in a binding preservation order to undertake the criminal penalty. The first circumstance is that the liable person refuses to obey the preservation order; the second situation is that a liable person commits unlawful conduct to the subject of a preservation order, such as selling the preserved property, destroying the preserved property.

3.276 First, refusing to obey a preservation order may lead to a criminal penalty, pursuant to the Criminal Law of the People's Republic of China 1980 (2020 Amendment) (hereinafter referred to as "Criminal Law (2020 Amendment)"), and it provides that:

> Whosoever has the ability to execute the judgment or ruling (order) made by a People's Court but refuses to do so shall, if the circumstances are serious, be sentenced to fixed-term imprisonment of not more than three years, to criminal detention, or to be fined; if the circumstances are extremely serious, he shall be sentenced to a fixed term of imprisonment of between three years and seven years and at the same time be fined.
>
> When a legal entity or organisation commits this crime, such legal entity or organisation shall be fined and the penalty for the direct principal and other directly responsible person shall be by reference to the first section.[299]

3.277 As early as 1980, Article 157 of the Criminal Law 1980 introduced criminal penalties against a natural person who refused to execute a court's judgment or order. However, the maximum penalty that could be given was simply detention for three years. Also, the issue of a similar penalty against a legal entity or against an organisation or its relevant principal was not incorporated into these provisions. In 2015, the amendment to the Criminal Law revised this provision, which was followed by the Criminal Law (2020 Amendment), which incorporated various amendments.

3.278 In practice, for many years it has been very difficult to enforce effective judgments or orders in China. It is quite common for the respondents/

298 CPL 1991 (as amended until 2020), Article 117.

299 Criminal Law of the People's Republic of China was adopted by the Second Session of the Standing Committee of the Fifth National People's Congress of the People's Republic of China on 1 July 1979 and came into effect on 1 January 1980. The latest amendment was adopted by the 24th Session of the Standing Committee of the 13th National People's Congress of the People's Republic of China on 26 December 2020; Criminal Law (2020 Amendment), Article 313.

losing parties to adopt various methods to avoid obeying effective judgments and orders. Even when such incidents were so widespread, the Chinese courts did not activate legal measures that were available to them – for example, fines, detaining parties who were disobeying the order, or transferring their cases to the people's prosecutor.[300] There were many reasons for this lack of initiative on the part of the courts to ensure that their judgments and orders were obeyed.[301]

3.279 In addition, most Chinese courts are unable to confirm whether preservation orders may come within the ambit of Article 313 of the Criminal Law (2020 Amendment). It was therefore likely that criminal penalties could not play a proper role in securing the enforcement of preservation orders.[302]

3.280 Since 2011, in order to address the situation as discussed in the previous paragraph and to maintain the legitimacy and credit of the Chinese courts, the SPC has taken different actions to strengthen the enforcement of preservation orders. For example, in *Some Opinions of the Supreme People's Court on Punishment of Evasion of Enforcement 2011*, the SPC stressed the need to "intensify property preservation" and to "promptly take enforcement measures on preserved property and secured property".[303]

3.281 In 2015, the Criminal Law was revised to increase the fixed-term sentence from three years to seven years and to increase the penalty that may

300 The general procedure is that, if a respondent's behaviour constitutes a criminal offence, then a competent court will collate evidence to prove his illegal behaviour. After collating all the evidence, it will transfer the evidential materials to the corresponding people's prosecutor.

301 For example, it is difficult for a court to collate evidence of a respondent's actions as most of the measures taken by them are evasive and carried out in secret. See also, 'Achieving the Enforcement of an Effective Judgment and Refraining from the Negative Effect of Evasion of Enforcement: Answer of the Responsible Judge in the Executive Bureau of the SPC to the Reporter' on 27 May 2011 <www.gongshu.gov.cn/art/2012/1/21/art_1235142_2715699.html> accessed 15 July 2021. Any further discussion of the topic is beyond the scope of the book.

302 Guixiang Liu and Huizhuo Liu, 'Understanding and Application of *Interpretation of the Supreme People's Court on Several Issues Concerning the Application of Law in the Trial of Criminal Cases of Refusing to Satisfy a Judgment or Ruling*' (2015) 13 The People's Judicature (Applied) 11.

303 *Some Opinions of the Supreme People's Court on Punishment of Evasion of Enforcement* (Fa [2011] No 195), Article 7 provides that "intensify property preservation" mechanisms that means "The courts in all places shall enhance their coordination in respect of property preservation in all respects, such as case initiation, hearing and enforcement, increase their efforts in carrying out property preservation in accordance with law, strengthen the cohesion between the trial and enforcement divisions in respect of property preservation, and reduce the risk of debtors or persons subject to enforcement concealing or transferring property". Additionally, its Article 8 provides for "promptly taking enforcement measures on preserved property and secured property. After entering the enforcement process, the courts in all locations must increase their efforts in relation to enforcement of their preservation orders against preserved property and secured property, conduct timely reviews on any objection raised by any party concerned, guarantor or any third person, take controlling measures on the relevant property in accordance with law during the review period, and increase the enforcement efforts on the relevant property after dismissing the objection".

be given to the relevant legal entity or organisation and its relevant principal who is responsible.

3.282 In the same year, the SPC issued *Interpretation on Several Issues Concerning the Application of Law in the Trial of Criminal Cases of Refusing to Satisfy a Judgment or Ruling*, which clarified that any court's order that includes a preservation order will put the onus on parties to the dispute and on the relevant parties, including any guarantor or any other party, who should assist in the enforcement process, also being liable for enforcement.[304] This therefore means that the sanctions regarding not obeying orders containing preservation measures are now governed by this interpretation as well.

3.283 At the end of 2016, the SPC published the guidance case concerning the criminal penalty for refusing to obey a judgment or order and, accordingly, instructed the Chinese courts to apply criminal penalties.[305] Although this guidance case is not relevant to a preservation order, it is expected by the stakeholders that the enforcement of preservation orders will become more efficient in China.

3.284 Secondly, as regards the preserved subject matter described by a preservation order, if someone took certain improper measures on those preserved property, his conduct may constitute the criminal penalty. Article 314 of the Criminal Law (2020 Amendment) provides that

> Whoever conceals, transfers, sells or intentionally destroys or damages the property sealed up, detained or frozen by judicial organs, if the circumstances are serious, shall be sentenced to fixed-term imprisonment of not more than three years, criminal detention or be fined.[306]

3.285 This provision expressly provides that all properties which have been sealed up, detained or frozen by judicial authorities shall not be hidden, transferred, sold or destroyed intentionally. In this context, there is no doubt that, after a court has sealed up, detained or frozen the property in light of a

---

304 *Interpretation of the Supreme People's Court on Several Issues Concerning the Application of Law in the Trial of Criminal Cases of Refusing to Satisfy a Judgment or Ruling* (2020 Amendment) (Fa Shi [2015] No 16) (superseded by Fa Shi [2020] No 21), Article 1; see also, Guixiang Liu and Huizhuo Liu, 'Understanding and Application of *Interpretation of the Supreme People's Court on Several Issues Concerning the Application of Law in the Trial of Criminal Cases of Refusing to Satisfy a Judgment or Ruling*' (2015) 13 The People's Judicature (Applied) 11.

305 Guiding Case No 71: Case regarding Jianwen Mao's Refusal to Satisfy a Judgment or Order (case on refusal to perform a judgment or order) [2014] Wen Ping Criminal Chu Zi No 314 (the Primary People's Court of Pingyang County of Wenzhou City of Zhejiang Province, first instance and binding judgment), the key point of the judgment is that "after a judgment or ruling/order comes into force, where the liable person in this binding judgment or ruling/order hides, transfers, deliberately damages the property, or commits any other act of refusing to perform the judgment or ruling/order, causing the failure to enforce the judgment or ruling/order, and the circumstances are serious, the person shall be convicted and punished for the crime of refusing to satisfy a judgment or ruling/order".

306 Criminal Law (2020 Amendment), Article 314.

preservation order, if a person commits unlawful conduct on the preserved property described by the Criminal Law (2020 Amendment), a criminal penalty will be applied

3.286 Unlike the first circumstance, there is no guiding case reported. Nonetheless, in legal practice, different courts in recent years have tended to apply criminal law to punish the liable person who disposes of property sealed up and detained so that the serious consequence has arisen/happened.[307]

Discharge of Orders[308]

General Rules

3.287 After rendering a preservation order, a court that has rendered the order may, under certain circumstances prescribed by law, issue a new order to discharge the previous preservation order. However, according to the kind of preservation order and taking into account the facts of the case, the circumstances under which the preservation order can be discharged may differ.

3.288 When any of the following circumstances apply, the court may discharge the preservation order:

(a) With regard to a pre-action preservation order, where the applicant fails to institute a lawsuit or apply for arbitration in accordance with the law *within 30 days* after the court has adopted preservation measures.[309]

(b) With regard to a preservation order rendered after a legal instrument comes into effect but before its enforcement procedure could commence, the winning party fails to apply for enforcement *within five days* upon the expiration of the performance period specified in the legal instrument.[310]

(c) With regard to a case arising from a property dispute, a respondent provides security and the preserved property is not the disputed

307 For example, *Chen **'s crime of illegal disposal of property* (Case on illegal disposal of property sealed up) [2017] Jin 08 Criminal Final No 103 (Yuncheng Intermediate People's Court of Shanxi Province, second instance and binding judgment); in this case, after land was sealed up in accordance with a ruling, Chen ** had sufficient knowledge of the land which was sealed up by the court, but he still constructed a building on this land so that the land could not be delivered to a buyer. Therefore, the court applied Article 314 of the Criminal Law to punish Chen **; see also, *Zhou *A and Zhou*B' s crime of illegal disposal of property* (Case on illegal disposal of property sealed up, distrained or frozen by judicial organs) [2015] He Ba Criminal Chu Zi No 653 (the Primary People's Court of Hezhou Babu District of Guangxi Zhuang Autonomous Region, first instance and binding judgment); see also, *Liu*'s crime of illegal disposal of property* (Case on illegal disposal of property sealed up, detained or frozen by judicial organs) [2015] Ju Criminal Chu Zi No 93 (the Primary People's Court of Ju County of Shandong province, first instance and binding judgment).

308 Format of Application for Discharging the Preservation Order, see Annex 2.

309 CPL 1991 (as amended until 2020), Article 101.

310 Interpretation of CPL 2015 (2020 Amendment), Article 163.

property of the case;[311] but as regards the intellectual property behaviour preservation, even if the respondent provides security, the order will not be discharged without an applicant's permission.[312]

(d) With regard to a property preservation or the pre-action behaviour preservation of a trademark dispute, if the applicant does not provide top-up security to make up the originally insufficient amount after a request from the court.[313]

(e) Where the preservation order issued earlier is erroneous.

(f) Where the applicant seeking preservation measures withdraws the application.

(g) Where the filing of an action or the claim of a preservation applicant is dismissed by a binding judgment/order; for example, the court had made an order supporting the objection application of an interested party.

(h) Where there are any other circumstances under which the people's court is of the opinion that the preservation order shall be discharged.[314]

An Applicant's Liability

3.289 Although the discharge of a preservation order is sometimes based on a competent court's legal duty, an applicant is also obliged, under certain circumstances, to apply for the court to seek discharge of an existing preservation order. Pursuant to the Interpretation of Property Preservation (2020 Amendment), under any of the following circumstances, the applicant must promptly apply to seek discharge of the property preservation order:

311 CPL 1991 (as amended until 2020), Article 104; see also, 3.136–3.137; in the field of maritime law, a similar requirement for a discharge can be applied to a preservation in respect of a maritime claim. Article 18 of SMPL 2000 provides that "where a person against whom a claim is made provides security or a party applies for discharge of preservation of the maritime claim on justified grounds, the maritime court shall discharge the preservation promptly". Additionally, preservation measures can be taken against the vessel owner's property or in respect of the return of the security provided for lifting the preservation measures, in accordance with Articles 23 and 24 of the "Provisions of the Supreme People's Court on Several Issues Concerning the Trial of Cases of Disputes over Compensation for Vessel-induced Oil Pollution Damage" (2020 Amendment) (*Fa Shi* [2011] No 14) (superseded by *Fa Shi* [2020] No 18). Such measures would be similar to the case of oil pollution damage caused by persistent oil carried by oil tankers, after the fund for limitation of liability for oil pollution damage is constituted.

312 Interpretation of IP Behaviour Preservation 2018, Article 12; see also, 8.143.

313 Article 5 of the Interpretation of Property Preservation (2020 Amendment) provides that "during the period of a property preservation, where the current security provided by an applicant is not sufficient to compensate the loss of the respondent, the court may order the applicant to supplement the corresponding amount of security. Further to that request, if the applicant refuses to supplement the security, the court may render an order wholly or partially to discharge the preservation order".

314 From (e) to (h), see Interpretation of CPL 2015 (2020 Amendment), Article 166.

(a) With regard to a pre-action preservation order, where the applicant does not institute a lawsuit or apply for arbitration in accordance with the law within 30 days after the court has adopted preservation measures.
(b) The arbitration institution does not accept the application for arbitration, or allows for its withdrawal.
(c) Another court does not accept the lawsuit, or allows for its withdrawal.[315]
(d) The lawsuit or claim is rejected by an effective judgment made by other courts.
(e) Any other circumstance where the applicant should apply for discharging the property preservation.[316]

3.290 It can be seen that from the above circumstances that it is very difficult for the court to second-guess them, unless the applicant keeps the court informed of such circumstances. It is therefore reasonable to assume that the applicant is under the obligation to keep the court fully informed of any change of circumstances or new circumstances. Furthermore, the applicant should be responsible for the loss caused to the respondent/any third party if he does not apply to the court in time to discharge the preservation order.[317]

3.291 Although the applicant's obligation is highlighted in the Interpretation of Property Preservation (2020 Amendment), which is relevant to the preservation of property, it is the authors' contention that these are applicable to other types of preservation orders as well.

Compensation: Legal Remedy from Substantive Law Perspective

General Rules

3.292 Under the CPL 1991 (as amended until 2020) and the relevant interpretations, where an application seeking a preservation measure is successful, but the measure is subsequently proved to be erroneous, the applicant must compensate the respondent for any losses incurred as a result of this error.[318] The purpose of this provision is to allow respondents, interested parties or outside parties under any types of preservation orders to claim compensation pursuant to liability in tort.

315 Because a court that makes a preservation order might not be the same court where the applicant lodges a case, in this context, if the application for case-filing is not accepted by the latter court, or after the case has been accepted, the applicant wants to withdraw the case, the applicant has an obligation to give notice to the court that made the preservation order.

316 Interpretation of Property Preservation (2020 Amendment), Article 23.

317 ibid.

318 CPL 1991 (as amended until 2020), Article 105; see also, Provisions on Evidence 2019, Article 28.

3.293 However, the CPL 1991 (as amended until 2020) does not clarify the liability principle governing the applicant's conduct. Pursuant to the Civil Code 2020, there are three types of liability principle – fault-based liability, the presumption of fault and non-fault liability.[319]

3.294 Even if tortious conducts under three types of preservation measures have been incorporated into one provision under the CPL 1991 (as amended until 2020), this does not mean that the liability principles are consistent in governing the issue of an applicant's conduct. In light of the different types of preservation measure, the liability principles and categorisation and identification of erroneous preservation measures will be specifically discussed in Chapters 6, 8 and 10.

3.295 It should be noted that a court's conduct that turns out to be erroneous may give rise to the issue of state compensation to the party that has suffered loss due to the error of the court. Furthermore, all persons who are affected by the court's order are entitled to claim state compensation, provided that their claims are prescribed by law.[320] Any further discussion on this topic will be beyond the scope of this book, and this book will focus simply on the issue of civil compensation.

Party Liable to Compensate an Injured Party

3.296 The party that is liable to compensate the injured party that has suffered loss due to an erroneous preservation order or due to the improper conduct of any party is normally referred to as the claimant and the defendant in a claim or a counterclaim. However, as discussed in 3.226–3.231, a preservation order can also impact on the lawful rights and interests of the parties that are not involved in the main civil dispute. These parties may also be named in the lawsuit as the interested party or the outside party. They may join such lawsuits as an injured party having their own claim for damages.

3.297 In accordance with the *Interpretation of the SPC on the Issue Concerning Whether the Parties Concerned Shall Be Liable for the Damage of Any Outsider Caused by Their Falsely Applying for Property*

319 Civil Code 2020, Articles 1165 (fault-based liability and the presumption of fault) and 1166 (non-fault liability); see also, Article 6 of the Tort Law 2010 (expired on 1 January 2021) which provides the fault-based liability and the presumption of fault and Article 7 which provides the non-fault liability.

320 For example, Article 3(2) of *Interpretation of the Supreme People's Court on Several Issues Concerning the Application of Law in the Trial of Judicial Compensation Cases in Civil and Administrative Lawsuits* (Fa Shi [2016] No 20) provides that the applicant is entitled to claim "if preservation measures that shall not be removed according to the law are removed", and Article 3(5) allows an outside party to claim if his property is preserved illegally; see also, State Compensation Law (2012 Amendment), Article 28 in relation to the issue of the state compensation.

Preservation,[321] the third party is entitled to claim against the applicant in the context of a property preservation order. Furthermore, there is a series of cases where this Interpretation has been applied to protect the third party's interests. These courts instruct the parties concerned, that is, the applicants in the preservation applications, to compensate these third parties.[322] The court will allow the claim for compensation, provided that the facts and evidence of a case satisfy the elements of infringement of rights pursuant to the Civil Code 2020.[323]

Difference between Procedural Remedy and Substantive Remedy

3.298 In the context of preservation orders, this book has divided the legal remedies into two types – procedural remedies and substantive remedies. The procedural remedies comprise the reconsideration of and objection to a preservation order and have been discussed in 3.232–3.265. The main function of the procedural remedy is to discharge the preservation order from the perspective of civil procedure law.[324] Even if the litigation in relation to an objection arises due to the infringement of a substantive right of a third party, the judicial decision regarding litigation of the objection to the preservation order will still be considered as a procedural remedy.

3.299 In contrast, in the context of preservation measures, the substantive remedies will allude to claims seeking damages arising from preservation orders. The purpose of this substantive remedy is to compensate losses of parties that arise from preservation orders. The court will evaluate the causative link between the alleged losses and preservation orders.

3.300 The two types of remedies therefore belong to different categories of remedy. The parties concerned, interested parties or outside parties are entitled to choose any of the legal remedies as based on their objectives. In legal practice, it has been observed that the parties regularly prefer at the first

321 *Interpretation of the Supreme People's Court on the Issue Concerning Whether the Parties Concerned Shall Assume Compensation Liability for the Damage of Any Outsider Caused by Their Falsely Applying for Property Preservation* (Fa Shi [2005] No 11).

322 *Laijiang Lai v Fuqing Chen and Other* (dispute over damages for a property preservation order) [2017] Yue Civil Retrial No 505 (the High People's Court of Guangdong Province, retrial and binding judgment); see also, *Shufang Sun v Shiping Li and Other* (dispute over damages for a property preservation order) [2016] Yun No 31 Civil Final No 284 (the Intermediate People's Court of Dehong Daizu Jingbozu Autonomous Prefecture of Yunnan Province, second instance and binding judgment); see also, *Tengzhou Runde Trade Co Ltd v Changxing Branch of Industrial and Commercial Bank of China* (dispute over damages for a property preservation order) [2017] Zhe No 05 Civil Final No 36 (the Intermediate People's Court of Huzhou of Zhejiang Province, second instance and binding judgment).

323 See Generally, Civil Code 2020, Part VII "Tort Liability". There is no fundamental difference as compared to the Tort Law 2010 on the elements.

324 *Cheng Liu and Other v Mingxiao Li* (dispute over the litigation of objection to enforcement) [2017] Jing No 02 Chu No 165 (the Second Intermediate People's Court of Beijing Municipality, first instance and binding judgment).

stage to seek a procedural remedy from the courts. If they cannot achieve their objectives through the pursuit of procedural remedies, they will then attempt to invoke one of the available substantive remedies.

3.301 However, a few Chinese courts cannot differentiate between these two categories of remedy. It is usual for many Chinese courts to insist that the claimant who has suffered losses as a result of a preservation order should first seek a procedural remedy and only then may he apply for a substantive remedy to claim compensation.

3.302 For example, in *Laijiang Lai v Fuqing Chen and Another*,[325] Laijiang Lai (a retrial applicant who was a third party to the original preservation application) claimed that he was not the party concerned in a debt dispute, but Fuqing Chen and another (two respondents in the retrial application) in the debt dispute had erroneously applied for preservation measures on his own property. Accordingly, Laijiang Lai contended that he was the third party who was entitled to claim compensation due to the erroneous preservation order.

3.303 In the first and second instances, both the primary court and the intermediate court respectively held that the claim of a third party was actually to seek a procedural remedy of an objection against the original preservation order. Laijiang Lai, as the third party, therefore had to first apply for an objection to a preservation order (a procedural remedy). Going further, the two courts held that, only after that route had been followed and order obtained, was he entitled to file a lawsuit to claim compensation (a substantive remedy).

3.304 As a result, the two courts commented that Laijiang Lai did not follow the correct procedure to obtain the procedural remedy and accordingly they disallowed his application.

3.305 Subsequently, that third party applied for a retrial at the High People's Court of Guangdong Province. The High Court clarified that the primary purpose of the third party in this retrial case was to claim compensation. The High People's Court of Guangdong Province overruled the intermediate court's ruling and allowed the claim in the third party's (the claimant in the retrial) favour.

3.306 In this case, although the High People's Court of Guangdong Province did not directly hold that the procedural remedy was a mandatory procedure prior to applying for a substantive remedy, it is noteworthy that the judges, in an *obiter dictum* remark, did not accept the opinion presented by the first instance and second instance courts that the third party must first apply for the procedural remedy seeking an objection to a preservation order.

325 *Laijiang Lai* v *Fuqing Chen and Other* (dispute over damages for a property preservation order) [2017] Yue Civil Retrial No 505 (the High People's Court of Guangdong Province, retrial and binding judgment).

Annex 1

Application for Reconsideration

Applicant: the full name of the company, organisation or other legal entities; a Unified Social Credit Code or the Registration Code.

Legal representative/principal: name, address, contact telephone number (optional), Identification Card Number (optional).

Authorised legal agent: XXXXX Law Firm, the lawyer's name, gender, Identification Card Number, contract number, lawyer's licence number, the lawyer's address.

Respondent: the full name of the company, organisation or other legal entities; a Unified Social Credit Code or the Registration Code.

Legal representative/principal: name, address, contact telephone number (optional), Identification Card Number (optional).

Authorised legal agent: XXXXX Law Firm, the lawyer's name, gender, Identification Card Number, contract number, lawyer's licence number, the lawyer's address.

Item to be requested:

To request the court to revoke the order granting property/behaviour/evidence preservation measures (the exact number of the order)

Facts and grounds:

The court rendered a property/behaviour/evidence order on XXXX (exact date). The number of this order is XXXX In light of this order, the court will take measures on XXXX (specify the exact content and measure of the order). The applicant contends that the purpose of taking the preservation measures is to secure the enforcement of the future judgment/award or to avoid the XXXX possible loss. However, according to the current scenario… (specify the exact facts and reasons). In accordance with Article 108 of the CPL 1991 (as amended until 2020), Article 108 and Interpretation of the CPL 2015, Articles 171 and 172, the applicant hereby applies for the reconsideration of the order granting preservation measure.

Regards

XXXX People's Court

Applicant (signature or stamp)

Date

Attachment: the property/behaviour/evidence order rendered by XXXX People's Court (XXXX).

Note:

1) This format can be used for a reconsideration application in arbitration proceedings.
2) If either the applicant or the respondent is an individual, the information should contain full name, gender, date of birth, ethnicity, employer and occupation, address, contact information.
3) This sample is provided for the reconsideration to revoke the order. In this scenario, the applicant in this form is the respondent of the application seeking the preservation measure. If the court does not approve an application seeking preservation measures, the applicant in the preservation application equally may file a reconsideration to request the court to relook at the application and render a preservation order. In this case, the applicant in the reconsideration form should stress the necessity and importance of the preservation order based on the purpose and requirements of the preservation measures in the circumstances of the case.

Annex 2

Application for Discharging the Preservation Order

Applicant: the full name of the company, organisation or other legal entities; a Unified Social Credit Code or the Registration Code.

Legal representative/principal: name, address, contact telephone number (optional), Identification Card Number (optional).

Authorised legal agent: XXXXX Law Firm, the lawyer's name, gender, Identification Card Number, contract number, lawyer's licence number, the lawyer's address.

Respondent: the full name of company, organisation or other legal entities; a Unified Social Credit Code or the Registration Code.

Legal representative/principal: name, address, contact telephone number (optional), Identification Card Number (optional).

Authorised legal agent: XXXXX Law Firm, the lawyer's name, gender, Identification Card Number, contract number, lawyer's licence number, the lawyer's address.

Items to be requested:

To request the court to discharge the order of property/behaviour/evidence preservation (the exact number of the order).

Facts and grounds:

The court rendered a property/behaviour/evidence order on XXXX (exact date). The number of this order is XXXX. In light of this order, the court takes measures on XXXX (specify the exact content and measure of the order). Currently, the prerequisite of the discharge of this order has been satisfied (specify the exact facts that can satisfy the requirement prescribed by law). The applicant hereby applies for discharging the preservation order.

Regards

XXXX People's Court

Applicant (signature or stamp)

Date

Attachment: the property/behaviour/evidence order rendered by XXXX People's Court (XXXX).

Note:

1) This format can be used for an application in arbitration proceedings.
2) If either the applicant or the respondent is an individual, the information should contain full name, gender, date of birth, ethnicity, employer and occupation, address, contact information.
3) After the applicant submits a preservation application, it is possible for him to withdraw the application. In this case, the application for withdrawing the applicant can refer to this form.
4) The requirement for discharging the preservation order has been provided by the different provisions; the applicant should apply the proper law. Refer to Chapter 3, 288.

PART 2

INTERIM MEASURES IN ARBITRATION

CHAPTER 4

Interim Remedies in Support of Arbitration

Introduction

4.1 London is a leading international centre for commercial arbitration, and English law has long supported arbitration as a form of commercial dispute resolution. In keeping with that approach, English law offers a suite of interim remedies which are designed to support arbitration agreements, the arbitral process and the enforcement of arbitral awards. Certain of these remedies may be granted by the arbitral tribunal itself, but these are often of limited practical use. The English court also has the power to grant a wider range of remedies, including the freezing injunction, the mandatory stay of English court proceedings brought in breach of an arbitration agreement and the interim antisuit injunction to restrain foreign proceedings brought in breach of an arbitration agreement. These court remedies are of much greater utility than ones which can be granted by an arbitral tribunal; but many of them are only available in very limited circumstances, in accordance with English law's policy of respecting party autonomy and restricting the role of the courts in the arbitral process.[1]

The New York Convention

4.2 In keeping with its support for arbitration as a dispute resolution mechanism, the UK is a party to the New York Convention.[2] It currently gives effect to the convention in domestic English law through the Arbitration Act 1996 ("the 1996 Act").[3]

---

1 Departmental Advisory Committee on Arbitration Law (DAC) report on the Arbitration Bill, February 1996, paras 19–22. *Cetelem SA v Roust Holdings Ltd* [2005] EWCA Civ 618 per Clarke LJ at [61].

2 United Nations Convention on the Recognition and Enforcement of Foreign Arbitral Awards; refer also, Chapter 1, 1.9–1.13, for discussion on various issues pertaining to interim measures during arbitration.

3 In particular sections 9, 10, 66 in Part I of the 1996 Act, and sections 100–104 in Part III, which is entitled "Recognition and Enforcement of Certain Foreign Awards". The 1996 Act applies to the whole of the UK apart from Scotland.

DOI: 10.4324/9781003000310-6

4.3 Pursuant to Articles I.1 and III of the New York Convention,[4] the 1996 Act contains several provisions which distinguish between domestic and international arbitration awards.[5] Those provisions of the 1996 Act have never been brought into force,[6] and there is no prospect that they ever will be. In practice, therefore, English domestic law does not recognise any distinction between domestic and international awards.

Part I of the Arbitration Act 1996

4.4 The 1996 Act replaced three earlier Arbitration Acts of 1950, 1975 and 1979.[7] It was enacted principally in response to international criticism that the English court intervened more than it should do in the arbitral process, thereby tending to frustrate the choice the parties had made to use arbitration rather than litigation as the means for resolving their disputes.[8]

4.5 The modern, hands-off, approach of English law is embodied in Part I of the 1996 Act, entitled "Arbitration pursuant to an arbitration agreement". This part contains the bulk of English arbitral procedural law,[9] i.e. the rules of English law governing the arbitration process, including the powers of arbitral tribunals to grant interim remedies. It also contains many of the rules comprising the supervisory jurisdiction of the English court in relation to arbitrations and arbitration agreements, including the power to grant a number of important interim remedies in support of arbitration.

4.6 The structure and content of Part I owe much to the UNCITRAL Model Law on International Commercial Arbitration 1985, although there

---

4 Article I.1 provides: "This Convention shall apply to the recognition and enforcement of arbitral awards made in the territory of a State other than the State where the recognition and enforcement of such awards are sought, and arising out of differences between persons, whether physical or legal. It shall also apply to arbitral awards not considered as domestic awards in the State where their recognition and enforcement are sought". Article III provides: "Each Contracting State shall recognize arbitral awards as binding and enforce them in accordance with the rules of procedure of the territory where the award is relied upon, under the conditions laid down in the following articles. There shall not be imposed substantially more onerous conditions or higher fees or charges on the recognition or enforcement of arbitral awards to which this Convention applies than are imposed on the recognition or enforcement of domestic arbitral awards".

5 Sections 85–88 of the 1996 Act.

6 See section 109 of the 1996 Act and the Arbitration Act 1996 (Commencement No.1) Order, SI 1996/3146, article 3. The distinction between domestic and international arbitration was formerly recognised in English law by section 1 of the Arbitration Act 1975, which was in force between 1975 and 1997.

7 Certain provisions of these earlier statutes remain technically in force, such as Part II of the Arbitration Act 1950 which continues to apply in relation to the enforcement of awards under the Geneva Convention on the Execution of Foreign Arbitral Awards 1927 (see section 99 of the 1996 Act); but their practical relevance is now extremely limited.

8 DAC report on the Arbitration Bill, February 1996, para 21.

9 Sometimes referred to as the *lex arbitri* or curial law; although those expressions are also used to refer to the law of the seat of the arbitration which exercises supervisory jurisdiction over the arbitration and the arbitration agreement.

are some significant differences. A number of provisions in Part I of importance to interim remedies are directly influenced by provisions of the Model Law.[10]

4.7 The general approach of Part I of the 1996 Act (and of English law more broadly towards arbitration) is reflected in section 1, entitled "General principles", which provides that:

a. the object of arbitration is to obtain the fair resolution of disputes by an impartial tribunal without unnecessary delay or expense;
b. the parties should be free to agree how their disputes are resolved, subject only to such safeguards as are necessary in the public interest; and
c. in matters governed by Part I, the English court should not intervene except as provided by Part I.

4.8 Not all of the powers of the English court to grant interim remedies in relation to arbitration arise under the 1996 Act. Of those that do not, the most important by far is the power to grant an interim antisuit injunction restraining a person from bringing foreign proceedings in breach of an arbitration agreement.[11]

Relevance of English Law

4.9 Before examining the availability of interim remedies under English law in the context of arbitration in more detail, it is worth first considering when and how English law applies in relation to arbitration.

4.10 Where a dispute arises under a contract containing an arbitration agreement, a number of different systems of national law may potentially be engaged.[12] These include (i) the law which applies to the substance of the dispute; (ii) the law which governs the agreement to arbitrate;[13] (iii) the law governing the process and procedure of the arbitration (the "curial law"); and (iv) the law of the juridical seat of the arbitration.[14] It is often the case that a

10 See in particular section 9 of the 1996 Act and Article 8 of the Model Law; section 43 and Article 27; section 44 and Article 9. No changes have been made to the 1996 Act in light of the amendments which were made to the Model Law in 2006.

11 *AES Ust-Kamenogorsk Hydropower Plant LLP v Ust-Kamenogorsk Hydropower Plant JSC* [2013] UKSC 35 per Lord Mance JSC at [48].

12 David St John Sutton, Judith Gill, Matthew Gearing, *Russell on Arbitration* (24th Edn, Sweet & Maxwell, 2015) §7-036, §2-113 identifies as many as eight.

13 This may be different from the law governing the substantive dispute. In accordance with the doctrine of separability enshrined in section 7 of the 1996 Act, an arbitration clause which appears in a contract is regarded, for the purposes of validity, as a distinct agreement from the rest of the contract, and is capable of being governed by a different law from the rest of the contract: *Enka Insaat ve Sanayi AS v OOO "Insurance Company Chubb"* [2020] UKSC 38 per Lord Hamblen JSC at [40]–[42].

14 *Enka Insaat ve Sanayi AS v OOO "Insurance Company Chubb"* [2020] UKSC 38 per Lord Hamblen JSC at [1].

single system of national law will govern all of these matters, but that is not always so, especially in international commercial contracts.

4.11 The question of which national law governs each of these matters is a question of conflicts of law, which falls to be determined in accordance with the conflict of laws rules of the court or tribunal which has to determine the question. Thus, the English court will apply English conflict of laws rules when determining these matters.

4.12 In the context of interim remedies, the seat and the procedural law of the arbitration are of primary importance. Under English law:

a. Every arbitration must have a juridical seat.[15] The seat of an arbitration is distinct from the geographical venue at which hearings physically take place, and also from the location where the arbitral award is physically signed. The significance of the seat is not practical but legal. It determines where an arbitral award is made, for the purposes of determining whether it is an award governed by the New York Convention. It also determines, for most purposes, which country's courts have power to exercise supervisory and supporting jurisdiction in relation to an arbitration and an arbitration agreement.[16]
b. The seat of an arbitration may be designated by the parties to the arbitration agreement, or by a person or institution chosen by the parties, or by the arbitral tribunal if the parties so agree. Where the seat is not designated in one of these ways, the seat is determined having regard to the parties' agreement and all the relevant circumstances.[17]
c. Where the seat of an arbitration is in England and Wales, the English court has the power to exercise supervisory and supporting jurisdiction over the arbitration and the arbitration agreement, including the power to grant interim remedies, including antisuit injunctions and remedies governed by Part I of the 1996 Act.[18] The parties can exclude some, but not all, of the court's supervisory and supporting powers by agreement.[19]
d. The parties to an arbitration are, for the most part, free to choose the procedural law of the arbitration. Where the seat of the arbitration is

15 *Arab National Bank v El-Abdali* [2004] EWHC 2381 (Comm) per Morison J at [14].

16 See generally *Enka Insaat ve Sanayi AS v OOO "Insurance Company Chubb"* [2020] EWCA Civ 574 per Popplewell LJ at [42]–[53]; [2020] UKSC 38 per Lord Hamblen JSC at [174] & [179], and see Lord Burrows (dissenting) at [193(ii)(e)] where he referred to the court's "curial or supervisory jurisdiction".

17 Section 3 of the 1996 Act.

18 *Enka Insaat ve Sanayi AS v OOO "Insurance Company Chubb"* [2020] UKSC 38 per Lord Hamblen JSC at [174].

19 Where the powers arise under "non-mandatory" provisions in Part I of the 1996 Act, the parties can exclude them by agreement under section 4(2)–(5) of the 1996 Act: see below.

in England, Wales or Northern Ireland, most of the rules of English arbitral procedural law contained in Part I of the 1996 Act apply unless the parties otherwise agree.[20] The provisions of the 1996 Act which contain these rules are referred to as "non-mandatory" provisions. Some provisions allow the parties to make their own arrangements by agreement but provide rules which apply in the absence of such agreement. Others simply set out what matters the parties are free to agree, but provide no default rules in the absence of such agreement.

e. Part I of the 1996 Act also contains a number of rules of English arbitral procedural law which apply compulsorily, whenever the seat of the arbitration is in England, Wales or Northern Ireland.[21] The parties cannot contract out of these "mandatory" provisions, either by specific agreement or by choosing a procedural law of the arbitration other than English law.

f. Finally, Part I of the 1996 Act contains a number of provisions which apply even where the seat of the arbitration is not in England, Wales or Northern Ireland, or where no seat has been designated or determined.[22] These include provisions which give the English court the power to grant interim remedies in relation to arbitrations. Most of these provisions, including those which govern the mandatory stay of English proceedings brought in breach of an arbitration agreement, are themselves mandatory, meaning that the parties are unable to contract out of them. But the most important provision, which governs the English court's power to grant freezing injunctions and other interim remedies in support of arbitration proceedings, is non-mandatory, meaning that the parties are free to agree to exclude the power of the English court to grant those remedies if they so choose.[23]

4.13 Where the parties are free to choose matters such as the seat of the arbitration, the procedural law of the arbitration and the application of non-mandatory provisions of Part I of the 1996 Act, that choice is generally to be found in their arbitration agreement, or in the rules of any arbitration body or institution to which they have agreed to refer their dispute, such as the International Chamber of Commerce, the London Court of International Arbitration or one of the many other regional or industry-specific arbitration bodies that have been established around the world in the past half-century.

20 Sections 2(1) and 4(2) of the 1996 Act.
21 Sections 2(1), 4(1) and Schedule 1 of the 1996 Act.
22 See section 2(2)–(5) of the 1996 Act.
23 Section 44 of the 1996 Act.

Power of Arbitral Tribunals to Grant Interim Remedies

4.14 English law recognises three forms in which an arbitral tribunal can grant a remedy in an arbitration: (i) an **order**, (ii) a **provisional award**, which determines an issue provisionally, subject to the tribunal's later final adjudication, and (iii) a **final award**, which determines an issue with final and binding effect.[24]

4.15 Under English law, an arbitral tribunal may, depending on the agreement of the parties, have the power to grant interim remedies in the form of an order.[25] It may also have the power to grant certain types of interim remedy in the form of a provisional award,[26] again depending on the agreement of the parties. It cannot, however, grant interim remedies in the form of a final award.[27] The practical significance of this is explained below.[28]

Orders

4.16 The power of an arbitral tribunal to grant interim remedies in the form of an order depends on the agreement of the parties, which in practice usually means the terms of whichever arbitral rules which the parties have agreed upon. Section 38(1) of the 1996 Act provides that the parties are "free to agree on the powers exercisable by the arbitral tribunal for the purposes of and in relation to the proceedings", without imposing any explicit limits on those powers. Many sets of arbitral rules confer very broad powers on arbitral tribunals to grant interim remedies by order. In some cases, the powers conferred by the arbitral rules are ostensibly unlimited. Thus, for example, Article 28 of the ICC Arbitration Rules 2021 provides that, unless the parties have otherwise agreed, the arbitral tribunal may, by order, grant "any interim or conservatory measure it deems appropriate"; and Article 29 of those Rules provides that an Emergency Arbitrator may be appointed and may exercise the same power, where a party needs urgent interim or conservatory measures that cannot await the constitution of an arbitral tribunal.

24 See sections 20–22, 38, 39, 47 and 58 of the 1996 Act. The 1996 Act also refers to a fourth type of act, a decision (see sections 20–22, 33, 47 and 54), but for that to be capable of enforcement, it must be embodied in an award or an order.

25 Under sections 38 and/or 39 of the 1996 Act.

26 Under section 39 of the 1996 Act.

27 David St John Sutton, Judith Gill, Matthew Gearing, *Russell on Arbitration* (24th Edn, Sweet & Maxwell, 2015) §7-036, §5-082; *Ronly Holdings Ltd v JSC Zestafoni G Nikoladze Ferroalloy Plant* [2004] EWHC 1354 (Comm) per Colman J at [23]. This is subject to one possible exception: in *Kastner v Jason* [2004] EWHC 592 (Ch) Lightman J suggested *obiter* at [27] that, where an arbitral tribunal made a final award granting substantive relief on the merits of the dispute (e.g. damages), it could also include in the final award an interim remedy such as a freezing injunction, to apply pending the satisfaction or the securing of the award of substantive relief, much like a freezing injunction granted by a court post-judgment.

28 See 4.25 below.

4.17 In the absence of a specific agreement, section 38 of the 1996 Act contains a suite of default powers to make orders, which an arbitral tribunal can exercise for the purposes of and in relation to arbitral proceedings. These include the power to order security for costs, powers relating to the examination of witnesses and the power to order two other important forms of interim relief:

a. The power to give directions in relation to any property which is the subject of the proceedings or as to which any question arises in the proceedings, and which is owned by or is in the possession of a party to the proceedings, (i) for the inspection, photographing, preservation, custody or detention of the property by the tribunal, an expert or a party, or (ii) ordering that samples be taken from, or any observation be made of or experiment conducted upon, the property.[29] These powers resemble the powers of the English court in relation to court proceedings under CPR 25.1(1)(c)(ii)–(iv), but they are more limited in a number of respects. In particular, the power of the arbitral tribunal only extends to property which is owned by or in the possession of a party to the proceedings; it does not extend to property which is merely within the custody or control of a party. Nor is there any power in the tribunal equivalent to CPR 25.1(d), to authorise a person to enter premises for the purposes of carrying out such an order.
b. The power to give directions to a party for the preservation for the purposes of the proceedings of any evidence in his custody or control.[30] This power bears some resemblance to the English court's powers under CPR 25.1(1)(c)(i) and 25.1(1)(h), but without any power to authorise a person to enter premises.

Provisional Awards

4.18 The power of an arbitral tribunal to grant interim remedies by way of a provisional award is also, in part, dependent on the agreement of the parties. That power is derived from section 39 of the 1996 Act which is entitled "Power to make provisional awards". Subsection 39(1) provides that the parties are free to agree that the tribunal shall have "power to order on a provisional basis any relief which it would have power to grant in a final award".[31] Subsection 39(2) contains two examples of the power which the parties can agree to confer on the arbitral tribunal under that section: the power to make a provisional order for the payment of money or the disposition of property

29 Subsection 38(4) of the 1996 Act.
30 Subsection 38(6) of the 1996 Act.
31 It appears that the parties can confer the power on an arbitral tribunal to make both orders and provisional awards under this provision: Robert Merkin QC, Louis Flannery QC, *Merkin and Flannery on the Arbitration Act 1996* (6th Edn, Informa Law, 2019) §39.1.

as between the parties, and an order to make an interim payment on account of the costs of the arbitration.

4.19 The scope of section 39 is not well worked out in the authorities. It is clear, however, that any power to make provisional awards which the parties can agree to confer on the arbitral tribunal under that section is limited to provisional versions of relief which the tribunal would have power to grant in a final award.[32] That seems to include the power to grant an interim injunction,[33] at least where the injunction is a temporary or provisional version of one which the arbitral tribunal would have power to grant as the final, substantive relief in the proceedings (such as an interim injunction temporarily restraining a Respondent from committing an allegedly unlawful act while the arbitral tribunal determines the Claimant's substantive claim for a final injunction restraining the Respondent permanently in the same terms). There is no consensus on whether it would also include forms of interim relief that can only ever be granted on an exclusively interim basis, such as freezing injunctions.[34]

4.20 Subject to these possible legal limitations, many sets of arbitral rules give the arbitral tribunal broad powers to grant interim remedies by way of provisional award. A well-known example is Article 28 of the ICC Arbitration Rules 2021, referred to above, which empowers an arbitral tribunal to grant any interim or conservatory measures, either in the form of an order "or of an award, as the arbitral tribunal considers appropriate".

Limitations of the Power of Arbitral Tribunals

4.21 Regardless of the apparent breadth of the parties' agreement, the powers of an arbitral tribunal to grant interim remedies, whether in the form of an order or a provisional award, are inherently limited. The private and consensual nature of arbitration means that an arbitral tribunal can never grant an interim remedy against a person who is not a party to the arbitration.[35] Of more practical significance, it also means that an arbitral tribunal lacks any effective means to enforce compliance with its interim remedies, such as by imposing penal sanctions on a party[36] for breach of its orders, such as fines, confiscation of assets or imprisonment.[37]

---

32 The power of an arbitral tribunal to grant remedies by way of final award is governed by section 48 of the 1996 Act.

33 See subsection 48(5) of the 1996 Act which, in default of agreement by the parties, gives the arbitral tribunal the same powers as the court to make a final award ordering a party to do or refrain from doing anything.

34 See generally *Kastner v Jason* [2004] EWCA Civ 1599 per Rix LJ at [15]–[19].

35 *Pacific Marine (Asia) Ltd v Holystone Overseas Ltd* [2007] EWHHC 2319 (Comm) per Christopher Clarke J at [80].

36 Still less can it do so against a non-party who aids and abets a breach of its orders by a party, or who deliberately subverts its orders.

37 That is so despite the ostensibly unfettered right of the parties in section 41(1) of the 1996 Act to agree on the powers of the tribunal "in case of a party's failure to do something

4.22 The problem of enforcement has a partial solution, in that the party seeking to enforce an interim remedy granted the arbitral tribunal may be able to apply to the English court for assistance. As we shall see, however, this solution is not particularly effective in practice in most cases.

4.23 An order of an arbitral tribunal granting an interim remedy can be enforced by applying to the English court for an order under section 42 of the 1996 Act. Under that provision, the court has the power to make its own order requiring the party against whom enforcement is sought (the Respondent) to comply with the tribunal's order. Failure to comply with the court's order can then be punished as a contempt of court. The section 42 procedure is, however, only available if the seat of the arbitration is in England, Wales or Northern Ireland; and the parties can exclude it altogether by agreement. Where the procedure is available, it is slow and cumbersome, and of limited usefulness, particularly in cases where the interim remedy is required urgently. It can only be used where the Respondent has failed to comply with the tribunal's order within the time prescribed in that order or, if no time was prescribed, within a reasonable time. The party seeking to enforce the order (the Applicant)[38] may have to obtain the permission of the tribunal before applying to the court. He will have to issue a Part 8 Claim Form claiming the relief sought, together with evidence in support, and serve it on the Respondent, who will then be entitled to serve evidence in response in the usual way, before the court determines the application.[39] In order to succeed, the Applicant will also have to satisfy the court that he has exhausted any available arbitral process in respect of failure to comply with the tribunal's order.

4.24 Similarly, a provisional award of an arbitral tribunal granting an interim remedy can be enforced in the English court by applying for permission to enforce the award in the same manner as a judgment or order of the court to the same effect, under section 66 of the 1996 Act. This provision is available for both provisional and final awards, and regardless of where the award was made.[40] Once again, however, the applicable procedure is not well suited to situations involving urgency. The Applicant must issue a Part 8 Claim Form together with written evidence as required by CPR 62.18(6), and the court may require him to serve it on the Respondent. If the application succeeds and the court grants permission to enforce the award under section 66, the Applicant cannot enforce the award in that manner for at least 14 days after the order granting permission has been served on the Respondent.[41]

necessary for the proper and expeditious conduct of the arbitration".

38 For an explanation of the terms Claimant, Defendant, Applicant and Respondent, see Chapter 2, 2.29–2.30.

39 CPR 62.4–7, CPR PD 62 §6.1–6.7.

40 Section 2(2)(b) of the 1996 Act; CPR 62.18(4).

41 CPR 62.18.

4.25 It may be also possible to enforce orders and provisional awards granting interim remedies, made by arbitral tribunals in England, in the courts of other countries. That will depend upon the domestic law of the country where enforcement is sought, and upon the ability to found jurisdiction there. It is, however, clear that enforcement is not available under the New York Convention, as that convention only applies to final awards.[42] Accordingly, if such orders and provisional awards can be enforced at all in the courts of other countries, the applicable procedures are likely to be even slower and more cumbersome than those required for enforcement in the English court.

4.26 A further practical problem with seeking interim remedies from an arbitral tribunal is that an arbitral tribunal can only grant a remedy once it has been properly constituted. Depending on the terms of the arbitration agreement, constituting the tribunal may take some time, and may require the cooperation of the party against whom an interim remedy is sought. In most cases, this will effectively preclude a party from applying for urgent interim relief from the tribunal at the very start of arbitral proceedings. Some sets of arbitral rules, such as the ICC Arbitration Rules 2021 and the LCIA Arbitration Rules 2020, seek to alleviate this problem by providing a mechanism for the appointment of an Emergency Arbitrator to deal with very urgent applications prior to the constitution of the main tribunal. However, both the ICC and LCIA procedures require an application to an Emergency Arbitrator to be made on notice to the Respondent,[43] which means that even this mechanism will be ineffective where there is very great urgency or where there is a need for secrecy, as is often the case with interim remedies.

Powers of the English Court to Grant Interim Remedies in Relation to Arbitration

4.27 The 1996 Act gives the English court the power to grant a range of interim remedies in relation to arbitration. The most important source of these powers is section 44, entitled "Court powers exercisable in support of arbitral proceedings".

Section 44 of the 1996 Act

4.28 Section 44 is a non-mandatory[44] provision of the 1996 Act, meaning that the parties can contract out of it if they choose. It gives the English court,

---

42 See generally Robert Merkin QC, Louis Flannery QC, *Merkin and Flannery on the Arbitration Act 1996* (6th Edn, Informa Law, 2019) §§39.1, 101.13.1.

43 ICC Arbitration Rules 2021, Appendix V, Articles 1.5, 2.3, 3.1 and 5.2; LCIA Arbitration Rules 2020, Article 9.5. David St John Sutton, Judith Gill, Matthew Gearing, *Russell on Arbitration* (24th Edn, Sweet & Maxwell, 2015) §7-036, suggests at §5-080 that arbitral tribunals cannot grant without notice applications under English law, even if the parties agree to confer the power on them to do so.

44 See section 4 and Schedule 1 of the 1996 Act.

in certain narrowly defined circumstances, the same power to make orders for the purposes of and in relation to arbitral proceedings, as it has for the purposes of and in relation to legal proceedings. The English court can exercise that power in relation to arbitral proceedings which have England, Wales or Northern Ireland as their seat; and also, under certain conditions, where the seat of the arbitration is outside England and Wales or Northern Ireland or no seat has been designated or determined.[45]

4.29 The English court's power under section 44 is limited to making orders about five categories of "matter".[46] These are:

a. The taking of evidence of witnesses.[47]
b. The preservation of evidence.[48] This is wide enough to cover search orders, which the English court has the power to grant for the purposes of and in relation to legal proceedings under section 7 of the Civil Procedure Act 1997and CPR 25.1(1)(h).
c. Making orders relating to property which is the subject of the proceedings or as to which any question arises in the proceedings:[49]
   i. For the inspection, photographing, preservation, custody or detention of the property.
   ii. Or ordering that samples be taken from, or any observation be made of or experiment conducted upon, the property ("and for that purpose authorising any person to enter any premises in the possession or control of a party to the arbitration").
d. The sale of any goods the subject of the proceedings.[50]
e. The granting of an interim injunction or the appointment of a receiver. This is wide enough to cover ordinary interim injunctions

45 Section 2(3) of the 1996 Act. This provision and its effect are discussed in Chapter 2, 2.71(c).

46 See section 44(2)(a)–(e) of the 1996 Act.

47 The English court can grant an order under this provision against a person who is not a party to the arbitration: **A v C** [2020] EWCA Civ 409 per Flaux LJ at [35] and per Males LJ at [57]. The court's power to make orders about these matters for the purposes of and in relation to legal proceedings is contained in CPR Part 34, entitled "Witnesses, Depositions and Evidence for Foreign Courts".

48 Section 38(6) of the 1996 Act confers a similar power on the arbitral tribunal, unless otherwise agreed by the parties, to give directions to a party for the preservation for the purposes of the proceedings of any evidence in his custody or control. The corresponding power of the English court under section 44 is not limited to evidence in a party's custody and control. There is conflicting authority at first instance over whether the English court can make an order under this provision against a person who is not a party to the arbitration: in *Assimina Maritime Ltd v Pakistan Shipping Corp (The Tasman Spirit)* [2004] EWHC 3005 (Comm) Colman J held at [14]–[15] that it can; whereas in *DTEK Trading SA v Morozov* Sara Cockerill QC held that it cannot. In light of the Court of Appeal's decision in *A v C* [2020] EWCA Civ 409, *The Tasman Spirit* appears more likely to be correct on this point.

49 The power of the English court to make orders about these matters in relation to legal proceedings is contained in CPR 25.1(1)(c).

50 This refers to the power in CPR 25.1(1)(c)(v).

and freezing injunctions, which the English court has power to grant for the purposes of and in relation to legal proceedings under section 37 of the Senior Courts Act 1981 and CPR 25.1(1)(a) and (f).

4.30 The power to grant orders under section 44 is also limited in a number of other ways. These limitations are designed to uphold the principles of party autonomy and judicial non-interference which underpin English arbitration law.

4.31 First, the English court can only act if or to the extent that the arbitral tribunal, and any arbitral or other institution or person vested by the parties with power in that regard (such as an Emergency Arbitrator, where one is available under the applicable arbitral rules), either has no power to act effectively, or is unable to act effectively for the time being.[51]

4.32 This requirement may be satisfied in a number of ways:[52] the arbitral tribunal may not yet have been constituted at the time when the interim remedy is required; there may be a need for the interim remedy to bind a third party and/or to be backed by coercive powers in order to ensure compliance, which is beyond the power of any arbitral tribunal; the interim remedy may be one which this particular arbitral tribunal lacks the power to grant, or which no arbitral tribunal would ever have power to grant (such as a freezing injunction); there may be a need for urgency or secrecy requiring that the application for the interim remedy be made without notice, which the arbitral tribunal has no power to entertain.

4.33 Secondly, if the case is not one of urgency, the English court can only act once the arbitration proceedings have been commenced, and then only with the permission of the tribunal or the written agreement of the other parties.[53]

4.34 Thirdly, if the case is one of urgency, the English court can act either before or after the commencement of arbitration proceedings, and it does not need the permission of the tribunal (if constituted) or the agreement of the other parties to do so; but in such circumstances it can only grant orders which it considers necessary for the purposes of preserving evidence or assets.[54] This is important as it means that the English court can grant urgent freezing injunctions and search orders, in support of pending or proposed arbitration proceedings, and can do so on a without-notice application where necessary for reasons of urgency and/or secrecy.

---

51 Subsection 44(5) of the 1996 Act.

52 See David St John Sutton, Judith Gill, Matthew Gearing, *Russell on Arbitration* (24th Edn, Sweet & Maxwell, 2015) §7-036, §5-080; Robert Merkin QC, Louis Flannery QC, *Merkin and Flannery on the Arbitration Act 1996* (6th Edn, Informa Law, 2019) §44.8; Steven Gee QC, *Gee on Commercial Injunctions* (7th Edn, Sweet & Maxwell, 2020) §6-046.

53 Subsection 44(4) of the 1996 Act.

54 Subsection 44(3) of the 1996 Act.

4.35 The procedure for applying for an interim remedy under section 44 of the 1996 Act is set out in CPR Part 62 and the accompanying Practice Direction. The application is made by issuing a Part 8 Claim Form. Where the person against whom the remedy is sought (the Defendant) is not amenable to service of the Claim Form within England and Wales, the English court can grant permission to serve it out of the jurisdiction under CPR 62.5(1)(b).

Section 44 and Non-Parties

4.36 The precise scope of the English court's jurisdiction under section 44 of the 1996 Act is still being worked out by the authorities. Two questions which have given rise to controversy are:

a. When, if ever, can the English court make an order under section 44 against a person who is not a party to the arbitration (or, where arbitral proceedings have not yet been commenced at the time of the application, a party to the arbitration agreement)? This is a question of subject-matter jurisdiction.[55]
b. When, if ever, can the English court grant permission to serve a Claim Form claiming relief under section 44 out of the jurisdiction on a non-party? That is a question of personal jurisdiction, which goes to the width of the jurisdictional gateway in CPR 62.5(1)(b).

4.37 These questions arise most acutely in relation to the English court's so-called ***Chabra*** jurisdiction.[56] That refers to the power of the English court to grant a freezing injunction against a person (Defendant 2) in support of a substantive claim by the Claimant against another person (Defendant 1), even though the Claimant asserts no substantive claim against Defendant 2. The basis of this power is that Defendant 2 holds assets which ought to be available to satisfy the Claimant's claim against Defendant 1. That may be because the assets belong in reality to Defendant 1, and Defendant 2 holds them simply as nominee or trustee for the benefit of Defendant 1; or because Defendant 2 is under some other kind of obligation to restore the assets or their value to Defendant 1.[57]

---

55 See Chapter 2, 2.65.

56 This takes its name from the case of *TSB Private Bank International SA v Chabra* [1992] 1 WLR 231, where existence of this jurisdiction was confirmed by the English Court of Appeal.

57 As in the leading Australian case of *Cardile v LED Builders Pty Ltd* [1999] HCA 18, in which Defendant 2 was under an obligation to restore the value of assets which he had removed from Defendant 1 (a company which he had controlled, and which was now insolvent), under the provisions of an Australian insolvency statute.

4.38 In ***Cruz City 1 Mauritius Holdings v Unitech***,[58] Males J considered a number of previous authorities and concluded, *obiter*, that section 44 of the 1996 Act does not give the English court power to grant an interim injunction, or any other kind of order, against a non-party to the arbitration or arbitration agreement.[59] It followed, in his view, that CPR 62.5(1)(b) did not permit a Claim Form seeking section 44 relief against a non-party to be served out of the jurisdiction; but he accepted that, if he was wrong on the first point, then CPR 62.5(1)(b) would permit service out against a non-party.[60]

4.39 More recently, however, in ***A v C***,[61] the English Court of Appeal has confirmed that the English court does have the power to make an order against a non-party under section 44(2)(a) of the 1996 Act, which covers orders about the taking of evidence of witnesses. One of the judges of the Court of Appeal in that case was Males LJ, now promoted. Although the court was careful to confine its decision to the scope of subsection 44(2)(a), it seems likely that the English courts will now move away from the position stated in ***Cruz City*** and accept that interim remedies including ***Chabra*** freezing injunctions are available against non-parties under section 44, and that permission to serve out can be granted under CPR 62.5(1)(b), subject to considerations of discretion and comity.[62]

Stay of English Court Proceedings

4.40 Article II.3 of the New York Convention requires the courts of a Contracting State, when seized of an action in a matter in respect of which the parties have made an agreement in writing to submit differences to arbitration, to refer the parties to arbitration if one of them requests it, unless it finds that the arbitration agreement is null and void, inoperative or incapable of being performed.

4.41 Pursuant to the UK's obligations under that provision, section 9 of the 1996 Act gives a party to an arbitration agreement the right to seek a mandatory stay of English court proceedings (including a counterclaim) brought in breach of that arbitration agreement, in favour of arbitration, by issuing an application under CPR Part 23 in those proceedings.[63] An application may not be brought by a person after he has taken any step in the English court proceedings to answer the substantive claim.[64] For these purposes, a

58 [2014] EWHC 3704 (Comm).

59 See [46]–[50].

60 At [51].

61 [2020] EWCA Civ 409.

62 That development will be welcomed by leading commentators. See in particular Steven Gee QC, *Gee on Commercial Injunctions* (7th Edn, Sweet & Maxwell, 2020) §§6-039 to 6-045; Merkin & Flannery on the Arbitration Act 1996, 6th Ed 2020, §44.7.5.

63 CPR 62.3(2).

64 Subsection 9(3) of the 1996 Act.

relevant step is one which invokes the jurisdiction of the court and demonstrates an election to abandon the right to a stay. Where the conditions of section 9 are satisfied, the English court must grant a stay,[65] unless satisfied that the arbitration agreement is null and void, inoperative or incapable of being performed.[66]

4.42 Section 9 of the 1996 Act applies, not only as between original parties to an arbitration agreement, but also as between persons claiming under or through an original party,[67] such as the subrogated insurer of a party to a contract containing an arbitration clause who takes a legal assignment of the assured's claim under the contract and brings proceedings in his own name in the English court to enforce that claim.[68]

4.43 Section 9 of the 1996 Act applies regardless of whether arbitration proceedings have been, or ever will be, commenced in relation to the dispute, and regardless of where the seat of any such arbitral proceedings is or may be situated. This reflects the fact that, unlike the English court's powers in section 44 of the 1996 Act, section 9 exists, not "for the purposes of and in relation to arbitral proceedings", but for the purposes of and in relation to the "negative promise" contained in the arbitration agreement, whereby each party undertakes not to bring proceedings in respect of disputes which are covered by the arbitration agreement otherwise than by arbitration in accordance with that arbitration agreement. This negative promise applies and is enforceable regardless of whether or not arbitral proceedings are under way or proposed.[69]

Interim Antisuit Injunctions in Support of Arbitration

4.44 The reasoning which underpins section 9 of the 1996 Act also forms the rationale for the English court's discretionary power to grant antisuit injunctions restraining a party to an arbitration agreement from commencing

65 *JSC Aeroflot Russian Airlines v Berezovsky* [2013] EWCA Civ 784 per Aikens LJ at [98] The English court also has an inherent power, rarely exercised, to grant a discretionary stay of court proceedings where the requirements of section 9 are not (or not yet) satisfied, for example where the interests of justice are best served by allowing the putative arbitral tribunal to determine, in the first instance, whether or not there really is a concluded arbitration agreement between the parties: *Microsoft Mobile Oy (Ltd) v Sony Europe Ltd* [2017] EWHC 374 (Ch) per Marcus Smith J at [84].

66 Subsection 9(4) of the 1996 Act: these words mirror those of Art II.3 of the New York Convention.

67 Such persons are regarded as parties to the arbitration agreement for the purposes of Part I of the 1996 Act: see section 82(2).

68 *Schiffahrtsgesellschaft Detlev von Appen GmbH v Voest Alpine Intertrading GmbH (The Jay Bola)* [1997] 2 Lloyd's Rep 279 (CA), per Hobhouse LJ at page 285, discussing the corresponding provisions of the Arbitration Acts 1950 and 1975.

69 *AES Ust-Kamenogorsk Hydropower Plant LLP v Ust-Kamenogorsk Hydropower Plant JSC* [2013] UKSC 35 per Lord Mance JSC at [48] and [60], discussing the English court's power to grant antisuit injunctions to restrain foreign court proceedings brought in breach of an arbitration agreement.

or pursuing foreign court proceedings in breach of the arbitration agreement. Indeed, these two powers have been described as two "opposite and complementary" sides of the same coin.[70]

4.45 The discretionary power to grant such antisuit injunctions forms part of the English court's supervisory and supporting jurisdiction over arbitrations and arbitration agreements.[71] It arises, not under the 1996 Act, but under section 37 of the Senior Courts Act 1981, which confirms that the English court can grant an injunction in all cases in which it appears to be just and convenient to do so.[72] As this type of antisuit injunction is aimed at preventing a breach of the negative promise in the arbitration agreement, it is available regardless of whether or not arbitral proceedings are under way or even proposed.

4.46 Where it is shown that the foreign proceedings are brought in breach of an arbitration agreement, the Court will ordinarily exercise its discretion to restrain those proceedings by an antisuit injunction, provided that it is sought promptly and before the foreign proceedings are too far advanced, unless the Defendant can show strong reasons for the court to refuse the relief.[73]

4.47 As with section 9 of the 1996 Act, the English court's power to grant antisuit injunctions on this basis is not limited to cases involving the original parties to the arbitration agreement. It applies equally to cases involving persons claiming under or through an original party as a legal assignee or transferee[74] of the original party's contractual rights. It also applies to cases where a third party T, who has a claim against an assured A, seeks to enforce A's contractual rights under his insurance policy with insurer I (which contains an arbitration clause) by bringing proceedings directly against I, under a so-called "direct action" statute.[75] In these and similar situations, English law treats the "remote party" bringing the claim as effectively bound by the

70 *AES Ust-Kamenogorsk Hydropower Plant LLP v Ust-Kamenogorsk Hydropower Plant JSC* [2013] UKSC 35 per Lord Mance JSC at [60].

71 *Enka Insaat ve Sanayi AS v OOO "Insurance Company Chubb"* [2020] UKSC 38 per Lord Hamblen JSC at [174].

72 *AES Ust-Kamenogorsk Hydropower Plant LLP v Ust-Kamenogorsk Hydropower Plant JSC* [2013] UKSC 35 per Lord Mance JSC at [48].

73 *Aggeliki Charis Compania Maritima SA v Pagnan SpA (The Angelic Grace)* [1995] 1 Lloyd's Rep 87 (CA) per Millett LJ at page 96.

74 Such as a person who becomes the lawful holder of a bill of lading containing an arbitration agreement, and so has all rights of suit under the bill of lading contract transferred to him under section 2(1) of the UK Carriage of Goods by Sea Act 1992: *Sea Master Shipping Inc v Arab Bank (Switzerland) Ltd* [2018] EWHC 1902 (Comm) per Popplewell J at [39]–[42].

75 Such statutes exist under a number of national laws, but not under English law. The person bringing a claim under such a direct-action statute is effectively bound by the arbitration clause in the insurance policy, despite not being a party to that agreement "in the full sense": *London Steam-Ship Owners' Mutual Insurance Association Ltd v Kingdom of Spain* [2013] EWHC 3188 (Comm) per Hamblen J at [136].

negative promise in the arbitration agreement, in much the same way as the original party would be.[76]

4.48 Prior to 2021, the scope of the power of the English court to grant antisuit injunctions was restricted by European Union law, which prevents the courts of an EU member state from granting an antisuit injunction to restrain proceedings in the courts of another EU or EFTA member state in civil or commercial matters.[77] This restriction disappeared when the UK ceased to be bound by EU law, on 31 December 2020. It may make a comeback, if the UK is permitted to rejoin the 2007 Lugano Convention as an independent state; but at the time of writing, that looks unlikely.[78]

4.49 The preceding paragraphs have discussed antisuit injunctions generally, rather than **interim** antisuit injunctions in particular. It is important to recognise that antisuit injunctions are not granted for the purposes of and in relation to arbitral proceedings, or substantive proceedings in a foreign court. Rather, they are available from the English court as a final, substantive, remedy for an actual or threatened breach of contract (the negative promise contained in an arbitration agreement) or for actual or threatened vexatious oppressive conduct.[79] The English court has power to grant antisuit injunctions on an **interim** basis as well as on a final basis; and indeed, most antisuit injunctions in support of arbitration are initially granted on an interim basis. But unlike interim injunctions under subsection 44(2)(e) of the 1996 Act, an **interim** antisuit injunction cannot be granted by way of final relief. It can only be granted by way of **interlocutory** relief, in proceedings in which the Claimant claims a substantive antisuit injunction by way of final relief.[80]

4.50 On an interlocutory application for an interim antisuit injunction, the Claimant must demonstrate to a high degree of probability that there is an arbitration agreement which governs the dispute in question and that

---

76 *Shipowners' Mutual Protection and Indemnity Association (Luxembourg) v Containerships Denizcilik Nakliyat Ve Ticaret AS (The Yusuf Cepnioglu)* [2016] EWCA Civ 386 per Longmore LJ at [21], [24], [32]–[35], and per Moore-Bick LJ at [50]–[55]. The precise juridical basis for treating a "remote party" in this way is still under debate: see the discussion in *Times Trading Corp v National Bank of Fujairah (Dubai Branch)* [2020] EWHC 1078 (Comm) per Cockerill J at [51]–[78].

77 *West Tankers Inc v Allianz SpA (The Front Comor)*, CJEU Case C-185/07, [2009] 1 AC 1138.

78 See the European Commission communication to the European Parliament and Council, "Assessment on the Application of the United Kingdom of Great Britain and Northern Ireland to Accede to the 2007 Lugano Convention", COM(2021) 222 final, dated 4 May 2021, which suggests that the EU is unlikely to forgive the UK for Brexit any time soon.

79 Thus, a final antisuit injunction granted to restrain proceedings in breach of an arbitration agreement gives rise to an issue estoppel *per rem judicatam* in future proceedings on the issue of the existence of the arbitration agreement: *AES Ust-Kamenogorsk Hydropower Plant LLP v Ust-Kamenogorsk Hydropower Plant JSC* [2013] UKSC 35 per Lord Mance JSC at [18].

80 See Chapter 2, 2.33–2.40 and 2.79.

the Defendant is bound[81] by the negative promise which it contains.[82] This is a much more exacting standard than the standard of serious question to be tried,[83] which applies to most applications for ordinary interim injunctions. It reflects the fact that the English court approaches the granting of antisuit injunctions with circumspection, for reasons of international comity. This arises from the fact that, although an antisuit injunction is addressed to the Defendant and not to the foreign court, it may be seen by the foreign court as an unwarranted interference with its right to control its own jurisdiction.[84]

4.51 If this standard is met, the English court may nevertheless refuse to grant an interim antisuit injunction if the Defendant shows strong reasons not to grant it. The primary considerations here will be the extent of any delay in seeking the injunction, the justifications for that delay, the effect of that delay on the Defendant and on the foreign proceedings and whether the Claimant has voluntarily taken any substantive steps to defend the foreign proceedings beyond simply challenging the jurisdiction of the foreign court.[85]

4.52 The English court has power to permit service of a Claim Form claiming an antisuit injunction out of the jurisdiction under CPR 62.5(1)(c). This provision requires that the seat of the arbitration is or will be in England and Wales. But, as an antisuit injunction is available even where the Claimant has no intention of ever commencing arbitration, this requirement is treated as being satisfied if the seat of any arbitration, "if any were to be commenced or proposed under the arbitration agreement", would be in England and Wales.[86] Where the arbitration agreement is governed by English law, permission to serve out may also be granted under CPR PD 6B §3.1(c). In either case, the English court will inevitably be the appropriate forum for seeking the antisuit injunction.[87]

---

81 Or that he is to be treated as bound: see 4.47 above.

82 *Michael Wilson & Partners Ltd v Emmott* [2018] EWCA Civ 51 per Sir Terence Etherton MR at [39].

83 *American Cyanamid Co v Ethicon Ltd* [1975] AC 396 per Lord Diplock at page 407.

84 This sentiment lies at the heart of the reasoning of the Court of Justice of the European Union in *West Tankers Inc v Allianz SpA (The Front Comor)*, CJEU Case C-185/07, [2009] 1 AC 1138.

85 *Qingdao Huiquan Shipping Co v Shanghai Dong He Xin Industry Group Co Ltd* [2018] EWHC 3009 (Comm) per Bryan J at [29]; *SAS Institute Inc v World Programming Ltd* [2020] EWCA Civ 599 per Males LJ at [113]–[115].

86 *AES Ust-Kamenogorsk Hydropower Plant LLP v Ust-Kamenogorsk Hydropower Plant JSC* [2013] UKSC 35 per Lord Mance JSC, exercising his judicial creativity, at [50].

87 *Enka Insaat ve Sanayi AS v OOO "Insurance Company Chubb"* [2020] UKSC 38 per Lord Hamblen JSC at [179].

CHAPTER 4A

Interim Measures in Arbitration (China)

Introduction

4.a.1 International arbitration has a long history, as one of the most important dispute resolution mechanisms, and without any doubt, it is an important mode for resolving commercial disputes. In China, however, it was not until the Arbitration Law of the People's Republic of China (hereinafter referred to "Arbitration Law 1995 (as amended until 2020)") was promulgated on 31 August 1994[1] that the Chinese arbitration system was fully established.[2]

4.a.2 Before drafting the Arbitration Law 1995, Chinese legislators took guidance from the UNCITRAL Model Law on International Commercial Arbitration 1985 (hereinafter referred to as "UNCITRAL Model Law 1985").[3] However, the UNCITRAL Model Law 1985 was not fully adopted in the Arbitration Law 1995. It can be observed that some features of the UNICTRAL Model Law 1985 that were adopted by many jurisdictions were in fact not incorporated into the Chinese Arbitration Law 1995.

4.a.3 For example, as far as seeking preservation measures during arbitration proceedings is concerned, the UNCITRAL Model Law 1985 provides the power to arbitral tribunals to grant interim measures. This power of the

1 The Arbitration Law came into effect in 1995, and the latest amendment to it was introduced in 2017. It hereinafter will be referred to as "Arbitration Law 1995 (as amended until 2020)".

2 It may be argued that international commercial arbitration in China appeared in the 1950s, but the corresponding legal system to support the arbitration was absent; see also, Hu Zhang, 'Reconstruct the Procedure of Recognition and Enforcement of Foreign Arbitral Award in China' (2018) 10 Law Science Magazine 106, 107; although in legal practice, the commercial arbitration is regarded as a dispute resolution mechanism, the completion of the enabling mechanism has always been through legislation, in this case, the promulgation of the Arbitration Law 1995 just provided the legal system to support arbitration in China.

3 Xiuwen Zhao, 'Development of Modernization and Internationalization of Chinese International Arbitration System in 21st Century' (2001) 3 Journal of Henan Administrative Institute of Politics and Law 31, 31; see also, the UNCITRAL Model Law 1985 on International Commercial Arbitration New York was adopted by the United Nations Commission on International Trade Law on 21 June 1985 and was further amended in 2006; , for more detailed provisions on interim remedies in the context of international arbitration, see < www.uncitral.org/pdf/english/texts/arbitration/ml-arb/07-86998_Ebook.pdf> accessed 15 June 2021.

DOI: 10.4324/9781003000310-7

arbitral tribunal to grant interim remedies in the jurisdiction of England & Wales has been discussed earlier.[4] On the other hand, in accordance with Articles 101 and 272 of the Civil Procedure Law 1991 (hereinafter referred to as "CPL 1991 (as amended until 2020)") and Articles 28, 46 and 68 of the Arbitration Law 1995 (as amended until 2020),[5] arbitration institutions/appointed arbitrators in China merely play transmitters' roles for arbitral preservation applications.[6] This means that there is no legal mechanism by which arbitration institutions or appointed arbitrators may directly issue effective preservation measures.

---

4 The UNCITRAL Model Law (2006 Amendment), Article 17; refer also, Chapter 1, 1.10–1.13 and 1.74–1.75.

5 Article 101 of the CPL 1991 (as amended until 2020) provides that "if the party fails to petition for property preservation promptly, may, before instituting a lawsuit or applying for arbitration, apply to the people's court at the locality of the property"; see also, Article 272 of the CPL 1991 (as amended until 2020) provides that "If a party applies for preservation, the arbitration institution of the People's Republic of China for foreign-related disputes shall submit the application to the intermediate people's court of the place where the domicile of the person against whom the application is made is located or where the property is located"; see also, Article 28 of the Arbitration Law 1995 (as amended until 2020) provides that "If a party applies for property preservation, the arbitration commission shall submit the party's application to the people's court in accordance with the relevant provisions of the Civil Procedure Law"; see also, Article 46 of the Arbitration Law 1995 (as amended until 2020) provides that "Under circumstances where the evidence may be destroyed or lost or difficult to obtain at a later time, a party may apply for preservation of the evidence. If a party applies for preservation of the evidence, the arbitration commission shall submit his application to the primary people's court in the place where the evidence is located"; see also, Article 68 of the Arbitration Law 1995 (as amended until 2020) stipulates that "If a party to a foreign-related arbitration applies for preservation of the evidence, the foreign-related arbitration commission shall submit his application to the intermediate people's court in the place where the evidence is located".

6 It should be noted that, unlike in England & Wales, the only type of arbitration available in China is an institutional arbitration, and there is no concept of an *ad hoc* arbitration except for the *ad hoc* arbitrations conducted in Pilot Free Trade Zone. In accordance with the *Letter of Ministry of Commerce of the People's Republic of China and General Administration of Customs of the People's Republic of China Concerning Regulating of the Concept of Free Trade Zone* (Shang Guo Ji Han [2008] No 15), the Free Trade Zone, also named the Pilot Free Trade Zone, refers to a particular area in the territory of China where preferential tax rates and special regulatory policy are implemented. In 2013, the Chinese government launched a scheme to set up the China Pilot Free Trade Zone in Shanghai. There are currently 18 Free Trade Zones in total in mainland China. The Supreme People's Court issued *Opinions of the Supreme People's Court on Providing Judicial Guarantee for the Building of Pilot Free Trade Zones* (Fa Fa [2016] No 34) on 30 December 2016. Article 9 (3) of the Opinions provides that "where enterprises registered in the Pilot Free Trade Zone agree to arbitrate a dispute by specific persons at the specific location in the Mainland China in accordance with a specific arbitration rules, such an arbitration agreement may be deemed to be valid". It is generally accepted that behind this Article the Supreme People's Court officially recognises *ad hoc* arbitration in the Pilot Free Trade Zone. Further to the Opinions, *Ad Hoc* Arbitration Rules in Hengqin Free Trade Zone came into effect on 15 April 2017 and was issued by the Zhuhai Court of International Arbitration, <www.zhac.org.cn/?p=434> accessed 6 June 2021. In addition, the Ministry of Justice of the People's Republic of China on 30 July 2021 issued the Revision of the Arbitration Law (Draft for Comments); in this draft, Articles 90–93 of Chapter VII "Special Provisions on Foreign-Related Arbitration" allow ad hoc arbitration. Nonetheless, when the revision will be approved by the National People's Congress can only be speculated at the time of publication of this book.

4.a.4 By the end of 2019, China established 260 arbitration institutions that disposed of more than 480,000 disputes involving RMB 762 billion in 2019,[7] but all these arbitral institutions still have to rely on the Chinese courts, as these courts can only grant arbitral preservation measures. In addition, where a dispute based on an arbitration clause or agreement should be or has been resolved by a tribunal outside China, the application to Chinese courts seeking arbitral preservation measures is not possible unless this is a maritime dispute.[8]

4.a.5 Under these circumstances, the need for improvement of the arbitral preservation mechanism has attracted the Supreme People's Court's attention (hereinafter referred to as "SPC") and that of some research organisations,[9] so that the judicial interpretations of the arbitral preservation orders given in the course of the arbitrations by Chinese courts have considerably improved in the last few years.[10] In particular, the Ministry of Justice of the People's Republic of China on 30 July 2021 issued the Revision of the Arbitration Law (Draft for Comments). In order to keep pace with the international arbitration rules, this revision supplements Section IV "Interim Remedies" in Chapter II "Arbitral Procedure" to empower an arbitrator to render a preservation order.[11] Nonetheless, after the Ministry of Justice receives further proposals and feedback from the public for the current draft revisions, it is likely to spend time reviewing those proposals in detail. To the authors' knowledge, the second revision for comments will be released again to receive further feedback. Following the review of such proposals, how long after the revised Arbitration Law will be issued and to what extent the arbitration tribunals may enjoy the power to render preservation orders can only be speculated at this stage. Accordingly, this chapter will simply focus on the current existing law.

4.a.6 All in all, this chapter will provide a review of the status of the preservation measures obtained from the Chinese courts in support of arbitrations. It will also examine the development, if any, of preservation orders in support of arbitrations in China.

---

7 The Supreme People's Court 'Annual Report on International Commercial in China 2019' <www.court.gov.cn/zixun-xiangqing-281031.html> accessed 9 June 2021.

8 See 4.a.59–4. a.72

9 For example, China Arbitration Institute established by Chinese University of Politics and Law recently created a questionnaire online and Chinese practitioners are welcome to complete this survey. One of the questions is about whether it is necessary to grant the arbitral tribunal the necessary power to order preservation measures; see also, China Arbitration Institute, 'Questionnaires on Some Important Issues Concerning the Revision of Arbitration Law' < https://wj.qq.com/s2/5236531/ab86/?from=timeline&isappinstalled=0> accessed 6 June 2021.

10 For example, the first and only legal document, an *Arrangement Concerning Mutual Assistance in Court-Ordered Interim Measures in Aid of Arbitral Proceedings by the Courts of the Mainland and of the Hong Kong Special Administrative Region* was signed by the SPC and the Government of the Hong Kong Special Administrative Region and came into effect on 1 October 2019, see 4.a.82–4.a.97.

11 Arbitration Law (Revision) (Draft for Comment) 2021, Articles 43–49.

Jurisdiction over Arbitral Preservation Measures in China

Legal Foundation of Chinese Exclusive Jurisdiction

4.a.7 First, as discussed in 4.a.3, there are no available legal mechanisms by which Chinese arbitration institutions can directly issue effective preservation orders via these arbitral institutions or via arbitrators pursuant to Chinese law. Furthermore, there is no general mechanism by which foreign arbitration institutions/arbitrators can directly issue enforceable preservation measures for enforcement in China.[12] It follows that courts in China, rather than arbitration institutions/arbitrators, have exclusive jurisdiction over an application seeking arbitral preservation orders.

4.a.8 In addition, even if parties in their arbitration clauses choose any of the Chinese arbitral institutions and a foreign law as the governing law, the procedural law governing arbitrations will still be Chinese law. The reason for applications of Chinese law is pursuant to Article 4 of the CPL 1991 (as amended until 2020) providing that:

> All those who are engaged in civil actions within the territory of the People's Republic of China shall abide by Law (Civil Procedure Law).[13]

4.a.9 It follows that the methodology of obtaining preservation measures and the procedures required to obtain them must comply with the CPL 1991 (as amended until 2020) and the Arbitration Law 1995 (as amended until 2020), even if the substantive law is subject to the agreed foreign law in the relevant contracts.

4.a.10 In *Hemofarm DD and Others v Jinan Yongning Pharmaceutical Co Ltd*,[14] the SPC affirmed the legal foundation in relation to the exclusive jurisdiction of Chinese courts over an application seeking arbitral preservation

12 It should be noted that, in general, Chinese law does not allow a foreign institution arbitration to establish its branch in mainland China. However, in those special zones, such as in Pilot Free Trade Zones, legal services are planned to be more international in character to attract arbitration business to China. For example, *Administrative Measures on Business Offices Established by Foreign Arbitration Institutions within the Lin Gang Area of China (Shanghai) Free Trade Zone* (Hu Si Gui [2019] No 5) issued by the Shanghai Municipal Bureau of Justice on 19 October 2019 provides that foreign arbitration institutions' business offices may be established within the Lin Gang area. Those foreign arbitration institutions refer to non-profit-making arbitration institutions legally established in the jurisdictions outside China. These foreign arbitral jurisdictions will include Hong Kong, Macau and Taiwan, as well as institutions established by international organisations that China has joined and is co-operating with. It is currently not clear whether the preservation order issued by these institutions in their branches in Free Trade Zones located in China based on their own rules may be recognised and enforced by the Chinese courts. However, the Free Trade Zone opens the door to a few foreign arbitral institutions and provides business opportunities to them in the field of arbitration.

13 CPL 1991 (as amended until 2020), Article 4.

14 *Letter of Reply of the Supreme People's Court to a Request for Instructions on the Non-Recognition and Non-Enforcement of an Arbitration Award of the ICC International Court of Arbitration* ([2008] Civil Si Ta Zi No11); see also, *Hemofarm DD and Others v Jinan Yongning Pharmaceutical Co Ltd* (an application seeking recognition and enforcement of a foreign

measures regardless of domestic arbitration or foreign arbitration. The legal foundations are as follows:

> Property preservation measure is governed by the civil litigation legal relationship. Any disputes over the legality and legitimacy of the preservation applications are based on the litigation legal relationships that is not relevant to contractual disputes and other disputes over rights and interests in property which can be arbitrated *[pursuant to Article 2 of the Arbitration Law_1995]*, and also do not belong to the contractual and non-contractual commercial legal relationships *[pursuant to the commercial reservation statement of the Chinese government on the Convention on the Recognition and Enforcement of Foreign Arbitral Awards 1958]*. Therefore, Chinese courts have exclusive jurisdiction over the dispute over applications seeking preservation measures and the tribunal has no jurisdiction over it *[and tribunals have to pass the applications to the relevant Chinese courts]* [added by authors].[15]

4.a.11 The above legal foundation actually stresses that the application seeking arbitral preservation measures belongs to the civil litigation procedural issue. Pursuant to the parties' arbitration clause/agreement, even if an arbitral tribunal chosen by the arbitration clause/agreement applies its own arbitration rules to dispose of the dispute, the procedural disputes, such as the preservation application procedure, must abide by the Chinese procedure law. Therefore, any preservation orders that are rendered by any tribunals are null and void.

4.a.12 It should be emphasised that although Chinese courts have exclusive jurisdiction over applications seeking arbitral preservation measures, this does not mean that the Chinese courts are willing to accept all applications from foreign arbitral tribunals located outside China. This will be discussed in 4.a.59.

arbitral award) ([2007] Lu Civil Si Ta Zi No 12) (the High People's Court of Shandong Province, binding order).

15 ibid. The original version is Chinese, and the English translation is carried out by the authors. It was determined at the 18th session of the Standing Committee of the 6th National People's Congress on 2 December 1986 that China should enter the Convention on the Recognition and Enforcement of Foreign Arbitral Awards (hereinafter referred to as "the New York Convention 1958") adopted in 1958 in New York. This Convention came into effect in China on 22 April 1987. The Chinese government made two reservations on this Convention before it came into effect. One is about the commercial reservation statement that "this Convention shall only apply to the disputes arising from contractual and non-contractual commercial legal relationship. 'Contractual and non-contractual commercial legal relationship' specifically refers to the economic rights and obligations resulted from contract, infringement or arising according to law, such as sale of goods, lease of property, project contracting, processing, technology assignment, joint adventure, joint business operation, exploration and development of natural resources, insurance, credit, labor service, surrogate, consultation service, marine/civil aviation/railway/road passenger and cargo transportation, product liability, environment pollution, marine accident, dispute over ownership, etc., and it does not include the dispute between foreign investors and the host government". See, *Circular of Supreme People's Court on Implementing Convention on the Recognition and Enforcement of Foreign Arbitral Awards Entered by China* (Fa (Jing) Fa [1987] No 5), Article 2.

4.a.13 The legal foundation stated above, equally, applies to the arbitral preservation measures in maritime disputes. Furthermore, compared with the court's jurisdiction in non-maritime arbitral disputes, the maritime court's jurisdiction is broader, which will be discussed in 4.a.61–4.a.72.

Tier Jurisdiction in Non-Maritime Disputes

4.a.14 Pursuant to Provisions of the Supreme People's Court on Some Issues Concerning the Enforcement by the People's Court (for Trial Implementation) (2020 Amendment) (hereinafter referred to as "Provisions on Enforcement (2020 Amendment)")[16] and *Notice of the SPC on Several Issues Concerning Enforcement of Arbitration Law of the People's Republic of China (2008 Adjustment)* (hereinafter referred to as "Notice on Enforcement of Arbitration Law (2008 Adjustment)"),[17] there are different tier jurisdictions in the context of a domestic or a foreign-related arbitration.

Domestic Arbitration in Non-Maritime Disputes

4.a.15 An application seeking pre-arbitral or post-arbitral property preservation measures should be made to the primary people's court located in the area where the respondent is domiciled; or the place where the property to which the dispute relates is located.[18] In addition, this primary court will have jurisdiction over the enforcement of the relevant preservation order.[19]

4.a.16 An application and enforcement for the pre-arbitral or post-arbitral evidence preservation measures should be made to the primary people's court located in the area where the evidence is located or in the domicile of the respondent.[20]

16 Provisions of the Supreme People's Court on Some Issues Concerning the Enforcement by the People's Court (for Trial Implementation) (2020 Amendment) (Fa Shi [1998] No 15) (superseded by Fa Shi [2020] No 21).

17 Notice of the Supreme People's Court on Several Issues Concerning Enforcement of Arbitration Law of the People's Republic of China (2008 Adjustment) (Fa Fa [1997] No 4) (superseded by Fa Shi [2008] No 18).

18 Article 9 of Provisions on Enforcement (2020 Amendment) provides that "In the domestic arbitration proceedings, if a party applies for property preservation and is submitted to the people's court by an arbitration institution, such application shall be ruled and enforced by the primary people's court in the location where the respondent is domiciled, or where the property is located; an application seeking evidence preservation shall be ruled and enforced by the primary people's court where the evidence is located"; see also, Notice on Enforcement of Arbitration Law (2008 Adjustment), Article 2; see also, CPL 1991 (as amended until 2020), Article 101; it should be noted that Article 101 of the CPL 1991 (as amended until 2020) does not clarify the tier of the court rendering a preservation order, but simply provides the competent court that has power to render an order.

19 Provisions on Enforcement (2020 Amendment), Article 9.

20 ibid; see also, CPL 1991 (as amended until 2020), Article 81; it should be noted that Article 81 does not stipulate the tier of the court rendering a preservation order, but simply provides the competent court that has power to render an order.

4.a.17 With regard to an application seeking behaviour preservation measures, in accordance with the existing law, in an intellectual property and/or an unfair competition dispute, there is an express provision allowing an applicant to file an application seeking arbitral behaviour preservation measures.[21] An application for pre-arbitral behaviour preservation measures should be filed before the corresponding local people's court having jurisdiction over intellectual property and unfair competition disputes in the place of the respondent[22] or before a people's court having jurisdiction over the case.[23] In terms of the jurisdiction over an application for post-arbitral behaviour preservation measures, there is no express provision. But the Supreme People's Court's judges opine that no matter whether the express provision is absent, the competent court to accept post-arbitral behaviour preservations may be compatible with the court to accept an application for pre-arbitral behaviour preservation measures.[24] It must be stressed that, with regard to an application seeking behaviour preservation measures in non-IP and non-unfair competition disputes, further discussion will be found in 4.a.38.

Foreign-Related Arbitration in Non-Maritime Disputes

4.a.18 There is no exact definition of a foreign-related arbitration pursuant to the Arbitration Law 1995 (as amended until 2020). Chapter Seven "Special Provisions for Foreign-Related Arbitration" of the Arbitration Law merely provides the scope of arbitrability for foreign-related arbitrations including foreign economic cooperation and trade, transportation and maritime

---

21 See 4.a.36–4.a.38.

22 *Provisions of the Supreme People's Court on Several Issues Concerning the Application of Law in Cases Involving the Review of Behaviour Preservation in Intellectual Property Disputes* (Fa Shi [2018] No 21) (hereinafter referred to as "Interpretation of IP Behaviour Preservation 2018"), Article 3; Xiaoming Song, Chuang Wang, Junli Xia and Guimei Lang, 'Understanding and Application of *Provisions of the Supreme People's Court on Several Issues Concerning the Application of Law in Cases Involving the Review of Behaviour Preservation in Intellectual Property Disputes*' [2019] 7 The People's Judicature 19, 21; the local people's court having jurisdiction over intellectual property and unfair competition disputes refers to the Intellectual Property Courts located in Beijing, Shanghai and Guangzhou. In terms of the specialised court, namely the intellectual property court, it can be found in Chapter 3, 3.30–3.31.

23 Interpretation of IP Behaviour Preservation 2018, Article 3; Xiaoming Song, Chuang Wang, Junli Xia and Guimei Lang, 'Understanding and Application of *Provisions of the Supreme People's Court on Several Issues Concerning the Application of Law in Cases Involving the Review of Behaviour Preservation in Intellectual Property Disputes*' [2019] 7 The People's Judicature 19, 21; a people's court having jurisdiction over the case refers to any courts located outside Beijing, Shanghai and Guangzhou, having jurisdiction over intellectual property and unfair competition disputes according to the rules of the tier and territorial jurisdictions discussed in Chapter 3, 3.56–3.60 and 3.64–3.70.

24 Xiaoming Song, Chuang Wang, Junli Xia and Guimei Lang, 'Understanding and Application of *Provisions of the Supreme People's Court on Several Issues Concerning the Application of Law in Cases Involving the Review of Behaviour Preservation in Intellectual Property Disputes*' [2019] 7 The People's Judicature 19, 21.

matters. In addition, matters not covered by this special chapter shall be handled pursuant to other relevant provisions of this arbitration law.[25] In accordance with the above scope of arbitrability and Article 271 of the CPL 1991 (as amended until 2020), a foreign-related arbitration means that before or after arbitral disputes arising from foreign economic, trade, transport or maritime activities, parties to disputes have agreed to include an arbitration clause or subsequently reached a written arbitration agreement that provides for their disputes to be submitted to a Chinese arbitration institution for foreign-related disputes or to other arbitral institution located in China.[26]

4.a.19 Applications seeking pre-arbitral or post-arbitral property preservation measures must be made to the intermediate people's court located in the area where the respondent is domiciled; or the property to which the dispute relates is located.[27] Meanwhile, this intermediate people's court has jurisdiction over the enforcement of a preservation order.[28]

4.a.20 The application and enforcement of pre-arbitral or post-arbitral evidence preservation measures must be made to the intermediate people's court located in the area where the evidence is located or in the area where the respondent is domiciled.[29]

4.a.21 With regard to an application seeking behaviour preservation measures, it can be by reference to the jurisdiction in 4.a.17.

Conflicts and Development of Jurisdiction in Non-Maritime Disputes

4.a.22 Even though the tier jurisdiction of an arbitral preservation application differs depending on whether it is a domestic arbitration or whether it is a foreign-related arbitration as discussed in 4.a.15–4.a.20, in accordance with *Interpretation of the Supreme People's Court Concerning Some Issues on Application of the Arbitration Law of the People's Republic of China (2008 Adjustment)* (hereinafter referred to as "Interpretation of Arbitration Law (2008 Adjustment)"), the intermediate people's court has jurisdiction over the enforcement of all arbitral awards.[30] To be clear, both Provisions on

---

25 Arbitration Law 1995 (as amended until 2020), Article 65.

26 CPL 1991 (as amended until 2020), Article 271.

27 Article 10 of Provisions on Enforcement (2020 Amendment) stipulates that "In the foreign-related arbitration proceedings, if a party applies for property preservation and is submitted to the people's court by an arbitration institution, such application shall be ruled and enforced by the primary people's court in the location where the respondent is domiciled, or where the property is located; an application seeking evidence preservation shall be ruled and enforced by the primary people's court where the evidence is located"; see also, Notice on Enforcement of Arbitration Law (2008 Adjustment) Article 2; see also, CPL 1991 (as amended until 2020), Article 272.

28 Provisions on Enforcement (2020 Amendment), Article 10.

29 ibid; see also, CPL 1991 (as amended until 2020), Article 272.

30 *Interpretation of the Supreme People's Court Concerning Some Issues on Application of the Arbitration Law of the People's Republic of China (2008 Adjustment)* (Fa Shi [2006] No 7), Article 29.

Enforcement (2020 Amendment) and Notice on Enforcement of Arbitration Law (2008 Adjustment) provide the different tier requirements for domestic or foreign-related arbitration as to the enforcement of the preservation order,[31] while Interpretation of Arbitration Law (2008 Adjustment) does not make a distinction between domestic and foreign-related arbitration. It should be noted that all three judicial interpretations were originally issued in 1998. The relevant tier jurisdiction over arbitration has never been rectified. From this point of view, it is not reasonable to argue that Provisions on Enforcement (2020 Amendment) will prevail on the grounds that 2020 Amendment is the updated version. As mentioned just now, the substantive content about the jurisdiction over arbitration is never updated. In this context, in order to address this controversial issue, in the past years, some high people's courts try to adjust and unify the jurisdiction of the court with respect to their territorial jurisdiction, irrespective of whether the dispute is domestic or foreign-related.[32]

4.a.23 For example, with respect to the property preservation measures, the main solution devised in Beijing is to request the intermediate people's courts to dispose of the applications seeking arbitral preservation measures in the location where the respondent is domiciled, or where the property is located,[33] while the High People's Court of Jiangsu Province simply provides that the intermediate people's courts will have jurisdiction over the applications seeking arbitral preservation measures in the location where the property is located.[34]

4.a.24 In this regard, prior to the submission of an application seeking pre-arbitral preservation measures, it is necessary for an applicant to work out whether the local high court has provided a unified jurisdiction over an arbitral preservation. Even though, in most situations, the applicants cannot communicate with the courts directly as they have to submit applications through the arbitral institutions, it is advisable for the authorised legal agent of the applicants to carry out sufficient research as to the formal requirements for

31 Provisions on Enforcement (2020 Amendment), Articles 9 and 10; Notice on Enforcement of Arbitration Law (2008 Adjustment), Article 2.

32 Qi Zhao, Hui Zhan and Huihua Wang, 'Improvement of Property Preservation Mechanism in Commercial Arbitration' (2019) 1 (107) Beijing Arbitration Quarterly 34, 38.

33 *Notice of the Beijing High People's Court on Jurisdiction of the Intermediate People's Court Concerning Enforcement of an Arbitration* (Jing Gao Fa Fa [2006] No 357). It should be noted that the Fourth Intermediate People's Court in Beijing territorial jurisdiction has exclusively been provided with the jurisdiction over the recognition and enforcement of foreign arbitral awards (including Macau, Hong Kong and Taiwan), but there are no specific provisions on the recognition and enforcement of foreign arbitral preservation orders because China, in general, does not recognise preservation orders rendered in foreign jurisdictions; see also, *Provisions of Beijing High People's Court on Jurisdiction over Cases of the Fourth Intermediate People's Court* (2018 Amendment).

34 *Opinions of the Jiangsu High People's Court on Some Issues Concerning Judicial Examination of Civil and Commercial Arbitration* (2010 Amendment), Article 46; see also, Article 44 stipulates that the primary people's court in the place where the evidence to be preserved is located has the jurisdiction over an application for seeking the evidence preservation.

seeking preservation applications. Sufficient research can be pursued through the courts' official guidance that is usually posted online.[35] Routinely, the arbitral institutions also advise applicants to pursue further research on such applications that are to be submitted to the courts seeking preservation measures.[36]

Maritime Courts' Jurisdiction for Arbitral Preservation Applications

4.a.25 Compared with the courts' jurisdiction in non-maritime disputes over applications seeking arbitral preservation measures, the important difference in maritime disputes is that all applications seeking maritime arbitral preservation measures must be submitted to the competent maritime courts. As discussed in Chapter 3, 3.30–3.31, maritime courts, as one of the specialised courts in the Chinese court system, are equivalent to the level of the local Intermediate People's Court. This means that, in both domestic arbitral and foreign-related arbitral disputes, the maritime courts should accept applications seeking arbitral preservation measures uniformly without considering the issues of tier divergence.

4.a.26 Another difference is that pursuant to the Arbitration Law 1995 (as amended until 2020), there are no available rights for the parties to apply to the courts seeking arbitral behaviour preservation measures except for intellectual property and unfair competition disputes,[37] though these rights would have been available if the parties were to go through litigation.[38] However, in maritime arbitrations in China, all three types of preservation measures are available either through pre-arbitral or post-arbitral preservation applications.

4.a.27 Based on this, the discussion of the maritime courts' jurisdiction, in both domestic and foreign-related arbitration, will be divided into the pre-arbitral and the post-arbitral stages according to the different types of preservation measures that parties can request from the courts.

4.a.28 Before initiating the arbitration, an applicant by its own initiative should submit an application to a competent people's court. In accordance with the Special Maritime Procedure Law 2000 (hereinafter referred to as "SMPL 2000"), an application seeking property preservation measures

---

35 For example, *Guidance of the First Intermediate People's Court of Beijing Municipality on Property Preservation at the Case-Filing Stage* (16 October 2019) <http://bj1zy.chinacourt.gov.cn/article/detail/2019/12/id/4746705.shtml> accessed 15 June 2021; see also, *Guidance of the Tianjin High People's Court on Examination of Property Preservation* (Jin Gao Fa Fa [2019] No 28); *Instruction of the Guangzhou Intermediate People's Court on Pre-Action Preservation* (25 July 2019).

36 For example, Beijing Arbitration Commission, 'General Issues on Arbitration Preservations' <https://www.bjac.org.cn/page/zc/zcbq.html> accessed 15 June 2021.

37 In certain disputes, the parties are entitled to apply for an arbitral behaviour preservation; see 4.a.36–4. a.39.

38 See generally, Chapter 8.

should be made to the maritime court of the place where the property to be preserved is located;[39] an application seeking maritime injunctions should be made to the maritime court of the place where the maritime dispute arises;[40] an application seeking evidence preservation measures must be made to the maritime court of the place where the evidence is to be preserved.[41]

4.a.29 After instituting the arbitration, the SMPL 2000 and its Interpretation[42] do not provide a clear answer to jurisdiction over applications for post-arbitral preservation measures. Based on requirements that an applicant should first submit an application to the agreed arbitral institution, and then this arbitral institution transfers the party's application to a competent Chinese court. As a result, the competent court that has jurisdiction over the application seeking arbitral preservation measures is customarily provided by rules of the agreed arbitral institution.

4.a.30 For example, if parties were to have agreed to submit their disputes to the China Maritime Arbitration Commission (hereinafter referred to as "CMAC"), pursuant to the Arbitration Rules of CMAC 2018,

(a) CMAC shall submit the party's application seeking post-arbitral preservation of maritime claim or preservation of other property to the maritime court or other people's court at the place of the respondent's domicile or at the place of the property.[43]
(b) CMAC shall submit the party's application seeking post-arbitral evidence preservation measures to the maritime court or other people's court at the place where the evidence to be preserved is located.[44]
(c) CMAC shall submit the party's application seeking post-arbitral maritime injunctions to the maritime court at the place where the maritime dispute arises.[45]

4.a.31 Where an arbitral dispute will be or has already been submitted to a foreign arbitration outside China, the relevant discussion can be found in 4.a.61–4.a.62.

Emergency Arbitrators and Preservation Orders

4.a.32 To keep pace with the development of international commercial arbitration, an arrangement for emergency arbitrators has been adopted by

39 SMPL 2000, Article 13.
40 ibid Article 52.
41 ibid Article 63.
42 *The Supreme People's Court Interpretations on the Application of the Special Maritime Procedure Law of the People's Republic of China (2008 Adjustment)* (Fa Shi [2003] No 3) (hereinafter referred to as "Interpretation of SMPL 2008").
43 Arbitration Rules of CMAC 2018, Article 23.
44 ibid Article 24.
45 ibid Article 25.

the main Chinese arbitration institutions,[46] such as the China International Economic and Trade Arbitration Commission (hereinafter referred to as "CIETAC"),[47] Beijing Arbitration Commission (hereinafter referred to as "BAC"),[48] Shanghai International Arbitration Centre (hereinafter referred to as "SIAC"),[49] the CMAC[50] and Shenzhen Court of International Arbitration (hereinafter referred to as "SCIA").[51]

4.a.33 One main purpose of emergency arbitrators has been to issue preservation orders before the arbitration tribunal can be assembled as announced by BAC as follows:

> Existing Chinese laws are silent as to whether an arbitral tribunal has the authority to order any interim measures. However, laws in some jurisdictions grant arbitral tribunals the power to make such orders, which are also enforceable before the local courts. On the purpose of a broader protection of the parties' legal rights, the New Rules confirm the arbitral tribunal's power to order any interim measures it deems proper in accordance with the applicable law. To support this provision, the New Rules also provide for "Emergency Arbitrator"

---

46 The emergency arbitrator procedure was applied for the first time in the International Arbitration Rules of the American Arbitration Association (2009) and over ten years most of the leading "international commercial arbitration" institutions have adopted this procedure; see also, Xuehua Wang, Jing Liu and Yuan Xing, 'Annual Review on Commercial Arbitration in China (2019)' in Beijing Arbitration Commission and Beijing International Arbitration Centre (eds), *Commercial Dispute Resolution in China: An Annual Review and Preview 2019* (China Legal Publishing House 2019) 23; see also, Ian Gaunt, 'Innovation of Maritime Dispute Resolution Mechanisms' (Paper 47, page 615, the Ninth International Conference on Maritime Law, Shanghai November 2018).

47 China International Economic and Trade Arbitration CIETAC Arbitration Rules (2015), Article 23 (2) and Appendix III 'Emergency Arbitrator Procedures' <http://www.cietac.org/Uploads/201902/5c6148b100105.pdf> accessed 10 June 2021.

48 Beijing Arbitration Commission Arbitration Rules (2019), Article 63 'Emergency Arbitrator' <https://www.bjac.org.cn/english/page/zc/guize_en.html> accessed 10 June 2021.

49 Shanghai International Economic and Trade Arbitration Commission (Shanghai International Arbitration Center) Arbitration Rules (2018), Article 68 'Interim Measures' and Article 69 'Emergency Arbitrator', see <www.accsh.org/uploadfile/2018/0930/20180930111411955.pdf> accessed 10 June 2021; it should be noted that the official English version issued by Shanghai International Arbitration Center applies the 2015 Rules which did not provide for an emergency arbitrator <www.shiac.org/upload/day_141230/SHIAC_ARBITRATION_RULES_2015_141222.pdf> accessed 10 June 2021; the China (Shanghai) Pilot Free Trade Zone Arbitration Rules (2015) issued by the Shanghai International Economic and Trade Arbitration Commission (Shanghai International Arbitration Center) stipulate the establishment and rights to interim measures of emergency tribunal in details at Article 21, see <www.shiac.org/upload_files/file/2020/20200813142126_1384.pdf> accessed 10 June 2021.

50 China Maritime Arbitration Commission Arbitration Rules (2018), Article 27 'Interim Measures' and Appendix III 'Emergency Arbitrator Procedures' <www.cmac.org.cn/en/quick-link/1684.html> accessed 10 June 2021.

51 Arbitration Rules of Shenzhen Court of International Arbitration (2020), Article 26 'Emergency Arbitrator', see <www.scia.com.cn/upload/20201027/5f97bf7833c8c.pdf> accessed 10 June 2021.

mechanism, in response to any possible request for interim measures before the constitution of the arbitral tribunal. Both provisions show exactly the BAC's close attention to the newly arising practice and its open mind to embrace the trend (Article 62 and Article 63).[52]

4.a.34 Even so, the Arbitration Law 1995 (as amended until 2020) and the relevant judicial interpretations do not adopt this scheme of emergency arbitrators. Therefore, unless further amendments to the Arbitration Law or the judicial interpretations clarify that the preservation orders issued by emergency arbitrators will become effective in China, the orders by emergency arbitrators in some arbitral institutions are really not recognised by the Chinese courts. However, it is worth noting that in the current draft of the revision of Arbitration Law 2021 (draft for Comment), the rule of "Emergency Arbitrator" has been stipulated.[53] Furthermore, this new revision empowers both an emergency arbitrator and an arbitration tribunal to render a preservation order.[54] On the ground that this draft needs much more time to be further revised and thereafter to be approved by the Standing Committee of the National People's Congress in the near future, this book will not discuss more.

4.a.35 In addition, it should be highlighted that these preservation orders from emergency arbitrators can be recognised and enforced in the jurisdiction where the orders of emergency arbitrators are recognised and enforced.[55] For instance, an emergency preservation order in BAC issued in *the GKML Case* in 2017 was recognised and enforced in the Hong Kong High Court.[56] Ironically,

---

52 Zhiwei Lin, 'A Brief Introduction of Beijing Arbitration Commission Arbitration Rules 2015' <www.bjac.org.cn/english/page/ckzl/gzsm2015.html> accessed 2 January 2020; in 2019, BAC issued the Rules 2019; see also, Qiuju Jiang, 'A Brief Introduction to the BAC Arbitration Rules 2019 and Annexes Concerning Schedules of Fees' <www.bjac.org.cn/english/news/view?id=3535> accessed 15 June 2021. In terms of the emergency arbitrator's procedure, the Rules 2019 improved the emergency arbitrator procedure and adopted a new fee schedule for appointing emergency arbitrators and thereafter to seek interim measures from the appointed emergency arbitrators. Further discussion of the topic is beyond the scope of the book.

53 Article 49 of Arbitration Law of the People's Republic of China (2021 Revision) (Draft for Comment) provides that "Prior to the formation of the arbitration tribunal, if the parties need to appoint an emergency arbitrator to take interim measures, they may apply to the arbitration institution for the appointment of an emergency arbitrator in accordance with the arbitration rules. The powers of emergency arbitrators are reserved until the arbitration tribunal is formed".

54 Arbitration Law of the People's Republic of China (2021 Revision) (Draft for Comment), Article 43; see 4.a.5.

55 Xuehua Wang, Jing Liu and Yuan Xing, 'Annual Review on Commercial Arbitration in China (2019)' in Beijing Arbitration Commission and Beijing International Arbitration Centre (eds), *Commercial Dispute Resolution in China: An Annual Review and Preview 2019* (China Legal Publishing House 2019) 23.

56 Terence Xu, 'Emergency Arbitrator Proceedings and the GKML Case' (*China Business Law Journal*, 14 November 2014) <www.vantageasia.com/emergency-arbitrator-proceedings-gkml-case> accessed 15 June 2021.

as mentioned in 4.a.34, the same preservation order from the arbitral institution based in China could not have been recognised in the Chinese courts.

Types of Preservation Measures in Arbitration

4.a.36 Three types of preservation measures are available in litigation proceedings, pursuant to the CPL 1991 (as amended until 2020). In contrast to litigation, there are no specific behaviour preservation provisions that are available to the parties to arbitration pursuant to the CPL 1991 (as amended until 2020) or the Arbitration Law 1995 (as amended until 2020). One reason for this anomaly may be that for many years in China the behaviour preservation measure has been utilised by parties in disputes over the infringement of rights; conversely, pursuant to the Arbitration Law 1995 (as amended until 2020), only contractual disputes and other disputes over rights and interests in property can be arbitrated.[57] In addition, the behaviour preservation measures became part of the mainstream civil procedural law of China only after the 2012 revisions/amendments to the CPL 1991. Therefore, a long-term controversial issue that has been debated is whether the issues involving the infringement of rights can be arbitrated pursuant to Chinese law. The majority view amongst legal scholars is inclined towards the view that arbitration is not possible when the issues concern the infringement of rights.[58]

4.a.37 The breakthrough needed to clarify the issue is provided by *Provisions of the SPC on Several Issues Concerning the Application of Law in Cases Involving the Review of Behaviour Preservation in Intellectual Property Disputes* (hereinafter referred to as "Interpretation of IP Behaviour Preservation 2018").[59] Article 5 (3) of this Interpretation provides:

> Where a party applies for behaviour preservation during arbitration, it shall submit an application form, an acceptance notification of the *arbitration*, and other relevant materials to the people's court via the arbitral authority [emphasis added].[60]

57 Article 2 of the Arbitration Law 1995 (as amended until 2020) provides that "Contractual disputes and other disputes over rights and interests in property between citizens, legal persons and other organisations that are equal subjects may be arbitrated".

58 Article 43 of the Arbitration Law of the People's Republic of China (2021 Revision) (Draft for Comment) has provided all three types of preservation measures. Meanwhile, if necessary, a court or an arbitration tribunal may render a short-term interim remedy. Again, because this is simply a draft, there is no space to discuss more.

59 *Provisions of the Supreme People's Court on Several Issues Concerning the Application of Law in Cases Involving the Review of Behaviour Preservation in Intellectual Property Disputes* (Fa Shi [2018] No 21).

60 Interpretation of IP Behaviour Preservation 2018, Article 5 (3).

4.a.38 Based on this, the understanding and application of this Interpretation issued by senior judges of the SPC also affirm the legality of behaviour preservation in intellectual property and unfair competition disputes during arbitration proceedings.[61] Therefore, during arbitration proceedings, the types of preservation measures that are available are property preservation, evidence preservation and IP and unfair competition behaviour preservation measures. At present, there is no clarity whether in non-maritime and non-IP disputes, the parties to arbitrations may seek behaviour preservation measures in Chinese courts.

4.a.39 In the maritime law domain, pursuant to the SMPL 2000 and its Interpretation, a maritime applicant is entitled to apply for pre-arbitral or post-arbitral injunctions and evidence preservations, preservation of maritime claims for all maritime disputes.[62]

Jurisdiction and Types of Preservations in the CICC

4.a.40 The Chinese International Commercial Court (hereinafter referred to as "CICC"), as a permanent adjudication organ of the SPC was conceptualised as a legal institution for resolving global disputes. The CICC was launched in 2018.[63] With many China-led international projects around the world, this development of the CICC is in a timely manner to resolve international commercial disputes and for ensuring preservation measures are available to the parties.

4.a.41 Although the CICC is subject to the rules governing the SPC, its aim is to create a "one-stop" international commercial dispute resolution mechanism together with the selected international commercial mediation and arbitration institutions.[64] This means that where the parties have agreed to submit their disputes to arbitration proceedings governed by an international arbitral

61 Xiaoming Song, Chuang Wang, Junli Xia and Guimei Lang, 'Understanding and Application of *Provisions of the Supreme People's Court on Several Issues Concerning the Application of Law in Cases Involving the Review of Behaviour Preservation in Intellectual Property Disputes*' [2019] 7 The People's Judicature 19, 22; it is emphasised that, pursuant to Article 1 of Interpretation of IP Preservation 2018, "intellectual property disputes" include disputes over intellectual property rights and unfair competition under the *Provisions on Causes of Action of Civil Cases* (Fa [2011] No 42).

62 SMPL 2000, Article 64; see also, Interpretation of SMPL 2008, Articles 21, 41 and 47; see 4.a.26.

63 *Provisions of the Supreme People's Court on Several Issues Regarding the Establishment of the International Commercial Court (Fa Shi [2018] No 11)* (hereinafter referred to as "Provisions on the CICC"), Article 1.

64 Provisions on the CICC 2018, Article 11 provides that "The Supreme People's Court will set up an International Commercial Expert Committee and select international commercial mediation institutions and international commercial arbitration institutions that meet certain conditions to build up together with the International Commercial Court a dispute resolution platform on which mediation, arbitration, and litigation are efficiently linked, thereby creating a 'one-stop' international commercial dispute resolution mechanism".

institution that has been preselected by the CICC, if they, before or after the arbitration proceedings have commenced from the CICC, applied for preservation orders such as the preservation of property, evidence or behaviour, the application may directly be submitted to the CICC.[65] However, it has not yet been seen how the preservation orders issued through the system of the CICC can be enforced in other countries.

4.a.42 Pursuant to *Notice of the General Office of the Supreme People's Court on the Determination of the First Batch of International Commercial Arbitration and Mediation Institutions* included in the "One-Stop" Mechanism for the Diversified Resolution of International Commercial Disputes, a few of the arbitral institutions selected in the system of the CICC for ensuring the "one-stop" approach to resolving international commercial disputes are the CIETAC, the BAC, the CMAC, the SIAC, the SCIA, the China Council for the Promotion of International Trade Mediation Center and the Shanghai Economic, Trade and Commercial Mediation Center.[66]

4.a.43 In an international commercial case, where the amount of the disputed subject matter is not less than RMB 300 million or where an international commercial case may possibly cause a significant impact, the parties may choose one of institutions stated above to file an application to commence the arbitration. The parties may also submit applications for arbitral preservations of evidence, property or behaviour to the CICC via the selected arbitral institution. The CICC should then receive and accept this preservation application and will thereafter make a preservation order.[67]

4.a.44 At this stage, the CICC has selected international arbitral institutions that are all located in mainland China. With the development of the CICC, the list may be expanded in the future. The reason is that although there is no foreign arbitration institution (including Hong Kong, Macau and Taiwan) for now, the CICC has invited foreign experts including a British judge, an American arbitrator and some other jurisdictions' professors and practitioners to participate in international commercial dispute resolution. If the CICC follows through on its aim to dispose of international commercial disputes, in the future, there will be opportunities for foreign arbitral institutions to transfer preservation applications to the CICC directly, and then it is very likely for the CICC to approve those applications.

---

65 Provisions on the CICC 2018, Article 14.

66 *Notice of the General Office of the Supreme People's Court on the Determination of the First Batch of International Commercial Arbitration and Mediation Institutions Included in the 'One-Stop' Mechanism for the Diversified Resolution of International Commercial Disputes* (Fa Ban [2018] No 212).

67 *Notice of the General Office of the Supreme People's Court on Issuing the Procedural Rules for the China International Commercial Court of the Supreme People's Court (for Trial Implementation)* (Fa Ban Fa [2018] No 13), Article 34.

Procedure for Applications[68]

4.a.45 Since to seek arbitral preservation measures, applicants still have to apply to the courts, so fundamentally, there is no significant difference in the written format of applications, the legal tests to obtain preservation orders, security and countersecurity and so forth between preservation applications arising from litigation and those applications arising out of arbitral proceedings.[69] Furthermore, the online preservation system of the people's court (www.baoquan.court.gov.cn) operated by the SPC and/or an online trial system established by the different courts can not only apply a litigation preservation application, but can also apply an arbitral preservation application.[70] However, from a practical point of view, online applications may need much more time to be operated well. The forthcoming section merely provides a brief account of preservation procedures in arbitration practice.

Procedural Step of Pre-Arbitral Preservations in Practice

4.a.46 Regarding pre-arbitral preservations, theoretically, in the light of Article 101 of the CPL 1991 (as amended until 2020),[71] an applicant may directly submit his application to a competent court on his own initiative, because at this stage there is no institution arbitration assisting the applicant to transfer the documents to the court. However, in legal practice, most Chinese courts are reluctant to accept applications seeking pre-arbitral preservation measures, or to put it lightly Chinese judges are not comfortable receiving pre-arbitral applications.[72]

4.a.47 In this situation, most Chinese lawyers have adopted a litigation tactic to file preservation applications together with arbitration applications to commence the arbitration. After arbitral institutions have preliminarily examined the types of applications for both commencing arbitration and seeking arbitral preservation measures, they will evaluate and determine whether the arbitration applications can be accepted. If so, they will further consider whether the preservation applications have met the formal requirements that are associated with these applications. After deciding to transfer

68 It is worth noting that the Arbitration Law of the People's Republic of China (2021 Revision) (Draft for Comment) has improved the procedure of the preservation measure in Articles 43–49. But the final draft will take some more time before it is approved and then implemented in China. To the authors' knowledge, at least in the forthcoming several years, the current procedure still stands. Therefore, any further discussion on the revision of the Arbitration Law (Draft for Comment) is beyond the scope of the book.

69 See Chapter 3, 3.117–3.129 in Format of Applications section; legal tests to obtain the orders, security and countersecurity and other rules, see generally, in Chapters 3, 6, 8 and 10.

70 See Chapter 3, 3.47–3.48 in Online Preservation System of the People's Court.

71 CPL 1991 (as amended until 2020), Article 101.

72 Qi Zhao, Hui Zhan and Huihua Wang, 'Improvement of Property Preservation Mechanism in Commercial Arbitration' (2019) 1 (107) Beijing Arbitration Quarterly 34, 40.

preservation applications to Chinese courts, the role of the arbitral bodies in relation to preservation measures will end at this stage.

Procedural Step after Submitting an Application

4.a.48 The documents pertaining to preservation applications will be transferred to competent courts from arbitral institutions after the preliminary examination by the arbitral institutions. It is not necessary for applicants to contact the relevant courts directly. However, in arbitration practice, to confirm the jurisdiction of a court and the requirements associated with the preservation applications, the applicants are routinely advised by the arbitral institutions to directly consult with the competent courts.

4.a.49 After receiving the documents for applications seeking preservation orders from the arbitral institutions, if the courts are not satisfied with the applications, they will then refuse to accept the preservation applications and accordingly will inform the arbitral institutions. There could be numerous circumstances due to which the Chinese courts may not be satisfied with information contained in the documents attached to a preservation application. For example, the courts may hold that the documents have not satisfied even the first test that the circumstances surrounding the applications do come within the meaning of "urgent circumstances". The arbitral institution will thereafter give the applicants notifications that have been received from the relevant Chinese courts.

4.a.50 Following the courts' notifications, it is expected that the applicants provide supplementary documents or evidence to meet the requirements of the preservation applications, such as drafting an explanation as to why the circumstances surrounding their applications are urgent. The arbitral institutions will then transfer all supplementary documents to the courts. After reviewing all the documents, the courts may issue relevant preservation orders.[73]

73 This strategy is generally observed in China in many arbitrations and is based on experiences of lawyers dealing with the China International Economic and Trade Arbitration Commission, Beijing Arbitration Commission and Shanghai International Arbitration Centre. Different institutions and courts may have different ways of dealing with arbitral preservation applications. For example, an arbitration institution in Chongqing may send an official letter to an applicant after this institution has examined the documents for the preservation applications. The applicant by himself may apply for arbitral preservation measures in a competent court depending on this official letter issued by the arbitration institution. Another example to highlight is from the Primary People's Court of Futian District of Shenzhen City of Guangdong Province, where it requests the applicant's lawyer to contact the clerk of the court to submit the application seeking property preservation measures after the arbitration has been commenced (instead of interacting with the arbitral institution in relation to arbitral preservation applications); see also, Guangzhou Nine Lawyers Team (eds) 'Notice on Case-Filing and Preservation of Shenzhen Intermediate and Primary People's Court' <www.zylawyera.com/gonggao/12.html> accessed 15 June 2021.

Underlying Issues Affecting Preservation Applications

4.a.51 There are two legal issues in arbitration practice that should be noted. First, Article 25 of the Arbitration Law 1995 (as amended until 2020) provides that:

> after an arbitration institution accepts an application for arbitration, it shall, within the time limit specified in the rules of arbitration, deliver a copy of the rules of arbitration and the register of arbitrators to the claimant, and serve one copy of the application for arbitration together with the rules of arbitration and the register of arbitrators to the respondent.[74]

4.a.52 It follows that it is necessary for arbitral institutions, based on their own rules, to keep respondents informed with regard to specific dates that need to be complied with by them, for example dates by which the defence statement needs to be provided to tribunals. However, different arbitral institutions can have different procedural rules and are not uniform. The lawyers need to consult the procedural rules of arbitral institutions carefully and should never assume that the rules will be uniform throughout China.

4.a.53 For example, Article 11 of the Rules of SIAC 2018 provides that the tribunal must inform the respondent within seven days of sending an acceptance notification to the respondent.[75] However, the Rules of BAC 2019 stipulate that the tribunal must inform the respondent within ten days.[76] The Rules of CMAC 2018 and the Rules of SCIA 2020 do even not provide time limits during which the respondent needs to be informed.[77]

4.a.54 In this context, it is to be noted that, even before the arbitral preservation applications can be transferred by arbitral institutions to the courts, the respondents have already received the acceptance notification of the commencement of an arbitration from the arbitral institutions. Under these circumstances, it is quite feasible that the respondents during arbitration proceedings could devise plans to transfer property that may be the subject matter of any preservation order by the courts in the near future. It is therefore important and prudent for the applicants to communicate with the arbitral institutions in advance as to the possibility of this scenario. The purpose is to ensure that the preservation orders are made before the respondents receive the acceptance notification from the arbitral institutions.

4.a.55 In practice, a tribunal will normally consider an applicant's request to transfer the application to a court as soon as possible and will endeavour to send the Notice of Acceptance to the respondent pursuant to the arbitral

74 Arbitration Law 1995 (as amended until 2020), Article 25.

75 Shanghai International Economic and Trade Arbitration Commission (Shanghai International Arbitration Center) Arbitration Rules (2018), Article 11.

76 Rules of Beijing Arbitration Commission 2019, Article 10.

77 See general, Rules of China Maritime Arbitration Commission 2018; Arbitration Rules of Shenzhen Court of International Arbitration (2020).

institution's rules on the last day of the requested period. As for the applicant, it is important to contact the court to purse the process of preservation measures in a timely manner.

4.a.56 Another problem is that even though Article 101 of the CPL 1991 (as amended until 2020) provides that the court, after receiving the application seeking pre-arbitral preservation measures, must render an order within 48 hours, and Article 4 of *Provisions on Several Issues Concerning the Handling of Property Preservation Cases by the People's Courts* (2020 Amendment) (hereinafter referred to as "Interpretation of Property Preservation (2020 Amendment)") provides that the order for a post-arbitral property preservation must be made within five days of receiving the application,[78] the Arbitration Law 1995 (as amended until 2020) has left a few procedural gaps.

4.a.57 For example, the Arbitration Law 1995 (as amended until 2020) does not stipulate the time frame within which the arbitral institutions have to submit applications to the courts seeking arbitral preservation measures after they have received the materials of applications from the applicants and so forth.[79]

4.a.58 In the context of the scenario highlighted in the preceding paragraph, and in the absence of relevant rules in most arbitral institutions, the efficiency of the transfer of the arbitral preservation applications from the arbitral institutions to the courts will solely be dependent on (i) the work efficiency of an arbitration tribunal, and (ii) the communication between the applicant and the tribunal. In most situations, the arbitral institutions would like to assist applicants to speed up the procedure. However, it is prudent to confirm beforehand with the relevant arbitral institutions as to this aspect of procedure pursuant to their arbitration practice.

Preservations for Foreign Arbitrations in China

4.a.59 A foreign arbitration refers to a dispute disposed of by an international arbitral tribunal, with the seat of the arbitration located outside mainland China. In accordance with the CPL 1991 (as amended until 2020) and the Arbitration Law 1995 (as amended until 2020), an arbitral institution with its seat outside China is in practice not entitled to transfer an application for preservation orders to a Chinese court. There is no express provision on whether a party during foreign arbitration proceedings is entitled to submit

78 Provisions of the Supreme People's Court on Several Issues Concerning the Handling of Property Preservation Cases by the People's Courts (2020 Amendment) (Fa Shi [2016] No 22) (superseded by Fa Shi [2020] No 21); it should be noted that there is no time limit to make an order for a post-arbitral behaviour or evidence preservation measure under the existing law if the circumstances are not urgent; see Chapter 8, 8.158 and Chapter 10, 10.135.

79 Interpretation of Property Preservation (2020 Amendment), Article 4.

applications seeking preservation measures to the Chinese court. There is also no express provision prohibiting applications, in such scenarios, seeking preservation measures. Nevertheless, Chinese courts are currently not inclined to accept preservation applications associated with foreign arbitration because these courts are of the view that there is no legal foundation to accept the application.[80]

4.a.60 This section will give a brief account of four exceptional regions where Chinese courts may assist foreign arbitrations to obtain preservation orders. Due to the limited space, there are no detailed guidance and practical strategies discussed in this chapter.

Preservations for Foreign Arbitrations in China (I):

Maritime Arbitration

4.a.61 Unlike other fields of laws where behaviour preservation, except for in IP and unfair competition disputes, cannot be accepted, in accordance with Articles 21, 41 and 47 of the Interpretation of SMPL 2008, Chinese maritime courts must accept applications seeking all three types of arbitral preservations. Furthermore, these maritime courts will accept applications, even if these disputes are heard by foreign courts or international arbitral institutions, whose seat of arbitration is outside China. The relevant Articles are as follows:

> **Article 21**: Where a foreign court has already accepted a related maritime case, or the relevant dispute has already been submitted for arbitration, but the involved property is within the People's Republic of China, if a party applies for a maritime claim preservation with the maritime court of the place where the property is located, the maritime court shall accept the application.
>
> **Article 41**: Where a foreign court has already accepted the relevant maritime case, or the relevant dispute has already been submitted for arbitration, if a party applies for a maritime injunction with a

80 For example, in *DONGWON F&B v Shanghai Lehan Commercial Co Ltd* (recognition and enforcement of a property preservation order issued by a foreign arbitration) [2014] Hu Yi Zhong Shou Chu Zi No 2 (the First Intermediate People's Court of Shanghai Municipality, first instance and binding order), due to the dispute over a sale of goods contract between DONGWON F&B and Shanghai Lehan Commercial Co Ltd, DONGWON F&B (applicant) instituted an arbitration to the Korean Commercial Arbitration Board. After the Korean Commercial Arbitration Board accepted this case, DONGWON F&B (applicant) filed an application seeking property preservation measures with the First Intermediate People's Court of Shanghai Municipality and requested the court to take measures over property belonging to Shanghai Lehan Commercial Co Ltd (respondent). The court held that the applicant did not commence arbitration in any of the Chinese arbitral institutions. Therefore, there was no legal foundation to approve this application seeking property preservation measures.

maritime court of the People's Republic of China, and furnishes to the court the relevant evidence for enforcement of the injunction, the maritime court shall accept the case.

Article 47: Where a foreign court has already accepted the relevant maritime case, or the relevant dispute has already been submitted for arbitration, if a party applies for preservation of maritime evidence with a maritime court of the People's Republic of China and furnishes relevant evidence proving the evidence within the People's Republic of China to be preserved, the maritime court shall accept the application.[81]

4.a.62 It can be seen that the parties that have filed their applications with international arbitral institutions, which have their seat of arbitration located outside China, are still entitled to apply for preservation applications to Chinese maritime courts.

Test Case for Post-Arbitral Maritime Preservation

4.a.63 There is no doubt that Chinese maritime courts are willing to assist applicants to obtain preservation measure orders even if the applicants have brought the disputes to foreign arbitration. For example, in one case, after a dispute over a ship sale contract had been brought to the London Maritime Arbitrators Association (hereinafter referred to as "LMAA"), an applicant filed an application seeking a post-arbitral property preservation with the Ningbo Maritime Court. The Ningbo Maritime Court located in Zhejiang Province accepted the application and made a preservation order to freeze RMB 40 million belonging to the respondent.[82]

4.a.64 Similarly, in E 72 Cai Bao No 427, after the arbitral institution, the Hong Kong International Arbitration Centre (hereinafter referred to as "HKIAC"), had accepted the application to commence the arbitration, the applicant filed an application seeking property preservation measures with the Wuhan Maritime Court. Similarly, the Wuhan Maritime Court located in Hubei Province allowed the application in favour of the applicant.[83] The latest application seeking property preservation during HKIAC proceedings was also accepted by the Xiamen Maritime Court.[84]

---

81 Interpretations of SMPL 2008, Articles 21, 41 and 47.

82 [2010] Yong Hai Fa Zhong Bao Zi No 1 (an application seeking a post-arbitral property preservation) (Ningbo Maritime Court, binding order).

83 [2016] E 72 Cai Bao No 427 (an application seeking a post-arbitral property preservation) (Wuhan Maritime Court, binding order).

84 *China Resource Chartering Limited v Fuqing Tianyi Building Material Co., Ltd.* (an application seeking a post-arbitral property preservation order) [2020] Min 71 Cai Bao No.17 (Xiamen Maritime Court, binding order).

Test Case for Pre-Arbitral Maritime Preservation

4.a.65 Articles 21, 41 and 47 of the Interpretations of the SMPL 2008 do not clarify whether an application for pre-arbitral preservations can be accepted by maritime courts to assist maritime arbitrations, where the seat of arbitration is not in China. In legal practice, many maritime courts and judges are inclined towards accepting applications seeking pre-arbitral maritime preservation measures.[85]

4.a.66 For example, in the *M/V NERISSA* case, before Tianji International Group Co (applicant) could bring a case to commence an arbitration in the LMAA, they filed an application seeking pre-arbitral property preservation with the Qingdao Maritime Court. Through this application, Tianji International Group Co requested the court to arrest the *M/V NERISSA*. The Qingdao Maritime Court thereafter allowed the pre-arbitral preservation application.[86]

4.a.67 Nonetheless, in certain disputes, the maritime courts have also rejected applications seeking pre-arbitral preservation measures. However, with regard to the reasons for dismissing the applications, it seems that the maritime judges have mainly considered that the subject matter of the applications did not satisfy the pre-requisites for maritime preservation measures. For example, in *China National Chartering Co Ltd v Tsingshan Holding Group Co Ltd*,[87] parties chose the HKIAC to dispose of their dispute via arbitration. Prior to the submission of the application to the HKIAC to commence an arbitration, China National Chartering Co Ltd (applicant) filed a pre-arbitral property preservation application with the Ningbo Maritime Court. The Ningbo Maritime Court held that the application seeking the pre-arbitral property preservation measures in China lacked legal foundation. Although the binding order issued by the Ningbo Maritime Court rejected the application, thereafter, one of the judges hearing this case further explained in his article that the subject matter of the property preservation application in this specific case did not abide by the law leading to the refusal of the application. This outcome did not mean that the pre-arbitral preservation application was

85 Shengli Wu, 'The Restriction of the Preservation of Non-Maritime Claim of Overseas Arbitration' (2015) 3 Chinese Journal of Maritime Law 68, 69.

86 *Arrest of M/V NERISSA* (an application seeking a pre-arbitral property preservation) [2019] Lu 72 Cai Bao No 108 (Qingdao Maritime Court, first instance and binding order); during the arrest of the ship, the parties reached a settlement. Therefore, no further facts of the dispute were disclosed; see also, *Jit International Corporation Ltd v Shanghai Greenroad International Logistics Co Ltd* (an application seeking pre-arbitral property preservation measures) [2010] Hu Hai Fa Hai Bao Zi No 105, Shanghai Maritime Court approved the application seeking the pre-arbitral property preservation measure.

87 *China National Chartering Co Ltd v Tsingshan Holding Group Co Ltd* (an application seeking pre-arbitral property preservation) [2010] Yong Hai Fa Wen Bao Zi No 7 (Ningbo Maritime Court, binding order).

not accepted by the court, and the detailed argument will be discussed later in 4.a.69–4.a.72.[88]

4.a.68 As far as a pre-arbitral application seeking maritime preservation measures is concerned, it can be argued that many Chinese maritime courts are willing to approve applications. However, due to the absence of express provision in law, whether the maritime courts will definitely accept these applications cannot be assumed with certainty.

Limitation of Property Preservations Measure in Maritime Disputes

4.a.69 In the maritime law domain, according to the kinds of property that may be the subject matter of preservation measures, the property can be divided into two types, namely (i) maritime property that refers to the vessel, the cargo on the vessel, the vessel's fuel and supplies, and (ii) other general types of property. It follows that the property preservation measures for the first type of property are subject to the SMPL 2000 while the preservation measures for the latter kind of property must abide by the CPL 1991 (as amended until 2020).[89] Because the two types of property are governed by the two different legislations, a controversial legal issue arises whether the parties are entitled to apply for property preservation measures from Chinese Maritime Courts if the property refers to the general property rather than the maritime property. At this stage, there is no uniform answer on this issue that would be applicable to all maritime courts.

4.a.70 In legal practice, most maritime courts are inclined to approve applications without the divergence between maritime property and other property to be preserved. For example, in Yong Hai Fa Bao Zi No 12,[90] the Ningbo Maritime Court accepted an application seeking property preservations and then held that five houses belonging to Wuyi Jiayuan Real Estate Development Co Ltd (respondent) would not be transferred and/or mortgaged within the next two years.[91] In this application, the respondent's houses obviously belonged to non-maritime property.

88 ibid; see also, Shengli Wu, 'The Restriction of the Preservation of Non-Maritime Claim of Overseas Arbitration' (2015) 3 Chinese Journal of Maritime Law 68, 69.

89 Interpretation of SMPL 2008, Article 18.

90 *Parties undisclosed* [2010] Yong Hai Fa Bao Zi No 12 (Ningbo Maritime Court, first instance and binding order); because this was an arbitral preservation, no detailed information on the facts of the case was disclosed; see also, in *Jit International Corporation Ltd v Shanghai Greenroad International Logistics Co Ltd* (an application seeking pre-arbitral property preservation measures) [2010] Hu Hai Fa Hai Bao Zi No 105 (Shanghai Maritime Court, first instance and binding order), an applicant requested the court to freeze the respondent's bank account; the Shanghai Maritime Court approved it; [2009] Jin Hai Fa Bao Zi No 17-1 (an arbitral application seeking property preservation) (Tianjin Maritime Court, first instance and binding order); see also, Shengli Wu, 'The Restriction of the Preservation of Non-Maritime Claim of Overseas Arbitration' (2015) 3 Chinese Journal of Maritime Law 68, 69.

91 ibid.

4.a.71 In contrast, certain maritime judges and courts are inclined to a viewpoint that the law expressly stipulates that the preservation measures in relation to non-maritime property must comply with the CPL 1991 (as amended until 2020) that in fact does not allow the parties to file applications seeking property preservation measures assisting foreign arbitrations. Accordingly, they are of the view that there is no legal foundation in such scenarios to approve applications seeking non-maritime property preservations.[92]

4.a.72 For example, as discussed in 4.a.67, in *China National Chartering Co Ltd v Tsingshan Holding Group Co Ltd*,[93] China National Chartering Co Ltd (applicant) filed an application seeking pre-arbitral property preservation with the Ningbo Maritime Court. However, on the ground that the subject matter of the property preservation measure was to freeze Tsingshan Holding Group Co Ltd (respondent)'s bank deposit, not its maritime property, the Ningbo Maritime Court held that the freezing of this subject matter lacked legal foundation, and the preservation application was therefore dismissed.[94]

Preservation for a Foreign Arbitration in China (II):

Macau and the Mainland

4.a.73 In Chapter 3, it was discussed that Macau and Taiwan, as special regions in China, enjoy their own independent legal systems, but like mainland China, both belong to the civil law tradition and the concept of "civil preservation procedure" is similar.[95] The difference is that the mainland and Macau reached a bilateral agreement for the recognition and enforcement of arbitral awards including arbitral preservations while the SPC promulgated a judicial interpretation to resolve the recognition and enforcement of arbitral awards including arbitral preservations associated with Taiwan.

4.a.74 *Arrangement between the Mainland and the Macau SAR on Reciprocal Recognition and Enforcement of Arbitration Awards 2007* (hereinafter referred to as "Mainland and Macau Arbitral Awards Arrangement 2007") came into effect on 1 January 2008.[96] Article 11 provides for the reciprocal application and enforcement of arbitral property preservations in both jurisdictions and it provides:

---

92 Shengli Wu, 'The Restriction of the Preservation of Non-Maritime Claim of Overseas Arbitration' (2015) 3 Chinese Journal of Maritime Law 68, 68–69; Chunlong Xu and Wenzhi Chen, 'Applicant's Right over the Application of Property Preservation Prior to the Recognition and Enforcement of a HK Arbitral Award' (2021) 2, The People's Judicature (Case) 79, 81.

93 *China National Chartering Co Ltd v Tsingshan Holding Group Co Ltd* (an application seeking a pre-arbitral property preservation) [2010] Yong Hai Fa Wen Bao Zi No 7 (Ningbo Maritime Court, first instance and binding order).

94 ibid.

95 See Chapter 3, 3.92.

96 Arrangement between the Mainland and the Macau SAR on Reciprocal Recognition and Enforcement of Arbitration Awards (Fa Shi [2007] No 17).

> Before or after the court has accepted an application for recognition and enforcement of arbitral awards, it may take preservation measures for the property of the party against whom the application is filed according to the provisions in the laws of the location of the court.[97]

4.a.75 This means that Chinese courts have the authority to accept property preservation applications and render preservation orders, as long as the applications comply with Chinese law, namely the CPL 1991 (as amended until 2020) and the relevant interpretations. The Chinese courts will accept these applications even though the disputes are brought to the Chinese courts from Macau arbitration institutions. Furthermore, this article expresses that regardless of whether it is before or during the period of recognition and enforcement of Macau arbitral awards, the parties are all entitled to apply for property preservation measures in the Chinese courts.

4.a.76 However, this Arrangement simply applies to property preservation measures, and does not govern applications seeking evidence or behaviour preservation measures. Furthermore, there is no specific provision on pre-arbitral property preservation in this Arrangement.

4.a.77 Nonetheless, along with the legal construction of the Greater Bay Area Initiative[98] and the Chinese judicial reform in different ways,[99] it is anticipated that the Mainland and Macau Arbitral Awards Arrangement 2007 might be revised to adopt the acceptance of evidence and behaviour preservation applications.

Preservations for Foreign Arbitrations in China (III):

Taiwan and the Mainland

4.a.78 The SPC promulgated *Provisions of the Supreme People's Court on Recognition and Enforcement of Arbitral Awards of the Taiwan Region*

97 Mainland and Macau Arbitral Awards Arrangement 2007, Article 11.

98 Qibo Jiang, Jiahai Zhou, Yanli Si and Kun Liu, 'Understanding and Application of *Arrangement Concerning Mutual Assistance in Court-Ordered Interim Measures in Aid of Arbitral Proceedings by the Courts of the Mainland and of the Hong Kong Special Administrative Region Mainland and Hong Kong Arrangement in Court-Ordered Interim Measures*' People's Court Daily (Beijing, 26 September 2019); see also, the Greater Bay Area Initiative released in the 13th Five-Year Plan for Economic and Social Development of PRC refers to the Guangdong-Hong Kong-Macau Greater Bay Area pursuing a marked increase in its economic strength and regional competitiveness.

99 This Arrangement was issued in 2007. However, until 2012, the amendment to the CPL provided for the behaviour preservation. It might be for this reason that the 2007 Arrangement only provided for property preservation applications. In 2015, the SPC issued the Provisions on Arbitral Awards Made by a Taiwan Court to provide for evidence and behaviour preservations and in 2019, the Arrangement between the mainland and Hong Kong also provided three types of preservations. The details are discussed in 4.a.79 (the mainland and Taiwan) and 4.a.88 (the mainland and Hong Kong).

(hereinafter referred to as "Provisions on Taiwan Arbitral Awards 2015") in 2015.[100] Article 10 of these Provisions provides that

> Before or after the [mainland] people's court has accepted an application for recognition and enforcement of the Taiwan Region arbitral awards, in the light of an applicant's application, it may take preservation measures in accordance with the CPL and the relevant judicial interpretations.[101]

4.a.79 Compared with the Mainland and Macau Arbitral Awards Arrangement 2007, due to the recent development of preservations in China, Provisions on Taiwan Arbitral Awards 2015 has expanded the scope of the arbitral preservation applications. It now encompasses all types of applications for preservation measures, namely, preservation of property, preservation of behaviour and preservation of evidence.

4.a.80 However, similar to the Mainland and Macau Arbitral Awards Arrangement 2007, Article 10 of Provisions on Taiwan Arbitral Awards 2015 does not clarify whether this Article may apply to applications for pre-arbitral preservation.

4.a.81 In these two judicial documents, either Macau arbitral preservation or Taiwan arbitral preservation applications will be regarded as foreign-related applications in the Chinese courts. Accordingly, the competent intermediate people's court has jurisdiction over the preservation application.

Preservation for a Foreign Arbitration in China (IV):

Hong Kong and the Mainland

Background

4.a.82 Unlike Macau and Taiwan, it is generally recognised that Hong Kong is one of the most important international commercial arbitration hubs which has attracted more international parties to choose an arbitration institution seated in Hong Kong to deal with commercial disputes. It has therefore been an important strategy to ensure that Hong Kong remains a popular destination to provide comprehensive legal services for international parties.[102]

4.a.83 In addition, as far as a foreign-related commercial contract is concerned, when arbitration is chosen as the dispute resolution mechanism, if it

100 *Provisions of the Supreme People's Court on Recognition and Enforcement of Arbitral Awards of the Taiwan Region* (Fa Shi [2015] No 14).

101 Provisions of Enforcement of Taiwan Judgment 2015, Article 10.

102 Further discussion on the issue of the Mainland China and Hong Kong Arrangement in Court-Ordered Interim Measures 2019 is beyond this book. See also, general read, Qibo Jiang, Jiahai Zhou, Yanli Si and Kun Liu, 'Understanding and Application of *Arrangement Concerning Mutual Assistance in Court-Ordered Interim Measures in Aid of Arbitral Proceedings by the Courts of the Mainland and of the Hong Kong Special Administrative Region Mainland and Hong Kong Arrangement in Court-Ordered Interim Measures*' (2019) 7 The People's Judicature (Applied) 30.

is not possible for a mainland party to choose a mainland arbitration institution, such parties are likely to be inclined to choose a qualified Hong Kong arbitration institution, such as Hong Kong International Arbitration Centre (HKIAC), rather than other international arbitration hubs such as London and Singapore. Furthermore, with the increase of the mainland party's bargaining power in recent years, according to the data provided by HKIAC, since 2010 the number of mainland-related arbitrations has dramatically increased.[103] HKIAC 2020 statistics show that, following Hong Kong, mainland China has become the top geographical region or nationality participating in arbitrations.[104]

4.a.84 Against the above background, the first and only legal document, an *Arrangement Concerning Mutual Assistance in Court-Ordered Interim Measures in Aid of Arbitral Proceedings by the Courts of the Mainland and of the Hong Kong Special Administrative Region* (hereinafter referred to as "Mainland and Hong Kong Arrangement in Court-Ordered Interim Measures 2019"), was signed by the SPC and the Government of the Hong Kong Special Administrative Region, and came into effect on 1 October 2019.[105] Subsequently, shortly after this Arrangement came into force for one year, *the Supplementary Arrangement Concerning Mutual Enforcement of Arbitral Awards between the Mainland and the Hong Kong Special Administrative Region 2021* (hereinafter referred to as "Supplementary Arrangement 2021") was promulgated by the Supreme People's Court on 26 November 2020[106] to fill in gaps which this Arrangement does not stipulate.

4.a.85 It is widely accepted that the main purpose of this Arrangement is to assist foreign parties who expect to address the issue of obtaining interim remedies/preservation measures in China due to the fact that many businessmen have assets or evidence in China. In accordance with the understanding and application of this Arrangement released by senior judges in the SPC, the

---

103 Ling Yang, 'HKIAC and the Mainland: Tendency and Challenge' *Legal Daily* (Beijing, 13 August 2018).

104 Hong Kong International Arbitration Centre, '2020 Statistics' <https://www.hkiac.org/about-us/statistics> accessed 15 June 2021.

105 *Arrangement Concerning Mutual Assistance in Court-Ordered Interim Measures in Aid of Arbitral Proceedings by the Courts of the Mainland and of the Hong Kong Special Administrative Region* (Fa Shi [2019] No 14).

106 *Supplementary Arrangement Concerning Mutual Enforcement of Arbitral Awards between the Mainland and the Hong Kong Special Administrative Region (2021)* (hereinafter referred to as "Supplementary Arrangement 2021") (Fa Shi [2020] No 13) was adopted at the 1815th meeting of the Judicial Committee of the SPC on 9 November 2020, with an announcement on 26 November 2020 that "Articles I and IV of this Judicial Interpretation shall come into force from 27 November 2020 and after the completion of the relevant procedures in HK, the SPC shall announce the effective date of Articles II and III thereof". At present, HK has completed the legal procedure. Hence, Articles II and III of the Supplementary Arrangement 2021 came into force on 19 May 2021.

authority similarly confirms that its main purpose is to reinforce and enhance Hong Kong's competitiveness in the Asia-Pacific as an important international dispute resolution centre and to contribute to the development of the Greater Bay Area Initiative.[107] It should be noted that this Arrangement also regulates parties involved in arbitral proceedings in mainland China seeking interim measures before a Hong Kong court. However, this issue is beyond the scope of this book, and accordingly, it is not discussed in detail.[108]

4.a.86 Because the applicable law for the examination of an application seeking preservation measures is the law of the requested place, Hong Kong arbitral preservation orders shall be subject to the law of mainland China, namely the CPL 1991 (as amended until 2020) and the relevant interpretations.[109] Therefore, for the detailed procedure and requirements of an application seeking Hong Kong arbitral preservation measures in mainland courts, one may look at other chapters of this book, including Chapters 6, 8 and 10 according to the types of preservation measures.

4.a.87 Compared with provisions applicable to domestic arbitration preservation in the mainland, there are several different key points provided by this Arrangement 2019, which will be discussed in the following paragraphs.

Types of Preservations

4.a.88 The Mainland and Hong Kong Arrangement in Court-Ordered Interim Measures 2019 expressly provides that both the pre-arbitral and post-arbitral preservations are accepted and recognised mutually by the courts in both jurisdictions.[110] Furthermore, Article 1 of this Arrangement provides that, in the case of the mainland, the types of preservations measures to which this Arrangement apply will include property, evidence and behaviour preservations.[111]

107 Qibo Jiang, Jiahai Zhou, Yanli Si and Kun Liu, 'Understanding and Application of *Arrangement Concerning Mutual Assistance in Court-Ordered Interim Measures in Aid of Arbitral Proceedings by the Courts of the Mainland and of the Hong Kong Special Administrative Region Mainland and Hong Kong Arrangement in Court-Ordered Interim Measures*' (2019) 7 The People's Judicature (Applied) 30, 30; the Greater Bay Area Initiative released in the 13th Five-Year Plan for Economic and Social Development of PRC refers to the Guangdong-Hong Kong-Macau Greater Bay Area pursuing a marked increase in its economic strength and regional competitiveness.

108 Unlike the Arbitration Law 1995 (as amended until 2020), the principles of the UNCITRAL Model Law are adopted in Hong Kong from which it follows that a Hong Kong court can grant interim measures on the application of a party to arbitration proceedings that have been or are to be commenced in or outside Hong Kong. Furthermore, the enforcement of interim measures granted by an arbitral tribunal outside Hong Kong is also accepted.

109 Mainland and Hong Kong Arrangement in Court-Ordered Interim Measures 2019, Article 8.

110 ibid Article 3.

111 ibid Article 1.

Qualified HK Institutions or Permanent Offices

4.a.89 With regard to Hong Kong arbitral proceedings, this Arrangement is first restricted to the arbitral institutions and is not applicable to *ad hoc* arbitrations. Secondly, not all arbitral institutions have the power to apply this Arrangement. The qualified arbitral institutions or other arbitral institutions with permanent offices in Hong Kong to which this Arrangement will be applicable are as follows:

(a) Hong Kong International Arbitration Centre.
(b) China International Economic and Trade Arbitration Commission Hong Kong Arbitration Centre.
(c) International Court of Arbitration of the International Chamber of Commerce – Asia Office.
(d) Hong Kong Maritime Arbitration Group.
(e) South China International Arbitration Centre (HK).
(f) eBRAM International Online Dispute Resolution Centre.[112]

4.a.90 At this stage, apart from the foregoing institutions, a dispute disposed of by other arbitral institutions or permanent offices of other arbitral institutions with seat of arbitration in Hong Kong cannot apply this Arrangement. In the near future, more institutions or permanent offices might become part of this Arrangement.

Jurisdiction over HK Arbitral Preservations

4.a.91 HK arbitral preservation measures are treated as foreign-related preservation orders. Therefore, the Intermediate People's Courts have jurisdiction over such applications for these arbitral preservation measures. Pursuant to this Arrangement, these Intermediate People's Courts having jurisdiction include the courts in the place of residence of the party against whom the application is made or the place where the property or evidence is situated.[113]

4.a.92 It must be emphasised that, generally speaking, if there are two or more courts having jurisdiction over the preservation applications, then the applicants may apply to any one of those people's courts that satisfies the jurisdiction requirements. However, unlike domestic arbitral preservation applications, it is not allowed for the applicants associated with preservation

112 Department of Justice (HK) '*Arrangement Concerning Mutual Assistance in Court-Ordered Interim Measures in Aid of Arbitral Proceedings by the Courts of the Mainland and of the Hong Kong Special Administrative Region Mainland and Hong Kong Arrangement in Court-Ordered Interim Measures* Result of Qualified Arbitration Institutions' <www.doj.gov.hk/chi/public/interim_measures_outcome.html> accessed 15 June 2021.

113 Mainland and Hong Kong Arrangement in Court-Ordered Interim Measures 2019, Article 3.

applications to apply to two or more Chinese courts.[114] Certainly, the positive aspect is that it is not necessary for an applicant to submit preservation applications to different courts. For example, in Min 02 Cai Bao No 207, a respondent's property was located in different areas including Xiamen, Beijing, Ningbo, Quanzhou and so on, but in accordance with Article 3 of the Mainland and Hong Kong Arrangement in Court-Ordered Interim Measures 2019, HKIAC simply transferred a property preservation application to the Intermediate People's Court of Xiamen City of Fujian Province on 23 October 2019. The court rendered the property preservation order to seal up, detain and freeze the corresponding property in the different cities on 25 October 2019.[115]

4.a.93 In addition, in terms of pre-arbitral preservation applications, an applicant may submit the application to the competent people's court on its own initiative. However, after the Chinese court has rendered the preservation orders, if this court does not receive an acceptance letter from the relevant HK institution or permanent office within 30 days, the court will discharge the preservation measure orders.

4.a.94 In terms of post-arbitral preservation measures, the application will be transferred by a competent HK institution or permanent office to the Chinese court. However, this does not mean that an applicant is not entitled to apply by himself. For example, in Hu 02 Cai Bao No 6, HKIAC issued a Letter on the Submission of Application Materials for Seeking an Arbitral Property Preservation to HKIAC on 26 January 2021. An applicant took this Letter and his application format to file a property preservation application with the Second Intermediate People's Court of Shanghai Municipality on his own initiative without being transferred by the HKIAC. At the same time, a security provider offered a house in his own name as the secured property. The Second Intermediate People's Court of Shanghai Municipality accepted and rendered a property preservation order on 12 March 2021.[116]

---

114 ibid. In terms of choice of venue in case there are two competent courts, see Chapter 3, 3.81–3.83.

115 [2019] Min 02 Cai Bao No 207 (an arbitral application seeking property preservation measures transferred by HKIAC) (the Intermediate People's Court of Xiamen City of Fujian Province, first instance and binding order); it should be noted that this case was disclosed by Ms Kun Liu, Deputy Director of the Hong Kong and Macau Judicial Affairs-Office of the SPC at the Conference of *Practical Implementation of the Arrangement Concerning Mutual Assistance in Court-Ordered Interim Measures in Aid of Arbitral Proceedings by the Courts of the Mainland and of the Hong Kong Special Administrative Region* on 17 August 2021. She stated that this disclosed case might become the reported case officially in the near future by the SPC, but currently she simply disclosed this case at this conference.

116 [2021] Hu 02 Cai Bao No 6 (an arbitral application seeking property preservation measures) (the Second Intermediate People's Court of Shanghai Municipality, first instance and binding order).

Status Quo

4.a.95 Since the Mainland and Hong Kong Arrangement in Court-Ordered Interim Measures became effective on 1 October 2019, this Arrangement has started to play a very positive role in the context of the applications for arbitral preservation measures in Chinese courts.

4.a.96 On the same day, when this Arrangement had become effective, a Hong Kong shipping company filed an application with the HKIAC seeking property preservation measures. This application was to be transferred to the Shanghai Maritime Court. In fact, prior to the Arrangement becoming effective, this Hong Kong shipping company had commenced arbitration in the HKIAC against a Shanghai-based company. Pursuant to the Mainland and Hong Kong Arrangement in Court-Ordered Interim Measures 2019 and the CPL 1991 (as amended until 2020), the Shanghai Maritime Court granted a property preservation order in support of an arbitration administered by the HKIAC under the new Arrangement on 8 October 2019.[117]

4.a.97 Up to 17 August 2021, the HKIAC had received 49 applications, 46 of them seeking property preservation orders, 2 seeking evidence preservation orders and 1 seeking a behaviour preservation order.[118] To assist foreign parties in understanding the procedure under the Mainland and Hong Kong Arrangement in Court-Ordered Interim Measures 2019, the HKIAC has even released an official guidance online[119] and also the Hong Kong Arbitration Centre and CIETAC issued "The Practical Guidance on the Application of Mainland and Hong Kong Arrangement in Court-Ordered Interim Measures" on 17 August 2021.[120] In addition, as discussed above, the Supplementary Arrangement 2021 has filled in certain gaps where Arrangement 2019 has

117 Hill Dickinson, 'Hill Dickinson Sets Legal Precedent as Shanghai Maritime Court Grants Interim Measures Application in Hong Kong Arbitration Case' <www.hilldickinson.com/insights/news/hill-dickinson-sets-legal-precedent-shanghai-maritime-court-grants-interim-measures> accessed on 15 June 2020; because of the confidentiality issue, the names of the parties are not mentioned in the court's order.

118 Ms Kun Liu (Deputy Director of the Hong Kong and Macau Judicial Affairs-Office of the SPC), 'Practical Implementation of the Arrangement Concerning Mutual Assistance Court-Ordered Interim Measures in Aid of Arbitral Proceedings by the Courts of the Mainland and of the Hong Kong Special Administrative Region' (Online Conference of Practical Implementation of the Arrangement Concerning Mutual Assistance Court-Ordered Interim Measures in Aid of Arbitral Proceedings by the Courts of the Mainland and of the Hong Kong Special Administrative Region, Hong Kong, 17 August 2021).

119 Hong Kong International Arbitration Centre, 'Hong Kong-Mainland China Arrangement on Interim Measures' <www.hkiac.org/arbitration/arrangement-interim-measures> accessed 2 June 2021; more details can be found at 'PRC-HK Arrangement Interim Measures Frequently Asked Questions' <www.hkiac.org/Arbitration/interim-measures-arrangement-faqs> accessed 2 June 2021.

120 The Practical Guidance on the Application of Mainland and Hong Kong Arrangement in Court-Ordered Interim Measures (17 August 2021) <www.cietachk.org.cn/portal/newsPage.do?pagePath=\zh_TW\news\47cda18ce6b6207f001&type=center> accessed 18 August 2021.

not provided. It is anticipated that this Arrangement will have an impact on the international parties to choose Hong Kong arbitration to address their China-related disputes.

Arbitral Preservation During Recognition and Enforcement of Foreign Arbitral Awards

4.a.98 China is a member of the Convention on the Recognition and Enforcement of Foreign Arbitral Awards 1958 (hereinafter referred to as the "New York Convention 1958").[121] However, both the New York Convention 1958 and existing Chinese law do not clarify whether parties are entitled to apply for preservation measures during the period of recognition and enforcement of foreign arbitral awards in China,[122] even if it is generally acknowledgeable that an application seeking preservations, particularly property preservations, is an effective measure to guarantee the enforcement of an arbitral award. In the current 39 bilateral judicial assistance treaties between China and 39 other states, among which 35 treaties are associated with judgment enforcement clauses, there is also no civil or commercial judicial assistance concerning the enforcement of foreign interim measures made by arbitral tribunals or courts.[123] Nonetheless, special Arrangements, including the Mainland and Macau Arbitral Awards Arrangement 2007 and Provisions on Taiwan Arbitral Awards 2015, provide that during the period of the recognition and enforcement of Macau or Taiwan arbitral awards, the parties are entitled to apply to the courts in order to seek preservation measures.[124] In the latest Supplementary Arrangement 2021 between the mainland and Hong Kong, the SPC also affirms that both mainland courts and Hong

121 Convention on the Recognition and Enforcement of Foreign Arbitral Awards 1958.

122 With regard to the issue as to whether or not interim measures can be ordered by an arbitral tribunal, it is always controversial in academic and practical circles. A few academics argue that an interim measure made by a tribunal is not a final and binding award under the New York Convention while others state that the "final" award is not the condition precedent of the recognition and enforcement of the arbitral award requested by the New York Convention. See Tijana Kojovic, 'Court Enforcement of Arbitral Decisions on Provisional Relief: How Final Is Provisional' (2001) 18 (5), Journal of International Arbitration 511, 523–524; see also, Ronald A Brand, 'Working Paper No. 2020-32: Provisional Measures in Aid of Arbitration' at 8, Social Science Research Network Electronic Paper Collection <https://papers.ssrn.com/sol3/papers.cfm?abstract_id=3708453> accessed 16 June 2021.

123 Ministry of Justice of the People's Republic of China, 'Civil and Commercial Judicial Assistance Treaties' <www.moj.gov.cn/Department/node_358.html> accessed 16 June 2021; see also Meng Yu, 'List of China's Bilateral Treaties on Judicial Assistance in Civil and Commercial Matters (Enforcement of Foreign and Judgments Included)' <www.chinajusticeobserver.com/a/list-of-chinas-bilateral-treaties-on-judicial-assistance-in-civil-and-commercial-matters> accessed 16 June 2021.

124 Mainland and Macau Arbitral Awards Arrangement 2007, Article 11 and Provisions on Taiwan Arbitral Awards 2015, Article 10.

Kong courts may grant preservation or mandatory measures after an arbitral award is made and before an enforcement action is instituted.[125]

4.a.99 In legal practice, there are some conflicting orders in relation to applications seeking property preservation measures.[126] A negative order was made by the Haikou Maritime Court during the reconsideration procedure for a preservation order. In 2016, the Korean Line Corporation filed an application for the recognition and enforcement of a LMAA arbitral award to the Haikou Maritime Court. Meanwhile, the Korean Line Corporation submitted an application seeking property preservation measures and the People's Insurance Company of China provided an irrevocable letter of guarantee to assist the application. The Haikou Maritime Court rendered an order to take a property preservation measure against the correspondent, HNA Group.[127] However, after HNA Group had filed an application for reconsideration, the Haikou Maritime Court discharged the previous order made by themselves on the ground that there was an absence of legal foundation for that preservation order and it should not have been rendered in the first place.[128]

4.a.100 In contrast, the Intermediate People's Court of Guangzhou City of Guangdong Province accepted the application seeking property preservation measures during the recognition stage of a HKIAC award. Accordingly, the Intermediate People's Court of Guangzhou City of Guangdong Province enforced the preservation measures against the respondent's equities in the third party's company.[129]

4.a.101 In face of the conflicting orders from different courts, the SPC resolved this issue through a legal process of "Reply" in 2017.[130] In the *Reply of the SPC to the Request of Hubei High People's Court for Application of Property*

125 Supplementary Arrangement 2021, Article IV; this Article has also been incorporated into Article 6 of 'Mainland and Hong Kong Arrangement in Court-Ordered Interim Measures 2019'. In practice, in accordance with the Arbitration Ordinance (Cap. 609), Hong Kong courts may grant preservation or mandatory measures. Therefore, this new Article empowers mainland courts to grant similar interim measures that are available in the Hong Kong courts. As a matter of fact, before this Supplementary Arrangement 2021 was issued, certain mainland courts have accepted applications seeking interim measures before the recognition of a Hong Kong arbitral award: see also, 4.a.100.

126 There is no evidence or behaviour preservation case disclosed.

127 *Korean Line Corporation v HNA* Group (a reconsideration for a preservation order) [2016] Qiong 72 Xie Wai Ren No 1 (Haikou Maritime Court, reconsideration and binding order).

128 ibid.

129 *Guangdong Yuehua International Trade Group Co v Sinotide Holdings Limited and Junxiang Ke* (an application for a post-arbitral property preservation) [2014] Sui Zhong Fa Civil Si Chu Zi No 42 (the Intermediate People's Court of Guangzhou City of Guangdong Province, first instance and binding order).

130 The legal effect of 'Reply' amounts to a judicial interpretation. Further discussion on this concept can be found in Chapter 3, 3.18.

Preservation during the Recognition and Enforcement of a Hong Kong Arbitral Award for Automotive Gate Fzco, the SPC contended that there was no specific provision related to applications seeking property preservation measures after an applicant had filed an application for the recognition and enforcement of a Hong Kong arbitral award. However, by reference to Article 100 of the CPL 1991 (as amended until 2020), the court then allowed an application seeking property preservation measures under the circumstances, where the applicant had provided adequate security with the preservation application.[131]

4.a.102 Subsequently, in the case of *Farenco Shipping Pte Ltd v Eastern Ocean Transportation Co Ltd* in 2018, Farenco Shipping Pte Ltd (applicant) filed an application for a property preservation measure to the Guangzhou Maritime Court prior to their application seeking the recognition of a Hong Kong arbitral award in China. Meanwhile, the applicant provided sufficient security. The Guangzhou Maritime Court upheld this application and accordingly froze the bank account that belonged to *Eastern Ocean Transportation Co Ltd* (respondent) for one year.[132]

4.a.103 After the Guangdong Maritime Court had issued the order, the chief judge in this case provided further legal reasoning to support this order. He stressed that the SPC's Reply *Automotive Gate Fzco* case was a crucial legal foundation to approve the applicant's request.[133]

4.a.104 Against the above discussion, it is observed by the authors that the SPC's Reply may become the legal foundation for approving applications seeking all three types of preservation measures during the recognition and enforcement of a foreign arbitral award.

---

131 *Reply of the Supreme People's Court to the Request of Hubei High People's Court for Application of Property Preservation during the Recognition and Enforcement of Hong Kong Arbitral Award for Automotive Gate Fzco* ([2017] SPC Civil Ta No 129).

132 *Farenco Shipping Pte Ltd v Eastern Ocean Transportation Co Ltd* (an application seeking a post-arbitral property preservation measure) [2018] Yue 72 Cai Bao No78 (Guangzhou Maritime Court, binding order).

133 Chunlong Xu and Wenzhi Chen, '*Farenco Shipping Pte Ltd* (Singapore)'s Property Preservation Case Prior to Recognition and Enforcement of a HK Arbitral Award' (Guangzhou Maritime Court Webpage, 8 July 2019) <www.gzhsfy.gov.cn/web/content?gid=90506&lmdm =1016> accessed 15 June 2021.

PART 3

INTERIM MEASURES FOR PROPERTY

CHAPTER 5

Freezing Injunctions

Introduction

5.1 A freezing injunction is an interim injunction restraining a person – the Respondent[1] – from removing from England and Wales assets which are located there, or from dealing with assets whether located within England and Wales or not.[2] It can be granted in respect of any kind of assets, including real property, chattels, money, bank accounts and other intangibles.[3]

Mareva Injunctions and Asset Preservation Orders

5.2 Freezing injunctions are granted in support of two distinct categories of claim: personal claims and proprietary claims. A proprietary claim is one in which the Claimant asserts a right of ownership over assets in the hands of the Defendant. A personal claim is one in which the Claimant asserts a claim (often but not always a monetary claim) against the Defendant personally, but does not assert any claim to ownership of any assets in the Defendant's hands. The vast majority of civil and commercial claims under English law are personal claims.

5.3 The English court has the power to grant freezing injunctions in support of proprietary claims ("proprietary freezing injunctions" or "asset preservation orders"[4]), restraining the Respondent from disposing of or dealing with the assets to which the Applicant asserts ownership rights in any way, until those rights can be finally determined. Asset preservation orders are granted in order to preserve the assets over which the Applicant asserts ownership pending trial, and to prevent the Respondent from taking steps in the meantime which might prejudice the enforcement of those rights if the Applicant succeeds at trial. They are governed by the principles set out in

---

1 For an explanation of the terms Claimant, Defendant, Applicant and Respondent, see Chapter 2, 2.29–2.30.

2 This is based on the definition in CPR 25.1(1)(f).

3 Steven Gee QC, *Gee on Commercial Injunctions* (7th Edn, Sweet & Maxwell, 2020) §3-041.

4 Steven Gee QC, *Gee on Commercial Injunctions* (7th Edn, Sweet & Maxwell, 2020) §1-036.

DOI: 10.4324/9781003000310-9

American Cyanamid Co v Ethicon Ltd,[5] just like any other ordinary interim injunction.[6]

5.4 The English court also has the power to grant freezing injunctions in support of monetary personal claims. These are often known as "Mareva injunctions", after the Court of Appeal decision in *Mareva Compania Naviera SA v International Bulkcarriers Ltd*, one of the first cases in which such relief was granted.[7] Mareva injunctions are granted on a different basis from asset preservation orders, and they are governed by a different set of principles.

5.5 The purpose of a Mareva injunction is to prevent the Respondent from dissipating his own assets,[8] so as to deny the Applicant the fruits of a judgment or arbitral award.[9] It is normally granted on terms which provide that the Respondent must not remove his assets from England and Wales, or dispose of, deal with or diminish the value of his assets,[10] up to a stated value,[11] usually calculated as the value of the Applicant's substantive claim assessed on his reasonably arguable best case, plus a reasonable allowance for interest and costs.[12]

5.6 The Mareva injunction is a relatively modern innovation. It was developed by the English courts in a series of cases beginning in the mid-1970s, taking inspiration from remedies available in civil law jurisdictions, such the French law remedy of *saisie conservatoire*.[13] In so doing, the English courts created an exception to the rule in *Lister v Stubbs*[14] which had stood

5 [1975] AC 396 (HL) per Lord Diplock at page 406.

6 *Polly Peck International plc v Nadir* [1992] 4 All ER 769 (CA) per Scott LJ at page 784, and per Lord Donaldson of Lymington MR at page 787.

7 [1975] 2 Lloyd's Rep 509 (CA), one of the earliest Court of Appeal decisions to recognise the jurisdiction.

8 Or, in some cases, assets belonging to a third-party Defendant: see paras 5.41–5.42 below.

9 In addition, where a Mareva injunction is sought post-judgment, its purpose is also to facilitate execution of the judgment: *Michael Wilson & Partners v Emmott* [2019] EWCA Civ 219 per Gross LJ at [53].

10 See paragraph 5 of the standard forms of freezing injunction appended to CPR PD 25A and in Appendix 11 of the Commercial Court Guide.

11 See paragraph 5 of the standard forms of freezing injunction appended to CPR PD 25A and in Appendix 11 of the Commercial Court Guide.

12 Compare *The Moschanthy* [1971] 1 Lloyd's Rep 37 per Brandon J at page 44.

13 Which means "conservatory seizure".

14 (1890) 45 Ch D 1 (CA). See in particular the judgment of Cotton LJ at page 14, where he said: "if the money sought to be recovered is not the money of the Plaintiffs, we should be simply ordering the Defendant to pay into Court a sum of money in his possession because there is a *prima facie* case against him that at the hearing it will be established that he owes the money to the Plaintiffs. In my opinion, that would be wrong in principle … if we were to order the Defendant to give the security asked for, it would be introducing an entirely new and wrong principle—which we ought not to do, even though we might think that, having regard to the circumstances of the case, it would be highly just to make the order". NB the other important point decided in *Lister v Stubbs* – that an agent who takes a secret commission in breach of his fiduciary duty to his principal does not hold the commission or its proceeds on trust for his principal – survived even longer, until being finally overruled in *FHR European Ventures LLP v Cedar Capital Partners LLC* [2014] UKSC 45.

for almost a century.[15] This new Mareva jurisdiction proved to be a runaway success, particularly in commercial disputes. It is now the most important specialised form of interim injunction, and perhaps the most important of all the interim remedies, available from the English court.

5.7 The remainder of this chapter is concerned solely with Mareva injunctions, and not with asset preservation orders, which are subject to the rules applicable to ordinary interim injunctions discussed in Chapter 7.

5.8 Since the introduction of the CPR, with its preference for everyday language that is accessible to non-lawyers, the expression "Mareva injunction" has fallen out of favour, and the English courts now usually refer to Mareva injunctions simply as freezing injunctions (or freezing orders[16]). Likewise, in the remainder of this chapter, we will use the expression "freezing injunction" to mean Mareva injunctions.

The Freezing Injunction – One of English Law's "Nuclear Weapons"

5.9 Freezing injunctions can be granted in any kind of case involving a monetary claim.[17] They can be granted before substantive proceedings are commenced, during those proceedings and post-judgment, in aid of enforcement. They can also be granted in support of arbitration proceedings, foreign court proceedings and the enforcement of arbitral awards and foreign court judgments.

5.10 Despite their ubiquity, freezing injunctions are rightly regarded by the courts as a Draconian form of interim relief. They have been characterised as one of the nuclear weapons in the court's arsenal,[18] immensely powerful but also capable of doing great harm if used inappropriately. Freezing injunctions are an exceptional interim remedy in as much as they restrict the Respondent from dealing with his own assets in ways which would otherwise be entirely lawful, under penalty of contempt of court.[19] In most cases, they are granted pre-judgment, before the merits of the underlying dispute have

15 For a characteristically pithy and readable account of these developments, see the passage headed "Historical and Comparative Survey" in the judgment of Lord Denning MR in *Rasu Maritima SA v Perusahaan Pertambangan* [1978] QB 644 (CA) at pages 657–659.

16 The CPR refers to freezing injunctions. The Commercial Court Guide uses the terms freezing injunction and freezing order interchangeably.

17 But not a non-monetary claim such as a claim for a declaration: *Steamship Mutual Underwriting Association (Bermuda) Ltd v Thakur Shipping Co Ltd* [1986] 2 Lloyd's Rep 439 (CA) per Sir John Donaldson MR at page 440.

18 The other being the search order: *Bank Mellat v Nikpour* [1985] FSR 87 (CA) per Donaldson LJ at page 92.

19 Another interim remedy which has a comparable effect is the so-called "springboard" interim injunction, which restrains a Respondent from making improper use of information or property belonging to the Applicant: *QBE Management Services (UK) Ltd v Dymoke* [2012] EWHC 80 (QB) per Haddon-Cave J at [240]–[247].

been determined. Applications for freezing injunctions are invariably made and granted without notice to the Respondent, and are heard in private, for reasons of urgency and secrecy, to avoid the Respondent seeking to dispose of his assets before a freezing injunction can be obtained. This runs counter to normal principles of justice, under which the court should not grant relief against a person in legal proceedings unless he has been notified of the proceedings and given a fair opportunity to be heard and to adduce evidence.[20] A freezing injunction may have the effect of crippling a Respondent's business; and when granted pre-judgment, this can create irresistible pressure upon the Respondent to settle the underlying dispute on disadvantageous terms that may not truly reflect the strength of the case against him.

5.11 For these reasons, the English court exercises its power to grant freezing injunctions with circumspection, particularly pre-judgment.[21] Freezing injunctions can only be granted by a full High Court Judge.[22] The form and the terms in which they are granted are tightly controlled,[23] in order to restrict the scope of the order to what is necessary and proportionate to achieve the ends of justice, to protect third parties who might suffer loss or be exposed to liability as a result of the order and, in the case of freezing injunctions with extraterritorial effect, so as to be consistent with principles of international comity.[24]

Freezing Injunctions as Security

5.12 A freezing injunction, like other forms of interim injunction, operates *in personam*, as an order addressed to a particular person or persons[25] (the Respondent), prohibiting him personally from dealing with assets in certain specified ways, and backed by the sanction of proceedings being brought against him[26] personally for contempt of court. In this way, it provides the

---

20 Granting a freezing injunction does not, however, engage the Respondent's right to a fair trial under Article 6 of the European Convention on Human Rights, as it does not involve determining his civil rights: *APIS v Slovakia* (2009) 29 EHRR CD105 (ECHR) at page 106, a case considering a similar interim remedy under Slovak law.

21 Somewhat different considerations apply post-judgment, as the underlying merits will by then have been finally determined against the Respondent, and as there is a strong public policy in favour of enforcing judgments and arbitral awards: *Maclaine Watson & Co Ltd v International Tin Council (No.2)* [1987] 1 WLR 1711 (Ch) per Millet J at page 1717; *Gidrxslme Shipping Co Ltd v Tantomar-transportes Maritimos Lda* [1995] 1 WLR 299 (QB) per Colman J at page 310.

22 CPR 2.3, CPR PD 2B § 2 and CPR PD 25A §1.1. This includes a judge exercising the function of a High Court Judge *pro tem*.

23 Unless good reason is shown, the court will only grant a freezing injunction in the terms of the approved standard forms of order appended to CPR PD 25A or, in the case of applications in the Commercial Court, Appendix 11 to the Commercial Court Guide.

24 See Chapter 2, para 2.70.

25 Including both natural and legal persons (companies).

26 Including third parties who knowingly assist or permit the Respondent to breach its terms.

Applicant with a measure of security against the risk that the Respondent will render himself "judgment proof"[27] by disposing of his assets or otherwise placing them out of reach, and thereby rendering any money judgment[28] which the Claimant may later obtain[29] against him practically valueless because there are no available assets against which to enforce it.

5.13 A freezing injunction does not, however, provide the Applicant with security for his claim in the conventional sense.[30] In particular, it gives him no proprietary or other form of security interest in the assets which are caught by the injunction, as it imposes no obligation on the Respondent to satisfy any judgment the Applicant may obtain out of those assets.[31] Nor does it give the Applicant any priority over those assets ahead of other unsecured creditors in the event of the Respondent's insolvency.[32]

5.14 In this respect, the freezing injunction differs fundamentally from forms of pre-judgment attachment which are available in some other jurisdictions, which give the claimant a security interest in the attached property.[33] It also differs from ship arrest, an interim remedy which is available to a Claimant in certain types of proceedings in the English Admiralty Court:

14.1. Ship arrest is an interim remedy by which a Claimant can obtain security for certain types of maritime claim,[34] which can be enforced by bringing *in rem* proceedings against a ship itself. These claims fall into three categories: (i) claims which give the Claimant a maritime lien[35] over the ship in respect of which the claim arises; (ii) claims to enforce a mortgage on the ship or proprietary rights of

27 *Z Ltd v A-Z* [1982] QB 558 (CA) per Kerr LJ at page 584.

28 Or arbitral award, in the case of a freezing injunction granted in support of arbitration proceedings.

29 Or which he has already obtained, in the case of a freezing injunction granted post-judgment.

30 To that extent, the rule in *Lister v Stubbs* (1890) 45 Ch D 1 (CA) survives.

31 *Flightline Ltd v Edwards* [2003] EWCA Civ 63 per Jonathan Parker LJ at [47].

32 *Halifax plc v Chandler* [2001] EWCA Civ 1750 per Clarke LJ at [16].

33 A form of pre-judgment attachment which had that effect was at one time available, in limited circumstances, by custom in London and certain other English cities. The custom died out over a century ago. See *Rasu Maritima SA v Perusahaan Pertambangan* [1978] QB 644 (CA) per Lord Denning MR at pages 657–658.

34 Senior Courts Act 1981 sections 20(2) and 21(2)–(4).

35 A maritime lien is a security interest in a ship, which arises by operation of law and is enforced by bringing proceedings *in rem* against the ship. It attaches to the ship at the moment that the claim accrues, and is not defeated by subsequent transfers of ownership of the ship. See *The Bold Buccleugh* (1851) 7 Moo PC 267 (PC) per Sir John Jervis at pages 284–285. Five types of claim give rise to a maritime lien under English law: claims for damage done by a ship, claims for salvage (a monetary reward payable to a person who renders assistance to a ship or other property in danger at sea), claims for seamen's wages, claims for disbursements made by the ship's Master (the captain) on account of the ship and claims for bottomry and respondentia (obsolete forms of mortgage where the hull of the ship is pledged as security for a loan of money to the shipowner to fit out the ship or buy cargo): see generally Meeson and Kimbell on *Admiralty Jurisdiction and Practice*, 5th Ed (2017), Chapter 2.

possession or ownership of the ship; and (iii) claims which give rise to a so-called statutory lien[36] over the ship in respect of which the claim arises and also, in certain circumstances, a statutory lien over other ships in the same beneficial ownership.[37]

14.2. In contrast to a freezing injunction, where a ship is arrested on the application of a Claimant in *in rem* proceedings which are brought to enforce a maritime lien or a statutory lien, the arrested ship becomes security in the hands of the court for the Claimant's claim in those proceedings, which cannot be defeated by the subsequent insolvency of the shipowner.[38] The court also has the power to grant an interim order under CPR 25.1(1)(v) for the sale of a ship which has been arrested[39] and for the proceeds of sale to be paid into court. Where it does so, the Claimant's security interest transfers from the ship to those proceeds.

14.3. Ship arrest differs from a freezing injunction in other important respects. A warrant for the arrest of a ship can only be issued after the *in rem* Claim Form has been issued,[40] whereas a freezing injunction may be granted before a Claim Form is issued.[41] Unlike a freezing injunction, ship arrest is not a discretionary remedy, but is available as of right when the statutory requirements are satisfied.[42] As ship arrest is non-discretionary, the court has no power to attach conditions to the grant of a warrant of arrest; so it cannot require the Claimant to give an undertaking in damages as the price of arresting a ship,[43] as is invariably required of an Applicant seeking a freezing

36 A statutory lien is a procedural right of action *in rem* which arises by statute and enables the Claimant to acquire real security in a ship by commencing proceedings *in rem* against it. The right of action is defeated by a change in ownership of the ship before the commencement of proceedings: Senior Courts Act 1981 section 21(4): *The Carmania II* [1963] 2 Lloyd's Rep 152 (Admlty) per Hewson J at page 154. The claims which give rise to a statutory lien are listed in Nigel Meeson and John A Kimbell, *Admiralty Jurisdiction and Practice* (5th Edn, Informa Law from Routledge, 2017) §3.39.

37 Senior Courts Act 1981 section 21(4). Claims that give rise to a maritime lien over a ship also give rise to a statutory lien over other ships in the same beneficial ownership: Nigel Meeson and John A Kimbell, *Admiralty Jurisdiction and Practice* (5th Edn, Informa Law from Routledge, 2017) §3.40.

38 *The Cella* (1888) 13 PD 82 (CA) per Lopes LJ at page 88.

39 Known as a sale *pendente lite*, which is Latin for during the proceedings. See *The Myrto* [1977] 2 Lloyd's Rep 243 (Admlty) per Brandon J at page 261.

40 CPR 61.5(1).

41 CPR 25.2(1)(a).

42 *The Alkyon* [2018] EWCA Civ 2760 per Sir Terence Etherton MR at [43]. This is subject to a very limited exception in CPR 61.5(4), which provides that a warrant of arrest will not be issued as of right in the case of property in respect of which the beneficial ownership, as a result of a sale or disposal by any court in any jurisdiction exercising admiralty jurisdiction in rem, has changed since the claim form was issued.

43 *Willers v Joyce* [2016] UKSC 43 per Lord Clarke JSC at [68]; *The Alkyon* [2018] EWCA Civ 2760 per Sir Terence Etherton MR at [43]. CPR 61.5(2) and CPR PD 61.5(1) do, however, require an application for a warrant of arrest to be made on form ADM4, which contains a

injunction or other discretionary interim remedy. For the same reason, there is no duty on a Claimant to give full and frank disclosure when applying for a warrant of arrest.[44]

5.15 Despite this, freezing injunctions frequently do have the practical effect of giving an Applicant security for his claim, as they invariably contain a provision that the order will cease to apply upon the Respondent providing security for the Applicant's claim, either by paying a specified sum into Court or by some other method agreed with the Applicant.[45] Respondents often avail themselves of that provision in order to free their other assets from the shackles of the freezing injunction.

Sources of Law in Relation to Freezing Injunctions

5.16 The English court's power to grant freezing injunctions forms part of its inherent jurisdiction, which is confirmed by section 37 of the Senior Courts Act 1981.

5.17 When the court's power to grant freezing injunctions was first recognised in the 1970s, it was limited to cases where the Respondent was not within England and Wales but had assets there: in such cases the court could grant a freezing injunction restraining the foreign Respondent from removing those assets from England and Wales (a "domestic freezing injunction") so as to frustrate enforcement of a future judgment against him.[46] That limitation was a judge-made rule of principled discretion,[47] governing the way in which the court could exercise its otherwise unfettered power to grant injunctive relief whenever it appeared just and convenient to do so.

5.18 Part of this limitation was removed by statute, in section 37(3) of the Senior Courts Act 1981, which expressly permitted domestic freezing injunctions to be granted against Respondents who were domiciled, resident or present in England and Wales, as well as foreign Respondents. The remainder of the limitation was removed by the courts themselves, in a series of decisions in the 1980s and 1990s. The effect of these decisions is that the court may now grant a domestic freezing injunction restraining a Respondent from disposing of or dissipating assets within England and Wales as well as removing assets from the jurisdiction;[48] and also, in an appropriate case, from disposing

---

mandatory undertaking to pay the fees and expenses of the Admiralty Marshal in relation to the arrest, care and custody and release of the ship.

44 *The Varna* [1983] 2 Lloyd's Rep 253 (Admlty) per Scott LJ at page 257.

45 See paragraph 11(4) of the standard forms of freezing injunction appended to CPR PD 25A and in Appendix 11 of the Commercial Court Guide.

46 *Rasu Maritima SA v Perusahaan Pertambangan* [1978] QB 644 (CA) per Lord Denning MR at pages 659–660.

47 See Chapter 2, para 2.67(b).

48 *Z Ltd v A-Z* [1982] QB 558 (CA) per Lord Denning MR at page 571 and per Kerr LJ at page 584.

of or dissipating assets anywhere in the world (a "worldwide freezing injunction" or "WWFO"), both pre- and post-judgment.[49]

5.19 The practice of the English court on applications for freezing injunctions is governed by CPR Parts 23 and 25, including in particular CPR 25.1(1)(f) and (g), CPR PD 25A §6 and specialist court guides such as the Chancery Guide and the Commercial Court Guide. An officially sanctioned example of a freezing injunction is annexed to CPR PD 25A. A modified version, adapted for use in the Commercial Court, is contained in Appendix 11 of Commercial Court Guide. Each of these standard forms includes a penal notice, and specific provisions about which assets are covered, what the Respondent is restrained from doing with those assets and for how long, what he is permitted to do, how the order affects third parties and how it may be varied or discharged. The standard forms also contain sets of standard undertakings that the court will require of the Applicant as the price of the freezing injunction, including an undertaking in damages. The standard forms have been formulated to reflect the law and best practice as developed by the courts over the past 45 years. Applications for freezing injunctions must be based on these standard forms, modified as appropriate to suit the circumstances of the particular case. Any material departure from the standard terms should be expressly referred to the judge's attention at the without-notice hearing.[50]

Jurisdiction and Discretion

5.20 As with other types of interim injunction, the freezing injunction is a discretionary remedy which the court "may make" if it considers it just and convenient to do so in all the circumstances.[51]

5.21 Before seeking to engage the court's discretion, the Applicant must first establish that it has jurisdiction to grant the relief sought, and that it is appropriate to exercise that jurisdiction in this case. That may involve applying for permission from the court to serve originating process on the Respondent out of the jurisdiction.[52] Where the injunction is sought in support of foreign court proceedings, under section 25 of the Civil Jurisdiction and Judgments Act 1982, or in support of arbitration proceedings under section 44 of the Arbitration Act 1996, the Applicant must satisfy additional jurisdictional and discretionary requirements.[53]

---

49 *Babanaft International Co SA v Bassatne* [1990] Ch 13 (CA) per Kerr LJ at page 28, Neill LJ at page 40 and Nicholls LJ at page 43 (post-judgment); *Derby v Weldon (No.1)* [1990] Ch 48 (CA) per May and Parker LJJ at page 56 and Nicholls LJ at pages 58–59.

50 Commercial Court Guide §15.7.

51 Steven Gee QC, *Gee on Commercial Injunctions* (7th Edn, Sweet & Maxwell, 2020) §12-033; *Finurba Corporate Finance Ltd v Sipp SA* [2011] EWCA Civ 645 per Lord Neuberger MR at [30].

52 See Chapter 2, paras 2.68–2.89.

53 See Chapter 2, para 2.72.

5.22 Then, in all cases, the Applicant must satisfy the court in relation to the following matters: (i) good arguable case on the merits, (ii) risk of dissipation, (iii) assets to be caught and (iv) justice and convenience.

(i) Good Arguable Case on the Merits

5.23 The Applicant must show a good arguable case on the merits of his substantive claim, in support of which the freezing injunction is being sought.[54] This is the same test as the court applies when considering whether to grant permission to serve originating process out of the jurisdiction.[55] A good arguable case is one which is more than barely capable of serious argument, but not necessarily one that the court considers more likely than not to succeed.[56] The central concept at the heart of the test is the need for a plausible evidential basis for the claim.[57] This reflects the fact that freezing injunctions are usually sought at a very early stage, often before proceedings have been commenced, when not all of the relevant evidence may be available and none of it has yet been tested, as would be the case at trial. Nevertheless, good arguable case is a higher standard than serious issue to be tried, which applies to other ordinary interim injunctions. This reflects the stringent nature of freezing injunctions.

5.24 The substantive claim relied upon must exist and be immediately enforceable at the time when the application is made. The court will generally not, as a matter of principled discretion, grant a freezing injunction on a *quia timet* basis in support of a claim which has not yet arisen, for example, where the Applicant anticipates that a breach of contract is about to be committed, and wants to prevent the Respondent from dissipating assets which might be used satisfy a judgment for damages for that breach.[58]

---

54 *Rasu Maritima v Perusahaan Pertambangan* [1978] QB 644 (CA) per Lord Denning MR at page 661. Where the freezing injunction is being sought post-judgment, the test will automatically be satisfied. The same is invariably the case where the freezing injunction is sought in support of proceedings to enforce a foreign judgment or an arbitral award.

55 See Chapter 2, para 2.87.

56 *Ninemia Maritime Corp v Trave Schiffahrtsgesellschaft GmbH (The Niedersachsen)* [1983] 2 Lloyd's Rep 600 (QB) per Mustill J at page 605.

57 *Kaefer Aislamientos SA de CV v AMS Drillnig Mexico SA de CV* [2019] EWCA Civ 10 per Green LJ at [73]–[80].

58 *Steamship Mutual Underwriting Association (Bermuda) Ltd v Thakur Shipping Co Ltd* [1986] 2 Lloyd's Rep 439 (CA) per Sir John Donaldson MR at page 440; *Siporex Trade SA v Comdel Commodities Ltd* [1986] 2 Lloyd's Rep 428 per Bingham J at page 437; *Veracruz Transportation v VC Shipping Co Inc* [1992] 1 Lloyd's Rep 353 (CA) per Beldam LJ at pages 357–359, and Nourse LJ at page 360. This rule is based on Lord Diplock's dictum in *The Siskina (Owners of Cargo Lately Laden on Board) v Distos Compania Naviera SA (The Siskina)* [1979] AC 210 (HL) at page 256, that an interim injunction can only be granted on the basis of a pre-existing cause of action against the defendant arising out of an invasion, actual or threatened by him, of a legal or equitable right of the claimant; but that dictum no longer represents an accurate statement of the law. The courts have from time to time found their way around the rule in the *Veracruz* line of cases, see e.g. *Rowland v Gulfpac Ltd* [1999] 1 Lloyd's Rep Bank 86 (Rix J). The rule itself has been the subject of strong criticism, as in *Kazakhstan Kagazy*

(ii) **Risk of Dissipation**

5.25 The Applicant must demonstrate a real risk that a judgment or award would go unsatisfied by reason of the Respondent dissipating assets – placing them out of reach, by transferring or concealing them – unless restrained by the court from doing so.[59] Again the standard of proof is a good arguable case, which must met by adducing solid evidence rather than mere inference or generalised assertion.[60] Plausible evidence of dishonesty on the part of the Respondent may be sufficient to discharge this burden, but only if it points to the conclusion that assets may be dissipated.

5.26 Moreover, the threatened dissipation must be **unjustifiable.**[61] A freezing injunction is not intended to provide the Applicant with security for his claim; and nor is it intended to stop a Respondent from dealing with assets in the normal course of business (or, in the case of a Respondent who is an individual, from conducting his personal affairs in the way he would normally do), provided that such conduct is legitimate, even if it would be likely to result in the Applicant being unable to enforce a judgment or award.[62]

5.27 This important principle is reflected in the approved standard forms of freezing injunction, which provide that the order "does not prohibit the Respondent from dealing with or disposing of any of its, her or his assets in the ordinary and proper course of business",[63] the so-called Angel Bell exception.[64]

5.28 For much the same reasons, a freezing injunction will invariably contain a provision permitting the Respondent to spend a reasonable sum on legal advice and representation, and (in the case of a Respondent who is an individual) a reasonable sum on living expenses.[65]

5.29 What is legitimate will, however, depend on the circumstances of each individual case. In particular, where a freezing injunction is sought

---

plc v Zhunus [2016] EWHC 1048 (Comm) at [48] where Leggatt J said that it was "ripe for consideration". See generally Steven Gee QC, *Gee on Commercial Injunctions* (7th Edn, Sweet & Maxwell, 2020) §§12-001 to 12-004.

59 *Lakatamia Shipping Co Ltd v Morimoto* [2019] EWCA Civ 2203 per Haddon-Cave LJ at [33]. This applies whether the freezing injunction is sought pre- or post-judgment: *Les Ambassadeurs Club Ltd v Songbo Yu* [2021] EWCA Civ 1310 per Andrews LJ at [17].

60 *Lakatamia Shipping Co Ltd v Morimoto* [2019] EWCA Civ 2203 per Haddon-Cave LJ at [35].

61 *Ketchum International plc v Group Public Relations Holdings Ltd* [1997] 1 WLR 4 (CA) per Stuart-Smith LJ at page 10. Some authorities refer to "illegitimate" dissipation.

62 *Fundo Soberano de Angola v Dos Santos* [2018] EWHC 2199 (Comm) per Popplewell J at [86(6)].

63 See paragraph 11(2) of the standard forms of freezing injunction appended to CPR PD 25A and in Appendix 11 of the Commercial Court Guide.

64 This takes its name from the decision of Robert Goff J in *Iraqi Ministry of Defence v Arcepey Shipping Co SA (The Angel Bell)* [1981] 1 QB 85 (QB).

65 See paragraph 11(1) of the standard forms of freezing injunction appended to CPR PD 25A and in Appendix 11 of the Commercial Court Guide.

post-judgment,[66] the court will usually regard it as illegitimate for a judgment debtor to continue in business paying one lot of creditors, but not the judgment creditor. For that reason, freezing injunctions granted post-judgment do not usually contain the Angel Bell exception.[67]

(iii) **Assets to Be Caught**

5.30 The Applicant must demonstrate that the Respondent has assets which will be caught by the freezing injunction, as otherwise the injunction would serve no useful purpose and would be oppressive. The Applicant demonstrates this by adducing evidence to show there are grounds for belief that such assets exist.[68] The test of grounds for belief is probably a little easier to satisfy than the test of good arguable case, but both require the Applicant to adduce plausible evidence. Where the Applicant seeks a domestic freezing injunction, limited to assets within England and Wales, that evidence must show that there are grounds for belief that the Respondent has assets in England and Wales.

(iv) **Justice and Convenience**

5.31 The Applicant must satisfy the court that it is just and convenient to grant the relief sought.[69] This requirement covers a multitude of potential factors, depending on the individual circumstances of each case.

Worldwide Freezing Injunctions

5.32 Worldwide freezing injunctions covering assets outside England and Wales were at one time regarded as exceptional forms of relief.[70] They are now the norm. The requirements which an Applicant must satisfy in order to obtain worldwide relief are no different from those required for a domestic freezing injunction.[71]

5.33 Unlike domestic freezing injunctions, however, worldwide freezing injunctions raise issues of comity,[72] generally and in respect of their

---

66 Or where it is sought in support of the enforcement of a foreign judgment or an arbitral award.

67 *Mobile Telesystems Finance SA v Nomihold Securities Inc* [2011] EWCA Civ 1040 per Tomlinson LJ at [33]–[34]; *Michael Wilson & Partners v Emmott* [2019] EWCA Civ 219 per Gross LJ at [53]–[57]. This is why the Angel Bell exception appears in square brackets in the standard forms of freezing injunction appended to CPR PD 25A and in Appendix 11 of the Commercial Court Guide. Naturally, this reasoning does not apply to the exceptions for reasonable legal expenses and an individual Respondent's reasonable living expenses.

68 *Ras al Khaimah Investment Authority v Bestfort Development LLP* [2017] EWCA Civ 1014 per Longmore LJ at [39].

69 Senior Courts Act 1981 section 37(1).

70 *Derby & Co Ltd v Weldon (Nos. 3 and 4)* [1990] Ch 65 (CA) per Neill LJ at 93.

71 Steven Gee QC, *Gee on Commercial Injunctions* (7th Edn, Sweet & Maxwell, 2020) §12-048.

72 See Chapter 2, para 2.70(b).

potential effect on third parties in particular. These issues arise because a worldwide freezing injunction is an order of the English court which compels the Respondent to conduct himself in particular ways within the sovereign territory of another state, in relation to property which is also within that territory, under threat of quasi-criminal punishment for contempt if he disobeys.[73]

5.34 The English court must, of course, establish personal jurisdiction over the Respondent in order to grant a worldwide freezing injunction against him, and the rules governing personal jurisdiction are framed so as to be consistent with principles of comity. Third parties, however, are not subject to the personal jurisdiction of the English court. The court therefore takes particular care to avoid imposing obligations on such persons in respect of conduct abroad, regarding property which is outside England and Wales.

5.35 The standard forms of worldwide freezing injunction contain two provisions which are designed to address these comity issues by limiting the extraterritorial effect of the order. They are commonly referred to as the Babanaft proviso[74] and the Baltic proviso.[75]

5.36 The Babanaft proviso is entitled "Persons outside England and Wales" and reads as follows:[76]

> (1) Except as provided in paragraph (2) below, the terms of this order do not affect or concern anyone outside the jurisdiction of this Court.
> (2) The terms of this order will affect the following persons in a country or state outside the jurisdiction of this Court—
> a. the Respondent or its officer or its, her or his agent appointed by power of attorney;
> b. any person who—
> i. is subject to the jurisdiction of this Court;
> ii. has been given written notice of this order at it, her or his residence or place of business within the jurisdiction of this Court; and
> iii. is able to prevent acts or omissions outside the jurisdiction of this Court which constitute or assist in a breach of the terms of this order; and
> c. any other person, only to the extent that this order is declared enforceable by or is enforced by a Court in that country or state.

73 See Chapter 2, para 2.126.

74 This takes its name from the Court of Appeal decision in *Babanaft International SA v Bassatne* [1990] Ch 13 (CA), the first case in which a worldwide freezing injunction was granted, which contained the prototype of this proviso.

75 The prototype of this proviso was first ordered by Clarke J in *Baltic Shipping Co v Translink Shipping Ltd* [1995] 1 Lloyd's Rep 673 (QB).

76 See paragraph 19 of the standard forms of freezing injunction appended to CPR PD 25A and in Appendix 11 of the Commercial Court Guide.

5.37 The Baltic proviso is entitled "Assets Located outside England and Wales" and reads as follows:[77]

> Nothing in this order shall, in respect of assets located outside England and Wales, prevent any third party from complying with—
>
> (1) what it reasonably believes to be its obligations, contractual or otherwise, under the laws and obligations of the country or state in which those assets are situated or under the proper law of any contract between itself and the Respondent; and
> (2) any orders of the Courts of that country or state, provided that reasonable notice of any application for such an order is given to the Applicant's solicitors.

5.38 In addition, where the court grants a worldwide freezing injunction, it will generally require the Applicant to give an undertaking not to seek to enforce the injunction in any country outside England and Wales, without the permission of the court.[78] The court will only grant such permission where it is just and convenient to allow the injunction to be enforced abroad for the purpose of ensuring its effectiveness, and then only on terms which avoid oppression and provide suitable protections for the Respondent and third parties.[79]

Ancillary Orders

5.39 The court has power to grant ancillary interim remedies in order to ensure the effectiveness of a freezing injunction, and to enable the court to police the Respondent's compliance with it.[80] The most important of these is the power to order the Respondent to provide information and disclose documents about his assets, including their value, location and details.[81] A provision to this effect is included in the official standard forms of freezing injunction.[82] This power derives from the same source as the court's power to grant interim injunctions including freezing injunctions.[83] In the case of

77 See paragraph 20 of the standard forms of freezing injunction appended to CPR PD 25A and in Appendix 11 of the Commercial Court Guide.

78 See Schedule B, paragraph 10, of the standard forms of freezing injunction appended to CPR PD 25A and in Appendix 11 of the Commercial Court Guide.

79 See the guidelines set out by Arden LJ in *Dadourian Group International Inc v Simms (No.1)* [2006] EWCA Civ 399 at [25].

80 *House of Spring Gardens Ltd v Waite* [1985] FSR 173 (CA) per Cumming-Bruce LJ at page 183.

81 CPR 25.1(1)(g).

82 See paragraph 20 of the standard forms of freezing injunction appended to CPR PD 25A and in Appendix 11 of the Commercial Court Guide. The standard provision contains an exception in respect of material covered by the privilege against self-incrimination, which is discussed more fully at Chapter 9, 9.42–9.44, in the context of search orders.

83 *A J Bekhor & Co Ltd v Bilton* [1981] QB 923 (CA) per Ackner LJ at page 940. Indeed, an ancillary order for the provision of information can be conceptualized as a form of mandatory interim injunction.

a Respondent which is a corporation, this order will be directed to a proper officer, such as a director. The court will usually require the Respondent to provide information about his assets immediately upon being served with the freezing injunction, and to confirm that information by affidavit a few days later. Where there is justifiable concern that the Respondent (or its officer who provided the affidavit) has failed to disclose his assets in full as required by the order, the court has the power to order him to attend court in order to be cross-examined on the contents of his affidavit, for the purpose of revealing further assets which might otherwise be dissipated.[84] The court has no power, however, to compel an officer of a Respondent to attend court if that officer is not in the UK.[85]

5.40 The court also has the power to grant a number of other ancillary interim remedies, which are not granted as a matter of course:

40.1. Appointing a receiver to take control of the Respondent's assets on behalf of the court.[86] The court may grant this form of relief where there is serious concern that the Respondent will not comply with the freezing injunction. In such a case, the order will expressly require the Respondent to give up possession of his assets and do all that may be necessary to vest them in the receiver.[87] If the assets covered by the freezing injunction include a business, the court may also authorise the receiver to act as manager, with power to continue trading in order to preserve its goodwill and its value as a going concern.[88]

40.2. Ordering a Respondent, or an officer of a corporate Respondent, who is in the UK not to leave the country and to surrender his passport.[89] The court may make this order where there is justifiable concern that the Respondent (or its officer who provided the affidavit) has failed to provide full information about the Respondent's assets and that he may abscond in order to avoid being cross-examined.[90] Orders of

---

84 *Otkritie Investment Management Ltd v Urumov* [2012] EWHC 3106 (Comm).

85 Compare *Masri v Consolidated Contractors International (UK) Ltd (No.4)* [2009] UKHL 43.

86 As with injunctions, the appointment of a receiver is equitable remedy whose existence is confirmed by section 37(1) of the Senior Courts Act 1981. See generally John McGhee QC and Steven Elliott QC, *Snell's Equity* (34th Edn, Sweet & Maxwell, 2019) §§19-001, 003, 007-008, 016.

87 *Derby v Weldon (Nos. 3 and 4)* [1990] Ch 65 per Lord Donaldson of Lymington MR at pages 84–85.

88 *In re Newdigate Colliery Ltd* [1912] 1 Ch 468 at p 472 per Cozens-Hardy MR; *JSC BTA Bank v Ablyazov* [2012] EWHC 648 (Comm) at [14] per Hamblen J.

89 *Bayer AG v Winter* [1986] 1 WLR 479 per Fox LJ at pages 501–503. Again, this is a form of interim injunction. It has superseded the old procedure of issuing a Writ *ne exeat regno*: see David Bean, Isabel Parry, Andrew Burns, *Injunctions* (13th Edn, Sweet & Maxwell, 2018) §§7.42–7.44.

90 *In re Oriental Credit* [1988] Ch 204 per Harman J at page 208.

this nature are rare. They can only be granted where necessary to give effect to an order for the provision of information, and only on terms which are proportionate,[91] having regard to the Respondent's right to respect for privacy and family life under Article 8 of the European Convention on Human Rights. They cannot be used as a form of house arrest post-judgment, to compel the Respondent to satisfy a judgment against him.[92]

Chabra Injunctions

5.41 The court's jurisdiction to grant freezing injunctions extends to cases where the assets to be frozen are not in the hands of the person against whom the Applicant has a substantive monetary claim ("the substantive Defendant"). They may, for example, be granted against a Respondent who holds assets which belong in law or in equity to the substantive Defendant, such as a bailee in possession of personal property, or a trustee or nominee. The paradigm case for this is where the substantive Defendant seeks to make himself judgment-proof by transferring assets into the name of his spouse, while remaining the true owner in the eyes of the law.[93] If the Applicant can demonstrate good reason for supposing that identifiable assets in the hands of the Respondent belong to the substantive Defendant, the Court may grant a so-called Chabra[94] freezing injunction directly against that Respondent, restraining him from dealing with those particular assets, provided that the Applicant also satisfies the other requirements for the grant of a freezing injunction.[95] The applicable standard of proof on this issue is a good arguable case.[96] The evidence which the Applicant will need to adduce in order to meet that standard will need to be cogent, in order to persuade the court to grant a freezing injunction against a Respondent against whom the Applicant has no substantive cause of action. It is not, however, necessary for the Applicant to identify specific assets which belong to the substantive Defendant: where the Applicant shows that the Respondent has been mixed up in the substantive Defendant's attempts to make himself judgment-proof, the court may grant a freezing injunction over the Respondent's general assets.[97] Where the court

91 *Lakatamia Shipping Co Ltd v Su* [2021] EWCA Civ 1187 per Sir Nicholas Patten at [7].

92 *B v B (Injunction: Restraint on Leaving Jurisdiction)* [1998] 1 WLR 329 per Wilson J at page 334.

93 See e.g. *Mercantile Group AG v Aiyela* [1984] QB 366 (CA), where the court upheld a freezing injunction against the wife of a judgment creditor, into whose name he had transferred valuable assets in an attempt to frustrate enforcement of any judgment against him.

94 Named after the decision of Mummery J in *TSB Private Bank v Chabra* [1992] 1 WLR 231 (Ch).

95 *SCF v Masri* [1985] 1 WLR 876 (CA) per Lloyd LJ at page 884.

96 *TSB Private Bank v Chabra* [1992] 1 WLR 231 (Ch) per Mummery J at page 238.

97 *Yukong Line Ltd v Rendsburg Investments Corp* [2001] 2 Lloyd's Rep 113 (CA) per Potter LJ at [44].

grants a Chabra injunction on this basis, it may require the Respondent to provide information and disclosure to reveal the true beneficial ownership of the assets covered by the injunction.

5.42 Chabra injunctions are granted against the Respondent as an interim remedy ancillary and incidental to the Applicant's substantive claim against the substantive Defendant.[98] The Chabra jurisdiction is not, however, confined to cases where the Respondent holds assets which belong to the substantive Defendant.[99] It extends to cases where the substantive Defendant has some right in or in respect of, or control over, or other rights of access to, assets in the hands of the Respondent, from which the Respondent may be obliged to contribute to the assets of the substantive Defendant.[100] This principle was first recognised in the Australian decision of *Cardile v LED Building Proprietary Ltd*,[101] where the court granted a freezing injunction against the shareholders of the substantive Defendant, on the basis that they had received dividends in an asset stripping exercise designed to render the substantive Defendant judgment-proof. The court reasoned that, in the event of the substantive Defendant's insolvency, those sums would be recoverable by a liquidator acting on behalf of its creditors, including the Applicant; the sums recovered by the liquidator would be available to satisfy the Applicant's judgment against the substantive Defendant; and it was just and equitable to grant a freezing injunction against the Respondents to prevent them from dissipating their own assets so as to render themselves unable to satisfy the liquidator's claims. Chabra relief has, for example, been granted in cases where the Respondent was a wholly owned subsidiary of the Defendant.[102] There is no need to show a causal link between the Applicant's claim against the substantive Defendant and the basis on which the Respondent may be liable to contribute to the assets of the substantive Defendant.[103]

The Standard Form of Order

5.43 The structure and content of the standard forms of freezing injunction appended to CPR PD 25A and in Appendix 11 of the Commercial Court Guide reflect the fact that applications for freezing injunctions are invariably

98 *Yukong Line Ltd v Rendsburg Investments Corp* [2001] 2 Lloyd's Rep 113 (CA) per Potter LJ at [37].

99 *HM Revenue & Customs v Egleton* [2006] EWHC 2313 (Ch) per Briggs J at [41].

100 *Yukos Capital Sarl v OJSC Rosneft Oil Co* [2010] EWHC 784 (Comm) per David Steel J at [16]–[22].

101 [1999] HCA 18.

102 *Parbulk II AS v PT Humpuss Intermoda Transportasi TBK* [2011] EWHC 3143 (Comm) (Gloster J). Under English law, the assets of a company do not belong in law or in equity to its shareholders: *Salomon v A Salomon & Co Ltd* [1897] AC 22 HL(E).

103 *New York Laser Clinic Ltd v Naturastudios Ltd* [2020] EWHC 560 (QB) per Clive Sheldon QC at [82].

made without notice, and often on a very urgent basis, as well as the serious and Draconian nature of freezing injunctions. The following paragraphs refer to the version in Appendix 11 of the Commercial Court Guide. [104]

5.44 The standard form is headed "FREEZING INJUNCTION". It sets out the name of the court, the judge who made the order and the parties, followed by a prominent penal notice warning the Respondent, and any other person who knowingly helps or permits him to breach the order, that they may be imprisoned, fined or have their assets seized for disobeying the order.

5.45 Thereafter the main body of the order is set out under a series of sub-headings. The first of these is entitled "THIS ORDER", and contains the following key information:

45.1. The date when the order was made, the judge who made it and the Applicant who applied for it.
45.2. The evidence on which judge relied, and the undertakings he accepted from the Applicant (in each case by reference to Schedules attached to the order).
45.3. That the order was made at a hearing without notice to the Respondent.
45.4. That the Respondent has the right to apply to the court to vary of discharge the injunction, in accordance with more detailed provisions later in the order.
45.5. The Return Date on which there will be a further hearing in respect of the order, at which the Respondent may adduce evidence and make submissions.
45.6. That, where there is more than one Respondent, the order is effective against any Respondent on whom it is served or who is given notice of it.

5.46 The next section of the order is entitled "FREEZING INJUNCTION" and constitutes the central core of the freezing injunction. The operative provision is paragraph 5. Two alternative wordings are provided in the standard form of order, one for use in domestic freezing injunctions, the other for worldwide freezing injunctions. In each case, the provisions state that, until after the Return Date or further order of the Court,[105] the Respondent must not deal with his assets in the manner specified:

46.1. For domestic freezing injunctions, paragraph 5 states that Respondent must not "**remove** from England and Wales or in any way **dispose of, deal with or diminish the value of** any of its, his or her assets which are in England and Wales up to the value of" a

104 The general version appended to CPR PD 25A is in very similar terms.

105 This wording allows for the possibility that the court may vary freezing injunction prior to the Return Date, on the application of the Applicant, the Respondent or a third party.

stated figure determined by the Court, usually reflecting the value of the Applicant's substantive case assessed on his reasonably arguable best case, plus a reasonable allowance for interest and costs (emphasis added).

46.2. For worldwide freezing injunctions, paragraph 5 states that the Respondent must not (1) **remove from England and Wales** any of its, her or his assets which are in England and Wales, up to the stated value; or (2) "in any way **dispose of, deal with or diminish the value of** any or any of its, her or his assets **whether they are in or outside England and Wales** up to the same value" (emphasis added).

5.47 The standard order then contains two provisions, paragraphs 6 and 7, which clarify which assets are covered by the freezing injunction.

47.1. Paragraph 6 states that the freezing injunction applies to all the Respondent's assets whether or not they are in its, her or his own name, and whether they are solely or jointly owned.

47.2. It contains optional additional wording stating that the freezing injunction covers the Respondent's assets whether the Respondent is interested in them legally, beneficially or otherwise.[106] It may be inappropriate to include that wording in cases where it is clear that the Respondent genuinely holds some assets as trustee for the benefit of third parties who have no involvement in the underlying dispute: such assets are not available to satisfy the Applicant's substantive claim, which is the underlying purpose of a freezing injunction.[107]

47.3. Paragraph 6 then explains what count as the Respondent's assets for the purposes of the order: they include any asset which the Respondent has the power, directly or indirectly to dispose of or deal with as if it were his own; and the Respondent is to be regarded as having such power if a third party holds or controls the asset in accordance with the Respondent's instructions.

47.4. Paragraph 7 identifies any specific assets covered by the injunction. The Applicant will usually be in a position to identify some specific assets, but he need not do so, provided that he can satisfy the court that there are grounds for belief that the Respondent has assets that will be caught by the order.

5.48 Finally in this section of the order comes paragraph 8, which clarifies the respects in which the Respondent is free to deal with his assets above the value limit stated in paragraph 5 of the order. Again, two versions are

---

106 *JSC BTA Bank v Ablyazov (No.10)* [2015] UISC 64 per Lord Clarke of Stone-cum-Ebony at [46].

107 *JSC BTA Bank v Solodchenko* [2010] EWCA Civ 1436 per Patten LJ [49].

provided in the standard form of order, for domestic and worldwide freezing injunctions respectively.

5.49 The next section is entitled "PROVISION OF INFORMATION" and contains two provisions, paragraphs 9 and 10.

49.1. Paragraph 9 requires the Respondent to inform the Applicant's solicitors, within the time specified "and to the best of his ability", of all his assets, either in England and Wales (in the case of a domestic freezing injunction) or worldwide (for a worldwide freezing injunction), including the value, location and details of all such assets. The provision will usually specify a minimum asset value, so that the Respondent is not required to provide information about low-value items, as that would be disproportionately onerous compared with the benefit to the Applicant.

49.2. The time limit for providing the information required by paragraph 9 may be as little as a matter of hours. More often it will be measured in days. The court should in any case give careful consideration to ensuring that the period is realistic in the particular circumstances of the case, given the likely nature and volume of material that may have to be disclosed, and the resources which are likely to be available to the Respondent in order to discharge this obligation.[108]

49.3. Paragraph 9 also contains a proviso stating the Respondent is entitled to refuse to provide information covered by the privilege against self-incrimination.[109]

49.4. Paragraph 10 of the standard order requires the Respondent to swear and serve an affidavit verifying the information provided pursuant to paragraph 9, within a specified number of working days. The court has the power to order the Respondent (or, in the case of a corporate Respondent, the officer who makes the affidavit on its behalf) to attend court to be cross-examined on the affidavit if it appears that the Respondent has failed to disclose all the required information.[110]

5.50 The next section of the standard form order is entitled "EXCEPTIONS TO THIS ORDER" and contains paragraph 11, which provides as follows:

50.1. That the order does not prohibit the Respondent from spending a stated amount on ordinary living expenses (which may be dispensed with in the case of a corporate Respondent), and a stated amount (or the court may order "a reasonable sum" without specifying the

108 See the footnote to this paragraph of the standard draft order in Appendix 11 to the Commercial Court Guide.

109 See Chapter 9, 9.42–9.44, where this is discussed in detail in the context of search orders.

110 See 5.39 above.

amount) on legal advice and representation. The court may supplement this with a requirement that the Respondent informs the Applicant's legal advisers before spending any money.

50.2. That the Respondent may agree in writing with the Applicant's solicitors to vary the amounts which he is permitted to spend.

50.3. That the freezing injunction will cease to have effect if the Respondent provides security in a specified amount.[111]

5.51 Paragraph 11 also contains the Angel Bell provision, discussed earlier in this chapter.[112] This may be dispensed with where the freezing injunction is granted post-judgment.

5.52 Next come sections entitled "COSTS", "VARIATION OR DISCHARGE OF THIS ORDER" and "INTERPRETATION OF THIS ORDER", which are largely self-explanatory.

5.53 These are followed by the important section entitled "PARTIES OTHER THAN THE APPLICANT AND RESPONDENT". This section contains the Babanaft and Baltic provisos discussed earlier in this chapter,[113] which are designed to ensure that the order is consistent with principles of comity when granted on a worldwide basis. It also contains two important provisions designed to protect the position of banks with whom the Respondent may have monies on account, which are covered by the freezing injunction.

53.1. Paragraph 17 of the standard form order is entitled "Set off by banks" and provides that the freezing injunction does not prevent any bank from exercising any right of set off it may have in respect of any facility which it gave to the respondent before it was notified of the order. This is designed to ensure that the freezing injunction does not impair the bank's security over the Respondent's accounts.

53.2. Paragraph 18 is entitled "Withdrawals by the Respondent" and provides that no bank need enquire as to the application or proposed application of any money withdrawn by the Respondent if the withdrawal appears to be permitted by this order. This is designed to give banks comfort that they are not exposing themselves to liability for contempt proceedings if they allow the Respondent to withdraw funds for purposes which are not permitted by the terms of the order, save in clear cases.

5.54 The final section of the standard form order is entitled "COMMUNICATIONS WITH THE COURT" and contains the court's contact details and opening hours.

111 See 5.15 above.
112 See 5.27 above.
113 See 5.35–5.37 above.

5.55 Attached to the standard form order are two schedules. The first, Schedule A, lists the affidavit evidence presented to the Court at the without-notice hearing. The second, Schedule B, sets out a set of standard undertakings which the Court will normally require from the Applicant at that hearing. These include:

55.1. An undertaking in damages, in terms that if the court later finds that the order has caused loss to the Respondent, and decides that the Respondent should be compensated for that loss, the Applicant will comply with any order the court may make.[114] The court may, in its discretion, require the Applicant to fortify this by giving a further undertaking to provide security in a specified amount, within a specified period, in a form satisfactory to the court. If the Respondent fails to comply with this undertaking, the freezing injunction will cease to have effect.

55.2. An undertaking to issue and serve a Claim Form. This reflects the fact that applications for freezing injunctions are usually made before the commencement of proceedings.

55.3. An undertaking to swear and file an affidavit containing the evidence relied upon at the without notice hearing if, as is often the case, the application was made on the basis of a draft affidavit or without an affidavit at all.[115]

55.4. An undertaking to serve the order, copies of the evidence relied upon, the Claim Form and an application notice for continuation of the freezing injunction,[116] on the Respondent. The court may also require an undertaking to provide a copy of the order on anyone who is notified of it, such as a bank.

55.5. An undertaking to pay the reasonable costs incurred by any third party in finding out whether they hold assets of the Respondents that are covered by the freezing injunction, and to comply with any order the court may make requiring them to compensate such person for any loss they suffer as a result of the freezing injunction.

55.6. An undertaking immediately to take all reasonable steps to inform anyone who has been notified of the order, or who may act on the order, if the order ceases to have effect.

55.7. An undertaking not to use information obtained as a result of the order for the purposes of any other proceedings without the permission of the court.

---

114 This undertaking is the only basis on which the Applicant can be made liable to compensate the Respondent for losses caused by a freezing injunction being wrongly granted: see Chapter 2, 2.119–2.120.

115 See Chapter 2, 2.100.

116 This application will be determined at the Return Date hearing: see Chapter 2, 2.107.

55.8. An undertaking not to seek to enforce the order or seek any order of a similar nature outside England and Wales without the permission of the court.[117]

Claim No ____________

IN THE HIGH COURT OF JUSTICE
BUSINESS AND PROPERTY COURTS OF ENGLAND AND WALES
COMMERCIAL COURT (QBD)
The Honourable Mr(s) Justice______________

B E T W E E N:

QUATRO CANCAN AB

Applicant

-and-

TINY CROCODILE LIMTED

Respondent

____

Draft / ORDER

____

PENAL NOTICE

If you TINY CROCODILE LTD. disobey this Order you may be held to be in contempt of court and may be imprisoned, fined or have your assets seized. Any other person who knows of this order and does anything which helps or permits the Respondent to breach the terms of this Order may also be held to be in contempt of court and may be imprisoned, fined or have their assets seized.

THIS ORDER

1. This is a Freezing Injunction made against Tiny Crocodile Ltd. ("the Respondent") on 31 May 2022 by Mrs/Mr Justice on the application of Quatro Cancan AB ("the Applicant"). The Judge read the Affidavits listed in Schedule A and accepted the undertakings set out in Schedule B at the end of this Order.
2. This order was made at a hearing without notice to the Respondent. The Respondent has a right to apply to the Court to vary or discharge the order – see paragraph 13 below.

117 See 5.38 above.

3. There will be a further hearing in respect of this order on ("the return date").
4. If there is more than one Respondent –
   a. Unless otherwise stated, references in this order to "the Respondent" mean both or all of them; and
   b. This order is effective against any Respondent on whom it is served or who is given notice of it.

FREEZING INJUNCTION

5. Until the return date or further order of the Court, the Respondent must not –
   a. Remove from England and Wales any of its, her or his assets which are in England and Wales up to the value of USD 1,200,000; or
   b. In any way dispose of, deal with or diminish the value of any of its, her or his assets whether they are in or outside England and Wales up to the same value.
6. Paragraph 5 applies to all the Respondent's assets whether or not they are in its, her or his own name, whether they are solely or jointly owned and whether the Respondent is interested in them legally, beneficially or otherwise. For the purpose of this order the Respondent's assets include any asset which it, she or he has the power, directly or indirectly, to dispose of or deal with as if it were its, her or his own. The Respondent is to be regarded as having such power if a third party holds or controls the asset in accordance with its, her or his direct or indirect instructions.
7. This prohibition includes the following assets in particular –
   a. The property known as Rodent House, 291 Rat Street, London.
   b. Any money in the account numbered 123456789 at the First Erehwon Bank, 14 Utopia Plaza, New York, USA.
   c. Any interest under any trust or similar entity including any interest which can arise by virtue of the exercise of any power of appointment, discretion or otherwise howsoever.
8.
   a. If the total value free of charges or other securities ("unencumbered value") of the Respondent's assets in England and Wales exceeds USD 1,200,000, the Respondent may remove any of those assets from England and Wales or may dispose of or deal with them so long as the total unencumbered value of the Respondent's assets still in England and Wales remains above USD 1,200,000.

b. If the total unencumbered value of the Respondent's assets in England and Wales does not exceed USD 1,200,000, the Respondent must not remove any of those assets from England and Wales and must not dispose of or deal with any of them. If the Respondent has other assets outside England and Wales she, he or it may dispose of or deal with those assets outside England and Wales so long as the total unencumbered value of all its, her or his assets whether in or outside England and Wales remains above USD 1,200,000.

PROVISION OF INFORMATION

9.
   a. Unless paragraph b. applies, the Respondent must within 48 hours of service of this order, and to the best of his ability inform the Applicant's solicitors of its, her or his assets worldwide, exceeding USD 1,000 in value, whether in its, her or his own name or not and whether solely or jointly owned, giving the value, location and details of all such assets.
   b. If the provision of this information is likely to incriminate the Respondent, she or he may be entitled to refuse to provide it, but is recommended to take legal advice before refusing to provide the information. Wrongful refusal to provide the information is contempt of Court and may render the Respondent liable to be imprisoned, fined or have its, her or his assets seized.

10. Within seven working days after being served with this order, the Respondent must swear and serve on the Applicant's solicitors an affidavit setting out the above information.

EXCEPTIONS TO THIS ORDER

11.
   a. This order does not prohibit the Respondent from spending £15,000 on legal advice and representation.
   b. This order does not prohibit the Respondent from dealing with or disposing of any of its, her or his assets in the ordinary and proper course of business.
   c. The Respondent may agree with the Applicant's legal representatives that the above spending limits should be increased or that this order should be varied in any other respect, but any agreement must be in writing.
   d. This order will cease to have effect if the Respondent –

i. Provides security by paying the sum of USD 1,200,000 into Court, to be held to the order of the Court; or
ii. Makes provision for security in that sum by another method agreed with the Applicant's legal representatives.

COSTS

12. The costs of this application are reserved to the Judge hearing the application on the return date.

VARIATION OR DISCHARGE OF THIS ORDER

13. Anyone served with or notified of this order may apply to the Court at any time to vary or discharge this order (or so much of it as affects that person), but they must first inform the Applicant's solicitors. If any evidence is to be relied upon in support of the application, the substance of it must be communicated in writing to the Applicant's solicitors in advance.

INTERPRETATION OF THIS ORDER

14. A Respondent who is an individual who is ordered not to do something must not do it herself or himself or in any other way. She or he must not do it through others acting on her or his behalf or on her or his instructions or with her or his encouragement.
15. A Respondent which is not an individual which is ordered not to do something must not do it itself or by its directors, officers, partners, employees or agents or in any other way.

PARTIES OTHER THAN THE APPLICANT AND RESPONDENT

16. **Effect of this order**

    It is a contempt of Court for any person notified of this order knowingly to assist in or permit a breach of this order. Any person doing so may be imprisoned, fined or have their assets seized.
17. **Set off by banks**

    This injunction does not prevent any bank from exercising any right of set off it may have in respect of any facility which it gave to the Respondent before it was notified of this order.
18. **Withdrawals by the Respondent**

No bank need enquire as to the application or proposed application of any money withdrawn by the Respondent if the withdrawal appears to be permitted by this order.

19. **Persons outside England and Wales**
   (1) Except as provided in paragraph (2) below, the terms of this order do not affect or concern anyone outside the jurisdiction of this Court.
   (2) The terms of this order will affect the following persons in a country or state outside the jurisdiction of this Court –
      a. The Respondent or its officer or its, her or his agent appointed by power of attorney;
      b. Any person who –
         i. Is subject to the jurisdiction of this Court;
         ii. Has been given written notice of this order at its, her or his residence or place of business within the jurisdiction of this Court; and
         iii. Is able to prevent acts or omissions outside the jurisdiction of this Court which constitute or assist in a breach of the terms of this order; and
      c. Any other person, only to the extent that this order is declared enforceable by or is enforced by a Court in that country or state.

20. **Assets Located outside England and Wales**
   Nothing in this order shall, in respect of assets located outside England and Wales, prevent any third party from complying with –
   a. What it reasonably believes to be its obligations, contractual or otherwise, under the laws and obligations of the country or state in which those assets are situated or under the proper law of any contract between itself and the Respondent; and
   b. Any orders of the Courts of that country or state, provided that reasonable notice of any application for such an order is given to the Applicant's solicitors.

COMMUNICATIONS WITH THE COURT

All communications to the Court about this order should be addressed to the Admiralty and Commercial Court Listing Office, 7 Rolls Building, Fetter Lane, London EC4A 1NL, quoting the case number. The telephone number is (+44) (0) 20 7947 6826.

The offices are open between 10 am and 4.30 pm Monday to Friday.

SCHEDULE A – AFFIDAVITS

The Applicant relied on the following affidavits –

First affidavit of Gary Foxman Feld, sworn 31 May 2022, filed on behalf of the Applicant.

SCHEDULE B – Undertakings given to the Court by the Applicant

(1) If the Court later finds that this order has caused loss to the Respondent, and decides that the Respondent should be compensated for that loss, the Applicant may comply with any order the Court may make.

(2) The Applicant will –
   a. On or before 4 June 2022 cause a written guarantee in a form satisfactory to the Court in the sum of £ to be issued from a bank with a place of business within England or Wales in respect of any order the Court may make pursuant to paragraphs (1) above and (6) below.
   b. Immediately upon issue of the guarantee, cause a copy of it to be served on the Respondent.

(3) As soon as practicable the Applicant will issue and serve a claim form claiming the appropriate relief.

(4) The Applicant will serve upon the Respondent together with this order as soon as practicable –
   a. Copies of the affidavits and exhibits containing the evidence relied upon by the Applicant, and any other documents provided to the Court on the making of the application;
   b. The claim form; and
   c. An application notice for continuation of the order.

(5) Anyone notified of this order will be given a copy of it by the Applicant's legal representatives.

(6) The Applicant will pay the reasonable costs of anyone other than the Respondent which have been incurred as a result of this order including the costs of finding out whether that person holds any of the Respondent's assets, and if the Court later finds that this order has caused such person loss, the Applicant will comply with any order the Court may make.

(7) If this order ceases to have effect (for example, if the Respondent provides security or the applicant does not provide a bank guarantee as provided for above) the Applicant will immediately take all reasonable steps to inform in writing anyone to whom he has given notice of this order, or who she, he or it has reasonable grounds for supposing may act upon this order, that it has ceased to have effect.

(8) The Applicant will not without the permission of the Court use any information obtained as a result of this order for the purpose of any civil or criminal proceedings, either in England and Wales or in any other jurisdiction, other than this claim.

(9) The Applicant will not without the permission of the Court seek to enforce this order in any country outside England and Wales or seek an order of a similar nature including orders conferring a charge or other security against the Respondent or the Respondent's assets.

NAME AND ADDRESS OF APPLICANT'S LEGAL REPRESENTATIVES

The Applicant's solicitors are:
Rex Hoople & Co LLP: Gary Feld (partner).
Correspondence address: No.14 Tiger Square, London, England, EC1X 9LP
Telephone: +44 (0)20 9099 9999 (24 hours)
Email: g.feld@rexhooplelegal.com

G.F. Feld
First affidavit
31.5.2022
For Applicant
Exhibit GFF1

Claim No ____________

IN THE HIGH COURT OF JUSTICE
BUSINESS AND PROPERTY COURTS OF ENGLAND AND WALES
COMMERCIAL COURT (QBD)

B E T W E E N:

QUATRO CANCAN INC

Applicant

-and-

TINY CROCODILE LIMITED

Respondent

AFFIDAVIT OF GARY FOXMAN FELD

I, Gary Foxman Feld, MAKE OATH and say as follows:

1. I am a solicitor and partner in the firm of Rex Hoople & Co LLP of No.14 Tiger Square, London EC1X 9LP, solicitors for the Applicant. I have the conduct of this case on behalf of the Applicant. I am duly authorised by the Applicant to make this witness statement.

2. The facts and matters to which I shall hereafter depose are known to me from my conduct of this case and from documents and from information provided to me by David Jones, the Applicant's managing director. Insofar as the contents of this affidavit are within my own knowledge, they are true. Otherwise they are true to the best of my knowledge, information and belief.
3. I swear this affidavit in support of the Applicant's application for an urgent worldwide freezing injunction against the Respondent, Tiny Crocodile Ltd.
4. There is now produced and shown to me and exhibited hereto marked "GFF1" a paginated bundle of true copy documents to which I shall hereinafter refer by page numbers in square brackets: [#].
5. This application is being made without notice to the Respondent for reasons of secrecy and urgency.

Background

6. The Applicant is a commodity trading company based in New York. By a contract dated 1 April 2022, the Respondent agreed to sell and the Applicant agreed to buy 60,000 mt +/– 5% in seller's option unobtainium ore, containing minimum 0.4% unobtainium by weight, FOB Valparaiso, Chile, for shipment between 24 and 28 April 2022. The agreed price was USD 28 per mt, payable by letter of credit against documents including a bill of lading, commercial invoice and assay certificate from the Asociación de Ensayadores de Minerales de los Andes (AEMA) based in Santiago, Chile, confirming that a representative sample of the cargo as shipped contained a minimum of 0.4% unobtainium by weight.
7. A copy of the sale contract is at [1–14]. By clause 12, it expressly provides for English law and the exclusive jurisdiction of the English High Court.
8. Pursuant to the sale contract, on 3 April 2022 the Applicant chartered the Ultramax bulk carrier "NOSFERATU" to carry the cargo from Valparaiso to 1–2 safe ports in China [15–41] and nominated that vessel to lift the cargo under the sale contract [42]. On 19 April 2022 the Applicant opened a letter of credit in favour of the Respondent for the purchase price with the Hesperides Bank [43–45].
9. The vessel arrived at Valparaiso on 24 April 2022. Between 24 and 26 April she loaded 60,231 mt of unobtainium ore, as evidenced by the bill of lading issued on behalf of the Master, dated Valparaiso 26 April [44].

10. During loading, cargo sampling was conducted by a surveyor from Ebeneezer & Co, Mr Goode, under the supervision of the Applicant's local representative, Mr Rodolpho, and representatives of the Respondent and the shipowners. Mr Goode prepared five sets of composite samples: one for each of the Applicant, the Respondent and the shipowners, one to be sent by Ebeneezer & Co for analysis by AMEA and one to be retailed by Ebeneezer & Co. I attach a copy of the joint sampling report prepared by Mr Goode of Ebeneezer & Co which explains these matters [45–76].
11. On the morning of 27 April 2022, the Vessel sailed from Valparaiso bound for Ningbo, China, as confirmed by the Master's noon report which was sent to the Applicant that day by email [77].
12. On 28 April 2022 the Respondent presented the Hesperides Bank with the documents required by the letter of credit, including an assay certificate which appeared to be issued by AMEA, stating that the cargo contained 0.421% unobtainium by weight. On 28 April the Hesperides Bank remitted the sum of USD 1,686,468 to the Respondent's account number 123456789 at the First Erehwon Bank, 14 Utopia Plaza, New York, USA, in accordance with the Respondent's instructions, and debited the Applicant's account with the Hesperides Bank by the same amount. I attach an email from Mr Velasquez of the Hesperides Bank to Mr Jones of the Applicant sent yesterday, 30 April, in which he confirmed this information and sought the Applicant's instructions in relation to the bill of lading.
13. The Applicant's representatives at Valparaiso, Mr Rodolpho, sent the Applicant's sample to the Laboratorio Analítico Bolivariano (LAB) in La Paz for analysis. On 28 April, LAB sent Mr Rodolpho its assay report on that sample, stating that it contained just 0.2001% unobtainium by weight [78–82].
14. Mr Rodolpho emailed the LAB report to Mr Jones on the morning of 30 April [83]. Mr Jones immediately contacted Mr Velasquez at Hesperides Bank, who emailed him a copy of the assay certificate which had been presented to the bank in order to obtain payment under the letter of credit. I attach a copy of the certificate at [83–84]. The certificate purports to be signed by a Pedro Montero.
15. I forwarded a copy of that certificate by email to AEMA on 29 April asking them to confirm that it was genuine and accurate. I attach AEMA's reply at [85–87]. It confirms that Pedro Montero is an assay technician employed at AEMA, and that he performed an assay on a sample of the cargo on 27 April 2022 and issued a certificate for it, but that his certificate stated that the sample contained 0.221% unobtainium by weight. He also sent me a copy of the true AEMA certificate [88–89].

16. I therefore believe that the Applicant, and the Hesperides Bank, have been the victims of a fraud, in which the Respondent, having shipped a cargo which does not comply with the specifications in the sale contract, has dishonestly forged an assay certificate and presented it to the Hesperides Bank in order to obtain payment of the purchase price under the letter of credit, knowing that it was not entitled to that payment.

Good Arguable Case on the Merits

17. Based on the matters which I have set out above, I believe that the Applicant has a good arguable case on the merits of a claim against the Respondent for breach of the contract of sale.
18. The *prima facie* measure of damages for that breach is the difference between the value of the cargo at the time of delivery to the Applicant and the value it would have had if it had contained the contractual minimum quantity of unobtainium. I attach a copy of a market report published by the Shanghai Metal Exchange, for the week in which the cargo was loaded, which states that the average market price of minimum 0.2% unobtainium ore shipped on the east coast of South America during that week was USD 14 per metric tonne, compared with USD 28 per mt minimum 0.4% ore. Accordingly I believe that that the Applicant has a good arguable case on the merits of a claim for damages for USD 843,234.
19. I also believe, based on the matters which I have set out above, that the Applicant may have a good arguable case on the merits of claims against the Respondent for similar amounts, for deceit and unjust enrichment.

Risk of Dissipation

20. I believe that there is a real risk that, unless restrained by a freezing injunction, the Respondent will take illegitimate steps to dissipate its assets, so as to frustrate the enforcement of any judgment the Applicant may obtain against it hereafter. I base that belief on the Respondent's apparently fraudulent conduct, in procuring a forged assay certificate and dishonestly presenting it to the Hesperides Bank to obtain payment under the letter of credit to which it was not entitled.

Respondent's Assets

21. I believe that the Respondent has assets within and outside the jurisdiction that would be caught by a freezing injunction. In particular:

a. The Respondent's registered address is Rodent House, 291 Rat Street, London. An online search of the property at the Land Registry reveals that the Respondent is the sole freehold proprietor, but that there is a charge on the property in favour of the First Erehwon Bank (UK) Ltd [90–95]. I do not know the unencumbered value of the property, or the value of the Respondent's equity in that property. The Respondent is unlikely to be able to sell the property quickly, particularly in light of the existing mortgage, but it may be able to dispose of the remaining equity quickly by borrowing against it. In particular, it may be able to do so quickly by borrowing further from the First Erehwon Bank (UK) Ltd, if the existing charge on the property is an all monies charge.

b. The Respondent has a bank account numbered 123456789 at the First Erehwon Bank, 14 Utopia Plaza, New York, USA. The sum of USD 1,686,468 was remitted into that account on 28 April 2022, and so I believe that the account is likely to be in credit. The Respondent may, however, have transferred that money to another account or accounts.

Just and Convenient

22. I believe that, in all the circumstances, it is just and convenient to grant the relief sought.
23. The Applicant offers the usual undertakings, including an undertaking to fortify its undertaking in damages if the Court so requires. I attach a copy of the Applicant's latest annual report and accounts [96–147], which show that the Applicant has total assets of USD 37 million, albeit not within England and Wales.

SWORN by the above-named Gary Foxwell Feld

This 1st day of May 2022

at

Before me

CHAPTER 6

Preservation Measure of Property in China

Introduction

Definition of Property Preservation and Its Purpose

6.1 A preservation measure of property (hereinafter referred to as "property preservation measure") enjoys the most comprehensive and developed system compared with other preservation measures available in China. The other two prominent preservation measures are "preservation measure of behaviour" and "preservation measure of evidence".[1] However, in accordance with the existing law, there is no direct definition of the property preservation measure that can be cited here.

6.2 By reference to Articles 100, 101, 102 and 103 of the Civil Procedure Law of the People's Republic of China (hereinafter referred to as "CPL 1991 (as amended until 2020)"),[2] the property preservation measure can be defined as follows:

> In the light of the application of an interested party or any concerned party to a competent court, then that court can take compulsory measures against the respondent's property or the disputed subject matter by means of pre-sealing,[3]

1 Refer to Chapter 1, 1.83–1.87 and 1.98–1.100 in relation to the evolution of property preservation measures in China. In addition, the other two preservation measures are discussed in Chapters 8 and 10 respectively.

2 Civil Procedure Law of the People's Republic of China 1991 was amended in 2005, majorly revised and amended in 2012. After the amendments of 2017, there has been no further amendment to it.

3 The validity of the "pre-sealing" of a subject matter is considered as equivalent to sealing up the same subject matter. Pursuant to *Notice on Some Issues Concerning Regulating the Execution by the People's Courts and the Assistance in Execution by the Departments of Land, Resources and Real Estate Administration According to Law* (Fa Fa [2004] No 5), the enforcement measure of "pre-sealing" is available in the context of the property preservation measure when the subject matters of enforcement are real estate, including land and houses, and such "pre-sealing" subject matters have not been registered in the name of the respondent. In other words, when the respondent has practically not completed the formalities for registration of the ownership, for example, where the full or partial transaction price has been paid for the transferred land but the formalities for registration of the ownership have not been fully completed.

DOI: 10.4324/9781003000310-10

sealing up, detaining, freezing of property or any other means prescribed by law, for the purpose of ensuring the enforcement of a future court judgement or an arbitral award, or preventing from the other loss of parties concerned.

6.3 An application seeking property preservation measures can be made either in pre-action or post-action proceedings or even in support of arbitration proceedings.4 In addition, a Chinese judge, without any party seeking such preservation order, can *ex officio* implement preservation of property measures. Regardless of the pre-action or post-action property preservation applications, the main purpose of such preservation is to secure the enforcement of future judgments or arbitral awards, or to avoid the applicant's underlying loss arising from the dispute.

Applicable Laws

6.4 The CPL 1991 (as amended until 2020), *Interpretations of the Supreme People's Court on Application of the Civil Procedure Law of the People's Republic of China 2015 (2020 Amendment)* (hereinafter referred to as "Interpretation of CPL 2015 (2020 Amendment)")5 and *Provisions of the Supreme People's Court on Several Issues Concerning the Handling of Property Preservation Cases by the People's Courts (2020 Amendment)* (hereinafter referred to as "Interpretation of Property Preservation (2020 Amendment)")6 have played an important role in providing guidelines for property preservation.

6.5 In order to apply these laws effectively and to bridge the gap between the legislation and the practice in courts, many regional local courts have taken initiatives to issue regional interpretations and legal guidance documents to address legal issues in practice. For this reason, the regional interpretations and guidance issued by these local courts in different provinces of China for property preservation measures cannot be overlooked.

6.6 Among the local courts' interpretations and legal guidance documents, this chapter will primarily examine guidelines provided by the courts

---

In such scenarios, these subject matters can be pre-sealed by the court order. See also, *Notice on Some Issues Concerning Regulating the Execution by the People's Courts and the Assistance in Execution by the Departments of Land, Resources and Real Estate Administration According to Law* (Fa Fa [2004] No 5), Articles 13–15.

4 Refer to Chapters 3 and 4.

5 *Interpretations of the Supreme People's Court on Application of the Civil Procedure Law of the People's Republic of China (2020 Amendment)* (Fa Shi [2015] No 5) (superseded by Fa Shi [2020] No 20).

6 *Provisions of the Supreme People's Court on Several Issues Concerning the Handling of Property Preservation Cases by the People's Courts (2020 Amendment)* (Fa Shi [2016] No 22) (superseded by Fa Shi [2020] No 21).

of Beijing,[7] Shanghai,[8] Guangdong,[9] Jiangsu,[10] Chongqing[11] and Sichuan.[12] All these regional courts are located in major commercial centres in China, and each of these locations can boast of considerable gross domestic product ("GDP").

6.7 There are a further two main reasons to concentrate on these regions stated above. First, from a regional point of view, compared with many other regions, the legal service systems in these regions are relatively well-developed, and they are harbingers to test grounds for many of the recent Chinese legal reforms and thereafter the implementation of such reforms.

6.8 Secondly, these regional courts are well-versed in handling different kinds of disputes due to the level of development in such regions. As a result, these courts dispose of a great number of commercial disputes, particularly disputes encompassing foreign elements.

6.9 Based on this, it is meaningful to examine the provisions of the property preservation prescribed by these regional interpretations and guidance.

---

7 For example, *Some Provisions of the Beijing High People's Court on Property Preservation During the Case-Filing Procedure* (hereinafter referred to as "Provisions on Beijing Property Preservation During the Case-Filing Procedure 2012") (Jing Gao Fa Fa [2012] No 405).

8 For example, *Provisions of the Shanghai High People's Court on Property Preservation (2017 Amendment)* (hereinafter referred to as "Provisions on Shanghai Property Preservation 2017") (Hu Gao Fa (Shen) [2014] No 3).

9 For example, *Opinions of the Guangdong High People's Court on Protecting Legal Interests of Private Enterprises and Standardizing Property Preservation* 2019 (hereinafter referred to as "Opinions on Guangdong Standardizing Property 2019"); see also, *Guidance of Shenzhen Intermediate People's Court on Pre-Action Property Preservation* (6 December 2018) (hereinafter referred to as "Guidance on Shenzhen Pre-Action Property Preservation 2018"); this Guidance on Shenzhen Pre-Action Property Preservation 2018 was endorsed by the Civil Enforcement Specialised Committee of the No 9 Trial Commission of Shenzhen Intermediate People's Court on 6 December 2018; see also, *Provisions of the Primary People's Court of Qianhai Cooperation Zone of Shenzhen City on Property Preservation (Trial)* 2018 (hereinafter referred to as "Provisions on Shenzhen Qianhai Property Preservation 2018").

10 For example, *Implementation Opinions of the Nanjing Intermediate People's Court on Establishing a Centralized Management System for Property Preservation* (1 June 2017) (hereinafter referred to as "Opinions on Nanjing Property Preservation 2017").

11 For example, *Opinion of Chongqing High People's Court on the Exact Enforcement of the Civil Property Preservation 2020* (Yu Gao Fa [2020] No 82) (hereinafter referred to as "Opinion on the Chongqing Property Preservation 2020") *Guidance of Chongqing High People's Court on the Evaluation of the Subject Matter Concerning the Property Preservation (Trial)* 2017 (hereinafter referred to as "Guidance on the Evaluation of Chongqing Property Preservation 2017"); *Notice of Chongqing High People's Court on Further Norm of Property Preservation 2018.*

12 For example, *Opinions of the Sichuan High People's Court on Corporation Property Preservation for Serving New Normal for Economic Development* (hereinafter referred to as "Opinions on Sichuan Property Preservation 2015").

6.10 Nonetheless, other regional guidance documents, from courts such as Hunan[13] and Tianjin,[14] will be also involved. However, purposefully, due to the limited space, not all such regional divergences will be included in this chapter. For the sake of completeness, it does not mean that other regional guidances which have not been discussed are not important.

Definition of Preservation of Maritime Claims and Its Purpose

6.11 In the maritime law domain, Article 12 of the Special Maritime Procedure Law of the People's Republic of China 2000 (hereinafter referred to as "SMPL 2000") provides:

> Preservation of maritime claims means the compulsory measures taken by a maritime court on the application of a maritime claimant against the property of the person against whom a claim is made, for the purpose of ensuring fulfillment of the claim of the maritime claimant.[15]

6.12 It is generally accepted in legal practice that "preservation of maritime claims" in China is equivalent to the property preservation measure in the CPL 1991 (as amended until 2020). Similarly, the main purpose is to secure the enforcement of future maritime judgments and arbitral awards, and to prevent the applicant's loss.

Applicable Laws in the Maritime Law Domain

6.13 With regard to applicable laws, the preservation of maritime claims is governed by both the SMPL 2000 and the CPL 1991 (as amended until 2020). According to the kinds of property that would be the subject matter of preservation measures, for example, when the property refers to the vessel, the cargo on the vessel and the vessel's fuel and supplies belonging to the respondent, the governing law in preservations of maritime claims is the SMPL 2000. As for other types of property belonging to the respondent, they should be governed by the CPL 1991 (as amended until 2020).[16]

6.14 Against the above background, the structure of this chapter will generally comply with the steps involved in the preservation procedure as set out

---

13 *Procedure of the Hunan High People's Court on Property Preservation* (Xiang Gao Fa Ban Fa [2015] No 3) (hereinafter referred to as "Procedure on Hunan Property Preservation 2015").

14 For example, *Guidance of the Tianjin High People's Court on Examination of Property Preservation (Trial)* (Jin Gao Fa Fa [2019] No 28) (hereinafter referred to as "Provisions on Tianjin Property Preservation 2019"); see also, Rules of Primary People's Court of Hexi District of Tianjin Municipality on Property Preservations (Trial) 2017.

15 SMPL 2000, Article 12.

16 *The Supreme People's Court Interpretations on the Application of the Special Maritime Procedure Law of the People's Republic of China (2008 Adjustment)* (Fa Shi [2003] No 3) (hereinafter referred to as "Interpretation of SMPL 2008"), Article 18.

in Chapter 3. The guidelines for property preservation and for the preservation of maritime claims will be examined separately in this chapter. However, the primary focus of this book is to evaluate the preservation of property measures in the context of civil/commercial disputes rather than maritime disputes, and accordingly the discussion on the SMPL 2000 is limited as it provides for special rules for the preservation of maritime property, particularly for the arrest of ships.

Format of Preservation Applications[17]

6.15 In accordance with Article 1 of the Interpretation of Property Preservation (2020 Amendment), in order to apply for property preservation, an interested party or a party concerned must file a written application and the relevant evidential materials with a competent court.[18] There is no standard precedent format for the application, but pursuant to the Interpretation of Property Preservation (2020 Amendment), the format of the application must set out the following compulsory elements that are required by the courts:

(a) The identity, delivery addresses and contact information of the preservation applicant and the respondent.
(b) The application must contain the facts and reasons on which the claims are based.
(c) The amount or the subject matter to be preserved.
(d) The exact information or specific pointers about the property for which the preservation is requested.
(e) For the application, detailed information on security that can be provided by the applicant, such as a secured property or a credit certification or a liability insurance for preservation applications. Alternatively, the applicant must provide reasons for not providing security.[19]
(f) Other matters which need to be stated.[20]

6.16 Some regional judicial interpretations and legal guidance documents from courts, such as Shanghai Municipality,[21] Sichuan Province[22] and Qianhai Cooperation Zone of Shenzhen City,[23] also provide their own guidance to applicants and the local courts. However, the compulsory features required

17 See Annex 1.
18 Interpretation of Property Preservation (2020 Amendment), Article 1.
19 The types of security and the relevant discussions can be found in Chapter 3, 3.130–3.194.
20 Interpretation of Property Preservation (2020 Amendment), Article 1.
21 Provisions on Shanghai Property Preservation 2017, Article 11.
22 Opinions on Sichuan Property Preservation 2015, Article 2.
23 Provisions on Shenzhen Qianhai Property Preservation 2018, Article 10.

in any application are in tune with the provisions of the Interpretation of Property Preservation (2020 Amendment).

6.17 The compulsory features required in any application will remain the same at the pre-action or post-action stage of the civil litigation. The only noticeable difference is that in the context of pre-action preservation measures, at all times, the grant of a preservation measure by the court will follow the written application of the interested party. However, in the context of post-action preservation measures, the competent court may even implement preservation measures on its own initiative without waiting for any application from an applicant or any other interested party. Nonetheless, in most scenarios, the post-action preservation measures will only be accepted and enforced based on the parties' applications rather than on the courts' own initiative enforcement *ex officio*.

6.18 In legal practice, an applicant may either provide the exact amount of the dispute for which the application requesting preservation measures is submitted, or simply list the likely specific subject matter of preservation measures without stating the disputed amount. Either of those two methods for presenting the application is recognised by courts.[24] However, once the applications on the online preservation application system become commonplace; if now an applicant chose to file an online application, the lack of the specific subject matter will not be accepted, because the applicant and the judge have no opportunity to communicate about the reason for the unclear subject matter.[25]

6.19 In accordance with Article 12 of the SMPL 2000, a maritime court has no power to take the initiative to render a property preservation order without the application of a party concerned in any litigation or arbitration proceedings.[26] In terms of the format of applications seeking preservation measures in the case of maritime claims, the content of applications will be similar to that of property preservation applications pursuant to the Interpretation of Property Preservation (2020 Amendment).[27]

Applicants and Respondents of Applications

The Meanings of Applicant and Respondent

6.20 An applicant, as the name suggests, refers to the party who files an application for property preservation measures. He can also be called an

---

24 Guidance on Shenzhen Pre-Action Property Preservation 2018, Article 20.

25 In the authors' experience, any unclear statement in an online application may be questioned by a judge. Normally, the judge refuses to accept the application following the refusal reason. But meanwhile the judge will require the applicant to provide more sufficient evidence or a further statement if the applicant wants to obtain the court's approval.

26 SMPL 2000, Article 12.

27 Article 15 of the SMPL 2000 provides that "in the application the particulars of the maritime claim, reasons for the application, subject-matter to be preserved and the amount of security required shall be specified with relevant evidence attached".

interested party in a pre-action preservation or a party concerned in a post-action preservation application. In the context of the pre-action preservation application, the applicant will become the future claimant in the disputed matter. On the other hand, the respondent in the pre-action preservation application will likely be the defendant in the disputed matter.

6.21 However, it is clearly feasible that the defendant in the post-action preservation application can also be the applicant in certain scenarios. For example, the defendant could have his own counterclaim and accordingly may wish to seek preservation measures from the courts for his own claims.

6.22 In accordance with the CPL 1991 (as amended until 2020) and its Interpretation, a defendant should have the right to institute a counterclaim as long as the claims of the original lawsuit and those of the counterclaims are based on the same legal relation or the claims of the original lawsuit and those of the counterclaims are based on the same facts.[28] The defendant of a case can therefore file a counterclaim in the ongoing civil litigation, and accordingly the defendant is also entitled to file an application seeking preservation measures. It can be argued whether a defendant is entitled to apply for applications seeking property preservation measures if he were not to institute a counterclaim. In consideration of the purpose of the property preservation measures, which is to secure the enforcement of future judgments or arbitral awards and to prevent the applicant's loss, it is obvious that such property preservations contribute to the claimant's claims against the defendant. It is reasonable that, when the defendant is absent of the items of claims in the dispute, there is no legal foundation to provide the provisional remedy to the defendant. For this reason, the defendant should file a property preservation application during counterclaim proceedings.

6.23 In this book, particularly for Chapters 6, 8 and 10, even though a party can play multiple roles in any civil litigation, the terminology of "applicant" and "respondent" will be used in the context of preservation applications rather than "claimant" and "defendant".

Information on an Applicant and a Respondent and Their Identifications

6.24 If an applicant and/or a respondent are individuals, the information of an application must include his full name, gender, age, nationality, domicile and contact number.[29]

28 CPL 1991 (as amended until 2020), Article 51 and Interpretation of CPL 2015 (2020 Amendment), Article 233.

29 The Interpretation of Property Preservation (2020 Amendment) and regional interpretations do not provide the details. By reference to Article 121 of the CPL 1991 (as amended until 2020), these items regarding an individual must be provided with bills of complaint. Accordingly, it is advisable to provide these details in the preservation application form.

6.25 The applicant must fill in his own Chinese identification card number or foreign passport number and a hard copy of this Chinese identification card or foreign passport will be attached to the letter of application.[30] Conversely, the applicant does not need to provide the respondent's Chinese identification card number or the foreign passport number, provided it is difficult to get this specific information, pursuant to the latest guidance by the SPC.[31]

6.26 If either of the parties is a legal entity or other organisation, the letter of the application must include its domicile in China, the contact number and the full name of the legal representative or the principal of that legal entity or organisation.

6.27 In addition, if the applicant is a legal entity or other organisation, they need to provide the business licence such as a Unified Social Credit Code or the registration code in China,[32] or a registration certificate in other countries. It is not necessary to provide the original documents with the application. However, the copy of the business licence should be stamped with an official seal.[33] If possible, the Chinese identification card or the foreign passport of the legal representative or the principal should be attached to the letter of the application. Nonetheless, the identification card and contact number of the legal representative or the principal are not mandatory according to the SPC's format.[34] Even so, the SPC's format is not a judicial guidance. In practice, the regional local courts may request the detailed information on the legal representative or the principal.

6.28 With regard to a respondent, if the respondent is a legal entity or other organisation, the applicant must submit the information of the respondent on the form. This information is usually collected by the National

30 The applicant must show the original identification card to a court when he brings the materials for the application to the court by himself. If his agent, on his behalf, brings the materials to the court, most Chinese courts will only check the agent's identification card or lawyer's licence. The Chinese courts will expect the agent/lawyer to have carried out due diligence with regard to the documents that are submitted with the applications.

31 *Reply of the Supreme People's Court on the Issue Concerning Whether a Defendant's Identification Card Information Must Be Provided for Case-Filing* (16 September 2019) <www.court.gov.cn/zixun-xiangqing-184581.html> accessed 15 July 2021. It must be highlighted that even though this Reply simply refers to the information regarding the *Chinese* Identification Card, it is reasonable for authors that the passport number of a foreign defendant is not mandatory as long as this foreign defendant can be identified.

32 In accordance with *Notice of the State Council on Approving and Forwarding the General Plan of the National Development and Reform Commission and Other Departments on the Development of a Unified Social Credit Code System for Legal Persons and Other Organisations* (The State Council, Guo Fa [2015] No 33), any legal entity or organisation registered in China must use this unified social credit code prior to 2021.

33 It should be noted that there is no common standard across China in all courts in relation to information and documents that need to be submitted with the applications. However, it is advisable to check the competent court's official webpage to seek guidance or seek more information from the local court to avoid delay, in particular for pre-action preservation applications.

34 Refer to Annex 1.

Enterprise Credit Information Publicity System to prove the legal status of the respondent.[35]

The Subject Matter of Applications: Property to Be Preserved

Category of Property

6.29 Nobody or no legislation may provide a perfect definition of property, which is a vague and ambiguous legal term. As Bentham contended, property is a pure creature of law.[36] It is thus impossible to list the property that can be preserved with certainty under the existing law.

6.30 However, pursuant to the Civil Code of the People's Republic of China 2020 (hereinafter referred to as "Civil Code 2020"), the property to be preserved can be segregated into real estate (immovable property) and movable property.[37]

6.31 Real estate or immovables generally include land and the fixtures on the land, such as a house or forest, and the above-ground fixtures over the land. The movables refer to any other property, except for real estate,[38] which includes movable tangibles and intangibles such as the rights arising from the property.

New Development of Property to Be Preserved

6.32 With the development of society and technology, in the past years, the meaning of property has been expanded. For example, both data and online virtual property have been recognised by the Civil Code 2020.[39] However, the Civil Code 2020 has not yet clarified the meaning of virtual property.

---

35 National Enterprise Credit Information Publicity System <www.gsxt.gov.cn/index.html> accessed 15 July 2021.

36 Thomas W Merrill and Henry E Smith, 'The Morality of Property' (2007) 48 William & Mary Law Review 1849, 1849, in which is cited Jeremy Bentham stating that "Property and law are born together and die together. Before laws were made there was no property; take away laws, and property cases", in *Theory of Legislation* (C K Ogden ed., Richard Hildreth trans., Harcourt, Brace & Co, 1931).

37 Civil Code of the People's Republic of China was adopted by the Third Session of the Standing Committee of the 13th National People's Congress of the People's Republic of China on 28 May 2020 and came into effect on 1 January 2021; Civil Code 2020, Article 115; this Article is the same as Article 115 of the General Rules of the Civil Law 2017 and Article 2 of Property Law 2007. Both General Rules of the Civil Law 2017 and Property Law 2007 were abolished on 1 January 2021.

38 Security Law 1995, Article 92. It should be noted that the Security Law 1995 was abolished after the Civil Code 2020 came into effect on 1 January 2021. The Civil Code does not list the scope of the real estate and movables. However, in accordance with Part II "Property Law" of the Civil Code 2020, the scope of the real estate and movables is broader than that provided by the Security Law 1995.

39 Article 127 of the Civil Code 2020 provides that "where the law has provisions on the protection of data or online virtual property, follow those provisions"; equally, this Article is the same as Article 127 of the General Rules 2017 (expired on 1 January 2021).

6.33 According to the published cases and general recognition, mobile numbers, QQ or WeChat accounts,[40] game accounts and similar online accounts can be regarded as virtual property.[41]

6.34 For example, in *Qiang Zhong v Hangzhou Netease Leihuo Techonology Co Ltd*,[42] the High People's Court of Guangxi Zhuang Autonomous Region affirmed that online game accounts and game currency were regarded as virtual property. In *Qingjian Wu v Shanghai Yaozhi Internet Technology Co Ltd and Other*,[43] the Hangzhou Internet Court held that Bitcoin constituted virtual property and could create the corresponding property right and interests.[44]

6.35 Similarly, this virtual property has been treated as the subject matter of property preservation by the Chinese courts. The Primary People's Court of Wuzhong District of Suzhou City of Jiangsu Province accepted an application for a property preservation to seal up a "lucky" mobile number 8888888 to prevent it from being transferred to another owner.[45]

6.36 Against the above background, it is observed that Chinese courts take a relaxed attitude toward the identification of new types of properties that could be the subject matter of preservation orders. If there are no express provisions in law preventing the recognition of a kind of property that can be preserved, then in that case, the new genre of properties, e.g. Bitcoin, online virtual accounts, can be regarded as the subject matter of property preservation.

Requirements of Preserved Property

6.37 Two requirements must be satisfied in order for the Chinese courts to evaluate the property that will become the subject matter of preservation orders.

---

40 Both QQ and WeChat are developed by Tencent. QQ is the most popular instant chat software on computer while WeChat is the most popular chat app on mobile phone in China.

41 Man Li, 'Internet Visual Property Preservation: Not Difficult at All' *Legal Weekly* (Beijing, 14 August 2019).

42 *Qiang Zhong v Hangzhou Netease Leihuo Techonology Co Ltd* (dispute over online infringement) [2019] Gan Min Shen No 634 (the High People's Court of Guangxi Zhuang Autonomous Region, retrial and binding judgment).

43 *Qingjian Wu v Shanghai Yaozhi Internet Technology Co Ltd and Other* (dispute over online infringement) [2019] Zhe 0192 Min Chu No 1626 (Hangzhou Internet Court, first instance and binding judgment).

44 ibid.

45 Jie He, 'Debt Is Not Repaid, Debtor's Mobile Phone Number Ending in 888888 Was Seized' *Xian Dai Kuai Bao* (Jiangsu, 22 November 2019). In practice, if a respondent loses the case but has no money left to perform the monetary obligation, then in that case the lucky number will be auctioned by the court to pay the monetary sum to the winning party. However, it is arguable whether the type of preservation measure required falls within the ambit of property preservation or behaviour preservation. If the purpose of the preservation measure was to forbid the respondent from transferring the mobile number, that is, not to do a certain thing, then in that case the purpose is akin to behaviour preservation measures; see also, Chapter 8, 8.97–8.99.

6.38 Firstly, the ownership of property must be clean, that is, the owner's title to that property is not disputed. Secondly, the value of property shall be compatible with the amount of the claim in dispute.[46] These two requirements are mainly to protect the respondents and the relevant parties' interests from the effects of any preservation orders.

6.39 Article 102 of the CPL 1991 (as amended until 2020) provides a general rule that "preservation shall be limited to the scope under the application or to the property related to the case in question".[47] It is generally recognised that "the property related to the case" refers to the scope of the preserved property.

6.40 According to the interpretation of the legislation, the preserved property refers to the disputed property and/or the property that is relevant to the enforcement of the future effective judgment or arbitral award.[48] The relevant property in some regional courts' guidance is often interpreted and referred to as "the respondent's property".[49] Based on this, the preserved property could contain the disputed property and the respondent's property.

6.41 To prevent the property preservation from infringing the rights of a third party or an outside party, Chinese courts in their guidance to an applicant may directly provide that "it is forbidden to apply for the property preservation measure over the outside party's property".[50] Alternatively, the courts insist that an applicant must clarify the ownership of the preserved property to the courts' satisfaction. However, it does not mean that no preservation measures are ever possible over the third party's property.

The Outside Party's Preserved Property

6.42 Under certain circumstances, an outside party's property can be the subject matter of preservation measures. To be precise, the outside party enjoys the right over the property, but the respondent, under certain conditions, may still have rights over such property filed.

6.43 The types of properties included are as follows:

(a) Matured claim: this means that, where a respondent's property is insufficient to meet the request for preservation measures, but the

46 Provisions on Beijing Property Preservation 2012, Article 9 (3); see also, Provisions on Shenzhen Qianhai Property Preservation 2018, Article 6.

47 CPL 1991 (as amended until 2020), Article 102.

48 Jianguo Xiao and Baocheng Zhang, 'Reconsideration on Specialization of Subject Matter of Property Preservation' (2017) 25 (3) Journal of National Prosecutors College 145, 145.

49 Provisions on Shanghai Property Preservation 2017, Article 7 (2); see also, Provisions on Beijing Property Preservation During the Case-Filing Procedure 2012, Article 9 (3); see also, Provisions on Shenzhen Qianhai Property Preservation 2018, Article 6 (2); see also, Guidance on Shenzhen Pre-Action Property Preservation 2018, Article 9 (3).

50 *Opinions of the Daya Bay Primary People's Court of Huizhou City of Guangdong Province on Some Issues Concerning Cases of Property Preservation* (2018), Article 5 (2).

respondent holds matured claims against other parties, a competent court may, according to the applicant's application, render an order that such other parties shall not repay their debts to the respondent. Where such other parties are required to repay debts, the court shall keep the property or amounts repaid in escrow on behalf of the debtor.[51]

(b) Receivables due: this means that if a respondent has receivables due, a court may take property preservation measures against the proceeds receivable by the respondent upon maturity, restrict the respondent from withdrawing such proceeds and notify relevant entities, such as a commercial bank, to provide assistance during enforcement.[52]

(c) The outside party's nominal property: this means that, where the land or house is registered under the name of an outside party, and the nominal person of registration (the outside party) recognises in writing that the land or house is actually owned by the respondent, the court may take preservation measures for sealing up the land or house.[53]

(d) The outside party's property, but the respondent has paid full or partial transaction price for such outside party's property, simply has practically/technically not completed the formalities for registration of the ownership or the sale contract provides the retention of title clause.[54]

6.44 It follows that the Chinese courts regularly issue notifications to the relevant outside party stated above requesting them to enforce the orders that have been granted by them. Such parties will be sanctioned for a failure to assist the courts in the enforcement of the preservation orders, as discussed in Chapter 3, 3.269.[55]

51 Interpretation of CPL 2015 (2020 Amendment), Article 159.

52 Interpretation of CPL 2015 (2020 Amendment), Article 158.

53 *Notice on Some Issues Concerning Regulating the Execution by the People's Courts and the Assistance in Execution by the Departments of Land, Resources and Real Estate Administration According to Law* (Fa Fa [2004] No 5), Article 7(1). In addition, Article 7(2) provides that if the nominal person under whose name the title is registered denies that the land or house or other immovable property is owned by the respondent, then even if the courts or applicants believe that the actual title registration does not reflect the actual ownership, the courts cannot take seizure measures against that property. In this scenario, the courts will have to wait to take seizure measures until the registration has been discharged by the authorities, such as a house registration department, and thereafter the ownership has been registered under the name of the respondent. This is generally by instituting a lawsuit separately, or through other procedures.

54 *Provisions of the Supreme People's Court on Seal-up, Detainment or Freezing of Property in the Civil Enforcement by the People's Courts* (2020 Amendment) (Fa Shi [2004] No 15) (superseded by Fa Shi [2020] No 21) (hereinafter referred to as "Provisions on Seal-up, Detainment or Freezing of Property (2020 Amendment)"), Articles 16 and 17.

55 On sanctions for not obeying preservation orders, a detailed discussion can be found Chapter 3, 3.266–3.286.

The Limitation of the Preserved Property

6.45 A few properties, or a specific property, under certain circumstances are not suitable to be preserved, although they are within a class of property that can suitably be subject to any preservation measure order from a court. There is no specific standard to clarify which kind of property can be regarded as the subject matter of the preserved property and which kind of property should not become the preserved subject matter, but by reference to 6.46, to the authors' observation, the standard is dependent on whether the preserved property may impact public policy or personal basic rights.

6.46 Under the existing law, the types of properties that are not suitable for preservation order are as follows:

(a) Hazardous goods or properties that could become major sources of danger, provided other property available is more suitable and does not have such issues.[56]

(b) Personal things for necessary living, necessary living expenses based on the local lowest living standard, unpublicised inventions or unpublished works, medals of honour or similar things that cannot be sealed up, detained or frozen.[57]

(c) Property that is immune from being sealed up, detained or frozen, as prescribed in a treaty, agreement or other legal documents signed by the People's Republic of China, the Government of the People's Republic of China or a governmental department of the People's Republic of China with a foreign country or an international organisation in accordance with the Law of the People's Republic of China on the Procedures for Conclusion of Treaties.[58]

(d) The respondent's social security fund, including endowment insurance fund, medical insurance fund, unemployment insurance fund, employment insurance fund and maternity insurance fund.[59]

---

56 *Urgent Notice by the General Office of the Supreme People's Court of Strengthening Safety Supervision on Hazardous Subject Matter in Attachment of Property and Enforcement of Judgment* (Fa Ban [2019] No 259), Article 1. In addition, its Articles 3 and 6 provide that if it is necessary to preserve hazardous goods or major sources of danger, a court granting such preservation order must report such circumstances to a higher court. In addition, such preservation measures must comply with Work Safety of the People's Republic of China and other relevant laws.

57 Provisions on Seal-up, Detainment or Freezing of Property (2020 Amendment), Article 3 (1) to (6). This judicial interpretation attempts to clarify the legal issue that may arise during the enforcement of a judgment or an order. On the other hand, Article 32 of these Provisions provides that during the enforcement stage, any order rendered against the property will also be subject to this interpretation from the courts. For this reason, its Article 3 (1) to (6) may apply to the legal issues that may arise during the enforcement of property preservation measures.

58 Provisions on Seal-up, Detainment or Freezing of Property (2020 Amendment), Article 3 (7).

59 *Notice of the Supreme People's Court on No Seal-up, Freezing and Deduction of Social Security Fund During the Trial and Enforcement of Civil and Economic Dispute* (Fa [2000]

(e) The remaining amount of the housing provident fund's account, unless this account meets the condition of withdrawal in accordance with the Regulation on the Administration of Housing Provident Fund.[60]

(f) Property belonging to an insolvent company, unless the receiver files a property preservation, or the insolvency court takes measures on its own initiative to avoid the impact of the relevant interested party's actions or other reasons.[61]

(g) Offices, buildings and armoured cash carriers belonging to a financial institution and its branches.[62]

(h) Reserve funds and supplies that financial institutions have stored in the People's Bank of China.[63]

(i) Deposits for capital recognizance of insurance companies.[64]

No 19); see also, *Administrative Supervision Measure of Social Security Fund* (Order of the Ministry of Labor and Social Security [2001] No 12), Article 2.

60 The housing provident fund does not belong to the social security fund pursuant to *Administrative Supervision Measure of Social Security Fund*. However, in practice, it is debatable whether the housing provident fund can be treated as the subject matter of property preservation. In this context, the Anhui High People's Court, based on debatable opinions, requested the SPC to provide a clear answer. In *Reply of the Supreme People's Court on the Issue Concerning the Enforceable Transfer of Obligee's Housing Provident Fund* ([2013] Zhi Ta Zi No 14), the SPC affirmed that the remaining amount of the housing provident fund's account can be subject to preservation orders, provided this account meets the conditions of the withdrawal in accordance with *Regulation on the Administration of Housing Provident Fund* (Order of the State Council [1999] No 262) (2019 Amendment). In any event, the withdrawal of the account should not in any way impact on the obligee's basic living conditions.

61 Article 19 of the Enterprise Bankruptcy Law of the People's Republic of China 2007 (hereinafter referred to as "Bankruptcy Law 2007") provides that "After the people's court accepts an application for bankruptcy, the relevant [preservation] measures for preserving the debtor's property shall be discharged and the procedures for execution shall be suspended"; see also, Article 6 of *Provisions (II) of the Supreme People's Court Concerning the Application of the Enterprise Bankruptcy Law* (Fa Shi [2013] No 22) provides that "where, after a bankruptcy petition is accepted, the conduct of bankruptcy procedures in accordance with the law may be affected by any conduct of the relevant interested party or for any other reason, the people's court accepting the bankruptcy petition may, upon application of the administrator or by exercising its powers, take preservation measures on all or part of the property of the debtor". It should be noted that there is no specialised insolvency court in China. In this context, the insolvency court merely refers to the court accepting the application of the insolvency.

62 *Provisions of the Supreme People's Court on Some Issues Concerning the Enforcement of an Effective Legal Document by the People's Courts* (2020 Amendment) (Fa Shi [1998] No15) (superseded by Fa Shi [2020] No 21) (hereinafter referred to as "Provisions on the Enforcement (2020 Amendment)"), Article 34. It should be noted that this interpretation simply provides for "offices of financial institutions"; see also, Article 4 (9) of *Notice of Chongqing High People's Court on Further Norm of Property Preservation 2018* provides that offices, buildings and armoured cash carriers belonging to the People's Bank of China and its branches cannot be subject to preservation measures.

63 Provisions on the Enforcement (2020 Amendment), Article 34.

64 Notice by the General Office of the China Banking and Insurance Regulatory Commission of Regulating the Matters Concerning Banking Financial Institutions' Assistance

(j) Money that has been stored in any tier's treasury.[65]

(k) Certain specialised property, such as migrant workers' wages and security deposits for wages,[66] funds belonging to trade unions,[67] the margin account of a futures company and negotiable securities submitted by a client to the futures company to offset the margin,[68] trust property[69] and death compensation for air crashes.[70]

---

in the Competent Authorities' Inquiry about, Freeze of and Deduction from Accounts of Deposits for Capital Recognizance of Insurance Companies (Order of the General Office of the China Banking and Insurance Regulatory Commission [2020] No 19). It is provided in Articles 1 and 4 that "in accordance with the Insurance Law of the People's Republic of China and Insurance Company Capital Guarantee Fund Management Measures, the deposit for Capital Recognizance refers to the drawn capital which amounts to 20% of the total registered capital of an insurance company after the establishment of the company. Such deposit for capital recognizance cannot be used except for specific purposes such as paying off debts during the liquidation of the insurance company. Accordingly, this capital recognizance cannot be frozen and transferred".

65 *Reply of the People's Bank of China on Enquiring, Freezing, Deducting Money in a Treasury* (Yin Han [1999] No 48) provides that unless otherwise prescribed by laws and regulations, departments, entities and individuals have no power to use or to take any measures on money that has been incorporated into the local treasury without permission of the local treasury; see also, *Notice of Chongqing High People's Court on Further Norm of Property Preservation* 2018, Article 4.

66 *Notice by the Supreme People's Court, the Ministry of Human Resources and Social Security, and the China Banking and Insurance Regulatory Commission of Effectively Conducting the Work Concerning Preventing Funds in Special Account for Migrant Workers' Wages and Security Deposits for Wages Being Seized, Frozen or Transferred* (Order of Ministry of Human Resources and Social Security [2020] No 93).

67 *Reply of the Supreme People's Court on Whether Industrial Union Trade and Primary Union Trade Belong to Qualified Social Organisations and Whether the Fund in These Union Trade Can be Frozen and Deducted* (Fa Fu [1997] No 6).

68 Article 4 of *Provisions of the Supreme People's Court on Several Issues Concerning the Trial of Futures Dispute Cases (II)* (Fa Shi [2011] No 1) (superseded by Fa Shi [2020] No 18) provides that "where a futures company is the debtor, and the creditor claims for freezing or transferring the following funds or negotiable securities in the account, the people's court shall not approve such claim: 1) funds of a client in the margin account of the company dealing with futures; or 2) negotiable securities submitted by a client to the company dealing with futures to offset the margin".

69 Article 95 of *Notice by the Supreme People's Court of Issuing the Minutes of the National Courts' Civil and Commercial Trial Work Conference* (Fa [2019] No 254) stipulates that trust property is classified as an independent property and this property should not be classified as a property belonging to an individual, a settlor, trustees and their beneficiary. Therefore, an applicant cannot be allowed to file an application seeking property preservation measures over trust property in an escrow account due to the dispute between the applicant and the settlor, trustee or beneficiary, unless the circumstances are compatible with those prescribed by Article 17 of the Trust Law. However, the beneficiary's usufruct arising from the trust property can also be preserved. Further discussion on this topic is beyond the scope of this book.

70 *Reply of the Supreme People's Court on Whether the Death Compensation Constitutes Heritage* ([2004] Civil Yi Ta Zi No 26) provides that the death compensation will belong to the close relative of a deceased person, rather than being classified as part of the estate of the deceased person. It means that the death compensation cannot be the subject matter of preservation measures.

The Necessity of Preserved Property Valuation

6.47 In a preservation application, it is advisable to clarify the value of the disputed subject matter, or to clarify the value of the property that needs to be preserved. The former is just the subject matter of the case while the latter is irrelevant to the claims in a case.

6.48 With regard to the subject matter of a case, if it is just a property that an applicant seeks to preserve, a court will grant a preservation measure on the disputed property directly. However, in the context of a pre-action preservation application, it is necessary to evaluate the value of the disputed property, because the value of the property has a close connection with the amount of security that the applicants must provide to the Chinese courts with their applications.

6.49 In contrast, in the context of post-action preservation applications, providing security is not a compulsory obligation for applicants. Seemingly, evaluating the value of the preserved property is not essential. However, it is still necessary to do so because it is unfair for the respondent to preserve excessive property. Furthermore, if the court requests the applicant to provide security for post-action preservation applications, or the respondent wants to provide countersecurity to discharge the preservation measure, it certainly becomes essential to evaluate the value of the property.

6.50 With regard to preserved property not belonging to the disputed subject, if, in the application, there is a request to preserve such specific property, unless this property comes under the category of bank accounts or similar specific accounts such as the respondent's share accounts, it is essential to appraise the property that needs to be preserved. In particular, if the property is in the class of real estate, vehicles, company equity and even virtual property, then, the property must go through the appraisal process.

Burden of Proof on Preserved Property Valuation

6.51 In the event that the applicants simply identify the relevant property that will become the subject matter of the property preservation order, but do not spell out the exact value of that property, no specific provision in any law or guidance from the local courts implies that there is a burden of proof on the applicants in relation to their obligation to provide the appraisal report for the preserved property through the preservation measures.

6.52 In order to further analyse the above issue, it is observed that Interpretation of Property Preservation (2020 Amendment) and most regional guidance issued by the local courts, such as Provisions on Beijing Property Preservation 2009, Provisions on Beijing Property Preservation During the Case-Filing Procedure 2012, Provisions on Shanghai Property Preservation 2017, Opinion on the Chongqing Property Preservation 2020 and Rules of the

Primary People's Court of Hexi District of Tianjin Municipality on Property Preservations (Trial) 2017, do not provide any guideline that deals with the burden of proof on the preserved property valuation.

6.53 However, pursuant to a general principle, that is, *semper necessitas probandi incumbit ei qui agit*, the burden of proof can be regarded to be on the applicants to provide appraisal reports of the properties with the application. To be clear, Article 64 of CPL 1991 (as amended until 2020) provides that

> a party shall be responsible for providing evidence in support of his or her allegations.[71]

6.54 It is generally recognised that this provision affirms the principle of burden of proof in China.[72]

6.55 Similar to the general principle stated above, Guidance on Shenzhen Pre-Action Property Preservation 2018 expressly provides that an applicant must submit evidence as to the value of the property that needs to be preserved.[73]

6.56 However, Guidance on Shenzhen Pre-Action Property Preservation 2018 further provides that, if the appraisal evidence, which is submitted with the application for the property, cannot corroborate the real value of the property, then in that case the court will estimate the value of the property, prior to granting the preservation measure against the property.[74]

6.57 On analysis, it seems that it is ultimately the Intermediate People's Court of Shenzhen City of Guangdong Province that is obliged to appraise the property that needs to be preserved, if the evidence provided by the applicant is inadequate.

6.58 Apart from the above guidance by the Intermediate People's Court of Shenzhen City of Guangdong Province, owing to the fact that the highest court, the SPC, is silent on the judicial interpretation of this issue, the different regional courts' guidance provides different views on this issue.

6.59 For instance, the High People's Court of Chongqing Municipality provides that the court must estimate the value of the properties based on the existing evidence and materials, prior to granting the preservation measures.[75] Furthermore, even if it is possible to easily appraise the property, the court cannot compel the party to provide the appraisal report.[76] As compared

71 CPL 1991 (as amended until 2020), Article 64.

72 It should be noted that according to the different causes of action and facts of cases, other rules in relation to burden of proof can be applied as well. Any further discussion on this topic is beyond the scope of this book.

73 Guidance on Shenzhen Pre-Action Property Preservation 2018, Article 22.

74 ibid.

75 Guidance on the Evaluation of Chongqing Property Preservation 2017, Article 3.

76 Interview Between Xiaofeng Wu (Legal Daily) and Fu Su, HongJun Wang (Chongqing High People's Court) 'Protection of Market Entity's Interests and Creation of Commercial

with Shenzhen's legal guidance, the Chongqing court's guidance document clearly emphasises that the obligation is on the court to appraise the property.

Approaches of Property Valuation

6.60 In order to avoid the high appraisal service fee, alternatively, the applicants may provide a reasonable and feasible appraisal approach to guide the courts appropriately.

6.61 By reference to Guidance on the Evaluation of Chongqing Property Preservation 2017, and Guidance on Shenzhen Pre-Action Property Preservation 2018,[77] according to the categories of property that need to be preserved, the appraisal process employed by the courts is as follows:

(a) With regard to a house, if the house is new (a first-hand house), the value of the house may refer to the estimated value of a similar house in the same area published by the real estate administrative bureau; if the house is second-hand, the value may refer to the surrounding market price of similar second-hand houses as estimated by the public offer of the housing transaction platform, or the approved price by the tax authorities.

(b) With regard to land, its price will be valuated based on the transferred amount recorded in the land transfer contract. If the land has been transferred over one year ago, its price may be appraised by reference to the surrounding land market price, or pursuant to the approved price by the tax authorities or pursuant to other factors such as the construction plan.

(c) With regard to a real estate project under construction, its value may be estimated by reference to various factors such as the investment amount of the project, the value of the completed project, the estimated expenses required for its demolition and resettlement, its sale price and so forth.

(d) With regard to a vehicle, if the vehicle has not been licensed, and the driving mileage is less than 100 kilometres, the value may be estimated by reference to the sale price of the same model announced by the manufacturer; if the vehicle has been licensed or the driving mileage is more than 100 kilometres, the value is by reference to the transaction price of the second-hand car. If the vehicle cannot be detained, which means that the respondent may continue to use it,

Environment: Interpretation of Chongqing High People's Court on Notice Concerning Further Norm of Property Preservation' (Legal Daily, 13 August 2018) <www.legaldaily.com.cn/index/content/2018-08/13/content_7617393.htm?node=20908> accessed 15 July 2021.

77 When reviewing different regional legal guidance documents, these two legal guidance documents may be the most comprehensive and feasible documents for the stakeholders to consider various issues.

then the value of the vehicle can be estimated at 20 per cent of the above value based on mileage.

(e) With regard to the freezing of equity in a limited liability company or a share of an unlisted limited company, the value of the equity or the share may be estimated by reference to the company's financial statements and the paid-up capital; if the subject matter of property to be preserved is the equity in a listed company, the appraisal value will be taken as 70 per cent of the closing price of the trading day before the date specified in the letter of preservation application.

(f) With regard to securities, fund shares, carbon emissions, land votes, trust interests, mining rights and so forth, the value can be appraised by reference to one of the following approaches – the par value, the public market price or other materials that may provide evidence for the value of the property.

(g) With regard to movables, such as machinery, equipment, products, semi-finished products and raw materials, if these movables have been detained, the value shall be estimated by reference to factors such as the purchased price of the invoice or the factory-gate price, the period that has been used and other relevant factors; if these movables are not detained and the respondent can continue to use or control the movables, then the value shall be estimated at 60 per cent of the above value.

(h) With regard to investment-type insurance products that are frozen, the amount of the preservation target is estimated by extractable policy dividends, the cash value of the policy or by consulting the institution which has issued that policy.

(i) With regard to other property rights, the value shall be estimated with relevant materials that can provide some clues as to the value that could be assigned to those property rights.[78]

6.62 In legal practice, the above appraisal approaches followed by the courts can in fact be employed by applicants. The respondents can also employ such property appraisal approaches to estimate the value of countersecurity they need to prepare for discharging the potential preservation orders against their property.

The Floating Value of Property to Be Preserved

6.63 In legal practice, the value of some property, such as the market value of a company's shares, is not steady. Therefore, either the applicant or the

78 Guidance on the Evaluation of Chongqing Property Preservation 2017, Article 7; see also, Guidance on Shenzhen Pre-Action Property Preservation 2018, Article 22.

respondent may apply for the discharge or the partial discharge of the property preservation order based on the fluctuation in the value of such property. However, in the context of applying for a discharge or partial discharge, the court is generally dependent on the appraisal report prepared by a qualified institution rather than the approaches suggested by the parties concerned in any preservation application.

6.64 Nonetheless, in order to avoid the discharge or partial discharge, some guidance, such as the Opinion on the Chongqing Property Preservation 2020, requests the court to sufficiently consider the underlying fluctuation of value of the preserved property while the court evaluates the floating property by reference to 6.61. It is provided that the preserved value of the floating property cannot exceed 20 per cent of the amount of the preservation.[79] It is supposed that the floating value of the property to be preserved is around RMB 100 million. When an applicant requires the preservation of RMB 10 million, the court may decide to preserve property amounting to RMB 12 million.

The Valuation of Excessive Property Preservation

6.65 Similar to the situation of the floating value, after the preservation orders have been rendered, including the seal-up, detainment or freezing of property, the modification or discharge of the preservation order might be needed. For example, if it comes to the notice of the court based on its own enquiries or on the application of the respondent or the interested party that the value of the preserved property has exceeded the amount of the claim, then that court will discharge or modify its preservation order in a timely manner.[80] This means that if the value of the preserved property, pursuant to the preservation orders, exceeds exorbitantly the value of claims in dispute, it will likely affect the respondents' and third parties' property rights in the future. This may even cause great financial losses far exceeding the value of the claim in the civil dispute. In addition, during the application of the respondent or the interested party, an appraisal report for the preserved property based on a unilateral request is effective and binding. In other words, as long as the appraisal report is made by a qualified verification organisation, the court will decide whether there is excessive property preservation.[81]

79 Opinion on Chongqing Property Preservation 2020, Article 3.

80 Article 19 of Provisions on Seal-up, Detainment or Freezing of Property (2020 Amendment) provides that the courts in ordering the sealing up, detaining or freezing of the property of a person subject to enforcement will ensure that the value of the property subjected to the preservation measure must be no more than the value of the dispute. The value of the property should be just sufficient to repay the creditor's rights determined in the future civil trial. However, the court will also take into account the enforcement expenses when analysing this issue, and these expenses will be added to the amount in dispute.

81 In *Daohai Xiong v Chongqing Jian'an Construction (Group) Co Ltd* (dispute over a construction contract) [2017] SPC Zhi Fu No 14 (the Supreme People's Court, reconsideration

6.66 In the context of excessive property preservation, the respondents will often claim against the applicants, irrespective of the fact that it is the court's obligation to properly appraise the property.[82] In legal practice, it is therefore prudent for applicants to provide property appraisal reports prepared by qualified evaluation institutions.

Pre-Action Property Preservations

6.67 Article 101 of the CPL 1991 (as amended until 2020) provides that:

> Any interested party whose lawful rights and interests, due to urgent circumstances, would suffer from irreparable harms if he fails to petition for preservation immediately, may, before filing the lawsuit, petition to the people's court with jurisdiction for the adoption of preservation measures.
>
> The applicant shall provide security; if the applicant fails to do so, his application shall be rejected.

6.68 This provision stipulates a general rule for pre-action property preservation applications. However, in legal practice, the general rule is not always operative when a specific issue should be addressed. For this reason, some regional courts have issued local legal guidance documents to guide the applicants in the context of pre-action preservation applications. In addition to discussion of the general rule, this section will mainly focus on regional courts' guidance documents that have provided detailed rules.

6.69 The formal requirements in any preservation application, such as the written format and the requirements of translation and of notarisation, have been discussed in Chapter 3, 3.117–3.129. This section will simply focus on the additional and substantive standards in the context of applications seeking pre-action property preservation measures.

---

and final ruling), Daohai Xiong, an applicant for reconsideration during the first instance, filed a property preservation application to preserve the property of the respondent, Chongqing Jian'an Construction (Group) Co Ltd. The High People's Court of Qinghai Province made a property preservation order ([2014] Qing Civil Bao Zi No 9) to seal up, detain and freeze Chongqing Jian'an Construction (Group) Co Ltd's property (RMB 26 million). Afterwards, an interested party, Guizhou Jian'an Real Estate Development Co Ltd, voluntarily provided the right of land (RMB 36 million) as the secured property for Chongqing Jian'an Construction (Group) Co Ltd. The High People's Court of Qinghai Province made an order ([2014] Qing Civil Yi Chu Zi No 17-1) to seal up the interested party's house. However, the interested party submitted an objection against [2014] Qing Civil Yi Chu Zi No 17-1 on the ground that an appraisal report provided by Guizhou Haotian Price Evaluation Judicial Institute had demonstrated that the evaluation price of the sealed house far exceeded Daohai Xiong's claim. In the end, both the High People's Court of Qinghai Province and the SPC upheld the interested party's argument to discharge the partial sealed house although the appraisal report by Guizhou Haotian Price Evaluation Judicial Institute was simply based on the interested party's unilateral request.

82 Pursuant to Article 28 of State Compensation Law of the People's Republic of China 1995 (2012 Amendment), if the court is at fault, the affected parties are entitled to commence an application to seek state compensation. Any further discussion on the topic is beyond the scope of the book.

Exact Information of Property in Applications

6.70 Providing exact information constitutes an additional requirement for a pre-action property preservation application in many regional courts' guidance documents. The Interpretation of Property Preservation (2020 Amendment) requires an applicant to provide exact information in applications seeking property preservation measures. However, it does not clarify the scope of the exact information that needs to be put into the written application.

6.71 Some regional guidance documents from local courts, such as Shanghai,[83] Shenzhen[84] and the Daya Bay Economic and Technological Development Zone,[85] provide detailed guidance to applicants on this issue.

6.72 By reference to Provisions of Shanghai Property Preservation 2017 and Guidance on Shenzhen Pre-Action Property Preservation 2018, the exact guidance can be summarised as follows:

(a) In terms of the bank deposit, the information should include the specific bank's name, the details of the bank account and the bank's address.
(b) In terms of the equity in a company, the information should include the shareholder's account, the capital account and the exact address of the securities company.
(c) In terms of real estates and specific movables that have been registered, the information should contain the certificate of registration provided by the registration authorities within one week prior to applying for the preservation of property; furthermore, the certificate should indicate the basic information of the property, such as the owner of the property, the number of certificate of ownership, the brand of property, the model of property (such as the model of

83 Provisions on Shanghai Property Preservation 2017, Article 14.

84 Provisions on Shenzhen Qianhai Property Preservation 2018, Article 12; see also, Guidance on Shenzhen Pre-Action Property Preservation 2018, Article 12; however, it should be emphasised that Article 12 does not treat providing exact information as a mandatory requirement in seeking pre-action preservations. It merely provides that either the exact information or some indications about the property for pre-action preservation applications is acceptable to the court.

85 *Opinions of People's Court of Daya Bay Economic and Technological Development Zone on Some Issues Concerning Property Preservation* (30 November 2018), Article 12. The Daya Bay Economic and Technological Development Zone is located in Huizhou, Guangdong Province. Because the People's Court of Daya Bay Economic and Technological Development Zone resolves a great number of foreign-related commercial cases, it is pertinent to look at the legal guidance documents provided by this court. It should be emphasised that Article 12 provides the criterion of exact information on property but does not stress that providing exact information is a mandatory requirement. It provides that the applicant should point out either the exact information or some indications regarding the property to be preserved. during the pre-action and post-action preservation applications by the courts.

a car), information on judicial restriction and information on the mortgage on the property.[86]

(d) In terms of the equity in a limited company or an unlisted public company, the information indicates the exact name of the company, the unified social credit code,[87] the amount of investment and equity shares and other information; if the preserved property is stocks of a listed company or other securities that can be preserved, the corresponding account information and the trading place or the name and address of the securities company shall be provided.

(e) In terms of the claims due, the names and addresses of the creditors and of debtors, the amount associated with the claims and the due date for payment of such claims.

(f) As for other property, the name of the property, its type, specification, quantity, value, owner, the storage location and other details and relevant evidence.[88]

6.73 In addition, the courts in order to avoid rendering the wrong preservation order will normally ask the applicant to provide evidence or information or other materials on the property indicated in the application.[89] In the absence of evidence or other relevant information, the court may determine whether the preservation order should be rendered in light of the property information that is available and the feasibility of enforcement of any preservation measure orders.[90]

6.74 It should be noted that Chinese courts will generally allow the applicants seeking post-action preservation measures to provide limited information about the property that would be subject to preservation measures.[91] This is in sharp contrast to the requirement on this aspect in the context of applications seeking pre-action measures, where the requirement is stringent in many courts.[92] For example, the Beijing High People's Court expressly

---

86 Provisions on Shanghai Property Preservation 2017, Article 14; see also, Guidance on Shenzhen Pre-Action Property Preservation 2018, Article 12.

87 The original version of Article 12 of Guidance on Shenzhen Pre-Action Property Preservation 2018 refers to "the registration code and the registration authorities". However, in accordance with *Notice of the State Council on Approving and Forwarding the General Plan of the National Development and Reform Commission and Other Departments on the Development of a Unified Social Credit Code System for Legal Persons and Other Organisations* (The State Council, Guo Fa [2015] No 33), any legal entity or organisation registered in China must use this unified social credit code prior to 2021. Therefore, apart from "unified social credit code", in the authors' experience, the traditional business licence is also operative.

88 Guidance on Shenzhen Pre-Action Property Preservation 2018, Article 12.

89 ibid Article 13; see also, Provisions of Beijing Property Preservation During the Case-Filing Procedure 2012, Article 8; see also, Provisions on Shenzhen Qianhai Property Preservation 2018, Article 10.

90 Guidance on Shenzhen Pre-Action Property Preservation 2018, Article 13.

91 Refer to 6.98.

92 For example, Article 12 of Guidance on Shenzhen Pre-Action Property Preservation 2018 provides that either the exact information or some indications about the property for

provides that an applicant seeking pre-action preservation measures must provide the exact property information of the respondent while the applicant seeking post-action property preservation measures can just provide some relevant information on the property that will become the subject matter of the preservation measure.[93] This means that in the territory of Beijing, all courts should comply with this rule.

6.75 Against the above discussion, even if not all regional court guidance documents require the applicant to provide exact information about the property, it is advisable for all applicants seeking pre-action preservation measures to spell out the exact information in their applications, if possible, on the property that will be the subject matter of any preservation.[94]

Substantive Prerequisites for Pre-Action Preservations

6.76 In light of the general rule in Article 101 of the CPL 1991 (as amended until 2020), some regional courts' guidance documents provide detailed standards to evaluate whether an application seeking pre-action preservation measures could be accepted by the courts. These detailed standards will constitute substantive prerequisites for pre-action preservation applications in different local courts.

6.77 By reference to different legal documents issued by Beijing,[95] Shanghai,[96] Sichuan[97] and Shenzhen,[98] there are three main prerequisites that any court looking into pre-action applications generally considers as follows:

(a) There is a legal relation between an applicant and a respondent.
(b) The circumstances are urgent; failure to grant a pre-action preservation measure immediately will lead to irreparable harms to the lawful rights of the applicant.
(c) The applicant must provide sufficient and flawless security.

pre-action preservation applications is acceptable to the court; see also, Article 12 of Opinions of the Daya Bay Primary People's Court of Huizhou City of Guangdong Province on Some Issues Concerning Cases of Property Preservation (2018) provides that the applicant should point out either the exact information or some indications regarding the property to be preserved during the pre-action and post-action preservation applications by the Chinese courts.

93 *Answer of Beijing High People's Court to Application of Some Issues of Case-Filing and Trial 2019 (II)* (20 November 2019), Item 36.

94 For example, Opinions on Sichuan Property Preservation 2015 and Opinions on Nanjing Property Preservation 2017, these legal guidance documents do not emphasise that the applicant for a pre-action property preservation must provide the exact information about property to be preserved.

95 Provisions on Beijing Property Preservation 2012, Article 9.

96 Provisions on Shanghai Property Preservation 2017, Article 9.

97 Opinions on Sichuan Property Preservation 2015, Article 3.

98 Guidance on Shenzhen Pre-Action Property Preservation 2018, Article 9.

6.78 The first prerequisite is dependent on the statements contained in the applicant's letter of the application. Also, the first prerequisite seems to point towards a need for a cause of action to exist between the parties to the preservation applications. However, if the applicant were to enunciate the legal relation, but was unable to postulate the cause of action in law, then in that scenario, the preservation application will still be accepted by the Chinese courts.[99] This section will not discuss the first prerequisite in detail and accordingly will focus on the second and third prerequisites.

Urgent Circumstances and Irreparable Harms

6.79 In legal practice, the term "urgent circumstances" refers to the facts surrounding the application at the time of filing of preservation applications, and "irreparable harms" may reflect the predicted consequences arising from those urgent circumstances. If analysed carefully, these two aspects to some extent can be very subjective and can vary from judge to judge. In order to restrict the judge's discretionary power, most local courts' guidance documents attempt to clarify what criteria will govern these two concepts of "urgent circumstances" and "irreparable harms".

6.80 By reference to Guidance on Shenzhen Pre-Action Property Preservation 2018 providing examples of "urgent circumstances" and Procedure on Hunan Property Preservation 2015 providing examples of "irreparable harms", the prerequisites for accepting a pre-action property preservation are as follows. Also, in authors' opinion, these following prerequisites might be applied by other courts that have not issued the similar guidance.

(a) The respondent has been sued in courts or in arbitrations by other creditors. Furthermore, this litigation or arbitration is under way or the respondent's liability has already been delineated by courts.
(b) All property or partial property belonging to the respondent has been preserved by courts based on other creditors' applications seeking property preservation measures.
(c) The disputed property or the property in the name of the respondent relating to the dispute is going through the formalities of transfer in real estate management, business administrative authorities or other departments; for example, an enquiry form provided by the real estate registration centre shows that a transaction related to the property is in progress.
(d) The applicant submits documentary evidence, such as contracts, agreements, minutes of meetings, correspondence signed by the

99 Refer to Chapter 1, 1.7.

respondent and so forth, demonstrating that a risk of harm to the interests of the applicant exists; nonetheless, the source of the evidence should be reliable and lawful.

(e) The applicant submits documentary or video evidence made by the public security bureau, the management committee or the village committee to prove that the respondent is transferring property, machines and other equipment; or to prove that the respondent, which is a company, has suspended production, has lost contact with the principal, is pursued by employees for wages and by suppliers for payment or other similar situations that may lead to the transfer of property.

(f) Generally, if a property that is the subject matter of preservation measures has in fact been mortgaged or pledged to the applicant and the registration procedure for such mortgage and pledge has already been completed, then in that case the circumstances surrounding the application will not be considered urgent circumstances by the courts. However, if the scope of the preserved property that the applicant applies for preservation is
   i) Not limited to the mortgaged or pledged property;
   ii) The value of the mortgaged or pledged property is not sufficient to pay off all claims to the applicant; or
   iii) The mortgaged or pledged property has been preserved by other courts in advance;

   then in such a scenario from (i) to (iii), it will not prevent the courts from recognising the circumstances as "urgent".[100]

(g) The disputed subject matter is seasonal, fresh, perishable goods or other things that are likely to be damaged or lost; or the long-term storage of the subject matter will lead to significant depreciation or other damages.

(h) The respondent is likely to encounter a financial crisis, and accordingly the respondent will not be able to fulfil the obligations to repay their debt.[101]

6.81 All in all, the applicant must shed light on both the urgent *circumstances* and the substantial impact on himself due to those urgent circumstances (irreparable harms). The court will reject the application if the applicant fails to convince the court on both prerequisites. In the end, it must be stressed that the purpose of the property preservation measure is to ensure that the enforcement of further court judgments or arbitral awards remains

100 Guidance on Shenzhen Pre-Action Property Preservation 2018, Article 10.
101 Procedure on Hunan Property Preservation 2015, Article 3.

achievable, or to prevent the applicant's loss. Therefore, apart from the two prerequisites above, it is necessary for the courts to examine whether future judgments or awards in the full civil trial could become impossible or could be difficult to enforce and whether the respondents' conduct or other factors may cause damage to the applicants.

Requirement of Security

6.82 The requirement of security is the third prerequisite for any application seeking pre-action preservation measures. Some general rules, particularly relating to the types of security and the exemptions for providing security, have been discussed at 3.139–3.194 in Chapter 3. In this section, only the supplementary provisions that are very specific to property preservation measures will be examined.

6.83 An applicant must provide evidence of adequate security with an application seeking a pre-action preservation order. This compulsory obligation is strictly enforced in any Chinese court. It is impossible for the court to accept an application for pre-action preservations without evaluating the applicant's evidence in relation to adequate security that the applicant must provide. If the court remains unconvinced that the applicant would be able to provide adequate security, then the court will not allow the application to go forward and file within the court system.

6.84 The Interpretation of Property Preservation (2020 Amendment) provides that the value of security to be furnished by the applicant must be at least equivalent in amount to the value of the property that will be the subject matter of the preservation order.[102] The value of the property put forward as security can be estimated by reference to the approaches used to calculate the value of the preserved property as discussed earlier in 6.60–6.62.

6.85 Under special circumstances, it is possible for the court to exercise its judicial discretion to either exempt the requirement of security that must be furnished by the applicant or to allow a lesser amount of security that must be furnished by the applicant,[103] as discussed in Chapter 3, 3.187–3.192.

---

102 The Interpretation of Property Preservation (2020 Amendment), Article 5(1).

103 Interpretation of Property Preservation (2020 Amendment), Article 5(2); in *Liupanshui Feida Real Estate Development Co Ltd v Luzhou Yinfeng Investment Management Co Ltd and Luzhou Jinhua Real Estate Development Co Ltd* (dispute over a pre-action property preservation) (2017) Chuan 05 Zhi Yi No 5 (the Intermediate People's Court of Luzhou of Sichuan Province, first instance, final and binding order), the court held that, in accordance with Article 5(2) of the Interpretation of Property Preservation (2020 Amendment), the court has the discretionary power to decide whether the value of the preserved property is adequate and how much the secured property should be provided; see also, Provisions on Shanghai Property Preservation 2017, Article 26; see also, Opinions on Sichuan Property Preservation 2015, Article 4.

Status Quo

6.86 In legal practice, the courts will generally adopt a vigilant approach when dealing with any pre-action applications seeking preservation measures. It's a fact that in comparison to the success rate of post-action preservation applications, the success rate of pre-action preservation applications is relatively low in Chinese courts. This has resulted in discontent and frustration among stakeholders.

6.87 It is the authors' submission that this relatively lower success rate for pre-action property preservation applications could be due to two main reasons as follows.

6.88 The first reason could be due to the fact that in accordance with Article 101 of the CPL 1991 (as amended until 2020), after the court has received the application seeking property preservation measures, the court must render the preservation order within 48 hours and then must also ensure that their order is enforced immediately.[104] In this very short time, the court must finish the full procedure associated with the application seeking pre-action preservation measures. For most Chinese courts, this is an impossible mission due to following situations – (i) generally Chinese courts are short staffed, (ii) Chinese courts are experiencing a great volume of cases and (iii) there are other invisible factors and contexts that could impact on the work of Chinese courts, and these factors are discussed later in Chapter 11,11.52–11.114.

6.89 Secondly, it has been observed that many applicants in China use the pre-action preservation orders only as a tactical step to negotiate with their counterpart. Many courts are fully aware of this so that they are concerned that applicants, after receiving preservation orders from the courts, will not submit a bill of complaint in a timely manner. The courts are therefore not keen to put all efforts into granting pre-action preservation measures. For the sake of completeness, interim remedies/preservation measures being used as a litigation tactic is not a new scenario in any jurisdiction as discussed in Chapter 1, 1.106–1.108.

6.90 To improve the situation as discussed in the preceding paragraphs, some of the regional people's courts, such as Beijing and Tianjin, have created a "one-stop legal service". Pursuant to this system, while applicants file applications seeking pre-action preservation measures, these applicants may at the same time submit their full applications with particulars of claims as a regular claim for the purpose of registering a full civil case.

6.91 In addition, as discussed in Chapter 3, 3.47–3.48, many courts now allow applicants to apply for preservation measures as online applications.[105] The purpose of these actions taken by the courts is to simplify the procedural

104 CPL 1991 (as amended until 2020), Article 101.

105 It is anticipated that online applications might be more commonplace after the COVID-19 pandemic.

steps required to seek preservation measures. This will ensure that the courts can finish the evaluation of materials in applications on time, and thereafter render the preservation orders on time as well. This will also ensure that enforcements of preservation orders are not delayed.[106] Nonetheless, in spite of these convenient measures adopted by the courts, these measures will not be able to dilute the stringent requirements and prerequisites of pre-action applications as mandated by the law and courts.

The Time Limit of Rendering Orders and Mode of Trials

6.92 The CPL 1991 (as amended until 2020) provides that the court must render a pre-action preservation order within 48 hours of receiving the application.[107] However, the CPL and its Interpretation have not provided any guidelines on whether the court can decide applications seeking property preservation measures just on the basis of documents or whether a quick interim hearing would need to be arranged.

6.93 In legal practice, it is observed that the courts determine the applications seeking pre-action property preservations just by the evaluation of evidence presented with the application. Also, the courts will largely not consider an interim hearing to hear the views of the two parties. The reasons for the approach adopted by the courts are discussed in the forthcoming paragraph.

6.94 First, the purpose of seeking pre-action preservations is to prevent the preserved property from being transferred or destroyed by the respondent. Organising a trial in these circumstances would be counterproductive for obvious reasons. Secondly, pursuant to the law, the courts must render an order within 48 hours of receiving a pre-action preservation application.[108] In a short period of 48 hours, it is impossible for the courts dealing with pre-action preservation applications to organise quick interim hearings in Chinese legal practice.

6.95 Therefore, it is the author's submission that it is reasonable and feasible for the Chinese courts to deal with pre-action preservation applications without interim hearings.

Post-Action Preservation Applications

6.96 A general rule for seeking post-action property preservation measures has been provided in Article 100 of the CPL 1991 (as amended until 2020) and it provides:

106 For example, Provisions on Tianjin Property Preservation 2019, Article 3; see also, Provisions on Shanghai Property Preservation 2017, Article 17.

107 CPL 1991 (as amended until 2020), Article 101.

108 ibid.

> In the event that, due to the conduct of one party to proceedings or other reasons, *it becomes impossible to enforce judgments* by, or *damage may occur to*, the other party to the same proceedings, the people's court may, upon the request of the other party, make an order to preserve the property of the party against whom the request is filed …; in the absence of such request, the people's court may, where necessary, also order the adoption of property preservation measures [emphasis added].
>
> When a people's court adopts any preservation measure, it may order the applicant to provide security; where the party refuses to provide such security, the court shall reject the application.
>
> *When a people's court receives an application for preservation in an emergency, it shall decide within forty-eight hours after the receipt of the application*; if the court accepts the application, such measures shall come into force immediately [emphasis added].[109]

6.97 In legal practice, post-action property preservation orders are widely pursued by stakeholders. During proceedings, if an applicant files for urgent property preservation orders, the requirements for seeking such orders are similar to the requirements in pre-action preservation applications.[110] If the applications are not urgent, then compared with the mandatory prerequisites for applications seeking pre-action and urgent post-action property preservation measures, the mandatory prerequisites for applying for post-action preservation measures are relatively flexible. The legal tests, pursuant to Article 100 of the CPL 1991 (as amended until 2020), will mainly focus on whether a future judgment or award will become impossible or difficult to enforce and whether the respondent's conduct or other factors may cause damage to the applicant. In addition, these flexible prerequisites are discussed in the forthcoming paragraphs.

Specific Indications of Property

6.98 During pre-action preservation applications, applicants are required by many Chinese courts to provide exact information about the property that is going to be preserved further to a preservation order.[111] However, in post-action preservation applications, the applicants may just provide some information about property that needs to be preserved. Article 10 of the Interpretation of Property Preservation (2020 Amendment) provides:

> During the action proceedings, where one party applying for the property preservation is unable to provide exact information of the property to be preserved due to objective reasons, however, if this party has provided specific clues of the property, the property preservation application may be adopted by the court.[112]

---

109 CPL 1991 (as amended until 2020), Article 100.

110 Refer to 6.79-6.81 for analysis of the requirements of "urgent circumstances" and "irreparable harms" in the context of pre-action preservation applications.

111 Refer to 6.70–6.75.

112 Interpretation of Property Preservation (2020 Amendment), Article 10.

6.99 This means that the applicants can just provide some indications of the property and it will be sufficient to persuade the Chinese courts in relation to one of the requirements for the post-action preservation. However, the Chinese courts can still demand exact information on the property while exercising their discretionary power.

Online Monitoring System for Property Information within China (I): Introduction

6.100 The full name of the online monitoring system is the "Network Enforcement Enquiry and Control system", established by the SPC and the China Banking Regulatory Commission in 2014. The purpose of the monitoring system is to encourage and support banking financial institutions, and to enable them to establish a network with Chinese courts through which enforcement enquiry, control and co-ordination mechanisms can be facilitated.

6.101 In addition, this network will support enquiries on the deposits and other financial assets of persons that are exposed to enforcement through the network, and simultaneously this network will facilitate the resolution of other issues which can assist the courts.[113]

6.102 Prior to 2016, this network system mainly served the enforcement of judgments or other rulings. However, due to the usual difficulty in providing exact information about property that is to be the subject matter of property preservation measures, Article 11 of the Interpretation of Property Preservation (2020 Amendment) stipulates that the applicant may instead file an application to request the court to take the assistance of an online monitoring system during enforcement of the preservation order. It is provided that, after the court has rendered a preservation order pursuant to Article 10(2),[114] then:

> The applicant may submit a written application to the court which has established an online monitoring system, in order to enquire about property of the respondent through the System.
>
> Where the applicant submits an application for enquiry, the court may make use of the System to enquire about property to be preserved pursuant to the order, or the property within the scope of the preservation amount, and take the corresponding measures of sealing-up, detaining and freezing.
>
> Where the court does not find any property available for preservation through the System, it shall notify the applicant in writing.[115]

---

113 *Opinions of the Supreme People's Court and the China Banking Regulatory Commission on Conducting Network Enforcement Enquiry and Control and Joint Credit Discipline by People's Courts and Banking Financial Institutions* (Fa [2014] No 266), Article 2.

114 Article 10(2) of the Interpretation of Property Preservation (2020 Amendment) provides that a court may render a property preservation order after an applicant has provided the specific indications of property to be preserved.

115 ibid Article 11; refer to Annex 2.

6.103 Currently, the cooperation with financial institutions is not limited to the SPC. By mid-2019, the SPC, together with 16 ministries including the Ministry of Public Security and over 3,900 financial institutions around China, set out a comprehensive monitoring system. The category of property or information about the property belonging to the citizens or the legal entities that can be investigated through this monitoring system. In a five-year (2019–2023) project launched by the SPC, it is stressed that the further step of the network system is to expand the scope of the property monitored and investigated and to enhance the interlink between the network monitoring system and internet finance in order for all kinds of insurance products including financial products to be incorporated within the scope of property monitored.[116] Following this guidance, the property or information investigated may include real estate, deposits, vehicles, securities, insurance, online assets, industrial and commercial registration and so forth.[117] Therefore, along with the expansion of the cooperation between the courts and other authorities, applicants may utilise this system to obtain more exact information about the respondent's property. The court will certainly decide whether it is necessary to accept the application of enquiry to assist applicants in finding property information utilising the online system.

6.104 In legal practice, it has been observed that an applicant seeking a property preservation application may also seek the court's legal assistance to find the exact property information by this network system, even if this network system provides for enforcement of a property preservation order. In particular, the online monitoring system is regularly useful to the applicant seeking post-action preservation orders.

6.105 In addition, the applicant seeking pre-action preservation measures from some local courts can also use this system to obtain information about property that is going to be the subject matter of the preservation order.

6.106 For example, in *Yurong Ma v Hong Pu and Others*,[118] Yurong, as an applicant, filed an application for a pre-action property preservation and meanwhile requested the court to employ the nationwide network enforcement investigation and control system to find the necessary information on the respondents' real estate or deposits. The disputed amount was RMB 4 million for which the preservation measure was requested.

6.107 Pursuant to Article 101 of the CPL 1991 (as amended until 2020) and Article 11 of the Interpretation of Property Preservation (2020 Amendment),

116 *Opinions of the Supreme People's Court on Deepening the Enforcement Reform and Improving the Long-Term Mechanism for Solving Enforcement Difficulties—the Outline of People's Courts' Enforcement Work* (2019–2023) (Fa Fa [2019] No16) (3 June 2019), Item 27.

117 Zhengzhou Intermediate People's Court of Henan Province, 'Opinions on Improvement of "Total-to-Total" Online Monitoring System' *People's Court Daily* (Beijing, 11 July 2019).

118 *Yurong Ma v Hong Pu and Others* (dispute over a private loan) [2018] Chuan 1921 Cai Bao No 74 (the primary People's Court of Tongjiang County of Sichuan Province, first instance and binding order).

the primary People's Court of Tongjiang County of Sichuan Province accepted the application and got access to the nationwide system to obtain information requested by the applicant.[119]

6.108 Nonetheless, a pre-action investigation for pre-action preservation applications is not common because of the absence of express provision in the judicial interpretation. However, as mentioned in 6.90, many courts can accept, at the same time, both applications, for the application seeking preservation measures as well as the application for full civil disputes. In this context, as long as the application seeking property preservation measures can explain the "urgent circumstances" and "irreparable harms", many Chinese courts, these days, are willing to use the online monitoring system to find the information on property that is going to be the subject matter of the preservation measures.[120]

Online Monitoring System for Property Information within China (II): Protection of Information

6.109 In order to protect the respondent's privacy, the Interpretation of Property Preservation (2020 Amendment) provides that:

> People's courts shall abide by law to keep confidential all the details of the respondent's property that has been investigated.[121]

6.110 Due to this obligation as to confidentiality, many courts adopt a restrained approach towards applications requesting the courts' assistance to utilise the online monitoring system to collate information on the respondents' property.

6.111 For example, the High People's Court of Guangdong Province will request a panel of judges rather than leaving the matter to a sole judge, in a

---

119 *Yurong Ma v Hong Pu and Others* (dispute over a private loan) [2018] Chuan 1921 Cai Bao No 74 (the primary People's Court of Tongjiang County of Sichuan Province, first instance and binding order); see also, *Gengwei He v Zhongsheng Guo* (dispute over a private loan) [2018] Chuan 1921 Cai Bao No 64 (the primary People's Court of Tongjiang County of Sichuan Province, first instance and binding order); the facts of the case are similar, and the primary People's Court of Tongjiang County of Sichuan Province made the same order as in Yurong. As a matter of fact, there are few published cases as to the application of the nationwide network enforcement investigation and control system. Perhaps disclosing such cases may involve personal information protection. Therefore, the courts are vigilant in releasing more information.

120 For example, in *Zhizhong Yan v Baoding Hongfu Real Estate Development Co Ltd* (an application for a property preservation) [2019] Ji 0635 Civil Chu No 2281 (the Primary People's Court of Li County of Hebei Province, first instance and binding order), a Chinese lawyer, on behalf of an applicant, filed an application for a property preservation, at the same time as he submitted a bill of complaint. In the letter of application seeking property preservation measures, the lawyer could not provide the exact information about the respondent's property. However, the Primary People's Court of Li County of Hebei Province utilised the online monitoring system to find the bank account of the respondent and accordingly froze the bank account of the respondent.

121 Interpretation of Property Preservation (2020 Amendment), Article 12.

scenario where an application for enquiry has been submitted along with the application seeking preservation of a property.[122]

6.112 Furthermore, there are restrictions pursuant to which the panel within the enforcement department of the court cannot give out the information about the respondent's property obtained after investigation to other departments of the courts, for example the trial department. However, the enforcement department within the court can in certain circumstance share the relevant information provided that information is limited to the scope of the preserved property.[123]

6.113 However, in practice, not every local court, like the High People's Court of Guangdong Province, provides an unambiguous procedure to protect the information of respondents. Furthermore, some courts, in order to avoid leaking information, are not willing to utilise the online monitoring system to assist applicants that are seeking property preservation measures. Based on this, the SPC in its five-year project has proposed not only to strengthen and guide the use of the online monitoring system, but also to regulate the entire process of the use of the online monitoring system to prevent the respondents' information from leaking out.[124] Currently, there are no more statistics available as to how the SPC and other local courts are taking measures to protect respondents' information. It is anticipated that the improvement of the protection of information may stimulate the use of the online monitoring system during the application stage.

Online Monitoring System for Property Information within China (III): Regional Online Monitoring System

6.114 Apart from the nationwide online monitoring system, some regional courts and local relevant authorities have established some "point-to-point"

122 *Some Provisions of the Enforcement Department of Guangdong High People's Court on Property Preservation* (25 October 2017), Article 9. In recent years, in order to efficiently secure the enforcement of preservation measures, many Chinese courts have requested their domestic enforcement department to accept applications seeking preservation measures, render an order and thereafter even enforce the preservation order. In the enforcement department of the court, which is a system similar to the civil trial system, whenever there is a simple case and where the amount of the claim involved is lower, the application will be heard by a sole judge, but for other cases, a panel made up of three judges will decide legal issues arising out of enforcement proceedings. In the context of deciding whether the application for enquiry should be accepted or not accepted, a panel of judges will decide this application. This demonstrates that the High People's Court of Guangdong Province is very cautious in dealing with this kind of enquiry application. Nonetheless, it should be noted that such Provisions simply apply in the High People's Court of Guangdong Province rather than other courts in the territory of Guangdong.

123 ibid.

124 *Opinions of the Supreme People's Court on Deepening the Enforcement Reform and Improving the Long-Term Mechanism for Solving Enforcement Difficulties—the Outline of People's Courts' Enforcement Work* (2019–2023) (Fa Fa [2019] No 16) (3 June 2019), Item 27.

online monitoring platforms that can be used in these regions. In the five-year (2019–2023) project launched by the SPC, it is also emphasised that a unified online monitoring system by the SPC should be treated as a general system to be applied around China and meanwhile to set out the local courts' online monitoring system as a supplement to the SPC's system.[125]

6.115 For example, the Intermediate People's Court of Nanjing City of Jiangsu Province and the PICC (Nanjing) Property and Casualty Company set up an online system to check respondents' information on insurance financial products and vehicle insurance.[126]

6.116 In addition, the High People's Court of Jiangsu Province and the Office of Jiangsu Housing and Urban-Rural Development in 2018 issued the guidance on building a platform for assisting a court to enquire/investigate, freeze and deduct the applied fund.[127] Pursuant to this Guidance, the Intermediate People's Court of Nanjing City of Jiangsu Province took the lead in working with the Nanjing Housing Fund Management Centre in order to complete the platform in 2018.[128] All the people's courts in the territory of Nanjing can utilise the above two systems to enquire about the relevant property information.

6.117 Apart from the territory of Jiangsu Province, similarly, in the territory of Guangdong Province, the High People's Court of Guangdong Province has also completed a regional network monitoring system.[129]

6.118 It can be seen from the above developments, which have been taking place locally and centrally in China, that in the future, there could be an elaborate mechanism to assist applicants in preservation applications.

6.119 However, for the time being, since not all the Chinese courts are willing to accept applications for enquiry, applicants cannot ignore various constraints.[130] Furthermore, pursuant to the Interpretation of Property Preservation (2020 Amendment), the court may exercise its discretionary power to determine whether it is even necessary to accept an application for enquiry. After all, in the light of Article 11 of this Interpretation, the main

125 ibid.

126 *Opinions of the Nanjing Intermediate People's Court and PICC (Nanjing) on the Establishment of Joint Enforcement and Cooperation Mechanism* (Ning Zhong Fa [2017] No 248).

127 *Guidance of Jiangsu High People's Court and the Office of Jiangsu Housing and Urban-Rural Development on the Establishment of Joint Enforcement Mechanism Concerning the Housing Fund* (23 July 2017).

128 *Notice of the Nanjing Intermediate People's Court on Open the "Point-to-Point" Online Monitoring System Concerning the Enquiry and Freezing of Housing Fund* (26 April 2018). It should be noted that the circumstances under which the housing fund can be frozen and deductions made from it have been discussed in 6.45.

129 Provisions on Guangdong Property Preservation 2017, Article 8.

130 After conducting field research, in Chinese legal practice, it is not uncommon that applications for enquiry are refused without any reasons by the Chinese courts. Therefore, the onus of providing property information will remain solely on the applicants in such instances.

function of this network monitoring system is to provide for the enforcement of a property preservation order. In practice, its extension function varies from court to court.

Security (I): Requirement

6.120 Unlike in pre-action preservation applications, furnishing security is not a mandatory obligation for an applicant in post-action preservation applications. However, in order to prevent the underlying risk of granting a wrong preservation order and to demonstrate the usual guarded approach, Chinese courts are likely to request security from applicants even in post-action preservation applications as well. In such instances, the Chinese courts will not insist on the full amount in security, which is a norm for pre-action preservation applications.

6.121 Article 5 of the Interpretation of Property Preservation (2020 Amendment) provides that:

> The security amount shall not exceed 30 per cent of the preservation amount requested; where the property to be preserved is a disputed subject matter, the security amount shall not exceed 30 per cent of the value of such disputed subject matter.[131]

6.122 However, the Interpretation of Property Preservation (2020 Amendment) does not provide the amount of security when it is difficult for the court to calculate the respondent's loss. By reference to Provisions on Shanghai Property Preservation 2017:

> The court may refer to the following standards to accumulate the amount of cash security in sections: the preservation amount is less than RMB 10 million as 20 per cent, the preservation amount is RMB 10 million to 100 million as 10 per cent, and the preservation amount is more than RMB 100 million as five per cent.[132]

Security (II): Exemptions from Providing Security

6.123 As discussed earlier, the requirement for applicants to furnish security is not compulsory during post-action preservation applications. However, whether the applicants must provide security will be dependent on the judge's exercise of discretion. Nonetheless, even if the judge were to request security, then subject to the applicant's state of affairs, the applicant can apply for an exemption or deduction from the amount of security as discussed in 3.187–3.192 of Chapter 3.

The Time Limit of Rendering Orders and Respondents' Defence

6.124 If an applicant files an application seeking post-action preservation measures under "urgent circumstances", the CPL 1991 (as amended until 2020) provides that a court must make an order within 48 hours.[133]

131 Interpretation of Property Preservation (2020 Amendment), Article 5.
132 Provisions on Shanghai Property Preservation 2017, Article 26.
133 CPL 1991 (as amended until 2020), Article 100.

6.125 If an applicant files an application seeking post-action preservation measures and there are no urgent circumstances, the Interpretation of Property Preservation (2020 Amendment) provides:

> After accepting an application for a property preservation, a court shall make an order within *five* days. If the security needs to be provided [by the applicant], it shall render an order within *five* days after the security is provided [by the applicant]. If the court renders an order to take a preservation measure, the enforcement of the order must commence within five days [emphasis added].[134]

6.126 Due to the above tight deadlines imposed on judges, it is very difficult for the courts to order interim hearings. In particular, courts are under similar deadlines when dealing with pre-action preservation applications; as these courts must render preservation orders within 48 hours of accepting applications, it is not feasible for the courts to organise interim hearings. Without interim hearings, respondents have no chance to defend against applicants seeking property preservation measures. However, the respondents can defend themselves during the countersecurity procedure by arguing that financial countersecurity could secure enforcement of future judgments and there is no scenario where the applicants could suffer loss as they have furnished countersecurity.

6.127 The procedure adopted by courts is slightly different in post-action preservation applications as compared to the procedure adopted in pre-action preservation applications. In most regional courts, where the applicants submit applications seeking post-action preservation measures, the disputes are likely to be transferred to the trial panel.[135] In this context, if analysed carefully, the respondents do have an opportunity to argue in the courts, even though the courts are under tight deadlines to issue an order within five days of the post-action preservation application. Similar to the argument during the countersecurity process mentioned in 6.126, the respondents in their defence can demonstrate that the future judgments can be enforced, and no other damage may occur without the preservation orders. In light of the subject matter of the property preservation measure requested by the applicants and the requirements of property applications, the respondents are entitled to argue: (i) the value of property to be preserved is excessive,[136] and/or (ii) the property is not suitable to preserve and/or (iii) there are no "urgent" cir-

134 Interpretation of Property Preservation (2020 Amendment), Article 4.

135 In some courts, all applications seeking pre-action or post-action property preservation measures are decided and enforced by the enforcement department of the court, for example, in the High People's Court of Guangdong Province; see also, Provisions on Guangdong Property Preservation 2019, Article 1.

136 Refer to 6.65. If a respondent provides an appraisal report by a qualified evaluation organisation to demonstrate the excessive preservation, it would be helpful to modify the preservation order; see also, *Daohai Xiong v Chongqing Jian'an Construction (Group) Co Ltd* (dispute over a construction contract) [2017] SPC Zhi Fu No 14 (the Supreme People's Court, reconsideration and final ruling).

cumstances and "irreparable damages" and so forth. Nonetheless, it is the authors' contention that in legal practice such arguments relating to the subject matter and requirements of the preservation application do not fundamentally impact on the courts' decision. The defence for the respondents must be to focus on the necessity of the applications from the perspective of the applicants' purposes.

The Possibility of Interim Hearing

6.128 There is no explicit provision that will clarify this issue. However, an interim hearing for the post-action preservation is still possible in certain cases. For example, when the value of the preserved property cannot be ascertained by two parties during a preservation application, in legal practice, the courts are generally inclined to hear the two parties' views. If so, the respondents' defence can refer to 6.126–6.127.

6.129 In addition, pursuant to the Opinions on Sichuan Property Preservation 2016, when an applicant contends that the amount of the preserved property is not sufficient and accordingly requests the court to increase the preservation measures, the High People's Court of Sichuan Province expressly provides that the court may organise an interim hearing to cater to such a scenario. On the other hand, when a respondent claims that the amount of the preserved property is excessive, the court may also organise an interim hearing to consider both parties' views on it.[137] Although this clear guidance is merely provided in the territory of Sichuan, to the authors' knowledge, this reasonable guidance in practice can be adopted by many local courts.

Protection of the Respondent's Interests

6.130 In the past few years, it has been observed by legal practitioners that Chinese courts are inclined to render property preservation orders as long as applicants can furnish sufficient and reliable security in any applications seeking preservation of property.

6.131 Furthermore, it has been observed that once preservation orders are enforced, the discharge of the preservation orders will not be allowed until the cases have reached the final stage in the civil proceedings, namely, the final and binding judgments have been pronounced by the courts.

6.132 As far as companies, especially private companies, are concerned, unlike state-owned companies, if these private companies' bank accounts have been frozen or the property for manufacturing and business operations,

137 Opinions on Sichuan Property Preservation 2016, Articles 23 and 24.

such as the factory, the machinery, the equipment or raw material, is under preservation measures, for example sealed up, there are possible ramifications. A few of the possible ramifications of such preservation measures will be the issue of cash flow problems or the preservation measures' impact on the daily operation of the going concern.

6.133 Against the above background, the deputies of the National People's Congress in recent years have regularly submitted proposals concerning the impact of property preservation measures on the corporations' business. These proposals are considered significant as they can affect the gross domestic product of a region.

6.134 Since 2018, the SPC has continuously focused on this issue, and further research and investigation have shown that the Interpretation of Property Preservation (2020 Amendment) should be improved.

6.135 Nonetheless, prior to the improvement of this Interpretation 2016, a few approaches have been devised to alleviate the concerns, for example, the Chinese courts may allow – (i) the substitution of property, (ii) the measures to be undertaken for enforcing property preservation would be broadened and could be flexible, and (iii) the issue of selection of property for enforcing preservation measures could be broadened within the existing law.[138]

Option of Multiple Properties

6.136 Article 13 of the Interpretation of Property Preservation (2020 Amendment) provides:

> Where the party subject to the preservation has multiple properties available for the preservation, subject to the prerequisite of fulfilling the purpose of preservation, the court shall choose to preserve property which has relatively smaller impact on the manufacturing and business operation of such party.[139]

6.137 This means that when an applicant applies for a property preservation measure over multiple properties, in the context of achieving the purpose of preservation, the court will have an option to preserve those property/properties, which may relatively have a lesser impact on the respondent or his businesses.

6.138 Furthermore, even if the applicant applies for the preservation of a specific property, but the respondent has multiple properties available for preservation, the court may choose the most appropriate property to preserve to alleviate the effects of preservation measures on the respondent.

138 *Reply of the Supreme People's Court to No 7882 Proposal of the First Session of the 13th National People's Congress* (8 August 2018); see also, *Reply of the Supreme People's Court to No 7974 Proposal of the Second Session of the 13th National People's Congress* (30 July 2019).

139 Interpretation of Property Preservation (2020 Amendment), Article 13.

6.139 This approach is strictly abided through many regional guidance documents issued by the local courts, such as Guangdong,[140] Sichuan[141] and Shanghai.[142]

6.140 Furthermore, the High People's Court of Sichuan Province has emphasised that, with regard to the respondent's basic bank account, the court should be cautious in freezing and accordingly will need to evaluate whether such bank account should be subjected to preservation measures.[143] In addition, although the applicant may apply for preserving a number of properties that belong to the respondent, he is not allowed to undervalue the respondent's properties.[144]

Use of Preserved Property

6.141 Where a court takes preservation measures on property used for the manufacturing and business operations (such as factory, machinery or equipment), the court may appoint a respondent as the custodian of property and allow this respondent to employ such property in his business during the enforcement of preservation measures.[145]

Sale of Preserved Property

6.142 Where a respondent requests a court to sell the preserved property while the enforcement of a preservation order is in progress, the court will consider and evaluate the request. The condition for considering such request is that this preserved property is not the disputed subject matter of the primary civil/commercial dispute. After taking into consideration such a request, if the court is of the view that this request will not damage the lawful interests of the applicants and other creditors, then the court may allow the request without seeking the applicant's consent.

6.143 However, after granting the request, the court will supervise the respondent's attempt to sell the preserved property while ensuring that the preserved property is sold at a reasonable price during the designated period. The court will also control the income of the transaction arising out of the disposal of the preserved property.

---

140 Opinions on Guangdong Standardizing Property 2019, Article 6.

141 Opinions on Sichuan Property Preservation 2015, Article 16.

142 Provisions on Shanghai Property Preservation 2017, Article 46.

143 Under Chinese law, a company is only allowed to open a basic bank account and a few general bank accounts. The basic bank account is used as a business account and is the most important account for the company. The company will use this basic account to withdraw cash; conversely, the general bank account of the company cannot be used to withdraw cash related to the company's business.

144 Opinions on Sichuan Property Preservation 2015, Article 18.

145 Interpretation of Property Preservation (2020 Amendment), Article 13.

6.144 In the above context, if an applicant were to not agree with the court allowing the respondent to sell the preserved property, then the applicant would have an option to file an application seeking procedural remedy of objection pursuant to Article 225 of the CPL 1991 (as amended until 2020). The procedural steps associated with any application seeking procedural remedy of objection have been discussed in Chapter 3, 3.247–3.257.

6.145 If the respondent were to seek the sale of preserved property that is the subject matter of the main dispute, then this is only possible with the consent of the applicant.[146]

Substitution of Property (Respondents' Countersecurity)

6.146 Article 104 of the CPL 1991 (as amended until 2020) provides:

> If the respondent provides [counter] security in a case concerning a property dispute, the people's court shall discharge the preservation order.[147]

6.147 Furthermore, Article 167 of the Interpretation of CPL 2015 (2020 Amendment) provides:

> Where the party against whom property preservation measures are to be taken provides other [counter] security such as property that are of equivalent value and are more convenient to enforce, the court may render an order to change the subject matter for preservation to the security property provided by the said party.[148]

6.148 The above provisions relating to a respondent's countersecurity mean that the respondent can provide, if he so wishes, other property to replace the preserved property.[149]

6.149 A few legal guidance documents from the local courts provide examples of property that can be used as substitute property instead of the preserved property. By reference to Guidance on Shenzhen Pre-Action Property Preservation 2018, the following categories of property can be considered by the courts as substitute property:

(a) Sufficient cash, deposits and securities.
(b) A letter of guarantee issued by a commercial bank.
(c) A letter of guarantee issued by an insurance company.
(d) Substituted property that belongs to a similar category as the preserved property.
(e) Other enforceable property with the applicant's consent.[150]

146 ibid, Article 20.
147 CPL 1991 (as amended until 2020), Article 104.
148 Interpretation of CPL 2015 (2020 Amendment), Article 167.
149 It must be noted that under certain circumstances, without the applicant's consent, the court cannot approve an application seeking the discharge of the order, even if the respondent provides countersecurity; see, Interpretation of Property Preservation (2020 Amendment), Article 22; see also Chapter 3, 3.136–3.138.
150 Guidance on Shenzhen Pre-Action Property Preservation 2018, Article 27.

Protection to Non-Profit Entity

6.150 Where some non-profit entities, such as hospitals, schools or nurseries, are involved in commercial disputes, prior to taking any preservation measures, a Chinese court is obligated to take a guarded approach towards the issue of whether the court can preserve property belonging to these non-profit entities.[151]

The Time Limit and Renewal of Preservation Orders

6.151 The property preservation measures cannot be enforced indefinitely. Pursuant to the existing law, any property preservation orders are subject to a time limit. If an applicant does not apply for renewal before the expiry of the time limit of a preservation order, the order will lapse automatically. Therefore, it is very important for any applicant to know the time limit of the preservation order that has been obtained from the court.

6.152 The time limit of the preservation order varies according to the categories of the preserved property. The time limits are as follows:

(a) No longer than one year for freezing of a bank deposit.
(b) No longer than two years for sealing up or detaining movables.
(c) No longer than three years for sealing up immovables and for freezing other property rights such as equity in a corporation.[152]
(d) No longer than one year for preservation of trademark rights.[153]
(e) No longer than six months for preservation of patent rights.[154]

---

151 For example, Opinions on Guangdong Standardizing Property 2019, Article 5; see also, in Chapter 11, 11.68 and 11.87, on the discussion that Chinese courts are obligated to take into account public interest issues.

152 From (a) to (c), see Interpretation of CPL 2015 (2020 Amendment), Article 487.

153 *Interpretation of the Supreme People's Court on Property Preservation of Trademark Rights by the People's Court (2020 Amendment)* (Fa Shi [2001] No1) (superseded by Fa Shi [2020] No 19). It should be noted that there is no exact meaning of "other property right" pursuant to Article 487 of the Interpretation of CPL 2015 (2020 Amendment). The trademark right belongs to the category of intangible property. In theory, trademark rights can be treated as "other property right". However, the Interpretation of CPL 2015 (2020 Amendment) simply provides for freezing "other property right" rather than other measures over "other property right". Conversely, *Interpretation of the Supreme People's Court on Property Preservation of Trademark Rights by the People's Court (2020 Amendment)* does not restrict measures of preservation. In this context, the preservation of trademark rights should be different from the general property right; see also, *Sichuan Weiyi Drink Foodstuff Co Ltd v Sale Centre of Weiyi Yinxiang Beverages in Chengdu Hi-tech Industrial Development Zone and Baiyu Chen* (a property preservation application arising from an infringement of trademark) [2017] Chuan 06 Zhi Bao No 78 (the Intermediate People's Court of Deyang City of Sichuan Province, first instance and binding order), where the Intermediate People's Court of Deyang City of Sichuan Province made an order to seal up the trademark belonging to Baiyu Chen for six months.

154 See, *Reply of the Supreme People's Court to National Intellectual Property Administration of PRC on How to Assist a People's Court to Enforce a Property Preservation Order* ([2000] Fa Zhi Zi No 3).

(f) No longer than six months for preservation of the application right of the patent.[155]

6.153 As discussed in the preceding paragraphs, the applicant must apply for the renewal of the order nearer to the expiry of the time limit according to the categories of the preserved property. The process is based on the Interpretation of CPL 2015 (2020 Amendment):

> In the case the applicant applies for extending the aforesaid time limit, the people's court shall go through extension formalities of seal-up, detainment and freezing prior to the expiration thereof...
>
> The people's court may go through extension formalities of seal-up, seizure and freezing *ex officio*.[156]

6.154 It should be noted that prior to the issue of the Interpretation of CPL 2015 (2020 Amendment), the Chinese judges on their own initiative could extend the preservation order nearer to the expiry of the time limit or the preservation order. The Chinese judges could take such an action even when the applicant had not requested the extension. Once the time limit had expired, the judges generally would have taken upon themselves the obligation to consider grant of extension.

6.155 However, since this Interpretation has been issued by the SPC, it is commonly recognised that the obligation to seek extension falls upon the applicant or his lawyers. It is therefore vital for an applicant to abide by the time limit of the preservation order to avoid forfeiting the preservation right.[157]

Compensation Caused by Wrongful Property Preservation

6.156 The general rules of compensation caused by unlawful/erroneous property preservation order were discussed in Chapter 3, 3.292–3.297. The forthcoming paragraphs will provide the specific rules in relation to the tortious liability principle and its elements in case of unlawful/erroneous property preservation. The extent of damages an aggrieved party can claim and how the Chinese courts will evaluate damages is a topic in itself and is beyond the scope of this book.

---

155 *Reply of the Supreme People's Court to National Intellectual Property Administration of PRC on How to Assist a People's Court to Enforce a Property Preservation Order* ([2000] Fa Zhi Zi No3) provides that the application right of patent belongs to a kind of property right that can be treated as the subject matter of a property preservation measure. The difference between the preservation of patent rights and the preservation of application rights of patent is that the former is derived from the patent right itself while the latter is not relevant to the patent right because no patent right exists at all at the time of enforcement of preservation measures.

156 Interpretation of CPL 2015 (2020 Amendment), Article 487.

157 Aaron Yizhou Deng, 'New Legal Risk for Applicants Seeking Property Preservation Measures' (Mondaq Connecting Knowledge and People, 25 September 2019) <https://www.mondaq.com/china/Real-Estate-and-Construction/848198/3613020135204452084030003358312015426032303402786124459391183850 5> accessed 15 July 2021.

Liability Principle of Wrongful Application

6.157 Article 105 of the CPL 1991 (as amended until 2020) provides:

> If an application [preservation] is made wrongfully, the applicant shall compensate the person against whom the application is made for any loss incurred as a result of the preservation of property.[158]

6.158 However, this Article does not clarify the liability principle that will be applicable to the applicant. Pursuant to the Civil Code 2020, the liability for tort can be divided into fault-based liability, the presumption of fault and non-fault liability.[159] With regard to the presumption of fault, it is provided:

> One who is at fault as construed according to legal provisions and cannot prove otherwise shall be subject to the tort liability.[160]

6.159 Similarly, with regard to non-fault liability, it is provided:

> One who shall assume the tort liability for infringing upon a civil right or interest of another person, whether at fault or not, as provided for by law, shall be subject to such legal provisions.[161]

6.160 It follows that the application of both the presumption of fault and non-fault liability are only dependent on the express provisions prescribed by law.

6.161 Accordingly, it is generally accepted in legal practice that the claim for damages caused by the wrongful application of preservation measures is subject to fault-based liability. In particular, the SPC in several cases held that the liability caused by an application for property preservation is subject to the principle of fault-based liability.[162] Correspondingly, the other lower people's courts in principle also follow fault-based liability and will evaluate

---

158 CPL 1991 (as amended until 2020), Article 105.

159 Civil Code 2020, Articles 1165 and 1166; see also Tort Law 2010 (expired on 1 January 2021), Articles 6 and 7.

160 Civil Code 2020, Article 1165 (2); see also Tort Law 2010 (expired on 1 January 2021), Article 6(2). These two items are exactly the same.

161 Civil Code 2020, Article 1166; see also, Tort Law 2010 (expired on 1 January 2021), Article 7; the difference between Article 1166 and Article 7 is that Article 1166 stresses that the person's conduct causes the consequence of damages.

162 For example, *Chongqing Wanzhou Suote Loading and Unloading Co Ltd v Yicheng Zong* (dispute over a pre-action property preservation) [2014] SPC Civil Retrial Zi No 2172 (the Supreme People's Court, retrial and binding judgment); see also, *Yinggui Chen and Other v Ninghua Yonglong Real Eastate Development Co* (dispute over a construction contract) [2015] SPC Civil Retrial Zi No 1147 (the Supreme People's Court, retrial and binding judgment); see also, *Zhoushan Penavico Freight and Forwarding v Dalian Fenghai International Fisheries Co Ltd* (dispute over damages caused by the application for property preservation) [2018] SPC Civil Retrial No 6289 (the Supreme People's Court, retrial and binding judgment); see also, *Qingdao Zhongjin Yuneng Real Estate Co Ltd v Qingdao Zhongjin Industrial Co Ltd and Other* (dispute over damages caused by the application for property preservation) [2017] SPC Civil Final No 118 (the Supreme People's Court, retrial and binding judgment).

whether the applicant should bear the loss of the respondent or the third party arising out of erroneous preservation measures.[163]

6.162 Although the mainstream liability regime in the compensation of wrongful property preservations complies with fault-based liability, in individual cases, some courts do not follow this liability. In contrast, non-fault liability is applied.

6.163 For example, in *Avnet (China) Technology Co Ltd v Beijing Ctrowell Technology Co Ltd*,[164] the Primary People's Court of Haidian District of Beijing Municipality, as the first instance court, held that, in accordance with Article 6 (1) of the Tort Law 2010 (fault-based liability), the applicant must bear the loss of the respondent on the ground that the application for preservation measures during litigation proceedings should consider the risk of failure and accordingly if the applicant felt that the evidence was against him, then the applicant must initiate steps to withdraw the application for property preservations in a timely manner to avoid unnecessary consequences for the respondent.[165]

6.164 After the case of Avent had been submitted to the second instance court, although the First Intermediate People's Court of Beijing Municipality affirmed the first instance judgment, the court overruled the applicable law of fault-based liability on which the judgment was granted by the first instance court.

6.165 It held that when the party concerned brought a case to court, that party must consider all risks based on the lawsuit including the failure of his preservation application or even overall case, the derivative risk, pursuant to a preservation order. If the party were subsequently to lose the case, it meant that the preservation order in an objective sense was erroneously granted regardless of the fact that the applicant in a subjective sense was at fault or not. Therefore, pursuant to Article 105 of the CPL 1991 (as amended until 2020), the First Intermediate People's Court of Beijing Municipality held that the applicant was liable for the loss to the respondent.[166]

---

163 For example, in *Wang Hucheng v Duan Junfeng* (dispute over damages caused by the application for property preservation) [2015] Jiao Civil Zai Er Final Zi No 00035 (the Intermediate People's Court of Jiaozuo City of Henan Province, second instance and binding judgment), where the Intermediate People's Court of Jiaozuo City of Henan Province held that the applicant simply undertook fault-based liability and had the duty of reasonable care before applying for preservation measures; see also, *Shenyang North Explosion-Proof Co Ltd v PICC (Liaoning) Property and Casualty Co Ltd* (dispute over damages caused by the application for property preservation) [2017] Liao 0102 Civil Chu No 9180; [2018] Liao 01 Civil Final No 3034.

164 *Avnet (China) Technology Co Ltd v Beijing Ctrowell Technology Co Ltd* (dispute over damages caused by the application of property preservation) [2016] Jing 01 Civil Final No 785.

165 *Beijing Ctrowell Technology Co Ltd v Avnet (China) Technology Co Ltd* (dispute over damages caused by the application of property preservation) [2015] Hai Civil (Commercial) Chu Zi No 7754 (the Primary People's Court of Haidian District of Beijing Municipality, first instance and first instance judgment).

166 *Beijing Ctrowell Technology Co Ltd v Avnet (China) Technology Co Ltd* (dispute over damages caused by the application of property preservation) [2015] Hai Civil (Commercial)

6.166 In fact, it can be analysed that the First Intermediate People's Court of Beijing Municipality contended that the applicant was liable for non-fault liability. On analysis, it also brings to the fore that the court is in fact considering the merits of the overall case even when considering and evaluating the preservation of property applications. If the liability regime can be based on the overall merit of the case, then the burden is immense on the applicant to evaluate the risk before even applying for preservation measures.

6.167 It is worth noting that the case pertaining to the issue of damages in the area of property preservation measure was heard in this particular area of Beijing in 2015. After that, the SPC's judgment discussed in 6.171–6.173 clarified the fault-based liability of the applicant. Although these authors do not find the latest judgment in the First Intermediate People's Court of Beijing Municipality Beijing to redress the verdict of non-fault liability, it is safe to state that the verdict of fault-based liability to the applicant seeking a property preservation measure should be followed by all Chinese courts.

Elements of Fault-Based Liability

6.168 In Chinese academic and legal practice, it is generally accepted that there are four elements to determine whether the applicant's preservation application shall be subjected to fault-based liability.

6.169 Firstly, the application seeking preservation measures is illegal; secondly, the respondent suffers a loss as a result of the granting of preservation measures; thirdly, there is a causative link between the applicant's conduct leading to a preservation order and the respondent's loss; and fourthly, the applicant is at fault in a subjective sense.[167]

6.170 While evaluating these four elements, the most controversial issue remains the relevant examination of the applicant's fault in the subjective sense. The reason is, in most situations, as long as the applicant loses the overall civil/commercial case and the respondent suffers from the loss, the respondent can easily claim damages caused by the preservation application. Considering this scenario, the first three elements in principle could easily be satisfied.[168] Therefore, the fourth element remains crucial and a bit controversial.

6.171 The SPC in 2017 provided an authoritative opinion on the applicant's erroneous preservation application in the case of *Qingdao Zhongjin Yuneng*

Chu Zi No 7754 (the First Intermediate People's Court of Beijing Municipality, first instance, final and binding judgment).

167 Lixin Yang, *Tort Law* (2nd Edn Peking University Press 2017).

168 In legal practice, the controversial issues arising out of these three elements are also very complex. Any further discussion is beyond the scope of this book.

Real Estate Co Ltd v Qingdao Zhongjin Industrial Co Ltd and Other.[169] By reference to this leading case, the standard of the applicant's fault can be revealed.

6.172 First, whether the applicant is at fault is not dependent on whether the applicant's claim is upheld by the court. The SPC, in *Qingdao Zhongjin Yuneng Real Estate Co Ltd v Qingdao Zhongjin Industrial Co Ltd and Other*,[170] clarified that whether the application for a property preservation was wrong depended on – (i) whether the applicant's claims for the case were upheld by the court, and (ii) whether the applicant's improper conduct in applying for the preservation measures was intentional or grossly negligent.[171]

6.173 Secondly, the standard of intentional or gross negligence will be examined on the basis of whether the overall lawsuit was reasonable on the basis of the facts of the case, legal arguments and fit within the ambit of relevant cause of action. In addition, whether the application seeking property preservation measures was appropriate would be evaluated on the basis of the amount of the property preservation requested, the subject matter of property preservation and the measures requested in the application for preservation of property.

Property Preservation Fees

6.174 Pursuant to Article 14 (2) of *Measures on Payment of Litigation Costs 2006*,[172] the application fees to seek property preservation measures should be paid on the basis of the actual amount of property to be preserved according to the following standards:

(a) Where the value of the property does not exceed RMB 1,000 or no amount of property is involved, RMB 30 shall be paid for each case.
(b) Where the disputed amount is between RMB 1,000 and RMB 100,000, 1 per cent thereof shall be paid.
(c) For an amount more than RMB 100,000, 0.5 per cent thereof on the amount above RMB 100,000 shall be paid.
(d) However, the maximum amount of the fees paid by a party concerned for applying for preservation measures shall not exceed RMB 5,000.

6.175 Other general rules regarding the property preservation fee can be located in Chapter 3, 3.195–3.221.

169 *Qingdao Zhongjin Yuneng Real Estate Co Ltd v Qingdao Zhongjin Industrial Co Ltd and Other* (dispute over damages caused by the application for property preservation) [2017] SPC Civil Final No 118 (the Supreme People's Court, second instance and binding judgment).

170 ibid.

171 ibid.

172 Measures on Payment of Litigation Costs 2006 (Order of the State Council No 481), Article 14(2).

Annex 1

Format of Application Seeking Property Preservation Measures (For Legal Entity or Organisation)[173]

Applicant: the full name of the company, organisation or other legal entities, a Unified Social Credit Code or the registration code.

Legal representative/principal: name, address, contact telephone number (optional), Identification Card Number (optional).

Authorised legal agent: XXXXX Law Firm, the lawyer's name, gender, Identification Card Number, contract number, lawyer's licence's number, the lawyer's address.

Respondent: the full name of company, organisation or other legal entities; a Unified Social Credit Code or the registration code.

Legal representative/principal: name, address, contact telephone number (optional), Identification Card Number (optional).

Authorised legal agent: XXXXX Law Firm, the lawyer's name, gender, Identification Card Number, contract number, lawyer's licence's number, the lawyer's address.

Items to be claimed/requested:

It is hereby requested that XXXXX people's court seals up (or freezes) the house (or other property) located in XXXXX (exact address) or deposited in XXXXX (exact bank name and bank account) within the amount of RMB XXXXX (exact amount).

Facts and grounds:

Due to XXXXX dispute between the applicant and the respondent, the applicant will bring the case to the court/XXXXX arbitration institution against the respondent or this case has been accepted by the court/XXXXX arbitration institution on XXXXX (the exact date). Because it is possible for the respondent to transfer (hide or destroy) the property and also the circumstances are urgent, thereby, in accordance with Article 101 or 100 of the Civil Procedure Law, the applicant hereby requests the court to take measures on the respondent's property (specify the exact measures).

The applicant will provide XXXXX property as the security (specify the name, nature, quantity, amount, location, etc., of the secured property).

Regards

XXXX People's Court

173 By reference to a sample provided by the Supreme People's Court at <www.court.gov.cn/susongyangshi-xiangqing-126.html>, a sample used in the territory of Nanjing at <www.njfy.gov.cn/www/njfy/sszy_mb_a39190118125076.htm> accessed 15 July 2021 and a sample used in the territory of Shenzhen, the authors have translated and thereafter drafted the current sample.

Applicant (stamp and/or legal representative signature)

Date

Attachment: specific indication of respondent's property
Holder of bank account
Name of bank
Bank account
House address

Note for the application seeking property preservation measures:

1) This format can be used for an application seeking arbitral property preservation measures.
2) If either the applicant or the respondent is an individual, the information of the individual should include the full name, gender, date of birth, ethnicity, employer and occupation, address and contact information. For other contents of the application form, refer to those of this sample.
3) Apart from a lawyer, the authorised legal agent could be an employee working for the applicant, such as in-house counsel, the principal.
4) The exact item can refer Chapter 6, 6.72. If the applicant cannot provide the exact property information in the "Item to be claimed", it is necessary to list the specific indication of the property that needs to be preserved.
5) In the section of Facts and Grounds, Article 101 is relevant for pre-action applications and Article 100 is relevant for post-action applications. The applicant should choose the proper article.
6) In different official samples, the facts and grounds are very simple. In accordance with the specific facts of a dispute, the applicant should provide more relevant facts and reasons to demonstrate that without the preservation measures, the future judgment/award will not be enforced, or cause substantial loss; the circumstances are urgent, for example, the property to be preserved will be transferred or destroyed immediately. All in all, in the light of the purpose and the requirements of the property preservation discussed in Chapter 6, the applicant should provide more exact facts and reasons to enhance the possibility of obtaining the order.
7) Security is mandatory for pre-action applications and optional for post-action applications. If not furnishing security for pre-action applications, the applicant must provide reasons for not providing security; refer to Chapter 3, 3.187–3.192, and Chapter 6, 6.123. The applicant should decide whether it is necessary to provide security for a post-action application. In legal practice, in order to alleviate

the court's concern, the applicant can voluntarily add the sentence "if an incorrect preservation application causes the respondent's unexpected loss, the applicant is willing to take responsibility for it".

8) When an application is submitted through an online preservation system and an applicant chooses an insurance liability policy provided online, the applicant simply follows the instruction online to pay the premium and then waits for the notification of the insurance company as to whether the policy is effective or not. If no refused policy were in existence, the court will accept this security.

Annex 2

Application for Online Inquiry[174]

In the case of the dispute over XXX between the claimant (applicant) XXX and the defendant (respondent) XXX, the claimant applies for preserving the property XXX under the name of the respondent.[175]

Given that the claimant can only provide the indications of the preserved property and cannot provide the exact information on the property, in accordance with *Provisions of the Supreme People's Court on Several Issues Concerning the Handling of Property Preservation Cases by the People's Courts*, the claimant applies for the court to inquire the property of the respondent though the Network Enforcement Inquiry and Control System.

Regards,

The Primary People's Court of Jiangning District of Nanjing City, Jiangsu Province

Applicant:

Date

Annex 3: Application for Reconsideration, Refer to Annex 1, Chapter 3

Annex 4: Application for Discharging the Preservation Order, Refer to Annex 2, Chapter 3

174 This sample is issued by the Primary People's Court of Jiangning District of Nanjing City, Jiangsu Province in *Provisions on Procedure of a Centralized Management for Property Preservation* (Jiang Ning Fa [2017] No 109).

175 The defendant to this case and the respondent may be the same person or legal entity; alternatively, they are different. Therefore, the respondent refers to the defendant to this case and/or the owner of the preserved property.

PART 4

INTERIM MEASURES FOR CONDUCT

CHAPTER 7

Interim Injunctions

Introduction

7.1 An injunction is a court order prohibiting a person from doing something (a "negative" or "prohibitory" injunction) or requiring a person to do something (a "positive" or "mandatory" injunction). An interim injunction is an injunction granted on an interim basis, at a stage when the full facts are not yet known and when the merits of the substantive dispute between the parties have not yet been finally determined.

7.2 The interim injunction is the most significant, and most fundamental, interim remedy available under English law. It is an important interim remedy in its own right. It also forms the basis of a number of other types of interim remedy which usually go by different names, but which are in reality specialised or modified forms of interim injunction. The most notable of these is the freezing order (otherwise known as a freezing injunction), which prohibits a Respondent from dissipating assets so as to frustrate enforcement of an actual or potential judgment or arbitral award.[1] The search order (formerly known as the Anton Piller order), which requires a person to permit a search party to enter premises and search for evidence or property in order to ensure its preservation, is also a specialised form of interim injunction;[2] as are its close cousins, the doorstep delivery-up order and the imaging order.[3] Many of the leading English cases which establish the key principles governing the granting of interim remedies in general are cases involving interim injunctions. The interim injunction also performs a crucial role as a supplemental interim remedy, granted alongside (or embedded within) other interim remedies in order to ensure their effectiveness.

7.3 Like all interim remedies under English law, the interim injunction is essentially temporary and provisional in its nature and effect. In principle, therefore, an application for an interim injunction does not involve the court determining the underlying dispute in a legally binding and conclusive way.

1 See Chapter 5.

2 Search orders now enjoy independent status under section 7 of the Civil Procedure Act 1997: see Chapter 9, 9.10–9.11.

3 See Chapter 9.

DOI: 10.4324/9781003000310-12

In practice, however, the court's decision to grant or refuse an interim injunction will often have the effect of disposing of the underlying dispute in favour of whichever party is successful on that application, as in many cases there will be nothing left worth fighting about afterwards. This practical reality is reflected in the fact that the majority of cases in which an interim injunction is sought never proceed to a trial of the underlying dispute.[4] In such cases, the application for the interim injunction becomes the decisive battleground on which the entire dispute is won and lost.

The Court's Power to Grant Interim Injunctions

7.4 The English court's legal power[5] to grant interim injunctions is of long standing. It is confirmed[6] for the present day by section 37(1) of the Senior Courts Act 1981, which covers both interim and final[7] injunctions, and provides as follows:

The High Court[8] may by order (whether interlocutory or final) grant an injunction or appoint a receiver in all cases in which it appears to the court to be just and convenient to do so.

7.5 In principle, the only limit on this legal power is that it must be "just and convenient" to grant injunctive relief.[9] The width and flexibility[10] of the court's legal power to grant injunctions reflects the fact that the origins of the remedy lie in equity, where the court is above all concerned to do justice in the particular circumstances of each case. It also reflects also the discretionary nature of the remedy.

7.6 As a matter of settled practice, however, the English courts will only grant injunctive relief in accordance with the CPR, and in accordance with rules of principled discretion[11] which have been established by judicial precedent over many years.[12] The authorities stress that the categories of case in which the court will grant injunctive relief are not closed,[13] and the courts

4 As observed by Lord Denning MR in *Fellowes & Sons v Fisher* [1976] QB 112 at page 129 – the observation remains true today.

5 I.e. the court's jurisdiction, in the strict sense of that word: see Chapter 2, 2.66-2.67.

6 *Fourie v Le Roux* [2007] UKHL 1 per Lord Scott at [25].

7 I.e. permanent – see Chapter 2, 2.34–2.38 and 2.42.

8 This work focuses on the High Court. The County Court's power to grant interim injunctions is more limited.

9 *Fourie v Le Roux* [2007] UKHL 1 per Lord Scott at [30].

10 See *British Airways Board v Laker Airways Ltd* [1985] AC 58 per Lord Scarman at page 95.

11 For an explanation of this phrase, and how it differs from jurisdiction, see Chapter 2, 2.67(b).

12 *Fourie v Le Roux* [2007] UKHL 1 per Lord Scott at [25]; *Broadmoor Special Hospital Authority v Robinson* [2000] QB 775 per Lord Woolf MR at [20].

13 *British Airways Board v Laker Airways Ltd* [1985] AC 58 per Lord Scarman at page 95; *South Carolina Insurance Co v Assurantie Maatshappij "De Zeven Provincien" NV* [1987] AC 24 per Lord Goff at page 44.

have from time to time, and with caution, been prepared to extend the types of situation in which injunctive relief can be granted, where that is necessary to avoid injustice.[14] Nevertheless, for most practical purposes, the court will only exercise its power to grant injunctive relief in two circumstances: [15]

a. To prevent an actual **or threatened**[16] infringement of a legal or equitable right.
b. To prevent unconscionable conduct.

7.7 Most injunctions fall into the first category: they are granted in order to prevent an actual or threatened infringement of a legal or equitable right. A typical example is where a Claimant brings a claim against a Defendant seeking a permanent injunction restraining the Defendant from committing, or continuing to commit, conduct which the Claimant alleges to constitute a tort[17] or a breach of contract; and where the Claimant (Applicant[18]) issues an interlocutory application in those proceedings seeking an interim injunction to restrain the Defendant (Respondent) from committing or continuing to commit the same conduct pending trial of the claim for the permanent injunction. In that example, both the permanent and the interim injunction are sought in order to prevent an actual or threatened breach of the Claimant's legal rights. Contractual and quasi-contractual anti-suit injunctions, which restrain a person from pursuing legal proceedings in a foreign court in breach of an exclusive English jurisdiction or arbitration agreement, are also granted on this basis.[19]

7.8 The second category, unconscionable conduct, is of particular importance in the field of interim remedies. For these purposes, unconscionable conduct includes conduct which is vexatious or oppressive, or which interferes with the due process of the English court.[20] Most freezing injunctions,

---

14 For the complete menu of the situations in which injunctions may currently be granted, see Spry on *Equitable Remedies*, 9th Ed 2013, pages 342–343, cited with approval by the Court of Appeal in *Cartier International AG v British Sky Broadcasting Ltd* [2016] EWCA Civ 658 at [48] per Kitchin LJ.

15 *South Carolina Insurance Co v Assurantie Maatshappij "De Zeven Provincien" NV* [1987] AC 24 per Lord Brandon at pages 39–40.

16 Injunctions granted on the basis of a threatened or apprehended infringement of rights are sometimes referred to as *"quia timet"* injunctions, which is Latin for "because he fears": *Redland Bricks Ltd v Morris* [1970] AC 652 per Lord Upjohn at page 664–665.

17 A tort is a civil wrong under English law consisting of a breach of a duty imposed on the defendant by law, without the need for a contract, which gives rise to liability to compensate the claimant by paying damages: see Professor Andrew Tettenborn, *Clerk & Lindsell on Torts* (23rd Edn, Sweet & Maxwell, 2020) §1-01 *ff.*

18 For an explanation of the terms Claimant, Defendant, Applicant and Respondent, see Chapter 2, 2.29–2.30.

19 They are granted in order to prevent the Defendant (Respondent) from infringing the Claimant's (Applicant's) right not to be sued anywhere other than the agreed forum. See 7.54 *ff* below.

20 *South Carolina Insurance Co v Assurantie Maatshappij "De Zeven Provincien" NV* [1987] AC 24 per Lord Brandon at page 41. For a discussion of the various types of conduct that

search orders, doorstep delivery-up orders and imaging orders – specialised forms of injunctive relief that are only ever available on an interim basis – fall into this second category.[21] So too do most non-contractual anti-suit injunctions (i.e. injunctions granted to restrain proceedings in a foreign court, where those proceedings have not been brought in breach of contract).[22]

7.9 In addition to these rules which limit the court's power to grant injunctions in general, the court's power to grant interim injunctions in particular is subject to the same principles that apply to all interim discretionary remedies:[23]

a. Interim injunctions cannot be granted in isolation, but are dependent on and ancillary to a substantive claim or cause of action, which itself arises out of an actual or threatened invasion of the Applicant's legal or equitable rights or unconscionable conduct.
b. That substantive claim or cause of action must either be one for the enforcement of which the Respondent is amenable to the jurisdiction of the English court; or, if it is to be determined by a foreign court or in arbitration, the requirements of section 25 of the Civil Jurisdiction and Judgments Act 1992 or section 44 of the Arbitration Act 1996 (as the case may be) must be satisfied.

American Cyanamid

7.10 In *American Cyanamid Co v Ethicon Ltd*[24] the House of Lords set out a three-stage test for the courts to apply when considering whether to grant an interim injunction in a standard case.[25] The test assumes that the court has

---

may be regarded as vexatious, oppressive or otherwise unconscionable, see Thomas Raphael QC, *The Anti-Suit Injunction* (2nd Edn, Oxford University Press, 2019) §§4.47–4.65.

21 These types of interim remedy may also fall into the first category. Thus, proprietary freezing injunctions (also known as asset preservation orders) are granted in order to prevent an actual or threatened infringement of the Applicant's legal or equitable rights in the property which is to be frozen (see Chapter 5, 5.2–5.3). Similarly, search orders and doorstep delivery-up orders fall into the first category where, and to the extent that, they are granted in order to preserve the Applicant's property (see Chapter 9).

22 Most non-contractual anti-suit injunctions are granted in "alternative forum" cases, where the remedy being sought in the foreign proceedings is also available in the English court. Much more rarely, non-contractual anti-suit injunctions are granted in "single forum" cases, where the remedy being sought in the foreign court is not available in the English court. In these rare cases, it seems that the court's power to grant an anti-suit injunction is based on the Claimant's/Applicant's equitable right not to be subjected to unconscionable foreign proceedings: *Masri v Consolidated Contractors International (UK) Ltd (No.3)* [2008] EWCA Civ 625 per Lawrence Collins LJ at [44]; but *c.f.* Thomas Raphael QC, *The Anti-Suit Inunction* (2nd Edn, Oxford University Press, 2019) §§3.09–3.26.

23 See Chapter 2, 2.71.

24 [1975] AC 396 (HL).

25 [1975] AC 396 at pages 408–409, in the judgment of Lord Diplock.

the power[26] to grant an interim injunction. As explained below, the American Cyanamid test applies in a modified form in certain types of case, and in some other types of case it does not apply at all.

7.11 In principle, *American Cyanamid* merely lays down a set of helpful guidelines[27] to assist the court when determining whether or not to exercise its discretion in favour of granting an interim injunction in the particular circumstances of the case before it.[28] In practice, the American Cyanamid test is treated more like a strict formula which the court is bound to apply unless there is a compelling reason not to.

7.12 The test is usually expressed as consisting of three stages, which is how it is treated in this work, although some authorities[29] treat the second stage as itself containing two separate stages, making a total of four. Even where the Applicant satisfies all three (or four) stages of the test, the court retains a general discretion to refuse relief where it considers that, in all the circumstances, it would not be just and convenient to grant it.

Stage 1 – Serious Issue to Be Tried

7.13 At the first stage, the court asks whether there is a serious issue to be tried on the merits of the substantive claim or cause of action, to which the interim injunction is ancillary. In order to meet this requirement, the Applicant must adduce evidence to demonstrate that the substantive claim is not merely frivolous or vexatious,[30] but rather that it has a real prospect of success.[31]

7.14 The requirement of a serious issue to be tried is a fairly easy one for an Applicant to satisfy. It reflects the fact that the court hearing the application for an interim injunction will not have before it all the relevant evidence

26 I.e. that the court has legal power (jurisdiction) to grant the relief, and that doing so is in accordance with the applicable rules of principled discretion.

27 As Captain Barbossa reminded Elizabeth Swann on the deck of the "Black Pearl", guidelines are not the same as actual rules.

28 See *Cayne v Global Natural Resources plc* [1984] 1 All ER 225 per Kerr LJ at page 234 and May LJ at page 237; *Cambridge Nutrition Ltd v BBC* [1990] 3 All ER 523 per Kerr LJ at page 535. These *dicta* reflect the unease of some of Lord Diplock's contemporaries at what they regarded as his tendency to over-systematise the law in the interests of legal certainty, and to create rules designed to trammel the judicial discretion of judges.

29 E.g. *Neurim Pharmaceuticals (1991) Ltd v Flynn Pharma Ltd* [2020] EWHC 1362 (Pat) per Marcus Smith J at [17].

30 *Draeger Safety UK Ltd v London Fire Commissioner* [2021] EWHC 2221 (TCC) per O'Farrell J at [23], a case involving an application for an interim order lifting an automatic suspension under the Public Contracts Regulations 2015 (SI 2015/102), to which the American Cyanamid test also applies.

31 *Protomed Ltd v Medication Systems Ltd* [2013] EWCA Civ 1205 per Lewison LJ at [9]–[11]. The test has been expressed in other ways, all of which are supposed to come down to the same thing: the substantive claim must carry some degree of conviction; it must have more than a fanciful prospect of success; it must be more than merely arguable; it must have some real substance: see *Easyair Ltd v Opal Telecom Ltd* [2009] EWHC 339 (Ch) per Lewison J at [15].

that would be adduced at trial, and that such evidence as is before the court will not have been tested by oral cross-examination, as would happen at trial. For those reasons, when determining whether the Applicant has succeeded in demonstrating a serious issue to be tried, the court will not attempt to resolve difficult issues of fact or law, but will leave them to be decided at trial.[32] As explained below, however, the court may sometimes consider the merits of the underlying claim in greater detail at a later stage of the American Cyanamid test.

7.15 If the Applicant fails to satisfy this first requirement, the interim injunction will be refused. If he succeeds, the court proceeds to the subsequent stages of the American Cyanamid test. These subsequent stages are designed to help the court to make a decision at an interlocutory stage of the proceedings, which will improve the chances of being able to do justice in the case after a full determination of the merits of the underlying dispute at trial, while at the same time minimising the risk of causing injustice to either party in the event that the court's decision at that interlocutory stage later turns out to have been the wrong decision. In general, the court will seek to take whichever course seems likely to cause the least irremediable prejudice to one party or the other.[33]

Stage Two – Adequacy of Damages to Each Party

7.16 At this second stage, the court begins by considering the hypothetical situation where (i) it refuses to grant an interim injunction; (ii) the Respondent continues to do what the interim injunction would have prevented him from doing up until trial; but (iii) the Applicant ultimately succeeds on his substantive claim or cause of action at trial. In other words, in this hypothetical situation, the court decides against granting an interim injunction at the interlocutory stage, and that decision is later proved wrong at trial.

7.17 The court has to consider whether the Applicant would be adequately compensated for the loss he would suffer as a result of the Respondent continuing with what, on this hypothesis, is wrongful conduct, in the period leading up to the trial, by an award of damages against the Respondent.

7.18 If the answer to that hypothetical is Yes – i.e. if (i) the damages which would be recoverable at trial would be an adequate remedy for the Applicant, and (ii) the Respondent would be in a financial position to pay those damages if they were awarded against him – then the court will invariably refuse to grant an interim injunction, regardless of how strong the Applicant's case on the underlying merits may appear to be.[34] This is because an interim

32 *American Cyanamid Co v Ethicon Ltd* [1975] AC 396 at page 407 per Lord Diplock.

33 *National Commercial Bank Jamaica Ltd v Olint Corp Ltd* [2009] UKPC 16 per Lord Hoffmann at [16]–[17].

34 *American Cyanamid Co v Ethicon Ltd* [1975] AC 396 at page 408 per Lord Diplock.

injunction is a form of equitable relief, and equitable relief is not usually available where damages are an adequate remedy.[35]

7.19 In some cases, the answer to this question will be a clear Yes. But in many cases the answer will be No, or there will at least be a significant doubt over whether damages would be an adequate remedy for the Applicant. That may be because the type of loss which the Applicant would suffer cannot be adequately compensated by an award of damages, e.g. in cases involving personal injury, loss of livelihood or invasion of privacy.[36] It may be because the type of loss the Applicant would suffer does not sound in damages;[37] or because the loss which the Applicant would suffer would be difficult to quantify with any accuracy, leading to the risk that any award of damages would leave him undercompensated;[38] or because the loss would be suffered by someone other than the Applicant, such as the wider public.[39] The courts have also held that damages are an inadequate remedy where the Applicant's right to recover damages is excluded or limited by contract.[40] But very often damages would be an inadequate remedy for the Applicant simply because the Respondent would not be in a financial position to pay those damages.

7.20 Where the answer is not a clear Yes, the court must go on to consider a second hypothetical situation, which is in many ways a mirror image of the first. In this second hypothetical situation (i) the court grants an interim injunction; (ii) the Respondent is prevented from doing what he would

35 *Lawrence v Fen Tigers Ltd* [2014] UKSC 13 per Lord Sumption JSC at [159]–[160], and per Lord Clarke of Stone-cum-Ebony at [171]. In rare cases, the court may be prepared grant an interim injunction even though damages would be an adequate remedy for the Applicant, if it considers that justice requires that the Respondent be compelled by injunction to comply with his obligations: see *AB v CD* [2014] EWCA Civ 299 per Underhill LJ at [29].

36 *PJS v News Group Newspapers* [2016] UKSC 26 per Lord Mance at [43].

37 For example, loss of reputation or standing: *Regent International Hotels (UK) Ltd v Pageguide Ltd* The Times, 13 May 1985. See also *LauritzenCool AB v Lady Navigation Inc* [2004] EWHC 2607 (Comm) per Cooke J at [39]. But where the loss is not recoverable by operation of the rules of remoteness of damage under English law (as to which see generally James Edelman, *McGregor on Damages* (21st Edn, Sweet & Maxwell, 2021), chapter 8) it seems that the court does not treat damages as an inadequate remedy: *Polaroid Corp v Eastman Kodak Co* [1977] RPC 379 per Goff LJ at pages 394–395, and per Buckley LJ at page 397.

38 *Bath & North East Somerset District Council v Mowlem plc* [2004] EWCA Civ 115 per Mance LJ at [16].

39 See e.g. *Bath & North East Somerset District Council v Mowlem plc* [2004] EWCA Civ 115 per Mance LJ at [21] (potential loss to the local economy and loss of public confidence, which the Applicant had a legitimate interest in avoiding); *Cambridge Nutrition Ltd v BBC* [1990] 3 All ER 523.

40 *Bath & North East Somerset District Council v Mowlem plc* [2004] EWCA Civ 115 per Mance LJ at [14]–[20]; *AB v CD* [2014] EWCA Civ 299 per Underhill LJ at [27]. In such cases, damages are an inadequate remedy only because the Applicant has agreed that he will not be entitled to damages. It might not seem unjust if the courts were to refuse injunctive relief to an Applicant who came to court complaining about a self-inflicted wound of that nature. The Court of Appeal sees the matter differently, however – see Laws LJ in *AB v CD* at [33]: "Where a party to a contract stipulates that if he breaches his obligations his liability will be limited or the damages he must pay will be capped, that is a circumstance which in justice tends to favour the grant of an injunction to prohibit the breach in the first place".

otherwise have been able to do up until the trial; but (iii) the Applicant ultimately fails in his substantive claim or cause of action at trial. In other words, in this second hypothetical situation, the court decides in favour of an interim injunction at the interlocutory stage, and that decision is later proved wrong at trial.

7.21 The court has to consider whether, in this second hypothetical situation, the Respondent would be adequately compensated for the loss he would suffer as a result of being prevented from continuing with what, on this hypothesis, is lawful conduct, in the period leading up to the trial, by an award of damages against the Applicant, taking into account the same sorts of factor as it does when considering the first hypothetical situation.

7.22 The Appellant commits no legal wrong against the Respondent simply by obtaining an interim injunction against him which later turns out to have been wrongly granted, so the court has no automatic basis on which to order the Appellant to compensate the Respondent for his resulting loss in that situation. Accordingly, the court will invariably require the Appellant to give an undertaking in damages, as the price of obtaining an interim injunction, and this undertaking becomes the source of the court's power to order the Appellant to compensate the Respondent.[41] If the Applicant is not prepared to give the undertaking, the court will invariably refuse to grant the injunction. Where there is a question mark over whether the Appellant would be in a financial position to honour his undertaking to compensate the Respondent, the court may, in its discretion, require the Appellant to fortify his undertaking by providing security,[42] where it considers that the Appellant[43] is, or ought to be, in a position to do so; and again, if the Applicant fails or refuses to do so, the court will refuse to grant the injunction.

7.23 If the answer to this second hypothetical is a clear Yes – i.e. if (i) the damages which the court could order the Appellant to pay to the Respondent would be an adequate remedy for the Respondent, and (ii) the Appellant would be in a financial position to pay those damages if they were awarded against him – then the court will normally grant an interim injunction, although it will still need to be persuaded that the terms of the injunction are appropriate and that it is just and convenient in all the circumstances to grant the relief, as a matter of general discretion.

7.24 In many cases, however, the answer to this second question will either be a clear No, or there may be significant doubt over whether damages would be an adequate remedy for the Respondent. In such cases, the court must proceed to the third stage of the American Cyanamid test.

---

41 See Chapter 2, 2.117–2.120.

42 See Chapter 2, 2.119.

43 The court will take account of whether the Applicant can provide security out of its own resources, and also whether it can do so from outside sources such as shareholders, affiliates, financial backers or others interested in the outcome of the legal proceedings.

Stage Three – Balance of Convenience

7.25 At the third stage, where there is doubt as to the adequacy of the respective remedies in damages available to either party or to both, the court seeks to determine where "the balance of convenience" lies.[44] This is a somewhat opaque expression. In plain English, it means that the court seeks to weigh up the risk of the injustice[45] to the Applicant if it refuses the injunction and that refusal turns out to be wrong at trial, against the risk of injustice to the Respondent if it grants the injunction and that decision turns out to be wrong at trial, as it were, in a balance,[46] and see which one is greater.[47] This is essentially the same exercise as the one which the court undertakes at stage two; but at stage three the court does not confine itself to considering whether damages would be an adequate remedy, and instead takes all the circumstances of the case into consideration. As a result, stage three is a highly fact-sensitive exercise, which requires the individual judge hearing the case to exercise his judgment.

7.26 One of the factors that the court may be entitled to take into account at this third stage is the strength of the parties' competing cases on the merits of the underlying dispute. In a standard case, the court should only take this factor into account where it is apparent on the facts disclosed by the evidence adduced on the application, as to which there is no credible dispute, that the strength of one party's case is disproportionate to that of the other.[48] The court should not embark on anything like a trial of the underlying dispute, and it should not attempt to resolve difficult or complex issues of fact or law.[49] This is the position in standard cases: as explained

44 *American Cyanamid Co v Ethicon Ltd* [1975] AC 396 at page 408 per Lord Diplock.

45 In *Cayne v Global Natural Resources plc* [1984] 1 WLR 225 May LJ at page 237 expressed the "balance of convenience" as the "balance of the risk of doing injustice".

46 As in the balance scales held by Lady Justice, a metaphor for justice dating from Ancient Rome, which is often rendered in statute form outside court houses such as the Old Bailey in London and the Court of Final Appeal in Hong Kong.

47 In other words, it seeks to compare the "uncompensatable disadvantage" to each party of granting or refusing the interim injunction, in order to work out which course of conduct is preferable in the interest of justice: *American Cyanamid Co v Ethicon Ltd* [1975] AC 396 at page 409 per Lord Diplock.

48 *American Cyanamid Co v Ethicon Ltd* [1975] AC 396 at page 409 per Lord Diplock.

49 *American Cyanamid Co v Ethicon Ltd* [1975] AC 396 at page 409 per Lord Diplock; *Sukhoruchkin v Van Bekestein* [2014] EWCA Civ 399 per Sir Terence Etherton C at [32]. The circumstances in which the court may have regard to the underlying merits on an application for an interim injunction has been the subject of disagreement in the authorities. In *Series 5 Software Ltd v Clarke* [1996] 1 All ER 853, Laddie J (who as Counsel had been largely responsible for the creation and development of the Anton Piller order, now called the search order) suggested that the court could take the underlying merits into account whenever it felt able to form a clear view that one party's case was stronger, and that it ought to express its provisional, non-binding, view of those merits where it was able to do so. Those *dicta* have been seen as in conflict with the position adopted by Lord Diplock in *American Cyanamid*, that the court should avoid expressing a view on the merits, and should only take them into account in the clearest of cases, and only where it was necessary to tip the balance of convenience. Despite

below, in certain categories of case the underlying merits may play a more important role.

7.27 Where the risk of injustice appears evenly balanced, the court will generally adopt whichever course will best preserve the *status quo*,[50] which is Latin for the situation which existed before. For these purposes, the relevant pre-existing situation is not necessarily the one which existed when the conduct which the interim injunction would prevent began to occur. Rather, the relevant situation is the one which existed immediately before the application for the interim injunction.[51] In order to qualify as the *status quo*, the pre-existing situation must have been settled rather than fleeting.[52]

7.28 In some cases, the *status quo* will be best preserved by refusing an interim injunction; but in others, especially where the injunction is sought to prevent the Respondent from committing a threatened or apprehended wrong (a *quia timet* injunction), the *status quo* will be best preserved by granting the injunction.

7.29 There will nevertheless be cases where the risk of injustice remains evenly balanced, and cannot be tipped in favour of one or other party by considerations such as preserving the *status quo*. In such cases, the court will refuse an interim injunction: it will not grant an order against the Respondent, backed by the threat of punitive sanctions for contempt of court, if the Applicant cannot demonstrate that the balance of convenience lies in favour of doing so.

---

support for Laddie J's *dicta* in some later authorities, the recent trend has been for the courts to reaffirm Lord Diplock's authoritative position: see e.g. *Epoch Co Ltd v Character Options Ltd* [2015] EWHC 3436 (IPEC) per HHJ Hacon at [5]; *In Re Brickvest Ltd* [2019] EWHC 2662 (Ch) per Marcus Smith J at [9]; *Neurim Pharmaceuticals (1991) Ltd v Flynn Pharma Ltd* [2020] EWHC 1362 (Pat) per Marcus Smith J, again, at [17(4)(b)]; "the court should not be sucked into a merits analysis *unless* the facts are so clear that 'there is no credible dispute' in relation to them", and at [26]: "The American Cyanamid test is extremely clear as the role of the merits. There is a threshold test of a 'serious issue to be tried'; and the possibility of taking the merits into account at Stage 4 [sic: he treated the second stage as consisting of two separate stages: are damages an adequate remedy for the Applicant, and are damages an adequate remedy for the Respondent?], provided the facts are unequivocal – and that is it … There is always a temptation to try to achieve at an earlier stage than trial the certainty that a trial is intended to achieve. But there is a reason we have trials: it is because many questions cannot be determined without consideration of all the evidence in light of the material *available at trial*" (emphasis in original).

50 *American Cyanamid Co v Ethicon Ltd* [1975] AC 396 at page 408 per Lord Diplock. It is often said that the purpose of an interim injunction is to preserve the *status quo*: *National Commercial Bank Jamaica Ltd v Olint Corp Ltd* [2009] UKPC 16 per Lord Hoffmann at [16].

51 *Garden Cottage Foods Ltd v Milk Marketing Board* [1984] AC 130 at page 140 per Lord Diplock.

52 It must have subsisted for a period which is "more than minimal, having regard to the total length of the relationship between the parties in respect of which the injunction is granted; otherwise the state of affairs before the last change would be the relevant status quo": *Garden Cottage Foods Ltd v Milk Marketing Board* [1984] AC 130 at page 140 per Lord Diplock.

Mandatory Interim Injunctions

7.30 The court's approach to stage three of the American Cyanamid test is modified where the Applicant seeks a mandatory interim injunction, i.e. one which requires the Respondent to take some positive step, as opposed to the more common negative injunction which merely requires the Respondent to refrain from certain conduct.

7.31 In the case of a mandatory interim injunction, the scope for injustice to a Respondent if the interim injunction later turns out to have been wrongly granted is usually greater than if he has merely been prohibited from doing something.[53] Therefore, where a court is asked to grant mandatory relief, and there is a risk of irremediable prejudice to the Respondent if the relief is wrongly granted which cannot adequately be compensated by an award of damages, the court will usually only be prepared to grant mandatory relief where it feels a high degree of assurance that, at trial, it will appear that the mandatory interim injunction was rightly granted.[54]

7.32 This means that, on an application for a mandatory interim injunction, the court will have to assess the underlying merits at stage three, even though it would not normally be permissible to do so in a standard case involving a negative interim injunction.

7.33 Where the court feels a high level of assurance that granting a mandatory interim injunction will turn out at trial to have been right, it may nevertheless conclude that the balance of convenience lies with refusing the injunction if, in all the circumstances, the risk of irremediable prejudice to the Respondent if the injunction is wrongly granted still outweighs the risk of irremediable prejudice to the Applicant if that injunction is wrongly refused.

Where the Outcome of the Application Will Determine the Overall Dispute

7.34 The American Cyanamid test assumes that there will be a proper trial at a later stage of the proceedings, at which the court will finally determine the rights of the parties. The test is designed to help the court to determine how best to hold the ring until that trial can take place, in a way which minimises the risk of injustice to either party, and without prejudging the outcome of that trial, at a stage when not all the relevant evidence is available, and none of the evidence has been properly tested.[55]

---

53 *National Commercial Bank Jamaica Ltd v Olint Corp Ltd* [2009] UKPC 16 per Lord Hoffmann at [19]–[20].

54 *Nottingham Building Society v Eurodynamics Systems plc* [1993] FSR 468 at page 474 per Chadwick J; *Zockoll Group Ltd v Mercury Communications Ltd* [1998] FSR 354 at page 366 per Phillips LJ.

55 *American Cyanamid Co v Ethicon Ltd* [1975] AC 396 at pages 407–409 per Lord Diplock; *Cayne v Global Natural Resources plc* [1984] 1 All ER 255 per May LJ; *Cambridge Nutritiuon Ltd v BBC* [1990] 3 All ER 523 per Kerr LJ.

7.35 But in many cases, the assumption that there will be a trial at a later date is unrealistic. This situation commonly arises where the subject-matter of the dispute is time-limited, so that there will be nothing left worth fighting about by the time any trial might take place.[56] Interim "springboard" injunctions, which are designed to deprive an alleged wrongdoer of the fruits of his allegedly unlawful acts, often fall into this category.[57] The situation may also arise in other circumstances, such as where the Respondent engages in conduct which is designed to exert short-term industrial or commercial pressure on the Applicant, but there is no real underlying dispute that the parties want to have resolved at a trial.[58]

7.36 In such cases, the court's decision to grant or refuse an interlocutory injunction will have the practical effect of determining the underlying dispute. Moreover, if that decision is wrong, it will inevitably cause irremediable harm to the unsuccessful party, as there will never be a trial where that error can be discovered, and where the court can make an award of damages to compensate that party for the loss he may have suffered as a consequence. The risk of injustice to one or other party if the court's decision is wrong is therefore much greater in this type of case, than in a standard case where a trial can be expected to take place at some future date.[59]

7.37 For these reasons, in this type of case the court must make an assessment of the underlying merits – i.e. the degree of likelihood that the Applicant would have succeeded in establishing his right to injunction if the case had proceeded to trial – when determining whether the balance of convenience

56 See for example *Lansing Linde Ltd v Kerr* [1991] 1 WLR 251, where the Applicant sought an interim injunction to restrain its former employee from breaching the restrictive covenant which prevented him from working for a competitor within 12 months of leaving the Applicant – a period which would expire well before the case was likely to reach trial.

57 *Aquinas Education Ltd v Dorian Miller* [2018] EWHC 404 (QB) per Nicholas Vineall QC at [25], [29]. A springboard injunction is granted to deprive the Respondent of an unfair head start he has obtained by improper use of information or property belonging to the Applicant. It is typically granted to an employer against a former employee who has allegedly committed breach of confidence, breach of contractual and fiduciary duty by misusing commercially sensitive material gained through his employment in order to obtain a competitive advantage. Unlike most injunctions, which restrain unlawful conduct, a springboard injunction usually restrains conduct which would otherwise be lawful. It can only be granted while the Respondent continues to enjoy his unfair advantage, and only where he will continue to do so for a significant time to come. See generally *QBE Management Services (UK) Ltd v Dymoke* [2012] EWHC 80 (QB) per Haddon-Cave J at [240]–[247].

58 See e.g. *NWL Ltd v Woods (No.2)* [1979] 1 WLR 1295 where a shipowner sought an interim injunction against a trade union official to restrain threatened industrial action against a ship which was due to call at a certain port, as part of a campaign by the union to pressurise this and other shipowners to employ European crews rather than cheaper workers from East Asia. In that case, Lord Diplock said at page 1306 that *American Cyanamid* had not been dealing with a case where the grant or refusal of injunction at the interim stage would, in effect, dispose of the matter finally in favour of whichever party was successful on that application.

59 *NWL Ltd v Woods* [1979] 1 WLR 1294 per Lord Diplock at page 1307; *Cayne v Global Natural Resources plc* [1984] 1 All ER 225 per Kerr LJ at page 235.

lies in favour of granting or refusing the injunction.[60] The considerations which prevent it from doing so in a standard case do not apply. There is no reason to avoid expressing a view on the merits at an interlocutory stage, and no reason to be cautious simply because the evidence is incomplete, as there will never be a trial at which fuller evidence will be available and subjected to greater scrutiny. If the court were to grant an interim injunction in this type of case without considering the merits more fully, it would in effect be giving the Applicant summary judgment on the underlying claim without him having to prove his claim to anything like the normal civil standard of proof,[61] and without the Respondent having any opportunity to defend the claim on its merits.[62]

7.38 Some authorities indicate that, in this type of case, the court should apply a modified version of the American Cyanamid three-stage test, taking the merits into consideration at stage three.[63] Others suggest that the American Cyanamid test is inapplicable, and that the court should first assess the likelihood that the Applicant would succeed at trial, and then consider the balance of convenience in the light of that assessment.[64]

7.39 This difference of approach makes no difference in practice. On either approach, the court must seek to assess the likely outcome of the Applicant's claim on the balance of probabilities. It should do so, not by conducting a mini-trial, but by undertaking a fair and reasonable evaluation of the available evidence, while always bearing in mind that there will have been no disclosure and that the witness evidence will be incomplete and untested by cross-examination.[65] If the Applicant fails to establish that his claim would probably have succeeded at trial, the court will generally

---

60 *NWL Ltd v Woods* [1979] 1 WLR 1294 per Lord Diplock at page 1307; *Tillman v Egon Zehnder Ltd* [2019] UKSC 32 per Lord Wilson at [14].

61 The balance of probabilities: more likely than not.

62 Some judges have expressed misgivings about the fact that granting an interim injunction in this type of case deprives the Respondent of the right to defend the underlying claim at trial. See e.g. May LJ in *Cayne v Global Natural Resources plc* [1984] 1 All ER 225 at page 238: "I think that it is, in general, an injustice to grant [an injunction] at an interlocutory stage if this effectively precludes a defendant from the opportunity of having his rights determined in a full trial. There may be cases where the plaintiff's evidence is so strong that to refuse an injunction and to allow the case to go through to trial would be a waste of time and expense and indeed do an overwhelming injustice to the plaintiff. But those cases would, in my judgment, be exceptional". See also the equally trenchant comments of Kerr LJ in the same case at page 236. Nevertheless, the European Court of Human Rights has held that an interim injunction which effectively determines the parties' rights and obligations is not inconsistent with the right to a fair trial in ECHR Article 6: *Micallef v Malta* (2009) 50 EHRR 920 at [78]–[85].

63 *NWL Ltd v Woods* [1979] 1 WLR 1294 per Lord Diplock at page 1307; *P14 Medical Ltd v Mahon* [2020] EWHC 1823 (QB) per Cavanagh J at [23]–[24].

64 *CEF Holdings Ltd v Mundey* [2012] EWHC 1524 (QB) per Silber J at [29]; *Aquinas Education Ltd v Dorian Miller* [2018] EWHC 404 (QB) per Nicholas Vineall QC at [29].

65 *Aquinas Education Ltd v Dorian Miller* [2018] EWHC 404 (QB) per Nicholas Vineall QC at [29]; *Forse v Xcina Ltd* [2019] EWCA Civ 215 per Sir Terence Etherton MR at [34].

conclude that the balance of convenience lies with refusing an interim injunction.[66]

Special Cases Where the American Cyanamid Test Is Modified

7.40 The standard American Cyanamid test is modified in a number of special cases, which are discussed below.

(i) Freedom of Expression

7.41 Where an interim injunction might affect the Respondent's exercise of her right to freedom of expression under Article 10 of the European Convention on Human Rights, such as an injunction restraining her from publishing material on the grounds that it would allegedly be a breach of confidence or infringe the Applicant's right to privacy under Article 8, a stricter standard applies at the first stage of the American Cyanamid test. The court cannot grant an interim injunction unless it is satisfied that the Applicant is likely to establish at trial that publication should not be allowed.[67] For these purposes, likely usually means more likely than not, on a balance of probabilities.[68]

(ii) Industrial Disputes

7.42 The court cannot grant an application for an interim injunction to restrain a Respondent from taking allegedly unlawful action in furtherance of a trade dispute without notice, and it must assess and take account of the likelihood that the Respondent would succeed in establishing a defence to the substantive claim at trial when considering where the balance of convenience lies.[69]

(iii) Public Bodies

7.43 On an application for an interim injunction to restrain a public body from exercising its public duties in an allegedly unlawful way, the court must take the interests of the wider public into account when considering the balance of convenience.[70]

66 *C.f. Lansing Linde Ltd v Kerr* [1991] 1 WLR 251 per Staughton LJ at page 259; *P14 Medical Ltd v Mahon* [2020] EWHC 1823 (QB) per Cavanagh J at [24].

67 Human Rights Act 1998 section 12(3).

68 *Cream Holdings Ltd v Banerjee* [2004] UKHL 44 per Lord Nicholls at [15]–[16] and [20]–[21].

69 Trade Union & Labour Relations (Consolidation) Act 1992 sections 219–221.

70 *Smith v Inner London Education Authority* [1978] 1 All ER 411 per Browne LJ at page 422.

Cases Where Interim Injunctions Are Generally Unavailable

7.44 The court will generally not grant an interim injunction in the following types of case, as a matter of principled discretion and/or public policy.

(i) Defamation

7.45 The court will not grant an interim injunction to restrain publication of material on the grounds that the publication would allegedly constitute the tort of defamation,[71] if the Respondent adduces evidence on the application to the effect that he will seek to justify (prove the truth of) the allegedly defamatory statement at trial.[72]

(ii) Performance Bonds and Irrevocable Letters of Credit

7.46 Special rules apply in relation to performance bonds and irrevocable letters of credit. These are unconditional undertakings to pay a specified amount to a named beneficiary, usually on demand and sometimes on the presentation of certain specified documents.[73] Performance bonds are typically issued at the request of one party to a commercial contract for a major construction, engineering or shipbuilding project (usually the main contractor), for the benefit of another party to that contract (usually the employer). Their purpose is to secure the beneficiary's right to compensation for failure of contractual performance[74] or, in the case of a refund guarantee, to secure his right to get his money back if the project is terminated before delivery.[75] Irrevocable letters of credit are typically issued by the buyer under an international commercial sale contract, for the benefit of the seller, as a means of effecting payment of the purchase price in a way which protects the seller from credit risk.

7.47 English law treats this type of instrument as an autonomous contract between the issuing bank and the beneficiary, wholly independent of the

---

71 Defamation consists of publishing an untrue statement which is likely to do substantial damage to the reputation of another person. There are two torts of defamation, depending on the form of publication, and whether it is permanent or not: where the defamatory statement is made in a non-permanent form, usually spoken words, but also sounds or gestures, that is slander; where it made in a permanent form, usually writing but also by pictures, statues, sound or video recordings and (increasingly important) online posts, that is libel. Both torts represent a derogation from the right to freedom of speech, and have long been controversial for that reason. See generally Professor Andrew Tettenborn, *Clerk & Lindsell on Torts* (23rd Edn, Sweet & Maxwell, 2020) §21-01 *ff.*

72 *Bonnard v Perryman* [1891] 2 Ch 269. An interim injunction is available, however, where the defamation is aimed at a candidate in an election: Representation of the People Act 1983, section 106(3).

73 Geraldine Andrews, Richard Millett QC, *Law of Guarantees* (7th Edn, Sweet & Maxwell, 2015) §16-001.

74 Steven Gee QC, *Gee on Commercial Injunctions* (7th Edn, Sweet & Maxwell, 2020) §15-001.

75 Simon Curtis, Ian Gaunt, William Cecil, *The Law of Shipbuilding Contracts* (5th Edn, Informa Law, 2020), page 301.

underlying commercial contract pursuant to which it is issued. As such, these instruments perform a critical role in international commerce: they enable the beneficiary to be completely satisfied that, whatever disputes may arise between him and the bank's customer who arranged for the instrument to be issued in his favour, in relation to the performance and even the existence of the underlying commercial contract, the bank is personally undertaking to pay the beneficiary, provided that conditions specified in the instrument are met.[76] By mercantile custom, the beneficiary's right to payment under this type of instrument is treated as the equivalent of cash-in-hand.[77]

7.48 For these reasons, as a matter of public policy, the court will generally not grant an interim injunction restraining a bank or other financial institution from paying on a performance bond (also known as a performance guarantee, demand guarantee or standby letter of credit) or an irrevocable letter of credit. Nor, generally, will it grant an interim injunction restraining a beneficiary from presenting a demand for payment under such an instrument.

7.49 In the case of an application against a bank or other financial institution, the only exception to this rule is the so-called fraud exception.[78] In order to bring the case within the exception, the Applicant must demonstrate that it is seriously arguable on the material available that the only realistic inference was that (i) the beneficiary of the instrument who presented the demand for payment could not honestly have believed in the validity of its demand[79] and (ii) the bank was aware of the beneficiary's fraud at the time of presentation.

7.50 This is a very difficult test to satisfy.[80] Even where it is met, the balance of convenience will almost always militate against the granting of injunction.[81] For these reasons, in practice the court does not grant interim

---

76 *Bolivinter Oil SA v Chase Manhattan Bank NA* [984] 1 WLR 392 at page 393 (a case on performance bonds). For this reason, they have been described as "the lifeblood of international commerce": *R D Harbottle (Mercantile) Ltd v National Westminster Bank Ltd* [1978] QB 146 at page 155 per Kerr J.

77 *R D Harbottle (Mercantile) Ltd v National Westminster Bank Ltd* [1978] QB at page 155 per Kerr J; *Solo Industries v Canara Bank* [2001] EWCA Civ 1059 per Mance LJ at [5] and [35].

78 *R D Harbottle (Mercantile) Ltd v National Westminster Bank Ltd* [1978] QB 146 at page 155 per Kerr J; *Edward Owen Engineering Ltd v Barclays Bank International Ltd* [1978] QB 159 per Lord Denning MR at page 171.

79 Presenting a demand for payment when one does not honestly believe that one is entitled to the payment is dishonest and constitutes fraud at common law: see generally Grant and Mumford on Civil Fraud (2018), Chapter 1.

80 The courts justify the strictness of this test by reference to the need to preserve the autonomy and independence of performance bonds and irrevocable letters of credit, and their status as equivalent to cash, and on the basis that banks and their customers accept the risks inherent in the terms of such instruments, including the risk that a beneficiary may make a demand which is unjustified or fraudulent but which has to be met because it cannot clearly be established to be so: *Solo Industries v Canara Bank* [2001] EWCA Civ 1059 per Mance LJ at [35].

81 *Alternative Power Solution Ltd v Central Electricity Board* [2015] UKPC 31 at [59] and [79]; *Tetronics (International) Ltd v HSBC Bank plc* [2018] EWHC 201 (TCC) per Fraser J at [23]–[29].

injunctions restraining banks from paying under performance bonds and irrevocable letters of credit.

7.51 The fraud exception also applies to applications for interim injunctions against the beneficiary of a performance bond or letter of credit.[82] In addition, the court may grant an injunction restraining a beneficiary from making a demand under such an instrument, in the absence of fraud,[83] where the demand would be in breach of a specific agreement with the Applicant.[84] The American Cyanamid principles apply to such an application, with the modification that the court must be satisfied to a high degree of assurance that the Respondent beneficiary is clearly precluded by her agreement with the Applicant from demanding payment under the instrument.[85]

Cases Where American Cyanamid Does Not Apply

7.52 The American Cyanamid test does not apply to a number of types of specialised forms of interim injunction:

a. Freezing injunctions.
b. Search orders, doorstep delivery-up orders and imaging orders.
c. Interim anti-suit injunctions.

7.53 Freezing injunctions are dealt with in Chapter 5. Search orders, doorstep delivery-up orders and imaging orders are dealt with in Chapter 9. Interim anti-suit injunctions are discussed below.

Interim Anti-Suit Injunctions

7.54 An anti-suit injunction is a court order restraining a person (the Respondent) from commencing or pursuing legal proceedings in a foreign court.[86] Anti-suit injunctions may also be granted in mandatory terms,

---

82 *Deutsche Rückversicherung AG v Walbrook Insurance Co Ltd* [1995] 1 WLR 1017 per Phillips J at page 1030.

83 See e.g. *ETC Export Trading Co SA v Aplas Importer and Berhan Bank SC* [2020] EWHC 3229 (QB).

84 See e.g. *Sirius International Insurance Co (Publ) v FAI General Insurance Ltd* [2003] EWCA Civ 470 per May LJ at [26]; *Simon Carves Ltd v Ensus UK Ltd* [2011] EWHC 657 (TCC) per Aikens J at [33].

85 *Simon Carves Ltd v Ensus UK Ltd* [2011] EWHC 657 (TCC) per Aikens J at [33(d)–(e)]; *Ouais Group Engineering & Contracting v Saipem SpA* [2013] EWHC 990 (Comm) per Popplewell J at [45]; *MW High Tech Projects UK Ltd v Biffa Waste Services Ltd* [2015] EWHC 949 (TCC) per Stuart-Smith J at [34].

86 A number of variants exist, including the anti-arbitration injunction which restrains a Respondent from commencing or pursuing arbitration proceedings, and the anti-anti-suit injunction which restrains a Respondent from seeking an anti-suit injunction in a foreign court. These exotic forms are relatively rare. Anti-suit injunctions are also available in certain domestic settings, e.g. to restrain a creditor from presenting a petition in the Companies Court to wind up a company, under sections 126 and 227 of the Insolvency Act 1986.

requiring the Respondent to take positive steps to discontinue foreign court proceedings which she has commenced. Anti-suit injunctions can be granted as final, substantive, relief (unlike freezing injunctions and search orders, which can only ever be granted on an interim basis), but they are very often granted on an interim basis.

7.55 Before addressing the topic of interim anti-suit injunctions, it may be helpful to provide a brief overview of the topic of anti-suit injunctions generally.[87]

7.56 In recent decades, the anti-suit injunction has emerged as one of the most important remedies available under English law, especially in the commercial context. The power to grant this type of relief has long been controversial, as it involves the English court making orders which, in substance if not in form, interfere with the right of foreign courts to control their own jurisdiction, and which therefore raise issues of comity.[88] Prior to Brexit,[89] the English court's power to grant anti-suit injunctions was a major source of contention with the Court of Justice of the European Union, which regarded it as an affront to the principles of mutual trust and respect between the national courts of member states and the rights of those courts to determine their own jurisdiction, as embodied in the instruments comprising the Brussels regime[90] governing the allocation of jurisdiction and the recognition and enforcement of judgments in civil and commercial matters.[91] While the UK was a member of the EU, the English court was prohibited from granting anti-suit injunctions to restrain legal proceedings in the courts of member states of the European Union and European Free Trade Area in civil and commercial matters.[92] With

87 For a comprehensive and authoritative review of this topic, see generally Thomas Raphael QC, *The Anti-Suit Injunction* (2nd Edn, Oxford University Press, 2019).

88 See Chapter 2, 2.70 and 2.72 for a discussion of comity.

89 The United Kingdom's ceasing to be a member state of the European Union, a seismic and highly divisive event in the recent political history of the UK.

90 The Brussels regime currently comprises the Judgments Regulation Recast, Regulation (EU) No 2015/2012 and the Lugano Convention 2007. The United Kingdom ceased to be bound by either instrument on 1 January 2021. It has applied to rejoin the Lugano Convention 2007 as an independent contracting state, but the EU, whose agreement is required, currently shows no sign of agreeing to that.

91 See *Turner v Grovit* (Case C-159/02) [2005] 1 AC 101 and *Allianz SpA v West Tankers Inc ("The Front Comor")* (Case C-185/07), [2009] 1 AC 1138. Anti-suit injunctions granted by an arbitral tribunal are outside the scope of the Brussels regime and can therefore be enforced within the EU and EFTA even where the tribunal has its seat in an EU / EFTA member state: *Gazprom OAO* (Case C-536/13) [2015] 1 WLR 4937.

92 It was suggested by Advocate General Wathelet in his Opinion for the *Gazprom OAO* case that this rule has been reversed, in relation to anti-suit injunctions restraining proceedings brought in breach of an arbitration agreement, by the amendments to the Brussels regime introduced by Recital 12 of the Judgments Regulation Recast. That suggestion was not considered by the CJEU in *Gazprom OAO*, and it was emphatically rejected by the English Commercial Court prior to Brexit in *Nori Holding Ltd v Public Joint-Stock Co Otkritie Financial Corp* [2018] EWHC 1343 (Comm) per Males J at [86]–[99]. See Thomas Raphael QC, *The Anti-Suit Injunction* (2nd Edn, Oxford University Press, 2019) §§12.18–12.27.

the UK's departure from the EU,[93] the English court's power to grant anti-suit injunctions again applies the world over; but it remains alert to the need to ensure that it exercises that power in a manner consistent with principles of comity.

7.57 English law usually classifies anti-suit injunctions in the following ways:

a. A **contractual** anti-suit injunction is one granted to enforce the Applicant's substantive contractual right not to be sued by the Respondent in the foreign court. Invariably, that contractual right arises under an exclusive jurisdiction or arbitration agreement, whereby the Applicant and the Respondent agree that their disputes shall be determined by an agreed court or arbitral tribunal to the exclusion of any other forum. Such agreements contain an implied negative promise, not to bring proceedings anywhere other than the chosen forum, which may be enforced by means of an anti-suit injunction.[94]
b. A **quasi-contractual** anti-suit injunction is one granted to enforce the Applicant's substantive contractual right not to be sued in a foreign court, where the Respondent is not herself a party to that contract, but brings proceedings to enforce a contractual right which has been transferred to her.[95] She may, for example, bring proceedings in a foreign court as the assignee of rights arising under a contract between the Applicant and the assignor of those rights; or under a statute which allows her to enforce contractual rights as a third party, such as the Contracts (Rights of Third Parties) Act 1999. In such cases the Respondent, although not strictly a party to the contract, is not entitled to enforce rights under the contract in

93 For practical purposes, this occurred at midnight GMT on 31 December 2020, at the end of the one-year transition period following the UK's formal departure from the EU at the end of 2019.

94 *AES Ust-Kamenogorsk Hydropower Plant LLC v Ust-Kamenogorsk Hydropower Plant JSC* [2013] UKSC 35 per Lord Mance JSC at [1] and [21]–[28].

95 If the Respondent is not an original party to the contract, but becomes a party by means of a novation (a new agreement between the original parties and the Respondent, whereby the Respondent takes the place of one of the original parties), then an anti-suit injunction to enforce an exclusive jurisdiction or arbitration clause in the contract against the Respondent is contractual, rather than quasi-contractual. The same is true of an anti-suit injunction to enforce an exclusive jurisdiction or arbitration clause in a bill of lading contract against a person who becomes the lawful holder the bill of lading under section 2 of the UK Carriage of Goods by Sea Act 1992: where that person demands delivery or makes a claim against the carrier under the bill of lading contract, she becomes subject to the liabilities under the contract as if she had been a party to it, under section 3(1) of the 1992 Act, including the obligation not to bring proceedings other than in the agreed forum: *Aline Tramp SA v Jordan International Insurance Co ("The Flag Evi")* [2016] EWHC 1317 (Comm) per Sara Cockerill QC at [34]–[40].

a manner which is inconsistent with the arbitration or jurisdiction clause contained in the contract.[96]

c. The expression "quasi-contractual anti-suit injunction" is also often used (perhaps incorrectly) to describe cases involving **inconsistent contractual claims**,[97] in which the Respondent brings proceedings against the Applicant to enforce rights under a contract, and the Applicant seeks to enforce an exclusive jurisdiction or arbitration clause in that contract by means of an anti-suit injunction while, at the same time, denying that she (the Applicant) is a party to that contract.[98] In that situation, the English court may grant an anti-suit injunction restraining the Respondent from pursuing a contractual claim in a foreign court while ignoring the contractual obligation to proceed in the contractual forum, even though the Applicant disavows any substantive contractual entitlement to enforce that obligation.[99]

d. A **non-contractual** anti-suit injunction is one granted to restrain foreign proceedings, not because they are brought in breach of contract, but on the grounds that they are vexatious, oppressive or unconscionable,[100] for example where the claim in the foreign

---

96 Generally, English law achieves this result by imposing an equitable duty on the Respondent to honour the negative promise which is an incident of the contractual right which she is seeking to enforce: *Shipowners' Mutual P&I Association (Luxembourg) v Containerships Denizcilik Nakliyat ve Ticaret AS (The "Yusuf Cepnioglu")* [2016] EWCA Civ 386 per Longmore LJ at [22]–[35]. Where the Respondent brings proceedings under the Contracts (Rights of Third Parties) Act 1999, sections 1(4) and 8 impose an equivalent statutory duty on the Respondent.

97 See Thomas Raphael QC, *The Anti-Suit Injunction* (2nd Edn, Oxford University Press, 2019) at §10.81 *ff*; *Times Trading Corp v National Bank of Fujairah (Dubai Branch)* [2020] EWHC 1078 (Comm) per Cockerill J at [60].

98 *Sea Premium Shipping Ltd v Sea Consortium* (unreported, David Steel J, 11 April 2011); *Jewel Owner v Sagaan Developments Trading (The "MD Gemini")* [2012] EWHC 2850 (Comm) per Popplewell J at [15]; *Shipowners' Mutual P&I Association (Luxembourg) v Containerships Denizcilik Nakliyat ve Ticaret AS (The "Yusuf Cepnioglu")* [2016] EWCA Civ 386 per Moore-Bick LJ at [49]; *Dell Emerging Markets (EMEA) v IB Maroc.com* [2017] EWHC 2397 (Comm) per Teare J at [24]; *Qingdao Huiquan Shipping Company v Shanghai Dong He Xin Industry Group Co Ltd* [2018] EWHC 3009 (Comm) per Bryan J at [31]; *XL Insurance Co v Little* [2019] EWHC 1284 (Comm) per Popplewell J at [15]–[17]; *Times Trading Corp v National Bank of Fujairah (Dubai Branch)* [2020] EWHC 1078 (Comm) per Cockerill J at [60]–[62].

99 In other words, the court allows the Applicant to have her cake and eat it, but not the Respondent. The juridical basis for this rule is not settled: see the discussion in Thomas Raphael QC, *The Anti-Suit Injunction* (2nd Edn, Oxford University Press, 2019) at §§10.85–10.87; and *Times Trading Corp v National Bank of Fujairah (Dubai Branch)* [2020] EWHC 1078 (Comm) per Cockerill J at [60]–[62].

100 There is a (somewhat abstruse) debate over the precise test, and over the juridical basis for granting an anti-suit injunction in a non-contractual case: see the discussion in *Masri v Consolidated Contractors International (UK) Ltd (No.3)* [2008] EWCA Civ 625 per Lawrence Collins LJ at [31]–[59].

proceedings is obviously hopeless, or on the grounds that they interfere unduly with the jurisdiction and due process of the English court.[101]

e. Non-contractual anti-suit injunctions are in turn subdivided into **alternative forum** cases, in which the remedy which the Respondent claims in the foreign proceedings would also be available in proceedings in the English court; and the much rarer category of **single forum** cases, where the foreign court alone has jurisdiction over the relevant dispute.[102]

7.58 All these classes of anti-suit injunction can be granted by way of final relief. The substantive and jurisdictional requirements which a Claimant must satisfy in order to obtain a final anti-suit injunction differ, depending on whether the injunction is sought on a contractual, quasi-contractual or non-contractual basis, and on whether it is an alternative or single forum case.

7.59 In a contractual or quasi-contractual claim to restrain foreign proceedings brought in breach of an exclusive English jurisdiction or arbitration clause:

a. The English court has jurisdiction to hear and determine the claim for a final anti-suit injunction by reason of the exclusive English jurisdiction or arbitration clause.[103]
b. It will exercise its discretion in favour of granting a final anti-suit injunction to restrain the foreign proceedings, if sought promptly, unless the Defendant can show strong reasons why it should not do so.[104]

7.60 In a non-contractual claim to restrain foreign proceedings on the grounds that they are vexatious, oppressive or unconscionable or interfere unduly with the jurisdiction or due process of the English court:

---

101 *Societe Nationale Industrielle Aerospatiale v Lee Kai Jak* [1987] AC 871 per Lord Goff of Chieveley at pages 892–893; *Star Reefers Pool Inc v JFC Group Co Ltd* [2012] EWCA Civ 14 per Rix LJ at [31] [32].

102 *Airbus Industrie GIE v Patel* [1999] 1 AC 119 per Lord Goff of Chieveley at page 134.

103 In cases covered by the Hague Convention 2005, and other cases involving an exclusive English jurisdiction clause, the Claim Form can be served out of the jurisdiction without permission under CPR 6.33(2B). In cases involving an English arbitration clause, the Claim Form can be served out of the jurisdiction with permission under CPR 62.5(1)(c): *AES Ust-Kamenogorsk Hydropower Plant LLP v Ust-Kamenogorsk Hydropower Plant JSC* [2013] UKSC 35 per Lord Mance JSC at [50].

104 *Aggeliki Charis Compania Maritima v Pagnan (The "Angelic Grace")* [1995] 1 Lloyd's Rep 87 per Millett LJ at page 96. In such cases, considerations of comity play little role, and the court has no need to exercise its power with caution, as it is "granting an injunction to restrain foreign proceedings on the clear and simple ground that the defendant has promised not to bring them". The expression "strong reasons" has largely superseded the formulation of "good reasons" used in *The Angelic Grace* itself: see e.g. *AES Ust-Kamenogorsk Hydropower Plant LLP v Ust-Kamenogorsk Hydropower Plant JSC* [2013] UKSC 35 per Lord Mance JSC at [25].

a. The English court will only have jurisdiction to hear and determine a claim for a final anti-suit injunction if (i) the Defendant is amenable to service of originating process there; or (ii) the claim can be brought within one of the jurisdictional gateways in CPR PD 6B §3.1,[105] and the court gives permission for the Claim Form to be served out of the jurisdiction; or (iii) the Defendant is already subject to the jurisdiction of the English court in other proceedings, and the anti-suit injunction is sought in order to protect the integrity of those proceedings, in which case the Claimant can seek an anti-suit injunction as a form of ancillary relief, by issuing an Application Notice in those proceedings rather than by issuing a separate Claim Form.[106]

b. The English court will grant a final anti-suit injunction to restrain the foreign proceedings only where (i) it has sufficient interest in the matter (which, in alternative forum cases, usually means that the English court is the natural forum for determining the underlying dispute[107]); (ii) the Claimant demonstrates that justice requires that the Defendant be restrained from exercising his right to pursue the foreign proceedings, taking account of any legitimate juridical advantages which the Defendant enjoys in those proceedings;[108] and (iii) granting an injunction is consistent with comity.[109]

7.61 On an application for an interim anti-suit injunction, the position appears to be as follows, reflecting the reality that, in most cases, there will be no trial of the Applicant's claim for a final anti-suit injunction (and indeed, where the Applicant applies for an anti-suit injunction as an ancillary order in existing proceedings before the English court, there may be no claim for

105 See in particular sub-paragraphs (1), (3) and (6).

106 *Masri v Consolidated Contractors International (UK) Ltd (No.3)* [2008] EWCA Civ 625 per Lawrence Collins LJ at [59] and [99]. Strictly speaking, if the Applicant seeks a final anti-suit injunction, he should apply to amend the Claim Form (or, if the Applicant is the Defendant, apply to plead/amend his counterclaim) in the existing proceedings in order to add a claim for a final anti-suit injunction; but that raises difficult jurisdictional issues: see Thomas Raphael QC, *The Anti-Suit Injunction* (2nd Edn, Oxford University Press, 2019) §13.28. Alternatively, he may be content simply to apply for an interim anti-suit injunction in those proceedings: see 7.61 *ff* below.

107 *Societe Nationale Industrielle Aerospatiale v Lee Kai Jak* [1987] AC 871 per Lord Goff of Chieveley at page 895; *Airbus Industrie v Patel* [1999] 1 AC 119 per Lord Goff of Chieveley at page 138. The need for a sufficient interest is a requirement of comity. Where the foreign claim is said to be vexatious because it is hopeless, the English court may have sufficient interest if it is the natural forum for determining whether the foreign claim is vexatious: *Shell International Petroleum Co v Coral Oil Co Ltd* [1999] 2 Lloyd's Rep 606 per Thomas J at page 610.

108 *Societe Nationale Industrielle Aerospatiale v Lee Kai Jak* [1987] AC 871 per Lord Goff of Chieveley at page 896.

109 For a fuller summary of the principles governing the granting of anti-suit injunctions, see Thomas Raphael QC, *The Anti-Suit Injunction* (2nd Edn, Oxford University Press, 2019) §4.05.

a final anti-suit injunction for the court to try) and that the outcome of the application for interim relief will, in practice, usually be decisive of whether the Respondent is permitted to pursue proceedings in the foreign court:

a. The American Cyanamid principles do not apply, save where the Applicant seeks a temporary injunction for a short period of time pending a fuller hearing of the application. Even in such cases, considerations of comity will generally require the court to take a cautious approach.
b. Where the application is made on a contractual or quasi-contractual basis, the Applicant must satisfy the court to a high degree of probability that there is a valid and applicable exclusive jurisdiction or arbitration agreement which is binding on the Respondent.[110]
c. Where the application is made on a non-contractual basis, the Applicant must show a *prima facie* right to a final anti-suit injunction or even that he would be actually entitled to a final injunction.[111]

Application Notice

- You must complete Parts A **and** B, **and** Part C if applicable.
- Send any relevant fee and the completed application notice to the court with any draft order, witness statement or other evidence.
- It is for you (and not the court) to serve this application notice.

You should provide this information for listing the application

Time estimate .... (hours) ....(mins)

Is this agreed by all parties? ......Yes [......]......No [......]

Please always refer to the Commercial Court Guide for details of how applications should be prepared and will be heard, or in a small number of exceptional cases can be dealt with on paper.

110 *Emmott v Michael Wilson & Partners Ltd* [2018] EWCA Civ 51 per Sir Terence Etherton MR at [39]; *Times Trading Corp v National Bank of Fujairah (Dubai Branch)* [2020] EWHC 1078 (Comm) per Cockerill J at [38(vi)].

111 *Sheffield United Football Club Ltd v West Ham United Football Club plc* [2008] EWHC 2855 (Comm) per Teare J at [10]; Thomas Raphael QC, *The Anti-Suit Injunction* (2nd Edn, Oxford University Press, 2019) §§13.39–13.43.

In the High Court of Justice **Business and Property Courts of England and Wales** **Commercial Court (QBD)** **Royal Courts of Justice**	
Claim No.	
Warrant no. (if applicable)	
Claimant(s) (including ref.)	**RHAPSODY CHAMPION LTD.**
Defendant(s) (including ref.)	**DANIEL ROCKETMAN S.A.**
Date	

Part A

1. Where there is more than one claimant or defendant, specify which claimant or defendant	(The claimant)~~(The defendant)~~(1)
2. State clearly what order you are seeking (if there is room) or otherwise refer to a draft order (which must be attached)	intend(s) to apply for an order (a draft of which is attached) that(2) see attached draft
3. Briefly set out why you are seeking the order. Identify any rule or statutory provision	because(3) for the reasons set out in the attached witness statement of Marcus Bolan dated 31 May 2022, it is just and convenient so to order.

Part B

*(The claimant)~~(The defendant)~~(1) wishes to rely on: *tick one:*

the attached (witness statement)~~(affidavit)~~ [√] ~~(the claimant)(the defendant)'s~~(1) ~~statement of case [ ] evidence in Part C overleaf~~ in support of this application [ ]

Signed	(Applicant)('s legal representative)	**Position or office held** (if signing on behalf of firm, company or corporation)	

Address to which documents about this claim should be sent (including reference if appropriate)[(4)]

4. If you are not already a party to the proceedings, you must provide an address for service of documents	Glammrokk LLP No.1 Blockbuster Street London		if applicable	
			Tel no.	+44 (0)20 9099 9999
			Fax no.	
			DX no.	
	Postcode	EC1X 9LP	e-mail	m.bolan@glammrokk.com

Claim No. | |

Part C

(Note: Part C should only be used where it is convenient to enter here the evidence in support of the application, rather than to use witness statements or affidavits)

*(The claimant)(~~The defendant~~)[(1)] wishes to rely on the following evidence in support of this application:

Statement of Truth

*[I believe] [The applicant believes] that the facts stated in this application notice are true.
[I understand] [The applicant understands] that proceedings for contempt of court may be brought against anyone who makes, or causes to be made, a false statement in a document verified by a statement of truth without an honest belief in its truth.

*I am duly authorised by the applicant to sign this statement

Full name...

Name of *(Applicant)('s litigation friend)('s legal representative)

....

Signed	[ ]	**Position or office held**	[ ]
*(Applicant) ('s legal representative)		(If signing on behalf of firm, company or corporation)	
delete as appropriate		**Date**	[ ]

Claim No ____________

IN THE HIGH COURT OF JUSTICE
BUSINESS AND PROPERTY COURTS OF ENGLAND AND WALES
COMMERCIAL COURT (QBD)
The Honourable Mr(s) Justice_____________

B E T W E E N:

RHAPSODY CHAMPION LIMITED

Claimant

-and-

DANIEL ROCKETMAN S.A.

Defendant

____

Draft/ORDER

____

PENAL NOTICE

If you DANIEL ROCKETMAN S.A. disobey this Order you may be held to be in contempt of court and may be imprisoned, fined or have your assets seized.

Any other person who knows of this order and does anything which helps or permits the Defendant to breach the terms of this Order may also be held to be in contempt of court and may be imprisoned, fined or have their assets seized.

UPON HEARING Counsel for the Claimant

AND UPON READING the Claimant's Application Notice dated 31 May 2022, the witness statement of Marcus Bolan dated 31 May 2021 and exhibit MHBB1 thereto

AND UPON the Claimant giving the undertakings set out in Schedule 1 hereto

IT IS ORDERED as follows:

1. Until further order, the Defendant must not, by itself, its servants or agents or otherwise howsoever cause or permit the m.v. TYRANNOSAURUS REX ("the Vessel") to sail away from the port of Felixstowe or employ the Vessel otherwise than in accordance with the orders of the Claimant given under the time charterparty dated 1 February 2022 between the Defendant as owner and the Claimant as charterer.
2. There will be a further hearing in respect of this Order on 7 June 2022 ("the Return Date").
3. The Defendant is at liberty to apply to discharge this Order at any time upon giving written notice to the Claimant's solicitors, whose contact details are set out in Schedule 2 hereto.
4. Costs reserved.

SCHEDULE 1

Undertakings given to the Court by the Claimant:

(1) If the court later finds that this order has caused loss to the Defendant, and decides that the Defendant should be compensated for that loss, the Claimant will comply with any order the Court may make.

(2) To fortify the undertaking in paragraph (1) above by paying the sum of US$500,000 into Court by 4 pm on 1 June 2022.
(3) The Claimant will as soon as practicable serve the Claim Form, Application Notice, witness statement of Marcus Bolan, exhibit MHBS1 and this Order on the Defendant.
(4) The Claimant will forthwith notify the Defendant of the making of this Order and provide the Defendant with a written note of the hearing.

SCHEDULE 2

The Claimant's solicitors are:
Glammrokk LLP: Marcus Bolan (partner).
Correspondence address: No.1 Blockbuster Street, London, England, EC1X 9LP
Telephone: +44 (0)20 9099 9999 (24 hours)
Email: m.bolan@glammrokk.com

M.H.B. Bolan
First witness statement
31.5.2022
For Claimant
Exhibit MHBB1

Claim No ____________

IN THE HIGH COURT OF JUSTICE
BUSINESS AND PROPERTY COURTS OF ENGLAND AND WALES
COMMERCIAL COURT (QBD)

B E T W E E N:

RHAPSODY CHAMPION LIMITED

Claimant

-and-

DANIEL ROCKETMAN S.A.

Defendant

WITNESS STATEMENT OF MARCUS HERCULES BULSARA BOLAN

1. I am a solicitor and partner in the firm of Glammrokk LLP of No.1 Blockbuster Street, London EC1X 9LP, solicitors for the Claimant. I have the conduct of this case on behalf of the Claimant. I am duly authorised by the Claimant to make this witness statement.

2. The contents of this witness statement are derived from my conduct of this case and from documents and information provided to me by Regina Dwight, the Claimant's Group Risk Manager. Insofar as the contents of this witness statement are within my own knowledge, they are true. Otherwise they are true to the best of my knowledge, information and belief.
3. I make this witness statement in support of the Claimant's application for an urgent injunction to restrain the Defendant, the owner of the m.v. TYRANNOSAURUS REX ("the Vessel") from causing or permitting her to sail away from the port of Felixstowe, where she is currently berthed, or from employing her otherwise than in accordance with the time charterparty between the Defendant as owner and the Claimant as charterer dated 1 February 2022 ("the Charterparty").
4. Attached to this witness statement is a paginated bundle of true copy documents marked "MHBB1" to which I shall hereinafter refer by page numbers in square brackets: [#].
5. This application is being made on short notice to the Defendants for reasons of urgency.

Background

6. The Claimant is the main contractor on the Krakken offshore wind farm ("Krakken"), which is currently under construction in the North Sea. The Claimant's employer is the energy company Ballroomblitz Energy Corp ("Ballroomblitz").
7. I attach a copy of the contract between the Claimant and Ballroomblitz, dated 1 April 2020 [1–183]. It requires the Claimant to install very large turbine blades on wind turbines at Krakken, in accordance with the programme set out in Schedule 15A of the contract. Clause 193 of the contract provides that the Claimant shall be liable to pay liquidated damages to Ballroomblitz at €21,500 per day for each day of delay in completing the installation of turbine blades beyond the dates set out in Schedule 15A.
8. The blades have been installed on all but one of the turbines. The deadline for installing the two remaining turbine blades in Schedule 15A of the contract is 14 May 2022.
9. Wind turbine blades of the type being installed at Krakken can only be carried by highly specialised ships. There are just three such ships operating in the Atlantic basin, one of which is the Vessel herself. These ships are in high demand during the summer months, when the weather is good, and their services need to be secured well in advance.

The Charterparty

10. By the Charterparty, a copy of which is at [184–245], the Defendant agreed to transport the two remaining wind turbine blades from Felixstowe to Krakken, in consideration of a payment of €1 million (clause 12.1), 50% of which was payable upon arrival at Felixstowe and the other 50% upon arrival at Krakken; plus an additional sum of €15,000 per day for each day the Vessel remained on site at Krakken until the Claimant declared that installation of the blades was complete (clause 12.2).
11. Clause 29.3 of the Charterparty provides that any additional insurance premium which Owners are required to pay by reason of being ordered into an area affected by war risks shall be for Charterers' account.
12. Clause 15 of the Charterparty provides that the Defendant's liability for loss or damage of whatsoever nature and howsoever caused, shall be limited to the sum of €250,000.

Events at Felixstowe

13. The Vessel arrived at Felixstowe on 28 April 2022, and the Claimant remitted the sum of €500,000 to the Defendant's nominated bank on the same day in accordance with clause 12.1 of the Charterparty. I attach a copy of the payment confirmation at [146].
14. Later that same day, the Claimant received an email from Roxy Ferreno of Ferreno Inc, the brokers on the Charterparty, containing a message from the Defendant [147]. It stated:

    We understand from the programming team at Ballroomblitz's Aberdeen office that the intended turbine blades are of non-standard design and materials. This creates additional risks for Owners, and we require additional insurance cover to load same. We attach quote for additional cover: premium of €1.1 million is for Charterers' account under clause 29.3 of Charterparty. Please remit same by close of business on 2 May 2021 or we will consider Charterparty at an end and the Vessel will depart from Felixstowe for other employment. In the meantime, no loading will take place.
15. On 29 April 2022 I wrote to the Defendant on behalf of the Claimant to explain that clause 29.3 has no application whatever to the current situation, calling upon the Defendant to withdraw its demand and its threat to withdraw the Vessel, and to commence loading [148]. I also stated that the Claimant reserved the right to take any necessary steps to protect its rights including making an application to the Court for urgent relief. The Defendant replied yesterday, 30 April

2022, flatly rejecting the Claimant's points and repeating its position [149].

16. None of the other specialist vessels which would be capable of carrying the turbine blades is available at present. According to market reports [150], the earliest that any of these vessels may be available is late September 2022.

The Relief Sought

17. The Claimant seeks an urgent interim injunction, restraining the Defendant from sailing the Vessel away from Felixstowe or employing her otherwise than in accordance with the Charterparty until further order. The Claimant's substantive claim, as set out in the draft Claim Form, is for a final injunction in similar terms, and for declaratory relief. The injunctive relief sought is negative, as I understand that the Court will not grant a mandatory injunction compelling a shipowner to perform a charterparty.
18. This case is one of urgency. The Defendant is demanding immediate payment and has threatened to sail the Vessel away if the Claimant does not comply within tomorrow. There is a very real risk that the Defendant will do tomorrow so unless restrained by injunction.

American Cyanamid Principles

19. I believe that the principles set out in ***American Cyanamid Co v Ethicon Ltd*** [1975] AC 396 are applicable to the granting of injunctive relief in this case.

Serious Issue to Be Tried

20. I respectfully submit that there is, at very least, a serious issue to be tried as to whether the Defendant is entitled to sail the Vessel away and/or refuse to load the turbine blades unless they receive the additional payment demanded, and as to whether it would be committing a repudiatory breach of the Charterparty by doing so. Indeed, I believe that the Claimant has a very strong case on the merits on those issues.

Adequacy of Damages

21. I do not believe that damages would be an adequate remedy for the Claimant if the Defendant were permitted to commit a repudiatory breach of the Charterparty. In particular, the Claimant would be

likely to suffer very substantial losses as a result, in the form of liability for liquidated damages under its contract with Ballroomblitz. I do not know whether the Defendant would be in a position to satisfy a judgment for the amount of those losses. But there is also a risk that it would be able to rely on the exemption clause in the Charterparty in order to limit its liability to the Claimant to just €250,000 (the Claimant's position is that that clause would not apply in the circumstances of this case).

22. In addition, I believe that the Claimant may suffer damage to its commercial reputation as a result of delays in the completion of the Krakken project, which would not be easily quantifiable and would not be readily compensable in damages.
23. Conversely, I believe that damages would be a perfectly adequate remedy for the Defendant, in the event that the Court later decided that that relief now sought should not have been granted. I attach a copy of the Claimant's latest annual report and accounts [151–186], which show that the Claimant has total assets of €481 million, including substantial cash and fixed assets within England and Wales. The Claimant is also willing to fortify its undertaking in damages if the Court so requires.

Balance of Convenience

24. If relevant, I believe that the balance of convenience lies with granting the Claimant the relief it seeks, as that will best preserve the *status quo*. I also believe that the merits of the Claimant's claim are very strong.

Discretion

I respectfully submit that, in all the circumstances, this is a proper case for the Court to exercise its discretion in favour of granting the relief sought.

I believe that the facts stated in this witness statement are true.

Signed

....

Dated

....

CHAPTER 8

Preservation Measure of Behaviour in China

Introduction

Terminology

8.1 The preservation measure of behaviour (hereinafter referred to as "behaviour preservation measure") is translated from the Chinese term "行为保全措施" (Xingwei Baoquan Cuoshi). Because of the absence of a uniform translation for this term, apart from being called "behaviour preservation", other translations by Chinese legal practitioners include the terms "conduct preservation", "act preservation", "prohibitory/mandatory injunctions" and so forth. There is no fundamental difference in concepts under Chinese law whenever any of these terms are used to describe this procedural remedy. In this chapter, the authors have adopted the term "behaviour preservation", except in the field of maritime law. In maritime law, traditionally, the term "maritime injunction" has been used since the Special Maritime Procedure Code 2000 (hereinafter referred to as "SMPL 2000") was promulgated.

8.2 It must be emphasised that the Civil Code of the People's Republic of China 2020 provides a new rule, entitled "injunction for infringement of personality rights", to strengthen the protection of personal rights.[1] The creation of such injunctions system has learned from other jurisdictions' similar system. Its function in effect amounts to the function of the behaviour preservation.[2] The reasonable ground why such procedural system has been provided in the substantive law, namely the Civil Code, is because the infringement

1 Article 997 of the Civil Code of the People's Republic of China provides that "if a party has evidence to prove that a perpetrator is committing or is going to commit the infringement of personality rights, and failure to stop this infringement may cause the irreparable harms, the party is entitled to apply for an order seeking measures to stop the infringement to the people's court". The third session of the 13th National People's Congress passed the Civil Code of the People's Republic of China on 28 May 2020 that came into effect on 1 January 2021.

2 The Leading Group of the Implementation of the Civil Code of the Supreme People's Court (ed.), *Understanding and Application of Part 'Personal Rights' of the Civil Code of the People's Republic of China* (People's Court Press 2020) 88.

DOI: 10.4324/9781003000310-13

of personal rights by way of the internet and of other high-end technology is getting worse; this procedural system incorporating into the Civil Code can demonstrate its importance.

Behaviour preservation measures are widely applied in intellectual property disputes rather than in the protection of personal rights. It is necessary to set out a unique rule to protect personal rights.[3] Although certain detailed analysis by the SPC was issued in late 2020 to instruct courts and stakeholders in understanding and applying this new rule, the application of this injunction is considered to abide by Article 101 of Civil Procedure Law of the People's Republic of China 1991 (hereinafter referred to as "CPL 1991 (as amended until 2020)").[4] Therefore, this chapter will not focus on it due to the limited space.

Evolution and History

8.3 The evolution of the behaviour preservation remedy in China was introduced in Chapter 1, 1.88–1.89. Accordingly, the history of the behaviour preservation measures is very short. Its evolution and later development are also as a result of legal transplants and adopting the best global practices in this field of law. Based on this, this area of law has benefited from work carried out by Chinese legal scholars and judges using legal transplants and taking ideas from various jurisdictions.

8.4 To understand the Chinese behaviour preservation system completely, it is essential first to understand the concept of "advance enforcement". The concept of "advance enforcement" provided by the CPL 1991 to some extent partially conveyed a concept of "behaviour preservation" in the civil procedure system.[5] However, it would not be wrong to suggest that in China, a comprehensive system for behaviour preservation measures was absent in the civil procedure law for many years.

8.5 The first procedure law that introduced the system of the behaviour preservation was the SMPL 2000. As mentioned in 8.1, behaviour preservation measures are called "maritime injunctions" pursuant to the SMPL 2000 that adopted the concept of injunctions available in English law.[6]

3 Liming Wang, 'Preliminary Injunction of the Infringement of Personality Rights' 2019(4) Law and Economy 3, 3–19; it should be noted that the first draft of the Civil Code simply provided "preliminary injunction", but the final draft does not limit this system to being employed during the pre-action proceedings.

4 The Leading Group of the Implementation of the Civil Code of the Supreme People's Court (ed.), *Understanding and Application of Part 'Personal Rights' of the Civil Code of the People's Republic of China* (People's Court Press 2020) 92–94.

5 A further discussion can be found in 8.9–8.54; here Civil Procedure Law 1991 does not refer to the revised CPL 1991 (as amended until 2020).

6 Refer to Chapter 1, 1.35–1.70.

8.6 Subsequently, intellectual property (IP) laws including the Patent Law of the People's Republic China 1985 (2020 Amendment) (hereinafter referred to as "Patent Law 1985 (2020 Amendment)"),[7] the Copyright Law of the People's Republic China 1991 (2020 Amendment) (hereinafter referred to as "Copyright Law (2020 Amendment)")[8] and the Trademark Law of the People's Republic China 1983 (2019 Amendment)[9] provided the behaviour preservation measures to match the TRIPS Agreement.[10]

8.7 In 2012, the general rules governing the procedural remedy of the behaviour preservation measures were established through the revision to the CPL 1991. This 2012 revision to the CPL 1991 ensured that behaviour preservation measures are now available not only in IP infringement disputes and maritime disputes, but also are available in other types of civil and commercial cases.

8.8 Against the above background, this chapter will first provide a brief overview of the traditional procedural remedy of "advance enforcement" that includes the special concept of the behaviour preservation measures. This analysis of advance enforcement will be followed by a general overview of the behaviour preservation measures applicable to all types of disputes that came into existence through the 2012 amendment to the CPL 1991. Thereafter, the authors have examined in detail the rules, which are outside of the CPL 1991 regime, that govern the similar preservation measures for IP and unfair competition behaviour preservation measures.

---

7 Patent Law of the People's Republic China was passed by the Fourth Session of the Standing Committee of the Sixth National People's Congress of the People's Republic of China on12 March 1984 and came into effect on 1 April 1985. The latest amendment was adopted by the 22nd Session of the Standing Committee of the 13th National People's Congress of the People's Republic of China on 17 October 2020.

8 The Copyright Law of the People's Republic China was adopted by the 15th Session of the Standing Committee of the 7th National People's Congress of the People's Republic of China on 7 September 1990 and came into effect on 1 June 1991. The latest amendment was adopted by the 23rd Session of the Standing Committee of the 13th National People's Congress of the People's Republic of China on 11 November 2020.

9 The Trade Law of the People's Republic China was passed by the 24th Session of the Standing Committee of the 15th National People's Congress of the People's Republic of China on 23 August 1982 and came into effect on 1 March 1983. The latest amendment was adopted by the 10th Session of the Standing Committee of the 13th National People's Congress of the People's Republic of China on 23 April 2019.

10 The Agreement on Trade-Related Aspects of Intellectual Property Rights was in force from 1995 ("TRIPS"); the TRIPS Agreement was contained in the Appendixes to World Trade Organization's Protocol on Accession of China to WTO. In order to join the WTO, China had to amend the Patent Law in 2000, and the Copyright Law and the Trademark Law in 2001 to comply with the Protocol. Currently, the latest versions of the three laws were amended in 2008, 2010, 2019 and 2020 respectively. The behaviour preservation measures were contained in Article 72 of the Patent Law 1985 (2020 Amendment), Article 50 of the Copyright Law (2020 Amendment) and Article 65 of the Trademark Law 1983 (2019 Amendment); see also, Xiaoming Song, Chuang Wang, Junli Xia and Guimei Lang, 'Understanding and Application of *Provisions of the Supreme People's Court on Several Issues Concerning the Application of Law in Cases Involving the Review of Behaviour Preservation in Intellectual Property Disputes*' (2019) 7 The People's Judicature (Applied) 19, 19.

Advance Enforcement

Meaning and Evolution of Advance Enforcement

8.9 In various debates initiated by legal scholars in China, the system of advance enforcement in the Chinese civil preservation system is regarded as the combination of both property preservation and behaviour preservation.[11] Precisely speaking, the procedural remedy of advance enforcement can be divided into two types of measures. The first type of measure will address the payment obligation of the respondent that should be incorporated into the preservation procedure together with the property preservation measures. The second type of measure will involve orders against a party such as "to do" or "not to do" and is more akin to the post-2012 behaviour preservation measures and related to procedures.[12]

8.10 No uniform explanation has yet been clarified in law or expressed by legal scholars on the issues discussed in the preceding paragraphs. In most scenarios, the system of advance enforcement can be treated as an independent system of seeking measures akin to the preservation measures.

8.11 From a practical point of view, the second type of "advance enforcement" as discussed in 8.9 and the "behaviour preservation" measures introduced through the 2012 amendment to the CPL 1991 are similar.[13]

8.12 However, the analysis on the evolution of the concept of advance enforcement alongside the development of the modern behaviour preservation measures has certainly shown their differences. It is the authors' contention that to some extent these differences have improved the system of the behaviour preservation measure in China. It is therefore necessary first to provide a brief introduction to the concept of advance enforcement.

---

11 The system of the advance payment was first provided by Article 95 of Civil Procedure Law of the People's Republic China (for Trial Implementation) 1982; see also, Shichun Li, 'Research on General Issues of Civil Preservation Procedure' (2005) 17 (1) Peking University Law Journal 43, 48; see also, Yiqiang Fan, 'Civil Preservation Procedure' (PhD Thesis, Southwest University of Political & Science 2008) 13 and 91; see also, Fuhua Wang, 'Research on Civil Preservation System' (PhD Thesis, China University of Political Science and Law 2005) 57–59.

12 Shichun Li, 'Studies on the Civil Securing Judgement Procedure' (PhD Thesis, China University of Political Science and Law 2002) 74.

13 These two concepts are certainly different from the notion of "interim injunctions" under English law. Nonetheless, there are a few similarities between the interim injunctions and behaviour preservation measures as well, in particular, the purpose of applicants seeking such remedies from the courts is similar in both jurisdictions; see also, Xun Yang, 'Development of "Interim Injunction" in IPR Cases in China' (17 January 2019) <https://wemp.app/posts/abbd7327-2d61-4546-8b23-a71f2b2b38e4?utm_source=latest-posts> accessed 30 July 2021; see also, Chapter 1, 1.14–1.22 for examination of purposes of interim remedies/preservation measures.

Scope of Application of Advance Enforcement

8.13 As early as 1982, the Civil Procedure Law of the People's Republic China (for Trial Implementation) provided the concept of "advance payment".[14] Its purpose was simply to satisfy the demand for advance payment. It is generally recognised that the system of advance payment has its origins in the advance enforcement system.[15]

8.14 In 1988, the *Opinion of the SPC on Questions Concerning the Implementation of the General Principles of Civil Law (for Trial Implementation)* provided that the concept of advance enforcement was similar to the modern behaviour preservation system. It provided:

> If in the course of a lawsuit there is a need to *stop an infringement, eliminate an obstruction, or remove a danger* [emphasis added], the People's Court may issue a decision before the conclusion of the lawsuit based on the application of a party or on its own initiative.[16]

8.15 The above interpretation deals with the General Principles of Civil Law 1986,[17] which is within the domain of substantive law rather than procedural law. Therefore, the requirements and standards required in any application seeking the procedural law remedy of advance enforcement are not clear.

8.16 Until 1991, the Civil Procedure Law of People's Republic of China 1991 clarified the legal terminology of "advance enforcement" and its scope. Accordingly, all disputes involving the payment obligation and certain behaviour obligations that required a party "to do" or "not to do" certain acts may invoke this concept of advance enforcement.

8.17 Through the amendments and revisions to the CPL in 2007, 2012 and 2017, the system of advance enforcement has evolved gradually. These days, subsequent to applications seeking behaviour preservation orders, it refers to orders made by courts that direct respondents "to do" or "not do" certain acts. Such orders are made after the cases have been accepted by the courts but prior to the final judgments on merits.[18]

8.18 However, there are lots of conflicting opinions on the procedural remedy of advance enforcement. These conflicting opinions are emanating from various courts and commentaries by legal scholars in China. In fact, these

---

14 Civil Procedure Law of the People's Republic China (trial) 1982, Article 95.

15 Refer to Chapter 1, 1.85 to 1.87, for discussion on the evolution of property preservation measures in China.

16 *Opinion of the Supreme People's Court on Questions Concerning the Implementation of the General Principles of Civil Law (for Trial Implementation) 1988* (Fa (Ban) Fa [1988] No 6), Article 162.

17 General Principles of the Civil Law of the People's Republic of China 1986 expired on 1 January 2021 when the Civil Code 2020 came into effect.

18 Yang Li, 'What Rules on Intellectual Property Behaviour Preservations Should Be Demanded in China' (2019) 5 Intellectual Property 3, 14.

conflicting opinions have made the task of clearly deciphering the theory of advance enforcement even more difficult for any stakeholder.

8.19 On one hand, the traditional viewpoint is that advance enforcement is only operative in cases involving advance payment obligations, such as the payment of a sum of money or in relation to property.[19] For this reason, some legal scholars have contended that this system is not available in infringement cases in general or infringement in IP disputes.[20]

8.20 On the other hand, the CPL 1991 (as amended until 2020) and cases published so far on this subject have demonstrated that the opinions stated above in fact narrow the relevance of the procedural remedy of advance enforcement in most civil and commercial disputes. The authors will analyse the wordings of relevant provision from the CPL 1991 (as amended until 2020).

8.21 First, Article 106 of the CPL 1991 (as amended until 2020) provides:

> According to the application of a party concerned, a court may make an order for *advance enforcement* [emphasis added] in the following cases:
>
> (a) those involving claims for payment of alimony, maintenance, child support, pensions for the disabled or the family of the deceased, or medical expenses;
> (b) those involving claims for remuneration for labour; and
> (c) those involving urgent circumstances that require advance enforcement.[21]

8.22 It follows that the meaning of "urgent circumstances" in the context of subparagraph (c) of Article 106 of the CPL 1991 (as amended until 2020) has been clarified through Article 170 of *Interpretations of the Supreme People's Court on Application of the Civil Procedure Law (2020 Amendment)* (hereinafter referred to as "Interpretation of CPL 2015 (2020 Amendment)").[22] This Interpretation provides that the term "urgent" can be considered in any of the following circumstances:

> (a) Where infringement needs to be immediately stopped, or obstruction needs to be immediately eliminated;
> (b) Where a certain act needs to be immediately stopped;

19 Yiwei Pu, Xuemian Wang and Xiaodong Guo, *Course of Civil Procedure Law* (Peking University Press 2016), Part V, Chapter 13 and Section 3 'Advance Enforcement'; see also, Xun Yang, 'Development of "Interim Injunction" in IPR Cases in China' (17 January 2019) <https://wemp.app/posts/abbd7327-2d61-4546-8b23-a71f2b2b38e4?utm_source=latest-posts> accessed 30 July 2021.

20 ibid.

21 CPL 1991 (as amended until 2020), Article 106; the formats of applications seeking advance payment and advance enforcement can be found Annex 2 and Annex 3.

22 *Interpretations of the Supreme People's Court on Application of the Civil Procedure Law of the People's Republic of China (2020 Amendment)* (superseded by Fa Shi [2015] No 5) (Fa Shi [2020] No 20).

(c) Where insurance benefits urgently needed for resuming production or operation need to be recovered;
(d) Where social insurance funds or social assistance funds need to be immediately returned; or
(e) Where the failure to immediately return relevant funds will seriously affect the daily life or production and operations of right holders.[23]

8.23 Based on the above provisions, it is clear that the CPL 1991 (as amended until 2020) and its Interpretation (2020 Amendment) have no intention of restricting the application of advance enforcement to the payment obligation. In fact, subparagraphs (a) and (b) of Article 170 of the Interpretation of CPL 2015 (2020 Amendment) explicitly stipulate that the infringement cases may specifically apply the system of advance enforcement and therefore it can be invoked by the applicants. Accordingly, pursuant to the above legal analysis, the traditional viewpoint of limiting the concept of advance enforcement to the payment obligations is no longer convincing.

Requirements of Advance Enforcement

8.24 As far as the requirements of advance enforcement are concerned, it is provided that there are two conditions that must be satisfied before any advance enforcement order can be granted:

(a) The relationship of rights and obligations between the parties concerned is evident and, without advance enforcement, the life, production activities or business operations of the applicant would be seriously affected.
(b) The person against whom the application is made is capable of performing the order for advance enforcement.[24]

8.25 Apart from the above two prerequisites, the courts may request the applicants to provide security as part of the procedure to seek the remedy of advance enforcement, even though the advance enforcement procedure is available only during post-action proceedings, which usually do not mandatorily require the applicants to provide security. If the applicants cannot furnish security, their applications seeking the remedy of advance enforcement will be rejected by the courts.

8.26 If the applicant were to lose the final civil trial, then the applicant must compensate the respondent for any losses as a result of application of advance enforcement.[25] For further guidance on the issues of security and

23 Interpretation of CPL 2015 (2020 Amendment), Article 170.
24 CPL 1991 (as amended until 2020), Article 107.
25 ibid.

compensation, the reader may refer to Chapter 3, 3.130–3.194, "Security" section, and 3.292–3.306, "Compensation" section.

Reconsideration and Objection

8.27 After a court renders an order on an application seeking advance enforcement, this order can be enforced immediately against the respondent. If either the applicant or the respondent is dissatisfied with the order, that party can apply to the court for reconsideration of the order. The application for reconsideration must be made to the same court that rendered the order of advance enforcement.[26] Further details about the procedure of reconsideration can be found in Chapter 3, 3.232–3.246 "Reconsideration". Similarly, the procedure of objection can be found in Chapter 3, 3.247–3.265 "Objection".

"Converse" Behaviour Preservation

8.28 As discussed earlier, the traditional purpose of an advance enforcement is to address the advance payment issue,[27] but Chinese courts in recent years have ventured out to apply this system of advance enforcement to address infringement disputes as well.

8.29 Pursuant to subparagraphs (a) and (b) of Article 170 of the Interpretation of CPL 2015 (2020 Amendment), where the remedy of advance enforcement is available, Article 100 of the CPL 1991 (as amended until 2020) may also provide for the behaviour preservation measures to be applicable to the same issues. It is therefore possible that the two remedies may overlap; however, it is the authors' view that each of the remedies can in fact fill the gaps that may exist in the other remedy.

8.30 A general view is that advance enforcement can be regarded as the "converse" behaviour preservation measures.[28] Specifically speaking, during civil proceedings, the advance enforcement order aims to prevent loss to the defendant due to the claimant's behaviour. Accordingly, as a result of this concept of converse behaviour preservation, defendants can also file applications to the courts to allow them to act in a particular way without intervention.[29]

26 ibid Article 108.

27 Shichun Li, 'Studies on the Civil Securing Judgement Procedure' (PhD Thesis, China University of Political Science and Law 2002) 88.

28 Jing Wang, 'A Court Upheld an Accused Infringer's Application for Advance Enforcement to Recover the Deleted Link' (*Legal Daily*, 16 July 2019) <www.legaldaily.com.cn/IT/content/2019-07/16/content_7935264.htm> accessed 30 July 2021.

29 Liwei Jiang, 'On the Capacity to Apply for Preliminary Injunction in IP Cases: Comments on the First Item of Draft Judicial Interpretation on Preliminary Injunction' (2016) 2 Journal of Science, Technology and Law 372, 374.

8.31 For example, in *Zhengzhou Yetou Internet Technology Co Ltd (Zhenghzou Yetou) v Zhejiang Tmall Network Co Ltd (Zhejiang Tmall), Xiaomei Ding and Other*,[30] Xiamen Ding (a claimant to the original dispute and the second respondent to an advance enforcement application) claimed that Zhengzhou Yetou (a defendant to the original dispute and an applicant to an advance enforcement application) had infringed her exterior design patent. After the Intermediate People's Court of Nanjing City of Jiangsu Province accepted this case, Zhejiang Tmall (the second defendant to the original dispute and the first respondent to an advance enforcement application), that had provided the online platform to the infringer, Zhengzhou Yetou, then deleted Zhengzhou Yetou's link at the online sale platform of Zhejiang Tmall on the ground of Xiamen Ding's complaint.

8.32 Zhengzhou Yetou, during the trial proceedings, submitted sufficient evidence to demonstrate the fact that any infringement of patent, if it did happen, was in effect lacking the basic legal foundation of the cause of action. Meanwhile, Zhengzhou Yetou claimed that the removal of the online sale link caused them irreparable damages, because during the period when they were removed from the link, the online sale platform was supposed to organise the "6.18" sale festival.[31] Without Zhengzhou Yetou being on the online link, it meant that Zhengzhou Yetou was deprived suddenly of an opportunity to earn huge economic benefits as they could not participate in the second biggest sale festival of that year.

8.33 Following the civil lawsuit, Zhengzhou Yetou decided to file an application to require Zhejiang Tmall to reinstate Zhengzhou Yetou on the online platform. To satisfy the requirement of advance enforcement, Zhengzhou Yetou furnished adequate security to the court.

8.34 The Intermediate People's Court of Nanjing City of Jiangsu Province considered the application for the advance enforcement. Pursuant to Articles 106 (c) "urgent circumstances" and 107 of the CPL 1991 (as amended until 2020),[32] the court held that the legal relationship between Xiaomei Ding and Zhengzhou Yetou was clear and Zhengzhou Yetou might suffer serious loss, if the online sale link was not restored immediately. Therefore, the court upheld Zhengzhou Yetou's application and requested Zhejiang Tmall (the second defendant to the original dispute and the first respondent to an

30 *Zhengzhou Yetou Internet Technology Co Ltd v Zhejiang Tmall Network Co Ltd and Other* (dispute over advance enforcement arising from the IP infringement case) [2019] Su 01 Civil Chu No 687 (the Intermediate People's Court of Nanjing City of Jiangsu Province, first instance and binding order).

31 In order to explain to readers unfamiliar with China, the "6.18" sale festival is the second biggest sale festival every year following the biggest sale festival "11.11". Both online festivals result in billions of dollars of turnover for various sellers participating on online platforms.

32 Refer to 8.21–8.22 for discussion on "urgent circumstances".

advance enforcement application) to recover the link to online platform immediately.[33]

8.35 Two crucial points come to the fore in this case. First, the removal of Zhengzhou Yetou's online sale link was based on the voluntary behaviour of one of the defendants to the original dispute, Zhejiang Tmall, rather than depending on Xiamen Ding's application for a behaviour preservation order against Zhengzhou Yetou. It means that there was no behaviour preservation order made by the court against Zhengzhou Yetou. Accordingly, Zhengzhou Yetou could not apply for reconsideration to discharge an "order" that was not yet made against them. Under these circumstances, this route of the procedural remedy of reconsideration was not available to Zhengzhou Yetou.

8.36 Secondly, in accordance with CPL 1991 (as amended until 2020), if Zhengzhou Yetou were to apply for a counterclaim against Xiamen Ding's claim, it was quite possible for Zhengzhou Yetou, as a claimant, in a counterclaim and accordingly file an application seeking behaviour preservation measures. In this context, then, Zhengzhou Yetou could have requested the behaviour preservation order stating that Zhejiang Tmall must "not" delete the online sale link or must "reinstate" the link for them on the online platform.

8.37 However, in this case, no counterclaim was filed by Zhengzhou Yetou and the route of seeking behaviour preservation measures was not adopted. It is arguable whether Zhengzhou Yetou, if he was simply one of the defendants in this case, could have been entitled to file an application, in the first place, to prevent Zhejiang Tmall from deleting the online sale link.

8.38 In contrast to such a specific scenario, as discussed in the preceding paragraphs, the order made by the Intermediate People's Court of Nanjing City of Jiangsu Province is regarded as the first case of "converse" behaviour preservation through the system of advance enforcement.[34]

8.39 It should be noted that the order of the "converse" behaviour preservation was not accepted by some legal scholars. One legal scholar contended that the system of "converse" behaviour preservation was not officially incorporated into Chinese law. Therefore, the only remedy that was available to Zhengzhou Yetou was to submit a bill of complaint (as a counterclaim). In other words, Zhengzhou Yetou should have filed a new case to request the recovery of the link to the online platform.[35]

---

33 *Zhengzhou Yetou Internet Technology Co Ltd v Zhejiang Tmall Network Co Ltd and Other* (dispute over advance enforcement arising from the IP infringement case) [2019] Su 01 Civil Chu No 687 (the Intermediate People's Court of Nanjing City of Jiangsu Province, first instance and binding order).

34 Jing Wang, 'A Court Upheld an Accused Infringer's Application for Advance Enforcement to Recover the Deleted Link' (*Legal Daily*, 16 July 2019) <www.legaldaily.com.cn/IT/content/2019-07/16/content_7935264.htm> accessed 30 July 2021.

35 Yin INT'LIP Firm, 'Different Comment on a Ruling to Recover Link' (*Yin INT'LIP Firm*, 23 July 2019) <www.suncrt.com/English/Newsen/NR5.asp?ID=909> accessed 30 July 2021.

8.40 Other legal scholars have claimed that the defendant is entitled to file an application for reinstating the online link, because the application seeking behaviour preservation measures is not the exclusive right of the claimant.[36] In other words, according to the scholars, this case was not relevant to the application seeking advance enforcement. They argued that an application seeking a behaviour preservation measure from the defendant should have been sufficient. However, in the authors' opinion, this argument that both the claimants and the respondents can seek behaviour preservation measures from the court is weak and lacks legal foundation. In consideration of the purpose of the behaviour preservation measures to secure the enforcement of the future judgment or to avoid the substantial loss of the applicant, such preservations serve the claimant's claims against the defendant. When the defendant does not file the items of claims in a dispute, there is no legal foundation to provide the provisional remedy to the defendant. Accordingly, the defendant must file a preservation application during counterclaim proceedings.[37]

8.41 There is no further official guidance available on the concept of "converse" behaviour preservation. Nonetheless, on the ground that some claimants make use of the system of behaviour preservation to obtain an order, and then employ these measures against the defendants to extract compromises, it is generally recognised that the application of "converse" behaviour preservation constitutes a kind of legal remedy for the defendants in such circumstances. Particularly, in infringement disputes, this system may prevent the claimants from abusing the procedural rights of other parties.

Advance Enforcement v Advance Judgment

8.42 An advance judgment as early as 1982 was provided by the Civil Procedure Law (for Trial Implementation) 1982.[38] The CPL 1991 (as amended until 2020) remains the complete provision. It provides:

> If some of the facts of a case being tried are evident already, the people's court may make a judgment on those facts first.[39]

---

36 Xiaohong Fang, 'The First Case "Converse Behaviour Preservation": The Wrong Nature Made by Court' (*Kuaibao*, 14 July 2019) <https://kuaibao.qq.com/s/20190714AZO09T00?refer=spider>; see also, IP Editor Team, 'A Ruling to Recover the Tmall Link: Advance Enforcement or Converse Behaviour Preservation' (*China Law Information*, 26 July 2019) <https://new.qq.com/omn/20190726/20190726A0QKZ900.html?pc> accessed 30 July 2021.

37 The discussion on the qualification of a respondent in a property preservation application can be found in Chapter 6, 6.22.

38 Civil Procedure Law of the People's Republic China (trial) 1982, Article 121.

39 CPL 1991 (as amended until 2020), Article 153.

8.43 While an advance judgment is similar to the procedural remedy of advance enforcement, it has different features. As far as the advance judgment is concerned, although this procedure does not address all the claims between parties, it can indeed make a partial judgment on the ground that a few facts of the case are evident, and it is necessary to do so. The advance judgment is therefore a final judgment made by the court on its own initiative, even if it is merely a partial judgment. In the event that the party is not satisfied with such partial judgment, that party can appeal the advance judgment to a higher court.

8.44 Conversely, an advance enforcement is a procedural remedy where urgent situations may affect the case. The order for the advance enforcement is a provisional decision rather than a substantive decision. There is no legal foundation for the losing party to appeal the advance enforcement order against them. The only remedy for the losing party is to apply for reconsideration of the procedural order. Alternatively, the party can invoke the objection procedure.[40]

8.45 In addition, the advance judgment must be able to separate other issues in a case. Otherwise, it would become impossible for the Chinese courts to apply this system of advance judgment. In terms of the application of advance judgment in practice, the SPC provides a sample with a reported case as follows.

8.46 In *Valeo Systemes D'essyage (Valeo Systems) v Xiamen Lukasi Automobile Parts Co Ltd, Xiamen Fuke Automobile Parts Co Ltd and Shaoqiang Chen*,[41] there were two main claims. First, Valeo Systems (claimant) argued that all the defendants had infringed upon its patent right; secondly, all defendants should be liable for the damages suffered as a result of this infringement.

8.47 During the civil proceedings, the Shanghai Intellectual Property Court considered that Valeo Systems (claimant) submitted sufficient evidence to demonstrate that this company was the patent owner of the invention patent, and without the procedural remedy of the advance judgment, the company would suffer irreparable damages. Pursuant to Article 153 of the CPL 1991 (as amended until 2020),[42] the Shanghai Intellectual Property Court rendered an order for advance judgment.[43]

---

40 Refer to Chapter 3 for "Reconsideration" in 3.232–3.246 and "Objection to Enforcement of a Preservation Order" in 3.247–3.257.

41 *Valeo Systemes D'essyage v Xiamen Lukasi Automobile Parts Co Ltd, Xiamen Fuke Automobile Parts Co Ltd and Shaoqiang Chen* (dispute over infringement upon invention patent) [2016] Hu 73 Civil Chu No 859 (Shanghai Intellectual Property Court, first instance court and judgment).

42 Refer to 8.42 for discussion on concept of advance judgment.

43 *Valeo Systems D'essyage v Xiamen Lukasi Automobile Parts Co Ltd, Xiamen Fuke Automobile Parts Co Ltd and Shaoqiang Chen* (dispute over infringement upon invention

8.48 Afterwards, the defendants submitted an appeal to the SPC against the advance judgment. The SPC upheld the advance judgment of the Shanghai Intellectual Property Court.[44]

8.49 It is worth noting that in this case, the SPC held that behaviour preservation measures for intellectual property disputes were an independent system and distinct from the civil procedure system. When the party filed an application seeking advance judgment to stop infringement of intellectual property rights, that party was entitled to apply to the courts simultaneously seeking the behaviour preservation measures to stop infringement.[45]

Advance Enforcement v Behaviour Preservation

8.50 Although the functions of the advance enforcement and the behaviour preservation measures to some extent seem similar, these two systems are still different.

8.51 First, the purpose of the advance enforcement is to address the urgent demand of an applicant's business and day to day needs prior to the final decision made by the court for the civil dispute on merits. It cannot be applied before the case is docked within the court system. The procedural remedy of the advance enforcement is therefore not available to parties seeking a pre-action behaviour preservation measure.

8.52 In contrast, the purpose of the procedural remedy of a behaviour preservation is to secure the enforcement of the future judgment or mitigate the applicant's loss through behaviour preservation measures against a respondent through "to do" or "not to do" orders.[46] It is available both as a pre-action as well as a post-action remedy.

8.53 Secondly, the applicants in two systems could be different. In most situations the applicants of the two systems are seeking orders against the defendants. However, as discussed in *Zhengzhou Yetou Internet Technology Co Ltd (Zhenghzou Yetou) v Zhejiang Tmall Network Co Ltd (Zhejiang*

patent) [2016] Hu 73 Civil Chu No 859 (Shanghai Intellectual Property Court, first instance court and judgment).

44 Guiding Case No 115: *Valeo Systemes D'essyage v Xiamen Lukasi Automobile Parts Co Ltd, Xiamen Fuke Automobile Parts Co Ltd and Shaoqiang Chen* (dispute over infringement upon invention patent) [2019] SPC IP Civil Final No 2 (the Supreme People's Court, second instance court and final judgment).

45 ibid, in this case, Valeo Systems had also applied for behaviour preservation measures. Since the second instance court (the SPC) made a final and binding partial judgment immediately after hearing the case, the SPC held that it was not necessary to request any behaviour preservation measure after the infringement was affirmed by the judgment. Therefore, the SPC, under these circumstances, was not in favour of granting behaviour preservation measures. However, in order to avoid misunderstanding, the SPC clarified that the behaviour preservation procedure is an independent system.

46 In terms of the purpose of the behaviour preservation measure, refer to at 8.55.

Tmall), Xiaomei Ding and Other,[47] the advance enforcement also provides an opportunity to a defendant to file an application for a "converse" behaviour preservation. In this context, the applicant is seeking order against the claimant under the main civil or commercial dispute.

8.54 All in all, the system of advance enforcement, along with its development, has achieved certain functions of behaviour preservation measures in China.

Behaviour Preservation Measures

Definition and Purpose of Behaviour Preservations

8.55 In accordance with Articles 100 and 101 of the CPL 1991 (as amended until 2020), the behaviour preservation measure can be understood as:

> In the light of the application of an interested party or a party concerned in the pre-action and post-action proceedings, a competent court makes an order to compel a respondent to do or not to do certain things, so as to ensure the enforcement of the further court judgement or the arbitral award, or preventing from the other loss of parties concerned due to the respondent's acts or other reasons.

8.56 It follows that, like the purpose of the property preservation measure, the main purpose of such preservation is to secure the enforcement of future judgments or arbitral awards, or to prevent the applicant from suffering other loss.

Definition and Purpose of Maritime Injunctions

8.57 The concept of the behaviour preservation measure is not completely equivalent to that of maritime injunction pursuant to the SMPL 2000, but the connotations associated with the two procedural systems are nearly the same. In accordance with Article 51 of the SMPL 2000, the maritime injunction can be understood as:

> The compulsory measures adopted on the application of a maritime claimant by the maritime court to compel the person against whom a claim is made to do or not to do certain things, so as to prevent the lawful rights and interest of the claimant from being infringed upon.[48]

8.58 It follows that this definition does not emphasis the purpose of the preservation of maritime injunction. Nonetheless, it is generally acknowledged

---

47 *Zhengzhou Yetou Internet Technology Co Ltd v Zhejiang Tmall Network Co Ltd and Other* (dispute over advance enforcement arising from the IP infringement case) [2019] Su 01 Civil Chu No 687 (the Intermediate People's Court of Nanjing City of Jiangsu Province, first instance and final order); refer to 8.30–8.41 for discussion on the procedural remedy of advance enforcement.

48 SMPL 2000, Article 51.

that the ultimate purpose of such preservation, like that of the behaviour preservation, is to assist the enforcement of the future judgment, if the applicant wins the case.[49]

Overview of Applicable Laws

8.59 The procedural remedy of the maritime injunction, pursuant to the SMPL 1999 and *Interpretations on the Application of the Special Maritime Procedure Law of the People's Republic of China* (2008 Adjustment) has been well-developed over the years. Nonetheless, if on some issue no relevant provision can be found in the SMPL 2000 and its Interpretation, then in that case, the CPL 1991 (as amended until 2020) and its Interpretation (2020 Amendment) will be applied to fill the gaps. In this book, the authors will only briefly discuss the SMPL 2000.

8.60 Apart from maritime injunctions, the general rules applicable for the behaviour preservation measures are currently incorporated alongside those of property preservation in the CPL 1991 (as amended until 2020).[50] This means that, in a wider sense, the requirements and standards of two types of preservation applications are the same, even if the measures for which the behaviour preservations are requested are different from those of the property preservations.

8.61 On top of the general rules provided by legislations, unlike the property preservation measure, there is no judicial interpretation on the behaviour preservation measure that has been provided by the SPC. Also, few regional interpretations from the local courts are available for the stakeholders. For example, among the regional courts discussed in Chapter 6, only Shanghai and Hunan have clarified the requirements and prerequisites for behaviour preservation measures in *Provisions of the Shanghai High People's Court on Property Preservation* (2017 amendment) (hereinafter referred to as "Provisions on Shanghai Property Preservation 2017")[51] and *Procedure of the Hunan High People's Court on Property Preservation* 2015 (hereinafter referred to as "Procedure on Hunan Property Preservation 2015").[52] It is provided that applications for behaviour preservation measures may refer to the guidance of the property preservation measure in the CPL 1991 (as amended until 2020) in scenarios where no suitable guidance or interpretation is

49 Liang Zhao and Lianjun Li, *Maritime Law and Practice in China* (1st Edn, Informa Law from Routledge 2017) para. 21.6.

50 CPL 1991 (as amended until 2020), Articles 100 and 101.

51 *Provisions of the Shanghai High People's Court on Property Preservation (2017 amendment)* (hereinafter referred to as "Provisions on Shanghai Property Preservation 2017") (Hu Gao Fa (Shen) [2014] No 3).

52 *Procedure of the Hunan High People's Court on Property Preservation* (Xiang Gao Fa Ban Fa [2015] No 3).

available.[53] Because most local courts do not provide similar guidance, how it is that these local courts resolve the issues arising from the behaviour preservation application is not clear if the CPL 1991 (as amended until 2020) and the relevant interpretations are silent.

8.62 Unlike the above scenario, five years after the introduction of the procedural remedy of behaviour preservation measures in the CPL 1991 (as amended until 2020), and taking into account the complexity of IP and unfair competition disputes, the SPC issued *Provisions on Several Issues Concerning the Application of Law in Cases Involving the Review of Behaviour Preservation in Intellectual Property Disputes 2018* (hereinafter referred to as "Interpretation of IP Behaviour Preservation 2018")[54] to provide specific guidance to stakeholders seeking behaviour preservation measures in IP and unfair competition disputes. It is emphasised that, pursuant to Article 1 of Interpretation of IP Behaviour Preservation 2018, "intellectual property disputes" include disputes over intellectual property rights and unfair competition under the *Notice of the Supreme People's Court on Issuing the Revised Provisions on Causes of Action in Civil Cases.*[55] Therefore, the IP behaviour preservation in this chapter will refer to IP and unfair competition behaviour preservation measures, unless otherwise described by the authors.

8.63 In Chinese legal practice, the guidance available from the courts for behaviour preservation measures in IP disputes may also be employed in non-IP disputes pursuant to the CPL 1991 regime. This will remain the case until a separate guidance or set of interpretations for obtaining behaviour preservation measures is provided by the courts for non-IP disputes.

Applicable Law of Intellectual Property Disputes

8.64 Under the circumstances stated above, with regard to the applicable law for seeking IP behaviour preservation measures, there are three IP laws that specifically provide the rules for obtaining behaviour preservation measures. Therefore, applicants in IP disputes seeking behaviour preservation measures must first comply with the three specific IP laws including the Patent Law 1985 (2020 Amendment), the Copyright Law 1991 (2020 Amendment) and the Trademark Law 1983 (2019 amendment). These laws will prevail over the CPL 1991 (as amended until 2020). If the above three laws in the domain of IP are silent on the specific legal issues, then the applicants can

---

53 Provisions on Shanghai Property Preservation 2017, Article 119; see also, Procedure on Hunan Property Preservation 2015, Article 27.

54 *Provisions of the Supreme People's Court on Several Issues Concerning the Application of Law in Cases Involving the Review of Behaviour Preservation in Intellectual Property Disputes* (Fa Shi [2018] No 21).

55 *Notice of the Supreme People's Court on Issuing the Revised Provisions on Causes of Action in Civil Cases* (Fa [2011] No 42).

seek guidance from the judicial interpretations including the Interpretation of IP Behaviour Preservation 2018, other two IP interpretations stated below and the Interpretation of CPL 2015 (2020 Amendment).

8.65 The three IP laws are not examined in this book in great detail. The order of applicable law in IP disputes is first to refer to the CPL 1991 (as amended until 2020), the Interpretation of IP Behaviour Preservation 2018, the two interpretations on patent rights and trademark rights and the Interpretation of CPL 2015 (2020 Amendment). If there is no local courts' guidance concerning IP behaviour preservation measures, the interpretations and guidance available for seeking property preservations measures will be considered by the legal practitioners. However, the guidance on property preservation measures is applicable only when there is no equivalent guidance available to seek behaviour preservation measures in those circumstances.

Applicable Law of Non-Intellectual Property Disputes

8.66 As discussed in 8.61, there is no interpretation on the behaviour preservation measures in non-IP disputes handed down by the SPC. Therefore, the applicable laws would be the CPL 1991 (as amended until 2020). For such applications, the guidance that is applicable for seeking property preservation orders can be utilised to fill in the gaps in law due to the fact that both property and behaviour preservation measures are stipulated in the same provision under the CPL 1991 (as amended until 2020). In addition, in legal practice, the Interpretation of IP Behaviour Preservation 2018 is also considered even in applications concerning non-IP disputes. Furthermore, as discussed in 8.61, certain regional guidance, such as Provisions on Shanghai Property Preservation 2017 and Procedure on Hunan Property Preservation 2015, has authorised the local courts to apply these rules in the context of applications seeking behaviour preservation measures.

8.67 In the above scenario, in legal practice, it is advised that the first step is to distinguish between the procedural issue and the substantive issue in the context of behaviour preservation measures. In the context of the procedural issues, such as the format of the application, and the time limit of a behaviour preservation order, the Interpretation of IP Behaviour Preservation 2018 can be applied directly, unless the procedural issue in IP disputes is not suitable for non-IP disputes. For example, there is an interim hearing procedure for IP disputes due to the fact that the IP disputes are complex;[56] thereby, this procedure is not suitable for non-IP disputes.[57] As far as the substantive issue is concerned, such as the prerequisites for an application, the Chinese courts may first examine the nature of the dispute and the exact measures

56 Refer to 8.149.
57 Refer to 8.155.

required pursuant to the behaviour preservation order. Thereafter, certain regional courts may choose to abide by the local legal guidance documents as long as such guidance does not violate the primary law. In addition, the local courts may determine which of the two interpretations, that is, for the property preservation measure or the IP behaviour preservation measure, is more suitable for an application seeking behaviour preservation measures in non-IP disputes.

8.68 However, in practice, how a local court applies the relevant legislation, interpretations and local guidance to examine an application seeking non-IP behaviour preservations is uncertain and not clear. Thus, applicable laws and their operation in non-IP practice are merely based on the authors' consideration.

Format of the Preservation Applications

8.69 In accordance with Article 4 of the Interpretation of IP Behaviour Preservation 2018, in order to apply for the behaviour preservation measures, an applicant, namely an interested party or a party concerned, must file an application accompanied by relevant evidential materials to the competent court.[58] The application must set out the following compulsory elements that are required by the courts:

(a) The identity, delivery addresses and contact information of the applicant and the respondent.
(b) The content and time limit of the preservation measure.
(c) The facts and reasons on which the application is based, including the specific description of, for example, the irreparable loss in the lawful rights and interests to be suffered by the applicant and the potential difficulty in the enforcement of the judgment of the case due to the respondent's behaviour.
(d) The information of the secured property or credit certification for application of behaviour preservation, or reasons for not providing security.
(e) Other matters which need to be stated.[59]

8.70 The compulsory features required in any application to seek behaviour preservation measures will remain the same at both the pre-action and post-action stages, and are not restricted in IP disputes. At the post-action stage, the competent court may even render the behaviour preservation measures on

58 In terms of how an applicant including a maritime applicant can find a competent court, refer to Chapter 3, 3.51–3.91. In terms of an application seeking IP behaviour preservation measures, if an applicant wants to apply for them in Beijing, Shanghai and Guangzhou, the Intellectual Property Courts in these three areas prevail.

59 Interpretation of IP Behaviour Preservation 2018, Article 4.

its own initiative without even waiting for an application to be brought by the applicant or any other interested party.

8.71 In terms of a maritime injunction, the SMPL 2000 does not provide that a maritime court can grant maritime injunction measures on its own initiative.

Meaning and Qualification of an Applicant

8.72 The general information required of an applicant for any letter of application seeking behaviour preservation measures is similar to the one discussed in the context of property preservation measures in Chapter 6, 6.20–6.28. If a defendant does not institute a counterclaim, whether he is entitled to file a behaviour preservation measure can be found 8.40. In this section, further analysis is done with regard to the scope and qualification of an applicant in an intellectual property dispute.

8.73 In any intellectual property dispute, some parties that are not the owner of the intellectual property often enjoy or use rights of the intellectual property based on a contract or other legal relationship with the actual owner. These parties are additional authorised parties in these intellectual property disputes. However, the rights of such additional authorised parties will hinge on the category of authorisation and accordingly their powers will be different.

8.74 In this context, in an IP infringement dispute, whether these authorised parties are entitled to file an application seeking behaviour preservation measures will depend entirely on the category of the IP contract. These IP contracts will generally grant a licence to the authorised parties according to the original right holder's will in relation to the subject matter of the contract, that is, the intellectual property rights.

8.75 As prescribed by Article 2 of the Interpretation of IP Behaviour Preservation 2018, it is stipulated that

> Where a licensee of an intellectual property license contract applies for an order to stop the infringement of intellectual property rights before trial, a licensee of an exclusive license contract may apply to the court separately; a licensee of a sole license contract may apply separately if the right holder does not apply to the court; a licensee of an ordinary license contract may, when explicitly authorised by the right holder to file a lawsuit in his own name, apply to the court separately.[60]

8.76 There is no specific provision on the issue in relation to other terms of IP disputes, such as a contract and declaratory judgment for a title to IP rights. However, in light of the opinion by the senior judges of the SPC, whether an authorised party is suitably qualified to file an application for

60 Interpretation of IP Behaviour Preservation 2018, Article 2.

behaviour preservation measures will depend entirely on whether the party can come within the ambit of the dispute as a connected party.[61] In other words, if the authorised party is a claimant, a defendant or a third party litigant in a dispute, then that party can file an application to seek behaviour preservation measures.

Meaning of Respondent

8.77 At 6.20–6.28 of Chapter 6, in the context of property preservation measures, it has been discussed that a respondent is a party connected to a dispute. This section will compare a few issues in the case of property preservation measures.

8.78 An outside party may be involved in seeking the property preservation measures as a result of the outside party's property which may become the subject matter of the property preservation measure.[62] However, such instances are rare in legal practice. Alternatively, an outside party, such as the housing registration department or the respondent's debtor, may assist in the enforcement of the property preservation order. However, in general, the outside party cannot generally become the respondent in applications seeking property preservation measures.

8.79 In the context of the behaviour preservation measure, the situation is very different. An applicant may directly request such measures against the outside party. In other words, even if the outside party is not the defendant in a dispute, an applicant may request such outside party "to do" or "not to do" certain things. Nonetheless, in legal practice in China, the applicant regularly lists the outside party not only as the respondent in an application seeking behaviour preservation measures, but also as the third party litigant in the bill of complaint.

8.80 For example, in *SINOHYDRO Engineering Bureau 4 Co Ltd v China CAMA Engineering Co Ltd and China Construction Bank (Xining Railway Branch)*,[63] due to a dispute concerning fraud associated with independent letters of guarantee, SINOHYDRO Engineering Bureau 4 Co Ltd (applicant),

61 Xiaoming Song, Chuang Wang, Junli Xia and Guimei Lang, 'Understanding and Application of Provisions of the Supreme People's Court on Several Issues Concerning the Application of Law in Cases Involving the Review of Behaviour Preservation in Intellectual Property Disputes' (2019) 7 The People's Judicature (Applied) 19, 21.

62 The meaning of an outside party can be found in Chapter 3, 3.226–3.231; the scope of the "outside party's" property can be found in Chapter 6, 6.42–6.43.

63 *SINOHYDRO Engineering Bureau 4 Co Ltd v China CAMA Engineering Co Ltd and China Construction Bank (Xining Railway Branch)* (an application for a behaviour preservation order) [2015] Qing Civil Bao Zi No 29 (the High People's Court of Qinghai Province, first instance and binding order); *SINOHYDRO Engineering Bureau 4 Co Ltd v China Construction Bank (Xining Railway Branch) and China CAMA Engineering Co Ltd* (a dispute over fraudulent independent letters of guarantee) [2019] SPC Civil Final No 349 (the Supreme People's Court, second instance and binding judgment).

filed an application for a pre-action behaviour preservation measure to stop China Construction Bank (respondent) from paying two letters of guarantee (RMB 66,315,000 and RMB 23,210,247) issued to *China CAMA Engineering Co Ltd*. The High People's Court of Qinghai Province was in favour of this application.

8.81 With regard to the legal status of China Construction Bank, when the applicant first submitted a bill of complaint to the court, China Construction Bank was not named as the respondent in the application seeking preservation measures but was instead included in the application as the third party litigant.[64]

8.82 The above cases demonstrate that, pursuant to Articles 100 and 101 (behaviour preservation measures) of the CPL 1991 (as amended until 2020), an applicant in legal practice may directly request a third party, as a respondent, "to do" or "not to do" certain things.

Scope of Behaviour Preservation Measures

8.83 The property preservation measures are regarded as the most important preservation measures in the Chinese legal system, but their disadvantage stems from the fact that the application is simply restricted to disputes arising from the payment or the delivery of property. Other types of actions, such as a declaratory judgment, an action for performance or an action for formation, cannot invoke the application for the property preservation measures.[65] From this point of view, the establishment of the behaviour preservation system through the amendment to the CPL in 2012 was a major step forward. The behaviour preservation system filled the gaps in situations arising from the discussed disadvantages associated with the property preservation measures.

64 ibid. It must be emphasised that in the final judgment made by the SPC, the SPC did not confirm that this preservation measure order constituted a behaviour preservation order, but instead they opined that the order granted was a property preservation measure. However, in the final judgment, the SPC also did not negate the Qinghai High People's Court's behaviour preservation order in the first instance; see also, *Huyuan Tongtai(Cambodia)Agricultural Technology development Co Ltd and Bank of China (Jiangsu Branch) v High Hope Int'l Group Jiangsu Champion Holdings Ltd* (an application for a behaviour preservation order) [2016] Su 01 Civil Chu No 849 (the Intermediate People's Court of Nanjing City of Jiangsu Province, first instance and binding order), [2016] Su Xing Bao Fu No 1 (the High People's Court of Jiangsu Province, second instance, final and binding order), where in a similar case, both the Intermediate People's Court of Nanjing City of Jiangsu Province and the High People's Court of Jiangsu Province held that an application for stopping the bank (the third party litigant) performing the letter of guarantee constituted a behaviour preservation measure. It can thus be seen that the area of behaviour preservation measures generates lots of debates.

65 Shaoping Zhang, Jiangming Li and Tufeng Zhu, 'Understanding and Judicial Application of the Behaviour Preservation System: Judges Forum No 73' (*Trial Research*, 16 July 2014) <https://mp.weixin.qq.com/s/JPq1XyjDnyNEkjIBr6Ankg> accessed 30 July 2021.

8.84 In terms of the scope of the application of the behaviour preservation measures, apart from IP and maritime disputes, they are available according to the category of the causes of action in other civil or commercial disputes including personality rights, marriage and family disputes, succession disputes, real rights, contractual disputes, *negotiorum gestio*, unjust enrichment and so forth.[66] In other words, there is no limitation on disputes in which the procedural remedy of behaviour preservation measures could be available to the parties to disputes.[67]

8.85 In this context, since the amendment to the CPL 2012, the behaviour preservation measure has been to a great extent applied in such disputes as discussed in the preceding paragraphs. The positive effects have been noticed by various stakeholders.

Positive Effect (I): Behaviour Preservation Measures in Family Disputes

8.86 In a marriage and family dispute, prior to 2012, even though a few Chinese courts had issued "personal safety protection orders" on the ground that a spouse suffered from domestic violence, the explicit legal foundation for such orders was in reality absent.[68]

8.87 After the establishment of the behaviour preservation system in 2012, the Primary People's Court of Shunyi District of Beijing Municipality issued China's first pre-action personal safety protection order on 12 August 2013, pursuant to Article 101 of the CPL 1991 (as amendment until 2020). This order was rendered after an applicant had submitted relevant evidence to prove the existing domestic violence but before she had brought the divorce case to the court.[69] Accordingly, these days, the applicant can apply to the

66 *Notice of the Supreme People's Court on Issuing the Revised Provisions on Causes of Action in Civil Cases* (Fa [2011] No 42); it should be noted that in theory there is no limitation of disputes; in practice because of the absence of knowledge on the behaviour preservation application, some scholars consider that this preservation may not operate well in all disputes. For this reason, the Civil Code (expected to come into effect on 1 January 2021) stipulates a new rule, "injunction for infringement of personality rights" (Article 997 of the Civil Code); refer to 8.2.

67 Shaoping Zhang, Jiangming Li and Tufeng Zhu, 'Understanding and Judicial Application of the Behaviour Preservation System: Judges Forum No 73' (*Trial Research*, 16 July 2014) <https://mp.weixin.qq.com/s/JPq1XyjDnyNEkjIBr6Ankg> accessed 30 July 2021.

68 The first personal safety protection order in China was issued by Jiangsu Wuxi Chong'an District People's Court on 6 August 2008; but the legal foundation on which order was founded actually relied on *Guidance for Hearing Marriage Cases Involving Domestic Violence* by the China Institute of Applied Jurisprudence of the Supreme People's Court (March 2008); see also, Chen Jinhong and Yang Huiyu, 'An Analysis of Civil Protection Order System in China' (*China Social Science University Humanity*, 2015) <sinoss.net/uploadfile/2015/0513/20150513085357381.pdf> accessed 15 July 2021.

69 Jingxia Guo and Xiuzhi Yang, 'Beijing Issued the First Pre-Action "Personal Safety Protection Order"' *People's Court Daily* (Beijing, 17 August 2013).

courts seeking behaviour preservation orders against domestic violence. Furthermore, in such cases no behaviour preservation fee is charged and even no security is requested by the court from the applicants.[70]

Positive Effect (II): Behaviour Preservation Measures in Commercial Disputes

8.88 Another positive effect is to provide more remedies to the parties to commercial contracts. For example, prior to the establishment of the behaviour preservation system, in the face of legal issues concerning the suspension of a letter of credit, the SPC had to expand the scope of the application of property preservation measures in the CPL 1991[71] and then allowed the party concerned to apply for a "Suspension Order of Letter of Credit" pursuant to *Provisions of the Supreme People's Court on Some Issues Concerning the Trial of Cases of Disputes over Letter of Credit (2020 Amendment)*.[72] However, this Suspension Order not only lacked legal foundation, but it also granted the courts wide discretionary power as the issues were not clear-cut without any intervention of legislation.

8.89 After the establishment of behaviour preservation in the CPL 2012, as discussed in 8.80–8.81, in a dispute over a letter of guarantee, an applicant as a creditor may directly file an application seeking pre-action behaviour preservation measures against a bank. The order would seek to stop the bank from performing the payment obligation based on the letter of guarantee provided by the debtor. This situation fills in the gaps in the Suspension Order.

Current Issues (I): Lack of Unified Standard of Subject Matter

8.90 In general, the subject matter of the behaviour preservation measure only refers to a kind of behaviour or conduct that a respondent "must do" or "not do" pursuant to the behaviour preservation order. Due to the absence of detailed guidance handed down by the SPC on behaviour preservation measures, in legal practice, as long as the application for a behaviour preservation is relevant and satisfies the requirements of law, there is no restriction on the subject matter where behaviour preservation measures can be applied. However, owing to lack of guidance, two legal issues arise.

8.91 First, there is no unified standard to identify the subject matter of the behaviour preservation measures. In certain disputes, for example, in an

70 *Official Reply of the Supreme People's Court Regarding Certain Procedural Issues in Personal Safety Protective Order Cases* (Fa Shi [2016] No 15).

71 In the CPL 1991, Article 94 merely provides the property preservation measure.

72 *Provisions of the Supreme People's Court on Some Issues Concerning the Trial of Cases of Disputes over Letter of Credit (2020 Amendment)* (Fa Shi [2005] No 13) (superseded by Fa Shi [2020] No 18), Article 11.

infringement dispute, it is relatively easy for lawyers and judges to evaluate the subject matter of the behaviour preservation measure. In other disputes, as long as an applicant in a letter of application states a kind of tortious behaviour that he was facing, such as invading the rights of the applicant or seizing the property belonging to the applicant,[73] impeding the applicant's work,[74] such kinds of tortious behaviour can straightaway become the subject matter of the behaviour preservation order.

8.92 However, it's not always easy to determine the subject matter of the behaviour preservation measure. For example, in contractual disputes, the answer might not be clear-cut in all cases.

8.93 For example, in a contract related to the sale and purchase of a hotel, a seller (applicant) could apply to stop the renovation of the hotel after a dispute between the seller (applicant) and the buyer (respondent) arose. The court assessed the application on the ground that the behaviour preservation measure directly aimed at the subject matter of the contract, namely the hotel, had left the court in no doubt that the requested order was to stop the decoration of the hotel by the buyer.[75]

8.94 However, if the application is not directly against the subject matter of the contract, it is arguable in legal practice whether an application

---

73 For example, in *Yuqing Zhang and Others v Binzhou Zhanhua District Xiawa County Village Committee and Zhanmin Qi* (an application for a behaviour preservation) [2019] Lu 1603 Zhi Bao No 181 (the Primary People's Court of Binzhou District of Zhanhua of Shandong Province, first instance and binding order), on the ground that Village Committee and Zhanmin Qi (respondents) collected the soil from the applicants' contracted land, several applicants filed an application seeking behaviour preservation measures that could end the practice of respondents freely collecting the soil. The court's behaviour preservation order was in favour of the applicants.

74 For example, in *Ankang Garden Construction Engineering Co Ltd (Zhenping Branch) v Changbing Li and Zhuoyuan Li* (an application seeking a behaviour preservation order) [2014] Zhen Ping Civil Chu Zi No 00087 (the Primary People's Court of Zhenping County of Ankang City of Shaanxi Province, first instance and behaviour preservation order), Ankang Garden Construction Engineering Co Ltd (Zhenping Branch) (applicant) claimed that the applicant's construction project was impeded by Changbing Li's and Zhuoyua Li's conduct (respondents). Therefore, the applicant filed an application to prevent the two respondents from their impeding the construction project. The court upheld the application and accordingly granted the behaviour preservation order. However, it should be noted that the court later discharged the order on the ground that the applicant could not provide a construction permit as evidence. Nonetheless, the reason for discharging this order is not associated with the reasonableness of seeking such a behaviour preservation order; see also, *Ankang Garden Construction Engineering Co Ltd (Zhenping Branch) v Changbing Li and Zhuoyuan Li* (an application seeking a behaviour preservation order) [2014] Zhen Ping Civil Chu Zi No 00087-1 (the Primary People's Court of Zhenping County of Ankang City of Shaanxi Province, reconsideration and binding order).

75 For example, in *Liuzhou Jianyu Real Estate Development Co Ltd (Jianyu) v Liuzhou City Investment and Construction Development Co Ltd (Liuzhou City)* (dispute over a contract) [2017] Gui Civil Chu No 7 (the High People's Court of Guangxi Zhuang Autonomous Region, first instance and binding order), Jianyu filed an application for a behaviour preservation measure to prevent Liuzhou City from further decorating the hotel and to prevent them from promoting the hotel. The High People's Court of Guangxi Zhuang Autonomous Region granted the preservation order allowing Jianyu's application.

will reasonably be accepted by the courts. There is no unified standard on this issue. Some courts take a flexible attitude toward such applications. For example, in *Sujing Wang v Zhihua Liao*,[76] during negotiation of a sale and purchase agreement, Sujing Wang (the seller), promised not to use the student enrolment quota that was registered in the name of house. The purpose of Sujing Wang (the buyer) in purchasing this house was to use this quota for his child. The buyer relied on the seller's promise and signed the contract to purchase the property. Thereafter, the seller attempted to terminate the contract by using the quota for his own child. As a result, the buyer filed an application seeking behaviour preservation measures to prevent the seller from using the quota associated with the house.[77]

8.95 In this case, the subject matter of the application seeking behaviour preservation measures was not just the subject matter of the contract. It raised the question whether the behaviour preservation application could be reasonable. The Primary People's Court of Haidian District of Beijing Municipality held that the buyer could not use the student quota again according to the educational policy, if the seller had already used the student enrolment quota. Accordingly, the buyer would have suffered irreparable harms. Pursuant to Article 100 of the CPL 1991 (as amended until 2020), the buyer's application satisfied the court with the twin requirements of "irreparable harms" and "urgent circumstances". Therefore, the court rendered an order that prohibited the seller from using the student enrolment quota associated with the property.[78]

8.96 However, the above order to take measures on the indirect subject matter of the contract is not commonplace because the order rendered had to rely on the substantive examination of the merit of the fact. The absence of any common standard means that the identification of the subject matter of the behaviour preservation measure must heavily rely on the court's exercise of its discretionary power. This in effect raises some uncertainty for

76 *Sujing Wang v Zhihua Liao* (dispute over a sale and purchase agreement) [2016] Jing 0108 Civil Chu No 16170 (the Primary People's Court of Haidian District of Beijing Municipality, first instance and binding order).

77 ibid.

78 *Sujing Wang v Zhihua Liao* (dispute over a sale and purchase agreement) [2016] Jing 0108 Civil Chu No 16170 (the Primary People's Court of Haidian District of Beijing Municipality, first instance and binding order); see also, Geng Zhao and Yang Xu, 'A Student Enrollment Quota Depending on Housing Register Can Be the Subject Matter of the Behaviour Preservation Measure' in the China Institute of Applied Jurisprudence of the Supreme People's Court (ed.), *China Law Reports (2017) 2* (People's Court Press, 2017) 109. According to Beijing educational policy, the location of the housing register may decide whether a child has qualification to enrol in a particular local school. For this reason, housing prices near a highly regarded school are relatively expensive, compared with prices of houses near an ordinary school. In order for the child to register at a highly regarded school, the parents are willing to buy an expensive house nearby a famous school. However, in order to control the abuse of enrolment, only one student can utilise the enrolment quota every six years. For this reason, in this case, if the seller used the quota, the buyer could not have used it for the next six years. Therefore, due to the seller's conduct, the main purpose of buying the house would have gone to waste.

stakeholders as to whether they could seek an appropriate behaviour preservation order from the courts.

Current Issues (II): Confusion between the Behaviour and Property Preservation Measures

8.97 The second issue arises from the confusion of the subject matter between the behaviour preservation and property preservation measures. In China, the length of judicial experience in the area of behaviour preservation measures pursuant to the CPL 1991 (as amended until 2020) amounts to just eight years from 2012 to 2020. Therefore, it is a fact that some Chinese courts lack experience in distinguishing the subject matter of the behaviour preservation measures from that of the subject matter of the property preservation measures.

8.98 For example, in the "lucky" mobile number 8888888 case introduced in 6.35 of Chapter 6, the Jiangsu Wuzhong People's Court accepted an application seeking property preservation measures to seal up a "lucky" mobile number 8888888 to prevent it from being transferred to another owner. The key legal issue in this case was that the court treated the lucky mobile number as the respondent's virtual property.[79] In this context, when the preservation measure was clearly directed at the virtual property, it was reasonable to argue that the relevant subject matter for preservation measures was the property.

8.99 While the court granted the property preservation measure for sealing up the "lucky" mobile number, it could equally be argued that the fundamental purpose was to prevent the respondent from transferring the telephone number. Accordingly, the applicant was in fact seeking a preservation order to prevent the respondent from doing a certain thing.

8.100 Another example is in *Haibo Shi v China Mobile Zhejiang Co Ltd* (Jinyun Branch),[80] where China Mobile contended that Haibo Shi, holder of a mobile phone number, did not perform registration obligations in relation to the Identification Card and accordingly Haibo's number was cancelled. In other words, Haibo could not hold this mobile number anymore. In this context, Haibo (applicant) filed an application to prevent China Mobile (respondent) from disposing of a mobile number that Haibo had been using. The Intermediate People's Court of Lishui City of Zhejiang Province ruled in favour of the applicant and also treated this application as a behaviour preservation measure.[81]

79 Jie He, 'Debt Is Not Repaid, Debtor's Mobile Phone Number Ending in 888888 Was Seized' *Xian Dai Kuai Bao* (Jiangsu, 22 November 2019).

80 *Haibo Shi v China Mobile Zhejiang Co Ltd* (Jinyun Branch) (dispute over telecommunication service contract) [2016] Zhe 1122 Civil Chu No 3552 (the Intermediate People's Court of Lishui City of Zhejiang Province, first instance and binding order).

81 ibid.

Requirements for Behaviour Preservation Applications in Non-IP Disputes

8.101 As discussed in 8.66–8.68, the requirements relevant for applications seeking behaviour preservation measures in non-IP disputes may apply the following laws and Interpretations – the Interpretation of IP Behaviour Preservation 2018, *Provisions of the Supreme People's Court on Several Issues Concerning the Handling of Property Preservation Cases by the People's Courts (2020 Amendment)* (hereinafter referred to as "Interpretation of Property Preservation (2020 Amendment)"),[82] the Interpretation of Property Preservation (2020 Amendment) or regional legal guidance documents.[83] The application of one of the Interpretations will depend on the nature of the disputes and the exact measures of behaviour preservation that are requested through the applications. If the Interpretation of Property Preservation (2020 Amendment) is more suitable, the reader can refer to "substantive requirements" in Chapter 6, 6.76–6.85 of the book. If the application for the behaviour preservation in non-IP disputes involves a similar nature and measure as the application in IP disputes, the rules in IP disputes will be applied to the non-IP preservation applications as well. It must be emphasised that the purpose of the behaviour preservation measure is to ensure the enforcement of further court judgments or arbitral awards, or to prevent loss to the applicants. Therefore, whether the dispute is non-IP or IP, in the context of the pre-action or post-action preservation applications, it is necessary for the courts to examine whether future judgments or arbitral awards will remain achievable or be difficult to enforce. At the same time, the courts will evaluate whether, due to the respondents' conduct or any other reasons, damage or loss may be caused to the applicant. In light of this, the applicants need to demonstrate that it is likely that the enforcement of future judgments or arbitral awards may become impossible, or damage or loss may occur to the applicants without behaviour preservation orders.

Requirements for Urgent Behaviour Preservation Applications in IP Disputes

8.102 Apart from the consideration of whether a future judgment will become impossible or difficult to enforce and whether the respondent's conduct or other reasons may cause damage to the applicant, and the requirement of security in IP and non-IP disputes which will be discussed in 8.138–8.142,

82 *Provisions of the Supreme People's Court on Several Issues Concerning the Handling of Property Preservation Cases by the People's Courts (2020 Amendment)* (Fa Shi [2016] No 22) (superseded by Fa Shi [2020] No 21).

83 For example, Provisions on Shanghai Property Preservation 2017 and Procedure on Hunan Property Preservation 2015.

there are mainly four requirements for urgent IP behaviour preservation measures provided by the Interpretation of IP Behaviour Preservation 2018 discussed in 8.104–8.134.

8.103 It should be noted that although these four requirements are stressed in the applications seeking the urgent preservation measures, they may also be applied during non-urgent application proceedings in 8.135–8.136 from case to case.

Requirement for Urgent Applications (I): Urgent Circumstances

8.104 Both Articles 100(c) for a post-action behaviour preservation application and 101(a) for a pre-action behaviour preservation application of the CPL 1991 (as amended until 2020) refer to the requirements of "urgent circumstances" that must be defined in the applications. For pre-action behaviour preservation applications, applicants must clarify the "urgent circumstances" that are deemed as a mandatory requirement. On the other hand, for post-action applications, clarifying urgent circumstances is only prerequisite in those circumstances where the applicants request the court through an application to grant a behaviour preservation order within 48 hours of submitting the application.

8.105 Article 6 of the Interpretation of IP Behaviour Preservation 2018 provides for five particular situations that will constitute "urgent circumstances". They are as follows:

(a) the applicant's trade secret is about to be illegally disclosed;
(b) the applicant's right of publication, privacy, etc. will be infringed upon;
(c) the intellectual property right involved in the dispute will soon be illegally disposed of;
(d) the applicant's intellectual property right is being or will be infringed upon at a time-sensitive occasion such as a trade fair;
(e) a time-sensitive hot-spot show is or will be infringed upon; or
(f) other circumstances requiring immediate act of preservation measures.[84]

8.106 The last broad circumstance pursuant to Article 6 (f) in the above Interpretation clearly grants the discretionary power to judges to determine whether the circumstances may be deemed "urgent" or "not urgent". Provisions of other urgent circumstances as categorised from paragraphs (a) to (e) of Article 6 have been employed often by judges during judicial practice before the issue of the Interpretation of IP Behaviour Preservation 2018.

8.107 For example, Article 6 (a) of the Interpretation requires an illegal disclosure of trade secrets to be classed as one of the "urgent circumstances". It

84 Interpretation of IP Behaviour Preservation 2018, Article 6.

is considered that this requirement can be stated in detail in the first application seeking the behaviour preservation measures arising from the infringement of know-how. In *Eli Lilly (US) Co and Eli Lilly (China) Co v Mengwei Huang*,[85] Mengwei Huang (respondent) downloaded 21 confidential documents belonging to Eli Lilly (US) Co and Eli Lilly (China) Co (two applicants) without the two companies' consent. The two companies then filed an application to stop Mengwei Huang disclosing their trade secrets, using or allowing others to use 21 confidential documents. The First Intermediate People's Court of Shanghai Municipality granted the behaviour preservation measures against Mengwei Huang.[86]

8.108 In the case of *Eli Lilly*, the two judges shed light on the legal reasoning before they granted the behaviour preservation order. They opined that how to evaluate the meaning of the "illegal disclosure" to arise "urgent circumstance" should mainly consider the following situation:

> The confidential documents had been under the control of the respondent. Once the respondent leaked the documents, the applicant's competitors might obtain them directly. Alternatively, after the documents were disclosed to the public, the confidentiality of these documents would be lost.[87]

8.109 Apart from the example of "the illegal disclosure", the consideration of "time-sensitive" circumstances in Articles 6 (d) and (e) of the Interpretation is relevant to the first application seeking the pre-action behaviour preservation arising from a copyright dispute.

8.110 In *Jikang Yang (pseudonym: Yang Jiang) v Sungari International Auction Co Ltd and Guoqiang Li*,[88] Jikang Yang (applicant) applied for behaviour preservation measures. The fact of the case was that Jikang Yang's husband, Zhongshu Qian (a famous writer and scholar in literature in China), and daughter, Yuan Qian, died a few years previously. Before they passed away, Zhongshu Qian, Yuan Qian and Jikang Yang (applicant) had frequently communicated with Guoqiang Li (one of the respondents) by written letters

85 *Eli Lilly (US) Co and Other v Mengwei Huang* (an application for a behaviour preservation measure arising from the infringement of know-how) [2013] Hu Yi Zhong Civil Wu (Zhi) Chu Zi No 119 (the First Intermediate People's Court of Shanghai Municipality, first instance and binding order); this case has been codified into Gazette Case of the Supreme People's Court in [2014] 5 (211).

86 ibid.

87 Zheng Tang and Changli Lv, 'The Application of a Behaviour Preservation in an Infringement of Know-How' (2013) 22 The People's Judicature (Case) 48, 49 (the original language is Chinese. The authors translated the Chinese into English).

88 No 3 of Top 10 IP Typical Disputes of Chinese People's Courts (2013): *Jikang Yang (pseudonym: Yang Jiang) v Sungari International Auction Co Ltd and Guoqiang Li* (dispute over a pre-action behaviour preservation order) [2013] Er Zhong Bao Zi Di No 9727 (the Second Intermediate People's Court of Beijing Municipality, first instance and binding order); *Sungari International Auction Co Ltd v Jikang Yang (pseudonym: Yang Jiang) and Other* (dispute over copyright and infringe) [2013] Go Civil Final Zi Di No 1152 (the High People's Court of Beijing Municipality, second instance and binding judgment).

in the past. The manuscripts of those private letters written were collated and preserved by Guoqiang Li.

8.111 However, in May 2013, it came to light that Sungari International Auction Co Ltd (Sungari company, one of the respondents), in its auction of 2013 (21 June), intended to make those manuscripts public, and as a result the Sungari company would auction hundreds of manuscripts of those private letters. Prior to the auction, the Sungari company had disclosed some details of private letters by way of photos for promotion (20 May 2013) and then organised a seminar on the content of the private letters (1 June 2013).

8.112 Jikang Yang asserted copyright on those letters and clarified that she did not agree to publish such manuscript of private letters. Owing to the fact that part of the private letters by way of photos had already been disclosed and in the forthcoming seminar the private letters would be made public, in the planned auction to be held on 21 June 2013, Jikang Yang (applicant) applied for pre-action preservation measures against Sungari Company and Guoqiang Li (two respondents) to restrain them from committing a tort on 21 June 2013.

8.113 On 3 June 2013, the Second Intermediate People's Court of Beijing Municipality held that without a behaviour preservation order from the court, Jikang's right would be infringed and irreparable damages would occur to Jikang. Accordingly, the appropriate preservation measures were immediately granted to stop public auctions, public exhibitions and publicity of private letters.[89]

8.114 This case was analysed by legal scholars in China who observed that a delay in granting the behaviour preservation order would have resulted in the letters being sold to a new owner on 21 June 2013.[90] Accordingly, this case provides guidance on "time-sensitive" circumstances that could be considered by the courts as "urgent" and thereby fulfilling one of the prerequisites in any application seeking pre-action behaviour preservation measures.

Requirement for Urgent Applications (II): Irreparable Harms

8.115 The Interpretation of IP Behaviour Preservation 2018 revealed what circumstances can be considered as satisfying the criterion of "irreparable

89 ibid. A distinguished Chinese scholar argued that the nature of this case was to infringe personal rights. After the Chinese Civil Code comes into effect, the applicant could apply for "preliminary injunction of personal rights" (Article 997 of the Civil Code); see also, Liming Wang, 'Preliminary Injunction of the Infringement of Personality Rights' 2019 (4) Law and Economy 3, 6.

90 Xun Yang, 'Development of "Interim Injunction" in IPR Cases in China' (*Links Law*, 17 January 2019) <https://wemp.app/posts/abbd7327-2d61-4546-8b23-a71f2b2b38e4?utm_source=latest-posts> accessed 30 July 2021.

harms" in an application seeking IP pre-action behaviour preservation measures:

(a) where the behaviour of the respondent will infringe upon the applicant's personal rights such as the right to goodwill or publication right, privacy, etc. and will cause irreparable harms;
(b) where the behaviour of the respondent will lead to uncontrollable infringement and significantly increase the loss suffered by the applicant;
(c) where the infringement of the respondent will result in a significant reduction in the relevant market share of the applicant; or
(d) where other irreparable harms are suffered by the applicant.[91]

8.116 According to the guidance available from senior judges, the circumstances stated above can equally be applied to deal with post-action behaviour preservation applications in the context of the prerequisite of "irreparable harms". This is in spite of the fact that the previous paragraph was apparently only applicable to applications seeking pre-action behaviour preservation measures.[92]

8.117 One legal practitioner was of the view that such a category of circumstances to evaluate the prerequisite of "irreparable harms" reflects that Chinese courts seem to be inclined to "provide stronger protections on moral rights", compared with the common law system.[93]

8.118 However, the proceeding opinion deviated from the meaning of the judicial interpretation. As early as 2009, the SPC has stressed that when determining whether an applicant for a pre-action behaviour preservation measure will suffer irreparable harms, the court should focus on two issues –

(a) whether the harm can be compensated by the way of monetary damages; and
(b) whether it is reasonable to expect that such damages can be enforced in future.[94]

91 Interpretation of IP Behaviour Preservation 2018, Article 10.

92 Xiaoming Song, Chuang Wang, Junli Xia and Guimei Lang, 'Understanding and Application of Provisions of the Supreme People's Court on Several Issues Concerning the Application of Law in Cases Involving the Review of Behaviour Preservation in Intellectual Property Disputes' (2019) 7 The People's Judicature 19, 24.

93 Xun Yang, 'Development of "Interim Injunction" in IPR Cases in China' (*Llinks Law*, 17 January 2019) <https://wemp.app/posts/abbd7327-2d61-4546-8b23-a71f2b2b38e4?utm_source=latest-posts> accessed 30 July 2021; refer to Chapter 11, 11.68, 11.77 and 11.89 for discussion on issues such as good faith, moral rights and so forth. They are also referred to as the invisible factors.

94 *Notice of the Supreme People's Court on Issuing the Opinions on Several Issues Concerning Intellectual Property Trials Serving the Overall Objective under the Current Economic Situation* (Fa Fa [2009] No 23), Item 14.

8.119 During the drafting steps that led to the Interpretation of IP Behaviour Preservation 2018, the above two issues concerning monetary damages were not overlooked by the SPC. As the SPC's judges have explained, Article 10 of the Interpretation of IP Behaviour Preservation 2018 primarily addresses the legal issues in various scenarios where the monetary damages cannot be calculated.[95]

8.120 In this context, the evaluation of irreparable harms will first calculate the estimated amount of monetary damages in the circumstances and then will evaluate the possibility of the respondent's enforcement of these monetary damages in the future.[96] When it is not possible for the courts to evaluate these two aspects, the four circumstances provided by Article 10 of the Interpretation will be followed by the Chinese judges. Among them, the fourth circumstance of Article 10 of the Interpretation of IP Behaviour Preservation 2018 belongs to a catch-all option available to judges, and in fact, it grants judges wide discretionary power to assess the facts of the case and act accordingly.[97]

Requirement for Urgent Applications (III): Stabilisation of Rights

8.121 The requirement of stabilisation, which cannot be applied to non-IP preservation applications, was added by the Interpretation of IP Behaviour Property 2018 to examine an application for IP behaviour preservation measures. To be precise, this requirement is applicable to the area of law of intellectual property, particularly, in utility model and exterior design patents. The Intellectual Property Administration in China empowers the registration of patent rights without substantive examination. This means, in practice, that the novelty and non-obviousness of the model and exterior design patents have not been examined thoroughly by the Patenting Authority.

8.122 In this context, the Interpretation of IP Behaviour Preservation 2018 provides that when a court examines whether the applicant's request is founded on law and facts, the validity of the IP right (utility model and exterior design patents) will also be examined at the same time by the judges.[98]

95 Xiaoming Song, Chuang Wang, Junli Xia and Guimei Lang, 'Understanding and Application of Provisions of the Supreme People's Court on Several Issues Concerning the Application of Law in Cases Involving the Review of Behaviour Preservation in Intellectual Property Disputes' (2019) 7 The People's Judicature 19, 23; refer also to 8.115.

96 In the Interpretation of IP Behaviour Preservation 2018, Article 7 (b) also provides that the possibility of future enforcement shall be one of the standards to evaluate the application for behaviour preservation measures.

97 The issue of discretionary power of Chinese judges in general is discussed in comparative context with the common law judges in Chapter 11, 11.3, 11.53, 11.60–11.61. 11.78–11.81 and 11.108–11.114.

98 Interpretation of IP Behaviour Preservation 2018, Article 7 (a).

8.123 Taking into consideration whether the validity of the IP right (utility model and exterior design patents) claimed by the applicants is stable, the courts will consider the factors stated below:

(a) The type or nature of the rights involved.
(b) Whether the grant of the rights has undergone the procedure of substantive examination.
(c) Whether the rights in question are in the process of invalidation or cancellation or have the possibility of being declared invalid or cancelled.
(d) Whether there is a dispute over the title of the IP.
(e) Other factors that may lead to instability of the rights in question.[99]

8.124 In order for applicants to provide concrete evidence in relation to the stabilisation of the utility model and exterior design patents, Article 9 of the Interpretation of IP Behaviour Preservation 2018 provides:

> The applicant must submit a search report, a patent right evaluation report issued by the patent administration of the State Council or a decision made by Patent Re-examination Board to maintain validity of the patent right. Where the applicant refuses to submit the above documents without justifiable reasons, the court shall decide to reject the application.[100]

8.125 It should be noted that the Patent Law 1985 (2020 amendment) provides for three types of patents, namely invention, utility model and exterior design patents.[101] Substantive examination by the Intellectual Property Administration is the prerequisite for granting an invention patent to applicants.[102] Thus, the reliability of the invention patent is sufficient and the requirement of stabilisation is then recognised by the Chinese judges directly.

8.126 Apart from the invention patent, the examination of stabilisation is not necessary for issues in unfair competition disputes, as the cause of action of unfair competition is different from that of the protection of IP rights. Even though the Interpretation of IP Behaviour Preservation 2018 governs IP and unfair competition, the two causes of action are based on different kinds

99 ibid Article 8.
100 ibid Article 9.
101 Patent Law 1985 (2020 amendment), Article 2.
102 ibid, Article 35 provides that "Upon the request of the applicant for a patent for invention, made at any time within three years from the date of filing, the patent administrative organ under the State Council will proceed to examine the application as to its substance. If, without any justified reason, the applicant fails to meet the time limit for requesting examination as to substance, the application shall be deemed to have been withdrawn. The patent administrative organ under the State Council may, on its own initiative, proceed to examine any application for a patent for invention as to its substance when it deems it necessary".

of disputes. It is not possible and not necessary to examine the stabilisation issue in disputes involving unfair competition.[103]

Requirement for Urgent Applications (IV): Balance of Interests and Protection of Public Interests

8.127 In judicial practice, an underlying rule adopted by Chinese judges to determine an application seeking behaviour preservation measures is to take into consideration whether on the available evidence the applicants have a "major possibility of winning the case", namely a strong likelihood of success on the merits.[104]

8.128 However, the Interpretation emphasises that Chinese judges need to maintain the balance of interests between the applicants and the respondents. Specifically, even if the applicant's claim is based on a strong legal foundation, the potential damages to the respondent that may arise due to the behaviour preservation order, if granted in favour of the applicant, may far outweigh the legitimate interests of the applicant. The courts in such a scenario will be restrained and will not likely grant the behaviour preservation order in favour of the applicant.

8.129 This rule for the courts to maintain a fine balance of interest between the parties to disputes is also relevant in the context of business infringement disputes.

8.130 As mentioned by the Chinese judges in *Eli Lilly (US) Co and Eli Lilly (China) Co v Mengwei Huang*,[105] from a practical point of view, the success rate for applicants is low in disputes concerning trade secrets in China. Therefore, it is difficult for any applicant seeking behaviour preservation measures to demonstrate in such circumstances that in all likelihood the applicant will win their case. For this reason, as suggested by the SPC's judges, the likelihood of the applicant winning a full civil trial could not

103 Xiaoming Song, Chuang Wang, Junli Xia and Guimei Lang, 'Understanding and Application of Provisions of the Supreme People's Court on Several Issues Concerning the Application of Law in Cases Involving the Review of Behaviour Preservation in Intellectual Property Disputes' (2019) 7 The People's Judicature (Applied) 19, 23.

104 Lihong Duan, 'Understanding and Application of *Interpretation of the Supreme People's Court on the Application of Law Concerning Pre-Action Behaviour and Evidence Preservations for Stopping the Infringement upon the Right of Trademark*' in the First Civil Division of the Supreme People's Court (ed.), *Reference and Guide to Civil Trial* (Law Press of China, 2002 (4) 12); refer to Chapter 11, 11.97–11.107, for comparative analysis of the concept of standards of proof between the common law and the Chinese legal systems.

105 Gazette Case of the SPC [2014] 5 (211): *Eli Lilly (US) Co and Other v Mengwei Huang* (an application for a behaviour preservation measure arising from the infringement of know-how) [2013] Hu Yi Zhong Civil Wu (Zhi) Chu Zi No 119 (the First Intermediate People's Court of Shanghai Municipality, first instance and binding order).

become a benchmark for Chinese judges to decide whether they could grant the behaviour preservation measure.[106]

8.131 It is worth noting that because IP disputes, at times, may impact on other stakeholders that are not parties to the dispute, therefore, apart from the consideration of stakeholders' interests (parties to disputes or parties having connection with the dispute), the Interpretation provides that the courts should consider whether the behaviour preservation measures may result in damaging public interests.[107]

8.132 However, the understanding of "public interests" is dependent on the specific context surrounding the facts of the case. A typical example is the case of *Qualcomm Incorporated v Apple Computer Trading (Shanghai) Co Ltd and Other*.[108] Qualcomm Incorporated (applicant), an American microchip maker, applied to the court to seek behaviour preservation measures against Apple's Chinese subsidiary companies (respondents) on the import and sale of iPhones using patented technology belonging to Qualcomm Incorporated. Meanwhile, Qualcomm Incorporated also provided a bank guarantee to the Chinese court.

8.133 The Intermediate People's Court of Fuzhou City of Fujian Province held that Qualcomm Incorporated (applicant) had submitted sufficient evidence to prove the alleged patent infringement on a *prima facie* basis and considered that the actual infringement on that basis would continue until the final judgment was rendered by that court. These were two important factors considered by the Chinese court; hence the Chinese court granted the behaviour preservation measure in favour of Qualcomm Incorporated. According to the preservation order, iPhones using Qualcomm Incorporated's patented technology could not be sold in the Chinese market. Furthermore, the respondents were not entitled to grant the third party any rights that would allow them to sell the above products in the vast Chinese market.[109]

8.134 It was observed that in the above case, the Chinese court did not consider whether the order for behaviour preservation measures could violate

106 Zheng Tang and Changli Lv, 'The Application of a Behaviour Preservation in an Infringement of Know-How' (2013) 22 The People's Judicature (Case) 48, 50.

107 Interpretation of IP Behaviour Preservation 2018, Article 7 (d); refer also to Chapter 11, 11.68, for discussion on Article 2 of Civil Procedural Law 1991 (as amended until 2020) of China that courts will have to consider that *social and economic order* is maintained and *guarantee the smooth progress of socialist construction.*

108 *Qualcomm Incorporated v Apple Computer Trading (Shanghai) Co Ltd and Other* (dispute over a post-action application for a behaviour preservation) [2018] Min 01 Civil Chu No1208-1 (the Intermediate People's Court of Fuzhou City of Fujian Province, first instance and binding order).

109 ibid; it should be noted that this order was not immediately executed in practice. The respondents continued to sell the forbidden iPhones in China; refer also to Chapter 11. 11.68, for discussion on Article 2 of Civil Procedural Law 1991 (as amended until 2020) of China and on how courts will have to consider that *social and economic order* is maintained and *guarantee the smooth progress of socialist construction.*

the public interests. However, a few legal scholars analysed whether forbidding the sale of iPhones in the Chinese market could be considered as against the rule of "public interests", as Apple was one of the biggest smartphone companies in China.[110] In the authors' experience, Chinese courts in the past few years have not overemphasised the rule of "public interests" in judicial practice even if this rule will always remain.

Requirements for Non-Urgent Post-Action Applications

8.135 All requirements discussed above mainly aim at pre-action or "urgent" post-action applications for obtaining behaviour preservation measures. As far as the "non-urgent" post-action application is concerned, there is no clear guidance prescribed by law.

8.136 However, as stressed in 8.101, regardless of the pre-action or post-action behaviour preservation measures, it is necessary for the courts to examine whether future judgments or arbitral awards will remain achievable or will be difficult to enforce. At the same time, the courts will evaluate whether due to the respondents' conduct, or any other reasons, damage or loss may be caused to the applicants. Furthermore, pursuant to Article 4 of the Interpretation of IP Behaviour Preservation 2018, the format for a letter of application should contain the specific facts and reasons such as what "irreparable harms" have arisen and the potential difficulty that could be envisaged at the time of application regarding the enforcement of the final judgment.[111] From this point of view, the applicants should stress the necessity of behaviour preservation measures in their letters of application and that, without the order, it is likely to become impossible to enforce future judgments, or damage or loss may occur for the applicants.

8.137 In addition, furnishing security along with the application could be advantageous, even though in post-action applications, furnishing security is not mandatory. However, the judges will inevitably exercise discretionary power and accordingly render their decisions on the applications.

110 Actually, the above issue was also litigated in the USA. Qualcomm Incorporated, based on the same argument, brought the case to the US courts (the US International Trade Commission (ITC)). Even though Judge Thomas Pender found that Intel-based technology used by Apple in its iPhones infringed one of three Qualcomm patents, he denied the application for ceasing importing iPhones with the Intel chips on the ground that such injunction order would go against the public interests. The evaluation of the public interest was argued on the basis that the majority of US residents use iPhones. On the contrary, in China, there were many competing smartphones. The argument of the public interest was held as not reasonable in the Chinese courts; see also, Shamita Etienne-Cummings and Kevin Trainer, '*Apple* v *Qualcomm*: Is Public Interest Apple's Best Defense in the ITC?' (White & Case, 18 October 2018) <www.whitecase.com/publications/alert/apple-v-qualcomm-public-interest-apples-best-defense-itc> accessed 30 July 2021.

111 Interpretation of IP Behaviour Preservation 2018, Article 4.

Requirement of Furnishing Security

8.138 Security is a prerequisite in any application that seeks pre-action behaviour preservation measures. The general rules, particularly relating to the types of security and the exemptions for providing security, have been discussed in Chapter 3, 3.130–3.194.

Rules Regarding Furnishing Security in IP and Non-IP Disputes[112]

8.139 Article 11 of the Interpretation of IP Behaviour Preservation 2018 provides that:

> Where an applicant applies for a behaviour preservation, it should provide security prescribed by law.[113]

8.140 This provision is interpreted as saying that the rule for furnishing security for an IP behaviour preservation application must abide by Articles 100 and 101 of CPL 1991 (as amended until 2020). That is to say that furnishing security for a pre-action application is mandatary, while for post-action applications, furnishing security is dependent on the exercise of judges' discretionary power.[114]

8.141 In terms of the amount of security, the Interpretation of IP Behaviour Preservation 2018 provides that the applicants must furnish security for the amount that is equivalent to the amount of possible loss that could be suffered by the respondent due to the IP preservation measures. The possible loss that could be suffered will include the reasonable loss of sale proceeds and custody expenses of the products involved in order to stop the infringement.[115]

8.142 There is no express provision available to govern the issue of furnishing security for applications seeking non-IP behaviour preservation measures. It is the authors' view that Articles 100 and 101 of CPL 1991 (as amended until 2020) are applicable to applications seeking non-IP behaviour preservation measures. Furthermore, the Chinese courts' evaluation process in relation to non-IP disputes may resemble the rules provided by the Interpretation of IP Behaviour Preservation 2018.

---

112 In this context, non-IP disputes do not include maritime disputes. Discussion of the rule of furnishing security in maritime disputes can be found in Chapter 3, 3.134–3.135.

113 Interpretation of IP Behaviour Preservation 2018, Article 11.

114 Xiaoming Song, Chuang Wang, Junli Xia and Guimei Lang, 'Understanding and Application of Provisions of the Supreme People's Court on Several Issues Concerning the Application of Law in Cases Involving the Review of Behaviour Preservation in Intellectual Property Disputes' (2019) 7 The People's Judicature 19, 24.

115 Interpretation of IP Behaviour Preservation 2018, Article 11.

Countersecurity Rules in IP and Non-IP Disputes

8.143 Pursuant to the Interpretation of IP Behaviour Preservation 2018, the countersecurity provided by the respondent does not inevitably lead to discharge of the court's order in IP behaviour preservation measures. However, with consent of the applicant, the court can thereafter discharge the preservation order.[116] In other words, whether it is necessary to provide countersecurity is dependent on the applicant's consent.

8.144 With regard to non-IP disputes, it is not clear whether the countersecurity provided by the respondent is sufficient to discharge the behaviour preservation order. According to the guidance available from senior judges of the SPC, the subject matter of the behaviour preservation order in IP disputes is closely related to the subject matter of the IP dispute. In other words, the respondent's behaviour directly impacts on the subject matter of the IP dispute. Thus, the court's IP behaviour preservation order instructs the respondent "to do" or "not to do" a certain thing, that is, to avoid affecting the subject matter of the dispute. In this context, the discharge of the preservation orders will impact discernibly on the subject matter of the IP dispute. Accordingly, whether providing countersecurity can be accepted is always dependent on the applicant's consent.[117] Similar legal reasoning is adopted by the Interpretation of Property Preservation (2020 Amendment) in respect of the discharge of property preservation measures. This means that with the applicant's consent the property preservation order may be discharged, if the property to be preserved is the subject matter of the dispute. Otherwise, providing countersecurity cannot lead to the discharge of the order.[118]

8.145 The above legal reasoning can be adopted in the context of the discharge of the behaviour preservation measures in non-IP disputes as well. In a scenario, if the respondent's behaviour were to target the subject matter of the dispute, then without the applicant's consent, providing countersecurity will not lead inevitably to the discharge of the behaviour preservation orders. On the contrary, if the subject matter of the respondent "should do" or "not to do" is not the same to the disputed subject matter in the case, then subject to the courts' exercise of their discretionary power, the order may be discharged after the respondent furnishes countersecurity.

116 ibid Article 12.

117 Xiaoming Song, Chuang Wang, Junli Xia and Guimei Lang, 'Understanding and Application of Provisions of the Supreme People's Court on Several Issues Concerning the Application of Law in Cases Involving the Review of Behaviour Preservation in Intellectual Property Disputes' (2019) 7 The People's Judicature 19, 24.

118 Interpretation of Property Preservation (2020 Amendment), Article 22; see also, 3.136–3.138 in Chapter 3.

8.146 For instance, in *Fujian Ganglong Concrete Co Ltd (Ganglong) v Putian Yongshengxin Industrial Co Ltd (Yongshengxin)*,[119] after the court had granted the behaviour preservation order ensuring Fujian Ganglong (respondent) halt ongoing construction on the contracted land, Fujian Ganglong (respondent) provided countersecurity to the court and hence requested the court to discharge the preservation order.

8.147 In the case of *Fujian Ganglong*, the court held that the applicant, pursuant to the CPL 1991 (as amended until 2020), had filed the behaviour preservation application and provided security as required by law. As per the courts' reasoning, the respondent's countersecurity did not constitute legal ground for discharging the preservation order granted against the respondent. Therefore, the court denied the respondent's application requesting the discharge of the preservation order as they were willing to provide countersecurity.[120]

8.148 It can be seen in the above case that the subject matter of the behaviour preservation measure is just the subject matter of the disputed contract. It means that furnishing countersecurity is no guarantee that courts will be willing to discharge the preservation order in non-IP disputes.

Inquiry Procedure or Interim Hearing and Respondent's Defence

Inquiry Procedure in IP Disputes and Respondent's Defence

8.149 Unlike the applications seeking property preservation measures, where an interim hearing is not mandatory, the Interpretation for IP Behaviour Preservation expressly stipulates the inquiry procedure should be conducted by similar judges to the interim hearing. Article 5 of this Interpretation provides:

> The court shall, before deciding to take behaviour preservation measures, *query* [emphasis added] the applicant and the respondent, except when the situation is urgent, or the inquiry may affect the implementation of the preservation measures.[121]

8.150 This requirement as to the interim hearing is considered necessary by the legal system because IP disputes are complex and an order for an IP behaviour preservation may impact on parties' interests to a large extent. Thus, the SPC looked into the best practices from Chinese judicial practice

119 *Fujian Ganglong Concrete Co Ltd v Putian Yongshengxin Industrial Co Ltd* (dispute over a land lease contract) [2017] Min 0303 Civil Chu No 151; [2017] Min 0303 Civil Chu No 151-1 (the Primary People's Court of Hanjiang District of Putian City of Fujian Province, first instance and reconsideration court, binding order).

120 ibid.

121 Interpretation of IP Behaviour Preservation 2018, Article 5.

and other jurisdictions, and accordingly set out the inquiry procedure.[122] The inquiry procedure provides an opportunity to all parties to present their arguments to the judges. In a way, it brings an element of procedural fairness in complex disputes. In this procedure, the respondents will have an opportunity to question the necessity of the application seeking the behaviour preservation measures and to challenge the applicants' motives. This will involve respondents arguing that, without the behaviour preservation order, future judgments can still be enforced, and the applicants will not suffer other loss. In addition, in light of the requirements of IP behaviour preservation applications, the possible defence for respondents may include that any behaviour preservation measures, if granted, will violate public interests and the non-stabilisation of the applicant's right in their applications which means that the applicant's right might be revoked in the future.

8.151 However, as a general rule, the inquiry procedure will be followed by the court during both the pre-action and post-action proceedings unless the court considers that the exceptional situations are involved pursuant to Article 5 of the Interpretation of IP Behaviour Preservation 2018. Firstly, if the situation is urgent; secondly, if the inquiry might affect the enforcement of the preservation order. Because the first situation "urgent" may be wrongly treated as the requirement of "urgent circumstances", the following paragraphs will focus on this exception.

8.152 In the authors' opinion, in a narrow sense, an urgent situation can be regarded as "urgent circumstances" for a pre-action or an urgent post-action application seeking behaviour preservation measures pursuant to Articles 100 and 101 of the CPL 1991 (as amended until 2020). It thus seems that the inquiry procedure will not apply to a pre-action or an urgent post-action application seeking behaviour preservation measures. However, in consideration of the purpose of this provision, the inquiry procedure during the pre-action or urgent post-action application proceedings may be recognised and accepted by the court. The reasons are as follows.

8.153 To start with, in any event, the urgent circumstances are a mandatory prerequisite for a pre-action or urgent post-action preservation application.[123] It can be argued that the meaning of "urgent situation" in the inquiry procedure, pursuant to Article 5 of this Interpretation, is equivalent to the meaning of urgent circumstances as a prerequisite for applications seeking pre-action or urgent post-action preservation measures. In that case, the Interpretation of IP Behaviour Preservation 2018 should have directly provided that the inquiry procedure is not applicable to pre-action or urgent post-

122 Xiaoming Song, Chuang Wang, Junli Xia and Guimei Lang, 'Understanding and Application of Provisions of the Supreme People's Court on Several Issues Concerning the Application of Law in Cases Involving the Review of Behaviour Preservation in Intellectual Property Disputes' (2019) 7 The People's Judicature 19, 22.

123 Refer to 8.104–8.114 for discussion on prerequisite of urgent circumstances.

action applications. However, obviously the Interpretation of IP Behaviour Preservation 2018 does not stress that the inquiry procedure is only suitable for post-action applications, or that it directly excludes pre-action or urgent post-action applications from applying the inquiry procedure.

8.154 Secondly, the SPC's judges have clarified that, pursuant to *Several Provisions of the SPC on Issues Concerning Applicable Laws to Acts of Stopping Aggressing Patent Right Before Trial 2001*[124] and *Interpretation of the Supreme People's Court on the Application of Law Concerning Pre-Action Behaviour and Evidence Preservations for Stopping the Infringement upon the Right of Trademark 2002*,[125] in pre-action behaviour preservation applications, the previous rule was to render the preservation order initially and then hear the legal arguments during the reconsideration procedure. However, after considering the complexity involved in most IP disputes, Article 5 of the Interpretation of IP Behaviour Preservation 2018 has designed the inquiry procedure. The purpose is to set out the general rule of the inquiry procedure and only when the exceptional circumstance has happened, then the inquiry may not be allowed.[126]

Inquiry Procedure in Non-IP Disputes and Respondents' Defence

8.155 As far as a behaviour preservation application in a non-IP dispute is concerned, there is no clear guidance available to stakeholders or even to courts concerning the requirement of inquiry for the parties before the behaviour preservation order can be granted. However, in legal practice, certain courts on their own initiative can arrange the inquiry before granting the behaviour preservation orders. For example, in *Chongqing Baoshi Property Co Ltd v Chongqing Tongda Investment Co Ltd and Other*,[127] the Second Intermediate People's Court of Chongqing Municipality emphasised the fact that there would not be a mandatory inquiry before granting the behaviour preservation order. However, the court clarified that the absence of clear

124 *Several Provisions of the SPC on Issues Concerning Applicable Laws to Acts of Stopping Aggressing Patent Right before Trial 2001* (Fa Shi [2001] No 20) (expired on 1 January 2021).

125 Interpretation of the Supreme People's Court on the Application of Law Concerning Pre-Action Behaviour and Evidence Preservations for Stopping the Infringement upon the Right of Trademark (Fa Shi [2002] No 2) (expired on 1 January 2021).

126 Xiaoming Song, Chuang Wang, Junli Xia and Guimei Lang, 'Understanding and Application of Provisions of the Supreme People's Court on Several Issues Concerning the Application of Law in Cases Involving the Review of Behaviour Preservation in Intellectual Property Disputes' (2019) 7 The People's Judicature 19, 22.

127 *Chongqing Baoshi Property Co Ltd v Chongqing Tongda Investment Co Ltd and Other* (an application for a behaviour preservation) [2017] Yu 02 Xing Bao Fu No 1 (the Second Intermediate People's Court of Chongqing Municipality, the first instance and reconsideration court, binding order).

procedural guidance by law on this matter would not prevent the court from organising the procedure of inquiry, if necessary.[128]

8.156 In terms of the respondents' defence during non-IP proceedings, first, if there were to be no inquiry procedure allowed by the courts, then the respondents would have no opportunity to state their argument. If they were given an opportunity to defend, then the respondents would argue that without the behaviour preservation orders, future judgments can still be enforced, and the applicants will not suffer other loss.

Inquiry Procedure for Maritime Injunction and Respondents' Defence

8.157 In the maritime injunction procedure, the SMPL 2000 does not provide for an interim hearing or inquiry procedure before courts can grant interim injunctions. A few legal scholars contend that it is necessary to organise interim hearings prior to the issue of maritime injunction orders.[129] In legal practice, some maritime courts, such as the Shanghai Maritime Court and the Dalian Maritime Court,[130] have adopted the procedure of interim hearings. However, this procedure is always based on the exercise of the judge's discretionary power.[131] Most cases in maritime courts concerning maritime injunctions exceed the legal time limit provided by the SMPL 2000 due to these interim hearings.[132] To the authors' knowledge, if respondents in a maritime dispute are given an opportunity to argue their defence in applications seeking maritime injunctions, the legal argument will be similar to the arguments for other non-maritime applications as discussed in 8.156.

---

128 ibid.

129 Xiaoru Zhang, 'Improvement of China's Maritime Injunction System' (2006) 4 The People's Judicature 79, 80; see also, Xiaofeng Li and Ping Guo, 'Comment on the Breakthrough and Deficiency of the Behaviour Preservation System under CPL (2012)' (2015) 6, Journal of Law Application 71, 75.

130 In *Nanning Branch of Guangxi Xijiang Modern International Logistics Holding Group v Tongling Huayuan Shipping Co Ltd* (an application for a maritime injunction) [2018] Liao 72 Xing Bao No 1 (Dalian Maritime Court, first instance and binding order), Nanning Branch of Guangxi Xijiang Modern International Logistics Holding Group (applicant) filed an application for a maritime injunction to the Dalian Maritime Court and requested Tongling Huayuan Shipping Co Ltd (respondent) to hand over bills of lading to the consignee. Furthermore, the applicant claimed that the urgent circumstances were applicable to their application. Without the maritime injunction, it was submitted by the applicant that they would suffer substantial loss. The Dalian Maritime Court organised an interim hearing and then upheld the applicant's request.

131 Xiaofeng Li and Ping Guo, 'Comment on the Breakthrough and Deficiency of the Behaviour Preservation System under CPL' (2015) 6, Journal of Law Application 71, 74–75; see also, Zhixian Shen (ed.) *Essentials of Maritime Justice* (Law Press of China 2011) 266–267.

132 Yongcan Chen, 'Data Report of Applications for Maritime Injunction' (Maritime Research Centre, 7 May 2019) <https://wemp.app/posts/095556d9-8e94-49cb-bfcd-8ec847bca332> accessed 15 July 2021; to the authors' knowledge, if the inquiry procedure in maritime injunction proceedings leads to the extension of the legal time limit, most maritime judges will not be inclined to hear the case.

The Time Limit of Rendering Post-Action Orders

8.158 As discussed in 3.222–3.325, if an applicant files an application seeking post-action preservation measures, under "urgent circumstances", the CPL 1991 (as amended until 2020) provides that the courts must render orders within 48 hours.[133] However, if there are no urgent circumstances, there is no exact time limit during which the courts have to render the post-action behaviour preservation orders provided by law from the time when the application seeking preservation measures has been submitted. The SPC's judges simply suggest that the courts should examine the requirements of the application and render an order in a timely fashion.[134] This means that the courts' discretionary power decides the length for rendering an order. Nonetheless, the Provisions on Shanghai Property Preservation 2017 expressly stipulate, by reference to the time limit for rendering a post-action property preservation order, that the courts should render preservation of behaviour orders within five days; if security is requested by the courts, then the orders can only be rendered after the security has been furnished by the applicants.[135]

Time Limit and Renewal of Preservation Orders

8.159 Unlike the time limit for the property preservation order, as discussed in 6.151 to 6.155 of Chapter 6, the time limit for the behaviour preservation orders is uncertain. Article 4 (b) of the Interpretation of IP Behaviour Preservation 2018 provides that the applicant should enunciate the time limit for the requested behaviour preservation measure in his letter of application.[136] Nonetheless, any time limit suggested by the applicant will not be inevitably considered and accepted by the court. Hence, the Chinese courts will exercise their discretionary power and decide on the issue of time limit accordingly. In accordance with Article 13 of this Interpretation, there are two types of time limit as follows observed by the authors.

First Type of Prescription of Time Limit

8.160 The first type of time limit will depend on the courts exercising their discretionary power to determine a reasonable duration for the behaviour preservation measures. The exercise of discretionary power will take

133 CPL 1991 (as amended until 2020), Article 100.

134 Xiaoming Song, Chuang Wang, Junli Xia and Guimei Lang, 'Understanding and Application of Provisions of the Supreme People's Court on Several Issues Concerning the Application of Law in Cases Involving the Review of Behaviour Preservation in Intellectual Property Disputes' (2019) 7 The People's Judicature 19, 22.

135 Provisions on Shanghai Property Preservation 2017, Articles 22 and 119.

136 Interpretation on IP Behaviour Preservation 2018, Article 4 (b).

into account the request of the applicant or the specific circumstances of the case.[137] The first type will be considered as a general rule for deciding the issue of the time limit of any behaviour preservation order. Furthermore, although this general rule is established in the Interpretation of IP Behaviour Preservation 2018, in non-IP disputes this rule is widely applied.

8.161 In this scenario, the time limit requested by the applicant will be considered by the court, but the court will also consider the specific or special circumstances of the case before it. In legal practice, applicants often do not request a specific time limit for behaviour preservation orders, as they are usually expecting a maximum time limit to be applicable. In these kinds of scenarios, due to the exercise of discretionary power, it has been observed that time limits have been inconsistent for similar orders in the Chinese courts.

8.162 For example, in two cases of *Chongqing Jiangjinqu Xiaqiang Construction Installation Engineering Co Ltd v Gaotang Jinhang Metal Welding Co Ltd*,[138] and *Baise Baian Driving Training Centre v Guangxi Yilai Trade Co Ltd*,[139] both applicants in these two cases applied for behaviour preservation measures in order to restrict or forbid respondents from changing the particulars in their industrial and commercial registration (including but not limited to the registration for change of name of shareholders, the change of legal representatives, the reduction of capital and the deregistration of the company).

8.163 In the former case, the Primary People's Court of Gaotang County of Liaocheng City of Shandong Province held that the respondent was forbidden from changing any particulars in the industrial and commercial registration for their company. Meanwhile, this behaviour preservation order was not rendered with any particular time limit.[140] It could be understood that the legal

137 ibid Article 13.

138 *Chongqing Jiangjinqu Xiaqiang Construction Installation Engineering Co Ltd v Gaotang Jinhang Metal Welding Co Ltd* (an application for a pre-action behaviour preservation) [2018] Lu 1526 Xing Bao No 1 (the Primary People's Court of Gaotang County of Liaocheng City of Shandong Province, first instance and binding order).

139 *Baise Baian Driving Training Centre v Guangxi Yilai Trade Co Ltd* (an application for a pre-action behaviour preservation order) [2018] Gui 1002 Cai Bao No 57 (the Primary People's Court of Guilin Baise Youjiang District of Guangxi Zhuang Autonomous Region, first instance and binding order).

140 *Chongqing Jiangjinqu Xiaqiang Construction Installation Engineering Co Ltd v Gaotang Jinhang Metal Welding Co Ltd* (an application for a pre-action behaviour preservation) [2018] Lu 1526 Xing Bao No 1 (the Primary People's Court of Gaotang County of Liaocheng City of Shandong Province, first instance and binding order); see also, in *Henan Tianpu Elevator Co Ltd v Henan Baiming Industrial Co Ltd* (an application for a pre-action behaviour preservation order) [2019] Yu 0102 Xing Bao No1 (the Primary People's Court of Zhongyuan District of Zhengzhou City of Henan Province, first instance and binding order), the court requested the respondent not to file the deregistration of the company. In practice, if there is no time limit, it is generally recognised that the valid period may last till the final judgment is effective.

effect of this order could last until the final judgment for the full civil trial became effective. However, in the latter case, although the Primary People's Court of Guilin Baise Youjiang District of Guangxi Zhuang Autonomous Region restricted (forbade) industrial and commercial registration, the prescribed time limit was only one year.[141]

8.164 After examining the cases for different causes of action, the result shows that the majority of the behaviour preservation orders do not clarify the time limit for the application of the orders. For example, in *Feixian Xinhao Yuanjingfa Board Mill v Linyi Lanshan Ourui Board Mill and Others*,[142] the Primary People's Court of Lanshan District of Linyi City of Shandong Province held that the respondents were prohibited from endorsing and transferring the commercial acceptance bill;[143] in *Qian'an Borui Ecological Agriculture Co Ltd v Kui Yu and Others*,[144] the Primary People's Court of Qian'an County of Jilin Province held that the respondent could not take any measures to prevent the applicant from constructing a vegetable greenhouse on the property.[145]

Second Type of Prescription of Time Limit

8.165 Pursuant to the second type of prescribed limit, it is provided that the behaviour preservation order to prevent the infringement of IP rights will be effective until the final judgment for the full dispute becomes effective.[146] In other words, where the cause of action is an IP infringement dispute, the prescribed time limit of a behaviour preservation will last automatically for the duration of civil proceedings.

8.166 Similar to the first type, the time limit for the non-IP order may apply this second type directly. There is no further discussion in this section.

---

141 *Baise Baian Driving Training Centre v Guangxi Yilai Trade Co Ltd* (an application for a pre-action behaviour preservation order) [2018] Gui 1002 Cai Bao No 57 (the Primary People's Court of Guilin Baise Youjiang District of Guangxi Zhuang Autonomous Region, first instance and binding order); see also, in *Weijie Gao v Henan Changxing Construction Group Co Ltd* (an application for a pre-action behaviour preservation order) [2017] Yu 0902 Cai Bao No 626 (the Primary People's Court of Hualong District of Puyang City of Henan Province, first instance and binding order), the court forbade the respondent from changing the registration of the company within one year.

142 *Feixian Xinhao Yuanjingfa Board Mill v Linyi Lanshan Ourui Board Mill and Others* (an application for a behaviour preservation order) [2019] Lu 1302 Civil Chu 14140-1 (the Primary People's Court of Lanshan District of Linyi City of Shandong Province, first instance and binding order), the court held that the respondents were forbidden from endorsing and transferring the commercial acceptance bill.

143 ibid.

144 *Qian'an Borui Ecological Agriculture Co Ltd v Kui Yu and Others* (an application for a pre-action behaviour preservation order) [2017] Ji 0723 Xing Bo No 1 (the Primary People's Court of Qian'an County of Jilin Province, first instance and binding order).

145 ibid.

146 Interpretation on IP Behaviour Preservation 2018, Article 13.

Renewal of Behaviour Preservation Order

8.167 With regard to the renewal of the behaviour preservation order, if the order does not provide for a time limit, it is not necessary for the applicant to apply for renewal of the order. If the order provides the valid period of the behaviour measure, by reference to the property preservation measure discussed in Chapter 6, 6.153–6.155, the applicant should apply for the renewal of the behaviour preservation order prior to the expiry of the order.

Compensation Caused by Wrongful Behaviour Preservations

Compensation Rules in IP Disputes

8.168 As discussed in Chapter 3, 3.294, even if the tortious conduct under the three types of preservation measures has been incorporated into one provision under the CPL 1991 (as amended until 2020),[147] this does not mean that the liability principles are inevitably consistent. An incorrect IP behaviour preservation is subject to non-fault liability. Non-fault liability is distinct from fault-based liability arising from the rendering of wrongful property preservation measures.

8.169 Article 16 of the Interpretation on IP Behaviour Preservation 2018 provides:

> Where any of the following circumstances occurs, it shall be deemed to fall within the circumstance of "wrongful application" under Article 105 of the Civil Procedure Law:
>
> (a) where the applicant does not file a lawsuit or apply for an arbitration within thirty days after taking the behaviour preservation measures;
> (b) where the behaviour preservation measures are improper from the beginning due to the invalidity of the intellectual property claimed to be protected;
> (c) where the application for a behaviour preservation is to cease the infringement upon intellectual property rights or upon unfair competition, yet the effective judgment holds that either infringement or unfair competition is not constituted;
> (d) other circumstances where the application is wrong.[148]

8.170 This provision has been interpreted by the SPC's judges, and their view is that when "wrongful application" for IP behaviour preservation is evaluated, it is not necessary to consider the element of fault of an applicant in a subjective sense. If only the behaviour preservation measure is proved to

147 CPL 1991 (as amended until 2020), Article 105.
148 Interpretation on IP Behaviour Preservation 2018, Article 16.

be wrong, the concept of "wrongful application" is then applicable based on the concept of strict liability.[149]

8.171 The adoption of strict liability is mainly founded on the ground that both Article 50 (7) of TRIPS[150] and interim injunctions provided by other jurisdictions apply the concept of strict liability under the tort law to such scenarios.[151] In addition, compared with the wrongful property preservation orders, a wrongful behaviour preservation measure may significantly impact the respondent's interests.[152]

The Retrospective Effect of Invalidity of Patent Rights in IP Compensation

8.172 With regard to Article 16 (b) of the Interpretation on IP Behaviour Preservation 2018, although any applicant's patent right that has been declared invalid is deemed to be non-existent from the beginning,[153] according to the stage of the dispute in civil proceedings, the retrospective effect of any order will be different for evaluating compensation.

8.173 In the event that the invalidity of patent right arises before the substantive judgment is rendered, the applicant's preservation application will be regarded as a wrongful behaviour preservation measure. In such a scenario, the applicant is liable for the respondent's loss.[154]

---

149 Xiaoming Song, Chuang Wang, Junli Xia and Guimei Lang, 'Understanding and Application of Provisions of the Supreme People's Court on Several Issues Concerning the Application of Law in Cases Involving the Review of Behaviour Preservation in Intellectual Property Disputes' (2019) 7 The People's Judicature 19, 25.

150 Article 50 (7) of TRIPS provides that "where the provisional measures are revoked or where they lapse due to any act or omission by the applicant, or where it is subsequently found that there has been no infringement or threat of infringement of an intellectual property right, the judicial authorities shall have the authority to order the applicant, upon request of the defendant, to provide the defendant appropriate compensation for any injury caused by these measures".

151 Xiaoming Song, Chuang Wang, Junli Xia and Guimei Lang, 'Understanding and Application of Provisions of the Supreme People's Court on Several Issues Concerning the Application of Law in Cases Involving the Review of Behaviour Preservation in Intellectual Property Disputes' (2019) 7 The People's Judicature 19, 25.

152 ibid.

153 Article 47 of the Patent Law 1985 (2020 Amendment) provides that "The decision on declaring a patent right invalid shall have no retroactive effect on any written judgment or written mediation on patent infringement that has been made and enforced by the people's court, or on any decision concerning the handling of a dispute over the patent infringement that has been performed or compulsively executed, or on any contract for permitted exploitation of the patent or for transfer of patent rights that has been performed—prior to the invalidation declaration of the patent right. However, compensation shall be made for the losses caused to another person mala fides by the patentee".

154 Xiaoming Song, Chuang Wang, Junli Xia and Guimei Lang, 'Understanding and Application of Provisions of the Supreme People's Court on Several Issues Concerning the Application of Law in Cases Involving the Review of Behaviour Preservation in Intellectual Property Disputes' (2019) 7 The People's Judicature 19, 26.

8.174 After the substantive judgment has been rendered and enforced, if the patent right is declared invalid, the legal effect of the invalidity cannot be traced back to the behaviour preservation application. In other words, the applicant will not be liable to the respondent for any compensation.[155]

Compensation Rules in Non-IP Disputes

8.175 Whether the non-fault liability regime may govern an applicant seeking a non-IP behaviour preservation measure is not clear from the existing jurisprudence. The authors are of the view that both the presumption of fault and non-fault liability regimes are only applicable provided the express provisions in relation to it are prescribed by law. Without the express provisions, the liability of applicants for a non-IP behaviour preservation measure should be based likely on the fault-based liability regime.[156]

Behaviour Preservation Fees

8.176 *Measures on Payment of Litigation Costs 2006* does not provide explicit guidance for seeking behaviour preservation fees. In legal practice, prior to the issue of the Interpretation of IP Behaviour Preservation 2018, the court generally applied Article 14 (2) of *Measures on Payment of Litigation Costs 2006*, which provides:

> Where … no amount of property is involved, RMB 30 shall be paid for each case.[157]

8.177 This means that the behaviour preservation application fee is in principle RMB 30.

8.178 After the issue of the Interpretation of IP Behaviour Preservation 2018, Article 20 provides:

> To apply for behaviour preservation, the applicant shall pay the application fee in accordance with the provisions of the *Measures on Payment of Litigation Costs* on the application for behaviour preservation measures.[158]

8.179 According to the understanding and application of the Interpretation of IP Behaviour Preservation 2018 stated by senior judges of the SPC,[159] this means that the IP behaviour preservation fee will be based on the standard of

155 ibid.

156 A detailed discussion can be found at Chapter 6, 6.156–6.173.

157 *Measures on Payment of Litigation Costs 2006*, Article 14 (2).

158 Interpretation of IP Behaviour Preservation 2018, Article 20.

159 Xiaoming Song, Chuang Wang, Junli Xia and Guimei Lang, 'Understanding and Application of Provisions of the Supreme People's Court on Several Issues Concerning the Application of Law in Cases Involving the Review of Behaviour Preservation in Intellectual Property Disputes' (2019) 7 The People's Judicature 19, 27.

fees as specified for obtaining maritime injunctions. It is set out at between RMB 1,000 and 5,000 pursuant to Article 14 (7) of *Measures for Payment of Litigation Costs 2006*.[160]

8.180 With regard to the criterion of the actual amount between RMB 1,000 and 5,000, the Interpretation of IP Behaviour Preservation 2018 does not provide a clear answer. According to legal practice, a reasonable approach is to follow the criterion for the similar issue in the case of seeking property preservation measures at 6.174 in Chapter 6.

8.181 However, in light of the criteria of property preservation, if the behaviour preservation fee calculated is below RMB 1,000, the applicant will be required to pay RMB 1,000. If the fee calculated exceeds RMB 5,000, only RMB 5,000 will be required for an application.

8.182 In terms of a non-IP behaviour preservation fee, it seems, by reference to Interpretation of IP Behaviour Preservation 2018, the application fee will be between RMB 1,000 and 5,000. This fee is applicable even if the judicial interpretation simply governs the application for seeking IP behaviour preservation fees.

8.183 However, in legal practice, there is no unified fee standard for seeking non-IP behaviour preservation measures in Chinese courts. For example, in *SINOHYDRO Engineering Bureau 4 Co Ltd v China CAMA Engineering Co Ltd and China Construction Bank (Xining Railway Branch)*,[161] an applicant, *SINOHYDRO Engineering Bureau 4 Co Ltd*, filed an application to stop *China Construction Bank* from paying RMB 89,525,247 prescribed by two letters of guarantee. The High People's Court of Qinghai Province held that an application fee was RMB 5,000.[162]

8.184 In *Huyuan Tongtai (Cambodia) Agricultural Technology Development Co Ltd and Bank of China (Jiangsu Branch) v High Hope Int'l Group Jiangsu Champion Holdings Ltd*,[163] the relevant application fee for

160 Measures on Payment of Litigation Costs 2006, Article 14 (7).

161 *SINOHYDRO Engineering Bureau 4 Co Ltd v China Construction Bank (Xining Railway Branch) and China CAMA Engineering Co Ltd* (an application seeking a behaviour preservation) [2015] Qing Civil Bao Zi No 29 (the High People's Court of Qinghai Province, first instance and binding order); *SINOHYDRO Engineering Bureau 4 Co Ltd v China Construction Bank (Xining Railway Branch) and China CAMA Engineering Co Ltd* (a dispute over fraudulent independent letters of guarantee) [2019] SPC Civil Final No 349 (the Supreme People's Court, second instance and binding judgment).

162 ibid, it should be emphasised that the losing party is liable for the preservation fee after the court renders a final and binding judgment. In this case, China CAMA Engineering Co Ltd (defendant) was liable for the behaviour preservation fee; see also, *SINOHYDRO Engineering Bureau 4 Co Ltd v China Construction Bank (Xining Railway Branch) and China CAMA Engineering Co Ltd* (a dispute over fraudulent independent letters of guarantee) [2019] SPC Civil Final No 349 (the Supreme People's Court, second instance and binding judgment).

163 *Huyuan Tongtai (Cambodia) Agricultural Technology development Co Ltd and Bank of China (Jiangsu Branch) v High Hope Int'l Group Jiangsu Champion Holdings Ltd* (an application for a behaviour preservation order) [2016] Su 01 Civil Chu No 849 (the Intermediate People's Court of Nanjing City of Jiangsu Province, first instance and binding order).

seeking behaviour preservation measures was confirmed as RMB 4,445 on the ground that the disputed amount was $1,196,000.[164]

8.185 On the other hand, in *Yingkou Aoxue Refrigerated Storage and Transportation Food Co Ltd (Yingkou) v Xiantao Shahu Chufeng Food Factory (Xiantao)*,[165] even though the cause of action was unfair competition, the Intermediate People's Court of Nanjing City of Jiangsu Province simply requested the applicant to pay the behaviour preservation fee of RMB 30.[166]

Annex 1

Format of Application for Seeking Behaviour Preservation Measures (for Legal Entity or Organisation)[167]

Applicant: the full name of the company, organisation or other legal entities; a Unified Social Credit Code or the registration code.

Legal representative/principal: name, address, contact telephone number (optional), Identification Card Number (optional).

Authorised legal agent: XXXXX Law Firm, the lawyer's name, gender, Identification Card Number, contract number, lawyer's licence's number, the lawyer's address.

Respondent: the full name of company, organisation or other legal entities; a Unified Social Credit Code or the registration code.

Legal representative/principal: name, address, contact telephone number (optional), Identification Card Number (optional).

Authorised legal agent: XXXXX Law Firm, the lawyer's name, gender, Identification Card Number, contract number, lawyer's licence's number, the lawyer's address.

Items to be claimed/requested:

It is hereby requested that XXXXX people's court compels the respondent "to do" or "not to do" certain things (specify the exact behaviour such as to stop circulating the applicant's articles XXXXX without the applicant's consent).

---

164 ibid, it should be noted that the case numbers for a behaviour preservation ruling and a final judgment by the Intermediate People's Court of Nanjing City of Jiangsu Province were the same in this dispute, but the preservation fee was specified and confirmed in the final judgment.

165 *Yingkou Aoxue Refrigerated Storage and Transportation Food Co Ltd v Xiantao Shahu Chufeng Food Factory* (an application seeking behaviour preservation measures) [2019] Su 01 Civil Chu No 1447-01 (the Intermediate People's Court of Nanjing City of Jiangsu Province, first instance and binding order).

166 ibid.

167 By reference to a sample provided by the Supreme People's Court at <http://www.court.gov.cn/susongyangshi-xiangqing-131.html> accessed 30 July 2021, this author drafts the current sample.

Facts and grounds:

Due to XXXXX dispute between the applicant and the respondent, the applicant will bring the case to the court/XXXXX arbitration institution against the respondent or this case has been accepted by the court/XXXXX arbitration institution on XXXXX (the exact date and exact case no.). Because the respondent's behaviour has serious consequences (exact facts), and also the circumstances are urgent, thereby, in accordance with Article 101 or 100 of the Civil Procedure Law, the applicant hereby requests the court to compel the respondent to do or not to do certain things (specify the exact measures).

The applicant will provide XXXXX property as security (specify the name, nature, quantity, amount, location, etc., of the secured property).

Regards

XXXX People's Court

Applicant (stamp and/or legal representative signature)

Date

Note for the application seeking behaviour preservation measures:

1) This format can be used for applications seeking arbitral behaviour preservation measures.
2) If either the applicant or the respondent is an individual, the information of the individual should include the full name, gender, date of birth, ethnicity, employer and occupation, address and contact information. Other contents of the application form can refer to those of this sample.
3) Apart from a lawyer, the authorised legal agent can be an employee working for the applicant, such as the in-house counsel, the principal.
4) In the section of Facts and Grounds, Article 101 is relevant for pre-action applications and Article 100 is relevant for post-action applications. The applicant should choose the proper article.
5) In different official samples, the facts and grounds are very simple. In accordance with the specific facts of a dispute, the applicant should provide more relevant facts and reasons to demonstrate that without the preservation measure, the future judgment/award will not be enforced, or cause substantial loss, the circumstances are urgent and so forth. All in all, in light of the purpose and the requirements of the behaviour preservation discussed in Chapter 8, the applicant should provide more exact facts and reasons to enhance the possibility of obtaining the satisfactory order.

6) Security is mandatory for pre-action applications and optional for post-action applications. The applicant should decide whether it is necessary to provide security for a post-action application. In legal practice, in order to assuage the court's concern, the applicant can voluntarily to add the sentence "if an incorrect preservation application causes the respondent's unexpected loss, the applicant is willing to take responsibility for it".

Annex 2

Application for Advance Enforcement[168]

(Advance Payment)

Applicant (individual): full name, gender, date of birth, ethnicity, employer and occupation, address, contact information.

Respondent (individual): full name, gender, date of birth, ethnicity, employer and occupation, address, contact information.

Items to be claimed:

In accordance with Article 57 of the Administrative Procedural Law of the People's Republic of China, we hereby apply for an order to request XXX (respondent) to pay a pension (or minimum living security, work injury insurance, medical social insurance) in the amount of RMB XXX.

Facts and grounds:

Due to XXXXX dispute between the applicant and the respondent, the court has accepted this case on XXXXX (the exact date). The relationship of rights and obligations between the applicant and the respondent is evident and, without advance enforcement, the daily life of the applicant would be seriously affected. Meanwhile, the respondent is capable of performing the order for advance enforcement. Therefore, prior to the final judgment, in order to secure the basic living expenses, the applicant applies for the advance enforcement order.

Regards

XXXX People's Court

168 This sample is provided by the SPC at <www.court.gov.cn/susongyangshi-xiangqing-770.html> accessed 30 July 2021. It should be noted that the pointers towards the section of Facts and Grounds are provided by the authors; in addition, although the concept of "advance payment" is close to that of "property preservation measure", for the sake of completeness in Chapter 8, the format of applications seeking advance payment is given here.

Applicant (stamp and/or legal representative signature)

Date

Note for applications seeking advance payment:

1) In most scenarios, the applicant seeking an advance payment order is an individual.
2) In the SPC's sample, Article 57 of the Administrative Procedural Law of the People's Republic of China is applied. However, the authors' contention is that it is feasible to apply Article 106 of the CPL 1991 (as amended until 2020) to file an application.
3) The applicant may refer to Article 170 of *Interpretations of the Supreme People's Court on Application of the Civil Procedure Law 2015 (2020 Amendment)* to explain why the reason/ground of the application abides by law. Refer to Chapter 8, 8.22.
4) The facts and grounds can refer to Chapter 8, 8.21–8.26.

Annex 3

Application for Advance Enforcement

Applicant: the full name of the company, organisation or other legal entities; a Unified Social Credit Code or the Registration Code.

Legal representative/principal: name, address, contact telephone number (optional), Identification Card Number (optional).

Authorised legal agent: XXXXX Law Firm, the lawyer's name, gender, Identification Card Number, contract number, lawyer's licence's number, the lawyer's address.

Respondent: the full name of the company, organisation or other legal entities; a Unified Social Credit Code the Registration Code.

Legal representative/principal: name, address, contact telephone number (optional), Identification Card Number (optional).

Authorised legal agent: XXXXX Law Firm, the lawyer's name, gender, Identification Card Number, contract number, lawyer's licence's number, the lawyer's address.

Items to be claimed:

In accordance with Article 106 of the CPL 1991 (as amended until 2020), the applicant hereby applies for an order to request XXXXX (respondent) to stop the XXXXX infringement immediately, or to eliminate the obstruction immediately (the exact conduct of the infringement).

Facts and grounds:

Due to XXXXX dispute between the applicant and the respondent, the court has filed this case on XXXXX (the exact date and case no.). The relationship of rights and obligations between the applicant and the respondent is evident and, without advance enforcement, the production activities or business operations of the applicant would be seriously affected. Meanwhile, the respondent is capable of performing the order for advance enforcement. Therefore, prior to the final judgment, in order to avoid further damage, the applicant applies for the advance enforcement order.

Regards

XXXX People's Court

Applicant (stamp and/or legal representative signature)

Date

Note for applications seeking advance enforcement:

1) If either the applicant or the respondent is an individual, the information can refer to the content of the application form seeking behaviour preservation orders.
2) The applicant may refer to Article 170 of *Interpretations of the Supreme People's Court on Application of the Civil Procedure Law 2015 (2020 Amendment)* to explain why the reason/ground of the application abides by law. Refer to Chapter 8, 8.22.
3) The facts and grounds can refer to Chapter 8, 8.21–8.26.

Annex 4: Application for Reconsideration, Refer to Annex 1, Chapter 3

Annex 5: Application for Discharging the Preservation Order, Refer to Annex 2, Chapter 3

PART 5

INTERIM MEASURES FOR EVIDENCE

CHAPTER 9

Search Orders

Introduction

9.1 A search order is an order requiring a person ("the Respondent")[1] to permit a search party consisting of specified persons – representatives of the Applicant, and an independent Supervising Solicitor appointed by the court – to enter the Respondent's premises and search for evidence or property, for the purpose of ensuring the preservation of that evidence or property. The search order may require the Respondent to permit the search party to inspect and take copies of the evidence or property. It may also require him to permit the search party to remove evidence or property from the premises for safekeeping, in which case it is often referred to as a "search and seizure order".

9.2 A search order is not the same thing as a search warrant.[2] It does not entitle anyone to enter premises against the Respondent's will, still less to force entry to the premises. If the Respondent, or any other person obliged to comply with the order,[3] refuses to comply and permit access to the premises, the search order cannot be executed, but he may be punished for contempt of court.[4] Nevertheless, in practical terms, search orders bear a close resemblance to search warrants, and the courts often describe the execution of a search order as a "raid".[5]

9.3 In principle, search orders can be granted in any kind of case. In practice, they tend only to be granted in certain specific categories of case,

1 For an explanation of the terms Claimant, Defendant, Applicant and Respondent, see Chapter 2, 2.29–2.30.

2 A search warrant is a document issued by a court to a police officer or other investigator, granting legal authority to enter premises to search for specified items. A person executing a search warrant may use reasonable force if necessary in order to gain entry and carry out the search.

3 Or any director, officer, partner or responsible employee of the Respondent; or, in the case of an individual Respondent, any other person having responsible control of the premises to be searched: see paragraph 5 of the standard form search order annexed to CPR PD 25A.

4 *Anton Piller KG v Manufacturing Processes Ltd* [1976] Ch 55 per Lord Denning MR at page 60.

5 See e.g. *Columbia Picture Industries Inc v Robinson* [1987] Ch 38 per Scott J at page 58.

DOI: 10.4324/9781003000310-15

involving claims for passing off[6] or infringement of intellectual property rights, claims by employers to enforce restrictive covenants against former employees and financial disputes between divorcing spouses.[7] They can also be granted post-judgment in any type of case, in aid of enforcement.[8]

9.4 Search orders can be granted in relation to any type of premises, including an office, a warehouse, a vehicle[9] or even a private residence. This intrusive nature of the remedy engages the Respondent's right to privacy under Article 8 of the European Convention on Human Rights (ECHR).[10]

9.5 Applications for search orders are invariably made without notice to the Respondent, and are heard in private, for reasons of secrecy, to prevent the Respondent from removing, hiding or destroying items which are the intended target of the search. To preserve the element of surprise, a search order is invariably executed without any warning, and without the Respondent having been given any prior notice of the existence of the order, or even of the fact that it has been applied for. Search orders thus run counter to normal principles of justice, under which the court should not grant relief against a person in legal proceedings unless he has been notified of the proceedings and given a fair opportunity to be heard and adduce evidence.

9.6 These features make the search order the most Draconian form of interim remedy available under English law, even more so than the freezing

---

6 A tort under English law in which a trader exploits the goodwill of another trader by misrepresenting to the public that his goods, services or business are those of that other trader. The British public was recently gripped by a dispute between two supermarkets, Marks & Spencer and Aldi, over whether Aldi committed the tort of passing off when they introduced a caterpillar-shaped children's birthday cake called "Cuthbert the Caterpillar", which bears a strong resemblance to Marks & Spencer's best-selling "Colin the Caterpillar" cake.

7 Civil Procedure ("The White Book") (2021), Vol. 2, §15–89.

8 *Abela v Baadarani (No.2)* [2017] EWHC 269 (Ch) per Nugee J at [15]–[22].

9 Subsection 7(8) of the Civil Procedure Act 1997.

10 But not, it seems, his right to a fair trial under Article 6: see the decision of the European Court of Human Rights in *Noviflora Sweden Aktiebolag v Sweden* (1993) 15 EHRR CD6, which concerned an equivalent form of interim remedy under Swedish law. English law gives effect to the ECHR through the Human Rights Act 1998. Article 8 of the ECHR contains the right to respect for a person's private and family life, his "home" and his correspondence. This right is engaged not only where a search order covers a private dwelling, but also where it covers professional premises: *Niemietz v Germany* (1993) 16 EHRR 97 at [59], a case about a criminal search warrant under German law. In either case, a search may be justified under Article 8(2), which permits a public authority (including a court granting a search order) to interfere with the right to privacy "in accordance with the law" where "necessary in a democratic society in the interests of national security, public safety or the economic well-being of the country, for the prevention of disorder or crime, for the protection of health or morals, or for the protection of the rights and freedoms of others": see *Chappell v United Kingdom* (1990) 12 EHRR 1 at [50]–[67]. Interference under Article 8(2) is only justifiable where it is proportionate, and a search order in relation to a family home is naturally harder to justify on this basis, because of the humiliation and family distress which it may cause. Such an order thus marks "the absolute extremity of the Court's powers": per Hoffmann J in *Lock International Plc v Beswick* [1989] 1 WLR 1268 at page 1281.

injunction,[11] which restricts the Respondent's ability to deal with his own property but does not violate his privacy.

9.7 Search orders are therefore only granted in exceptional circumstances, where the court is satisfied that there is a paramount need to prevent a denial of justice to the Applicant.[12] They can only be granted by a full High Court Judge.[13] Whenever they are granted, they are hedged about with strict terms governing the precise manner in which they are to be executed, for the benefit and protection of the Respondent. They are always granted on terms which limit the scope of the permitted search, and of any inspection, copying and removal of documents or articles found during the search, to what is strictly necessary for the preservation of evidence or property.

9.8 If the court considers that a search order is not justified in the circumstances of a particular case, it may instead grant a less intrusive form of without notice interim remedy, such as a doorstep delivery-up order – a form of mandatory interim injunction requiring the Respondent to deliver up property or evidence at the threshold to his premises, but without requiring him to allow anyone physically to enter the premises.[14] In such cases, the court may still choose to include detailed provisions for the benefit and protection of the Respondent in the order, similar to those which would be included in a true search order.[15] Furthermore, as electronic data storage becomes increasingly important, the courts have become increasingly ready to grant another form of mandatory injunction – the "imaging order" – either instead of or in addition to a search order, requiring the Respondent to permit the contents of electronic storage media incorporated in or associated with computers or other electronic devices to be imaged or copied, but without affecting the stored data.[16]

9.9 The court also has a general power to grant interim orders for the detention, custody preservation, inspection, sampling and experimentation of relevant property; and to authorise a person to enter any land or building in the possession of a party to the proceedings for that purpose.[17] An order under

---

11 Together, freezing injunctions and search orders have been described as the two "nuclear weapons" of English law: *Bank Mellat v Nikpour* [1985] FSR 87 (CA) per Donaldson LJ at page 92.

12 *Lock International Plc v Beswick* [1989] 1 WLR 1268 per Hoffman J at page 1281, deprecating the manner in which the courts had begun handing out search orders too freely in the late 1980s.

13 CPR 2.3, CPD PD 2 §2 and CPR PD 25A §1.1. This includes a judge exercising the function of a High Court Judge *pro tem.*

14 *Universal City Studios Inc v Mukhtar & Sons Universal City Studios Inc v Mukhtar & Sons* [1976] 2 All ER 330 per Templeman J at page 333; *Hyperama Plc v Poulis* [2018] EWHC 3483 (QB) per Pepperall J at [11]–[23].

15 CPR PD 25A §8.

16 See 9.66–9.69 below.

17 CPR 25.1(1)(c)(i)–(iv) and (d).

this general power cannot be granted before proceedings are commenced;[18] it is not normally available on a without notice application; and it cannot permit an unannounced, surprise raid on the Respondent's premises, which is the hallmark of a true search order.[19]

Sources of Law in Relation to Search Orders

9.10 The English court's power to grant search orders, like its power to grant interim injunctions, originally formed part of its inherent jurisdiction.[20] That power, and the rules of principled discretion governing its exercise, were developed by the courts in a series of cases beginning in the mid-1970s, including the celebrated Court of Appeal decision in *Anton Piller KG v Manufacturing Processes Ltd*,[21] which gave this form of relief the name by which it is still sometimes known: the Anton Piller order.

9.11 The power to grant search orders has since been clarified and placed on a statutory footing by section 7 of the Civil Procedure Act 1997. That provision does not, however, limit or reduce the court's inherent jurisdiction.[22]

9.12 The practice of the English court on applications for search orders is governed by CPR Parts 23 and 25, including in particular CPR 25.1(1)(h); and by the detailed rules in paragraph 7 of CPR PD 25A, one of the practice directions accompanying CPR Part 25. Annexed to that Practice Direction is an officially sanctioned "example" of a search order, which will invariably form the basis of any search order the court grants.[23] This standard form includes specific provisions about how the search order is to be executed, as well as the undertakings which the court will generally require, from both the Applicant and the Supervising Solicitor, as a condition of granting the order.

18 CPR 25.1(1)(d).

19 In other words, an Applicant cannot obtain what amounts to a search order, by applying to the court under this more general power.

20 *Anton Piller KG v Manufacturing Processes Ltd* [1976] Ch 55 per Lord Denning MR at page 61. A search order may, indeed, be conceptualised as specific type of mandatory interim injunction: Steven Gee QC, *Gee on Commercial Injunctions* (7th Edn, Sweet & Maxwell, 2020) §1-049. Moreover, search orders invariably include provisions which, on any view, amount to conventional negative interim injunctions, restraining the Respondent from taking steps which would frustrate the search order before it can be properly executed, such as by tipping others off about its existence or terms, or by removing hiding or destroying any of the items which are the target of the search: see paragraphs 20–22 of the standard form search order appended to CPR PD 25A.

21 [1976] Ch 55. For an authoritative account of the history and development of this jurisdiction, and of some of the uses and abuses of search orders, see *TDB (Owen Holland) Ltd v Andrew Simons* [2020] EWCA Civ 1182 per Arnold LJ at [127]–[175].

22 Steven Gee QC, *Gee on Commercial Injunctions* (7th Edn, Sweet & Maxwell, 2020) §17-002. The court's inherent jurisdiction is also preserved by CPR 25.1(3).

23 To this extent, the expression "example" is misleading: the court will not depart from the terms of the standard form unless there is good reason for doing so: *TDB (Owen Holland) Ltd v Andrew Simons* [2020] EWCA Civ 1182 per Arnold LJ at [173]–[174] and per David Richards LJ at [286].

9.13 The provisions of section 7 of the Civil Procedure Act 1997, paragraph 7 of CPR PD 25A, and the terms of the standard form search order annexed thereto, are at the same time both reflective of, and supplemented by, a substantial body of caselaw decided by the courts, both before and since the passing of the Civil Procedure Act 1997.

Section 7 of the Civil Procedure Act 1997

9.14 As indicated above, the power of the English court to grant a search order is, for most practical purposes, contained in section 7 of the Civil Procedure Act 1997, which provides as follows:

> **Power of courts to make orders for preserving evidence, etc.**
>
> (1) The court may make an order under this section for the purpose of securing, in the case of any existing or proposed proceedings in the court—
> (a) the preservation of evidence which is or may be relevant, or
> (b) the preservation of property which is or may be the subject-matter of the proceedings or as to which any question arises or may arise in the proceedings.
> (2) A person who is, or appears to the court likely to be, a party to proceedings in the court may make an application for such an order.
> (3) Such an order may direct any person to permit any person described in the order, or secure that any person so described is permitted—
> (a) to enter premises in England and Wales, and
> (b) while on the premises, to take in accordance with the terms of the order any of the following steps.
> (4) Those steps are—
> (a) to carry out a search for or inspection of anything described in the order, and
> (b) to make or obtain a copy, photograph, sample or other record of anything so described.
> (5) The order may also direct the person concerned—
> (a) to provide any person described in the order, or secure that any person so described is provided, with any information or article described in the order, and
> (b) to allow any person described in the order, or secure that any person so described is allowed, to retain for safe keeping anything described in the order, and
> (6) An order under this section is to have effect subject to such conditions as are specified in the order.
> (7) This section does not affect any right of a person to refuse to do anything on the ground that to do so might tend to expose him or his spouse or civil partner to proceedings for an offence or for the recovery of a penalty.

(8) In this section—
"court" means the High Court, and
"premises" includes any vehicle;

and an order under this section may describe anything generally, whether by reference to a class or otherwise.

9.15 A number of points arise from the wording of this provision, which are discussed below.

Discretionary Remedy

9.16 As with nearly all interim remedies available under English law, the search order is a discretionary remedy, which the court "may make" if it considers it just and convenient to do so in all the circumstances. Before the court's general discretion can be engaged, the Applicant must first satisfy the following preconditions,[24] which constitute rules of principled discretion:[25]

a. He must show an extremely strong *prima facie* case on the merits of the substantive claim, in support of which the search order is being sought. It is not enough to show merely a serious question to be tried.
b. He must show very serious damage, actual or potential, which will be avoided by the grant of the search order. If the purpose of the search order is to forestall the destruction of evidence, he must show that the evidence is not merely relevant, but of major importance, to the substantive dispute.
c. He must adduce clear evidence that the Respondent to whom the search order is addressed has incriminating material or important evidence in his possession.
d. He must demonstrate a real possibility that the material or evidence may be destroyed, hidden or removed if the search order is not granted.
e. He must satisfy the court that the harm which is likely to be caused, to the Respondent and his business affairs, by the execution of the search order, will not be out of proportion to the legitimate object of the search order.

9.17 Even where these preconditions are met, the court will only exercise its discretion to grant a search order if it is satisfied in all the circumstances that the risk of injustice to the Applicant, if the order is not granted, is greater

24 *Indicii Salus Ltd v Chandrasekaran* [2006] EWHC 521 (Ch) per Warren J at [85]; *Arcelormittal USA LLC v Essar Steel Ltd* [2019] EWHC 724 (Comm) per Jacobs J at [97]–[99].
25 See Chapter 2, 2.67(b) for an explanation of this term.

than the risk of injustice to the Respondent, if the order is wrongly granted. In weighing that balance, the court will also have regard to the fact that the order is to be granted without the Respondent having the opportunity to be heard by the court; the fact that it will be executed without prior warning, and without the Respondent having even been made aware of its existence, let alone its terms; the intrusive and mandatory nature of the order; and the shock, humiliation and distress which executing the order may cause.

Stage at Which a Search Order Can Be Granted

9.18 A search order can be granted in support of substantive proceedings which have already been commenced, or which are yet to be commenced ("proposed proceedings"). For obvious reasons, search orders are typically sought before the formal commencement of substantive proceedings.

Search Order in Support of Substantive Proceedings Elsewhere

9.19 Sub-section 7(1) of the Civil Procedure Act 1997 expressly provides that a search order can be granted in support of actual or proposed proceedings "in the court", i.e. the English High Court.[26]

9.20 The court also has power to grant search orders in support of actual or proposed substantive proceedings:[27]

a. In a foreign court, pursuant to section 25 of the Civil Jurisdiction and Judgments Act 1982.
b. In arbitration, pursuant to section 44 of the Arbitration Act 1996, provided that the strict conditions of that provision are satisfied.[28]

9.21 The English court may refuse to grant relief in support of substantive proceedings in a foreign court if it considers that the fact that it has no jurisdiction apart from section 25 of the Civil Jurisdiction & Judgments Act 1982 in relation to the subject-matter of the proceedings makes it "inexpedient" to do so.[29] Similarly, where the arbitration is outside England and Wales or Northern Ireland, the English court may refuse to grant such relief if it considers that the location of the seat of the arbitration makes it "inappropriate" to do so.[30]

---

26 See subsection 7(8).

27 Steven Gee QC, *Gee on Commercial Injunctions* (7th Edn, Sweet & Maxwell, 2020) suggests otherwise, at §§6-035, 036, 043, 068, 080. There is probably no power, at any rate under section 7 of the Civil Procedure Act 1997, to grant a search order post-judgment, in aid of enforcement of a judgment in another jurisdiction: *Arcelormittal USA LLC v Essar Steel Ltd* [2019] EWHC 724 (Comm) per Jacobs J *obiter* at [100]–[101].

28 See Chapter 4, 4.31–4.34.

29 See Chapter 2, 2.72(a).

30 See Chapter 2, 2.72(b)–(c).

Purpose of Search

9.22 A search order may be granted for the purpose of securing the preservation of evidence, property or both, to prevent the Respondent from altering, destroying or hiding such evidence or property.[31]

9.23 Where the purpose is to preserve evidence, that evidence must be relevant to the issues arising in the actual or proposed proceedings although, as explained above, something more than mere relevance must be demonstrated before the court will be prepared to exercise its discretion to grant a search order on this basis. Where the purpose is to preserve property, either the property must itself be the subject-matter of the substantive proceedings, or a question must arise (or be likely to arise) in relation to that property in those proceedings.

9.24 In either case, the purpose of the search order is always limited to securing the **preservation** of the evidence or property. It cannot be granted for any other purpose. Thus, a search order may require the Respondent to permit the Applicant to inspect documents during the search, but only for the purpose of identifying documents which need to be preserved. A search order does not entitle the Applicant to use the documents which are uncovered during the search, or the information which they contain, as he could if they belonged to him; or even to use them as he could if the Respondent had disclosed them to him in the proceedings.[32] The court may order the Respondent to disclose documents found during a raid to the Applicant, or permit the Applicant to treat those documents as if the Respondent had disclosed them, in which case the Applicant will be entitled to make use of those documents in the usual way; but that involves the court exercising a separate case-management power from the power to grant a search order itself.

Who Can Apply?

9.25 A search order may be granted on the application of a person who is, or is likely to be, a party to substantive proceedings, either in the English court or, where the application is made under section 25 of the Civil Jurisdiction and Judgments Act 1992 or section 44 of the Arbitration Act 1996, in a foreign court or in arbitration. That includes both a Claimant and a Defendant (or, indeed, a Part 20 Defendant) in court proceedings, and both a claimant or a respondent in arbitration. Where, as is very often the case, substantive proceedings have not yet been commenced at the time the application is made,

31 *TBD (Owen Holland) Ltd v Simons* [2020] EWCA Civ 1182 per Arnold LJ at [175].

32 The general rule in CPR 31.22(1) is that a party to whom a document has been disclosed may use the document only for the purpose of the proceedings in which it is disclosed. This rule is subject to exceptions set out in CPR 31.22(1)(a)–(c) and (2).

the court will require the Applicant to give an undertaking to commence those substantive proceedings as soon as practicable.[33]

Which Premises Can Be Searched?

9.26 Section 7 of the Civil Procedure Act 1997 empowers the court to grant a search order in respect of premises within England and Wales. Where the premises are a ship (a type of vehicle), it must be located within the territorial waters of the United Kingdom adjoining England and Wales.

9.27 In principle, the English court also has the power to grant a search order in respect of premises outside England and Wales, under its pre-existing inherent jurisdiction.[34] In practice, that power is rarely if ever exercised, for reasons of international comity.[35] There are no reported cases since the passing of the Civil Procedure Act 1997 in which the English court has exercised that power.

Against Whom Can a Search Order Be Granted?

9.28 The court may grant a search order addressed to any person (the Respondent) who appears to have the legal right or the power to grant access to the premises which are to be searched, provided that the court has personal jurisdiction over that Respondent.

9.29 Typically, the Respondent will be both the owner or occupier of the premises, and the person against whom the Applicant intends to bring the substantive claim (the "substantive Defendant"). But that will not always be the case. If so, the English court will often have the power to grant a search order addressed to a Respondent against whom the Applicant asserts no substantive cause of action.

9.30 Prior to the passing of the Civil Procedure Act 1997, the English court had power grant such relief on two bases:[36]

a. It could do so under its "Chabra" jurisdiction, in support of and ancillary to the Applicant's substantive claim against the substantive Defendant.[37] Most instances of the court exercising this jurisdiction involve the grant of freezing injunctions, and it is discussed

---

33 See Schedule C, para (2), to the standard form search order appended to CPR PD 25A.

34 *Cook Industries Inc v Galliher* [1979] Ch 439 per Templeman J at page 444.

35 A point reinforced by Parliament's decision not to include that power in section 7 of the Civil Procedure Act 1997.

36 Steven Gee QC, *Gee on Commercial Injunctions* (7th Edn, Sweet & Maxwell, 2020) §17-008.

37 See Chapter 2, 2.73; Chapter 4, 4.37–4.39; and Chapter 7, 7.41–7.42.

in detail in that context in Chapter 5; but the power also extends to search orders.[38]

b. It could also do so in support of and ancillary to a "substantive" claim by the Applicant for a Norwich Pharmacal order against the Respondent himself, brought on the basis that the Respondent had become mixed up in wrongdoing so as to give rise to a duty to assist the Applicant by providing information which would assist him in righting that wrong.[39]

9.31 These powers arise under the court's inherent jurisdiction,[40] and are limited by established rules of principled discretion. They have survived the passing of the Civil Procedure Act 1997.

9.32 Section 7 of the Civil Procedure Act 1997 ostensibly gives the court a wholly unfettered power to grant a search order against anyone it chooses, in relation to premises within England and Wales, regardless of whether it could grant such relief against that person under its inherent jurisdiction. In principle, this statutory power might permit the court to grant a search order addressed to an entirely innocent Respondent, who just happened to have access to the target premises, but who had no other involvement in the matters giving rise to the substantive dispute whatsoever.[41] Such a Respondent would not fall within the ambit of the court's inherent Chabra or Norwich Pharmacal jurisdictions.[42] In practice, given the Draconian nature of search orders, the court would be unlikely to grant relief against such a Respondent under section 7, in circumstances where it could not do so under its inherent jurisdiction.

Personal Jurisdiction over the Respondent

9.33 A search order can only be granted against a Respondent who is herself amenable to the personal jurisdiction of the English court. That in turn depends on whether the Respondent can lawfully be served with an

38 See e.g. *Mercantile Group (Europe) AG v Aiyela* [1993] FSR 745 per Hobhouse J at pages 747 and 752.

39 Chapter 2, 2.45; *Mercantile Group (Europe) AG v Aiyela* [1993] FSR 745 per Hobhouse J at pages 751–753; [1994] QB 366 (CA) per Steyn LJ at page 376. A Norwich Pharmacal order is technically a form of substantive relief, although it possesses many characteristics of an interim remedy.

40 The power to grant both forms of relief is confirmed by section 37 of the Senior Courts Act 1981: *Mercantile Group (Europe) AG v Aiyela* [1994] QB 366 (CA) per Hoffmann LJ at page 374.

41 Steven Gee QC, *Gee on Commercial Injunctions* (7th Edn, Sweet & Maxwell, 2020) §17-009.

42 Such a person would be regarded as a "mere witness or bystander" who could not be made the subject of Norwich Pharmacal relief: *Norwich Pharmacal Co v Customs & Excise Commissioners* [1974] AC 133 per Lord Reid at pages 174–175.

Application Notice containing an application for the search order.[43] This is so, notwithstanding that applications for search orders are invariably made without notice.[44]

9.34 In most cases, this requirement presents no difficulties, as the Respondent will very often be amenable to personal service in England and Wales, at the premises which are to be searched.[45]

9.35 But where the Respondent is not amenable to service in England and Wales, a search order can only be granted against her if she can lawfully be served out of the jurisdiction.[46] The position can be summarised as follows:

a. Where the search order is sought in support of substantive proceedings[47] in the English court, and the Respondent is the substantive Defendant[48] in those proceedings, she is subject to the personal jurisdiction of the English court if:
   i. The Claim Form containing the substantive claim can be served on her out of the jurisdiction without the court's permission under CPR 6.33, or
   ii. The substantive claim falls within one of the jurisdictional gateways in CPR PD 6B §3.1, and the court gives permission to serve the Claim Form on her out of the jurisdiction under CPR 6.36–37.
b. Where the search order is sought in support of substantive proceedings in the English court, and the Respondent is *not* the substantive Defendant in those proceedings, she cannot be made subject to the personal jurisdiction of the English court unless she voluntarily submits.[49]
c. Where the search order is sought in support of substantive proceedings in a foreign court, and the Respondent is the substantive

43 See Chapter 2, 2.68–2.69, 2.73–2.74. The Respondent will also be subject to the personal jurisdiction of the English court if she has submitted to the jurisdiction voluntarily, e.g. by commencing the substantive proceedings herself as Claimant, in which case the court has personal jurisdiction to grant a search order against her in support of a counterclaim or other additional claim made against her in the same proceedings under CPR Part 20.

44 See Chapter 2, 2.98.

45 The rules governing personal service in England and Wales are contained in CPR Part 6, Sections II and III, and CPR PD 6A.

46 See Chapter 2, 2.75–2.84.

47 This also applies where the only "substantive" claim in the English court proceedings is a claim for a Norwich Pharmacal order against the Respondent: see Chapter 2, 2.45.

48 Or the intended substantive Defendant.

49 See Steven Gee QC, *Gee on Commercial Injunctions* (7th Edn, Sweet & Maxwell, 2020) §13-051. Gee's view assumes that the decision of Aikens J in *C Inc plc v L* [2001] 2 Lloyd's Rep 459 on the scope of the jurisdictional gateway in CPR PD 6B §3.1(3) is wrong, and that it only applies where there is a substantive claim against the Respondent. But in any event, it would seem that that gateway can only apply if (i) an application for a search order is also being made against the Defendant to the substantive claim and (ii) the Respondent is, for some reason, a necessary or proper party to that application against the Defendant.

Defendant in those foreign proceedings, she is subject to the personal jurisdiction of the English court if the court gives permission to serve a Part 8 Claim Form on her out of the jurisdiction under CPR PD 6B §3.1(5), containing a claim for a search order as final relief under section 25 of the Civil Jurisdiction & Judgments Act 1982.

d. Where the search order is sought in support of substantive proceedings in a foreign court, and the Respondent is *not* the substantive Defendant to those foreign proceedings, she cannot be made subject to the personal jurisdiction of the English court unless she voluntarily submits.[50]

e. Where the search order is sought in support of substantive proceedings in arbitration, and the Respondent to the search order is also the respondent in the arbitration, she is subject to the personal jurisdiction of the English court if the court gives permission to serve a Part 8 Claim Form on her out of the jurisdiction under CPR 62.5, containing a claim for a search order as final relief under section 44 of the Arbitration Act 1996.

f. Where the search order is sought in support of substantive proceedings in arbitration, and the Respondent to the search order is *not* the respondent in the arbitration, English law is currently unclear as to whether she can be made subject to the personal jurisdiction of the English court, in the absence of a voluntary submission.[51]

Search Party

9.36 A search order must identify the members of the search party who must be permitted to enter the Respondent's premises, either by name or by description. The search party will invariably consist of the Applicant's solicitor, and one or more other representatives of the Applicant, and an independent Supervising Solicitor.[52] The search party should not contain any person who could gain personally or commercially from anything they might read or see on the premises, unless their presence is essential.[53]

9.37 The Supervising Solicitor is an independent solicitor, not acting for the Applicant or the Respondent,[54] who is experienced in the operation of

50 *Belletti v Morici* [2009] EWHC 2316 (Comm) per Flaux J at [38].

51 See Chapter 4, 4.36–4.39 discussing *Cruz City 1 Mauritius Holdings v Unitech* [2014] EWHC 3704 (Comm) and *A v C* [2020] EWCA Civ 409.

52 The court has a discretion not to require a Supervising Solicitor: CPR PD 25A §7.4(1).

53 See footnote 9 to the standard form search order appended to CPR PD 25A.

54 In particular, he must not be an employee or member of the Applicant's firm of solicitors: CPR PD 25A §7.6.

search orders.[55] He will invariably be identified by name in the search order. He does not participate in the search itself. Instead, his role is to attend the raid, serve the search order on the Respondent, and supervise the execution of the order, as discussed in more detail below.[56]

9.38 If the Respondent is likely to be an unaccompanied woman, the Supervising Solicitor must either be a woman, or must be accompanied on the raid by at least one woman, who must herself be named in the search order.[57]

Scope of the Search

9.39 A search order may require the Respondent to permit the search party, or a specified member of the search party, to do the following while on the premises:

a. Carry out a search for an item or items of property or evidence.
b. Perform an inspection on such items.
c. Make or obtain a copy, photograph, sample or other record of such items.
d. Remove such items from the premises and retain them for safekeeping.

9.40 In each case, the item or items of property or evidence must be described in the search order. It may be described specifically, or in more general terms, e.g. items of property which appear to infringe a particular trademark or intellectual property right of the Applicant, or documents which appear to contain confidential information belonging to the Applicant. The description must be clear enough to enable the Respondent to know what the search party is and is not entitled to do.

Respondent's Duty to Provide Assistance

9.41 In addition to requiring the Respondent to permit the search party to conduct the search, the search order may also contain a mandatory provision requiring the Respondent to provide the search party with any information or article described in the order. The court will typically order the Respondent to inform the Applicant's legal representatives of the location of all items listed in the search order.[58] In cases involving infringement of intellectual property rights, the court may also order the Respondent to provide information about third parties to whom he has supplied or offered to

55 CPR PD 25A §7.2.
56 See 9.53, 9.58–9.59, 9.62, 9.64–9.65 below.
57 CPR PD 25A §7.4(5).
58 See paragraph 18(a) of the standard form search order appended to CPR PD 25A.

supply items listed in the search order; and details of how many items he supplied or offered to supply to them, and when.[59] The Respondent's obligation to provide information is, however, subject to his right to invoke the privilege against self-incrimination.

The Privilege against Self-Incrimination

9.42 The privilege against self-incrimination is the right under English law of any person[60] to avoid providing any information or releasing any document or thing, if that would tend to expose him (or a spouse or civil partner) to criminal proceedings,[61] including proceedings for civil contempt of court.[62] The court will not grant a search order in terms which are likely to require the Respondent to incriminate himself, and the Respondent is entitled to invoke the privilege in order to avoid complying with a search order in whole or in part.[63]

9.43 On its face, the privilege against self-incrimination looks like a powerful weapon in the hands of a Respondent who wishes to withhold relevant material and information in the face of a search order. In practice, its scope and effect are much less far-reaching than might first appear:

a. The privilege is only available where there is a real and appreciable risk that the Respondent will be prosecuted in the UK.[64]
b. It does not entitle the Respondent to refuse access by the search party to his premises for the purposes of looking for property belonging to the Applicant, or to refuse to allow the Applicant to remove such property for safekeeping, where that is permitted by the search order.[65]
c. Nor does it entitle the Respondent to refuse to provide documents or things which exist "independently of the will of the Respondent"

59 See paragraph 18(b)–(c) of the standard form search order appended to CPR PD 25A. The court's power to grant this type of order arises under its Norwich Pharmacal jurisdiction: see Chapter 2, 2.45.

60 Including a company: *Triplex Safety Glass Co Ltd v Lancegaye Safety Glass (1934) Ltd* [1939] 2 KB 395 per Du Parcq LJ at pages 408–409.

61 CPR PD 25A §7.4(4)(b)(ii). See Charles Hollander QC, *Documentary Evidence* (13th Edn, Sweet & Maxwell, 2021) §21-02. The privilege against self-incrimination exists at common law. Its scope is confirmed by section 14 of the Civil Evidence Act 1968: *Rio Tinto Zinc Corp v Westinghouse Electric Corp* [1978] AC 547 per Lord Diplock at page 636. It is expressly preserved in the case of search orders by subsection 7(7) of the Civil Procedure Act 1997. It is closely related to aspects of the right to a fair trial conferred by Article 6 of the European Convention on Human Rights.

62 *Memory Corp Plc v Sidhu* [2000] Ch 645 per Arden J at [22].

63 Civil Procedure Act 1997 section 7(7).

64 *Rio Tinto Zinc Corp v Westinghouse Electric Corp* [1978] AC 547 per Lord Denning MR at page 574 (CA); and per Viscount Dilhorne at pages 627–628 (HL).

65 *Rank Film Distributors Ltd v Video Information Centre* [1982] AC 380 per Lord Wilberforce at pages 440–441.

to remain silent and not to incriminate himself.[66] In practice, this means that the Respondent cannot refuse to allow inspection and removal of, say, a computer on the basis that it contains incriminating evidence, even if he created the evidence himself, as that evidence exists entirely independently of his will not to incriminate himself. By contrast, he can refuse to make a statement which would incriminate himself, as that statement has no independent existence, and the court cannot compel him to make a statement (and in so doing, create evidence) in defiance of his will not to incriminate himself.

9.44 Furthermore, the privilege has been withdrawn altogether by statute in number of situations. Some of these are of real practical importance to search orders. In particular:

a. In proceedings for infringement of intellectual property rights,[67] or to obtain disclosure or information in relation to any infringement of such rights, or to prevent any apprehended infringement of such rights,[68] the Respondent cannot refuse to comply with a search order made in those proceedings on the grounds that doing so would tend to expose him to prosecution for:
   i. Any offence which he may have committed by, or in the course of, infringing the intellectual property rights; or
   ii. Any other offence which he may have committed in connection with that infringement, which involves fraud or dishonesty.[69]

66 *R (River East Supplies Ltd) v Crown Court at Nottingham* [2017] EWHC 1942 (Admin) per Simon LJ at [80] and [83]. We have the European Court of Human Rights to thank for this Delphic language: see *Saunders v United Kingdom* (1996) 23 EHRR 313 at [68]–[69], a case on Article 6 of the ECHR. The position has also been summarised somewhat differently, if no less clearly, by Popplewell J in *JSC BTA Bank v Ablyazov* [2014] EWHC 2788 (Comm) at [115] and [117], as follows: the privilege does not provide a Respondent with protection against the risk of incriminating himself by the provision of a document or documents which come into existence independently of any order, statute or other instrument of law which compelled their production; it does not normally cover documents other than those which come into existence by an exercise of will pursuant to a "testimonial obligation" imposed upon him; and what matters is whether the creation of the document which contains or evidences the communication in question was compelled by a relevant order of the court.

67 I.e. rights pertaining to any patent, trademark, copyright, design right, registered design, technical or commercial information or any other form of intellectual property: Senior Courts Act 1981 section 72(5).

68 Where the search order is sought in support of substantive proceedings for infringement of intellectual property rights in a foreign court or in arbitration, the English proceedings in which the search order is sought will generally qualify as proceedings to obtain disclosure or information in relation to any infringement of such rights or to prevent any apprehended infringement of such rights for these purposes.

69 Senior Courts Act 1981 section 72; CPR PD 25A §7.9(1).

b. In proceedings for the recovery of property,[70] the Respondent cannot refuse to comply with a search order on the grounds that doing so would tend to expose him to prosecution for:
   i. An offence under the Theft Act 1968 (including theft, robbery, burglary, false accounting, false statements by company directors, dishonest suppression of documents, blackmail and handling stolen goods).[71]
   ii. An offence under the Fraud Act 2006 (including fraud; conspiracy to defraud; possessing, making or supplying articles for use in fraud; and obtaining services dishonestly).
   iii. Any other offence involving any form of fraudulent conduct or purpose.[72]

Applying for a Search Order

9.45 Applications for a search order are invariably made without notice and heard in private. Nevertheless, save in cases of exceptional urgency, the Applicant must issue an Application Notice, setting out the order sought and brief reasons why it is sought. In practice, given the length and complexity of search orders, the Application Notice will invariably not contain the terms of the order sought but, rather, will refer to the terms of a draft order prepared by the Applicant's solicitors and attached to the Application Notice.

9.46 The application must be supported by evidence in the form of an affidavit – a witness statement is not sufficient.[73] The affidavit must disclose "very fully" the reasons the order is sought, including the probability that the material which the search is intended to reveal would disappear if the order were not made.[74] This is a reflection of the Applicant's duty of full and frank disclosure, which arises from the fact that the application is being made without notice to the Respondent. The affidavit must also give details of the Supervising Solicitor, including the name and address of his law firm, and of his experience in the operation of search orders, so that the court can determine whether he is a suitable person to perform the important functions of a supervising solicitor in that case. The affidavit must also give the address of the premises which are to be searched, and state whether it is a private or business address.[75] This is an important factor for the court to consider when deciding whether, and if so how, to exercise its general discretion to grant a search order.

---

70 This includes proceedings for the administration of property, for the execution of a trust or for an account of any property or dealings with property: CPR PD 25A §7.9(2).

71 Theft Act 1968 section 31(1); CPR PD 25A §7.9(2)(a).

72 Fraud Act 2006 section 13; CPR PD 25A §7.9(2)(b).

73 CPR PD 25A §3.1, CPR PD 32 §1.4.

74 CPR PD 25A §7.3(2).

75 CPR PD 25A §7.3(1).

9.47 The draft order accompanying the Application Notice should be based on the officially sanctioned example annexed to CPR PD 25A. The court can modify the terms of that standard form as appropriate in any particular case, but in practice it will not depart from those terms without good reason.[76] Where the court is asked to grant a search order in terms which differ from that standard form in any material (i.e. non-trivial) way, the Applicant's Counsel must bring the differences to the specific attention of the judge hearing the application, as part of the duty of full and frank disclosure, and explain why they are appropriate.[77]

Undertakings

9.48 The court will invariably require the Applicant, the Applicant's solicitors and the Supervising Solicitor each to give a set of undertakings to the court, as a condition of granting the search order. Typically, the Applicant's solicitors and the Supervising Solicitor will both require the Applicant to agree to indemnify them against any liability or loss they incur by reason of giving these undertakings, before they will agree to act; and they may also require the Applicant to secure that indemnity, by means of a cash deposit or a guarantee from a parent company or a bank or other financial institution. As with any other undertaking given to the court, breach of these undertakings may render the person who gave the undertaking liable to committal proceedings for contempt of court.

9.49 The Applicant will be required to give a wide-ranging undertaking in damages, to compensate the Respondent for any loss caused by the search order or its execution which the court orders him to compensate, and for any loss caused by executing the search order in a way which breaches the terms of the order or the duties of the Applicant's solicitors as officers of the court.[78] This undertaking is much wider than the undertaking which an applicant is typically required to give when applying without notice for other types of interim remedy. In particular, it is not limited to situations where the court later decides that the order ought not to have been made. The Applicant will often be required to fortify that undertaking by providing security to the court.[79]

9.50 The Applicant will also be required to undertake not to use any information or documents obtained during the search without the permission of

76 CPR PD 25A §7.11.

77 *The Gadget Shop Ltd v The Bug.Com Ltd* [2001] FSR 26 per Rimer J at [109]. The same principle applies to freezing injunctions: Commercial Court Guide §F15.7; *Frenkel v Lyampart* [2017] EWHC 312 (Ch) per Amanda Tipples QC at [90–91].

78 See Schedule C, paragraph (1) of the standard form search order appended to CPR PD 25A.

79 See Schedule C, paragraph (5) of the standard form search order appended to CPR PD 25A.

the court, except for specified purposes; to take out insurance on the items removed from the premises in the search; and to comply with any procedural steps which he did not have time to complete before making the without notice application, such as issuing the Claim Form and swearing the affidavit in support of the application.[80]

9.51 The Applicant's solicitors will be required to undertake to provide the Supervising Solicitor with a copy of the search order and all the other documents which will have to be served on the Respondent at the start of the raid,[81] including the Claim Form (or draft Claim Form if this had not yet been issued by the time of the application), the Application Notice, the affidavits (or draft affidavits) and exhibits shown to the court at the without notice hearing, a note of any other allegation of fact made orally to the court at the hearing which is not contained in those affidavits and the Applicant's skeleton argument provided to the court for that hearing.

9.52 They will also be required to undertake to answer at once to the best of their ability any question whether a particular item is one of the items of property or evidence listed in the search order; to retain in their own safekeeping all such items removed during the raid; and to return to the Respondent all documents removed during the raid (except documents which belong to the Applicant) as soon as possible and in any event within two days, which should give them time to make copies of the documents.[82]

9.53 The Supervising Solicitor will be required to give a number of independent undertakings of his own: to use his best endeavours to serve the search order and all other necessary documents on the Respondent; to explain to the person served with the order its meaning and effect fairly and in everyday language, and to inform him of his rights;[83] to retain in safe keeping all items which he retains as a result of the search order; not to disclose any information relating to those items unless required to do so by the court; and to make a written report of the raid within 48 hours of completion of the search, and serve it on the Applicant's solicitors, the Respondent and the court.[84]

The Format of the Search Order

9.54 The standard form of search order has a penal notice on the front page, warning the Respondent that, if he disobeys the order, he may be held

80 See Schedule C, paragraphs (2), (3), (4) and (6) of the standard form search order appended to CPR PD 25A.

81 See Schedule D, paragraph (1) of the standard form search order appended to CPR PD 25A.

82 See Schedule D, paragraphs (2), (3) and (4) of the standard form search order appended to CPR PD 25A.

83 See 9.56 below.

84 See Schedule E of the standard form search order appended to CPR PD 25A.

in contempt of court and punished accordingly, and that any other person who knows of the order and does anything which helps or permits the Respondent to breach the order may be treated in the same way.[85]

9.55 Then come the operative parts of the order, which are set out in a series of sections:

a. The first section, entitled "This Order", states when the search order was made and identifies the judge who made it, the Applicant who applied for it and the Respondent to whom it addresses and the persons who must comply with it. It states that the order was made on an application without notice, and that the Respondent has the right to apply to the court to set it aside or vary it. It also gives the Return Date on which the court will rehear the application, but this time on notice to the Respondent.
b. The next section, entitled "The Search", identifies the Supervising Solicitor and the other members of the search party, and sets out the scope of the search.
c. The section entitled "Restrictions on Search" set out a series of restrictions on when and how the search is to be carried out, and explains the Respondent's rights in relation to them.
d. The section entitled "Delivery of Articles/Documents" contains provisions requiring the Respondent to hand over items of property and evidence to the search party.
e. The section entitled "Provision of Information" contains provisions requiring the Respondent to provide information to the search party about the items which are the target of the search, and other related information.
f. The section entitled "Prohibited Acts" sets out various things which the Respondent is prohibited from doing, which would frustrate the purpose of the search.
g. Finally, there are short sections entitled "Costs", "Restrictions on Service", "Variation and Discharge of this Order", "Interpretation of this Order" and "Communication with the Court".

9.56 There are also five schedules attached to the order:

- Schedule A identifies the premises which are to be searched.
- Schedule B lists the items of property or evidence which are the subject of the search order.
- Schedule C records the undertakings given by the Applicant himself.
- Schedule D records the undertakings given by the Applicant's solicitors.

---

85 See generally Chapter 2, 2.128.

- Schedule E records the undertakings given by the Supervising Solicitor.

Executing the Search Order: Service

9.57 The raid commences when the search party arrives, unannounced, at the Respondent's premises and serves the search order on him. Unless the court orders otherwise, that can only be done between the hours of 9:30 am and 5:30 pm, Monday to Friday.[86] A search order must not be executed at the same time as a police search warrant.[87]

9.58 The person responsible for serving the search order is the Supervising Solicitor. He must personally serve the order on the Respondent.[88] At the same time he must explain the terms and effect of the order to the Respondent, using everyday language.[89] He must also advise the Respondent that he has the following rights:

a. The right to take legal advice.
b. The right to apply to the court to vary or discharge the order.[90] This right will also be set out expressly in the search order itself.
c. The right to avail himself of:
    i. The privilege against self-incrimination.[91]
    ii. Legal professional privilege, which is the right not to be required to disclose confidential communications between the Respondent and his lawyers in relation to the seeking or obtaining of legal advice ("legal advice privilege"), and confidential documents created for the dominant purpose of gathering evidence for use in existing or reasonably contemplated legal proceedings ("litigation privilege").[92]

9.59 Along with the search order, the Supervising Solicitor must also serve the Respondent with a copy of the affidavit evidence that was presented to the court by the Applicant in support of the application for the search order, any other documents that were provided to the court at the without

---

86 CPR PD 25A §7.4(6). It should normally be served on a weekday morning, but not before 9:30 am, to give the Respondent a proper opportunity to obtain legal advice: see footnote 12 to the standard form search order appended to CPR PD 25A.

87 CPR PD 25A §7.8.

88 CPR PD 25A §7.4(1). The court may order that this requirement be dispensed with, in which case the search order must set out the reasons why: CPR PD 25A §7.7.

89 CPR PD 25A §7.4(4).

90 CPR PD 25A §7.4(4)(a). This right arises from the fact that the search order will have been granted on a without notice application: CPR 23.10. The search order must state that the Respondent has this right: CPR 23.9(3).

91 See 9.42–9.44 above.

92 CPR PD 25A §7.4(4)(b)(i). See Charles Hollander QC, *Documentary Evidence* (13th Edn, Sweet & Maxwell, 2021) §13-02.

notice hearing, and a note of what was said at that hearing.[93] In some cases, the exhibits to the affidavit evidence may include confidential documents. In such cases, the Supervising Solicitor is not required to serve the confidential exhibits on the Respondent; but he must instead make them available for the Respondent to inspect, in the presence of the Applicant's solicitors, while the search is being carried out; and he must allow the Respondent's own solicitors to retain them afterwards, provided that they undertake not to permit the Respondent to see them or copies of them except in their presence, and not to make or take away any note or copy of them.[94]

9.60 From the moment that the search order is served, the Respondent is prohibited from informing anyone of the proceedings in which the search order has been made, or the contents of the search order, and he is prohibited from warning anyone that proceedings have been or may be brought against him by the Applicant. This prohibition continues in the first instance until 4:30 pm UK time on the Return Date. There is one exception to these prohibitions: the Respondent is permitted to inform his lawyers for the purpose of obtaining legal advice.[95]

9.61 The Respondent is also prohibited, from the moment the search order is served on him, from destroying, tampering with, cancelling or disposing of any of the items listed in the search order. Again, this prohibition continues in the first instance until 4:30 pm UK time on the Return Date.

Executing the Search Order: The Search

9.62 Once the Supervising Solicitor has served the search order on the Respondent, explained its meaning to him and advised him of his rights, the Respondent must immediately permit the Supervising Solicitor to enter the premises. Generally, however, he is not required to permit the rest of the search party to enter and start searching immediately:[96]

a. He is entitled to ask the Supervising Solicitor to delay the start of the search for a short time, so that he can seek legal advice and apply to the Court to vary or discharge the search order. The Supervising Solicitor is not obliged to agree but, if he does, the Respondent must not disturb or remove any of the items listed in the search order during the delay.[97]

---

93 CPR PD 25A §7.4(1).

94 CPR PD 25A §7.4(2).

95 See paragraph 20 of the standard form order annexed to CPR PD 25A.

96 This reflects the terms of the standard form of search order annexed to CPR PD 25A. The court can, in an appropriate case, depart from the terms of that standard form and require the Respondent to permit the whole of the search party to enter the premises and start searching immediately.

97 See paragraph 10 of the standard form search order appended to CPR PD 25A.

b. He is entitled to insist on an initial period of delay, usually of no more than two hours,[98] while he gathers together any documents that he believes may be covered by the privilege against self-incrimination or by legal professional privilege, and hands them to the Supervising Solicitor to assess whether they are indeed incriminating or privileged.[99]

9.63 Once these initial periods have ended,[100] the Respondent must permit the rest of the search party to enter the premises and search for, inspect, photograph or photocopy, and deliver into the safekeeping of the Applicant's solicitors, the documents and articles listed in the search order. He must allow them to remain on the premises until that search is complete. If any members of the search party need to leave before the search is complete, he must let them back in immediately, on the same day or the following day, to complete the search.[101]

9.64 The search itself is performed by the Applicant's representatives, including the Applicant's solicitor. It must be carried out in the presence, and under the supervision, of the Supervising Solicitor. The Supervising Solicitor does not participate in the search himself. He does, however, have a number of duties to perform during the search:

a. He must ensure that the search is conducted in the presence of the Respondent. He can, however, allow the search to proceed in the absence of the Respondent if he is satisfied that that is not practicable, such as where the Respondent refuses to remain on the premises during the search.[102]
b. If he concludes that any documents found on the premises are covered by the privilege against self-incrimination or legal professional privilege, he must exclude them from the search, make a list of them and give them back to the Respondent. This applies to documents which the Respondent gathers in the initial period before the search begins, and to documents which the search party uncovers during the search itself.[103]
c. If he merely **believes** that the Respondent **may be** entitled to withhold a document, or any part of the document, on the grounds of privilege against self-incrimination or legal professional privilege, or if the Respondent claims to be entitled to withhold documents on this basis and the Supervising Solicitor does not agree, the Supervising Solicitor must again exclude those documents from the

98 The Supervising Solicitor may agree a longer time.
99 See paragraph 11(1) of the standard form search order appended to CPR PD 25A.
100 And assuming that the court has not set aside the search order in the meantime.
101 See paragraphs 6 and 7 of standard form search order appended to CPR PD 25A.
102 See paragraphs 14 and 15 of the standard form search order appended to CPR PD 25A.
103 See paragraph 11(2) of the standard form search order appended to CPR PD 25A.

search and make a list of them. But instead of giving the documents back to the Respondent, the Supervising Solicitor must keep them in his possession, until such time as the court decides whether or not they are covered by privilege.[104]

d. He must ensure that no documents or articles are removed from the premises until the Applicant's representatives have prepared a list of those items, given a copy of the list to the Respondent and given the Respondent a reasonable opportunity to check it.[105]

9.65 The Respondent will also have a number of obligations to perform during the search. He will continue to be bound by the prohibitions on informing anyone about the search order and on destroying, interfering with or disposing of items listed in the search order. In addition, the search order may impose a number of positive obligations on him:

a. The search order will usually require the Respondent immediately to inform the Applicant's solicitors, in the presence of the Supervising Solicitor, of the whereabouts of all the items listed in the search order. It will usually also require the Respondent immediately to hand over to the Applicant's solicitors all such listed items which are in the Respondent's possession or control. If the Respondent does not accept that an item is covered by the search order, or if he claims privilege in respect of it, then he must immediately hand the item over to the Supervising Solicitor for safe keeping, until the court can resolve the dispute over that item.[106]
b. Where the search order is granted in support of a substantive claim for passing off, or for breach of trademark, copyright or other intellectual property rights involving dealing in physical goods, the search order will usually order the Respondent immediately to provide the Applicant's solicitors, in the presence of the Supervising Solicitor, with full details of his supply network, so that the Applicant can take legal action against them too.[107]

Imaging Orders

9.66 Documents and information are now very often created, processed and stored electronically. They may be held locally on the hard drives of

104 See paragraph 11(2) of the standard form search order appended to CPR PD 25A.

105 See paragraphs 13 and 15 of the standard form search order appended to CPR PD 25A. Again, the Supervising Solicitor can allow the Applicant's representatives to remove items without complying with these requirements, if he is satisfied that that is not practicable to do so.

106 See paragraphs 16 and 18(a) of the standard form search order appended to CPR PD 25A.

107 See paragraph 18(b)–(d) of the standard form search order appended to CPR PD 25A.

desktops, laptops, tablets, smartphones and other electronic devices; on local servers; or on removable storage devices such as flash drives and CD-ROMs. Electronic material is also increasingly stored or archived remotely in the "cloud", on servers owned and operated by third parties who provide email, social media or other online services.

9.67 These technology-driven developments have had a significant effect on the court's willingness to grant search orders, where the purpose of the order is the preservation of evidence rather than property. In such cases, the court may consider that a search order is not necessary at all, and that the appropriate order is an "imaging order",[108] in which the Respondent is ordered to permit an independent forensic computer expert[109] to copy or image the data stored on the Respondent's digital devices and cloud storage.[110] The court may, of course, consider that a search order is necessary alongside an imaging order, for two reasons: to ensure that the relevant digital devices are not wiped or tampered with before the Applicant's representatives can copy or image the data which they hold; and to preserve any relevant paper documents.

9.68 The practice of the English court in granting imaging orders is in a relatively early stage of development,[111] and there is, as yet, no officially approved standard form of imaging order, although one is currently being developed by the Civil Procedure Rules Committee.[112] The existing standard form of search order, which originated in 2005 and was last updated in 2017, contains some rudimentary provisions for the imaging and copying of electronic data. It provides that the Respondent must immediately to give the

---

108 *TBD (Owen Holland) Ltd v Simons* [2020] EWCA Civ 1182 per Arnold LJ at [176]–[180].

109 As with a Supervising Solicitor, the court will usually require an independent forensic computer expert to give appropriate undertakings to the court, as a condition of granting the imaging order: see footnote 10 to the standard form search order appended to CPR PD 25A.

110 See for example *Advetec Holdings Ltd v Shaw* [2020] EWHC 2660 (QB) at [9] recording that, earlier in the proceedings, the court granted an order (described as an "injunction") without notice, requiring the Respondents to immediately deliver up to the Supervising Solicitor "(1) any desktop or laptop computer, USB storage device, memory stick, disc, tablet device, mobile phone and any other electronic storage device or computer in each of their possession or control ('Devices') together with usernames, login details and passwords which are necessary to enable the contents of the devices to be copied or imaged; (2) names, login details and passwords for any account or medium held by the Respondents on which documents or information may be stored in an electronic format, including (but not limited to) any email account, webmail account, website, social networking site, online storage or backup facility or other remote storage facility ('Electronic Accounts')".

111 There are two leading cases at first instance: *CBS Butler Ltd v Brown* [2013] EWHC 3944 (QB) and *A v B* [2019] EWHC 2089 (Ch) (also referred to as *Hewlett Packard Enterprise Co v Manchester Technology Data (Holdings) Ltd*); and one in the Court of Appeal: *TBD (Owen Holland) Ltd v Simons* [2020] EWCA Civ 1182.

112 In *TBD (Owen Holland) Ltd v Simons* [2020] EWCA Civ 1182, Arnold LJ at [181] and David Richards LJ at [286] in both called upon the Civil Procedure Rules Committee to produce a standard form "as a matter of urgency". According to the minutes of the meeting of the Committee on 9 October 2020, the process of developing a standard form has begun, but no drafts have yet been published.

search party effective access to any "computers" on the premises, with all necessary passwords, to enable the computers to be searched; that he must cause any items listed in the search order which are stored on the computers to be displayed so that they can be read and copied; and that he must provide copies of all such items to the Applicant's solicitors. These provisions may be adequate for a narrowly defined search which aims to preserve a small number of discrete documents stored locally on a computer hard drive, but they are wholly inadequate for a more extensive search which aims to preserve a wider range of electronic data and material, and information which is stored remotely.[113]

9.69 As with search orders, imaging orders are granted for the purpose of preserving evidence. An imaging order does not, in and of itself, entitle the Applicant to use the data which is captured by the copying or imaging process. It does not even entitle the Applicant to search or inspect the data in order to find relevant documents and evidence contained with it. The court may, in due course, permit the Applicant to do so, pursuant to separate case management powers; but it will normally order that, at least during the period between the date of when the imaging and copying takes place and the Return Date of the application for the imaging order, all the material captured by the imaging and copying must be kept in the safekeeping of the independent forensic computer expert (or, where the imaging order is combined with a search order, by the Supervising Solicitor), and not searched or inspected by anyone in the meantime.[114]

Claim No _____________

IN THE HIGH COURT OF JUSTICE
BUSINESS AND PROPERTY COURTS OF ENGLAND AND WALES
COMMERCIAL COURT (QBD)
The Honourable Mr(s) Justice______________

B E T W E E N:

HIDEOUS TROLL GAMES INC

Applicant

-and-

GEOFFREY GENERIC LTD

113 Footnote 10 to the standard form order acknowledges this: it provides that if it is envisaged that the Respondent's computers are to be imaged – "i.e. the hard drives are to be copied wholesale, thereby reproducing listed items and other items indiscriminately" – special provision needs to be made and independent computer specialists need to be appointed, who should be required to give undertakings to the court.

114 *TBD (Owen Holland) Ltd v Simons* [2020] EWCA Civ 1182 per Arnold LJ at [193].

Respondent

Draft/ORDER

PENAL NOTICE

If you GEOFFREY GENERIC LTD disobey this Order you may be held to be in contempt of court and may be imprisoned, fined or have your assets seized.

Any other person who knows of this order and does anything which helps or permits the Respondent to breach the terms of this Order may also be held to be in contempt of court and may be imprisoned, fined or have their assets seized.

THIS ORDER

1. This is a Search Order made against Geoffrey Generic Ltd ("the Respondent") on 31 May 2022 by Mrs/Mr Justice on the application of Hideous Troll Games Inc ("the Applicant"). The Judge read the Affidavits listed in Schedule F and accepted the undertakings set out in Schedules C, D and E at the end of this Order.
2. This order was made at a hearing without notice to the Respondent. The Respondent has a right to apply to the Court to vary or discharge the order – see paragraph 25 below.
3. There will be a further hearing in respect of this order on ("the return date").
4. If there is more than one Respondent –
   a. Unless otherwise stated, references in this order to "the Respondent" mean both or all of them; and
   b. This order is effective against any Respondent on whom it is served or who is given notice of it.
5. This order must be complied with by –
   a. The Respondent;
   b. Any director, officer, partner or responsible employee of the Respondent; and
   c. If the Respondent is an individual, any other person having responsible control of the premises to be searched.

THE SEARCH

6. The Respondent must permit the following persons:
   a. Atticus Finch ("the Supervising Solicitor");
   b. William Tulkinghorn, a solicitor in the firm of Bleak Tulkinghorn LLP, the Applicant's solicitors; and
   c. Up to three other persons, being employees of the Applicant accompanying them,

   (together "the Search Party"), to enter the premises mentioned in Schedule A to this order and any other premises of the Respondent disclosed under paragraph 18 below and any vehicles under the Respondent's control on or around the premises ("the Premises") so that they can search for, inspect, photograph or photocopy and deliver into the safekeeping of the Applicant's solicitors all the documents and articles which are listed in Schedule B to this order ("the Listed Items").
7. Having permitted the Search Party to enter the Premises, the Respondent must allow the Search Party to remain on the Premises until the search is complete. In the event that it becomes necessary for any of those persons to leave the Premises before the search is complete, the Respondent must allow them to re-enter the Premises immediately upon their seeking re-entry on the same day or the following day in order to complete the search.

RESTRICTIONS ON SEARCH

8. This order may not be carried out at the same time as a police search warrant.
9. Before the Respondent allows anybody onto the Premises to carry out this order, he is entitled to have the Supervising Solicitor explain to him what it means in everyday language.
10. The Respondent is entitled to seek legal advice and to ask the court to vary or discharge this order. Whilst doing so, he may ask the Supervising Solicitor to delay starting the search for up to two hours or such longer period as the Supervising Solicitor may permit. However, the Respondent must:
    a. Comply with the terms of paragraph 25 below;
    b. Not disturb or remove any listed items; and
    c. Permit the Supervising Solicitor to enter, but not start to search.
11.
    (1) Before permitting entry to the premises by a person other than the Supervising Solicitor, the Respondent may, for a short time (not exceeding two hours, unless the Supervising Solicitor agrees to a longer period) –

a. Gather together any documents he believes may be incriminating or privileged; and
b. Hand them to the Supervising Solicitor for him to assess whether they are incriminating or privileged as claimed.

(2) If the Supervising Solicitor decides that the Respondent is entitled to withhold production of any of the documents on the ground that they are privileged or incriminating, he will exclude them from the search, record them in a list for inclusion in his report and return them to the Respondent.

(3) If the Supervising Solicitor believes that the Respondent may be entitled to withhold production of the whole or any part of a document on the ground that it or part of it may be privileged or incriminating, or if the Respondent claims to be entitled to withhold production on those grounds, the Supervising Solicitor will exclude it from the search and retain it in his possession pending further order of the court.

12. If the Respondent wishes to take legal advice and gather documents as permitted, he must first inform the Supervising Solicitor and keep him informed of the steps being taken.
13. No item may be removed from the premises until a list of the items to be removed has been prepared, and a copy of the list has been supplied to the Respondent, and he has been given a reasonable opportunity to check the list.
14. The premises must not be searched, and items must not be removed from them, except in the presence of the Respondent.
15. If the Supervising Solicitor is satisfied that full compliance with paragraphs 13 and 14 is not practicable, he may permit the search to proceed and items to be removed without fully complying with them.

DELIVERY UP OF ARTICLES/DOCUMENTS

16. The Respondent must immediately hand over to the Applicant's solicitors any of the listed items, which are in his possession or under his control, save for any computer or hard disc integral to any computer. Any items the subject of a dispute as to whether they are listed items must immediately be handed over to the Supervising Solicitor for safe keeping pending resolution of the dispute or further order of the court.
17. The Respondent must immediately give the search party effective access to the computers on the premises, with all necessary passwords, to enable the computers to be searched. If they contain any listed items the Respondent must cause the listed items to be displayed so that they can be read and copied. The Respondent must provide the

Applicant's Solicitors with copies of all listed items contained in the computers. All reasonable steps shall be taken by the Applicant and the Applicant's solicitors to ensure that no damage is done to any computer or data. The Applicant and his representatives may not themselves search the Respondent's computers unless they have sufficient expertise to do so without damaging the Respondent's system.

PROVISION OF INFORMATION

18. The Respondent must immediately inform the Applicant's Solicitors (in the presence of the Supervising Solicitor) so far as he is aware –
    a. Where all the listed items are;
    b. The name and address of everyone who has supplied him, or offered to supply him, with listed items;
    c. The name and address of everyone to whom he has supplied, or offered to supply, listed items;
    d. Full details of the dates and quantities of every such supply and offer.
19. Within seven working days after being served with this order the Respondent must swear and serve an affidavit setting out the above information.

PROHIBITED ACTS

20. Except for the purpose of obtaining legal advice, the Respondent must not directly or indirectly inform anyone of these proceedings or of the contents of this order, or warn anyone that proceedings have been or may be brought against him by the Applicant until 4.30 pm on the return date or further order of the court.
21. Until 4.30 pm on the return date the Respondent must not destroy, tamper with, cancel or part with possession, power, custody or control of the listed items otherwise than in accordance with the terms of this order.

COSTS

22. The costs of this application are reserved to the judge hearing the application on the return date.

RESTRICTIONS ON SERVICE

23. This order may only be served between 9 am and 5 pm on a weekday.

24. This order must be served by the Supervising Solicitor, and paragraph 6 of the order must be carried out in his presence and under his supervision.

VARIATION AND DISCHARGE OF THIS ORDER

25. Anyone served with or notified of this order may apply to the court at any time to vary or discharge this order (or so much of it as affects that person), but they must first inform the Applicant's solicitors. If any evidence is to be relied upon in support of the application, the substance of it must be communicated in writing to the Applicant's solicitors in advance.

INTERPRETATION OF THIS ORDER

26. A requirement that something shall be done to or in the presence of the Respondent means –
    a. If there is more than one Respondent, to or in the presence of any one of them; and
    b. If a Respondent is not an individual, to or in the presence of a director, officer, partner or responsible employee.
27. A Respondent who is an individual who is ordered not to do something must not do it himself or in any other way. He must not do it through others acting on his behalf or on his instructions or with his encouragement.
28. A Respondent which is not an individual which is ordered not to do something must not do it itself or by its directors, officers, partners, employees or agents or in any other way.

COMMUNICATIONS WITH THE COURT

All communications to the Court about this order should be addressed to the Admiralty and Commercial Court Listing Office, 7 Rolls Building, Fetter Lane, London EC4A 1NL, quoting the case number. The telephone number is (+44) (0) 20 7947 6826.

The offices are open between 10 am and 4.30 pm Monday to Friday.

SCHEDULE A – THE PREMISES

141 Ogre Street, London W88 9LP

SCHEDULE B – THE LISTED ITEMS

(1) All items of merchandise bearing the words "Hideous" or "Troll" or "HideousTroll" or the HideousTroll logo or any other registered trademark of the Applicant.
(2) All documents containing information relating to the sale, purchase, supply, storage, delivery of or payment for items listed in paragraph (1) of this Schedule.

SCHEDULE C – Undertakings given to the Court by the Applicant

(1) If the court later finds that this order or carrying out has caused loss to the Respondent, and decides that the Respondent should be compensated for that loss, the Applicant will comply with any order that the court may make. Further if the carryout out of this order has been in breach of the terms of this order or otherwise in a manner inconsistent with the Applicant's solicitors' duties as officers of the court, the Applicant will comply with any order for damages the court may make.
(2) As soon as is practicable the Applicant will issue a claim for the appropriate relief.
(3) The Applicant will not, without the permission of the court, use any information or documents obtained as a result of carrying out this order nor inform anyone else of these proceedings except for the purposes of these proceedings (including adding further Respondents) or commencing civil proceedings in relation to the same or related subject matter to these proceedings until after the return date.
(4) The Applicant will maintain pending further order the sum of £50,000 in an account controlled by the Applicant's solicitors.
(5) The Applicant will insure the items removed from the premises.

SCHEDULE D – UNDERTAKINGS GIVEN BY THE APPLICANT'S SOLICITORS

(1) The Applicant's solicitors will provide to the Supervising Solicitor for service on the Respondent
   a. A service copy of this order;
   b. The claim form (with defendant's response pack) or, if not issued, the draft produced to the court;
   c. An application for hearing on the return date;
   d. Copies of the affidavits and exhibits capable of being copied containing the evidence relied upon by the Applicant;

e. A note of any allegation of fact made orally to the court where such allegation is not contained in the affidavits or draft affidavits read by the judge; and

f. A copy of the skeleton argument produced to the court by the Applicant's counsel.

(2) The Applicant's solicitors will answer at once to the best of their ability any question whether a particular item is a listed item.

(3) Subject as provided below the Applicant's solicitors will retain in their own safe keeping all items obtained as a result of this order until the court directs otherwise.

(4) The Applicant's solicitors will return the originals of all documents obtained as a result of this order (except original documents which belong to the Applicant) as soon as possible and in any event within two working days of their removal.

SCHEDULE E – UNDERTAKINGS GIVEN BY THE SUPERVISING SOLICITOR

(1) The Supervising Solicitor will use his best endeavours to serve this order upon the Respondent and at the same time to serve upon the Respondent the other documents required to be served and referred to in paragraph (1) of Schedule D.

(2) The Supervising Solicitor will offer to explain to the person served with the order its meaning and effect fairly and in everyday language, and to inform him of his right to take legal advice (including an explanation that the Respondent may be entitled to avail himself of the privilege against self-incrimination and legal professional privilege) and to apply to vary or discharge this order as mentioned in paragraph 27 above.

(3) The Supervising Solicitor will retain in the safe keeping of his firm all items retained by him as a result of this order until the court directs otherwise.

(4) Unless and until the court otherwise orders, or unless otherwise necessary to comply with any duty to the court pursuant to this order, the Supervising Solicitor shall not disclose to any person any information relating to those items, and shall keep the existence of such items confidential.

(5) Within 48 hours of completion of the search the Supervising Solicitor will make and provide to the Applicant's solicitors, the Respondent or his solicitors and to the judge who made this order (for the purposes of the court file) a written report on the carrying out of the order.

SCHEDULE F – AFFIDAVITS

The Applicant relied on the following affidavits –

First affidavit of William Dickens Tulkinghorn, sworn 31 May 2022, filed on behalf of the Applicant.

NAME AND ADDRESS OF APPLICANT'S LEGAL REPRESENTATIVES

The Applicant's solicitors are:
Bleak Tulkinghorn LLP: William Tulkinghorn (partner).
Correspondence address: No. 99 Cornet Gardens, London, England, EC5X 9LP
Telephone: +44 (0)20 9099 9999 (24 hours)
Email: w.tulkinghorn@bleakhouselaw.com

W.D. Tulkinghorn
First affidavit
31.5.2022
For Applicant
Exhibit WDT1

Claim No ____________

IN THE HIGH COURT OF JUSTICE
BUSINESS AND PROPERTY COURTS OF ENGLAND AND WALES
COMMERCIAL COURT (QBD)

B E T W E E N:

HIDEOUS TROLL GAMES INC

Applicant

-and-

GEOFFREY GENERIC LIMITED

Respondent

AFFIDAVIT OF WILLIAM DICKENS TULKINGHORN

I, William Dickens Tulkinghorn, MAKE OATH and say as follows:

1. I am a solicitor and partner in the firm of Bleak Tulkingorn LLP of No. 99 Cornet Gardens, London, England, EC5X 9LP, solicitors

for the Applicant. I have the conduct of this case on behalf of the Applicant. I am duly authorised by the Applicant to make this witness statement.

2. The facts and matters to which I shall hereafter depose are known to me from my conduct of this case and from documents and from information provided to me by Zelda Zealous, the Applicant's general counsel, and Ken Sleuth, a private investigator engaged by Ms Zealous to investigate matters with which this case is concerned. Insofar as the contents of this affidavit are within my own knowledge, they are true. Otherwise they are true to the best of my knowledge, information and belief.
3. I swear this affidavit in support of the Applicant's application for an urgent search order against the Respondent, Geoffrey Generic Ltd, for a search of the Respondent's commercial premises at 141 Ogre Street, London.
4. There is now produced and shown to me and exhibited hereto marked "WDT1" a paginated bundle of true copy documents to which I shall hereinafter refer by page numbers in square brackets: [#].
5. This application is being made without notice to the Respondent for reasons of secrecy and urgency.

The Applicant

6. The Applicant is a computer game company. It produces and markets the well-known "HideousTrolls" family of computer games. It owns the UK copyright in the software of the games themselves, and UK registered trademarks in the word "HideousTrolls" and in a number of associated designs and logos. I attach a complete list of the Applicant's UK registered trademarks at [1–35].
7. As part of its business, the Applicant licenses the use of its trademarks on clothing, toys, stationery and other items of merchandise for sale within the UK. It does so by way of license agreements on standard terms, which provide that the Applicant shall be entitled to receive a lump sum per annum plus a royalty on retails sales of all merchandise covered by the license agreement. I attach an example of one such agreement (I have redacted the name of the licensee and the lump sum under the agreement for reasons of commercial confidentiality) at [36–88]. In the financial year ending on 31 April 2022, the Applicant's gross earnings on these royalties was £3.14 million.
8. The Applicant's business faces an ever-increasing threat from counterfeiting of merchandise bearing its trademarks. Counterfeiting reduces the amount of royalties which the Applicant earns under existing licensing agreement, and also reduces the lump sum

payments it can earn from future licensing agreements, by making the licenses less profitable for licensees. According to market research commissioned by the Applicant in 2019 [89–107], around 40% of all HideousTrolls-branded merchandise sold in London and the south-east of England at that time was reported to be counterfeit. Ms Zealous informs me, and I believe, that there is no reason to suppose that the problem is any less serious now.

The Counterfeit Merchandise

9. Ms Zealous regularly visits street markets in and around London to see if counterfeit merchandise is on sale there. On 24 April 2022 she visited a street market in Deptford, south-east London. She found a market stall selling a number of items bearing HideousTroll trademarks. She took a number of photographs with her telephone [108–123]. She purchased several items of merchandise from the stall, without revealing her identity, and brought them back to the office.
10. On inspection, all the items turned out to be counterfeit. In particular, none of the items bears a label stating that they are manufactured under license by any of the official licensees, and the some of the colours on the logos are wrong (brown instead of purple stripe).
11. Ms Zealous then instructed Mr Sleuth to investigate further. Mr Sleuth is a private investigator employed by the Applicant to investigate instances of counterfeiting and software piracy. Mr Sleuth's report dated 28 April 2022 is at [124–145]. In it, he explains that he attended the market at Deptford on 26 April and observed a Ford Transit van making deliveries to the market stall which Ms Zealous had previously identified. Mr Sleuth tailed the van over the following days. On 28 April, he observed it being emptied at another market, in Lewisham, and then driving to 141 Ogre Street, where a number of men loaded more boxes into the back of the van. The van then drove directly to the market in Deptford, where some of the boxes were unloaded and delivered to the same stall as before. Mr Sleuth observed the stallholder opening the boxes and removing HideousTroll-branded items, which he then displayed for sale at the stall. Mr Sleuth's report contains the photographs he took of these events.
12. Mr Sleuth approached the stallholder towards the end of the day on 28 April and asked about the HideousTroll-branded merchandise. He did not ask the stallholder's name. The stallholder said that HideousTroll merchandise was very hard to come by, but that he had a supplier who could get hold of it from time to time. He explained that

his supplier had received a large consignment a week or so before, and that it was selling out "like hot cakes" and would soon all be gone. He was at pains to point out that the merchandise was "good quality" and "indistinguishable from the real thing, but half the price".

The Premises

13. The address where Mr Sleuth observed the van being loaded with counterfeit merchandise, 141 Ogre Street, is a warehouse owned by the Respondent company. I attach a copy of the land registry entry for the property at [146–150], which confirms this. I also attach printouts from the Respondent's website at [151–154] which explain that it is a company formed in 2017 which operates an import-export and wholesale trading business from that address. I also attach a photograph of the front of the premises [155], taken by Mr Sleuth this morning, which shows the Respondent's name on a sign above the door.

Extremely Strong Prima Facie Case on the Merits

14. Based on the matters which I have set out above, I believe that the Applicant has an extremely strong prima facie case on the merits of a claim against the Respondent for infringement of its registered trademarks, by selling and distributing counterfeit merchandise bearing those trademarks without the Applicant's permission.

Very Serious Damage

15. I believe that a search order of the Respondent's premises would avoid very serious damage to the Applicant, by ensuring that counterfeit merchandise on the premises which bears the Applicant's trademark is preserved and cannot be destroyed or distributed for sale, and by ensuring that evidence on the premises of the Respondent's unlawful activities, and evidence which is likely to identify and implicate third parties involved in the unlawful manufacture and distribution of counterfeit merchandise bearing the Applicant's trademarks, cannot be destroyed, hidden or removed.

Respondent Has Relevant Material in Its Possession

16. I believe that the information which I have received from Ms Zealous and Mr Sleuth constitutes clear evidence that the Respondent has

incriminating material and important evidence in relation to these matters in its possession at its premises in Ogre Street.

Material May Be Destroyed, Hidden or Removed

17. I believe that there is a strong possibility that the counterfeit merchandise and the evidence which can identify and implicate third parties involved in the unlawful manufacture and distribution of that merchandise, will be destroyed, hidden or removed from the premises if the search order is not granted. The merchandise itself is likely to be distributed to retail sellers in the next few days. In any event, the Respondent would be likely to destroy, hide or remove the merchandise and the evidence, if it became aware that the Applicant had commenced, or was contemplating bringing, legal proceedings against it in relation to that material, because of the clandestine and unlawful nature of the activities concerned.

Harm Is Not Disproportionate

18. I believe that any harm which is likely to be caused to the Respondent and its business affairs by the execution of a search order would not be disproportionate to the legitimate object of the search order. The search order is likely to disrupt the Respondent's legitimate business activities at the premises for no more than one day, which is not disproportionate to the Applicant's legitimate interest in preventing the distribution of counterfeit merchandise and in obtaining evidence which is likely to identify and implicate third parties involved in the unlawful manufacture and distribution of that merchandise.

Discretion

19. In light of the matters set out above, I believe that it is just and convenient in all the circumstances for the Court to grant the relief sought.

Undertakings

20. The Applicant offers the usual undertakings, including an undertaking to fortify its undertaking in damages if the Court so requires. I attach a copy of the Applicant's latest annual report and accounts [156–197], which show that the Applicant has total assets of USD 37 million, albeit not within England and Wales.

21. I also offer the usual undertakings required of the applicant's solicitor.

Supervising Solicitor

22. Atticus Finch, of Atticus Finch & Partners, has agreed to act as Supervising Solicitor. Mr Finch informs me, and I believe, that he is experienced in the operation of search orders, having participated as Supervising Solicitor on three previous occasions and having been a member of search parties on a further four occasions, all in the past ten years. Mr Finch's CV, detailing his experience in these matters, is at [198–200].
23. Mr Finch offers the Court the usual undertakings required of a Supervising Solicitor.

SWORN by the above-named William Dickens Tulkinghorn

This 1st day of May 2022
at
Before me

CHAPTER 10

Preservation Measure of Evidence in China

Introduction

10.1 The modern Chinese legal system, in particular since the 1990s, has adopted many features from the civil law family with considerable influences from procedural law from countries such as Germany. Even so, it may be argued that the Chinese civil procedural system retains many elements of socialist legal families in the Civil Procedure Law 1991 (hereinafter referred to as "CPL 1991 (as amended until 2020)").[1] As part of the civil law family, Chinese procedural law has adopted an inquisitorial system for civil trials with Chinese characteristics and lately also adopted a few common law characteristics for civil trials.[2] In traditional civil law, as discussed at Chapter 1, 1.91–1.92, the preservation measure of evidence (hereinafter referred to as "evidence preservation measure") is generally not governed by the civil preservation procedure. However, this argument is simply raised by legal scholars in various academic debates. In Chinese legal practice, the procedural remedy of evidence preservation is always treated as an important type of preservation measure.

10.2 Prior to the 2012 amendment to the CPL 1991, pre-action evidence preservation measures were available, outside of the CPL regime, in particular, the Special Maritime Procedure Law 2000 (hereinafter referred to as "SMPL 2000") and the intellectual property laws.[3] The pre-action evidence

1 See Article 2 of the CPL 1991 (as amended until 2020) that provides that "it [civil procedural system] must maintain the smooth progress of the socialist construct"; see also, Vivek Jain, *Insight into China through Comparative Analysis of Invisible Factors and Contexts – Common Law v. Chinese Law* (1st Edn, Notion Press 2019) 25 for a discussion on legal families and the Chinese legal system; refer also to Chapter 11, 11.57 and 11.90 for a discussion on legal families.

2 ibid; refer also to Chapter 11, 11.82 and 11.92 for discussion on the concept of conservatism and the adoption of Chinese characteristics into a traditional civil law procedural system.

3 SMPL 2000, Article 63; see also, various laws in the area of intellectual property law, and it should be emphasised that there is no unified intellectual property law. Intellectual property (IP) laws include the Patent Law of the People's Republic China 1985 (2020 Amendment), Copyright Law of the People's Republic China 1991(2020 amendment) and Trademark Law of the People's Republic China 1983 (2019 Amendment). Prior to the 2012 amendment to CPL 1991, the provisions required to obtain pre-action evidence preservation measures were available in various laws such as Article 73 of the Patent Law 1985 (2020 Amendment), Article 57 of

DOI: 10.4324/9781003000310-16

preservation measures in other disputes in legal practice could be enforced by notary public offices in China.[4]

10.3 In the last few decades, alongside the parallel development and reforms of the Chinese civil litigation procedure including civil trials, the stakeholders have developed an appreciation for the utility of evidence preservation measures. This has led to the development of the concept of evidence preservation measures.[5] It is recognised that pre-action preservation of evidence measures are utilised *inter alia* to investigate the case, prepare for future civil trial and preserve the evidence from being destroyed and/or lost.[6]

10.4 Against the above background, the 2012 amendment to the CPL 1991 provided the systematic legal mechanism whereby a procedural remedy is available to applicants or interested parties to seek pre-action preservation of evidence measures from the courts.

Applicable Laws

Applicable Laws for General Disputes

10.5 A general rule of evidence preservation is provided by Article 81 of the CPL 1991 (as amended until 2020) as follows.

> Under the circumstances in which evidence is lost or it will be difficult to collect such evidence in the future, the party concerned may apply to the People's court for preservation of such evidence *in the juridical proceedings* [emphasis added], and the *People's court may also take* [emphasis added] the initiative to take preservation measures.
>
> Under the emergencies in which evidence is lost or it will be difficult to collect such evidence in the future, an interested party may, *before the case or arbitration is filed* [emphasis added], apply for preservation of such evidence with the People's court in the place where the evidence to be preserved is located or the place where the respondent is domiciled, or the people's court with jurisdiction over the case.
>
> With regard to other procedures for the preservation of evidence, the relevant provisions of Chapter 9 entitled "Preservation" herein shall apply as a reference.[7]

---

the Copyright Law 1991 (2020 Amendment) and Article 65 of the Trademark Law 1983 (2019 Amendment).

4 Lingzhang Kong, 'Pretrial Evidence Preservation: By Reference of German Independent Evidence Collection Procedure' (2011) 33 (3) Modern Law Science 124, 125; see also, Liu Jiang, Huimin Wang and Wenge Li, *Speech Concerning Civil Procedure Law* (People Daily Press 1991) 88.

5 Bixin Jiang and Xuelin Zheng, 'Press Conference of the Supreme People's Court on Amendment of Some Provisions of the Supreme People's Court on Evidence in Civil Procedures' <www.court.gov.cn/zixun-xiangqing-212691.html> accessed 26 December 2019.

6 Lingzhang Kong, 'Pretrial Evidence Preservation: By Reference of German Independent Evidence Collection Procedure' (2011) 33 (3) Modern Law Science 124, 126.

7 CPL 1991 (as amended until 2020), Article 81.

10.6 The general rule governs applications seeking either pre-action or post-action preservation of evidence measures. Courts on their own initiative may also take evidence preservation measures during civil proceedings.

10.7 From the point of view of the structure of the CPL 1991 (as amended until 2020), although the provisions of evidence preservation measures are codified into Chapter VI "Evidence" of the CPL 1991 (as amended until 2020) rather than the all-encompassing Chapter IX "Preservation and Advance Enforcement" that provides the preservation regime within civil procedure in China, the detailed rules on evidence preservation shall be by reference to the provisions of Chapter IX.[8]

10.8 It may be argued that the different features of evidence preservation measures are not suitable to be governed by the articles of Chapter IX "Preservation and Advance Enforcement". Chapter IX is more suited to applications seeking property/behaviour/conduct preservation measures.[9] A legal scholar, after comparing all articles of Chapter IX "Preservation and Advance Enforcement" with the applications seeking evidence preservation measures, has proposed that only Articles 100 (3), 101 (2) and 102 could be applied to evidence preservation measures.[10]

10.9 However, the latest judicial interpretation handed down by the SPC, *Some Provisions of the Supreme People's Court on Evidence in Civil Procedures* (2019 Amendment) (hereinafter referred to as "Provisions on Evidence 2019"), enunciates that if there are no specific provisions in Provisions on Evidence 2019 on evidence preservation measures, it is necessary to refer to the law and judicial interpretations on property preservation measures to resolve the legal issues arising from applications seeking evidence preservation measures.[11] Based on this, the ranking order of applicable laws in the context of evidence preservation measures is Article 81 of the CPL 1991 (as amended until 2020), Provisions on Evidence 2019, Articles of Chapter IX "Preservation and Advance Enforcement" of CPL 1991 (as

---

8 ibid.

9 Shangang Zhan, 'Question on Evidence Preservation with Reference to Preservation Procedure: Examination of Article 81 of CPL' (2015) 6 Journal in Law and Business 121, 128.

10 CPL 1991 (as amended until 2020), Article 100(3) provides that "When a people's court receives an application for preservation in an emergency, it shall decide within forty-eight hours after the receipt of the application; if the court accepts the application, such measures shall come into force immediately"; Article 101(2) provides that "When a people's court receives an application for preservation, it shall decide within forty-eight hours after the receipt of the application; if the court accepts the application, the preservation measures shall come into force immediately", and Article 102 provides that "Preservation shall be limited to the scope under the application or to the property related to the case in question"; see also, Shangang Zhan, 'Question on Evidence Preservation with Reference to Preservation Procedure: Examination of Article 81 of CPL' (2015) 6 Journal in Law and Business 121, 128.

11 Some Provisions of the Supreme People's Court on Evidence in Civil Procedures was originally issued in 2001 (Fa Shi [2001] No 33). By the end of 2019, the Amendment was promulgated by the SPC (Fa Shi [2019] No 19). This Amendment was issued on 25 December 2019 and came into effect on 1 May 2020; see also, Provisions on Evidence 2019, Article 99.

amended until 2020) and the corresponding interpretations, and *Provisions of the Supreme People's Court on Several Issues Concerning the Handling of Property Preservation Cases by the People's Courts (2020 Amendment)*.[12]

Applicable Laws for Intellectual Property Disputes

10.10 In intellectual property (IP) disputes, the most important judicial interpretation as to IP evidence preservation, namely *Several Provisions of the Supreme People's Court on Evidence in Civil Procedures Involving Intellectual Property Rights* (hereinafter referred to as "Provisions on IP Evidence 2020"), was newly issued by the SPC and came into force on 18 November 2020.[13] In accordance with Article 33 of Provisions on IP Evidence 2020, it is provided that "if the previous judicial interpretations issued were not compatible with this one, this shall prevail".[14] It follows that Provisions on IP Evidence 2020 will prevail if other judicial interpretations are in conflict.

10.11 In addition, it is articulated by the Leader of the Third Civil Division of the SPC that Provisions on IP Evidence 2020 abides by the legal foundation provided by Provisions on Evidence 2019 and meanwhile supplements some crucial issues which have not been addressed in other laws and judicial interpretations.[15] Based on this, if seeking evidence preservation measures in IP disputes one may first look into Provisions on IP Evidence 2020 and thereafter may apply Provisions on Evidence 2019.

10.12 Regional interpretations and guidance by local courts for applications seeking evidence preservation measures are absent. Nonetheless, the High People's Court of Chonqqing Municipality and the High People's Court of Zhejiang Province issue guidance for the evidence preservation measures in the area of intellectual property law that will be analysed later in this chapter.[16] Therefore, in the context of applications seeking evidence preservation measures for intellectual property disputes, if the judicial interpretations

12 *Provisions of the Supreme People's Court on Several Issues Concerning the Handling of Property Preservation Cases by the People's Courts (2020 Amendment)* (Fa Shi [2016] No 22) (superseded by Fa Shi [2020] No 21).

13 *Several Provisions of the Supreme People's Court on Evidence in Civil Procedures Involving Intellectual Property Rights* (Fa Shi [2020] No 12) was issued on 16 November 2020 and came into force on 18 November 2020.

14 Provisions on IP Evidence 2020, Article 33.

15 Hang Sun, 'To Address the Difficulty of Proof in Intellectual Property Disputes: Answer to Correspondent's Questions on "*Several Provisions of the Supreme People's Court on Evidence in Civil Procedures Involving Intellectual Property Rights" by the Leader of the Third Civil Division of the Supreme People's Court*' (*People's Court Daily*, 17 November 2020).

16 *Guidance of Chongqing High People's Court on Intellectual Property Civil Evidence* (Yu Gao Fa [2018] No 210); see also, *Opinion of the Third Civil Division of Zhejiang High People's Court on Intellectual Property Civil Evidence Preservation* (July 2014).

handed down by the SPC are not available, then the above two regional guidance may be consulted to seek further guidance.

Applicable Laws for Maritime Disputes

10.13 In the maritime law domain, maritime evidence is governed by Chapter 5 "maritime evidence" of the SMPL 2000 and its Interpretation 2008.[17] If the rules relating to the specific legal issues are silent, then, the CPL 1991 (as amended until 2020), its Interpretation (2020 Amendment) and the Provisions on Evidence 2019 will be applied to applications seeking evidence preservation measures in maritime disputes.[18]

Definition and Purpose of Evidence Preservation Measures

10.14 After the Provisions on Evidence 2019 was issued, the SPC provided a comprehensive definition for an evidence preservation measure in China:

> In order to prevent the possibility of destroying evidence or failing to collect evidence later on, the court should take measures to extract, save or sealing up the evidence prior to the lawsuit or before investigation of the evidence materials, based on the application of the interested party, the parties concerned or on their own initiative.[19]

10.15 It follows that the purpose of the evidence preservation measure, as compared with those of the other two preservation measures as discussed in Chapters 6 and 8, is to prevent the possibility of the destruction of evidence or a failure to collect evidence during proceedings.

Definition and Purpose of Maritime Evidence Preservation

10.16 Similarly, Article 62 of the SMPL 2000 provides:

> Preservation of maritime evidence means the compulsory measures imposed by the maritime court, upon the application by a maritime claimant, to take, preserve or seal up the evidence relating to a maritime claim.[20]

---

17 Interpretation refers to *The Supreme People's Court Interpretations on the Application of the Special Maritime Procedure Law of the People's Republic of China (2008 Adjustment)* (Fa Shi [2003] No 3) (hereinafter referred to as "Interpretation of SMPL 2008").

18 Article 97 of the Interpretation of SMPL 2008 provides that "Maritime litigations carried out within the People's Republic of China shall be governed by the Special Maritime Procedure Law. Matters not covered by the Special Maritime Procedure Law will be governed by the relevant provisions of the civil procedure law".

19 The First Civil Division of the Supreme People's Court (ed), *Understanding and Application of New Provisions of the Supreme People's Court on Evidence in Civil Procedures, Volume 1* (People's Court Press 2020) 270; see also, Yuqian Bi, *Essentials of Evidence Law* (Law Press of China 2003) 523.

20 SMPL 2000, Article 62.

10.17 It follows that this definition does not emphasise the purpose of the maritime evidence preservation measure. Nonetheless, maritime scholars have highlighted the scenarios where the maritime evidence preservation measure may be rendered by courts. Accordingly, a few of the purposes of such measures include the loss of evidence or the difficulty in obtaining evidence.[21]

Format of Preservation Applications and Key Points

10.18 Provisions on Evidence 2019 stipulates key points that need to be complied with in order to draft a letter of application seeking evidence preservation measures. In addition, *Interpretation of the Supreme People's Court on the Application of Law Concerning Pre-Action Behaviour and Evidence Preservations for Stopping the Infringement upon the Right of Trademark 2002*[22] clarifies several elements that must be included in the letter of application seeking trademark right evidence preservation measures. By reference to these two interpretations, the letter of application must set out the following elements:

- (a) The identity, delivery addresses and contact information of the preservation applicant and the respondent.
- (b) The claims for application, facts and reasons the claims are based on.
- (c) The list, basic situation, scope, holder and location of evidence to be preserved.
- (d) Preservation measure suggested.
- (e) The connection between the evidence listed and the claims and the purpose of the evidence preservation.
- (f) Information on the secured property for the application of preservation or credit certification, or reasons why it is not necessary to provide security.
- (g) Other matters which need to be stated.[23]

An Applicant and a Respondent

10.19 The general information required of an applicant for any letter of application seeking evidence preservation measures is similar to that discussed

21 Liang Zhao and Lianjun Li, *Maritime Law and Practice in China* (1st Edn, Informa Law from Routledge 2017) para. 22.30.

22 *Interpretation of the Supreme People's Court on the Application of Law Concerning Pre-Action Behaviour and Evidence Preservations for Stopping the Infringement upon the Right of Trademark* (Fa Shi [2002] No 2); it should be noted that this interpretation was just abolished on 1 January 2021 after the Civil Code 2020 came into effect. However, only this interpretation provides elements in detail and Provisions on IP Evidence 2020 does not stipulate the relevant provisions. In the authors' opinion, these elements provided by this interpretation are still operative.

23 ibid, Article 3 (2); see also, Provisions on Evidence 2019, Article 25 (1).

in the context of property preservation measures in Chapter 6, 6.20–6.28. However, it is different from the qualification of the respondent during applications seeking property and behaviour preservation measures discussed in Chapter 6, 6.22, and Chapter 8, 8.40; even if the defendant during applications seeking evidence preservation measures were not to institute a counterclaim, he is entitled to apply for an evidence preservation measure because the purpose of such evidence preservation is to prevent the loss of evidence no matter who controls this evidence. It is irrelevant to the legal status of the applicant who is the claimant or the defendant. With regard to a respondent, its meaning should follow the discussion in Chapter 8, 8.77–8.82. However, as the evidence could be held by any party and is not limited to the party to dispute, it is possible for any natural person, legal entity or organisation to become respondents.

10.20 A maritime applicant in maritime evidence preservation measures may follow the same rule that the applicant may include both the claimant and defendant. A maritime respondent of an application seeking maritime evidence preservation measures also follows the same rule in 10.19. Item 3 of Article 67 in the SMPL 2000 provides that

> (3) the person against whom the application is made is a party relevant to the evidence, preservation of which is requested.[24]

10.21 This means that the respondent is not restricted to the party in a dispute.

Evidence to Be Preserved

10.22 Article 63 of the CPL1991 (as amended until 2020) and Article 14 of Provisions on Evidence 2019 list eight types of evidence as follows:

(a) Statements of the parties concerned.
(b) Documentary evidence.
(c) Physical evidence.
(d) Audio-visual materials.
(e) Electronic data including information on the platform of a webpage, blog, Weibo and others; communication information through mobile messages, e-mails, instant messages and group chats; online records such as registration information, user verification information, transaction records, communication records and access journal; and electronic documents such as documents, images, data, electronic certificates, computer programmes and similar evidence.
(f) Witness testimony.
(g) Expert opinions.
(h) Written records for inspection.[25]

24 SMPL 2000, Article 67 (3).

25 CPL 1991 (as amended until 2020), Article 63; see also, Provisions on Evidence 2019, Article 14.

10.23 All above evidence can become the subject matter of evidence preservation measures in Chinese courts, including maritime courts. In addition, because it is impossible for all the scope and list of evidence preservation measures to be included in Article 63 of the CPL 1991 (as amended until 2020) and Article 14 of Provisions on Evidence 2019, the courts may therefore consider other kinds of evidence in specific cases.

10.24 In order to convince the courts that other evidence outside the above list in 10.22 can be regarded as "evidence" in evidence preservation applications, the applicants must provide specific information when seeking evidence preservation measures for such kinds of evidence. If the court deems that the applicants have provided sufficient information in relation to this kind of evidence and as long as this kind of evidence does not violate the provisions prescribed by law, any kinds of evidence will then be regarded as within the scope of the evidence preservation measures.[26]

10.25 It is worth noting that property, such as houses, securities, precious metals and so forth, may all become the subject matter of evidence preservation measures. In this context, such property will simply constitute the evidence in a dispute but cannot become the subject matter of the enforcement of the future effective judgment.

Measures of Preservation

10.26 The preservation measures on evidence requested by an applicant will include sealing up, detainment, taking photographs, making sound recordings or visual recordings, making reproductions, authentication, inspection and so forth.[27] Furthermore, where a court preserves the evidence, the court may request the parties concerned or their lawyers to be present on the scene of issues at hand.[28] Particularly, in an IP dispute, in light of the party's application, the court may appoint an expert or a technical investigation officer to participate in the work involving evidence preservation.[29] It is the authors' submission that the absence of the proper involvement of an expert in an IP dispute may lead, in future, the correspondent or the interested party to raise an objection to the preservation measure.

10.27 Subject to the purpose of seeking evidence preservation measures, as cited in the application, the courts may exercise their discretionary power

26 The First Civil Division of the Supreme People's Court (ed), *Understanding and Application of New Provisions of the Supreme People's Court on Evidence in Civil Procedures, Volume I* (People's Court Press 2020) 275.

27 Provisions on Evidence 2019, Article 27.

28 ibid.

29 Provisions on IP Evidence 2020, Article 15; it should be noted that the SPC does not provide the exact meaning and scope of the technical investigation officer. It depends on further clarification by the SPC.

to order a particular kind(s) of evidence preservation measures. This exercise of discretionary power will be carried out only after evaluating the legal effect of any kind of preservation measures on the respondents. The courts are likely to choose the evidence preservation measures that impact insignificantly on the interests of the respondents.[30] This means that the applicants should be prepared that the evidence preservation measures requested in the application may not be acceptable to the courts, even if their application seeking evidence preservation measures by itself were approved by these courts.

10.28 In addition, if it is difficult for the courts to obtain the original evidence during the enforcement of their evidence preservation orders, such as the original electronic data or video, the courts may take measures allowing the copy of that data or video or similar evidence. Accordingly, the copy will be considered as equivalent in validity to the original evidence pursuant to the courts' orders.[31]

10.29 It must be emphasised that the minimum impact on the interests of respondents that should be considered during the choice of preservation measures, as discussed in 10.27, has been treated as a general principle in the course of the evidence preservation application by the SPC.[32] Where a Chinese court examines whether it is necessary to approve an application seeking evidence preservation, which kind of preservation measure and how it should be taken, this principle should be always followed.[33] Further discussion can be found in 10.47–10.51.

Preliminary Procedural Examination

10.30 The rule of preliminary procedural examination should govern both pre-action and post-action applications seeking evidence preservation measures.

Test of Correlation and Necessity

10.31 The judges' examination of an application seeking evidence preservation measures does not amount to the substantive evaluation of the evidence that is relevant during civil action proceedings. Therefore, the primary focus in the applicant's letter of application must be to explain the correlation

30 Provisions on Evidence 2019, Article 27; see also, Provisions on IP Evidence 2020, Article 12 (1) provides that "evidence preservation shall be limited to fix evidence effectively, minimize the damages to the value of the preserved objects and the impact on the normal production and operations of the holder of the evidence".

31 Provisions on Evidence 2019, Article 23.

32 The First Civil Division of the Supreme People's Court (ed), *Understanding and Application of New Provisions of the Supreme People's Court on Evidence in Civil Procedures, Volume I* (People's Court Press 2020) 290.

33 ibid.

between the evidence and the disputed matter and why the applicant is of the view that the evidence preservation measure is necessary.[34]

10.32 In this context, the preliminary procedural evaluation of an application seeking evidence preservation measures will be carried out by courts. Any issue as to the legal effect of the evidence on the dispute between the parties will not be evaluated as this is the substantive issue that should be ascertained during the future civil trial.[35]

10.33 From the above analysis, it follows that the application must additionally emphasise that in the event of failure to preserve the evidence, the evidence will likely disappear or be destroyed, or it will be difficult to obtain it later. If the judges were to evaluate that these circumstances do not exist at the time of submitting the application, even if such evidence were to play a crucial role in addressing the civil/commercial dispute, then the judges are likely to dismiss the application seeking the evidence preservation measures.[36]

Case Test and Status Quo

10.34 For example, in *Guizhou Peninsula Hot Spring Real Estate Co Ltd (Guizhou Peninsula) v Guoji Construction Group Co Ltd (Guoji),*[37] Guizhou Peninsula (applicant) applied for the preservation of all construction materials whose custody Guoji was in charge of prior to filing a case in a Chinese court. Although the subject matter of the preservation application would have constituted important and relevant evidence for the future civil trial, the jurisdiction court held that under the circumstances as they were at the time of submitting the application, the court was not convinced that there was a likelihood of destruction of evidence or there could be a failure to obtain the same evidence at a later stage. The pre-action preservation application was thus denied by the court.[38]

10.35 However, for the stakeholders, the understanding of the preliminary procedural examination was recently clarified through the Provisions on Evidence 2019. In legal practice, more time is needed to observe how Chinese courts will apply this new rule. In particular, a few courts, prior to Provisions on Evidence 2019, had not applied the rule of the preliminary procedural examination.

34 The First Civil Division of the Supreme People's Court (ed), *Understanding and Application of New Provisions of the Supreme People's Court on Evidence in Civil Procedures, Volume I* (People's Court Press 2020) 273.

35 ibid.

36 ibid.

37 *Guizhou Peninsula Hot Spring Real Estate Co Ltd v Guoji Construction Group Co Ltd* (an application for a pre-action evidence preservation order) [2020] Qian 0524 Bao Zheng No 1 (the Primary People's Court of Zhijin County of Guizhou Province, first instance and binding order).

38 ibid.

10.36 For instance, in *Hangzhou Ai** Biotechnology Co Ltd v Hangzhou Weice Biotechnology Co Ltd and Hua**,[39] Ai** Company (applicant) claimed that Hua* obtained know-how based on his employment relationship with Ai** Company and as a result, Hua* and Weice Company (two respondents) acting together infringed the know-how that rightly belonged to the applicant. During the first instance proceedings, in order to prove to the court that two respondents infringed the know-how, Ai** Company filed an application seeking evidence preservation measures. However, the first instance court (the Primary People's Court of Yuhang District of Hangzhou City of Zhejiang Province) denied the application.

10.37 During the second instance proceedings, the applicant contended that the first instance court was not correct with regard to its refusal in the application seeking the evidence preservation measures. The second instance court (the Intermediate People's Court of Hangzhou City of Zhejiang Province) emphasised that the applicant did not provide the preliminary evidence to prove the respondent's infringement of know-how that belonged to the applicant. Therefore, the second instance court was of the view that the order to refuse the application seeking evidence preservation measures made by the first instance court was reasonable.[40]

10.38 It is apparent that certain courts in the territory of Zhejiang Province did not adopt the rule of preliminary evaluation during the course of the application seeking evidence preservation measures. On the other hand, these courts are usually inclined to adopt the standard of substantive examination of such applications which can cause considerable difficulty with regard to applications seeking evidence preservation measures.[41]

Tests in the SMPL 2000 Regime

10.39 Similarly, difficulty has been observed in the domain of maritime law. In a maritime evidence preservation application, the SMPL 2000 provides:

39 *Hangzhou Ai**Biotechnology Co Ltd v Hangzhou Weice Biotechnology Co Ltd and Hua** (dispute over an infringement of know-how) [2017] Zhe 01 Civil Final No 7141 (the Intermediate People's Court of Hangzhou City of Zhejiang Province, second instance and binding judgment); see also, [2016] Zhe 0110 Civil Chu No 17243 (the Primary People's Court of Yuhang District of Hanghzou City of Zhejiang Province, first instance and judgment); it should be noted that no order in relation to the evidence preservation application was reported online. The facts of this case and *obiter dictum* were, in fact, reported in the final judgment. Furthermore, due to the issues of confidentiality, the judgment did not disclose the full name of parties involved in the disputes and application, but the detailed facts of the case were clear from the report. The star (*) in the parties' names represents the name of a party that was not disclosed to maintain confidentiality.

40 ibid.

41 Refer to Chapter 11, 11.86, 11.97–11.107, for discussion on the comparative analysis of standards of proof in civil courts in China.

> The following conditions shall be met before preservation of maritime evidence is granted: (b) the evidence, preservation of which is requested, *substantiates* [emphasis added] the maritime claim.[42]

10.40 The above condition is understood by maritime judges and scholars as requiring that the evidence that needs to be preserved is capable of playing a role in substantially proving a maritime claim, apart from ensuring the correlation between the evidence that needs to be preserved and the maritime claim. It means that the court must examine whether the evidence to be preserved has an evidential effect on the actual situation of the case.[43] This leads to the evaluation of the application with great scrutiny and is much beyond the preliminary procedural examination that should have been the standard. Accordingly, the applicants should prepare for the substantial examination of their applications in certain maritime courts in China.

10.41 With the promulgation of Provisions on Evidence 2019, the view of the maritime court and the scholar is expected to gradually evolve regarding their insistence on substantively evaluating preservation applications. However, in the authors' view, it will take a few years before a substantive change becomes noticeable.

Pre-Action Evidence Preservations and Alternative Remedies

10.42 In this section, two main requirements – urgent circumstances and the minimum impact for applications seeking evidence preservation measures – will be discussed. Several more legal issues can refer to the requirements of post-action preservation measures in 10.81–10.97.

Requirement of "Urgent Circumstances"

10.43 Pursuant to Article 81 of the CPL 1991 (as amended until 2020), the purpose of both pre-action and post-action evidence preservation applications is the same. In the context of the satisfaction of the purpose,[44] the only different requirement between pre-action and post-action evidence preservation applications is that the pre-action application must emphasise the "urgent circumstances" surrounding the facts of the dispute. However, Article 81 has not elaborated on the meaning of "urgent circumstances". The detailed rules in relation to applications seeking evidence preservation measures should comply with the provisions of Chapter IX of the CPL 1991 (as amended until 2020) on the property and behaviour preservations. Accordingly, the

42 SMPL 2000, Article 67(2).

43 Weifeng Hu, 'Collection of Evidence by Maritime Evidence Preservation Prior to Maritime Arbitration' (*Xiamen Maritime Court*, 6 July 2017) <https://wemp.app/posts/0af7efcb-9e50-4b41-be5c-1c25a918d533> accessed 30 July 2021; Liang Zhao and Lianjun Li, *Maritime Law and Practice in China* (1st Edn, Informa Law from Routledge 2017) para. 22.25–22.28.

44 In terms of the legal test on the purpose, further discussion can be found in 10.82.

guidance on the standard of "urgent circumstance" relating to applications seeking evidence preservation measures can be obtained from Chapter 6, 6.79–6.81, and Chapter 8, 8.104–8.105, respectively. However, the guidance in these chapters has to be customised for three different types of preservation measures due to their own specific characteristics. It must be emphasised that these guidances in Chapters 6 and 8 have to be seen from the point of view that additionally, Chinese judges will exercise their discretionary power.

10.44 There is no standard rule that can decipher or predict the way that the discretionary power of the Chinese judges will be exercised. After reviewing a few reported Chinese evidence preservation orders, it is observed that the judicial orders do not provide detailed guidance in the context of the meaning of "urgent circumstances".[45]

10.45 First, there is no guidance case or gazette case reported by the SPC to clarify the meaning of "urgent circumstance" for evidence preservation measures. Secondly, the reported lower courts' orders for the pre-action evidence preservation measures do not provide detailed guidance as to how the application will be evaluated by the courts.

10.46 In the reported evidence preservation orders, the courts simply held that "the application complied with the Article 81 of the CPL 1991 (as amended until 2020). The applications were therefore accepted".[46] There was no further explanation that was provided with these preservation orders. Alternatively, in a very few orders, the legal reasoning provided by courts is along the lines that "due to urgent circumstances, in the context of the likelihood that the evidence may be destroyed or cannot be obtained in future, accordingly the applicant was entitled to apply for the pre-action evidence preservation measures".[47]

The Principle of the Minimum Impact

10.47 In order to balance the interests of an applicant and a respondent/an interested party involved in evidence preservation, in the recent

45 In property preservation or behaviour preservation orders, similarly, Chinese judges do not provide the legal reasoning in detail. However, the judicial interpretations in relation to those two types of preservation measures make up this gap.

46 For example, *Jiangxi Kete Investment Co Ltd v Shanghai Yizhou Asset Management Co Ltd* (an application seeking a pre-action evidence preservation in a loan contract dispute) [2019] Gan Civil Chu No 64-1 (the High People's Court of Jiangxi Province, first instance and binding order); *Ningbo Runjin Electromechanical and Technology Co Ltd v Ningbo Anmeida Numerical Control Technology Co Ltd* (an application seeking a pre-action evidence preservation in a patent dispute) [2017] Zhe 02 Zheng Bao No 22 (the Intermediate People's Court of Ningbo City of Zhejiang Province, first instance and binding order).

47 For example, *Shandong Laifang Surveying Co Ltd v Shandong Xincheng Geography Information Co Ltd* (an application seeking a pre-action evidence preservation measure in an infringement of know-how dispute) [2019] Lu 01 Zheng Bao No 49 (the Intermediate People's Court of Jinan City of Shandong Province, first instance and binding order).

interpretation, the new principle to examine the necessity of applications seeking evidence preservation measures is clarified. Article 27 of Provisions on Evidence 2019 provides that

> In the context of the satisfaction of the evidence preservation purpose, the courts should take preservation measures that cause the minimum impact on the respondents' interests.[48]

10.48 It follows that the SPC highlights that the principle of "the minimum impact on the respondents' interests" should be applied to examine whether and to what extent it is necessary and lawful to render an evidence preservation order.[49] In order to satisfy the principle of "the minimum impact", the SPC requests the courts to focus on the legality and necessity of the application. The legality of the application involves ascertaining the qualification of the applicant, the format of the application, the court's jurisdiction over the application and so forth. The necessity of the application involves looking at the purpose of the evidence preservation and whether other approaches, such as the notary public office or the applicant by himself, can obtain the evidence without the intervention of the courts.[50] This principle applies to the legal tests of post-action evidence preservation as well.

10.49 Following the Provisions on Evidence 2019, Provisions on IP Evidence 2020 also applies the same principle. It is provided that

> Evidence preservation shall be limited to fix evidence effectively, minimize the damages to the value of the preserved objects and the impact on the normal production and operations of the holder of the evidence.[51]

10.50 It is interpreted by the IP senior judges of the SPC that apart from the traditional principles regarding evidence preservation, namely, the principles of timeliness and necessity, two aspects should be highlighted.

10.51 First, it is necessary to take the most proper measure to preserve the evidence in order to reflect the condition of the evidence completely and authentically; secondly, as for the understanding of the principle of the minimum impact, according to the extent of the impact of the evidence preservation measure, it follows that the measure of sealing up the evidence is not necessary if taking photos is sufficient to keep the evidence; afterwards, if the measure of sealing up the evidence were sufficient, the detainment should

48 Provisions on Evidence 2019, Article 27.

49 The First Civil Division of the Supreme People's Court (ed), *Understanding and Application of New Provisions of the Supreme People's Court on Evidence in Civil Procedures, Volume 1* (People's Court Press 2020) 290–292.

50 ibid.

51 Provisions on IP Evidence 2020, Article 12.

not be taken, and so on, the fundamental purpose is to minimise the damage to the preserved evidence and disturb the holder of the evidence.[52]

Status Quo for Pre-Action Applications in Courts

10.52 It is not possible to state with certainty that the pre-action evidence preservation system has been functioning well in China. Just after the 2012 amendment to the CPL 1991, few applications seeking pre-action evidence preservation measures were submitted to courts between 2012 and 2015. These statistics were observed by a legal scholar in this area of law.[53] In addition, even if pre-action evidence preservation applications were submitted to the courts, the outlook of Chinese courts was downbeat towards such applications.[54]

10.53 By way of searching several authoritative webpages for providing Chinese judicial decisions including judgments, rulings and orders, such as China's Judicial Opinions webpage (中国裁判文书网www.wenshu.com),[55] Lawinfochina webpage (北大法宝www.lawinfochina.com)[56] and Itslaw webpage (无讼www.itslaw.com),[57] the number of reported cases of applications seeking pre-action evidence preservation measures is very low.

10.54 For example, after searching for key words such as "order", "pre-action evidence preservation", "after 2012 (including)" on three webpages

52 Guanghai Lin, Jian Li and Rong Wu, 'Understanding and Application of *Several Provisions of the Supreme People's Court on Evidence in Civil Procedures Involving Intellectual Property Rights*' (2021) 4 The People's Judicature (Applied) 24.

53 In Chinese academic circles, statistics and research in relation to evidence preservation applications are rare; the authors have only found one article; see also, Pengchao Ding, 'A Study on the System of Civil Pretrial Evidence Preservation' (2015) 6 Journal of Henan University of Economics and Law 113.

54 Pengchao Ding, 'A Study on the System of Civil Pretrial Evidence Preservation' (2015) 6 Journal of Henan University of Economics and Law 113, 115–116.

55 In 2013, the SPC issued *Provisions on the Issuance of Judgments on the Internet by the People's Courts*. It is provided that "The Supreme People's Court will set up a website for Judicial Opinions of China on the Internet, and uniformly issues the effective judgments of Chinese courts at all levels. The Chinese courts at all levels shall be responsible for the quality of judgments issued on the Internet"; see also, *Provisions of the Supreme People's Court on the Issuance of Judgments on the Internet by the People's Courts* (Fa Shi [2013] No 26), Article 2. This Interpretation has been replaced by *Provisions of the Supreme People's Court on the Issuance of Judgments on the Internet by the People's Courts* (Fa Shi [2016] No 19). The new Interpretation's Article 2 provides that "China's Judicial Opinions Webpage is a unified platform for national courts to report judicial decisions. Chinese courts at all levels should set up links to this webpage on the government affairs website and the judicial open platform of this court". This webpage is therefore the most authoritative webpage for providing judicial decisions including judgments, rulings and orders in China.

56 The Lawinfochina webpage was produced by the Law School of Peking University in 1985 and then in 2003 this webpage cooperated with the SPC to report judicial decisions, law and relevant judicial interpretations.

57 The Itslaw webpage serves Chinese lawyers by providing Chinese judicial decisions, legislations and articles.

as stated above, it is shown that the number of orders for pre-action evidence preservations rendered by the courts of all levels is – (i) 35 on China's Judicial Opinions webpage (中国裁判文书网),[58] (ii) 849 on Lawinfochina (北大法宝)[59] and (iii) 1,052 on Itslaw (无讼).[60] These evidence preservation orders are from different kinds of civil disputes including intellectual property disputes and maritime disputes and are from the year 2012 onwards. In addition, most of these orders belong to general cases rather than reference cases discussed in Chapter 3, 3.23–3.25, which means that those general cases cannot be treated as a source of law.

10.55 After one of the key terms is changed to "pre-action property preservation" from "pre-action evidence preservation", the number of orders is 32,124 on China's Judicial Opinions webpage (中国裁判文书网),[61] 121,131 on Lawinfochina (北大法宝)[62] and 494,563 on Itslaw (无讼) respectively.[63]

10.56 In the three webpages, how many evidence preservation orders from Chinese courts are overlapping and the exact number of orders as compared to the number of applications filed are not clear. Furthermore, many features in the applications seeking evidence and property preservation are different. Even so, in comparison with the results obtained from the webpages, it is safe to assume that the applications seeking pre-action evidence preservation measures have not been functioning well in comparison with the property preservation applications. The authors are expecting that, in the years to come, there will be more clarity and acceptance of such applications in Chinese courts.

---

58 <https://wenshu.court.gov.cn/website/wenshu/181217BMTKHNT2W0/index.html?pageId=842a2ffe2cb17f2ecfbbff795a279804&s1=诉前财产保全&cprqStart=2012-01-01&cprqEnd=2021-08-09> accessed 9 August 2021.

59 <https://bjlx.pkulaw.com/case/Search/FindByAnyou?QueryType=case-cause&ClassCodeKey=002100903,,,> accessed 9 August 2021.

60 <www.itslaw.com/search?searchMode=judgements&sortType=1&conditions=searchWord%2B诉前证据保全%2B1%2B诉前证据保全&conditions=caseType%2B1%2B10%2B民事&conditions=judgementType%2B2%2B9%2B裁定&searchView=text> accessed 10 March 2020; it should be noted that the update of the webpage is always under way before the authors submit the final draft of this book; therefore, the data were simply collected on 10 March 2020.

61 <https://wenshu.court.gov.cn/website/wenshu/181217BMTKHNT2W0/index.html?pageId=842a2ffe2cb17f2ecfbbff795a279804&s1=诉前财产保全&cprqStart=2012-01-01&cprqEnd=2021-08-09> accessed 9 August 2021.

62 <https://bjlx.pkulaw.com/case/Search/FindByAnyou?QueryType=case-cause&ClassCodeKey=002100903,,,> accessed 9 August 2021.

63 <www.itslaw.com/search?searchMode=judgements&sortType=1&conditions=searchWord%2B诉前财产保全%2B1%2B诉前财产保全&conditions=caseType%2B1%2B10%2B民事&conditions=judgementType%2B2%2B9%2B裁定&conditions=trialYear%2B2012%2B7%2B2012&conditions=trialYear%2B2013%2B7%2B2013&conditions=trialYear%2B2014%2B7%2B2014&conditions=trialYear%2B2015%2B7%2B2015&conditions=trialYear%2B2016%2B7%2B2016&conditions=trialYear%2B2017%2B7%2B2017&conditions=trialYear%2B2018%2B7%2B2018&conditions=trialYear%2B2019%2B7%2B2019&conditions=trialYear%2B2020%2B7%2B2020&searchView=text> accessed 10 March 2020; it should be noted that the update of the webpage was under way when the authors submitted the final draft of this book; therefore, the data were simply collected on 10 March 2020.

Alternative Remedy (I): Evidence Preservation by Notary Public Offices

10.57 Compared to the low number of applications seeking pre-action evidence preservation measures that are submitted to Chinese courts, the applications that are submitted to notary public offices in China are a matter of routine.[64] Prior to the 2012 amendment to the CPL 1991, the notary public offices fulfilled an important obligation in assisting parties in relation to the pre-action evidence preservation measures. Many Chinese practitioners and in-house lawyers in companies are familiar with the procedure of seeking the assistance of the notaries in relation to pre-action evidence preservation measures.

10.58 This method of obtaining pre-action preservation of evidence measures utilising the notarial services is different from the applications made to the court, pursuant to the CPL 1991 (as amended until 2020). The notary public offices, in practice, will not examine "whether the circumstances are urgent" and will not examine "whether the evidence will be destroyed or will become difficult to obtain in future". The notary public office accepts such requests from the parties and renders a notarial document, as long as the applications do not violate the laws in China.

10.59 Pursuant to Provisions on Evidence 2019, the legal effect of the notarial evidence preservation measures will be directly recognised by the courts without the party's further proof. Furthermore, notarial evidence preservation measures will be considered by the courts to examine whether the disputed fact has been proved by the effective notarial documents.[65] This means that the validity of pre-action evidence preservation measures by the notary public office is equivalent to that of the courts' evidence preservation measures, unless the evidence is presented to the courts to rebut the notarial documents.

---

64 In the past, notary public offices belonged to state offices representing the state in witnessing legal relations in civil matters. Although since 1 October 2000, the Ministry of Justice of PRC has implemented a plan to reform the notary system, that is to change notary public offices from administrative bodies to non-profit entities, their function in witnessing legal relations still stands. In accordance with Articles 2 and 6 of the Notarisation Law of the People's Republic of China 2006 (2017 Amendment), "Notarisation means an act performed by a notarial office, upon the application of a party concerned, to certify the authenticity and legality of a civil juristic act, a fact of legal significance and a document in accordance with the statutory procedures", and "A notarial office is a non-profit certification institution that is lawfully established and independently exercises the notarial functions and bear corresponding civil liabilities". Due to the duty of the notary public offices in witnessing legal relations, the disputed parties are used to seeking the remedy from the notary public offices; the Notarisation Law of the People's Republic of China, which was adopted at the 17th meeting of the Standing Committee of the National People's Congress of the People's Republic of China on 28 August 2005, came into effect on 1 March 2006. The latest amendment was adopted by the 29th Session of the Standing Committee of the 12th National People's Congress of the People's Republic of China on 1 September 2017.

65 Provisions on Evidence 2019, Article 10.

10.60 After the amendment to the CPL 2012, even if the applicants are entitled to submit pre-action evidence preservation applications to the court, the notarial preservation measures are still available throughout China. As discussed in 10.58, the procedure to obtain the notarial preservation measures is very flexible. Furthermore, many notary public offices have been innovative with regard to providing the service of notarial evidence preservation measures to enhance their practice.

10.61 For example, one of the prominent notary offices in Beijing has produced an electronic notary system to serve clients in the context of evidence preservation for copyright disputes.[66] Similarly, another prominent notary office in Shanghai set up an electronic evidence preservation platform in 2012.[67] The purpose of all such new measures is to facilitate a system to obtain pre-action evidence preservation through notaries, and it has been operating in parallel to the system pursuant to the CPL regime.

10.62 It has been observed that Chinese courts are generally very receptive of the notarial evidence preservation measures because this is an effective way to reduce the court's burden in dealing with evidence preservation applications. However, it should be kept in mind that whether the Chinese courts accept the evidence preservation granted by the notary or not will rely, in legal practice, on the exercise of judges' discretionary power.

10.63 For example, in *Guidance of Chongqing High People's Court on Intellectual Property Civil Evidence 2018*, if the courts require that the parties must provide the original data or the carrier of data or software and so on, even if the evidence preservation document is prepared by the notary public office, then the parties have to submit the original electronic evidence to the courts.[68]

Alternative Remedy (II): Online Preservation by Way of Blockchain Technology

10.64 In 10.61, the authors briefly introduced the use of the advanced technology by many notary public offices, and also these days, a few Chinese companies have set up "Preservation Network" by way of blockchain technology. The main purpose of "Preservation Network" is to preserve electronic data online. In cases involving infringement disputes, parties concerned may apply for online preservations of the relevant electronic data that is the subject

66 For example, Beijing Fangyuan Notary Public Office in 2012.

67 For example, Dongfang Notary Public Office in Shanghai; see also, Project Team of Shanghai Xujiahui Notary Public Office, 'Change and Development of Notary Institutions on Evidence Preservations in the Context of the Internet and Big Data' (2019) 5 China Notary Journal 40, 43.

68 *Chongqing High People's Court on Intellectual Property Civil Evidence 2018*, Article 14.

matter of infringement disputes.[69] After these data, which are the subject matter of infringement disputes, are saved on the "Preservation Network", then the procedure for evidence preservation measures is deemed completed.

10.65 For example, the first case from Zhejiang Province has recently confirmed the validity of online preservation measures using blockchain technology. In this case, Hangzhou Huatai (applicant) claimed that its company enjoyed the copyright over an online paper. However, without the applicant's permission, Shenzhen Tongdao (respondent) had uploaded this paper on the respondent's webpage. In order to preserve the evidence, the applicant had used the "Preservation Network" platform to preserve the relevant electronic data that was the subject matter of the infringement disputes. The Hangzhou Internet Court of Zhejiang Province ascertained that "Preservation Network" was a specialised qualified webpage to provide an online preservation platform by way of blockchain technology. The electronic data saved on this platform could not be changed, destroyed or disappeared. Thus, the court held that these evidence preservation measures were valid, and the evidence to be preserved could be used in the case before the court.[70]

10.66 Similarly, the first case in Beijing to confirm the evidence preservation by blockchain technology was disposed of by the Primary People's Court of Dongcheng District of Beijing Municipality in *COL Digital Publishing Group Co Ltd v Beijing JD 360 Electronic Commerce Co Ltd*.[71] The process of evidence preservation was similar to the process of the evidence measures in the case that was heard by the Hangzhou Internet Court of Zhejiang Province. Accordingly, the Primary People's Court of Dongcheng District of Beijing Municipality allowed the online evidence preservation as well.[72]

10.67 Following the above discussion, pre-action evidence preservation measures may not be functioning well in Chinese courts. As a result, applicants are trying to use different approaches to achieve the purpose of pre-action evidence preservation measures. Furthermore, many of these approaches, such as notarial preservation or online preservation measures using blockchain technology, are not only convenient and effective, but also such preserved evidence has been accepted and recognised by the Chinese courts during civil trials.

10.68 It is important to note that in the *Opinion of the Third Civil Division of the Zhejiang High People's Court on Intellectual Property Civil Evidence Preservation 2014* (hereinafter referred to as "Opinion on Zhejiang IP

---

69 Refer to 10.22 (e) for the scope of "electronic data".

70 *Hangzhou Huatai Yimei Culture Media Co Ltd v Shenzhen Tongdao Technology Development Co Ltd* (dispute over an internet infringement) [2018] Zhe 0192 Civil Chu No 81 (the Hangzhou Internet Court of Zhejiang Province, first instance and binding order).

71 *COL Digital Publishing Group Co Ltd* v *Beijing JD 360 Electronic Commerce Co Ltd* (dispute over an internet infringement) [2018] Jing 0101 Civil Chu No 6426 (the Primary People's Court of Dongcheng District of Beijing Municipality, first instance and binding order).

72 ibid.

Evidence Preservation 2014"), it is expressly stated that the courts may refuse to render evidence preservation measures if the requested evidence preservation measures could be obtained easily through any of the notary public offices.[73] Although this provision is only applied in intellectual property disputes in the territory of Zhejiang Province, it seem to highlight that a few Chinese courts are willing to depend on the assistance of the notary public offices in the context of evidence preservation measures. Also, it indirectly reveals the reason for the low number of pre-action evidence preservation applications in the Chinese legal system.[74]

10.69 In the end, notarial evidence preservation and online preservation are not restricted to pre-action preservation measures. Parties to a dispute during civil trials can also employ these approaches to achieve the function of evidence preservation measures. However, during the civil trial proceedings, it may be easier to obtain post-action evidence measures from the courts.

Time Limit of Post-Action Applications

10.70 In terms of the time limit of applications, there is no time limit of pre-action applications seeking all three types of preservation measures. Prior to filing a case, a party may apply for a preservation measure at any time. However, the application seeking post-action evidence preservation measures must strictly abide by the time limit for providing relevant evidence to the courts, while applications seeking post-action property or behaviour preservation measures may be submitted to the courts any time before the judgment is made.

10.71 The time limit for providing evidence refers to the period during which the concerned parties must provide evidence to the courts. Article 25 (2) of Provisions on Evidence 2019 stipulates that the parties concerned should file an application seeking evidence preservation measures prior to the time limit applicable for providing relevant evidence to the courts during civil proceedings.[75] It follows that beyond the expiry of that statutory time period, the Chinese courts are likely to disallow the applications seeking the preservation of post-action evidence without giving any further reasons.

Statutory Time Limit

10.72 In the pre-trial preparatory phase, in terms of the time limit that is applicable to the parties to disputes in relation to their obligations to submit

73 Opinion on Zhejiang IP Evidence Preservation 2014, Article 7.
74 Refer to 10.52–10.56.
75 Provisions on Evidence 2019, Article 25 (2).

the relevant evidence, the competent courts are entitled to determine the time period on the following basis:

(a) No less than 15 days for the first instance case under an ordinary procedure.
(b) No less than 15 days for a second instance case where the parties concerned provide new evidence.
(c) No more than 15 days under a summary procedure.
(d) No more than seven days for a small claim case.[76]

10.73 Prior to the expiry of the above time limits, the parties are allowed to apply to seek an extension of time from the courts in relation to their obligations to submit the relevant evidence with the prescribed time limits. After the expiry of the time period, in the absence of extension, parties can only request the court:

(a) To allow the provision of evidence to refute the evidence provided by the counterpart.
(b) To submit correction/supplementary materials for defects in terms of the sources, forms and other aspects of the evidence that was submitted by himself.[77]

10.74 If the courts approve the application seeking new time limits, then it is possible for the parties to apply for evidence preservation measures during these new time limits. In the absence of time extension, an application for evidence preservation measures will not be accepted by the courts after the expiry of the prescribed time limits.

10.75 It must be emphasised that, pursuant to Article 25 (2) of Provisions on Evidence 2019, it is provided that

> the applications seeking evidence preservation measures *must* [emphasis added] abide by the applicable time limits for providing evidence in the civil process.[78]

10.76 In contrast, Article 98 of the Interpretation of CPL 2015 (2020 Amendment) provides that

> the applications seeking evidence preservation measures *may* [emphasis added] be submitted prior to the expiry of the time limits for providing evidence.[79]

10.77 In accordance with the principles of *lex posterior derogat lex priori* and *lex specialis*, Provisions on Evidence 2019 will prevail over the

---

76 Interpretation of CPL 2015 (2020 Amendment), Article 99 and Provisions on Evidence 2019, Article 51.

77 Interpretation of CPL 2015 (2020 Amendment), Articles 99 and 100.

78 Provisions on Evidence 2019, Article 25 (2).

79 Interpretation of CPL 2015 (2020 Amendment), Article 98.

Interpretation of CPL 2015 (2020 Amendment).[80] This means that the applicants must abide by the time limit for submitting the evidence, even if the Interpretation of CPL 2015 (2020 Amendment) employs the term "may".

Agreed Time Limit

10.78 The time limit for providing evidence may be negotiated by the parties to disputes, and these parties may then take this consent agreement to Chinese courts for their approval.[81] However, it has been observed that such negotiated outcomes between the parties to disputes are very rare.

10.79 In legal practice, the alternative remedy is to seek the court's consent rather than negotiation between parties. The tactic is that after Chinese courts have docked the case within the civil legal system, both the claimant and the defendant will receive a notice of case-filing from the Chinese courts. In such notice, both parties will be requested to provide evidence within the prescribed time limits. If the parties are not satisfied with the prescribed time limit, it is feasible for them to apply for an extension of time.[82] Whether the application for extension can be approved by the courts will be dependent on the legal grounds stated in the application. If the Chinese courts consider that the legal grounds were sufficient, the application might be successful.

10.80 There is no express guidance on what may constitute proper legal grounds in the context of seeking time extension for providing evidence to the Chinese courts. A few legal scholars contend that the failure to collect evidence in time indicates the reasonable objective ground that the courts are likely to consider before granting extension of time.[83] However, due to the absence of guidance prescribed by law, in the end, the courts' exercise of discretionary power will determine whether the extension of time can be granted. If the extension is approved, the time limit for filing an application seeking evidence preservation measures is deemed extended automatically.

Requirement for Post-Action Evidence Preservations

10.81 Notarial preservations and advanced technology preservations cannot address all issues concerning the preservation of evidence, as many evidence preservation measures in light of the different categories of evidence

80 The 2020 Amendment to the Interpretation of CPL simply adjusted several provisions not associated with the preservation measure and the 2015 provisions relating to the preservation measure do not change; therefore, Provisions on Evidence 2019 still follows the rule of *lex posterior derogat lex priori*.

81 Interpretation of CPL 2015 (2020 Amendment), Article 99.

82 ibid Article 100.

83 Lin Wang, Renbo Wang and Others (eds), *Casebook on Civil Procedure Law* (China Democracy Legal System Publishing Home Co Ltd 2016).

may not be taken by the notary public offices or advanced technology. A few preservation of evidence measures, such as sealing up or detainment, must rely on the courts' orders. The forthcoming sections will focus on requirements that must be satisfied in post-action evidence preservation applications. In terms of pre-action applications, these requirements are equally valuable.

General Requirements

10.82 The only express guidance for the evidence preservation applications highlighted by the SPC is the principle of the minimum impact discussed in 10.47–10.51. In addition, Article 81 of the CPL 1991 (as amended until 2020) provides that the purposes of the evidence preservation measure are (i) to prevent the "likelihood of destruction of the evidence" and (ii) to avoid the "possibility of failing to obtain evidence in future". Such purposes actually reflect the principle of necessity. Certainly, they also constitute the legal requirements that the applicants must satisfy before their pre-action or post-action evidence preservation measures can be granted by the courts. If the applicant can prove that the existing circumstances satisfy the principle of the minimum impact and the purpose of the preservation (the principle of necessity), then it is likely that the applications seeking evidence preservation measures will be approved by the courts. Nonetheless, there is no guidance available on how and to what extent the judges shall evaluate the circumstances.

Requirements for IP Evidence Preservation and Its Understanding

10.83 Provisions on IP Evidence 2020 enunciates four requirements of evidence preservation which apply to pre-action and post-action applications. It is provided that

> The people's court shall review the application for evidence preservation by the parties or interested parties in combination with the following elements:
>
> (1) Whether the applicant has provided preliminary evidence for its claim;
> (2) Whether the evidence can be collected by the applicant itself;
> (3) The possibility that the evidence will be lost or will be difficult to obtain in the future and its impact on the facts to be proved;
> (4) The impact of possible preservation measures on evidence holders.[84]

10.84 It is observed that although the preceding requirements are provided in the judicial interpretation of IP disputes, the exact content may apply to other disputes. For example, the first requirement as to the preliminary evidence is basically compatible with the preliminary procedure examination

84 Provisions on IP Evidence 2020, Article 11.

discussed in 10.30–10.41 while the fourth requirement in effect amounts to the principle of the minimum impact in 10.47–10.51.

10.85 Furthermore, when the IP senior judges of the SPC provided the understanding and application of Provisions on IP Evidence 2020, these four requirements were clarified in this interpretation on the ground that Article 81 of the CPL 1991 (as amended until 2020) does not stipulate the uniform standard to guide the court, so that different courts apply different requirements.[85] In other words, these requirements provided by the new interpretation are to fill in the gaps. From this point of view, it is the authors' submission that the evidence preservation application for other disputes may be by reference to Article 11 of Provisions on IP Evidence 2020.

Other Considerations and Underlying Issues

10.86 Apart from the preceding requirements provided by the interpretation, taking into consideration the practical requirements, the authors also attempt to give some relevant guidance in the following paragraphs.

10.87 Firstly, the inherent nature of the evidence itself will provide clues whether such evidence needs the preservation measures. For example, the evidence might rot or perish in the short term and as a result, the cost of obtaining such evidence in the future might be substantially increased, or it even might be impossible to obtain in the future.

10.88 Secondly, according to the objective criterion, the measures that the applicants can take are restricted. In other words, the applicants subjectively expect to collect the evidence by themselves; but it is objectively impossible for them to obtain the evidence by themselves.

10.89 For example, where the relevant evidence is controlled by a respondent, and the evidence is likely to be destroyed by the holder. However, an applicant and his authorised legal agent cannot directly take any measures to obtain such evidence controlled by the respondent and have to seek assistance from the courts.

10.90 Certainly, the above suggestions or guidance for applicants are not always useful in the context of Chinese legal practice. Conflicting orders have been seen in the past years in the context of similar types of evidence that needs an evidence preservation order.

10.91 For example, in *Guizhou Peninsula Hot Spring Real Estate Co Ltd (Guizhou Peninsula) v Guoji Construction Group Co Ltd (Guoji Group)*,[86]

---

85 Guanghai Lin, Jian Li and Rong Wu, 'Understanding and Application of *Several Provisions of the Supreme People's Court on Evidence in Civil Procedures Involving Intellectual Property Rights*' (2021) 4 The People's Judicature (Applied) 24.

86 *Guizhou Peninsula Hot Spring Real Estate Co Ltd v Guoji Construction Group Co Ltd* (an application seeking pre-action evidence preservation measures) [2020] Qian 0524 Bao

Guizhou Peninsula (applicant) applied for evidence preservation measures relating to the documents of the construction project. These documents were controlled by Guoji Group (respondent). However, after evaluating the application, the court held that there was no risk for such evidence to be destroyed and it was not of the type that could not be obtained in the future. The application seeking preservation of evidence was therefore denied.[87]

10.92 In contrast, in the case of *Yanan Si v Sichuan Luzhou Yuhe Construction Engineering Co Ltd (Luzhou Yuhe) and Others*,[88] Yanan Si (applicant) filed an evidence preservation application for preserving the annual balance sheet, cash flow sheet, shareholders' registration list, shareholders' minutes and other files belonging to Luzhou Yuhe (respondent). The court accepted this application and accordingly sealed up all files on the ground that it was possible that these files could be lost or could not be obtained in the future.[89]

10.93 In these two conflicting evidence preservation orders, all evidence to be preserved was in fact original official files. If analysed objectively, in any event, it is difficult to revise the original files. Even if, due to the subjective reasons, the files were to be lost or destroyed or were to be unavailable, in accordance with Article 113 of the Interpretation of CPL 2015 (2020 Amendment) and Article 111 of the CPL 1991 (as amended until 2020), the holder of that evidence could have been fined or even detained among other sanctions.[90] These sanctions are in effect equivalent to that of disobeying the preservation orders granted by the courts which have been discussed in Chapter 3, 3.266–3.274. The only difference is that Article 113 of the Interpretation of CPL 2015 (2020 Amendment) does not provide for the criminal penalty.[91]

10.94 Furthermore, pursuant to Article 95 of Provisions on Evidence 2019, it is provided:

> If a party refuses to submit the evidence in his possession without the justifiable reason, and the other party who undertakes the burden of the proof claims that such evidence is against the party taking control of the evidence, the court may uphold the other party's allegation.[92]

Zheng No 1 (the Primary People's Court of Zhijin County of Guizhou Province, first instance and binding order).

87 ibid.

88 *Yanan Si v Sichuan Luzhou Yuhe Construction Engineering Co Ltd (Luzhou Yuhe) and Others* (an application for an evidence preservation) [2019] Chuan 05 Civil Chu No 49 (the Intermediate People's Court of Luzhou City of Sichuan Province, first instance and binding order).

89 ibid.

90 Interpretation of CPL 2015 (2020 Amendment), Article 113; CPL 1991 (as amended until 2020), Article 111.

91 Interpretation of CPL 2015 (2020 Amendment), Article 113.

92 Provisions on Evidence 2019, Article 95.

10.95 From the analysis of the above Article 95, if the evidence is revised, destroyed or lost without justifiable reasons, the holder of the evidence can be subjected to unfavourable consequences by Chinese courts. Therefore, it seems that in many cases the preservation of evidence measures may even not be required after the advent of Provisions on Evidence 2019.

10.96 In contrast, from another point of view, all original files are controlled by the respondents, who are likely to be the defendants in the main civil/commercial disputes. Indeed, in the context of failing to take evidence preservation measures, there is a risk that the original files will be destroyed or lost. If the respondents were to prove that they are not liable for the loss of the evidence, there is no ground to sanction them pursuant to the CPL (2020 Amendment) and Provisions on Evidence 2019. Based on this, it is still necessary for applicants to seek evidence preservation.

10.97 It can be observed that both conflicting orders can be explained from different angles. The absence of clear guidance from the courts may therefore lead to similar conflicting orders in legal practice and create uncertainty in the minds of stakeholders before approaching the courts.

Documentary Evidence Disclosure Order

General Rule

10.98 Where applicants, during the post-action proceedings, expect to preserve the documentary evidence, then the applicants can rely on an alternative course available to the applicants pursuant to the documentary evidence disclosure system. The new documentary evidence disclosure system is available pursuant to the Interpretation of CPL 2015 (2020 Amendment), Provisions on Evidence 2019 and Provisions on IP Evidence 2020. In this scenario, the applicants may request the courts to order the respondents to submit the documentary evidence.[93]

10.99 Article 112 of the Interpretation of CPL 2015 (2020 Amendment) provides:

> Where a piece of documentary evidence is under the control of the opposite party, the party bearing the burden of proof may, prior to the expiration of the time limit for producing evidence, apply to the competent people's court

93 During the process of the 2012 amendment to the CPL 1991, the SPC submitted a proposal to set out the order of the documentary evidence disclosure and the search order systems in the CPL 2012, but this proposal was not accepted by the legislator. Thereafter, the SPC issued the Interpretation of CPL 2015 (2020 Amendment) to devise a general rule for the order of the documentary evidence disclosure. Nonetheless, the Interpretation did not provide clear guidance. Until 2019, the detailed rules were provided in Provisions on Evidence 2019, Articles 45–48; see also, the First Civil Division of the Supreme People's Court (ed), *Understanding and Application of New Provisions of the Supreme People's Court on Evidence in Civil Procedures, Volume I* (People's Court Press 2020) 433–435.

> in writing to request the latter to order the opposite party to submit the said evidence.
> Where the reasons for the application are reasonable, the people's court shall order the opposite party to submit the piece of documentary evidence.[94]

10.100 It follows that the courts allow applicants to apply for an order seeking the disclosure of documents in civil proceedings when the evidence holder is the opponent in the civil/commercial action. Such opponent includes the defendant/claimant to the dispute and the third party who enjoys an independent or non-independent claim against both the claimants and the defendants to the dispute but will not include an outside third party to the dispute.[95]

10.101 In Provisions on Evidence 2019, detailed guidance on this rule has been further provided by the SPC.[96] First, similar to the format of applications seeking preservations of evidence, the applicants should submit their applications seeking documentary evidence disclosure orders. The mandatory elements in the format of the applications include the exact name and content of the document to be disclosed, the necessity and importance of the disclosure, the ground that the respondent is holding the documentary evidence and the reasonable ground of the disclosure.[97]

10.102 Secondly, the scope of the document to be disclosed may include (i) the documentary evidence of the respondent's statement; (ii) the produced evidence in support of the applicant; (iii) accounting books, original receipts and so forth; (iv) any documents that the applicant is legally entitled to review or obtain, such as the annual balance sheet, cash flow sheet, shareholders' registration list, shareholders' minutes; and (v) other documents depending on the courts' discretionary power. If the documentary evidence relates to state or company confidential issues, personal privacy or similar situations, the cross-examination will not be carried out in public.[98]

10.103 Thirdly, during this application, it is necessary for the court to hear both the applicants' and the respondents' opinions. Where a request is not specific or is irrelevant or immaterial to the consequence of the case, or where the document to be disclosed is not within the control of the respondents, then the court will likely be minded to refuse the application.[99]

---

94 Interpretation of CPL 2015 (2020 Amendment), Article 112.

95 The First Civil Division of the Supreme People's Court (ed), *Understanding and Application of New Provisions of the Supreme People's Court on Evidence in Civil Procedures, Volume I* (People's Court Press 2020) 435–436.

96 Provisions on Evidence 2019, Articles 45–48.

97 Provisions on Evidence 2019, Article 45; see also, the First Civil Division of the Supreme People's Court (ed), *Understanding and Application of New Provisions of the Supreme People's Court on Evidence in Civil Procedures, Volume I* (People's Court Press 2020) 433–439.

98 Provisions on Evidence 2019, Article 47; see also, the First Civil Division of the Supreme People's Court (ed), *Understanding and Application of New Provisions of the Supreme People's Court on Evidence in Civil Procedures, Volume I* (People's Court Press 2020) 449–457.

99 Provisions on Evidence 2019, Article 46; see also, the First Civil Division of the Supreme People's Court (ed), *Understanding and Application of New Provisions of the Supreme People's*

10.104 Finally, the legal consequences of refusing to disclose the evidence will cause the court to support the applicant's allegation in relation to the fact to be proved by the covered document. To be clear, if the applicant has proved that the respondent is taking control of the documentary evidence and meanwhile alleges that such document demonstrates a specific fact of the case, but the respondent refuses to submit such document in its possession, it will be deemed that the respondent has admitted to the allegation against him.[100]

10.105 It is anticipated that if this new rule can function well, in the future, the conflicting orders in *Guizhou Peninsula Hot Spring Real Estate Co Ltd (Guizhou Peninsula) v Guoji Construction Group Co Ltd (Guoji Group)*[101] and *Yanan Si v Sichuan Luzhou Yuhe Construction Engineering Co Ltd (Luzhou Yuhe) and Others*[102] discussed in 10.91–10.92 will be resolved.

10.106 However, this rule is available only against the defendant and the involved third party in a civil/commercial case but not outside third parties who may be in possession of evidence. Furthermore, because the detailed rules are simply provided in Provisions of Evidence 2019, the function of the disclosure of documentary evidence order leaves more time to examine how this new system may play a role in the evidence preservation domain in the future.

The Extension of the Documentary Disclosure Order in IP Disputes

10.107 As discussed in 10.102, the scope of the disclosure order is merely restricted to documentary evidence. However, taking into consideration the fact that apart from the documentary evidence, a great number of material objects and the place of the infringement in IP disputes should be regarded as important evidence controlled by the infringing party, the SPC contends that it is necessary to extend the application of the disclosure order in order to address the difficulty of the submission of evidence by the aggrieved party.[103] Therefore, Article 24 of the Provisions on IP Evidence 2020 extends the

Court on Evidence in Civil Procedures, Volume I (People's Court Press 2020) 441–447.

100 Provisions on Evidence 2019, Article 48; see also, the First Civil Division of the Supreme People's Court (ed), *Understanding and Application of New Provisions of the Supreme People's Court on Evidence in Civil Procedures, Volume I* (People's Court Press 2020) 458–464.

101 Refer to 10.91; *Guizhou Peninsula Hot Spring Real Estate Co Ltd v Guoji Construction Group Co Ltd* (an application for a pre-action evidence preservation) [2020] Qian 0524 Bao Zheng No 1 (the Primary People's Court of Zhijin County of Guizhou Province, first instance and binding order).

102 Refer to 10.92; *Yanan Si v Sichuan Luzhou Yuhe Construction Engineering Co Ltd (Luzhou Yuhe) and Others* (an application for an evidence preservation) [2019] Chuan 05 Civil Chu No 49 (the Intermediate People's Court of Luzhou City of Sichuan Province, first instance and binding order).

103 Guanghai Lin, Jian Li and Rong Wu, 'Understanding and Application of *Several Provisions of the Supreme People's Court on Evidence in Civil Procedures Involving Intellectual Property Rights*' (2021) 4 The People's Judicature (Applied) 24.

scope of the disclosure order from documentary evidence to all evidence. It is provided that

> Where the party who undertakes the burden of proof files a written application for seeking the evidence controlled by the counterpart, if the ground were reasonable, the people's court shall render an order to request the counterpart to submit the evidence.[104]

10.108 Following Article 24, in order to ensure the implementation of the disclosure order, Article 25 of Provisions on IP Evidence 2020 further stipulates as follows:

> When a people's court requires a party to submit relevant evidence in accordance with the law, and such party refuses to do so without justifiable reasons, submits false evidence, destroys the evidence, or commits any other acts that causes the evidence unusable, the people's court may presume that the other party's claim about the facts involving the evidence is established.
>
> If the party's behaviour stated above constitutes the circumstance provided in Article 111 of the Civil Procedure Law, such person will be prosecuted accordingly, as prescribed by law.[105]

10.109 It is observed that as compared with the Interpretation of CPL 2015 (2020 Amendment) and Provisions on IP Evidence 2020, to address the difficulty of the submission of evidence, the new judicial interpretation makes great progress by way of the extension of the application of the disclosure order. It is anticipated that this extension may be applied in all types of disputes. Nonetheless, whether outside parties to the dispute are entitled to file an application is still in question.

Collection of Evidence by Courts

10.110 Apart from the above alternative legal remedy wherein the applicant is entitled to file an application to disclose the documentary evidence, there is another route available to the applicant. In this route, the applicants could request the courts to investigate and to collate evidence (hereinafter referred to "collecting of evidence"). However, this remedy is operative in limited circumstances only provided it can be shown to the courts by objective reasoning that the applicants are unable to collect the relevant evidence. It is clear that the courts must be satisfied that there are objective reasons for the applicants' inability to collect evidence and not subjective reasons, which the applicants subjectively consider as applicable to the circumstances surrounding the applications.

10.111 Collecting of evidence can be carried out by the Chinese courts in two instances. In the first instance, the courts can determine to collect

104 Provisions on IP Evidence 2020, Article 24.
105 ibid Article 25.

evidence on its own initiative. In the second instance, in light of the application of the party concerned, the courts can determine to assist the party to collect the evidence. Both instances, where the courts will get involved will not assist the parties seeking the pre-action preservation or evidence remedy.

Courts' Power to Collect Evidence on Its Own Initiative

10.112 Like the property and behaviour preservation measures,[106] the Chinese courts may take evidence preservation measures on its own initiative without a need for applications from the applicants during civil action proceedings.[107] The SPC has provided guidance on the principles of collecting evidence in the context of the Chinese courts' legal duty to collect evidence.

10.113 The legal circumstances under which the court on its own initiative will decide to collect evidence are limited. Under the existing law, there are only five circumstances in which the court will decide to collect evidence and they are as follows:

(a) Evidence that points to possible damage to national interests or public interests.
(b) Evidence that involves personal status relationship.
(c) Evidence that involves litigations prescribed by Article 55 of the Civil Procedure Law.
(d) Evidence that points to the possibility that the parties concerned may have maliciously colluded with each other to prejudice the legitimate rights and interests of others.
(e) Evidence that involves procedural matters, such as adding parties concerned ex officio, suspending litigation proceedings, terminating litigation proceedings and recusal.[108]

Maritime Courts' Power to Collect Evidence

10.114 There is no equivalent duty on the Chinese maritime courts for collecting evidence as there is no similar provision available in the SMPL 2000. A legal scholar has therefore commented that in the area of maritime law, maritime evidence may only be collated by the court after the application has been submitted to the maritime court.[109]

10.115 Nevertheless, in accordance with Article 97 of the Interpretation of SMPL 2008, if there are no provisions under the SMPL 2000 concerning any

---

106 Refer to Chapter 6, 6.17, and Chapter 8, 8.70.

107 CPL 1991 (as amended until 2020), Article 81.

108 Interpretation of CPL 2015 (2020 Amendment), Article 96.

109 Liang Zhao and Lianjun Li, *Maritime Law and Practice in China* (1st Edn, Informa Law from Routledge 2017) para. 22.4.

legal issues before the maritime courts, then, those unsolved issues will be governed by the relevant provisions of the CPL 1991.[110] In this regard, in the light of Article 64 of the CPL 1991 (as amended until 2020), it can be argued that the maritime courts are also under an obligation to collect the evidence prescribed by law.[111] However, this is only available when the full maritime case is part of the Chinese civil process, and accordingly the Chinese maritime courts will not assist international stakeholders, where the dispute has no connection with the Chinese courts, in collecting evidence on its own initiative.

Collecting of Evidence on Parties' Applications

10.116 Item 2 of Article 94 of Interpretation of CPL 2015 (2020 Amendment) provides:

> The party concerned and the agent *ad litem* thereof may, prior to the expiration of the time limit for producing evidence, apply to the competent people's court in writing to request the latter to investigate and collect the evidence that they are unable to collect on their own due to objective reasons.[112]

10.117 It follows that the party concerned is entitled to request the assistance of the court to obtain certain evidence that cannot be collected due to objective reasons.

10.118 This mode is quite different from a scenario where courts decide to collect evidence on their own initiative. The procedure to seek courts' assistance to collate the evidence is through a written letter of application. The format of the letter of application is similar to that of a letter of application seeking the preservation of evidence.[113] However, in this letter of application, the applicants must explain to the judge their inability to obtain evidence through objective factors surrounding the circumstances of the dispute.

10.119 The legal circumstances for collecting evidence on parties' applications are limited as provided in Article 94 of the Interpretation of CPL 2015 (2020 Amendment). This is not very different from the legal circumstances

110 The Supreme People's Court Interpretations on the Application of the Special Maritime Procedure Law of the People's Republic of China (2008 Adjustment) (Fa Shi [2003] No 3), Article 97.

111 Article 64 of the CPL 1991 (as amended until 2020) provides that "where the people's court deems that the evidence is necessary for the trial of the case, the people's court shall investigate and collect the evidence". In addition, Article 15 of the Provisions on Evidence 2019 clarifies that "the evidence is necessary for the trial of the case' refers to – a) the facts of a case that may damage the national interest, the public interest or the lawful interest of other people; b) the procedural matters that have nothing to do with the substantial dispute such as adding parties concerned, suspending the litigation, ending the litigation, withdrawing from the litigation, etc. on the basis of authority of the courts".

112 Interpretation of CPL 2015 (2020 Amendment), Article 94(2); see also, CPL 1991 (as amended until 2020), Article 64.

113 Refer to 10.18.

in which a court could collate the evidence on its own initiative.[114] Item 1 of Article 94 of the Interpretation of CPL 2015 (2020 Amendment) provides:

(a) Evidence kept by relevant State departments which the party concerned and the agent *ad litem* thereof are not entitled to access and retrieve;
(b) Evidence involving State secrets, trade secrets or personal privacy; and
(c) Other evidence that the party concerned and the agent ad litem thereof are unable to collect on their own due to objective reasons.[115]

10.120 The third circumstance above is a catch-all clause depending on the court's discretionary power.

Security for Evidence Preservation Applications

10.121 Furnishing security is not a mandatory requirement for obtaining pre-action evidence preservation orders except under certain circumstances.[116] This is quite different from the requirement for obtaining pre-action property and behaviour preservation measures, where security has to be furnished mandatorily by the applicants. However, according to the categories of disputes, the rules of providing security are somewhat different. In IP and maritime disputes, the existing law stresses the courts' discretionary power, while in other disputes there is no similar provision.

Rule of Security for IP and Maritime Pre-Action Applications

10.122 In intellectual property and maritime disputes, the law empowers Chinese judges to determine whether or not applicants seeking pre-action evidence preservation measures should furnish security. If the applicants were not to furnish security after the judges have requested it, then in those instances the applications will be dismissed.[117]

10.123 In relation to the requirement of security that need to be furnished by the applicants, on the one hand, the expression in the IP laws and the SMPL 2000 just states that "the court *may* request security [emphasis added]" for an evidence preservation measure.[118] The wordings clearly specify that the requirement to furnish security is optional rather than mandatory.

114 Refer to 10.113.

115 Interpretation of CPL 2015 (2020 Amendment), Article 94.

116 The First Civil Division of the Supreme People's Court (ed), *Understanding and Application of New Provisions of the Supreme People's Court on Evidence in Civil Procedures, Volume I* (People's Court Press 2020) 279.

117 SMPL 2000, Article 66; see also, Patent Law 1985 (2020 Amendment), Article 73; see also, Copyright Law 1991 (2020 Amendment), Article 57; see also, Chapter 3, 3.134–3.135.

118 ibid.

10.124 On the other hand, the provision expressly stipulates the furnishing of security when seeking property and behaviour preservation measures through application. For the sake of completeness, the provision pertaining to applications seeking property and behaviour preservation measures provide that "the applicant *must* provide security [emphasis added]".[119]

10.125 Accordingly, furnishing security with applications seeking pre-action preservation of evidence for IP and maritime disputes can be considered as exceptional. This exception will be operative according to the courts' exercise of their discretionary power.

Exception for Furnishing Security for Pre-Action and Post-Action Applications

10.126 Unlike the IP and maritime disputes, there is no provision granting discretionary power to the Chinese courts in other disputes to determine whether the applicant should provide security in applications seeking the preservation of evidence. However, pursuant to the express provisions, there are two circumstances in which the courts can require applicants to furnish security as a prerequisite for seeking evidence preservation measures.

10.127 The first circumstance in which applicants can be required to furnish security is when the applicants request the courts to take certain preservation measures on the evidence, such as sealing up, detaining and so forth, or to restrict the use and circulation of the subject matter of the evidence preservation measures.[120]

10.128 For example, when an application seeking evidence preservation measures also involves a request to seal up and detain a house or other property, such requested measure may result in damage to the preserved evidence. The courts may therefore request the applicants to furnish security before an order can be granted.[121] In legal practice, it is the authors' view that the courts are very likely to instruct the applicant to furnish security in such cases.

10.129 The second circumstance in which the applicants can be required to furnish security is when the evidence preservation measures are likely to result in loss to the parties who are in control of the subject matter of preservation measures.[122] In legal practice, the judges will generally exercise their discretionary power to evaluate the underlying consequence and then make a decision.

119 CPL 1991 (as amended until 2020), Article 101(1); see also, Chapter 3, 3.131; Chapter 6, 6.82–6.85 and Chapter 8, 8.138–8.140.

120 Provisions on Evidence 2019, Article 26.

121 The First Civil Division of the Supreme People's Court (ed), *Understanding and Application of New Provisions of the Supreme People's Court on Evidence in Civil Procedures, Volume I* (People's Court Press 2020) 280.

122 Interpretation of CPL 2015 (2020 Amendment), Article 98; see also, Provisions on Evidence 2019, Article 26.

10.130 The above two circumstances, in which courts may instruct the applicants to furnish security, are also applicable to post-action applications seeking evidence preservation measures. Furthermore, regardless of the pre-action or post-action preservation measure, as long as the applicants do not furnish security pursuant to the Chinese courts' requirement, the courts are likely to dismiss the applications.[123]

Amount of Security

10.131 Evidence that needs to be preserved can be of different categories.[124] For some types of evidence, the market price cannot be calculated, for example electronic data. Alternatively, even if the market price of the evidence can be calculated, the value of security that needs to be furnished may not simply be decided by the value of the preserved evidence. This is quite different from the issue regarding calculation of the value of security that needs to be provided for applications seeking property preservation measures.[125] This difference exists due to the fact that the character of the property preservation measures is different from that of the evidence preservation measures.

10.132 In this context, Provisions on Evidence 2019 merely provides general guidance as follows:

> The amount of security is comprehensively determined by the court in the light of factors such as the impact of the preservation measures on the evidence holder, the value of the preserved evidence, and the disputed amount of the case.[126]

10.133 Since Provisions on Evidence 2019 has recently been issued in China, its application on the issue of the amount of security that needs to be furnished is still unclear. This area of law may develop in the next two to three years.

10.134 The other guidance in the context of furnishing security, including the types of security, is similar and has been discussed in Chapter 3, 3.130–3.194.

Time Limit of Rendering Post-Action Orders

10.135 Similar to the time limit for rendering a post-action behaviour order discussed in Chapter 8, 8.158, there is no exact time limit during which the courts have to render the evidence preservation orders provided by law from the time when the application seeking evidence preservation measures

123 The First Civil Division of the Supreme People's Court (ed), *Understanding and Application of New Provisions of the Supreme People's Court on Evidence in Civil Procedures, Volume I* (People's Court Press 2020) 283.

124 Refer to 10.22.

125 Refer to Chapter 6, 6.47–6.50.

126 Provisions on Evidence 2019, Article 26.

has been submitted. In theory and practice, the order must be rendered and enforced before the completion of the "cross-examination" of the parties, because the evidence to be preserved needs to be used during the "cross-examination" proceedings.[127] Although the legislation and judicial interpretations do not specify the exact time limit, a local guidance, titled Provisions on Shanghai Property Preservation 2017, expressly stipulates that by reference to the time limit for rendering a post-action property preservation order, the courts should render preservation of behaviour orders within five days; if security is requested by the courts, then the orders can only be rendered after the security has been furnished by the applicants.[128] It is advisable that the parties concerned do some investigations on the local court's guidance before or after submitting post-action applications.

Time Limit of Evidence Preservation Orders

10.136 In property preservation orders as discussed in Chapter 6, 6.151–6.155, the standard time limits of orders vary according to the categories of the preserved property. However, there is no time limit applicable to evidence preservation orders. In legal practice, the courts will ensure the time limit in light of the principle of the minimum impact on the respondents' interests.[129] This means that the court may decide the time limit of the evidence preservation order depending on the specific evidence to be preserved. Nonetheless, it is generally acknowledged that the courts' orders are likely to follow the process of the "cross-examination" of the concerned parties; after the completion of the "cross-examination", the time limit lapses.[130]

Discharge of Evidence Preservation Orders

10.137 The general rules concerning the discharge of the preservation orders have been discussed in Chapter 3, 3.287–3.291. Additionally, there

127 The "cross-examination" proceedings in China refer to the "质证 (Zhi Zheng)" procedure in which, under the auspices of the judges, litigants to a case testify to the authenticity, relevance and legitimacy of the evidential materials submitted to the court by way of hearing, reviewing, verifying, identifying and other methods. If there is no objection to the evidence, such evidence will be recognised directly by the litigants; if there is an objection to the evidence, the litigants should raise questions and inquire in person in the court; see also, the First Civil Division of the Supreme People's Court (ed), *Understanding and Application of New Provisions of the Supreme People's Court on Evidence in Civil Procedures, Volume 1* (People's Court Press 2020) 346.

128 *Provisions of the Shanghai High People's Court on Property Preservation (2017 Amendment)* (Hu Gao Fa (Shen) [2014] No 3), Articles 22 and 119.

129 Provisions on Evidence 2019, Article 27.

130 The First Civil Division of the Supreme People's Court (ed), *Understanding and Application of New Provisions of the Supreme People's Court on Evidence in Civil Procedures, Volume 1* (People's Court Press 2020) 292.

are two further ways in which the evidence preservation orders can be discharged. If the evidence preservation measures were to involve creating a record, taking a video, surveying or copying the evidence, then after the completion of the "cross-examination", the preservation of evidence order will be discharged automatically without the party's application and without requiring any formalities.[131]

10.138 If the preservation measures were to involve sealing up, detainment, authenticating and so forth, or the measure of the evidence preservation needs a third party's assistance, then the court will render a discharge order immediately after the completion of the "cross-examination" of the parties and along with sending the relevant notices to the related parties.[132]

Compensation Caused by Wrongful Evidence Preservation

10.139 Article 28 of Provisions on Evidence 2019 provides:

> Where an application for an evidence preservation is wrongfully filed leading to the property damages, the party concerned requests the applicant to compensate the damages, the court should support it.[133]

10.140 Based on this, there are several issues that need to be analysed in the forthcoming paragraphs.

Liability Principle

10.141 A claim for damages caused by a wrongful application seeking evidence preservation measures is subject to fault-based liability. This is similar to the liability principle in case of wrongful property preservation.[134] The identification of fault-based liability is not just based on whether or not the application was accepted by the court, but also on whether the applicant's improper conduct in relation to applications was intentional or grossly negligent.

Principle of Common Evidence

10.142 According to the principle of common evidence during civil/commercial proceedings in China,[135] the evidence that has been preserved can be

131 ibid.

132 ibid.

133 Provisions on Evidence 2019, Article 28.

134 Refer to Chapter 6, 6.157–6.173.

135 The principle of common evidence in civil litigation means that the results of the investigation by way of sealing up or detaining evidence can be used to prove the facts of the case claimed by both parties. In other words, the evidence sealed up or seized by the court can not only be used to support the applicant's claim, but also can be used to support the respondent's

utilised by the applicant, as well by other litigants, including the respondent and the third party joining the trial. In any event, it is therefore likely that the ultimate winner of the civil trial would have benefited from the preserved evidence. Following this principle, as long as the applicant has exercised a duty of care in relation to the preserved evidence, even if the holder of evidence has suffered damages as a result of the preservation measures, the applicant will not be held liable for such loss.

Causative Link and Burden of Proof

10.143 It is a requirement that there be a causative link between the applicant's conduct leading to the preservation evidence order and the respondent's property loss.[136]

10.144 In most scenarios, the legal consequences arising out of evidence preservation measures are not likely to cause property loss. On the one hand, the subject matter of the evidence preservation does not always involve property or things that may closely relate to the value; while on the other hand, during the enforcement of evidence preservation measures, the Chinese courts should abide by the principle that there needs to be minimum impact on the evidence holder's interests as a result of such measures. Based on this, the evidence that is preserved would be released from any measures immediately after the "cross-examination" of the parties.

10.145 Against the above analysis, whether a respondent has suffered any loss due to the evidence preservation measures must be proved by the respondent. For example, an applicant may requests the court to preserve and authenticate valuable items. According to this application, the court approves of authenticating the value of the items. Thereafter, the respondent claims the devaluation of the items as a result of the court's order. In this context, the respondent has the burden of proof to prove his losses.

Actual Property Damages

10.146 The damages principle that the compensation arising from tortious conduct should be paid in full is undisputed.[137] However, the SPC has emphasised the principle of fairness and also advised to comply with the indemnity principle. In the light of these guidelines, the SPC has affirmed that the scope

argument; see also, Shangang Zhan, 'Question on Evidence Preservation with Reference to Preservation Procedure: Examination of Article 81 of CPL' (2015) 6 Journal in Law and Business 121, 128.

136 The First Civil Division of the Supreme People's Court (ed), 'Understanding and Application of New Provisions of the Supreme People's Court on Evidence in Civil Procedures' (People's Court Press 2020) 297.

137 Junju Ma and Tingman Yu, *Principles of Civil Law* (Law Press of China 2016) 1027.

of compensation is merely restricted on actual property damages, and will not include indirect damages, the expectation interests of the evidence holder and so forth.[138]

10.147 The actual damages arising from the implementation of the evidence preservation measures are dependent on various factors, such as the impact of the preservation measures on the business operations, the period for which evidence preservation measures are in operation, the impact on the function of evidence in the future and so forth.[139]

10.148 However, in the Opinion on Zhejiang IP Evidence Preservation 2014, the High People's Court of Zhejiang Province contends that the scope of damages should include both the direct and indirect loss.[140] For example, if the evidence is just the subject matter of a contract between the evidence holder and the buyer, the evidence preservation measures may lead to the evidence holder's failure to deliver the goods pursuant to the sale contract. The applicant will be liable for any damages arising out of breach of contract that the evidence holder will have to undertake under that contract.

10.149 After Provisions on Evidence 2019 has come into effect, it is likely the regional guidance from the local courts will be revised in the near future. However, in the authors' experience in China, a few Chinese judges may still consider indirect losses in such cases unless the SPC's judicial interpretation or guidance provides the express compensation principle in the evidence preservation measures.

Evidence Preservation Fees

10.150 The application fees regime applicable to preservation applications is set out in *Measures on Payment of Litigation Costs 2006*. However, there is no explicit provision that provides for fees applicable to evidence preservation measures.

10.151 By reference to Article 14 of the Measures, if the evidence to be preserved is not relevant to the category of property, RMB 30 shall be paid for each application.[141] If the evidence that needs to be preserved belongs to the category of property and meanwhile the value of property can be calculated, then the fee applicable for an evidence preservation application would be the same as that for applications seeking property preservation measures as discussed in Chapter 6, 6.174.

---

138 The First Civil Division of the Supreme People's Court (ed), *Understanding and Application of New Provisions of the Supreme People's Court on Evidence in Civil Procedures, Volume I* (People's Court Press 2020) 298.

139 ibid.

140 Opinion on Zhejiang IP Evidence Preservation 2014, Article 33.

141 *Measures on Payment of Litigation Costs 2006*, Article 14.

10.152 Other rules regarding the fee applicable to property preservation applications can be found in Chapter 3, 3.195–3.221.

Annex 1

Format of Application Seeking Evidence Preservation Measures[142]

(for Legal Entity or Organisation)

Applicant: the full name of the company, organisation or other legal entities; a Unified Social Credit Code or the registration code.

Legal representative/principal: name, address, contact telephone number (optional), Identification Card Number (optional).

Authorised legal agent: XXXXX Law Firm, the lawyer's name, gender, Identification Card Number, contract number, lawyer's licence's number, the lawyer's address.

Respondent: the full name of company, organisation or other legal entities; a Unified Social Credit Code or the registration code.

Legal representative/principal: name, address, contact telephone number (optional), Identification Card Number (optional).

Authorised legal agent: XXXXX Law Firm, the lawyer's name, gender, Identification Card Number, contract number, lawyer's licence's number, the lawyer's address.

Items to be claimed/requested:
It is hereby requested that XXXXX people's court takes measures to preserve the evidence (specify the exact evidence to be preserved and the preservation measures).

Facts and grounds:
Due to XXXXX dispute between the applicant and the respondent, the applicant will bring the case to the court/XXXXX arbitration institution against the respondent or this case has been accepted by the court/XXXXX arbitration institution on XXXXX (the exact date and exact case no.). The evidence to be preserved will play a crucial role in witnessing the fact of the case and is likely to be destroyed or lost anytime in the future. Under this circumstance, this evidence may be lost, or it will be difficult to collect such evidence in the future; in accordance with Article 81 of the CPL 1991 (as amended until

142 The author has drafted the current sample by reference to a sample provided by the Supreme People's Court at <http://www.court.gov.cn/susongyangshi-xiangqing-98.html> accessed 30 July 2021.

2020), the applicant hereby applies for the evidence preservation measures (specify the exact measure and the location of the evidence or the holder of the evidence).

The applicant will provide XXXXX property as the security (specify the name, nature, quantity, amount, location, etc., of the secured property).

Regards

XXXX People's Court

Applicant (stamp and/or legal representative signature)
Date

Note for applications seeking evidence preservation measures:

1) This format can be used for applications seeking arbitral evidence preservation measures.
2) If either the applicant or the respondent is an individual, the information of the individual should include the full name, gender, date of birth, ethnicity, employer and occupation, address, contact information. Other contents of the application form can refer to those of this sample.
3) Apart from the lawyer, the authorised legal agent may be an employee working for the applicant, such as the in-house counsel, the principal.
4) In different official samples, the facts and grounds are very simple. In accordance with the specific issue of a dispute, the applicant should provide more relevant facts and reasons to demonstrate that without the grant of preservation measures, the evidence will be destroyed or lost which will directly impact on the investigation of the facts that are relevant to the case and so forth. All in all, in light of the purpose and the requirements of evidence preservation discussed in Chapter 10, the applicant should provide more exact facts and grounds to enhance the possibility of obtaining a satisfactory order.
5) Security is not mandatory for either pre-action applications or for post-action applications except for the special circumstances. Refer to Chapter 10, 10.121–10.130. The applicant should decide whether it is necessary to provide security for a post-action application. In legal practice, in order to assuage the court's concern, the applicant can voluntarily to add the sentence "if an incorrect preservation application causes the respondent's unexpected loss, the applicant is willing to take responsibility for it".

6) In terms of the application for a documentary evidence disclosure order, it may refer to this form. However, the applicable law in the Facts and Grounds should point out Article 112 of the Interpretation of CPL 2015 (2020 Amendment). In addition, the applicant should explain that why he claims that the respondent is controlling the evidence. The scope of the documentary evidence should comply with Article 47 of Provisions on Evidence 2019.

Annex 2: Application for Reconsideration, Refer to Annex 1, Chapter 3

Annex 3: Application for Discharging the Preservation Order, Refer to Annex 2, Chapter 3

PART 6

COMPARATIVE ANALYSIS OF INTERIM MEASURES IN THE TWO JURISDICTIONS

CHAPTER 11

Comparative Analysis of Interim Measures on Visible and Invisible Factors

England & Wales v China

Overview of the Chapter

Summary

11.1 In the previous chapters, the authors have separately discussed three interim remedies/preservation measures in England & Wales and China from Chapters 5–10. Accordingly, in this chapter, the authors have compiled six comparative tables for pre-action and post-action stage applications seeking three key interim remedies and preservation measures in the English and Chinese jurisdictions respectively. These six tables will enable readers to compare these procedural interim remedies/preservation measures in both jurisdictions. It is hoped that these tables will shed light on the similarities and differences between the interim measures in both jurisdictions.

11.2 In this chapter, the comparison of the interim measures in these jurisdictions is carried out at two levels. At the first level, the authors have selected a few well-researched parameters in the comparative tables and carried out the juxtaposition of the interim remedies with the preservation orders on these selected parameters. In this chapter, the authors will uniformly employ the term "order", as this term is commonplace in common law while there is no such term in the Chinese civil procedure system.[1] These parameters from the external law in form of the Civil Procedure Law of China ("CPL 1991 (as amended until 2020)"), the Civil Procedure Law of England & Wales ("CPR 1998", and amendments until 2020 are taken into account), caselaw, local courts' guidance documents, in particular, in China and so forth are clearly *visible* to readers from their analysis in Chapters 5–10. Therefore, the comparative analysis of the interim measures on these *visible factors* in both jurisdictions will give a fairly reasonable idea of similarities and differences.[2]

1 The First Civil Division of the Supreme People's Court (ed), *Understanding and Application of New Provisions of the Supreme People's Court on Evidence in Civil Procedures, Volume I* (People's Court Press 2020) 446.

2 Pursuant to Eberle's Comparative Law Methodology, in which he referred to external law as the comparison of laws in the form of legislations, codes, practice directions, cases, circulars, provisions, interpretations and so forth. The authors have referred to the same concept of external law in the context of the comparative analysis of interim measures as *visible factors*;

DOI: 10.4324/9781003000310-18

However, unquestionably, the interim measures are procedural remedies in both jurisdictions, and therefore, the exercise of the discretionary power of judges in granting these pre-judgment remedies is an essential feature in both jurisdictions. In this chapter, the issue of the discretionary power of judges will also be examined a bit later.[3]

11.3 In both English law and Chinese law, the need for judges to exercise their discretionary power in granting such remedies invariably will involve the impact of lots of "*invisible factors and contexts*",[4] which are germane to a particular jurisdiction. The application of these invisible factors and contexts and their impact on the possibility of successfully seeking interim measures from the courts can alter the analysis of lawyers in cross-border litigation and arbitration. This analysis can even force the managers and in-house lawyers of organisations to rethink options and tactics. The knowledge of these issues will also assist expert lawyers within these specific jurisdictions to ensure the

---

see also, Edward J Eberle, 'The Method and Role of Comparative Law' (2009) 8 (3) Wash U Global Stud L Rev 451, 451–486 to fully comprehend the comparative methodologies that are relevant to comparative law; see also, Bernhard Grossfeld and Edward J Eberle, 'Patterns of Order in Comparative Law: Discovering and Decoding Invisible Powers' (2003) 38 (2) Tex Int'l LJ 291, 291–316. Discussion in detail on relevant theories and methodologies of comparative law in the context of the comparison of interim remedies in England & Wales with preservation measures in China is beyond the scope of the book. It is recommended that readers refer to specialist text books on comparative law studies to fully discern the theories relevant to the study of comparative law. In this chapter, the authors have simply applied such well-established methodologies for comparing the interim measures in the jurisdictions of England & Wales and China.

3 Refer to 11.60–11.62, 11.65, 11.78–11.82, 11.96, 11.108–11.114.

4 A few of the invisible factors that can impact on the *law in action and practice* are custom, evolution of law and procedural law, history, religion, ethics, geography, language, philosophy, interpretation or translation, concept of discretionary power, concept of standard of proof, evolution of law and jurisprudence and so forth. For discussion on the comparative methodologies, in particular the methodologies that are relevant to the issue of impact of these invisible factors and contexts on various issues in law, see Edward J Eberle, 'The Method and Role of Comparative Law' (2009) 8 (3) Wash U Global Stud L Rev 451, 462–463, and issue of translations in comparing laws in 463, fn 26; see also, John C Reitz, 'How to Do Comparative Law' (1998) 46(4) Am J Comp L, 620, 620—621 <www.jstor.org/stable/840981> accessed 15 November 2016; see also, V V Palmer, 'From Lerotholi to Lando: Some Examples of Comparative Law Methodology' (2004) 4(2) Global Jurist Frontiers 1, 1–29 <53.261-290. 10.1093/ajcl/53.1.261> accessed 15 November 2019, where he highlighted that that there was no single method of carrying out comparisons of laws from different jurisdictions and in particular advised specific approaches that need to be considered in the legal practice due to costs that may be involved in pursuing such comparative analysis; see also, Janet E Ainsworth, 'Categories and Culture: On the "Rectification of Names" in Comparative Law' (1996) 82 (1) CLR 19, 19–42 <http://scholarship.law.cornell.edu/clr/vol82/iss1/3> accessed 20 November 2019; see also, the issue of invisible factors and contexts in relation to procedural laws as opposed to substantive laws, James R Maxeiner, 'Legal Methods as a Point of Reference for Comparative Studies of Procedural Law' (XIIIth World Congress on Procedural Law, Salvador Bahia, 16–22 September 2007) 2–3 <https://ssrn.com/abstract=1232579> accessed 18 November 2019; see also, Vivek Jain, *Insight into China through Comparative Analysis of Invisible Factors and Contexts – Common Law v. Chinese Law* (1st Edn, Notion Press 2019) for very detailed analysis of various invisible factors and contexts affecting the law in practice or law in action in England & Wales and China.

objectives of clients are attained effectively. These invisible factors and contexts could also be considered as the reasons for similarities and differences as observed in the comparative analysis using the six tables on visible facts for each of the three key interim measures.

Major Conclusions after Comparative Analysis

11.4 The purposes of the interim remedies as well of the preservation measures are nearly same in both jurisdictions albeit with minor differences.[5] However, after observing and analysing the comparative tables for juxtaposing these interim measures individually, the authors have reached the following conclusions:[6]

- In general, the English jurisdiction is applicant-/claimant-friendly in the context of seeking interim measures.
- In general, the Chinese jurisdiction is respondent-/defendant-friendly in the context of seeking interim measures.

Comparative Analysis of Interim Measures on Visible Factors

Visible Factors

11.5 In the first step, the authors will just focus on comparison of the interim measures in both jurisdictions based on legislation and adjective law including procedural laws in both jurisdictions, including practice directions, purposes, relevant procedural principles, tests governing applications seeking these pre-judgment remedies and associated issues concerning these applications.

Warning on Comparative Analysis Pursued on Visible Factors

11.6 While the authors have tried in this chapter to compare the interim remedies in England & Wales with preservation measures in China, it is important to appreciate that though they seem to be similar remedies, the comparison between the two is not that simplistic. It will be prudent for readers to bear in mind that these jurisdictions do not use the same terminologies or even sub-text behind those terminologies, and in fact terminologies differ from one jurisdiction to another jurisdiction. This is the only way to appreciate fully the similarities and dissimilarities between the interim measures

---

5 Refer to Chapter 1, 1.14–1.22.

6 Vivek Jain, 'Sufficiency of Court's Pre-Judgment Power in Commercial Litigation: A Comparative Study Assessing the Law and Practice in PRC and England & Wales' (PhD Thesis, China University of Political Science and Law 2017) 401–485.

in the two jurisdictions.[7] This warning is important for readers before they plunge deeper into the comparative analysis of interim measures in both jurisdictions.

Comparative Analysis of Working Methods of Courts for Seeking Interim Measures

11.7 Before discussing the key similarities and differences between interim remedies and preservation measures, it is important to discuss initially the subtle working methods of the courts in the context of interim measures in both jurisdictions. The working methods in the context of the procedural remedies will be determined by the relevant adjective law comprising procedural law and administrative practices of courts relevant to law in action. These working methods must be appreciated by the stakeholders when they plan tactics to seek these procedural remedies from courts in either of the two jurisdictions. These working methods are discussed in the forthcoming paragraphs, and a comparative analysis is pursued in Table 11.1.

11.8 In England & Wales, interim injunctions can be obtained *quia timet*, just based on the fear that some wrong may be done to the applicant, and damages cannot be an adequate remedy.[8] In China, still certain circumstances must exist to qualify as the breach of some substantive law before the courts are minded to grant preservation measures.[9]

7 See Janet E Ainsworth, 'Categories and Culture: On the "Rectification of Names" in Comparative Law' (1996) 82 (1) CLR 19, 20 <http://scholarship.law.cornell.edu/clr/vol82/iss1/3> accessed 20 November 2019, for examination of issues that are relevant in relation to the sub-contexts behind the visible factors. In this article, Ainsworth explained the issue of sub-context by an example, where the development of promissory estoppel was linked to the development of concepts in contract law. This development was itself linked to the common law concept of consideration in the field of contract law. In other jurisdictions, similar development of concept of promissory estoppel along with the other evolution of concepts in contract law cannot be assumed. Therefore, the sub-context behind the laws is crucial to understand the issues in greater depth. Ainsworth has also suggested that terminologies from one jurisdiction cannot be assumed for understanding similar concepts in another jurisdiction because terminology may differ in another jurisdiction. Such assumptions can lead the stakeholders to the wrong course; see also, Vivek Jain, *Insight into China through Comparative Analysis of Invisible Factors and Contexts – Common Law v. Chinese Law* (1st Edn, Notion Press 2019), where Jain was of the view that in the rapidly changing society of China in the last 30 years, knowing sub-contexts behind codes and laws fully is difficult for any researcher/practitioner, even for researchers/practitioners that have lived in China for all their lives.

8 Refer to Chapter 7, 7.16.

9 For example, refer, in order to seek property preservation measures, to Chapter 6, 6.79–6.81, for the requirements of "urgent" circumstances and "irreparable harms"; refer also, in order to seek behaviour preservation measures – (Chapter 8, 8.104–8.114) for the requirement of "urgent" circumstances, (Chapter 8, 8.115–8.120), for requirement of "irreparable harms" (Chapter 8, 8.121–8.126), for requirement of "stabilization right" and (Chapter 8, 8.127–8.134) for requirement of "balance of interests" and protection of public interests in only intellectual property disputes; refer also, in order to seek preservation of evidence measures – (Chapter 10,

TABLE 11.1 Comparative analysis – general procedural rules for interim applications

	English law	*Chinese law*
Formal requirements	1) Generally, a written application notice must be issued in the prescribed form, supported by written evidence (either in the application notice or a separate witness statement), verified by a signed statement of truth, accompanied by a draft order and served on the respondent. 2) Freezing injunctions and search orders require written evidence in an affidavit, verified by a sworn oath or an affirmation. 3) All documents must be in English. 4) In exceptionally urgent cases, the application may be made orally on unsigned/unsworn drafts or even without documents. 5) In cases of urgency or where secrecy is needed, the application may be made without notice to the respondent. (See Chapters 2, 5, 7 and 9.)	1) As a general rule, a written application is required; see Chapter 3, 3.117–3.119. 2) In exceptional circumstances, for example in maritime disputes, applications can be made in first instances via fax, e-mails; see Chapter 3, 3.120. 3) Requirement of Mandarin except in the CICC; see Chapter 3, 3.121–3.124. 4) Requirements of notarisation and legalization; see Chapter 3, 3.125–3.126. 5) Flexible requirements as to notarisation and legalisation in IP disputes; see Chapter 3, 3.127–3.129.

(Continued)

TABLE 11.1 *(Continued)*

	English law	*Chinese law*
Time period to render interim orders	1) No formal time limits apply. 2) Ordinarily applications will either be determined on paper or listed for oral hearing at the first available date the court can offer following service of evidence (see CPR PD 58 §13). 3) In cases of urgency, the application may be dealt with immediately, or as soon as a judge can be made able to consider it. 4) Where there is an oral hearing, the court will render its decision at the end of the hearing, which will be immediately effective. (See Chapters 2, 5, 7 and 9.)	1) Interim orders rendered within 48 hours after the courts have received the pre-action applications; see Chapter 3, 3.222. 2) If the applications are urgent, even in post-action applications, the courts will render orders within 48 hours after the courts have received the post-action applications; see Chapter 3, 3.222. 3) If the applications are not urgent during the post-action stage, the courts will render preservation of property orders within five days; if security is requested by the courts, then the orders can only be rendered after the security has been furnished by the applicants; see Chapter 6, 6.125. 4) If the applications are not urgent, then there are no mandatory time limits applicable to the courts in which they have to render post-action behaviour orders; only certain courts provide for a period of five days; see Chapter 8, 8.158. 5) If the applications are not urgent, then there are no mandatory time limits applicable to the courts during which they have to render post-action evidence orders; but the orders must be rendered before the completion of a process similar to "cross-examination"; see Chapter 10, 10.135.

		6) In maritime disputes, the courts are obliged to render orders within 48 hours after they have received pre-action or post-action applications; see Chapter 3, 3.224. 7) In the online preservation system, the period is not very clear. It might be by reference to offline applications; see Chapter 3, 3.225.
Procedural remedies against an interim order	1) Where an application is granted without notice, the respondent may apply to vary or set the order aside at any time, or as provided in the order. 2) Where an application is granted on notice, the respondent must seek permission to appeal to the Court of Appeal. 3) A third party affected by the order may apply to vary or set the order aside at any time. (See Chapters 2, 5, 7 and 9.)	1) An application for reconsideration to be dealt with within five days of receiving the order; see Chapter 3, 3.232–3.246. 2) An application for objection to the enforcement of a preservation order, prior to the termination of the execution of the order; see Chapter 3, 3.247–3.257. 3) Objection to the subject matter of a preservation order; see Chapter 3, 3.258–3.265.
Sanctions for not obeying the interim orders rendered by the courts	1) Quasi-criminal proceedings for contempt of court for the respondent and third parties who knowingly assist a breach of the order, resulting in a fine, seizure of assets or imprisonment. 2) Adverse costs orders. (See Chapters 2, 5, 7 and 9.)	1) Sanctions for certain behaviour and parties; see Chapter 3, 3.266–3.269. 2) Fine and detention penalty; see Chapter 3, 3.270–3.274. 3) Criminal penalty; see Chapter 3, 3.275–3.286.

11.9 In England & Wales, the courts will require the applicants to disclose all material facts to the courts in urgent and on notice hearings, and will also require various further undertakings from the applicants in the urgent hearings.[10] On the other hand, in China, the format of the applications must include the compulsory features, which are required mandatorily by the courts.[11] In addition, there are detailed rules on requirements of security that needs to be furnished by the applicants with their applications seeking pre-action or post-action preservation orders.[12] Apart from the mandatory features that are disclosed within the format of applications submitted to the courts, various legal tests also need to be passed in order to obtain preservation measures. Various evidence that is enclosed with the applications will be examined by the courts.[13]

11.10 In England & Wales, there are various tests of standards of proof that are applicable to applications seeking different kinds of interim remedies.[14] On the other hand, in the Chinese courts, it appears to be the case that the standards of proof are constant or if there are any variations in the tests for overall civil trials, they are not delineated in the relevant codes.[15] The threshold for standards of proof in China is set higher relative to similar tests in England & Wales, and it seems, in practice, as a result of this, the defendants/respondents have a bit of advantage over claimants/applicants in China to counter such applications seeking preservation measures. The Supreme People's Court is even willing to suggest on their own to the lower courts that they must recommend the preservation orders to creditors as discussed

10.30–10.41) for the Supreme People's Court emphasis on a need for the preliminary procedural examination and (Chapter 10, 10.42–10.46) for the requirement of "urgent" circumstances.

10 Refer to Chapter 2, 2.88–2.89, 2.109–2.124.

11 With respect to an application seeking property preservation measures, the features that must be part and parcel of the format for any pre-action or post-action applications and must be disclosed (refer to Chapter 6, 6.15–6.16) and the highlighted features for the pre-action application should be provided (refer to Chapter 6, 6.77); with respect to an application seeking behaviour preservation measures, the features highlighted earlier in Chapter 8 through an example for the format of application must be disclosed to the court (refer to Chapter 8, 8.69–8.70); with respect to an application seeking evidence preservation measures, the features highlighted earlier in Chapter 10 regarding necessary features required in the application must be disclosed to the court (refer to Chapter 10, 10.18).

12 Refer to Chapter 3, 3.130–3.194.

13 Refer to fn 9 of this chapter with regards to various legal tests that are required to obtain preservation remedies. For example, when seeking preservation of property measures, "urgent circumstances" and "irreparable harms" need to be proved (refer to Chapter 6, 6.79–6.81); when seeking preservation of behaviour measures, in addition to providing the evidence for "urgent" circumstances and "irreparable harms" for seeking preservations in all disputes (refer to Chapter 8, 8.104–8.120), the applicants must also provide evidence of the "stabilization right" (refer to Chapter 8, 8.121–8.126); when seeking preservation of evidence measures, the applicant needs to provide materials to prove "urgent circumstances" (refer to Chapter 10, 10.42–10.46).

14 Refer to Chapter 5, 5.23, 5.25, 5.30; Chapter 7, 7.13–7.14, 7.31–7.33, 7.51, 7.61; Chapter 9, 9.16. See also 11.97–11.105 for comparative analysis of standard of proof in both jurisdictions.

15 Refer to 11.97–11.105 for comparative analysis of standards of proof in both jurisdictions.

in Chapter 1, 1.25. However, it will depend largely on balancing the test of standards of proof to evaluate quickly the facts in any application without turning the interim hearings into mini-trials in China, and to a large extent, the Chinese courts have prevented interim hearing from becoming mini-trials.[16] The authors have discussed and carried out the comparative analysis of the invisible factor of standards of proof a little later in this chapter (refer to 11.97–11.107) , as it distinctly affects the exercise of discretionary power in relation to the grant of interim measures in both jurisdictions.

11.11 Additionally, Chinese judges can grant preservation orders on their own, provided they are necessary, without the parties seeking them through applications, although, in practice, this is seen rarely. The Chinese judges in non-maritime disputes could grant such interim orders pursuant to the statutory powers under the *CPL 1991 (as amended until 2020).*[17] However, it has been observed that the grant of preservation orders is usually limited to post-action preservation measures only. On the other hand, without the parties' applications, English judges are not known to grant interim orders on their own accord.[18]

11.12 In both jurisdictions, the interim applications can be submitted in courts before the claim forms are issued to commence litigation for the main disputes.[19] In English law, there is a requirement for additional undertakings to be provided by the applicants in such cases,[20] whereas in the Chinese courts there are demanding requirements for the applicants to furnish security for pre-trial preservation measures.[21]

11.13 In English law, the judges will evaluate evidence using general principles such as inconsistent evidence relative to other evidence,

16 In terms of the procedure for interim hearings in China, detailed discussion can be found in Chapter 6, 6.92–6.95 and Chapter 8, 8.149–8.157. In particular, an application seeking intellectual property behaviour preservation measures will go through an inquiry procedure (refer to Chapter 8, 8.149–8.154). See also, 11.106–11.107.

17 Refer to Chapter 6, 6.17; refer also to Chapter 8, 8.70; refer also to Chapter 10, 10.112–10.113; see also, CPL 1991 (as amended until 2020), Articles 81 and 100; see also, Articles 12, 51 and 62 of the Special Maritime Procedure Law of the People's Republic of China 2000 ("SMPL 2000"), where the maritime courts in China have no power to take the initiative to render a preservation order without the application of a party concerned in any litigation/arbitration. The rules in SMPL 2000 will also act as an exception to the general rule; refer also to 6.1, 8.71 and 10.114–10.115.

18 They nevertheless have the power to do so: CPR 3.3(1).

19 In relation to applications in England and Wales see Chapter 2, 2.30, 2.56. With respect to China the meaning of pre-action has been given in Chapter 3, 3.43.

20 See Chapter 2, 2.118–2.125.

21 On the other hand in China, for general rules of security, refer to Chapter 3, 3.130–3.194, for the specific provisions with regards to evaluation of pre-action security in applications for property preservation measures, refer to Chapter 6, 6.83–6.85, for the evaluation of post-action security, refer to Chapter 6, 6.120–6.122, for exemptions from furnishing security, refer to Chapter 6, 6.123, for the specific provisions on behaviour preservation applications such as the amount of security in disputes, refer to Chapter 8, 8.141–8.142, and for the specific provisions on evidence preservation measures, refer to Chapter 10, 10.121–10.130.

self-contradictory evidence and so forth to prevent the interim hearings from becoming mini-trials.[22] On the other hand, in China, judges are reluctant to handle the evidence at the lower standard of proof.[23] These aspects will be considered in more detail in the discussion of the invisible factors affecting interim applications in both jurisdictions. Nonetheless, in legal practice, there seems to be a tendency observed in the Chinese courts to allow applications seeking preservation measures as long as the applicants are able to furnish security prescribed by law or as requested by the courts.

11.14 In English law, interim applications will be considered "urgent" where it is impossible for the applicants to give three clear days' notice. The administration of English courts will list these urgent applications before other cases highlighting immense flexibility in the administration of the courts. Such interim applications can be dealt with by judges even after office hours.[24] On the other hand, in China, judges will deal with interim applications within 48 hours.[25] In the authors' view, in the current business environment, there are many steps that innovative respondents can take during the 48 hours to render any interim orders toothless.[26]

11.15 Interim hearings are shorter hearings with discretion available to the English judges in relation to evidence, duration of interim hearings that need to be organised, whether the hearings can be conducted on phone or video conference and whether the interim applications can be conducted on documents alone provided that the parties can agree to it.[27] On the other hand, in China with regards to applications seeking property and evidence preservation measures, there are no mandatory interim hearings and preservation measures can be rendered by the courts on documents alone.[28] However, in legal practice, Chinese judges do display the tendency to go deeper into the civil disputes on jurisprudential grounds to seek truth in the disputes before them.[29] In addition, the Interpretation for IP behaviour preservation expressly stipulates that the inquiry procedures should be conducted by the judges, and such inquiry procedures are similar to interim hearings.[30]

22 Refer to Chapter 2, 2.47 (discussing CPR Part 32), 2.125.

23 Refer to Chapter 11.62–11.114 for discussion on invisible factors and contexts and their impact on seeking interim measures from the courts.

24 Refer to Chapter 2, 2.103 and the Commercial Court Guide §P.1.

25 In non-maritime disputes, applications seeking pre-action preservation measures must be dealt with by the courts within the first 48 hours of docketing them in the court system, or if there are urgent circumstances in the applications seeking post-action preservation measures, courts must also deal with those applications in the first 48 hours. In maritime disputes, all applications seeking preservation measures must also render interim orders within 48 hours; see also, Chapter 3, 3.222 and 3.225.

26 Refer to Chapter 1, 1.14–1.17 for discussion on role and need of interim measures.

27 Refer to Chapter 2, 2.96–2.108.

28 Refer to Chapter 6, 6.92–6.95.

29 Refer to 11.90–11.96.

30 Refer to 11.106–11.07 on issue of standard of proof in interim hearings; see also, *Provisions of the Supreme People's Court on Several Issues Concerning the Application of Law*

11.16 Strict undertakings provided by the applicants are attached to the injunctive orders in English law. These undertakings are not ordinarily required to be fortified by the courts unless these courts consider the issues of claimants to be impecunious or other extraordinary issues are relevant to the applications.[31] These undertakings will generally cover the potential damages to the respondents and third parties.[32] In the authors' view, flexibility exists with regard to the issue of furnishing security in interim applications made to the English courts. This is one of the key factors in the popularity of the English jurisdiction among stakeholders that are seeking interim remedies. Additionally, undertakings for ancillary orders such as disclosure orders may be required.[33] On the other hand, in China, there are strict requirements for security that needs to be furnished during pre-action preservation applications except for pre-action evidence preservation applications.[34] Generally speaking, the types of security that can be furnished comprise property security,[35] cash security[36] and a letter of guarantee.[37] In recent years, the development with regard to the furnishing of security in the form of a credit guarantee has been remarkable. Additionally, the Chinese courts have accepted the concept of property preservation liability insurance. To be precise, insurance companies will provide letters of guarantee to applicants based on insurance policies. Nonetheless, such letters of guarantee are mainly utilised for applications seeking property preservation measures.[38] In addition, an online guarantee system is gradually being employed in a few Chinese courts.[39] Compared to other types of security where the Chinese courts normally spend a huge amount of time dealing with the issue of security that needs to be furnished by the applicants, the online guarantee system along with an online preservation system is more convenient and economical. It is anticipated that this kind of guarantee will be greatly employed.

11.17 In case of pre-action preservation applications, the parties in China will have to file their main claims in the civil action within 30 days after the courts have rendered the preservation orders.[40] On the other hand, in England

in Cases Involving the Review of Behaviour Preservation in Intellectual Property Disputes (Fa Shi [2018] No 21) ("The Interpretations of IP Behaviour Preservation 2018"), Article 5; refer also to Chapter 8, 8.149–8.156, where in addition, there are no mandatory requirements for the interim hearings in non-IP behaviour preservation applications.

31 Refer to Chapter 2, 2.120.

32 Refer to Chapter 2, 2.119.

33 Refer to Chapter 2, 2.21(b).

34 Refer to Chapter 10, 10.121–10.131 for specific provisions regarding the pre-action evidence preservation applications, where security is not mandatory except in certain circumstances as decided by the Chinese court.

35 Refer to Chapter 3, 3.142–8.153.

36 Refer to Chapter 3, 3.154–8.159.

37 Refer to Chapter 3, 3.160–3.174.

38 Refer to Chapter 3, 3.175–3.183.

39 Refer to Chapter 3, 3.184–3.186.

40 See CPL 1991 (as amended until 2020), Article 101.

& Wales, the judges will give directions with the interim orders in this regard and accordingly, there is no set fixed time period during which the civil actions have to be commenced in the courts.[41]

11.18 In the English courts, a Penal Notice is inserted with the interim orders to give power and enforceability to the injunctions. The purpose of such a Penal Notice is to make respondents aware of the repercussions for not obeying the orders.[42] Similarly, in China, in order to maintain the legitimacy of the Chinese preservation orders, the existing law provides for different sanctions for non-obeying the preservation orders, including fines, detention[43] and criminal penalties.[44] The sanctioned party could not only be a natural person, a principal or the direct responsible person of a legal entity or an organisation, but also could be the legal entity or the organisation itself.[45]

11.19 In England & Wales, in without notice hearings, costs orders are reserved until the next hearings. In general, for most interim applications, the English judges have considerable discretion to award costs by observing the conduct of the parties, including that of the parties that have successfully obtained the interim orders.[46] On the other hand, in China, when the applicants submit interim applications seeking preservation measures, they need to pay for the costs of interim applications. After the final and binding judgment is made, the legal costs are usually borne by the losing party. The allocation of costs will be calculated proportionally following the judgment.[47]

11.20 In the English courts, evidence in support of an application for an interim remedy must be in writing, and contained either in the Application Notice itself, or in a separate witness statement, or in an affidavit (the latter is required for applications for freezing injunctions and search orders). Application notices and witness statements must be verified by a signed statement of truth; affidavits must be sworn or affirmed before an authorised person.[48] On the other hand, in China, applications in a written format are requested by the Chinese courts.[49] However, for urgent interim applications, fax, e-mails and other modes can be accepted by Chinese maritime courts.[50] In addition, if the applications and/or the relevant evidence are not in Mandarin, the general rule is to translate the documents in the foreign language into Mandarin.[51] If the evidence is collected from outside mainland

---

41 Refer to Chapter 2, 2.123(a). Typically, the applicant will be required to undertake to commence substantive proceedings forthwith, or within a specified time.

42 Refer to Chapter 2, 2.129.

43 Refer to Chapter 3, 3.270–3.274 for discussion on fine and detention penalty.

44 Refer to Chapter 3, 3.275–3.286 for discussion on criminal penalty.

45 Refer to Chapter 3, 3.266–3.269.

46 Refer to Chapter 2, 2.47 (discussing CPR Part 44).

47 Refer to Chapter 3, 3.216–3.221.

48 Refer to Chapter 2, 2.47 (discussing CPR Part 32).

49 Refer to Chapter 3, 3.117–3.119.

50 Refer to Chapter 3, 3.120.

51 Refer to Chapter 3, 3.121–3.124.

China, notarisation and legalisation are mandatory,[52] although in certain circumstances involving IP disputes, the courts may waive the requirements pertaining to notarisation and legalisation.[53] Therefore, English judges will focus on concepts such as full and frank disclosure, affidavits and a good record of representations from the parties' counsels during hearings, whereas in China, the judges will expect the details from the applicants, and at times the exact information must be in the form of documentary evidence.

11.21 Where the English court grants an interim remedy on an application heard without notice, the respondent has a right to apply to the court that made the order to have it varied or set aside; otherwise the respondent must seek permission to appeal to the Court of Appeal.[54] In China, there are three types of procedural remedies if the parties concerned or third parties are not satisfied with the preservation orders rendered by the courts. The parties concerned or the interested parties are entitled to submit applications for reconsideration against the rendered preservation orders,[55] or file an objection against the enforcement of preservation orders,[56] or an outside party can apply for an objection against the subject matter of the preservation orders.[57]

11.22 Legal costs in England & Wales for any interim application need to be planned properly because high legal costs are associated with litigation in the English courts. Such high costs could be considered as a major impediment to seeking justice. On the other hand, in the Chinese legal system, though the litigation costs are gradually increasing, this factor is not yet as intractable as in England & Wales.[58]

11.23 Third parties may be able to claim compensation as a result of the loss arising from interim orders. Under English law their ability to do so will depend on whether the applicant was required to give an undertaking in damages as a price of the order, and whether the terms of the undertaking extend to third parties.[59] In China, either the parties concerned or the third party who suffered a loss due to the preservation orders is entitled to claim compensation against the applicants.[60] The liability principles to decide compensation can vary depending on the type of preservation measure and the identification of the error(s) in the rendered preservation measures. Claims

---

52 Refer to Chapter 3, 3.125–3.126.
53 Refer to Chapter 3, 3.127–3.129.
54 Refer to Chapter 2, 2.60–2.65, 2.106.
55 Refer to Chapter 3, 3.232–3.246.
56 Refer to Chapter 3, 3.247–3.257.
57 Refer to Chapter 3, 3.258–3.265.
58 In terms of legal costs in China, the relevant law is *Measures on Payment of Litigation Costs 2006* (Order of the State Council No 481); see also, Chapter 3, 3.197–3.221.
59 Refer to Chapter 2, 213(b).
60 Refer to Chapter 3, 3.296–3.297. It should also be emphasised that conduct of the courts that turns out to be erroneous may give rise to the issue of state compensation to the party that has suffered loss due to the error of the court. However, this book focused simply on the issue of the civil compensation. Refer to Chapter 3, 3.295.

for damages caused by wrongful non-IP behaviour preservation applications or property/evidence preservation measures are subject to fault-based liability.[61] On the other hand, wrongful IP behaviour preservation measures are subject to non-fault liability.[62]

Comparative Analysis – Freezing Orders (England & Wales) v Preservation of Property Measures (China)

11.24 The very apparent similarities and differences between freezing orders in English law and property preservation measures in Chinese law on the key parameters are delineated in the tables for both stages – pre-action and post-action. The readers are guided to Table 11.2 and Table 11.3 for comparative analysis of the pre-action and post-action stages between the interim measures for both jurisdictions.

11.25 In order to obtain a domestic freezing injunction covering only assets within England & Wales, the applicants will have to demonstrate grounds for belief that the respondents have assets in the jurisdiction that will be caught by the injunction.[63] In England & Wales, an ancillary order called a disclosure order along with the freezing order can also be granted, the purpose of which is to provide the applicant and the court with information about the respondent's assets in order to ensure the effectiveness of the freezing injunction and to enable the court to police it effectively.[64] On the other hand, in China, according to the different stages of applications, the burden of proof on the applicants can vary. In pre-action property preservation applications, applicants are normally required to provide exact information on property, otherwise their preservation applications will not be successful.[65] However, during post-action applications seeking property preservation measures, applicants may just be required to provide specific information about of property(ies) that is going to be the relevant subject matter of the property preservation order, if granted.[66] Furthermore, applicants seeking post-action preservation measures are entitled to request the courts to employ the online monitoring system to find the respondent's property.[67]

11.26 World-wide freezing injunctions are available in England & Wales even when the assets of the respondents are not present in England & Wales, provided the applicants can provide additional undertakings.[68] On the other

61 Refer to Chapter 6, 6.157–6.167; Chapter 8, 8.175 and Chapter 10, 10.141–10.142.
62 Refer to Chapter 8, 8.168–8.171.
63 Refer to Chapter 5, 5.30.
64 Refer to Chapter 2, 2.21(b), 2.44(c); Chapter 5, 5.39.
65 Refer to Chapter 6, 6.70–6.75.
66 Refer to Chapter 6, 6.98–6.99.
67 Refer to Chapter 6, 6.100–6.108.
68 Refer to Chapter 5, 5.38.

TABLE 11.2 Comparative analysis (pre-action) – freezing injunctions (England & Wales) v preservation of property measures (China)

	English law	*Chinese law*
Purpose	Monetary personal claims: to prevent the illegitimate dissipation of assets so as to prevent the enforcement of a judgment or arbitral award. (Proprietary claims: to preserve the assets to which the applicant claims ownership ("asset preservation orders").) (See Chapters 2 and 5.)	To ensure the enforcement of a further court judgment or an arbitral award remains achievable, or to prevent loss to parties concerned; see Chapter 6, 6.2–6.3 and 6.11–6.12.
The scope of the property to be preserved	Monetary personal claims: 1) Any assets of any kind belonging to the respondent, where the respondent is the defendant to the substantive claim. 2) Where the respondent is not the defendant to the substantive claim, any assets in the hands of the respondent to which the substantive defendant is beneficially entitled, or which the respondent may otherwise be obliged to make available to satisfy the applicant's claim. 3) Value of assets limited to the applicant's reasonably arguable best case plus interest and costs. (Asset preservation orders may be granted in respect of any assets over which the applicant asserts a proprietary claim, and are not limited in amount.) (See Chapters 2 and 5.)	1) There are no specific restrictions on the property that can be preserved, except for some properties that are not suitable for preservation, and third parties' property; see Chapter 6, 6.29–6.31, 6.37–6.45. 2) Property to be preserved can include data and online virtual property; see Chapter 6, 6.32–6.33. 3) If there are multiple properties available for the preservation order, the courts will have an option to select a property to preserve; see Chapter 6, 6.136–6.140. 4) Based on the respondents' request, the courts may choose the more convenient property to preserve; see Chapter 6, 6.146–6.149.

(*Continued*)

TABLE 11.2 *(Continued)*

	English law	*Chinese law*
Legal tests to obtain interim orders	Monetary personal claims: 1) Good arguable case on the merits of the applicant's substantive claim. 2) Good arguable case of a real risk of unjustifiable dissipation of assets. 3) Grounds for belief that assets exist that will be caught by the freezing injunction – no need for assets to be specifically identified or located. 4) Just and convenient to grant the freezing injunction. (Asset preservation orders: (i) serious issue to be tried on the merits of applicant's proprietary claim to the assets, and either (ii) damages are an inadequate remedy for the applicant but would be an adequate remedy for the respondent if the injunction was wrongly granted, or (iii) the balance of convenience is in favour of granting the injunction.) (See Chapters 2 and 5.)	1) Exact information on property to be preserved is required by the courts; see Chapter 6, 6.70–6.75. 2) The subject matter of an application: (i) the clean title of the property to be preserved; (ii) the value of property to be preserved; see Chapter 6, 6.37–6.50. 3) Requirements of "urgent circumstances" and "irreparable harms", such as the possible transfer of the property by the respondent and the possible damage to the property; see Chapter 6, 6.79–6.81. 4) The requirement that the applicant must furnish security; see Chapter 6, 6.82–6.91. 5) To examine "whether a future judgment may become impossible or may be difficult to enforce", or "whether the respondent's conduct or other reasons may cause the loss or damage to the applicant"; see Chapter 6, 6.81.
Security to be provided by the applicants to obtain interim orders	1) Undertaking in damages to the respondent and, at the court's discretion, to third parties. 2) At the court's discretion, fortification of undertaking by provision of security in cash or another form acceptable to the court. (See Chapters 2 and 5.)	1) Furnishing security is mandatory for pre-action preservation measures in non-maritime disputes; see Chapter 3, 3.130–3.31. 2) Furnishing security is non-mandatory for pre-action preservation measures in maritime disputes; see Chapter 3, 3.134–3.135. 3) Types of security; see Chapter 3, 3.139–3.141. a) Property security; see Chapter 3, 3.142–3.153. b) Cash security; see Chapter 3, 3.154–3.159. c) A letter of guarantee; see Chapter 3, 3.160–3.186.

		4) Evaluation of security; see Chapter 6, 6.83–6.85. 5) Exemptions from furnishing security; see Chapter 3, 3.187–3.192.
Countersecurity and the respondents	Respondent has the option to provide security for the applicant's claim to discharge freezing injunction, in cash or other form acceptable to the court or to the applicant. (See Chapters 2 and 5.)	1) Furnishing countersecurity to seek the discharge of preservation orders; see Chapter 3, 3.136–3.138. 2) As a general rule, the types of countersecurity are the same as those of security that could be provided by the applicants; see 3.139–3.186. 3) Some specific requirements for types of countersecurity; see Chapter 6, 6.146–6.149.
Defences available to respondents	Respondent may apply to set aside an order made without notice, by demonstrating that any of the requirements for granting the interim remedy are not made out, or on discretionary grounds including the applicant's failure to give full and frank disclosure on the without notice application. (See Chapters 2 and 5.)	Without interim hearings, respondents will have no opportunity to defend against applicants, who are seeking property preservation measures; see Chapter 6, 6.126.
Procedure for interim hearings	Standard procedures apply where an application is not urgent. On urgent applications, the court may dispense with most procedural requirements. (See Chapters 2 and 5.)	No mandatory interim hearing procedure is prescribed by law; see Chapter 6, 6.92–6.95.
Burden and standard of proof	Applicant bears burden of proof. A range of different standards apply, from very low (serious issue to be tried) to very high (high degree of assurance), depending on the nature and practical effect of the interim remedy sought and the particular requirement of that remedy under consideration. (See Chapters 2 and 5.)	In all applications there is a hurdle of very high standard of proof on the applicants or whosoever is initiating the applications; see 11.97–11.107.

(Continued)

TABLE 11.2 *(Continued)*

	English law	*Chinese law*
Discharge of interim orders	1) If an interim remedy is granted without notice, the respondent has the right to apply to the court which granted it to set it aside. 2) Third parties may also apply to vary or discharge orders that affect them. 3) The respondent can discharge a freezing injunction by providing security. 4) Otherwise, and where an interim remedy is granted on notice, the respondent must seek permission to appeal. (See Chapter 2 and 5.)	1) Under certain circumstances, an interim order can be discharged; see Chapter 3, 3.287–3.288. 2) Under certain circumstances, an applicant's liability to file for a discharge; see Chapter 3, 3.289–3.291. 3) A respondent provides countersecurity; see Chapter 3, 3.136–3.138 and Chapter 6, 6.146–6.149.
The time limit and renewal of interim orders	The order will state its duration, which may be for a specific time or until a specified event, e.g. judgment or further order. (See Chapters 2 and 5.)	Without the renewal of an interim order prior to the expiry of the time limit, the interim order will lapse. The time limit is different based on the preserved property; see Chapter 6, 6.151–6.155.
Substantive remedy: compensation	At the discretion of the court, the applicant may be ordered to compensate the respondent for proven losses pursuant to its undertaking in damages. (See Chapters 2 and 5.)	1) The scope of the compensation to the injured party; see Chapter 3, 3.296–3.297. 2) The fault-based liability principle; see Chapter 6, 6.157–6.167. 3) Elements of fault-based liability; see Chapter 6, 6.168–6.173.
Costs	At the discretion of the court. The general rule is that the loser pays the winner's costs. (See Chapters 2 and 5.)	1) Application fee: on the basis of the actual value of property; see Chapter 6, 6.174. 2) The underlying other fees such as storage fee, custodian fee, appraisal fee and transport fee, insurance fee and lawyer's fee; see Chapter 3, 3.197–3.215. 3) The burden of the legal costs; see Chapter 3, 3.216–3.221.

TABLE 11.3 Comparative analysis (post-action) – freezing injunctions (England & Wales) v preservation of property measures (China)

	English law	*Chinese law*
Purpose	Refer to Table 11.2.	To ensure the enforcement of a further court judgment or an arbitral award, or to prevent the other loss of parties concerned; see Chapter 6, 6.2–6.3 and 6.11–6.12.
The scope of property to be preserved	Refer to Table 11.2.	Refer to Table 11.2, as they are similar for both pre-action and post-action applications.
Legal tests to obtain interim orders	Refer to Table 11.2.	1) Specific evidence of property; see Chapter 6, 6.98–6.99. 2) The subject matter of an application: (i) clean title of the property to be preserved; (ii) the value of property; see Chapter 6, 6.37–6.50. 3) Requirements of "urgent circumstances" and "irreparable harms", if the applicants are requesting urgent orders; see Chapter 6, 6.79–6.81. 4) Security requested by the courts under certain circumstances; see Chapter 6, 6.120–6.122. 5) To examine "whether a future judgment may become impossible or difficult to enforce", or "whether the respondent's conduct or other reasons may cause the damage or loss to applicant"; see Chapter 6, 6.96–6.97.
Security to be provided by an applicant to obtain interim orders	Refer to Table 11.2.	1) Furnishing security by applicants is not mandatory and depends on the courts' discretionary power; see Chapter 3, 3.132–3.135. 2) Types of security; see Chapter 3, see 3.139–3.141. a) Property security; see Chapter 3, 3.142–3.153. b) Cash security; see Chapter 3, 3.154–3.159. c) A letter of guarantee; see Chapter 3, 3.160–3.186. 3) Amount of security; see Chapter 6, 6.120–6.122. 4) Exemptions from furnishing security; see Chapter 3, 3.187–3.192 and Chapter 6, 6.123.

(*Continued*)

TABLE 11.3 (*Continued*)

	English law	*Chinese law*
Countersecurity and respondents	Refer to Table 11.2.	1) Furnishing countersecurity seeking the discharge of the preservation orders; see Chapter 3, 3.136–3.138. 2) As a general rule, the types of countersecurity are the same as that of security that could be provided by the applicants; see Chapter 3, 3.139–3.186. 3) Some specific requirements for types of countersecurity; see Chapter 6, 6.146–6.149.
Defences available to the respondents	Refer to Table 11.2.	The defence for the respondents must be able to focus on the necessity of the applications from the perspective of the applicants' purposes; see Chapter 6, 6.126.
Procedure for interim hearings	Refer to Table 11.2.	1) No mandatory interim hearing procedure is prescribed by law; see Chapter 6, 6.92–6.95. 2) No express requirement for interim hearings prescribed by law, but in practice, it is possible during civil trials to do so and certain regional legal documents guide the courts to organise the interim hearings; see Chapter 6, 6.128–6.129.
Burden and standard of proof	Refer to Table 11.2.	In all applications there is a hurdle of very high standard of proof on the applicants or whosoever is initiating the applications; see 11.97–11.107.
Discharge of interim orders	Refer to Table 11.2.	Refer to Table 11.2, as they are similar for both pre-action and post-action applications.
Costs	Refer to Table 11.2.	Refer to Table 11.2, as they are similar for both pre-action and post-action applications.

hand, in China, the remedy of worldwide preservation measures is not yet available to applicants.

11.27 In England & Wales, receivers can be appointed by the court to manage the property subject to freezing orders,[69] whereas in China there is no similar rule to assist judges in managing preservation orders. Nonetheless, the Chinese courts regularly issue notifications to the relevant authorities, such as commercial banks, property registration departments and so forth, requesting them to manage preservations granted by them. The responsible person or the relevant legal entities can be sanctioned, if there is any failure to assist the courts in the enforcement of the preservation orders.[70] In addition, the courts may appoint the respondents as custodians of the property and allow these respondents to employ such property in their business during the enforcement stage of the preservation measures.[71]

11.28 In England & Wales, the freezing orders are a remedy *in personam* and do not grant any security or right under a pledge over the assets,[72] and the concept is similar in China.[73] In England & Wales, as well as in China, personal expenses and in certain cases trade debts may be allowed from the preserved property.[74] However, post-judgment, in England and Wales the court will generally not allow the respondent to pay other creditors.[75] In England & Wales, the third parties without notice of freezing injunction orders can get a good title to the assets that are subjected to the freezing injunctions.[76]

11.29 There are various methods pursuant to which third parties are affected or included as defendants in applications seeking freezing orders.[77] *Chabra injunctions* are available in England & Wales where third parties' assets can be frozen where there is evidence that they are in possession or control of respondents' assets, and such third parties could even be spouses.[78] However, the English court's power to grant *Chabra injunctions* in support of arbitration proceedings in England & Wales, against persons who are outside England and Wales, is doubtful.[79] In China, to prevent property preservation orders from infringing the rights of third parties, the Chinese courts may directly forbid

69 Refer to Chapter 2, 2.21(a), 2.45; Chapter 5, 5.40.

70 Refer to Chapter 3, 3.269–3.286; refer also to Chapter 6, 6.13.

71 *Provisions of the Supreme People's Court on Several Issues Concerning the Handling of Property Preservation Cases by the People's Courts* (220 amendment) (Fa Shi [2016] No 22) (superseded by Fa Shi [2020] No 21) ("Interpretation of Property Preservation 2016"), Article 13; refer to Chapter 6, 6.141.

72 Refer to Chapter 5, 5.13.

73 In China, generally speaking, only action *in personam* is approved by law. An exception is available in the domain of maritime law, where both action *in rem* and action *in personam* are recognised by law.

74 Refer to Chapter 5, 5.25–5.29; refer to Chapter 6, 6.43.

75 Refer to Chapter 5, 5.29

76 Refer to Chapter 5, 5.13.

77 Refer to Chapter 5, 5.31–5.32.

78 Refer to Chapter 5, 5.41–5.42.

79 Refer to Chapter 4, 4.36–4.4.39

the applicants from applying for property preservation measures over such outside parties' property.[80] Nevertheless, this does not mean that no preservation measures are ever possible over the third party's property. Such property preservation measures are available in circumstances where the assets of the third parties can be preserved on the basis that this third party is in "control" of the assets of respondents. The exception to the general rule will work only in circumstances where the third party enjoys the rights over the property, but the respondent, under certain conditions, still has rights over such properties.[81] However, in legal practice in China, the evidential burden is enormous on applicants to obtain such preservation orders on third parties' properties. Since, these days, complex company structures are common in disputes, the unavailability of a well-defined *Chabra injunction* is major handicap in China; however, the above discussed exceptions can operate, to some extent, in a way not very different from the *Chabra injunctions*.

11.30 In England & Wales, where the applicant claims an ownership interest in specific property in the hands of the respondent, he can cost-effectively obtain a freezing injunction over that property by means of a proprietary freezing injunction or asset preservation order.[82] Proprietary injunctions are available against a particular property, and therefore, these are not available to freeze the assets in general.[83] In China, there are no available equivalent special property preservation measures that are relatively cost-effective in preserving a specific property.

11.31 In China, in order to protect the respondent's interests and to ease the burden on the respondent, the Chinese courts may allow various options such as multiple properties,[84] the use of reserved property,[85] the sale of preserved property[86] and the substitution of property subject to order with another property.[87] In addition, some properties, or a specific property, under certain circumstances are unsuitable to be preserved pursuant to preservation orders.[88]

Comparative Analysis – Interim Injunctions (England & Wales) v Preservation of Behaviour Measures (China)

11.32 The apparent similarities and differences between interim injunctions in English law and behaviour preservation measures in Chinese law on

80 Refer to Chapter 6, 6.37–6.41.

81 Refer to Chapter 6, 6.42–6.43. In addition, before the respondent takes the clean title of the real estate, Chinese law allows a "pre-sealing" measure over such real estate.

82 Refer to Chapter 5, 5.2–5.3.

83 Refer to Chapter 5, 5.4.

84 Refer to Chapter 6, 6.136–6.140.

85 Refer to Chapter 6, 6.141.

86 Refer to Chapter 6, 6.142–6.145.

87 Refer to Chapter 6, 6.146–6.149.

88 Refer to Chapter 6, 6.44–6.45.

the key parameters are delineated in the tables for both stages – pre-action and post-action. The readers are guided to Table 11.4 and Table 11.5 for comparative analysis of the pre-action and post-action stages of the interim measures for both jurisdictions.

11.33 Prior to 2012, the concept of "advance enforcement" provided by the Civil Procedure Law 1991, to some extent, included partially a concept of "behaviour preservation" in the civil procedure system.[89] The behaviour preservation measures were available initially only in intellectual property and maritime disputes.[90] Therefore, it is safe to say that the preservation measures as interim measures were not widely available until the 2012 revision and amendment to the Civil Procedure Law 1991.[91] On the other hand, the procedural remedy of interim injunctions in England & Wales has a long history, and English judges are well-versed in rendering such interim orders.[92]

11.34 In English law, applicants have to prove that damages will not be an adequate remedy at the end of civil trials, and in some cases, test of balance of convenience and test of relative strength as well.[93] On the other hand, in China, pursuant to Article 100 of the CPL 1991 (as amended until 2020), the legal tests to obtain behaviour preservation measures that are necessary for the applicants to overcome include the examination of whether future judgments will remain achievable or if it will be difficult for the courts to enforce their order and whether the respondents' conduct or any other factors may damage or cause further loss to the applicants.[94] In addition, due to the absence of the judicial interpretation in non-IP disputes, according to the nature of the disputes and the exact measure of the behaviour preservation that is requested from the courts, the legal tests will involve the application of the following laws and Interpretations: the *Provisions of the Supreme People's Court on Several Issues Concerning the Application of Law in Cases Involving the Review of Behaviour Preservation in Intellectual Property Disputes* (Fa Shi [2018] No 21), *Provisions of the Supreme People's Court on Several Issues Concerning the Handling of Property Preservation Cases by the People's Courts* (2020 amendment) (Fa Shi [2016] No 22) (superseded by Fa Shi [2020] No 21), regional courts' legal guidance documents such as *Procedure of the Hunan High People's Court on Property Preservation* (Xiang Gao Fa Ban Fa [2015] No 3) and *Provisions of the Shanghai High People's Court on Property Preservation (2017 Amendment)* (Hu Gao Fa

89 Refer to Chapter 1, 1.85–1.92; refer also to Chapter 8, 8.4; refer also to Chapter 8, 8.9–8.54, for more discussion on applications and requirement of advance enforcement and the relationship between advance enforcement and behaviour preservation measures.

90 Refer to Chapter 1, 1.86–1.88 and Chapter 8, 8.5–8.6.

91 Refer to Chapter 1, 1.99–1.100; refer also to Chapter 8, 8.7.

92 Refer to Chapter 1, 1.65–1.67 and Chapter 2, 2.21; Chapter 7, 7.10.

93 Refer to Chapter 7, 7.13–7.29.

94 Refer to Chapter 8, 8.101; refer also to Chapter 6, 6.76–6.85.

TABLE 11.4 Comparative analysis (pre-action) – interim injunctions (England & Wales) v behaviour preservation measures (China)

	English law	*Chinese law*
Purpose	To restrain the respondent from certain conduct, or to compel the respondent to take a certain action, before the merits of the underlying claim have been determined, so as to minimize the risk of irremediable injustice to either the applicant or the respondent. (See Chapters 2 & 7.)	To compel a respondent "to do" or "not to do certain things", so as to ensure that the enforcement of court's judgment or the arbitral award remains achievable, or prevent loss to parties concerned; see Chapter 8, 8.55–8.56.
Legal tests to obtain interim orders	1) Serious issue to be tried on the merits of the underlying claim – a higher standard may be imposed where the injunction is mandatory or where grant or refusal of the injunction will determine the underlying dispute. 2) Damages an inadequate remedy for the applicant and an adequate remedy for the respondent if the injunction later turns out to have been wrongly granted. 3) Where (2) is not satisfied, balance of convenience, which may involve consideration of the underlying merits. (See Chapters 2 and 7.)	1) "Urgent circumstances" in all disputes; see Chapter 8, 8.104–8.114 and Chapter 6, 6.76–6.85. 2) "Irreparable harms" in all disputes; see Chapter 8, 8.115–8.120 and Chapter 6, 6.76 - 6.85. 3) "Stabilization right" in IP disputes; see Chapter 8, 8.121–8.126. 4) "Balance of interests" and protection of public interests in IP disputes; see Chapter 8, 8.127–8.134. 5) The requirement that security be furnished by the applicants; see Chapter 8, 8.138–8.142. 6) To examine "whether a future judgment may become impossible or difficult to enforce", or "whether the respondent's conduct or other reasons may cause the loss or damage to the applicant"; see Chapter 8, 8.101–8.103.

Security to be provided by an applicant to obtain interim orders	1) Undertaking in damages. 2) At the court's discretion, fortification by provision of security in cash or another form permitted by the court. (See Chapters 2 and 7.)	1) Security needs to be furnished mandatorily in non-maritime disputes; see Chapter 8, 8.139–8.140 and Chapter 3, 3.130–3.131. 2) Furnishing security is not mandatory in maritime disputes and is dependent on the courts' discretionary power; see Chapter 3, 3.134–3.135. 3) Types of security; see Chapter 3, 3.139–3.141. a) Property security; see Chapter 3, 3.142–3.153. b) Cash security; see Chapter 3, 3.154–3.159. c) A letter of guarantee; see Chapter 3, 3.160–3.186. 4) Amount of security in IP disputes; see Chapter 8, 8.141; amount of security in non-IP disputes; see Chapter 8, 8.142. 5) Exemptions from providing security; see Chapter 3, 3.187–3.193.
Countersecurity and respondents	In cash or any other form permitted by the court. (See Chapters 2 and 7.)	1) As a general rule, the types of countersecurity are the same as that of security that needs to be furnished by the applicants; Chapter 3, 3.139–3.186. 2) An applicant's consent determines the necessity of countersecurity in IP disputes; see Chapter 8, 8.143. 3) Uncertainty about countersecurity in non-IP disputes; Chapter 8, 8.144–8.148.
Defences available to the respondents	Respondent may apply to set aside order made without notice, by demonstrating that any of the requirements for granting the interim remedy are not made out, or on discretionary grounds including the applicant's failure to give full and frank disclosure on the without notice application. (See Chapters 2 and 7.)	1) In IP disputes, if inquiry procedure is organized by courts, it is possible for the respondents to defend; for general guidance, see Chapter 8, 8.150. 2) Without inquiry procedure, the respondents will have no opportunity to defend. 3) In non-IP disputes, the general guidance; see Chapter 8, 8.56. 4) In maritime disputes; see Chapter 8, 8.56.

(Continued)

TABLE 11.4 (*Continued*)

	English law	*Chinese law*
Procedure for interim hearings	Standard procedures apply where application is not urgent. On urgent applications, the court may dispense with most procedural requirements. (See Chapters 2 and 7.)	1) Inquiry procedure for an application seeking IP behaviour preservations; see Chapter 8, 8.149–8.154. 2) No mandatory requirement for interim hearings in non-IP disputes; see Chapter 8, 8.155–8.156. 3) In practice, the interim hearing procedure in maritime disputes; see Chapter 8, 8.157.
Burden and standard of proof	Applicant bears burden of proof. A range of different standards apply, from very low (serious issue to be tried) to very high (high degree of assurance), depending on the nature and practical effect of the interim remedy sought and the particular requirement of that remedy under consideration. (See Chapters 2 and 7.)	In all applications there is a hurdle of very high standard of proof on the applicants or whosoever is initiating the applications; see 11.97–11.107.
Discharge of interim orders	1) If interim remedy is granted without notice, respondent has right to apply to the court which granted it to set it aside. 2) Third parties may also apply to vary or discharge orders that affect them. 3) If order permits, respondent can discharge injunction by providing security or by offering undertaking to the court. 4) Otherwise, and where interim remedy is granted on notice, respondent must seek permission to appeal. (See Chapters 2 and 7.)	1) Under certain circumstances, interim orders can be discharged; see Chapter 3, 3.287–3.288. 2) An applicant's liability to file for a discharge; see Chapter 3, 3.289–3.291. 3) A respondent provides countersecurity with an applicant's consent in IP disputes; see Chapter 8, 8.143. 4) A respondent provides countersecurity in non-IP disputes; see Chapter 8, 8.144–8.148.

The time limit and renewal of interim orders	The order will state its duration, which may be for a specific time or until a specified event, e.g. judgment or further order. (See Chapters 2 and 7.)	No statutory time limit is prescribed, so the expiry of the renewal time is uncertain; see Chapter 8, 8.159–8.167.
Substantive remedies: compensation	At the discretion of the court, the applicant may be ordered to compensate the respondent for proven losses pursuant to its undertaking in damages. (See Chapters 2 and 7.)	1) The scope of compensation to the injured party; see Chapter 3, 3.296–3.297. 2) The non-fault liability principle in IP disputes; see Chapter 8, 8.168–8.171. 3) The fault-based liability in non-IP disputes; see Chapter 8, 8.175.
Costs	At the discretion of the court. The general rule is that the loser pays the winner's costs. (See Chapters 2 and 7.)	1) Intellectual property application fee between RMB 1,000 and RMB 5,000; for details, see Chapter 8, 8.177–8.180. 2) Non-IP application fee: uncertainty in practice, but by reference to IP application fee; for details, see Chapter 8, 8.181–8.184. 3) The underlying other fees such as storage fee, custodian fee, appraisal fee and transport fee, insurance fee and lawyer's fee; see Chapter 3, 3.197–3.215. 4) The burden of the legal costs; see Chapter 3, 3.216–3.221.

TABLE 11.5 Comparative analysis (post-action) – interim injunctions (England & Wales) v behaviour preservation measures (China)

	English law	*Chinese law*
Purpose	Refer to Table 11.4.	To compel a respondent "to do" or "not to do" certain things, so as to ensure that the enforcement of court's judgment or the arbitral award remains achievable, or preventing loss of parties concerned; see Chapter 8, 8.55–8.56.
Legal tests to obtain interim orders	Refer to Table 11.4.	1) "Urgent" circumstances in all disputes for an urgent order; see Chapter 8, 8.104–8.114 and Chapter 6, between 6.76 and 6.85. 2) "Irreparable harms" in all disputes for an urgent order; see Chapter 8 8.115–8.120 and Chapter 6 between 6.76–6.85. 3) "Stabilization right" in IP disputes; see Chapter 8, 8.121–8.126. 4) "Balance of interests" and "protection of public interests" in IP disputes; see Chapter 8, 8.127–8.134. 5) Security requested by courts, if any; see Chapter 8, 8.138–8.142. 6) To examine "whether a future judgment becomes impossible or difficult to enforce", or "whether the respondent's conduct or other reasons may cause the loss or damage to the applicant"; see Chapter 8, 8.101–8.103 and 8.136.
Security to be provided by an applicant to obtain interim orders	Refer to Table 11.4.	By reference to the rules in pre-action behaviour preservation security in Table 11.4.
Countersecurity of respondents	Refer to Table 11.4.	By reference to the rules in pre-action behaviour preservation countersecurity in Table 11.4.
Defences available to the respondents	Refer to Table 11.4.	By reference to the rules in pre-action behaviour preservation security in Table 11.4.

Procedure for interim hearings	Refer to Table 11.4.	1) Inquiry procedure for an application seeking IP behaviour preservation; see Chapter 8, 8.149–8.154. 2) No mandatory requirement to have interim hearings in non-IP disputes; see Chapter 8, 8.155–8.156. 3) In practice, the procedure for interim hearings in maritime disputes; see Chapter 8, 8.157.
Burden and standard of proof	Refer to Table 11.4.	In all applications there is a hurdle of very high standard of proof on the applicants or whosoever is initiating the applications; see 11.97–11.107.
Discharge of interim orders	Refer to Table 11.4.	1) Under certain circumstances, interim orders can be discharged; see Chapter 3, 3.287–3.288. 2) A respondent provides countersecurity with an applicant's consent in IP disputes; see Chapter 8, 8.143. 3) A respondent provides countersecurity in non-IP disputes; see Chapter 8, 8.144–8.148.
The time limit and renewal of interim orders	Refer to Table 11.4.	No statutory time limit, so the expiry of the renewal order is uncertain; see Chapter 8, 8.159–8.167.
Substantive remedies: compensation	Refer to Table 11.4.	1) The scope of the compensation for the injured party; see Chapter 3, 3.296–3.297. 2) The non-fault liability principle in IP disputes; see Chapter 8, 8.168–8.171. 3) The fault-based liability in non-IP disputes; see Chapter 8, 8.175.
Costs	Refer to Table 11.4.	1) IP application fee between RMB 1,000 and RMB 5,000; for details, see Chapter 8, 8.177–8.180. 2) Non-IP application fee: uncertainty in practice, but by reference to IP application fee; for details, see Chapter 8, 8.181–8.184. 3) The underlying other fees such as storage fee, custodian fee, appraisal fee and transport fee, insurance fee and lawyer's fee; see Chapter 3, 3.197–3.215. 4) The burden of proving the legal costs; see Chapter 3, 3.216–3.221.

(Shen) [2014] No 3).[95] In the IP behaviour preservation measures, apart from the legal tests stated above, the Interpretations of IP Behaviour Preservation 2018 stipulates that judges need to ascertain whether the requirements of "urgent circumstances" and "irreparable harms" can be satisfied[96] and whether the subject matter of the protection in a behaviour preservation measure belongs to the "right of the stabilization"[97] and does not impact on public policy,[98] before they can grant the IP behaviour preservation orders. It must be emphasised that this Interpretation does not require judges to look into the merits of the case, but in pre-action IP preservations, the SPC has instructed the lower courts' judges to consider the prevailing merits of the case, before they grant behaviour preservation orders.[99]

11.35 From the above analysis, it is likely that on similar facts, the same applicant will be able to obtain an interim injunction under English law, while the same applicant will be unsuccessful in China in obtaining behaviour preservation measures. One major reason is that some Chinese judges will evaluate carefully the merits of the overall dispute, in particular, in applications seeking IP behaviour preservation measures.[100] Although in recent years, the "public interests" evaluation in commercial disputes has not been highlighted, *Provisions of the Supreme People's Court on Several Issues Concerning the Application of Law in Cases Involving the Review of Behaviour Preservation in Intellectual Property Disputes* (Fa Shi [2018] No 21) provides the requirement of "public interest". Even if this requirement is not applied widely, the issue of "public interest" in commercial disputes still seems to lead to complications.[101]

11.36 In certain scenarios, undertakings and in some cases fortifications may be required to ensure compensation for losses that may be suffered by the respondents in the future as a result of the interim injunctions.[102] Additionally, undertakings are mandatorily required in pre-action applications in England

95 These examples of local guidance will be referred hereinafter as Provisions on Shanghai Property Preservation 2017 and Procedure on Hunan Property Preservation 2015.

96 Refer to Chapter 8, 8.104–8.114 for the test of "Urgent circumstances" that the applicants must overcome in the courts; refer also to Chapter 8, 8.115–8.120 for the test of "irreparable harms" that the applicants must overcome in the courts.

97 Refer to Chapter 8, 8.121–8.126.

98 Refer to Chapter 8, 8.127–8.134.

99 Xiaoming Song, Chuang Wang, Junli Xia and Guimei Lang, 'Understanding and Application of *Provisions of the Supreme People's Court on Several Issues Concerning the Application of Law in Cases Involving the Review of Behaviour Preservation in Intellectual Property Disputes*' (2019) 7 The People's Judicature (Applied) 19, 23.

100 Refer to Chapter 8, 8.102–8.137. In general, IP disputes are very complex and accordingly, the courts have stipulated additional requirements to evaluate the behaviour preservation applications.

101 Refer to Chapter 1, 1.20 and 1.105; see also, Article 13 of the CPL 1991 (as amended until 2020), where principle of good faith is enshrined in the CPL 1991.

102 Refer to Chapter 2, 2.118–2.119.

& Wales.[103] However, in pre-action applications under Chinese law, mandatory security in non-maritime disputes needs to be furnished pursuant to Article 101 of the CPL 1991 (as amended until 2020),[104] while in post-action applications, the requirement of security will largely depend on the court's discretionary power in light of Article 100 of the CPL 1991 (as amended until 2020).[105]

11.37 Conversely, in maritime disputes, regardless of whether such applications are at the pre-action or post-action stage, applicants' obligation to furnish security will be dependent on the exercise of discretionary power by the courts.[106] Nonetheless, under certain circumstances, the Chinese courts may not request security even if Article 100 of CPL 1991 (as amended until 2020) provides for a need to obtain security.[107] In addition, in legal practice, it has been observed that many Chinese judges, depending on the exercise of discretionary power, are inclined to seek security from applicants even in post-action applications, especially for applications seeking property preservation measures.[108] However, in such instances, the Chinese courts will not insist on the full amount of security, which is generally a norm for pre-action preservation applications.[109] In England and Wales, the same rules regarding undertakings and security apply to discretionary interim remedies in maritime claims as to any other type of claim; but an applicant for a warrant of arrest of a ship is not required to provide either.[110]

11.38 The authors submit that the onerous requirements to furnish adequate security with applications in China can seriously affect the cash flow of businesses of applicants. These applicants are already affected by the behaviour of the respondents. However, the onerous requirements are a bit diluted owing to the fact that property liability insurance is widely accepted by the courts during applications seeking property preservation measures. In spite of this, it is still arguable that the Chinese jurisdiction is a more respondent-friendly jurisdiction as compared to the English jurisdiction.

11.39 *Provisions of the Supreme People's Court on Several Issues Concerning the Application of Law in Cases Involving the Review of Behaviour Preservation in Intellectual Property Disputes* (Fa Shi [2018] No 21) expressly stipulates that the inquiry procedure should be conducted by Chinese judges and such inquiry process is similar to the interim hearing

103 Refer to Chapter 5, 5.19.

104 See Article 101 of the CPL 1991 (as amended until 2020); refer to Chapter 3, 3.130–3.131.

105 See Article 100 of the CPL 1991 (as amended until 2020); refer to Chapter 3, 3.132.

106 See Special Maritime Procedure Law of the People's Republic of China 2000, Articles 16, 55 and 66; refer Chapter 3, 3.134–3.135.

107 Refer to Chapter 3, 3.187–3.192.

108 Refer to Chapter 6, 6.120.

109 Refer to Chapter 6, 6.121–6.122.

110 Refer to Chapter 5, 5.14.

except in certain circumstances.[111] As far as a behaviour preservation application in a non-IP dispute is concerned, there is no clear guidance available to stakeholders and even to courts concerning the requirement to conduct an inquiry process for the parties before the behaviour preservation order can be granted.[112] On the other hand, in England & Wales, interim injunctions can be obtained via telephone and so forth in urgent cases involving without notice applications.[113] However, interim hearings may be required for the renewal or setting aside of urgent orders within seven days.[114] But in many such interim orders, the co-operation of the respondents will be required in both jurisdictions, and therefore, *ex-parte* hearings are less likely.

11.40 In England & Wales, the merits of civil/commercial disputes are usually only considered in detail in exceptional cases.[115] The flexibility shown by English judges in granting interim injunctions has been admired by international stakeholders.[116] However, English judges will evaluate "whether a serious question to be tried" is present in the overall dispute to avoid granting interim injunctions for hopeless claims.[117] On the other hand, in China, *Provisions of the Supreme People's Court on Several Issues Concerning the Application of Law in Cases Involving the Review of Behaviour Preservation in Intellectual Property Disputes* (Fa Shi [2018] No 21) does not expressly require judges to look at the merits of the case, but in pre-action IP preservation applications, the SPC requires judges to consider the merits of the case.[118] Whether judges will consider the merits of the case before granting behaviour preservation measures in non-IP disputes is not well-defined. However, in legal practice, due to jurisprudential reasons, Chinese judges are likely to consider the merits of the case in considerable detail.[119]

11.41 In China, civil lawsuits must be commenced within 30 days of the grant of pre-action behaviour preservation orders; otherwise, the preservation order will be discharged. In England & Wales, there is no such

111 *Provisions of the Supreme People's Court on Several Issues Concerning the Application of Law in Cases Involving the Review of Behaviour Preservation in Intellectual Property Disputes* (Fa Shi [2018] No 21), Article 5; refer to Chapter 8, 8.149–8.154; and reference to "certain circumstances" will be those urgent scenarios, where analysis needs to be carried by courts for possible impacts arising from the enforcement of the potential preservation orders.

112 Refer to Chapter 8, 8.155.

113 Refer to Chapter 2, 2.96(e).

114 Refer to Chapter 2, 2.106.

115 Refer to Chapter 7, 7.14, 7.26, 7.32, 7.37–7.39.

116 Refer to 11.108–11.114 for discussion in detail on discretionary power of judges in particular in the comparative context between both jurisdictions.

117 Refer to Chapter 7, 7.13–7.15.

118 Xiaoming Song, Chuang Wang, Junli Xia and Guimei Lang, 'Understanding and Application of *Provisions of the Supreme People's Court on Several Issues Concerning the Application of Law in Cases Involving the Review of Behaviour Preservation in Intellectual Property Disputes*' (2019) 7 The People's Judicature (Applied) 19, 23.

119 Refer to 11.97–11.107.

requirement as to time limits. However, judges will require an undertaking to that effect.[120]

11.42 Interim injunctions as a procedural remedy have matured over the years in English jurisdiction, whereas the behaviour preservation remedy is a very new remedy in China. As a result, it is likely that the experience of judges in dealing with applications seeking behaviour preservation measures in China is still a work in progress.[121]

Comparative Analysis – Search Orders (England & Wales) v Preservation of Evidence Measures (China)

11.43 The very apparent similarities and differences between search orders in English law and evidence preservation measures in Chinese law on the key parameters are delineated in the tables for both stages – pre-action and post-action. Readers are guided to Table 11.6 and Table 11.7 for comparative analysis of the pre-action and post-action stages between the interim measures for both jurisdictions.

11.44 Under English law, a search order may be granted for the purpose of securing the preservation of evidence, property or both, to prevent the respondent from altering, destroying or hiding such evidence or property.[122] Under Chinese law, the purpose of the evidence preservation measure is to prevent the possibility of destruction of evidence or failing to collect evidence in the future during the proceedings.[123] Generally speaking, search orders in England and Wales are a much wider procedural remedy than the preservation of evidence measures in China. However, in order to address the issue of difficulty in collating evidence, Chinese law provides for two supplementary rules – the disclosure of documentary evidence[124] and collecting evidence by courts.[125] These two supplementary rules can be regarded as alternative remedies available to applicants. English law provides the courts with a wide range of powers to compel the disclosure and production of documents and evidence as part of the court's case management powers, which it may exercise alongside the power to grant emergency relief such as search orders or during the ordinary course of litigation. These case management powers are generally not regarded as interim remedies.[126]

120 Refer to Chapter 2, 2.123(a).

121 Refer to Chapter 1, 1.82–1.83, for discussion of the fact that the behaviour preservation remedy is a very new interim measure in China.

122 Refer to Chapter 9, 9.22.

123 Refer to Chapter 10, 10.14–10.17.

124 Refer to Chapter 10, 10.98–10.106; it is worth noting that in IP disputes the disclosure order is not simply limited to the documentary evidence; refer to Chapter 10, 10.107–10.109.

125 Refer to Chapter 10, 10.110–10.120.

126 Refer to Chapter 2, 2.43, 2.45, 2.47 (in relation to CPR Part 31).

TABLE 11.6 Comparative analysis (pre-action) – search orders (England & Wales) v preservation of evidence measures (China)

	English law	*Chinese law*
Purpose	To secure the preservation of evidence, property or both, to prevent the respondent from altering, destroying or hiding such evidence or property. (See Chapters 2 and 9.)	To prevent the possibility of destruction of evidence or failure to collate evidence in future; see Chapter 10, 10.14–10.17.
Legal tests to obtain interim orders	1) Extremely strong prima facie case on the merits of the underlying claim. 2) Very serious damage, actual or potential, which will be avoided by the grant of the order. 3) Clear evidence that the respondent has important material or evidence in his possession. 4) Real possibility that the material or evidence may be destroyed, hidden or removed. 5) Order will not cause disproportionate harm. (See Chapters 2 and 9.)	1) Preliminary procedural examination; see Chapter 10, 10.30–10.41. 2) "Urgent" circumstances; see Chapter 10, 10.42–10.46. 3) Principle of the minimum impact on the respondents' interests; see Chapter 10, 10.47–10.51. 4) "Likelihood of destruction of the evidence" or "possibility of failing to obtain evidence in future"; see Chapter 10, 10.82. 5) Requirements for IP evidence preservation; see Chapter 10, 10.83–10.85. 6) Security under certain circumstances; see Chapter 10, 10.126–10.130.
Security to be provided by an applicant to obtain interim orders	1) Undertaking in damages to the respondent and, at the court's discretion, to third parties. 2) At the court's discretion, fortification of undertaking by provision of security in cash or another form acceptable to the court. 3) Where required by the supervising solicitor in return for his agreeing to act, an indemnity and/or security in a form acceptable to the supervising solicitor. (See Chapters 2 and 9.)	1) As a general rule, no mandatory security needs to be furnished by the applicants; see Chapter 10, 10.121. 2) The court's discretionary power to request security in IP and maritime disputes; see Chapter 10, 10.122–10.125. 3) Requirement to furnish security is mandatory under certain circumstances; see Chapter 10, 10.126–10.130. 4) Types of security; see Chapter 3, 3.139–3.141. a) Property security; see Chapter 3, 3.142–3.153. b) Cash security; see Chapter 3, 3.154–3.159. c) A letter of guarantee; see Chapter 3, 3.160–3.186.

		5) Amount of security; see Chapter 10, 10.131–10.134. 6) Exemptions from providing security; see Chapter 3, 3.187–3.193.
Countersecurity of respondents	Not applicable. (See Chapters 2 and 9.)	No countersecurity system; see Chapter 3, 3.136.
Defences available to respondents	Respondent may apply to set aside order made without notice, by demonstrating that any of the requirements for granting the interim remedy are not made out, or on discretionary grounds including the applicant's failure to give full and frank disclosure on the without notice application. (See Chapters 2 and 9.)	Respondents can argue: 1) The evidence preservation application cannot achieve its purpose; see Chapter 10, 10.14–10.15. 2) The principle of the minimum impact cannot be satisfied; see Chapter 10, 10.47–10.51. 3) In IP disputes, several points as to requirements for IP evidence preservation can be in favour of respondents; see Chapter 10, 10.83–10.85.
Procedure for interim hearings	Standard procedures apply where application is not urgent. On urgent applications, the court may dispense with most procedural requirements. (See Chapters 2 and 9.)	No mandatory requirement to conduct interim hearings.
Burden and standard of proof	Applicant bears burden of proof. Standard is 1) Extremely strong prima facie case on the merits. 2) Clear evidence that the respondent has important material or evidence in his possession. 3) Real possibility that the material or evidence may be destroyed, hidden or removed. (See Chapters 2 and 9.)	In all applications there is a hurdle of very high standard of proof on the applicants or whosoever is initiating the applications; see 11.97–11.107.

(*Continued*)

TABLE 11.6 *(Continued)*

	English law	*Chinese law*
Discharge of interim orders	1) If interim remedy is granted without notice, respondent has right to apply to the court which granted it to set it aside. 2) Third parties may also apply to vary or discharge orders that affect them. 3) Respondent can discharge freezing injunction by providing security. 4) Otherwise, and where interim remedy is granted on notice, respondent must seek permission to appeal. (See Chapters 2 and 9.)	1) Under certain circumstances, an order can be discharged; see Chapter 3, 3.287–3.288. 2) An applicant's liability to file a discharge of interim order; see Chapter 3, 3.289–3.291. 3) After cross-examination; see Chapter 10, 10.137–10.138.
The time limit and renewal of interim orders	The order will state any applicable time limits for executing the order. (See Chapters 2 and 9.)	No statutory time limit, so the expiry of the renewal of order is uncertain; see Chapter 10, 10.136.
Substantive remedies: compensation	At the discretion of the court, the applicant may be ordered to compensate the respondent for proven losses pursuant to its undertaking in damages. (See Chapters 2 and 9.)	1) The scope of the compensation to the injured party; see Chapter 3, 3.296–3.297. 2) The fault-based liability principle; see Chapter 10, 10.141. 3) Principle of common evidence; see Chapter 10, 10.142. 4) Causative link and burden of proof; see Chapter 10, 10.143–10.145. 5) Actual property damages; see Chapter 10, 10.146–10.149.
Costs	At the discretion of the court. The general rule is that the loser pays the winner's costs. (See Chapters 2 and 9.)	1) Application fee: RMB 30. 2) The underlying other fees such as storage fee, custodian fee, appraisal fee and transport fee, insurance fee and lawyer's fee; see Chapter 3, 3.197–3.215. 3) The burden of legal costs; see Chapter 3, 3.216–3.221.
Other options to obtain evidence	1) Doorstep delivery up order. 2) Imaging order. 3) Other forms of disclosure order. (See Chapters 2 and 9.)	1) Evidence preservation by notary offices; see Chapter 10, 10.57–10.63. 2) Online preservation using blockchain technology; see Chapter 10, 10.64–10.69.

TABLE 11.7 Comparative analysis (post-action) – preservation of evidence (England & Wales) v preservation of evidence measures (China)

	English law	*Chinese law*
Purpose	Refer to Table 11.6.	To prevent the possibility of destruction of evidence or failure to collate evidence in future; see Chapter 10, 10.14–10.17.
Time limit for filing an application	Refer to Table 11.6.	1) For a general rule; see Chapter 10, 10.70–10.71. 2) Statutory time limit; see Chapter 10, 10.72–10.77. 3) Agreed time limit; see Chapter 10, 10.78–10.80.
Legal tests to obtain interim orders	Refer to Table 11.6.	1) General requirements; see Chapter 10, 10.82. 2) Preliminary procedural examination; see Chapter 10, 10.30–10.41. 3) Principle of the minimum impact on the respondents' interests; see Chapter 10, 10.47–10.51. 4) Requirements for IP evidence preservation; see Chapter 10, 10.83–10.85. 5) Security under certain circumstances; see Chapter 10, 10.126–10.130.
Security to be provided by an applicant to obtain interim orders	Refer to Table 11.6.	1) Mandatory security needs to be furnished by the applicants under certain circumstances; Chapter 10, 10.126–10.130. 2) Types of security; see Chapter 3, 3.139–3.141. a) Property security; see Chapter 3, 3.142–3.153. b) Cash security; see Chapter 3, 3.154–3.159. c) A letter of guarantee; Chapter 3, 3.160–3.186. 3) Amount of security; see Chapter 10, 10.131–10.134. 4) Exemptions from providing security; Chapter 3, 3.187–3.192.
Countersecurity of respondents	Refer to Table 11.6.	No countersecurity system; see Chapter 3, 3.136.
Defences available to respondents	Refer to Table 11.6.	Respondents can argue: 1) The evidence preservation application cannot achieve its purpose; see Chapter 10, 10.14–10.15. 2) The principle of the minimum impact cannot be satisfied; see Chapter 10, 10.47–10.51. 3) In IP disputes, several points as to requirements for IP evidence preservation can be in favour to respondents; see Chapter 10, 10.83–10.85.

(*Continued*)

TABLE 11.7 *(Continued)*

	English law	*Chinese law*
Procedure for interim hearings	Refer to Table 11.6.	No mandatory requirement.
Burden and standard of proof	Refer to Table 11.6.	In all applications there is a hurdle of a very high standard of proof on the applicants or whosoever is initiating the applications; see 11.97–11.107.
Discharge of interim orders	Refer to Table 11.6.	1) Under certain circumstances, the interim orders can be discharged; see Chapter 3, 3.287–3.288. 2) After cross-examination; see Chapter 10, 10.137–10.138.
The time limit and renewal of interim orders	Refer to Table 11.6.	No statutory time limit, so the expiry of the renewal is uncertain; see Chapter 10, 10.136.
Substantive remedies: compensation	Refer to Table 11.6.	1) The scope of the compensation to the injured party; see Chapter 3, 3.296–3.297. 2) The fault-based liability principle; see Chapter 10, 10.141. 3) Causative link and burden of proof; see Chapter 10, 10.143–10.145. 4) Actual property damages; see Chapter 10, 10.146–10.149. 5) Principles of common evidence; see Chapter 10, 10.142.
Costs	Refer to Table 11.6.	1) Application fee: RMB 30; see Chapter 10, 10.150–10.152. 2) The underlying other fees such as storage fee, custodian fee, appraisal fee and transport fee, insurance fee and lawyer's fee; see Chapter 3, 3.197–3.215. 3) The burden of proving legal costs; see Chapter 3, 3.216–3.221.
Other options to obtain evidence	Refer to Table 11.6.	1) Evidence preservation by notary offices; see Chapter 10, 10.57–10.63, 10.69. 2) Online preservation using blockchain technology; see Chapter 10, 10.64–10.69. 3) Applications seeking documentary evidence disclosure order; see Chapter 10, 10.98–10.106. 4) Applications seeking evidence disclosure order in IP disputes; see Chapter 10, 10.107–10.109. 5) Applications seeking collation of evidence by courts; see Chapter 10, (i) general rule (10.110–10.111), (ii) collecting evidence on the court's own initiative (10.112–10.113), (iii) maritime courts' power (10.114 - 10.115) and (iv) applicant's request (10.116–10.120).

11.45 Search orders, popularly called *Anton Pillar* orders, are orders that are rendered by judges after exercising a great deal of discretionary power.[127] They are available at both the pre-action and post-action stages. However, pursuant to the CPL 1991, until it was revised in 2012, the preservation of evidence was not available as a pre-action remedy in China. Before the 2012 revision to the CPL 1991, applicants routinely depended on notary public offices to achieve results similar to pre-action evidence preservation measures.[128] However, even after the 2012 revisions, the pre-action remedy via notary offices is still available and is quite popular with stakeholders.

11.46 In England and Wales until 2014, such remedy was available only at the High Court of London and not the County courts.[129] In China, such remedies are available in all courts.

11.47 In England and Wales a search order is only available if the applicant can show an extremely strong case on the merits, the risk of very serious damage if property or evidence is not preserved, clear evidence that the respondent has important material in his possession, a real possibility that the material will be destroyed, hidden or removed, and that any harm caused to the Respondent by a search order would not be disproportionate.[130] In China, the legal test to obtain evidence preservation measures is initially restricted to the preliminary procedural examination rather than the substantial examination of the evidence that needs preservation.[131] However, in the domain of maritime law disputes, judges and scholars have emphasised that evidence which requires preservation should have an evidential effect on the actual status of the case.[132] Following the preliminary procedural examination, the legal tests to obtain such measures must focus on the principle of the minimum impact on the respondents' interest,[133] "likelihood of destruction of the evidence" or "possibility of failing to obtain evidence in the future".[134] As for the pre-action application, one more requirement from the court is to examine whether the circumstances surrounding the applications are "urgent".[135] In IP disputes, the several legal tests are very detailed, but the general rules in such disputes are same as the general rules governing preservation measures.[136]

127 Refer to Chapter 9.

128 Refer to Chapter 10, 10.57.

129 Refer to Chapter 9, 9.7.

130 Refer to Chapter 9, 9.16.

131 The First Civil Division of the Supreme People's Court (ed), 'Understanding and Application of New Provisions of the Supreme People's Court on Evidence in Civil Procedures, Volume I' (People's Court Press 2020) 273; refer also to Chapter 10, 10.30–10.38.

132 Refer to Chapter 10, 10.39–10.41.

133 Refer to Chapter 10, 10.47–10.51.

134 Refer to Chapter 10, 10.81–10.97.

135 Refer to Chapter 10, 10.42–10.46.

136 Refer to Chapter 10, 10.83–10.85.

11.48 In England & Wales, there is a requirement that the evidence in support of an application for a search order take the form of a formal affidavit.[137] The applicant will also be required to give a series of onerous undertakings to the respondent, in damages and in relation to the use of material obtained as a result of the search. The search must also be supervised by a qualified independent solicitor, who is also required to give undertakings to the respondent in respect of his conduct, for which he will usually demand an indemnity from the applicant.[138] On the other hand, in China, pursuant to Article 26 of *Some Provisions of the Supreme People's Court on Evidence in Civil Procedures (2019 Amendment)* (Fa Shi [2001] No 33) (*superseded by* Fa Shi [2019]) ("Provisions on Evidence 2019"), it is not mandatory for the applicants to furnish security with pre-action or post-action applications; however in certain circumstances, security can still be requested by the courts.[139] In addition, in intellectual property and maritime disputes, the law empowers Chinese judges to determine whether or not applicants seeking pre-action evidence preservation measures should furnish security.[140]

11.49 In England and Wales, the nature of the search order and the very limited circumstances in which it is available mean that there is nothing a respondent can do to avoid it being granted and executed.[141] In addition, in China, the system of countersecurity does not apply to the evidence preservation measure.[142] Accordingly, respondents cannot depend on countersecurity to discharge the preservation of evidence orders in China.

11.50 There is a system of a supervisory solicitor and detailed guidelines in relation to the execution of search orders, to ensure that a search order is conducted in a fair and orderly manner, in accordance with the terms of the order, under the control of an independent officer of the court.[143] However, similar guidelines are missing for enforcing evidence preservation orders in China. Pursuant to Provisions on Evidence 2019, where the courts render preservation of evidence orders, the courts may request the parties or their lawyers to be present on the location of the evidence that needs to be preserved.[144] The purpose of requesting parties to be present at the location is to show the legality of the evidence collection procedure,[145] and this is quite dif-

137 Refer to Chapter 9, 9.46.

138 Refer to Chapter 9, 9.48–9.52.

139 Refer to Chapter 10, 10.126–10.130.

140 Refer to Chapter 10, 10.122–10.125.

141 Refer to Chapter 9 generally.

142 The First Civil Division of the Supreme People's Court (ed), 'Understanding and Application of New Provisions of the Supreme People's Court on Evidence in Civil Procedures Volume I' (People's Court Press 2020) 278.

143 Refer to Chapter 9, 9.37–9.38, 9.57–9.65.

144 *Some Provisions of the Supreme People's Court on Evidence in Civil Procedures (2019 Amendment)* (Fa Shi [2001] No 33) (*superseded by* Fa Shi [2019]), Article 27.

145 The First Civil Division of the Supreme People's Court (ed), 'Understanding and Application of New Provisions of the Supreme People's Court on Evidence in Civil Procedures

ferent from the English legal system of supervisory solicitors. Furthermore, in China, it is not necessary at all times to request the parties to applications and their lawyers to go to the scene.[146]

11.51 In England & Wales, in certain specific circumstances, applicants can also substitute search orders with cost-effective interim orders such as disclosure orders or orders against specific property for inspection or taking samples.[147] In China, the judicial interpretation provided the new rule of documentary evidence disclosure in 2015 and Provisions on Evidence 2019 stipulated detailed guidance.[148] However, applicants can only apply for orders against the defendants and third parties who may be involved in a civil/commercial dispute. Applicants cannot apply for such orders against outside third parties that may be in possession of evidence. Furthermore, the detailed guidance in relation to it has merely come into effect on 1 May 2020. The effects of the new rules can only be examined in the near future. Interim orders such as the *Norwich Pharmacal Order* obliging the third parties to a dispute to disclose the name of third party wrong-doers or Bankers Trust orders are available in England & Wales.[149]

Theory Relevant to Comparative Analysis of Interim Measures

Difference between Visible and Invisible Factors

11.52 It is the authors' contention that, although in the first part of this Chapter 11, the key similarities and differences along the selected parameters were delineated in tabular form, however, there are other *invisible factors and contexts* that can affect the grant of interim measures in these two jurisdictions. There are inherent dangers in analysing the similarities and differences along the selected parameters or relying only on the textual comparisons of laws and procedures as they exist in England & Wales and China.

Warning to Readers

11.53 Foreign lawyers will still need the assistance of local lawyers and in no way after reading this book should one feel that they know everything

Volume I' (People's Court Press 2020) 287.

146 ibid.

147 Refer to Chapter 2, 2.44(i), (j), 2.45.

148 *Interpretations of the Supreme People's Court on Application of the Civil Procedure Law of the People's Republic of China* (Fa Shi [2015] No 5) ("Interpretation of CPL 2015") (superceded by Fa Shi [2020] No 21), Article 112, *Some Provisions of the Supreme People's Court on Evidence in Civil Procedures (2019 Amendment)* (Fa Shi [2001] No 33) (*superseded by* Fa Shi [2019]), Articles 45–48; refer to Chapter 10, 10.98–10.109.

149 Refer to Chapter 2, 2.45.

about interim measures in another jurisdiction.[150] The reason for these warnings to readers is due to the fact that when comparing the laws in various jurisdictions, it is important to analyse the *sub-contexts* of the laws; such sub-contexts may be history, culture, language, evolution of the remedies, socio-cultural contexts and so forth.[151] In addition, the grant of interim measures in any jurisdiction requires the exercise of the discretionary power of judges, and therefore, these invisible factors and contexts can play a decisive role in the outcome of applications seeking interim measures.

Comparative Procedural Law Relevant to Interim Measures

11.54 There could be nuances in the language used for legislation and codes; it is the authors' contention that generally only a native speaker of that language living in that jurisdiction for years can clearly appreciate and clarify such nuances. In addition, there is always the possibility that there are no functional equivalents of concepts and terminologies in another jurisdiction to enable comparative analysis based entirely on terminology. To enable easy understanding of this issue, let us discuss it with an example. In the example, even within western jurisprudence, not all jurisdictions have a concept of pure economic loss, and a few others do not have this concept in law of tort.[152] There are similar issues in relation to other substantive and procedural issues, especially when divergences between English law and Chinese law are substantial. On one hand, English law is considered a pioneer in the development of common law and law of equity, while the Chinese jurisdiction is a socialist system with Chinese characteristics influenced by the civil law system, in particular, from the 1990s.[153]

11.55 The above highlighted issues are even more complicated when comparing the procedural laws between the two jurisdictions. In the comparison

---

150 Refer to Chapter 1, 1.12, where the authors warned the readers not to make assumptions about other jurisdictions based on legal practice in their own jurisdiction.

151 ibid 19–42. In relation to China, in fact, knowledge of any sub-contexts is impossible due to the size and constant changes within China; see also, Vivek Jain, *Insight into China through Comparative Analysis of Invisible Factors and Contexts – Common Law v. Chinese Law* (1st Edn, Notion Press 2019) 21–22.

152 See V V Palmer, 'From Lerotholi to Lando: Some Examples of Comparative Law Methodology' (2004) 4 (2) Global Jurist Frontiers 1, 17–18 <53.261-290. 10.1093/ajcl/53.1.261> accessed 15 November 2019. A renowned comparativist, Palmer used the example of the concept of pure economic loss to highlight the subtleness that is required in comparisons as the terminology may be different for the same issue even within western jurisdictions. When such substantial divergence could exist in concepts within substantive law amongst western jurisdiction, imagine how difficult it would be to compare procedural remedies between English law and Chinese law or between any two jurisdictions. It is submitted, in light of the fact that interim measures being procedural remedies; therefore the issue of pursuing comparative analysis of interim remedies from England & Wales with preservation measures from China will even be more difficult.

153 See Vivek Jain, *Insight into China through Comparative Analysis of Invisible Factors and Contexts – Common Law v. Chinese Law* (1st Edn, Notion Press 2019) 25.

of procedural laws, even the procedures within the courts must be analysed, and these procedures are at times centred on the administration of the courts and local practices within these courts that have evolved over the years. Within continent-sized China, courts' practices will vary from province to province so that similar applications seeking preservation measures can result in conflicting orders.[154] Alternatively, similar applications in courts can result in different measures being granted by local courts in China.[155] There is no equivalent of Practice Directions in China that would be applicable to all courts at all levels in all provinces. On the other hand, in England & Wales, there are succinct Practice Directions that are available and they are applied uniformly in courtrooms in England & Wales. However, as a matter of fact, the geographical area of England & Wales is limited as compared to China.

11.56 The practice of interim measures is even more complicated as this emanates in the procedural laws in both jurisdictions of England & Wales and China. In Chapter 1, the authors did consider the purpose of interim measures in both jurisdictions. Many purposes of interim measures in these two jurisdictions are similar, though the Chinese jurisdiction has additional reasons for which the Chinese courts may consider granting those pre-judgment remedies.[156] Even though the purposes are similar in both jurisdictions, it is important to note that the terminologies relevant for interim measures are different.[157] In essence, not only academics/research scholars, but also practitioners at times must analyse the issues and laws of another jurisdiction within the context of that jurisdiction's philosophy, culture, religion, language, evolution of substantive and procedural law, nuances and so forth. These contexts may even differ locally in the same jurisdiction.[158]

11.57 Similarly, as a jurisdiction, the reference point of England & Wales has always been property law and individual rights, whereas historically, the reference point of Chinese law and jurisdiction has always been state ownership and society.[159] It is the authors' contention that, without appreciating

---

154 For example, in the evidence preservation applications, the two conflicting orders are analysed in Chapter 10, 10.90–10.93.

155 For example, in an application seeking property preservation, one court rendered a property preservation order in Chapter 6, 6.35, while the other court rendered a behaviour preservation order on similar facts in Chapter 8, 8.97–8.99.

156 Refer to Chapter 1, 1.14–1.22.

157 Refer to Chapters 1, 2 and 3.

158 See Edward J Eberle, 'The Method and Role of Comparative Law' (2009) 8 (3) Wash U Global Stud L Rev 451, 453, 455 and 458–459. In this article, Eberle highlighted the need to dive deeper into various aspects of a foreign jurisdiction. This diving deep into understanding various facets was called cultural immersion, which is required of a researcher and was highlighted by comparativist Curran in Vivian Grosswald Curran, 'Cultural Immersion, Difference and Categories in U.S. Comparative Law' (1998) 46 (1) Am J Comp L 43 <www.jstor.org/stable/841076> accessed 24 October 2016. Curran was also quoted in Eberle on page 453, where it was highlighted that a comparativist needs to free themselves of "cognitive lock-in".

159 The comparativist approaches regarding reference points as expounded highlight the attitude of foreign jurisdictions towards law and assist in understanding the classification of

the reference points of jurisdictions, practicing lawyers and academics could have incorrect assumptions, patronising views, biases and in general half-hearted appreciation of other jurisdictions. The common law jurisdictions, in particular, are reluctant in general to carry out comparative law studies and in most universities in England & Wales, comparative law is not even taught as a subject on its own.

11.58 The comparison of substantive laws available in the two jurisdictions is relatively easier, but procedural law that supports the substantive law and its comparison creates its own issues.[160] Interim measures in almost all jurisdictions are a function of their procedural laws. The authors will discuss the key concepts that have been developed when comparing civil procedure systems, for example, a well-known comparativist expounded that in any jurisdiction, the civil process is an imitation of political, social and legal realities and the civil process within these jurisdictions will respond to and be affected by any changes in these realities.[161] These are the *invisible factors and contexts* that govern any jurisdiction, and they comprise current political philosophy, the origins of substantive law and procedural law, the development of jurisprudence, the concept of power, in particular, the discretionary power of judges, the willingness of judges to exercise their discretionary power, the training of judges, the development of judicial activities of judges, the legal philosophy of civil litigation, the philosophy of finding truth and so forth.[162]

groupings within legal families such as the common law family, civil law family, socialist law family and so forth; see J C Church and A B Edwards, 'Comparative Law/Comparative Method' in Hosten *et al* (eds), *Introduction to South African Law and Legal Theory* (Butterworths 1995) 1261–1270; see also, Vivek Jain, *Insight into China through Comparative Analysis of Invisible Factors and Contexts – Common Law v. Chinese Law* (1st Edn, Notion Press 2019) 25, for examination as to where exactly the Chinese legal system fits within the group of legal families. This issue regarding the Chinese legal system is a bit complicated as there have been influences from continental civil law jurisdictions from the 1990s along with socialist and Marxist-Leninist thoughts on the Chinese legal system from 1949. The issue is further complicated due to the influence of the traditional and ancient Chinese legal system on the current legal system (refer to concept of conservatism in fn 204 of this chapter). Therefore, comparative analysis of the common law system in England & Wales with China will span many features from different legal families.

160 Yikun Zhu, *Concise Chinese Law* (Law Press China 2003) 1, where the author clearly mentioned that "*substantive law is concerned with what, while procedural law is concerned with how*"; see also, Weizou Chen, *Chinese Civil Procedure and Conflict of Laws* (Tsinghua University Press 2011) 3 for examination of issues concerning the relationship between substantive law and procedural law.

161 Oscar G. Chase, 'Some Observations on the Cultural Dimension in Civil Procedure Reform' (1997) 45 (4) Am J Comp Law 861, 862. Oscar attempted to highlight the subtle relationship between society and civil procedure law, while at the same time gave due recognition in this respect to the ideas of famous proceduralists such as Piero Calamandrei and Chiovenda.

162 Vivek Jain, 'Sufficiency of Court's Pre-Judgment Power in Commercial Litigation: A Comparative Study Assessing the Law and Practice in PRC and England & Wales' (PhD Thesis, China University of Political Science and Law 2017), where the effects of invisible factors and contexts on the interim measures in legal practice were compared for England & Wales

11.59 In order to discuss the comparative civil procedure relevant to this book, it is important to appreciate from the start that the cultural dimensions of the civil procedure will affect the practice of procedural law; for example, even local practices in courtrooms can vary from region to region even within a jurisdiction. A well-known comparativist has discussed that it is very difficult to document culture, but it is a representation of the collective personality of a group of people within a boundary.[163]

Discretionary Power and Human Angle – A Key Factor Relevant to Interim Measures

11.60 In the context of interim measures, it is important to appreciate the concept of the discretionary power of judges and the way that judges exercise their discretionary power. Since the judges are involved in granting these interim remedies and preservation orders through the exercise of their discretionary power, there is clearly a human angle that is relevant to the issue of interim measures. This human angle that becomes relevant through the exercise of discretionary power could in fact bring out the judges' biases, perceptions, assumptions, culture, methodology of their training, concept of separation of power, political philosophy and so forth. As a result, the function of invisible factors and contexts needs to be analysed minutely in order to carry out any comparative studies that are relevant not just for academics, but also for legal practitioners in the context of interim measures.[164] The scope of the book does not allow consideration of all such invisible factors and contexts or discussion on any factor in considerable detail.[165] However, one particular invisible factor will be considered in detail a bit later;[166] that is, differences in judges' power in relation to their judicial activities such as the concept of burden and standards of proof and its relevance in the context of applications seeking interim remedies/preservation measures.

11.61 To conclude, in particular, in the context of comparative civil procedure law, Maxeiner has described how the two approaches are based on concepts of *functionalism* and *culturalism*. These two approaches to some extent represent the similarities and differences respectively among civil

---

and China. See also, Vivek Jain, *Insight into China through Comparative Analysis of Invisible Factors and Contexts – Common Law v. Chinese Law* (1st Edn, Notion Press 2019).

163 Oscar G Chase, 'Some Observations on the Cultural Dimension in Civil Procedure Reform' (1997) 45 (4) Am J Comp Law 861, 863.

164 Vivek Jain, *Insight into China through Comparative Analysis of Invisible Factors and Contexts – Common Law v. Chinese Law* (1st Edn, Notion Press 2019) 146–148.

165 See Vivek Jain, *Insight into China through Comparative Analysis of Invisible Factors and Contexts – Common Law v. Chinese Law* (1st Edn, Notion Press 2019), for theoretical study of invisible factors and contexts affecting common law system in England & Wales and Chinese law and detailed analysis of various invisible factors with examples.

166 Refer to 11.97–11.107 for examination of concept of standards of proof in both jurisdictions.

procedural systems.[167] In the context of the book, the concept of *functionalism* represents the purpose of interim measures in both England & Wales and China, whereas the concept of *culturalism* is represented by the invisible factors or cultural dimensions of the way such practice of interim measures has evolved in both jurisdictions. These invisible factors and contexts could also be additional reasons for similarities and differences between the pre-judgment remedies in both jurisdictions. These invisible factors and contexts lie in the background; therefore, they cannot be described with precision for any given set of circumstances in any jurisdiction. However, even though practitioners may be reluctant at times to appreciate them, those involved in cross-border litigations/arbitrations should recognise them in their legal practice. In particular, these invisible factors are relevant to all tasks carried out within the ambit of civil procedure of any jurisdiction, in particular, the grant of interim measures by judges.

Invisible Factors and Contexts – Comparative Analysis of Their Influence on Seeking Interim Measures from Courts

Effects on Legal Practice

11.62 The exercise of the discretionary power of judges is needed for the granting of interim measures that are available through civil procedural codes in both jurisdictions. The authors will consider various invisible factors and contexts acting in the background that lawyers qualified in a particular jurisdiction usually take for granted in that particular jurisdiction; however, the impact of different invisible factors and contexts cannot be recognised and appreciated that easily in another jurisdiction. The authors have compared these factors systematically in the context of interim remedies/preservation measures in both jurisdictions.

11.63 Although the concept of invisible factors is a very complicated and immense area of study, the authors have attempted to discuss and apply briefly these invisible factors and contexts to issues of the granting of interim remedies and preservation remedies in legal practice.[168] If one were

167 See James R Maxeiner, 'Legal Methods as a Point of Reference for Comparative Studies of Procedural Law' (XIIIth World Congress on Procedural Law, Salvador Bahia, 16–22 September 2007) 2–3 <https://ssrn.com/abstract=1232579> accessed 18 November 2019, where he seems to highlight that the discussion of "*culturalism*" in the context of comparative civil procedure is in many ways the same concept as that of analysing the invisible factors and contexts in general comparative law.

168 Vivek Jain, 'Sufficiency of Court's Pre-Judgment Power in Commercial Litigation: A Comparative Study Assessing the Law and Practice in PRC and England & Wales' (PhD Thesis, China University of Political Science and Law 2017), where a study of comparative analysis of interim measures in both jurisdictions on visible factors was followed by a comparative analysis in detail on the invisible factors and contexts. see also, Vivek Jain, *Insight into China through Comparative Analysis of Invisible Factors and Contexts – Common Law v.*

to solely observe visible factors such as legislation, codes and legal practice and the customs of courts, then these invisible factors and contexts could also be reasons for observable similarities and differences between interim remedies in England & Wales and preservation measures in China on standard parameters within the visible factors as discussed in 11.3. These differences were analysed in 11.7–11.51. It is beyond the scope of this book to discuss in detail all the invisible factors and contexts. However, the authors have considered in the forthcoming paragraphs a few of the invisible factors and their impact on applications seeking interim remedies/preservation measures.

11.64 Any practising lawyer who does not appreciate the impact of invisible factors and contexts in a foreign jurisdiction and in fact, relies solely upon legislations, codes, practice directions, local courts' guidance documents, caselaw and precedents, should be prepared for surprises in foreign jurisdictions. Therefore, in any cross-border litigation and arbitration when encountering foreign jurisdictions, comparative analysis pursued by taking into account the invisible factors and contexts can assist lawyers and legal consultants in moulding their legal strategy.

Invisible Factor of the Historical Evolution of Substantive and Procedural Law

11.65 First, common law has been in existence in England & Wales from the middle of the 11th century and has gradually evolved into a large body of law. The pre-judgment remedies, which are in the category of discretionary remedies, were developed over a long period of time. The principles of equity along with the intellect and willingness of common law judges to exercise their discretionary power over the years have a played a major role in the development of the interim remedies.[169] Civil procedure rules in England & Wales are ancient in origin, and the history of their evolution can be traced even to the Magna Carta, ACE 1215. However, over the years civil procedure rules have become complicated and the size of the famous *White Book* for Civil Procedure Rules is increasing even after the Woolf Reforms 1999.[170] This development has resulted in increased legal costs even for short interim hearings for parties that are seeking interim remedies in their civil/commercial disputes.

Chinese Law (1st Edn, Notion Press 2019), in order to analyse invisible factors at great length from the perspective of comparative law.

169 Refer to Chapter 2, 2.4–2.5, 2.38, 2.67(b), 2.71, 2.121; Chapter 5, 5.20; Chapter 7, 7.4–7.11; Chapter 9, 9.10, 9.16. Refer also to Chapter 1, 1.31–1.75.

170 See Déirdre Dwyer, 'What Is the Meaning of CPR r 1.1(1)?' in Dé irdre Dwyer (ed) *The Civil Procedure Rules Ten Years on* (Reprinted 2012, Oxford University Press 2009) 68.

11.66 On the other hand, ancient China, even though it was an economic power for centuries, focussed mainly on penal codes.[171] Trivial civil procedure law that was developed over centuries was in fact just developed out of concern to maintain harmony in society and was there to prohibit litigation. In fact, the first comprehensive substantive body of law in centuries was only introduced as recently in 1986 in the field of civil law (*Minfa Tongze*) describing various possible causes of action. In fact, in 2017, the more developed civil law, titled the General Principles of Civil Law (*Minfa Zongze*), was promulgated.[172] Currently, the first comprehensive and unified Civil Code just came into effect on 1 January 2021. Accordingly, the authors have discussed its effects on seeking preservation measures under procedural law in Chapters 6, 8 and 10. In terms of procedural law, a major body of civil procedure law was introduced in China as recently in 1991, which was majorly revised in 2012 and last amended in 2017, even if the Civil Procedure Law (for Trial Implementation) was issued as early as in 1982.[173]

11.67 From the above, if analysed carefully, the relevant Chinese law in the context of interim measures is very recent in its origins, as compared to the English law; it also has a less complicated body of procedure rules. However, it is also true that the current CPL 1991 (as amended until 2020), its *Interpretations of the Supreme People's Court on Application of the Civil Procedure Law of the People's Republic of China* (Fa Shi [2015] No 5) (superseded by Fa Shi [2020] No 21) and other relevant local guidance from local courts that are scattered all over can be overwhelming and complicated. The effects can be seen from the fact that the practice of such law and rules in

171 Geoffrey MacCormack, *The Spirit of Traditional Chinese Law*, The Spirit of the Laws (University of Georgia Press 1996) 8. MacCormak at page 23 further highlighted that most of the private or civil law in Chinese legal history was contained in *unofficial law*. He highlighted that throughout Chinese legal history, the main focus was on Penal Codes and on importance of family relationships. However, it is surprising that even within the family relationship, the law regarding inheritance, property and commerce in society was not as detailed as one would have expected in a substantial economy. The author highlighted that whatever rules that were present in ancient Chinese society, such as for a use of land, regulation of debt and transactions through the markets, were historically out of concern for the maintenance of good order in Chinese society.

172 The General Principles of Civil Law of the People's Republic of China (*Minfa Tongze*) was passed by the Fourth Session of the Sixth National People's Congress on 21 April 1986 and came into effect on 1 July 1987. The General Rules of the Civil Law of the PR China 2017 came into effect on 1 October 2017. Both laws were abolished after the Civil Code 2020 came into effect on 1 January 2021. In addition, the new General Rules will have priority over the earlier rules; see also, Albert H Y Chen, 'The Developing Chinese Law and the Civil Law Tradition' (1996) China Review 29, 31 <www.jstor.org/stable/23453139> accessed 24 September 2016, where the development of civil law and traditions was analysed in great detail.

173 Between 1949 and 1982, the Committee of Legal Affairs of Central Government and the SPC issued the Draft of General Rules of Civil Procedure 1950, the Civil Trial Procedure (draft) 1957 and Provisions for People's Court Civil Trial Procedure 1979, but these procedural codes were not comprehensive and were also not applied very well in legal practice throughout China; refer to Chapter 1, 1.82–1.103 for the evolution of civil procedure in detail.

courts differs from court to court in the different provinces in continent-size China, thereby bringing uncertainty for litigants/stakeholders. This book has attempted to bring the scattered guidance into one place, with regard to the practice of preservation measures.

11.68 One of the key principles that Chinese courts will always consider is that any grant of pre-judgment remedies does not fall foul of the "public interests" issue.[174] It is arguable as to why any court, anywhere in any jurisdiction, would consider such a principle in commercial and civil cases. In theory, there is always a need for the issues to remain only between the parties to the commercial/civil dispute and this issue of the need to include the influence of "public interests" seems to introduce a great amount of uncertainty for stakeholders. Foreign lawyers cannot fully anticipate such factors during the planning stage, but they should be prepared for such issues. This is also one of the reasons that obtaining preservation measures remains relatively difficult in China, and therefore, China can rightly be considered as an example of a respondent-/defendant-friendly jurisdiction. Nonetheless, in recent years, in commercial disputes, the role of the concept of "public interests" seems to be on the decline.

11.69 In addition, a few of the preservation measures were introduced just recently in 2012,[175] so in continent-size China, it may take some time before these interim measures are fully developed, and judges throughout China are consistent in their approach to applying the relevant rules and interpretations. Another factor is that local court rules and practices may differ from court to court in the different provinces.[176] In addition, there is not one thorough

174 Refer to Chapter 8, 8.127–8.134, for discussion with examples regarding the issues involving "public interests" in legal practice involving civil procedure. One of the reasons why the Chinese courts will always focus on public interests is primarily based on the principle of good faith that is enshrined in civil procedure law pursuant to Article 13 of the CPL 1991 (as amended until 2020). This principle forbids the courts, parties to a dispute and other involved parties from abusing the rights of the parties. Such abuses could have the potential to damage the state, public and other parties' interests. Accordingly, the issue of public interests turn out to be an important requirement and in a way is an additional invisible test to be passed before the preservation order can be rendered at all by the courts; see also, Shuju Ha and Yue Yu, *Interpretation of Civil Procedural System* (Intellectual Property Publishing House 2016) Section 1, Chapter II; Article 2 of Civil Procedural Law 1991 (amended until 2019) of China provides *inter alia* very similar objectives as *CPR 1998*, but with additional requirements that courts will have to consider the objectives of the civil procedural system in China: that *social and economic order* will be maintained and also *the smooth progress of socialist construction* will be guaranteed. These requirements could not be defined with precision and in the authors' view, in a way, are examples of extreme discretion available to the Chinese courts.

175 For example, the relevant codes for obtaining behaviour preservation in non-IP and maritime disputes (refer to Chapter 1, 1.88–1.90, Chapter 8, 8.7) along with provisions for seeking pre-action evidence preservation measures (refer to Chapter 10, 10.2–10.4) were provided recently in the 2012 revision to CPL 1991.

176 For example, in the context of burden of proof concerning preserved property's value, the different regional courts' guidance provides dissimilar views on this issue (refer to Chapter 6, 6.51–6.59). The other example is in respect to the behaviour preservation applications, whereby Shanghai and Hunan local courts have clarified that the requirements and prerequisites

Practice Direction that a lawyer can refer to in China, thereby making the task very complicated relative to the English jurisdiction for both judges and litigants to decipher the overall guidance or rules that will be applicable in one particular court in one particular province of China.[177] This book has attempted to fill the void caused by the lack of Practice Directions in China, in particular, for obtaining preservation measures.

11.70 Furthermore, in Chinese society, historically (over centuries) there has been distrust of litigation and lawyers, through the concept referred to as *sung kun*.[178] This may, to some extent, also explain why the Chinese jurisdiction is a more defendant-/respondent-friendly jurisdiction in the context of pre-judgment remedies. On the other hand, the common law has been developed inside courtrooms during arguments by barristers and questions from judges and thereafter judges feel confident to grant pre-judgment remedies; this is a quite distinct trait from that of China.[179] This feature seems to

---

for behaviour preservation measures are similar to those of property preservation measures, but other local courts elsewhere in China do not provide similar guidance. Therefore, how other local courts in China will resolve the issues arising from behaviour preservation applications is not clear to stakeholders. The lack of clarity is also due the fact that the main legislation, CPL 1991 (as amended until 2020), and the relevant interpretations are silent on such issues (refer to Chapter 8, 8.59).

177 Refer to Chapter 3, 3.5–3.26, where various source of laws in China were explored in detail.

178 See Geoffrey MacCormack, *The Spirit of Traditional Chinese Law*, The Spirit of the Laws (University of Georgia Press 1996) 10–11. For centuries, the development of civil law was neglected in ancient China; however the void was filled in 1986, when the General Principles of Civil Law 1986 was promulgated in China. It is argued that the lack of civil law for centuries could have been the result of the influence of Confucian jurisprudence on reflecting on one's conduct, and the general impetus to share resources between the people and accordingly a need to avoid civil disputes was justified historically. It was supplemented by a concept of "*Sung kun*", referred to as "litigation tricksters" or "pettifoggers" and as a result litigation of any kind was abhorred for centuries; see also, Cynthia Losure Baraban, 'Inspiring Global Professionalism: Challenges and Opportunities for American Lawyers in China' (1998) 73 (4) Ind L J 1247, 1252, where she discussed the philosophical reasons as to why lawyers were detested for centuries in China. In Mandarin, "Sung kun" is pronounced as "*Su Gun*".

179 Over the centuries, the personal independence of the judiciary has increased considerably and there is also a concept of separation of power of judiciary from the executive in England & Wales. This personal independence of the judiciary itself led to the development of judicial independence in England & Wales. On the other hand, in China, the Chinese judiciary is answerable to the National People's Congress or local provincial legislatures and strictly there is no concept of separation of power in China; see Art 67(6) of the *Constitution of PRC 1982* pursuant to which the Supreme People's Court is answerable to the National People's Congress; see also, Art 104 of the Constitution of PRC 1982 pursuant to which the People's Court is answerable to the Local People's Congress at the provincial level in the PRC; , Art 14 of CPL 1991 (as amended until 2020) provides for State Procuratorates with the authority to supervise trials. The system of Procuratorates has the power to interpret its own laws that are related to its own work and their work is not considered to be within the realm of the judiciary; see also, Margaret Woo, 'Law and Discretion in Contemporary Chinese Courts' (1999) 8 (3) Pacific Rim L & Pol'y J 581, 607, whereby it seems that the system comprising of Procuratorates may intervene in civil cases only when the state's interests are affected. In addition, there is a provision of supervision by the masses pursuant to Art 7(7) of *Judges Law 1995* (as revised in 2019) as part of the concept of democratic supervision *(mizhu jiandu)*. Accordingly, the National

explain why the English jurisdiction is a more applicant-/claimant-friendly jurisdiction.

11.71 It is to be appreciated that many laws are currently enforced in China by administrative organs of the legal system that are prone to unpredictability, and at times they may be inattentive. The system of supervision of judges and possible intervention by Procuratorates is discussed in detail in footnote 179 of this chapter. These features in China elevate the importance of issues such as impartial administration of justice along with principles of *judicial independence and judicial neutrality*.[180] These principles are needed by the stakeholders in any legal system, in particular, for resolving civil/commercial litigation, and are even more relevant in the context of the granting of preservation measures/interim remedies. Such invisible factors operating in China cannot be overlooked by foreign lawyers, even though there have been improvements in the system as can be seen from the rapid pace of reforms in the last few years.

Invisible Factor of the Historical Evolution of Injunctions and Preservation Measures

11.72 In England & Wales, injunctions were developed in the Chancery Courts as well as in the Court of Exchequer and Court of Requests, as these courts had equitable powers.[181] Further rules in relations to injunctions were developed in law of equity after a few years of a tussle with the common law courts, whereby a stage came where the power of courts of equity was reduced.[182] As a result of these developments over the years, it is characteristic of equitable remedies, and in particular, injunctions, that the courts have shown over the years a degree of flexibility[183] when granting them to customise them for the particular circumstances and taking into account the business environment surrounding the facts of the case before them.[184]

People's Congress (legislature) can seek a report from the system of Procuratorates and courts. At page 609, Woo highlighted that supervision of judges at multiple levels led to the situation in which Chinese judges are happy to remain embedded in administrative roles and accordingly seem to delegate decision-making to the adjudication committees within the court system. Therefore, the judges in Chinese courts submit themselves to the adjudication committees that in turn submit to Procuratorates. Procuratorates themselves submit to the National People's Congress. This process of multiple chains of command in relation to the working of Chinese courts is pursuant to Art 3 of the Constitution of PRC 1982 and is as a result of the principle *of democratic centralism* that is enshrined in the Constitution of China.

180 Huang Lie, 'Rule of Law in China: Ideal and Reality' in Buyun Li (eds), *Constitutionalism and China* (Law Press China 2006) 183–185.

181 David W Raack, 'A History of Injunctions in England before 1700' (1986) 61 (4) Ind LJ 539, 553–555 and 561 <www.repository.law.indiana.edu/cgi/viewcontent.cgi?article=2160&context=ilj> accessed 15 September 2019.

182 ibid 570–578 and 585.

183 ibid 570.

184 Refer to Chapter 1, 1.14–1.18.

11.73 It is important to appreciate that there are direct costs along with indirect costs of compliance that are associated with injunctions, and these can affect even the harmless activities of respondents.[185] Knowledge of the evolution of interim remedies historically and during the 1970s and 1980s[186] can certainly assist a good lawyer when seeking such interim remedies from the English courts.

11.74 On the other hand, in the relatively new legal system of China, the system of preservation measures is a few years old and has been developed largely due to China's accession to the World Trade Organization in 2001. In fact, newer preservation remedies were introduced in the legal system of China as recently in 2012 in CPL 1991 (as amended until 2020). This knowledge again would be useful to foreign lawyers in order to appreciate the invisible issues they may encounter in China in their applications seeking preservation measures.

Invisible Factor of Jurisprudence

11.75 Jurisprudence is a very wide topic and will be discussed briefly in respect of both jurisdictions.[187] In English law, the jurisprudence debate has always been between "*what law is*" and "*what law ought to be*".[188] On the other hand, a major debate in China for the last 2,400 years has been around Legalist jurisprudence (*Fa-Jia*) which provides a little flexibility to judges

185 Samuel L Bray, 'The System of Equitable Remedies' (2016) 63 (3) UCLA L Rev 532, 573.

186 Refer to Chapter 1, 1.44–1.75.

187 For further debate and comparative analysis of jurisprudence in both jurisdictions, see Vivek Jain, *Insight into China through Comparative Analysis of Invisible Factors and Contexts – Common Law v. Chinese Law* (1st Edn, Notion Press 2019) 99–106.

188 Gerald J Postema, 'Classical Common Law Jurisprudence (Part I)' (2002) 2 (2) OUCLJ 155; see also, Gerald J Postema, 'Classical Common Law Jurisprudence (Part II)' (2003) 3 (1) OUCLJ 1; see also, Lon L Fuller, *The Law in Quest of Itself* (Beacon Press 1940). Very briefly, in the beginning, the search was on for universal morality that could bind all the populace in terms of natural law. In practical terms, it was then understood on the basis of a social contract through the governance of rules between the governed and government. On the other end, there were positivists, who would not allow any space for morals or whether the enacted rules were liked by the populace. However, H L A Hart justified that the populace accept particular rules not due to sanctions but due to reason for their actions, and further he seemed to overlook and in fact tacitly approved the role of morals when judges are exercising their discretionary power in courtrooms; see also, H L A Hart, *The Concept of Law* (2nd Edn, Oxford University Press 1994); see also, Magna Carta 1215, Petition of Rights 1628, Habeas Corpus Act 1679 and Bill of Rights 1689 and legislations or declarations over centuries along with the development of jurisprudence from other Commonwealth countries, in particular due to the evolution of jurisprudence in the US which affected the underlying jurisprudence. Any further discussion on the topic is beyond the scope of the book. For further debate and comparative analysis of jurisprudence in both jurisdictions, see Vivek Jain, *Insight into China through Comparative Analysis of Invisible Factors and Contexts – Common Law v. Chinese Law* (1st Edn, Notion Press 2019), where the development of English jurisprudence was discussed for pursuing comparative analysis.

to circumvent the written law with a sanction-based approach built into the Chinese system.[189] This approach pursuant to Legalist jurisprudence was modified, to some extent, by Confucians' (*Ru-Jia*) approach over many centuries of regulating human behaviour. Confucians' approach was based on finding solutions based on compassion and benevolence (*ce yin zhi xin*), and social norms were considered higher than the written law.[190]

11.76 However, the Confucian approach also brought in within China for centuries a distaste for adversarial litigation, and it has been assumed that litigation can bring catastrophe (*song-ze zhong-xiong*).[191] Thus, a focus on issues of morality has been brought into legal practice in China over centuries and can be seen in principles such as good faith in the current civil procedural law.

11.77 Following the ancient traditions of Confucian jurisprudence spanning centuries, in current legislation, the moral standard for society has been codified into both substantive laws, such as the General Principles of Civil

189 Wejen Chang, 'Classical Chinese Jurisprudence and Development of Chinese Legal System' (2010) 2 (2) Tsinghua China L Rev 207, 250–261. In Legalist jurisprudence, all rules will come from the top (that is from the emperor); compassion and benevolence favoured by Confucians were to be discarded. There were two main proponents of this classical jurisprudence, that is, Yang Shang (390–338 BCE) and Fei Han (280–233 BCE). In this jurisprudence, the rules were to originate from the emperor, and there was no need for any discussion on morals and whether morals/compassion would govern any of these rules. The basic assumption in this jurisprudence was that humans are always looking for advantage and rules need to cater to the nature of humans. Any further discussion on this interesting topic is beyond the scope of the book; see also, Vivek Jain, *Insight into China through Comparative Analysis of Invisible Factors and Contexts – Common Law v. Chinese Law* (1st Edn, Notion Press 2019), where the development of the Chinese jurisprudence over the centuries has been discussed in great detail.

190 ibid 212–240. The main proponents of Confucian jurisprudence were Confucius (551–479 BCE), Mencius (390–305 BCE) and Xunzi (340–245 BCE). Briefly, the main characteristics *inter alia* of Confucians, who in fact predated Legalists, were – (1) emphasis on kindness, (2) emphasis on benevolence, (3) focussing on becoming a better persons, (4) the concept of morality will rank higher than any rules, (5) emphasis on focus on the good intention behind the rules, and (6) rulers need to lead by example. Any further discussion on this interesting topic is again beyond the scope of the book; see also, Vivek Jain, *Insight into China through Comparative Analysis of Invisible Factors and Contexts – Common Law v. Chinese Law* (1st Edn, Notion Press 2019), where the development of Chinese jurisprudence over the centuries has been compared systematically with the development in English jurisprudence.

191 ibid 217. Confucians' approach highlighted that the adversarial system is not the right way to resolve disputes within society. This approach had a profound effect over the years as it led to little development of civil law for centuries until in 1986 the General Civil Law was promulgated. In many ancient dynasties, the Confucian approach was preferred and civil servants at times would follow a mix of Legalist and Confucian approaches. In the current jurisprudence in China, the Communist and Marxist-Leninist philosophies have influenced the Chinese legal system along with Maoist philosophy where the collective good overrides the need of the individuals. The reasoning is that if the collective good were to increase, then the individuals within that collective would automatically benefit; see also, Ann D Jordan, 'Lost in Translation: Two Legal Cultures, Common Law Judiciary and the Basic Law of Hong Kong Special Administrative Region' (1997) 30 (2) Cornell Int'l L J 335, 338.

Law 1986 and the General Rules of the Civil Law of the PR China 2017; nowadays, both laws have been replaced by the Civil Code 2020, and it still includes the same Confucian jurisprudence.[192] Similarly the moral standard for society has been codified in procedure law such as the CPL 1991 (as amended until 2020)[193] to become the paramount principle – "the principle of good faith". The incorporation of the principle of good faith forbids courts, parties to disputes and other involved parties to abuse the right to damage the state, public and other parties' interests.[194] It is no surprise that the courts are willing to follow the stricter legal tests as a result of the test of good faith to render preservation orders and accordingly, the Chinese jurisdiction seems to be a more defendant-/respondent-friendly jurisdiction. Foreign lawyers cannot ignore these aspects when developing tactics for cross-border litigation or arbitration as this principle can give wide discretion to the Chinese courts. It should be emphasised that with the advent of recent Chinese legal reforms, the Chinese courts are gradually adopting a few positive features of the adversarial system that are available in the common law legal systems.[195]

11.78 In China, the reference point in jurisprudence is society as compared to individuals' property rights. In China the focus is more on sharing resources within society as compared to the strict individuals' rights approach observed in English jurisdiction.[196] This reference point leads to less reliance on debates in Chinese courts as compared to the English courts thus making it less of an adversarial system. The issue of the reference point is connected with the issue of the exercise of discretionary power by judges in both jurisdictions. Common law judges will exercise their discretionary power more willingly. On the other hand, in China, except for the judges in the Supreme People's Court (highest tier) who are relatively more confident in exercising their discretionary power, their colleagues in the lower courts are at times not willing or are not confident in exercising their discretionary power. If judges exercise discretionary power, and it were to result in incorrect interim orders, then in that scenario, the party that had suffered a loss may claim state compensation in China. In many scenarios, the judges might even be punished in accordance with the internal regulations of the courts, or even according to the Judges Law of the People's Republic of China 1995 (2019 Revision).

---

192 Civil Code 2020, Article 7.

193 CPL 1991 (as amended until 2020), Article 13.

194 Shuju Ha and Yue Yu, *Interpretation of Civil Procedural System* (Intellectual Property Publishing House 2016) Section 1, Chapter II.

195 The First Civil Division of the Supreme People's Court (ed), *Understanding and Application of New Provisions of the Supreme People's Court on Evidence in Civil Procedures, Volume I* (People's Court Press 2020) 82–83.

196 J C Church and AB Edwards, 'Comparative Law/Comparative Method' in Hosten *et al* (eds), *Introduction to South African Law and Legal Theory* (Butterworths 1995) 1261–1270 .

11.79 Pre-judgment remedies largely are based on the exercise of the discretionary power of judges, which means that judges subconsciously are bound to be affected by jurisprudential approaches incorporated into practice or law in action in their courtrooms. The issue of whether the discretionary power exercised by the judges in both jurisdictions falls within the customary judicial practice is beyond the scope of the book.[197]

11.80 In the English jurisdiction, the law has evolved over the years, as a result of which the population is happy to adopt law as a benchmark rather than something they are compelled to follow.[198] Accordingly, the English judges feel confident in exercising their discretionary power in the context of granting interim remedies. This can be clearly seen from the evolution of interim remedies as a result of the exercise of discretionary power in the English jurisdiction after the 1970s and 1980s,[199] and the English judges have maintained a fine balance between the parties by utilising the arguments presented by barristers/parties in the courtrooms. Over the years, various tests for standards of proof have been developed by judges on their own to maintain the balance of interests between the parties during interim applications.[200]

11.81 On the other hand, in China, at the moment the real issue in the practice of law is whether the populace should on their own consider that the implementation of law is in their interest, similar to the prevailing scenario in England & Wales, or if they should feel as if they are compelled to follow written law. This invisible factor has a direct effect on the practice of law in the context of interim measures as it affects, to some extent, even the willingness of judges in China to exercise their discretionary power.[201]

---

197 Vivek Jain, *Insight into China through Comparative Analysis of Invisible Factors and Contexts – Common Law v. Chinese Law* (1st Edn, Notion Press 2019) 185–200 for examination in detail on similar issues such as discretionary power, willingness of judges to exercise discretionary power and so forth.

198 H L A Hart, *The Concept of Law* (2nd Edn, Oxford University Press 1994) 79 for further examination in detail on the issues of "primary rules" and "secondary rules" and further examination in the same book on page 57 of "internal aspects of law".

199 Refer to Part I, Chapter 1, 1.44–1.75. Many of the leading judicial decisions which established the English court's power to grant the main forms of interim remedy, or which laid down the basic principles governing the exercise of that power, date from this era, including *American Cyanamid v Ethicon Ltd* [1975] AC 396 (HL) (interim injunctions), *Mareva Compania Naviera SA v International Bulkcarriers Ltd* [1975] 2 Lloyd's Rep 509 (CA) (freezing injunctions), *Anton Piller KG v Manufacturing Processes Ltd* [1976] Ch 55 (CA) (search orders), *The Siskina* [1979] AC 210 (HL) (interim relief generally), *Societe Nationale Industrielle Aerospatiale v Lee Kai Jak* [1987] AC 871 (PC) (interim antisuit injunctions), *Babanaft International SA v Bassatne* [1990] Ch 13 (CA) and *Derby v Weldon (Nos. 3 and 4)* [1990] Ch 65 (CA) (worldwide freezing injunctions). Refer to Chapter 5, 5.6, 5.32–5.37; Chapter 7, 7.10; Chapter 9, 9.10.

200 Refer to Chapter 5, 5.23, 5.25, 5.30; Chapter 7, 7.13–7.14, 7.31; Chapter 9, 9.16.

201 Due to the effects of thousand years of Legalist jurisprudence, Chinese judges are reluctant to exercise discretionary power in their courtrooms. The lack of initiative could also be due to the possibility of punishment if they deviate strictly from the ruling according to law. On the other extreme, judges in China are allowed in law to even investigate facts on their own (refer to 11.91 and Article 64 of CPL 1991 (as amended until 2020)). In practice, Chinese judges

11.82 In English law, the concept of procedural justice has greatly evolved over centuries. The concept of procedural justice phased in concepts such as fairness, justice, "equality of arms" and so forth along with a purposive approach that has been adopted by judges to fill in the gaps in legislation by way of reasons through the formulation of policy by judges, and lately through interdisciplinary approaches.[202] On the other hand, the current legal practice of China is still governed by the concept of *rule by law* instead of *rule of law*.[203] This has affected the evolution of the concept of procedural justice in China, and in addition, practice of old traditions from history also subtly impact the present practice of law and this practice is described as *conservatism*.[204] In addition, jurisprudence in China was further affected by the

---

may opt not to investigate the matter themselves due to the workload. These are two extremes in China that clearly can be distinguished from the English legal system, where English judges are known for their willingness to exercise discretionary power without fear. In fact, discretionary power in common law has been institutionalised and has even become part of the law for example in the Civil Procedural Law 1998.

202 The effects of the Magna Carta 1215, Petition of Right 1628, Habeas Corpus Act 1679 and Bill of Rights 1689 on English jurisprudence and the legal system are profound.

203 Roderick O'Brien, 'Survival of Traditional Chinese Law in the People's Republic of China' (2010) 40 (1) Hong Kong LJ 165, 167, where the author explained succinctly that the western concept of "*rule of law*" is bit different in China and the nearest meaning would be that all "*ruling according to the law*", which means that strict rule *by* law. It is to be noted that there is no concept of judicial separation in China and there are multiple reporting channels. There is no equivalent concept of separation of power in China and there is a Procuratorates system and reporting structure; see also, Dennis Chang, 'Towards a Jurisprudence of a Third Kind – "One Country, Two Systems"' (1988) 20 (1) Case W Res J Int'l L 99, 110; the discussion on the difference between *rule of law* and *rule by law* can be best demonstrated in Hong Kong because Hong Kong, being a former colony of the United Kingdom, has maintained its common law traditions along with the influence of mainland Chinese law; see also, Ann D Jordan, 'Lost in Translation: Two Legal Cultures, Common Law Judiciary and the Basic Law of Hong Kong Special Administrative Region' (1997) 30 (2) Cornell Int'l L J 335, 338 for examination of the Confucian approach combining with the Marxist-Leninist approach that results in a general lack of trust in law. This combination ensures the dominance of philosophies that locked in the general approach resulting in disregard for law. This general approach assumed that the laws were made by elites to control the masses. In addition, the influence of the socialist law has ensured the visibility of extreme discretion in the procedural aspects within the Chinese legal system.

204 Jerome Cohen (ed), *Essays on China's Legal Tradition* (Princeton University Press 1980) 4; see also, Roderick O'Brien, 'Survival of Traditional Chinese Law in the People's Republic of China' (2010) 40 (1) Hong Kong LJ 165, where he quoted Cohen. Cohen was of the view that modern Chinese law bears a resemblance to ancient Chinese law, as a result of which, the assumptions and traditions from ancient Chinese law seem to have been engraved in modern Chinese society. See also, Geoffrey MacCormack, *The Spirit of Traditional Chinese Law*, The Spirit of the Laws (University of Georgia Press 1996) 12, where he discussed the connection between ancient Chinese law, assumptions and practice in various ancient Chinese empires and the modern law, and it is these connections that are characterised as *conservatism* by many scholars. A few of the reasons for hesitation in changing the modern law are also influenced by the Confucian thoughts based on morals, whereby it is believed that universal morals are not bound to change with the passage of time; see also, Vivek Jain, *Insight into China through Comparative Analysis of Invisible Factors and Contexts – Common Law v. Chinese Law* (1st Edn, Notion Press 2019) 96, 192 and 196 for further discussion on this topic. Any further discussion is beyond the scope of the book.

influence of socialism, Marxism-Leninism and Maoist schools of thought.[205] However, it is debateable whether such traditions and philosophies are still relevant to the goal of market economy seen with the exponential rise of the Chinese economy and can still be considered as relevant to the current practice of law in China. All such factors make the Chinese jurisdiction a more respondent-/defendant-friendly jurisdiction and at times even unpredictable because the administrative organs within the Chinese legal system are susceptible to arbitrariness.[206]

Invisible Factor of the Legal Philosophy of Civil Litigation

11.83 Western legal philosophy in relation to civil litigation has equal commitment to *procedural justice* along with *substantive justice*,[207] whereas in China, the emphasis is on primarily ensuring *substantive justice* in cases before the judges.[208] The concept of "*overriding objectives*"[209] in English law in the new CPR 1999 (as amended until 2020) has ensured that an element of

205 These schools of thoughts further distanced "religion" from the concept of morality in laws. Maoist school of thought brought in the concept of *Legalism* that ensured that the state is the only party in the position to decide what is right and what is wrong and completely excluded any religion-based views in discourse within the society. In addition, the Marxist school of thought filtered out any ideas founded on feudalism in any law and ensured the upliftment of the working class within the population. On the timeline of China, the four Constitutions were adopted in 1954, 1975, 1978 and 1982 along with the 1949 Common Programme. Article 5 of the current Constitution of China 1982 provides for socialism as one of the pillars of the constitution. Article 3 of the 1993 amendments to Constitution of China 1982 though introduced the concept of a socialist economy with Chinese characteristics that according to a few Chinese scholars can be considered as a *market economy with Chinese characteristics*; see also, Guobin Zhu, 'Constitution Law and State Structure' in Guiguo Wang and John Mo (eds) in *Chinese Law* (Kluwer Law International 1999) 25 for discussion on Marxism and Leninism in detail and their influence in the Chinese legal system; see also, H Y Chen, 'The Developing Chinese Law and the Civil Law Tradition' (1996) China Review 29 <www.jstor.org/stable/23453139> accessed 24 September 2016.

206 Huang Lie, 'Rule of Law in China: Ideal and Reality' in Buyun Li (eds), *Constitutionalism and China* (Law Press China 2006) 183–184.

207 John Sorabji, 'The Road to New Street Station: Fact, Fiction and Overriding Objective' (2012) 23 (1) EBLR 77, 85; see also, Woolf, 'Access to Justice: Interim Report to the Lord Chancellor on the Civil Justice System in England and Wales' (1995) HMSO 216; see also, Woolf, 'Final Report to the Lord Chancellor on the Civil Justice System in England and Wales' (1996) HMSO.

208 Kristie Thomas, 'Dynamism in China's Civil Procedure Law: Civil Justice with Chinese Characteristics' in C Picker and G Seidman (eds) *The Dynamism of Civil Procedure: Global Trends and Developments* (Springer 2016) 119–121. See also, Margaret Y K Woo and Mary E Gallagher (eds), *Chinese Justice: Civil Dispute Resolution in Contemporary China* (Cambridge University Press 2011) 13, where Woo has discussed about the experience of the people that have encountered courts tends to have relatively more negative experience with the legal system in China. In addition, the *distribution of justice* was preferred over *procedural justice*.

209 CPR r.1.1 (1) states *inter alia* that "These Rules are a new procedural code with the *overriding objective* of enabling the court to deal with cases justly and at proportionate cost [emphasis added]".

procedural justice is introduced in order to balance the issues of substantive justice.[210] This invisible factor will also have a profound effect on interim applications and interim hearings in England & Wales.

11.84 In addition, China is a civil law jurisdiction following an inquisitorial system modelled on the continental traditions of Germany and other similar countries. In addition, China has adopted philosophies of *democratic centralism* (*min zhu ji zhong zhi)* and *socialism*. As a result, in theory, there is a requirement to establish a subtle balance between procedural justice and substantive truth, even though, in practice, the focus is predominantly still on obtaining substantive justice for parties in disputes. This requirement to maintain a balance between substantive and procedural rights is also due to the influence of the Soviet Union's theory of *binary right of action* on laws in China. China has adopted the right to debate in CPL 1991 (as amended until 2020), thus bringing their legal system nearer to the continental civil procedural system, but still Article 12 of the *CPL 1991 (as amended until 2020)* has not guaranteed such a right.[211]

11.85 Unlike in the English procedural system, the principle to debate as provided in the China's *CPL 1991 (as amended until 2020)* is a *non-binding debate system*, as a result of which Chinese judges are not constrained by the facts presented by the parties; in fact the Chinese judges can actively investigate the case themselves.[212] As a result, this invisible factor of judges' power to investigate the case in commercial cases could be a considerable barrier for litigants because interim hearings, in theory, can easily be converted into mini-trials in Chinese courts due to the possibility of judges trying to investigate the matter on merits. In addition, due to the adoption of the principle of *democratic centralism* in China, there are concepts unique to the Chinese legal system such as "re-trial" and "supervision of judges by the Procuratorate system", and interim hearings in the context of preservation measures would be no exception for application of unique concepts like Procuratorate system.[213] However, there has been a systematic approach in recent years to improve the eco-system surrounding preservation measures in China.

11.86 As a civil litigation philosophy, English law favours party-led case management and process of disclosure, whereas traditionally the Chinese

210 John Sorabji, 'The Road to New Street Station: Fact, Fiction and Overriding Objective' (2012) 23 (1) EBLR 77, 85.

211 Haihong Huo, 'Chinese Expression or Theory of Civil Procedure Law' (2013) 4 Legal System and Social Development 3, 3–9. The article is available in Mandarin and has been translated for this book. In this article, Huo has discussed the ideas of author Dobrovorsky from the erstwhile Soviet Union, in his edited book, *Civil Action*, that was translated by Li Yan into Mandarin; see also Dobrovorsky, *Civil Action* (trans into Mandarin from Russian by Li Yan, Beijing Law Press 1985).

212 Refer to 11.91.

213 Refer to fn 179 in relation to the Procuratorate system, multiple supervision and reporting system in China for judges; refer also to Chapter 3, 3.4(i), 3.36 and Figure 3.3.

procedural system is in a way a discovery model led by judges. However, a few reforms have been adopted recently to bring in common law concepts within the Chinese legal system. In addition, in China, there is a requirement for a higher standard of proof from the time applications seeking any remedy in the courts are submitted, and it will also involve a requirement in relation to the method of submitting applications following specific-fact pleading.[214]

11.87 As a result of the above, to some extent, Chinese judges mandatorily have to think of public interests as an objective.[215] This issue may create barriers during interim applications seeking preservation measures. If we combine this factor with the stringent countersecurity requirements in applications seeking preservation remedies in China, then these invisible and visible factors or legal philosophy can be problematic in commercial disputes. Another visible factor has already been highlighted, where there are more formal requirements in which the evidence needs to be presented in Chapter 3, 3.125–3.129. If we analyse this issue intensely, it seems in the Chinese legal system, the philosophy is that it is the state's responsibility through the judges to decipher what the parties have not said in their pleadings.

11.88 On the other hand, in English legal philosophy, the judges have no independent power to inspect the documents to find truth, except at the initiative of the parties. However, this part of the jurisprudence is slightly debatable in English law.[216] According to the authors, this invisible factor cannot be overlooked by practicing lawyers.

11.89 In England & Wales, any non-criminal matter can be brought to the civil courts.[217] China, an example of a civil law jurisdiction, until recently, with the arrival of the new comprehensive of Chinese Civil Code 2020, had

214 See *Provisions of the Supreme People's Court on Several Issues Concerning the Registration-Based Filing of Cases by People's Courts* (Fa Shi [2015] No 8), effective from 1 May 2015. In a way, these provisions attempted to improve the legal system, but it is still a very new system. However, the philosophical approach is a major impediment in China for its implementation in both letter and spirit, as higher standards of proof are usually required even at the time of filing of the cases. It is quite possible that, because of the requirements of higher standards of proof, a few cases might not even be allowed to go through the legal system.

215 Refer to Chapter 1, 1.20 and 1.105.

216 *Air Canada v Secretary of State for Trade (No 2)* [1983] 2 AC 394 (HL), 438 (Lord Wilberforce); see also, the dicta of Lord Edmund Davies in the same case at page 441 on similar lines; contrast this with the case of *Davies v Eli Lilly & Co* [1987] 1 WLR 428, 431 (Sir John Donaldson MR), where litigation being treated as a game was criticised and subtly a view was expressed that courts were there to find a truth, otherwise why would any party come to the courts; see also, *Jones v National Coal Board* [1957] 2 QB 55, 63 (Denning LJ), where there was a reference to the notion that judges are entitled to find the truth. All these cases are pre-CPR 1999, and it could very well be argued by the authors that considerably more written evidence is available to judges these days through the case management system and process of disclosure of documents pursuant to CPR 1998 (as amended until 2020).

217 *Re State of Norway's Application (Nos 1 and 2)* [1990] 1 AC 723, 806 (Lord Goff); see also, J A Jolowicz, Civil Litigation: What Is It for?' (2008) 67 (3) CLJ 508, 509–510.

separate systems of civil and commercial law.[218] However, with the advent of the comprehensive and unified Civil Procedure Code 2020 such difference will slowly wither away.[219] The new Chinese Civil Code 2020 still includes at the start the principles of good faith, fairness and obeying the public order and good customs that are applicable to civil cases, and it seems they would be equally applicable to commercial cases as well.[220] How suitable are these principles such as "good faith" or "maintaining public order" that are also enshrined in the new Civil Code 2020 for interim hearings for preservation orders in commercial cases, where the focus is on maximising profits/benefits in commerce, is not very clear logically. However, practising lawyers cannot ignore this invisible factor in the context of their blueprint for seeking preservation orders in China.

Invisible Factor of Philosophy of Finding Truth in Judicial Practice

11.90 As discussed earlier, the focus of common law is to maintain a subtle balance between procedural justice and substantive justice,[221] whereas in Chinese law, an inquisitorial civil law system containing influences from the socialist family of legal systems,[222] the focus remains primarily on finding the truth. Therefore, the Chinese courts will ensure the primacy of substantive justice in any matter in the Chinese courts. In China, the facts are divided into legal facts and objective facts. Even though Chinese judges are likely to focus on the legal facts based on evidence, they retain investigative power unlike English judges, who possess no such powers. Even though in interim

218 In the civil law tradition, there are two models that are relevant to the drafting of the civil code in any jurisdiction. One model is called "a unified mode of the civil and commercial law" which means that both the civil law and commercial law are incorporated into one civil code. On the other hand, there is another model, namely "the separation of civil and commercial law" model, which means that both the civil code and the commercial code exist separately in the legal system. In recent years, the majority of civil law countries are applying the unified model of civil and commercial law; see also, Huixing Liang, 'Issues on the Framework of the Civil Code' (40th Anniversary Colloquium of Chinese Academy of Social Sciences, Beijing, 11 May 2017); see also, Jianwei Li, 'Chinese Model Pertaining to the Legal Frame of a Unified Civil and Commercial Law', 2018 (3) Social Science Research 67, 67–68. The New Civil Code 2020 seems to suggest the China is now following the unified model.

219 Refer to Chapter 1, fn7.

220 Civil Code of the People's Republic of China 2020, Articles 6, 7 and 8.

221 Refer to 11.84.

222 Vivek Jain, *Insight into China through Comparative Analysis of Invisible Factors and Contexts – Common Law v. Chinese Law* (1st Edn, Notion Press 2019) 25, for examination on the issue "where exactly does the Chinese legal system fit into the established families of legal systems in the field of comparative law?" The socialist system of civil litigation as in China is considerably different from the common law and civil law continental systems. However, the Roman-Germanic family of civil procedure systems has influenced the Chinese system since the 1990s. Therefore, currently, the Chinese litigation system is an inquisitorial system with Chinese characteristics, though having also retained socialist construction in philosophy. Recently, the Chinese legal system has also adopted a few features of the adversarial legal system.

applications, full merits are not fully taken into account, the recognition of the philosophical background is essential for foreign lawyers.

11.91 While it is debatable within the community of scholars whether the adversarial system of common law is rational and logical,[223] or at the other end, whether the adversarial system is not at all perfect, in any event, it is difficult or even impossible to ascertain the absolute truth in any case.[224] Historically, the judges in England & Wales will decide cases based on the evidence before them as submitted by the parties in contrast to the power of Chinese judges to investigate the matter on their own.[225] Therefore, English judges have no duty philosophically to find the truth.[226] Foreign lawyers cannot ignore such invisible factors at the planning stage by overly focussing on written laws and cases.

11.92 As discussed previously, in the Chinese legal system, the judges' focus on finding the objective truth also stems from the concept of traditional jurisprudential *conservatism*, whereby a general impression exists about litigation. Pursuant to this impression, litigation is always supposed to bring disasters (*song ze zhong xiong*). Article 64 of the CPL 1991 (*as amended until 2020*) provides that the Chinese courts should examine and verify the evidence *comprehensively and objectively*.[227] This was further clarified through

---

223 Ann D Jordan, 'Lost in Translation: Two Legal Cultures, Common Law Judiciary and the Basic Law of Hong Kong Special Administrative Region' (1997) 30 (2) Cornell Int'l L J 335, 337.

224 R Finkelstein, 'The Adversarial System and the Search for the Truth' (2011) 37 (1) Monash U L Rev 135; see also, in Fabien Gèlinas, *et al*, *Foundations of Civil Justice: Toward a Value-Based Framework for Reform* (Springer 2015) 68, where Finkelstein's views were quoted and analysed. Finkelstein was of the view that the public expects the courts to find absolute truth, even though it may not be a sound approach or in a way even possible for the court to find truth.

225 Article 64 of CPL 1991 (as amended until 2020).

226 Further discussion on this issue is beyond the scope of the book and readers may refer to Vivek Jain, *Insight into China through Comparative Analysis of Invisible Factors and Contexts – Common Law v. Chinese Law* (1st Edn, Notion Press 2019) 160–183; refer also to fn 216 for discussion on the English courts' practice in the context of "finding the truth".

227 The focus on finding objective truth is exemplified even through Article 139 of the CPL 1991 (as amended until 2020), where the parties can request a new investigation from the court or present evidence anytime to the court. It should be noted that in accordance with Provisions of Evidence 2001, the evidence should be submitted prior to the expiration of the time limit for producing evidence; otherwise, parties generally forfeit the right to submit new evidence. However, Article 139 of the CPL 1991 (as amended until 2020) provides a flexible rule to submit the evidence even after the expiration of the time limit for producing evidence. Nonetheless, Provisions of Evidence 2019 following the CPL 1991 (as amended until 2020) has now revised the 2001 Provisions. Article 12 of the CPL 1991 (as amended until 2020) provides the right to debate, but it is not guaranteed in the CPL 1991 (as amended until 2020). It seems parties can also request the judge to investigate the facts pursuant to Article 139 of CPL 1991 (as amended until 2020). If cross-examination is allowed, it seems this concept is wider as compared to English law and is called *zhi zheng*. In the Chinese legal system pursuant to Article 68 of the CPL 1991 (as amended until 2020), parties can confront the other side's submitted evidence in courts in order to question the authenticity and relevance of submitted documents/ evidence. The full discussion on this concept is beyond the scope of book; see also, Lawrence

Article 105 of the *SPC's Interpretations of the Supreme People's Court on Application of the Civil Procedure Law of the People's Republic of China (2020 Amendment)* (Fa Shi [2015] No 5) (superseded by Fa Shi [2020] No 21) that provides that the courts shall

> [follow] statutory procedures, conduct comprehensive and objective examination of evidence, and according to provisions of law, judge whether a piece of evidence has probative force and the extent of its probative force, by logical reasoning and daily life experience, and then make public the reasons for, and the results of, such judgment.[228]

Article 7 of CPL 1991 (as amended until 2020) provides that "in trying civil cases, the People's Courts must base themselves on facts and take the law as the criterion". This philosophical approach as articulated in the above guidance and codes is actually rooted in the Marxist-Leninist template of jurisprudence that provides for the courts to proceed in reality.

11.93 As a result of the above, there are factors that can impact upon applications seeking preservation remedies in Chinese courts, for example, relatively inordinate reliance on documentary evidence,[229] and no clear rules for the parties to provide full and frank disclosure and material information for the judges. The lack of rules may be a result of the assumption that in any event, the judges will investigate the matter. In the authors' view, Chinese judges also exert a lot of effort in providing assistance to collate evidence rather than analysing the evidence in most cases.

11.94 However, the twin factors of the issue of costs and economic inequality between the parties to disputes do affect litigants in the adversarial system followed by the English courts. The possible reason is that a relatively wealthy party can employ costly procedural adversarial tactics to stonewall the whole process.[230]

B Solum, 'Procedural Justice' (2004) 78 (1) S Cal L Rev 181–322, 191, where Solum discussed two competing models in civil procedure – the *accuracy model* and the *participation model*. This comparison of civil procedural models is very relevant when we are comparing the procedural law of a common law system with the inquisitorial system with Chinese characteristics pursuant to Chinese procedural law. Further discussion on this topic is beyond the scope of the book; see also, James R Maxeiner, 'Legal Methods as a Point of Reference for Comparative Studies of Procedural Law' (XIIIth World Congress on Procedural Law, Salvador Bahia, 16–22 September 2007) 6 <https://ssrn.com/abstract=1232579> accessed 18 November 2019 for discussion on Solum's accuracy model; see also, Vivek Jain, *Insight into China through Comparative Analysis of Invisible Factors and Contexts – Common Law v. Chinese Law* (1st Edn, Notion Press 2019) 172 for further discussion on the concept of *zhi zheng* that is wider than the common law concept of cross-examination.

228 Refer to fn 205 for further details on the influence of the philosophy of Marxism and Leninism on the Chinese legal system.

229 Refer to Table 11.1 in this chapter on comparative formal requirements in both jurisdictions.

230 A D Kessler, 'Our Inquisitorial Tradition: Equity Procedure, Due Process, and the Search for an Alternative to the Adversarial' (2005) 90 (5) Cornell L Rev 1251. In this article, Kessler highlighted a few defects in the adversarial system by taking examples from the

Training of Judges

11.95 The above philosophical approaches in both jurisdictions have a considerable impact on the way judges are trained. Since there is an overwhelming focus on ensuring substantive justice in China, Chinese judges possess superior administrative skills to investigate the facts, but in the authors' view these administrative skills are obtained at the expense of superior legal and commercial training.[231] This view also arises from the fact that most of the codes in China are of recent origins, and the judges need constant training.[232]

11.96 Many preservation remedies require judges to analyse the commercial facts and then accordingly exercise their discretion power. The issues discussed in the previous paragraph 11.95 can have a profound effect on the issue of the exercise of discretionary power of judges. These are invisible factors that practising lawyers cannot lose sight of when seeking interim remedies/preservation measures in any jurisdiction. In addition, in China, the supervisory procedures under democratic supervision (*minzhu jiandu*) pursuant to which cases can be re-opened to check unjust judicial discretion is an invisible factor that needs to be factored into the overall analysis.

Invisible Factor of the Concept of Standards of Proof

11.97 It is easy to understand the procedural requirements and tests to obtain interim remedies/preservation measures in any jurisdiction. However, in any jurisdiction, how much evidence is required from a party to discharge the burden of proof is explained by the concept of standard of proof. These are key invisible factors and contexts when comparing the *law in action* between two jurisdictions. In any jurisdiction, all lawyers will try their best to present as much as evidence as possible. However, the issues are not as simple as just presenting the evidence. There could be issues as to any procedural rules in these courts in relation to the presentation of evidence such as relevancy, exclusionary principles, weight given to particular evidence, powers of judges to investigate on their own, nature of hearings, type of hearings such as interim hearings and other similar issues. The judges, however, will consider carefully the quality of evidence, and therefore, it is a complex exercise for judges, and it is considered one of the most important judicial activities. The concept of standard of proof varies considerably in common

---

common law system of the US. The issues highlighted are equally applicable to the legal system in England & Wales; see also, Fabien Gèlinas, *et al*, *Foundations of Civil Justice: Toward a Value-Based Framework for Reform* (Springer 2015) 70, where Kessler was quoted and analysed. Any further discussion on the topic is beyond the scope of this book.

231 Vivek Jain, 'Sufficiency of Court's Pre-Judgment Power in Commercial Litigation: A Comparative Study Assessing the Law and Practice in PRC and England & Wales' (PhD Thesis, China University of Political Science and Law 2017) 447.

232 Refer to 11.66–11.69.

law and civil law jurisdictions, and marked differences should be appreciated by the readers and in particular, practising lawyers.

11.98 For these reasons, as discussed in paragraph 11.97, the understanding of concepts from foreign jurisdictions is not a simple exercise of reading the codes/statutes and caselaw. Appreciation of the impact of invisible factors such as standard of proof is very important to contemplate any action in any foreign jurisdiction. Only then should practising lawyers contemplate the next step.

11.99 In England & Wales, in civil/commercial cases, the test for standard of proof is "balance of probabilities", which means that a party asserting something must prove that there is a higher probability something has happened as per their assertion.[233] However, in no jurisdiction does there exist mathematical formulas for deciding as to how much of a percentage above 50 per cent that the party must prove their case based on evidence. In civil cases, in common law jurisdictions, this burden on the litigants under the concept of standard of proof is much less as compared to the burden in criminal cases. In criminal cases, in common law, the criminal courts expect the prosecution to prove their case "beyond reasonable doubt".

11.100 In civil law jurisdictions, the standard of proof is stated in terms of "*moral certainty* or as *intime conviction*".[234] standard of proof in England & Wales is an objective concept, while in civil law jurisdictions, it is a subjective concept.[235] If the concept is subjective in civil law jurisdictions, then there is an argument that without proper checks, the requirements under standard of proof can vary from judges to judges in these jurisdictions. It could also mean, at times, that there is no clarity as to how much evidence needs to be provided to satisfy the judges in civil law jurisdictions. It is common to experience many interventions from judges in civil law jurisdictions during any kind of civil law trial, whereas, on the other hand, common law judges will

233 See Lord Denning's view in *Miller v Minister of Pensions* [1947] 2 All ER 372, 374 where the concept of standard of proof was stated as "more probable than not". In other common law jurisdictions, such as Canada, there is a similar test for standard of proof, whereby it would mean that "there is a higher probability for this to happen than not"; in that case the burden of proof of such party would be released. In English law, in the courts, it would mean that either the burden has been discharged or it is not discharged at the end of the trial; see also, In *Re H and Others (Minors) (AP) (Respondents)* [1995] UKHL 16, [73] (Lord Nicholls), where it has been clarified that the test for standard of proof is very flexible and requirements can be modified to the particular circumstances of a case, but the principle or the main rule will not change; see also, *Re B* (Children) [2008] UKHL 35, [2] (Lord Hoffmann) in relation to the legal rule in the context of standard of proof to prove fact in issue.

234 Dominique Demougin and Claude Fluet, 'Deterrence Vs Judicial Error: A Comparative View of Standards of Proof' (2004) 161 (2) Journal of Institutional and Theoretical Economics 193, 193–194 <https://ssrn/abstract=585770> accessed 16 November 2016.

235 In prominent civil law jurisdictions such as Germany, *German Code*, section 286 (1) of *Code of Civil Procedure 2005 (as amended)*, where it is stated in clear terms that the personal conviction of judges is important in relation to evidence presented to the judges.

let the parties or their lawyers present their cases to them.[236] Besides that, the common law system has many exclusionary principles that govern the issue of exclusion of evidence by the judges.[237]

11.101 Chinese jurisdiction, modelled on a civil law jurisdiction with socialist underpinnings affected by Marxist-Leninist ideology, will follow seemingly the concepts from civil law jurisdictions. The starting point to understand the test of standard of proof in China is to analyse the relevant codes from the CPL 1991 (as amended until 2020) and in particular, the prevailing Provisions on Evidence 2019 on issues of evidence which are as follows:

- Article 63 of *CPL 1991 (as amended until 2020)* provides:

  Evidence shall include as follows: (1) Statements of parties concerned; (2) documentary evidence; (3) material evidence; (4) audio-visual material; (5) testimony of witnesses; (6) statements of the parties; (7) expert conclusions; and (8) records of inspection.

  The above-mentioned evidence must be verified before it can be taken as a basis for ascertaining a fact [emphasis added].[238]
- Article 1 of *Some Provisions of the Supreme People's Court on Evidence in Civil Procedures (2019 Amendment)* (Fa Shi [2001] No 33) (*superseded by* Fa Shi [2019] No 19) provides:

  A Claimant filed a case or a Defendant filed a counterclaim in the people's court should submit the relevant evidence to meet the prerequisite of *case-filing* [emphasis added].
- Article 64 of *CPL 1991 (as amended until 2020)* provides:

  If, for objective reasons, a party and his agent are unable to collect the evidence by themselves or if the people's court considers the evidence necessary for the trial of the case, *the People's court shall investigate and collect it* [emphasis added].

  The People's court shall, in accordance with the procedure prescribed by the law, *examine and verify evidence comprehensively and objectively* [emphasis added].[239]

236 E Sherwin and K M Clermont, 'A Comparative View of Standards of Proof' (2002) 50 (2) Am J Comp L 243, 247.

237 Exclusionary principles in the English jurisdiction mean that the evidence can be excluded if its prejudicial value were to exceed the probative value, for example, confessions, improperly obtained evidence and so forth. Accordingly, the judges in England & Wales will focus on relevance, weight and probative effect of evidence in all matters.

238 See also, *Some Provisions of the Supreme People's Court on Evidence in Civil Procedures (2019 Amendment)* (Fa Shi [2001] No 33) (*superseded by* Fa Shi [2019]), Article 14 to comprehend the terms of the scope of evidence; refer also to Chapter 10, 10.22–10.23.

239 See also, *Some Provisions of the Supreme People's Court on Evidence in Civil Procedures (2019 Amendment)* (Fa Shi [2001] No 33) (*superseded by* Fa Shi [2019]), Article 2.

11.102 Article 1 of Provisions on Evidence 2019 has clarified the issue of burden of proof in a case. According to this Provision, the parties concerned should be liable to provide the evidence in favour of their own arguments for the case they put forward. Accordingly, Article 64 of *CPL 1991 (as amended until 2020)* clearly provides that the judges will examine the evidence "*comprehensively and objectively*". In the authors' view, this test in China is a combination of the common law test as in England & Wales and that of civil law jurisdictions such as Germany.[240] First, the standards of proof are very high as set in terms of "*comprehensively*" as in civil law jurisdictions. Therefore, the test for standard of proof in China is similar to that of the continental European jurisdictions' high standard of proof, but with a slight twist – in China any *subjectivity of the judges* is ruled out by using the word "*objectively*". This objective test seems to be similar to the common law test and thereby can be differentiated from the tests for standard of proof provided in the continental civil law jurisdictions. The same codes also allow Chinese judges to investigate and collate evidence.[241] Nonetheless, through the legal reforms that were started by the late 20th century in China, the Chinese courts are adopting many features from the adversarial system. Accordingly, these days, the Chinese courts are emphasising that it is the duty of the parties to provide evidence.[242] The collection of evidence by judges does not constitute a general rule in accordance with the CPL 1991 (as amended until 2020); however they retain the power to do so. Nonetheless, these days, it is only applied under certain circumstances.[243]

11.103 The authors have also discussed previously that there is always a focus on ensuring substantive justice in China.[244] In the authors' view, there are so many uncertainties in any factual story, human emotions, perceptions, prejudices and biases, and therefore, it is nearly impossible to find "absolute truth" not just in China but in any jurisdiction. Another factor, in the authors' view, is that the focus on such high standards of proof is bound to affect procedural justice in many dimensions.

11.104 Against this backdrop of differing concepts of standard of proof in England & Wales and China, there are two stages in the context of applications

---

240 Vivek Jain, 'Sufficiency of Court's Pre-Judgment Power in Commercial Litigation: A Comparative Study Assessing the Law and Practice in PRC and England & Wales' (PhD Thesis, China University of Political Science and Law 2017) 207–209.

241 See Article 2 of *Some Provisions of the Supreme People's Court on Evidence in Civil Procedures (2019 Amendment)* (Fa Shi [2001] No 33) (*superseded by* Fa Shi [2019]); see also, Article 64 of *CPL 1991 (as amended until 2020)*.

242 The First Civil Division of the Supreme People's Court (ed), 'Understanding and Application of New Provisions of the Supreme People's Court on Evidence in Civil Procedures, Volume I' (People's Court Press 2020) 82–83.

243 Refer to Chapter 10, 10.110–10.121.

244 Refer to 11.83–11.84.

seeking interim remedies/preservation measures that need to be analysed for the effects of this invisible factor:

- Submission of applications in courts seeking these interim measures.
- Interim hearings after the application stage.

Standard of Proof at the Time of Application

11.105 For many years, the requirement of standard of proof at the time of filing of a case in China was also high with a need to provide considerable documentary evidence for the case to be accepted by the administration of the courts.[245] Therefore, many cases could not even pass this initial test, and it is likely that many such cases might not even enter the legal process. Until 2014, the Fourth Plenary Session of the 18th Communist Party of China (CPC) Central Committee passed *Decision on Major Issues Pertaining to Comprehensively Promoting the Rule of Law* providing that

> with the reform of a case acceptance system, the examination system to accept a case should be changed into the registration system seeking the acceptance of the case. The court should accept the case prescribed by law in order to guarantee the right of claim [for the parties].[246]

Accordingly, the requirement of high standards of proof at the time of filing of a case in China was relaxed a bit. Nonetheless, in continent-size China, it is not easy to implement this fundamental change overnight, and many local courts will still insist on lots of documents even at the case-filing stage. One reason could be that administrators' focus on substantive truth will not go away overnight in spite of the 2014 Decision. This issue as an invisible factor can have devastating effects on parties seeking preservation measures. This issue is not that relevant in the English courts and as long as procedures are followed in submitting applications, including those relevant for seeking interim remedies, the administration of the courts will accept those applications.

During Interim Hearings

11.106 In the interim hearings, the disputes are not, in principle, finally resolved, although this will sometimes be the practical result, and judges do not like to convert interim hearings into mini-trials in order to resolve disputed issues of fact, although they will, where necessary, assess the likely outcome of the underlying claim by undertaking a fair and reasonable evaluation of the available evidence, while always bearing in mind that there has

245 In China, the courts adopt specific-fact pleadings, whereby a lot of evidence needs to be attached with the applications. Only then the administration of the courts will decide whether that case can be accepted for a civil trial or for seeking preservation measures.

246 *Decision of the CPC Central Committee on Major Issues Pertaining to Comprehensively Promoting the Rule of Law*, 4th Plenary Session, was promulgated on 23 October 2014.

been no disclosure and that the witness evidence is incomplete and untested by cross-examination.[247] As a result of the inherent flexibility in common law systems, English judges have devised various tests of standard of proof that the authors have discussed in previous chapters.[248] These tests devised by judges ensure that the absence of the fact finding process through cross-examination of the witnesses in the context of credibility, demeanour and answers does not affect the interim hearings. At the same time, these various tests of standards of proof for various applications balance the interests of applicants as well as the respondents.

11.107 In the interim hearings and inquiry process in China, there is no indication of any different test for standard of proof for interim hearings, and in fact, it seems the test is the same as that for the main civil trials.[249] Additionally, it seems that Chinese judges will still try to find the objective truth as their focus might be on substantive justice.[250] This is an important invisible factor that foreign lawyers at times do not even think about before planning to seek preservation applications from the Chinese courts.

Invisible Factor of the Discretionary Power of Judges

11.108 Interim remedies/preservation orders are discretionary in nature and are procedural remedies. The judges are required to exercise their discretion based on parties' presentation of cases usually in short interim hearings and other documentary evidence. As discussed previously in the context of various invisible factors, the underlying values, philosophical underpinnings, norms and principles are relevant in the exercise of discretionary power.

11.109 However, the utilisation of such principles in the granting of interim remedies/preservation orders will also be affected by the dominant jurisprudential thoughts, ideologies and constitutional principles and so forth.[251] There are also factors such as the number of judges per capita, wherein the civil law systems incorporating inquisitorial systems have an edge over common law systems in this respect. In addition, the training standards of judges vary between the two jurisdictions, but these two issues as to the number of judges per capita and the training of judges are beyond the scope of this book. However, in reality, these are also invisible factors and can affect applications seeking interim remedies/preservation measures.

---

247 Refer to Chapter 7, 7.39. Also, Chapter 1, 1.109–1.111, in relation to the issue of dispute of facts in the interim hearings.

248 Refer to Chapter 5, 5.23, 5.25, 5.30; Chapter 7, 7.13–7.14, 7.31–7.33, 7.51, 7.61; Chapter 9, 9.16.

249 Refer to 11.100–11.102.

250 Refer to 11.83–11.84.

251 Refer to examination of other invisible factors in this chapter.

11.110 The invisible factor of the discretionary power of judges is also affected by the fact that procedural codes for preservation measures are relatively very new in China,[252] and as a result, it will take time for Chinese judges in continent-size China to comprehend them fully and implement them consistently throughout China. In addition, only after fully comprehending these new codes can Chinese judges move to the second step of filling gaps in the legislations through discretionary power by seeking directions from the Supreme People's Court and so forth. Further, the social and economic changes are mind-boggling in recent years in China,[253] which renders it essential for readers to appreciate the role of the discretionary power of judges and its exercise in courtrooms in China. There is also another issue of the willingness of Chinese judges to exercise their discretionary power, and this invisible factor is important for readers to appreciate in the context of the role of Chinese judges in applications seeking preservation measures.[254]

11.111 Chinese courts are governed by the philosophy of *youti zhengti*,[255] which means that these courts are part of an entity, and the judges are just part of the whole legal system and any discussion of independence of individual judges is not relevant. In addition, the courts' independence as an entity is what needs to be discussed. Any judicial activity associated with the adjudication of disputes is carried out by the judges, but all such judicial activities are actually the part of the legal system as a whole.[256]

11.112 Any comparison of the discretionary power of Chinese judges with English judges has to keep this important concept of *youti zhengti* in mind. Currently, in this area, there is a huge work in progress and accordingly reforms are underway. Any further discussion on this topic is beyond the scope of the book.[257] In addition, the relatively brief reasoning in most of

---

252 Refer to 11.66–11.69 as to the examination of recent origins of most laws in China.

253 Guo Rongxing, *An Introduction to the Chinese Economy: The Driving Forces behind Modern Day China* (John Wiley & Sons (Asia) 2010) 11–13.

254 John Gillespie, 'Rethinking the Role of Judicial Independence in Socialist Transforming East Asia' (2007) 56 (4) ICLQ 837. The author explained the importance of judicial power and was of a view that the role of judicial power was more important than the issue of judicial independence in the socialist countries of the East Asia. This preference for judicial power is opposite to the primacy of judicial independence in western jurisprudence. These views are important to similar issues in continent-size China; refer also to fn 179 for discussion on issues of judicial independence, supervision and re-trials affecting the legal process in the Chinese courts.

255 Margaret Woo, 'Law and Discretion in Contemporary Chinese Courts' (1999) 8 (3) Pacific Rim L & Pol'y J 581, 604.

256 Again, the recent legal reforms have advocated and established the Chinese judges' role in the independent trial system, but the kind of judicial independence that was foreseen is different from that available in the English legal system; see also, *Decision of the Communist Party of China Central Committee on Some Major Issues Concerning Comprehensively Deepening the Reform* was promulgated by the Third Plenary Session of the 18th Communist Party of China (CPC) Central Committee on 12 November 2013.

257 ibid.

the Chinese judgments provides leeway for excessive discretionary power to Chinese judges as compared to English judges.

11.113 Therefore, there exist two extremes in the context of the exercise of discretionary power by Chinese judges – on one end of the spectrum, Chinese judges are unwilling to take any risk, and on the other end of the spectrum there exists an institutionalised system pursuant to which there exists considerable discretion within this system. This invisible factor can bring considerable uncertainty for the stakeholders in the context of applications seeking preservation measures.

11.114 Common law judges in England and Wales are accustomed to the exercise of discretionary power and more importantly judges have been willing to employ those powers for centuries and are also affected by the path of law of equity. In England & Wales, such discretionary power can even be considered as a law itself as this discretionary power employed by judges is now made part of law. From the above discussion, stakeholders should not presume, due to the impact of various invisible factors and contexts, when analysing the law in action, that Chinese judges' judicial acts will be similar to those of English judges.[258]

Concluding Remarks

11.115 The comparative analysis of visible similarities and differences along with the subtle understanding of the impact of invisible factors and contexts on applications seeking interim measures during law in action is key to appreciating and understanding foreign jurisdictions. The impact of these factors on workings inside the courtrooms in the context of applications seeking interim measures is quintessential for planning tactics for cross-border litigations and arbitrations. Ultimately, what matters for seeking procedural remedies such as interim measures in any court in any jurisdiction is the subtle understanding of the *law in action* and how *invisible factors and contexts* can impact the legal process of seeking such measures in courts. This must be in addition to the lawyers' focus on *visible factors* in respect of codes/statutes, caselaw, practice directions, local courts' directions and guidance and so forth. In addition, there could be different terminology altogether in another jurisdiction.

11.116 In addition to being a reference book for practitioners, the authors hope that this book can provide enough food for thought for practising

258 Vivek Jain, 'Sufficiency of Court's Pre-Judgment Power in Commercial Litigation: A Comparative Study Assessing the Law and Practice in PRC and England & Wales' (PhD Thesis, China University of Political Science and Law 2017). See also, Vivek Jain, *Insight into China through Comparative Analysis of Invisible Factors and Contexts – Common Law v. Chinese Law* (1st Edn, Notion Press 2019).

lawyers, academics, law students, comparative law scholars and other stakeholders that are interested in law in action. Hopefully, the comparative analysis pursued in this book will bring out unique characteristics of both jurisdictions, while also providing opportunities to lawyers from both jurisdictions to analyse how the existing laws and processes can be improved in the context of interim remedies/preservation measures in England & Wales/China.

REFERENCES

Aaron Yizhou Deng, 'New Legal Risk for Applicants Seeking Property Preservation Measures' (Mondaq Connecting Knowledge and People, 25 September 2019) <https://www.mondaq.com/china/Real-Estate-and-Construction/848198/361302013520445208403000335831201542603230340278612445939118385 05> accessed 15 July 2021

'Achieving the Enforcement of an Effective Judgment and Refraining from the Negative Effect of Evasion of Enforcement: Answer of the Responsible Judge in the Executive Bureau of the SPC to the Reporter' on 27 May 2011 <www.gongshu.gov.cn/art/2012/1/21/art_1235142_2715699.html> accessed 15 July 2021

A D Kessler, 'Our Inquisitorial Tradition: Equity Procedure, Due Process, and the Search for an Alternative to the Adversarial' (2005) 90 (5) Cornell L Rev 1251

Adams George Burton, 'The Origin of English Equity' (1916) 16 (2) Colum L Rev 87

Albert H Y Chen, 'The Developing Chinese Law and the Civil Law Tradition' (1996) China Review 29, 31 <www.jstor.org/stable/23453139> accessed on 24 September 2016

Andrews G and Richard Millett Q C, *Law of Guarantees* (7th edn, Sweet & Maxwell 2015)

Ann D Jordan, 'Lost in Translation: Two Legal Cultures, Common Law Judiciary and the Basic Law of Hong Kong Special Administrative Region' (1997) 30 (2) Cornell Int'l L J 335

Bean D, Parry I and Burns A, *Injunctions* (13th edn, Sweet & Maxwell 2018)

Beijing Arbitration Commission, 'General Issues on Arbitration Preservations' <www.bjac.org.cn/page/zc/zcbq.html> accessed 15 June 2021

Beijing No1 Intermediate People's Court, 'Online Application for a Letter of Guarantee' <http://bjbq.86court.com> accessed 15 July 2021

Bernhard Grossfeld and Edward J Eberle, 'Patterns of Order in Comparative Law: Discovering and Decoding Invisible Powers (2003) 38 (2) Tex Int'l LJ 291

Bigelow M M, *History of Procedure in England* (Reprint of Macmillan 1880, AMS Press 1983)

Birks Peter, 'Rights, Wrongs, and Remedies' (2000) 20 (1) OJLS 1

Bixin Jiang, 'Press Conference of the Supreme People's Court on Amendment of Some Provisions of the Supreme People's Court on Evidence in Civil Procedures' on 26 December 2019 <www.court.gov.cn/zixun-xiangqing-212691.html> accessed 15 July 2021

Bixin Jiang and Xuelin Zheng, 'Press Conference of the Supreme People's Court on Amendment of Some Provisions of the Supreme People's Court on Evidence in Civil Procedures' on 26 December 2019 <http://www.court.gov.cn/zixun-xiangqing-212691.html > accessed 30 July 2021

Blake Susan, *A Practical Approach to Effective Litigation* (8th edn, Oxford University Press 2015)

Bracton Hde, 'Bracton's Note Book' in Frederic William Maitland (ed), *Bracton's Note Book: A Collection of Cases Decided in the King's Courts during the Reign of Henry the Third*, vol 2 (Cambridge University Press 2010)

Brand Ronald A, 'Working Paper No. 2020-32: Provisional Measures in Aid of Arbitration' Social Science Research Network Electronic Paper Collection <https://papers.ssrn.com/sol3/papers.cfm?abstract_id=3708453> accessed 16 June 2021

Bray Samuel L, 'The System of Equitable Remedies' (2016) 63 (3) UCLA L Rev 530

Briggs A, *Civil Jurisdiction and Judgments* (7th edn, Sweet & Maxwell 2021)

Browne-Wilkinson Nicolas, 'Territorial Jurisdiction and the New Technologies' (1991) 25 (3) Israel L Rev 145

Burrow Andrew, 'We Do this at Common Law but that in Equity' 22 (1) (2002) OJLS 1

Byran Michael, 'Injunction and Damages – Taking Shelfer Off the Shelf' (2016) 28 SAcLJ 921

Chen Jinhong and Yang Huiyu, 'An Analysis of Civil Protection Order System In China' (China Social Science University Humanity, 2015) <sinoss.net/uploadfile/2015/0513/20150513085357381.pdf> accessed 30 July 2021

Chen Su and Tian He (eds.), *Annual Report on Informatization of Chinese Courts No.4 (2020)* (Translator: Liu Ying, Social Sciences Academic Press 2020)

China Arbitration Institute, 'Questionnaires on Some Important Issues Concerning the Revision of Arbitration Law' <https://wj.qq.com/s2/5236531/ab86/?from=timeline&isappinstalled=0> accessed 15 June 2021

China International Commercial Court, 'A Brief Introduction of China International Commercial Court' <http://cicc.court.gov.cn/html/1/219/193/195/index.html> accessed 15 July 2021

Chunlong Xu and Wenzhi Chen, 'Applicant's Right over the Application of Property Preservation Prior to the Recognition and Enforcement of a HK Arbitral Award' (2021) 2 The People's Judicature (Case) 79

Chunlong Xu and Wenzhi Chen, 'Farenco Shipping Pte Ltd (Singapore)'s Property Preservation Case Prior to Recognition and Enforcement of a HK Arbitral Award' (Guangzhou Maritime Court Webpage, 8 July 2019) '<www.gzhsfy.gov.cn/web/content?gid=90506&lmdm=1016> accessed 15 June 2021

Curtis S, Gaunt I and Cecil W, *The Law of Shipbuilding Contracts* (5th edn, Informa Law 2020)

Cynthia Losure Baraban, 'Inspiring Global Professionalism: Challenges and Opportunities for American Lawyers in China' (1998) 73 (4) Ind L J 1247

David W Raack, 'A History of Injunctions in England before 1700' (1986) 61 (4) Ind LJ 539, 553–555 & 561, <www.repository.law.indiana.edu/cgi/viewcontent.cgi?article=2160&context=ilj>, accessed on 15 September 2019

Dennis Chang, 'Towards a Jurisprudence of a Third Kind – "One Country, Two Systems"' (1988) 20 (1) Case W Res J Int'l L 99

Deyong Shen (ed.), *Understanding and Application of the Interpretation of the CPL* (People's Court Press 2015)

Ding Pengchao, 'A Study on the System of Civil Pretrial Evidence Preservation' [2015] 6 Journal of Henan University of Economics and Law 113

Dominique Demougin and Claude Fluet, 'Deterrence Vs Judicial Error: A Comparative View of Standards of Proof' (2004) 161 (2) Journal of Institutional and Theoretical Economics 193, 193–94, <https://ssrn/abstract=585770> accessed on 16 November 2016.

Edelman J, *McGregor on Damages* (21st edn, Sweet & Maxwell 2021)

Edward J Eberle, 'The Method and Role of Comparative Law' (2009) 8 (3) Wash U Global Stud L Rev 451

Eric C. Ip. 'The Supreme People's Court and the Political Economy of Judicial Empowerment in Contemporary China' (2011) 24 (2) Colum J. Asian L. 367

E Sherwin and K M Clermont, 'A Comparative View of Standards of Proof' (2002) 50 (2) Am J Comp L 243

Fan Yiqiang, 'Civil Preservation Procedure' (PhD Thesis, Southwest University of Political & Science 2008)

Fisher J and Herd A, *Arlidge, Heady & Smith on Contempt* (5th edn, Sweet & Maxwell 2019)

Fuhua Wang, 'Research on Civil Preservation System' (PhD Thesis, China University of Political Science and Law 2005)

Gard, 'LOI, LOU and BLG—Confused?' (Gard yourship, Loss Prevention Circular No.01-10) <www.gard.no/Content/503153/No%2001-10%20LOI%20LOU%20and%20BLG%20-%20Confused.pdf> accessed 15 July 2021

Gee S, *Gee on Commercial Injunctions* (7th edn, Sweet & Maxwell 2020)

Geng Zhang and Shujun Wang, 'The Limited Payment of Lawyer's Fee in the IP Dispute' (2014) 9 The People's Judicature (Applied) 97

Geng Zhao and Yang Xu, 'A Student Enrollment Quota Depending on Housing Register can be the Subject Matter of the Behaviour Preservation Measure' in The China Institute of Applied Jurisprudent of the Supreme People's Court (ed.), *China Law Reports (2017) 2* (People's Court Press 2017)

Gerald J Postema, 'Classical Common Law Jurisprudence (Part I)' (2002) 2 (2) OUCLJ 155

Gerald J Postema, 'Classical Common Law Jurisprudence (Part II)' (2003) 3 (1) OUCLJ 1

Gu Yun, 'Research on Preservation Procedure of Civil Litigation' (Master Thesis, Wuhan University 2005)

Guanghai Lin, Jian Li and Rong Wu, 'Understanding and Application of *Several Provisions of the Supreme People's Court on Evidence in Civil Procedures Involving Intellectual Property Rights*' (2021) 4 The People's Judicature (Applied) 24

Guangliang Luo, 'Study on Litigation Preservation Security Provided by Financial Guarantee Company Registered in Huizhou Province' (Guizhou People's Government Legal Information Platform) <sft.guizhou.gov.cn/ywgz_97/zfflgw/201905/t20190516_2548698.html> accessed 15 July 2021

Guangzhou Nine Lawyers Team (eds), 'Notice on Case-Filing and Preservation of Shenzhen Intermediate and Primary People's Court' <www.zylawyera.com/gonggao/12.html> accessed 15 June 2021

Guixiang Liu and Huizhuo Liu, 'Understanding and Application of *Interpretation of the Supreme People's Court on Several Issues Concerning the Application of Law in the Trial of Criminal Cases of Refusing to Satisfy a Judgment or Ruling*' (2015) 13 The People's Judicature (Applied) 11

Guixiang Liu and Xiangyang Fan, 'Understanding and Application of *Provisions of the Supreme People's Court on Several Issues Concerning the Handling of Enforcement Objection and Reconsideration Cases by People's Courts 2015*' (2015) 11 The People's Judicature (Applied) 23

Guo Rongxing, *An Introduction to the Chinese Economy: The Driving Forces Behind Modern Day China* (John Wiley & Sons (Asia) 2010)

Haihong Huo, 'Chinese Expression or Theory of Civil Procedure Law' (2013) 4 Legal System and Social Development 3

Hang Sun, 'To Address the Difficulty of Proof in Intellectual Property Disputes: Answer to Correspondent's Questions on "*Several Provisions of the Supreme People's Court on Evidence in Civil Procedures Involving Intellectual Property Rights" by the Leader of the Third Civil Division of the Supreme People's Court"' People's Court Daily* (Beijing, 17 November 2020)

Hill Dickinson, 'Hill Dickinson Sets Legal Precedent as Shanghai Maritime Court Grants Interim Measures Application in Hong Kong Arbitration Case' <www.hilldickinson.com/insights/news/hill-dickinson-sets-legal-precedent-shanghai-maritime-court-grants-interim-measures> accessed 15 June 2021

Holdsworth W S, 'The Early History of Equity' (1915) 13 (4) Mich L Rev 293

Hollander C, *Documentary Evidence* (13th edn, Sweet & Maxwell 2021)

Hong Kong International Arbitration Centre, '2019 Statistics', <www.hkiac.org/about-us/statistics> accessed 15 June 2021

Hong Kong International Arbitration Centre, '2020 Statistics', <www.hkiac.org/about-us/statistics> accessed 15 June 2021

Hong Kong Arbitration Centre, China International Economic and Trade Arbitration Commission, 'The Practical Guidance on the Application of Mainland and Hong Kong Arrangement in Court-Ordered Interim Measures' (17 August 2021)' <www.cietachk.org.cn/portal/newsPage.do?pagePath=\zh_TW\news\47cda18ce6b6207f001&type=center> accessed 18 August 2021

Hong Kong International Arbitration Centre, 'Hong Kong-Mainland China Arrangement on Interim Measures' <www.hkiac.org/arbitration/arrangement-interim-measures> accessed 2 June 2021

Hong Kong International Arbitration Centre, 'PRC-HK Arrangement Interim Measures Frequently Asked Questions' <www.hkiac.org/Arbitration/interim-measures-arrangement-faqs> accessed 2 June 2021

Hu Zhang, 'Reconstruct the Procedure of Recognition and Enforcement of Foreign Arbitral Award in China' (2018) 10 Law Science Magazine 106

Hua Chou and Yangyi Shi, 'Statistic Analysis of Ningbo Ninghai People's Court on Pre-Action Property Preservation' (Ningbo People's Court,8 June 2017) <http://www.nbcourt.gov.cn/art/2017/6/8/art_3414_73130.html> accessed 15 July 2021

H Y Chen, 'The Developing Chinese Law and the Civil Law Tradition' (1996) China Review 29 <www.jstor.org/stable/23453139> accessed on 24 September 2016

Ian Gaunt, 'Innovation of Maritime Dispute Resolution Mechanisms' (Paper 47, page 615, the Ninth International Conference on Maritime Law, Shanghai November 2018)

Interview Between Xiaofeng Wu (Legal Daily) and Fu Su, HongJun Wang (Chongqing High People's Court), 'Protection of Market Entity's Interests and Creation of Commercial Environment: Interpretation of Chongqing High People's Court on Notice Concerning Further Norm of Property Preservation' (Legal Daily, 13 August 2018) <www.legaldaily.com.cn/index/content/2018-08/13/content_7617393.htm?node=20908 > accessed 15 July 2021

IP Editor Team, 'A Ruling to Recover the Tmall Link: Advance Enforcement or Converse Behaviour Preservation' (*China Law Information*, 26 July 2019) <https://new.qq.com/omn/20190726/20190726A0QKZ900.html?pc> accessed 30 July 2021

J A Jolowicz, 'Civil Litigation: What is it For?' (2008) 67 (3) CLJ 508

Jain Vivek, *Insight into China through Comparative Analysis of Invisible Factors and Contexts – Common Law v. Chinese Law* (1st edn, Notion Press 2019)

Jain Vivek, 'Sufficiency of Court's Pre-judgment Power in Commercial Litigation: A Comparative Study Assessing the Law and Practice in PRC and England & Wales' (PhD Thesis, China University of Political Science and Law 2017)

James R Maxeiner, 'Legal Methods as a Point of Reference for Comparative Studies of Procedural Law' (XIIIth World Congress on Procedural Law, Salvador Bahia, September 16–22 2007) 2–3 <https://ssrn.com/abstract=1232579> accessed on 18 November 2019

Janet E Ainsworth, 'Categories and Culture: On the "Rectification of Names" in Comparative Law' (1996) 82 (1) CLR 19, 19–42 <http://scholarship.law.cornell.edu/clr/vol82/iss1/3> accessed on 20 November 2019

J C Church and A B Edwards, 'Comparative Law/Comparative Method' in Hosten et al (eds), *Introduction to South African Law and Legal Theory* (Butterworths 1995) 1261–1270

Jeremy Bentham, *Theory of Legislation* (CK Ogden ed., Richard Hildreth trans., Harcourt, Brace & Co 1931)

Jianguo Xiao and Baocheng Zhang, 'Reconsideration on Specialization of Subject Matter of Property Preservation' (2017) 25 (3) Journal of National Prosecutors College 145

Jianwei Li, 'Chinese Model Pertaining to the Legal Frame of a Unified Civil and Commercial Law' (2018) 3 Social Science Research 67, 67–68

Jiaxing Liu and Jianfeng Pan, *Civil Procedure Law* (5th edn, Peking University Press 2017)

Jie He, 'Debt Is Not Repaid, Debtor's Mobile Phone Number Ending in 888888 was Seized' *Xian Dai Kuai Bao* (Jiangsu, 22 November 2019)

Jing Wang, 'A Court Upheld An Accused Infringer's Application for Advance Enforcement to Recover the Deleted Link' (*Legal Daily*, 16 July 2019) <www.legaldaily.com.cn/IT/content/2019-07/16/content_7935264.htm> accessed 30 July 2021

Jingxia Guo and Xiuzhi Yang, 'Beijing Issued the First Pre-action "Personal Safety Protection Order"' *People's Court Daily* (Beijing, 17 August 2013)

John C Reitz, 'How to Do Comparative Law' (1998) 46 (4) Am J Comp L, 620, 620–21 <www.jstor.org/stable/840981> accessed on 15 November 2016

John Sorabji, 'The Road to New Street Station: Fact, Fiction and Overriding Objective' (2012) 23 (1) EBLR 77

Jun Wang, 'A Case over Obstructing the Enforcement of a Judicial Document' *People's Court Daily* (Beijing, 1 December 2020)

Junbo Liu, 'Interpretation and Restructure of Legal Remedy for Property Preservation' (2018) 12 (5) Tsinghua University Law Journal 178

Jungong Sun, *Statement Concerning Several Provisions of the Supreme People's Court on Issuing the Information on the List of Dishonest Judgment Debtors* (Press Conference of the Supreme People's Court, 19 July 2013)

Junju Ma and Tingman Yu, *Principles of Civil Law* (Law Press of China 2016)

Kennedy Kevin C, 'Equitable Remedies and Principled Discretion: The Michigan Experience' (1997) 74 (4) U Det Mercy L Rev 609

Kong Lingzhang, 'Pretrial Evidence Preservation: By Reference of German Independent Evidence Collection Procedure' (2011) 33 (3) Modern Law Science 124

Lawrence B Solum, 'Procedural Justice' (2004) 78 (1) S Cal L Rev 181–322

Lei Zhang, 'Memorandum of the Guangxi High Court and Guangxi Bureau of China Insurance Regulatory Commission to Recognition on a Letter of Guarantee for Litigation Property Preservation by Insurance Company' *People's Court Daily* (Beijing, 14 November 2015)

Li Shichun, 'Research on General Issues of Civil Preservation Procedure' (2005) 17 (1) Peking University Law Journal 43

Li Shichun, 'Studies on the Civil Securing Judgement Procedure' (PhD Thesis, China University of Political Science and Law 2002)

Li Xuan, 'The Revision of the Civil Procedure Law: From a Practitioner Perspective' (2011) 5 Journal of National Prosecutors College 51

Liang Zhao and Lianjun Li, *Maritime Law and Practice in China* (1st edn, Informa Law from Routledge 2017)

Lihong Duan, 'Understanding and Application of *Interpretation of the Supreme People's Court on the Application of Law Concerning Pre-action Behaviour and Evidence Preservations for Stopping the Infringement upon the Right of Trademark* in The First Civil Division of the Supreme People's Court (ed.), *Reference and Guide to Civil Trial* (Law Press of China 2002)

Liming Wang, 'Preliminary Injunction of the Infringement of Personality Rights' (2019) 4 Law and Economy 3

Lin Wang, Renbo Wang and Others (eds), *Casebook on Civil Procedure Law* (China Democracy Legal System Publishing Home Co Ltd 2016)

Ling Yang, 'HKIAC and the Mainland: Tendency and Challenge' Legal Daily (Beijing, 13 August 2018)

Lingzhang Kong, 'Pretrial Evidence Preservation: By Reference of German Independent Evidence Collection Procedure' (2011) 33 (3) Modern Law Science 124

Liu Jiang, Huimin Wang and Wenge Li, *Speech Concerning Civil Procedure Law* (People Daily Press 1991)
Liu Jiang, Huimin Wang and Wenge Li, *Speech Concerning Civil Procedure Law* (People Daily Press 1991) 88
Lixin Han, Shaochun Yuan and Weimin Yin, *Maritime Litigation and Arbitration* (1st edn, Dalian Maritime University Press 2007)
Lixin Yang, *Tort Law* (2nd edn, Peking University Press 2017)
Liwei Jiang, 'On the Capacity to Apply for Preliminary Injunction in IP Cases: Comments on the First Item of Draft Judicial Interpretation on Preliminary Injunction' (2016) 2 Journal of Science, Technology and Law 372
Lord Collins of Mapesbury, Harris J, *Dicey, Morris & Collins on the Conflict of Laws* (15th edn, Sweet & Maxwell 2018)
Malek H M, *Phipson on Evidence* (19th edn, Sweet & Maxwell 2017)
Man Li, 'Internet Visual Property Preservation: Not Difficulty at All' *Legal Weekly* (Beijing, 14 August 2019)
Margaret Woo, 'Law and Discretion in Contemporary Chinese Courts' (1999) 8 (3) Pacific Rim L & Pol'y J 581
Mark Jia, 'Chinese Common Law? Guiding Cases and Judicial Reform' (2016) 129 Harv. L Rev. 2213
McCaffrey Stephen C and Main Thomas O, *Transnational Litigation in Comparative Perspective: Theory and Application* (1st edn, Oxford University Press 2009)
McGhee J and Elliott S, *Snell's Equity* (34th edn, Sweet & Maxwell 2019)
Meeson N and Kimbell J A, *Admiralty Jurisdiction and Practice* (5th edn, Informa Law from Routledge 2017)
Meng Yu, 'List of China's Bilateral Treaties on Judicial Assistance in Civil and Commercial Matters (Enforcement of Foreign and Judgments Included)' <www.chinajusticeobserver.com/a/list-of-chinas-bilateral-treaties-on-judicial-assistance-in-civil-and-commercial-matters> accessed 16 June 2021
Merkin R and Flannery L, *Merkin and Flannery on the Arbitration Act 1996* (6th edn, Informa Law 2019)
Mingmin Pan, 'Study on Legislation Perfection of the Property Preservation: Comments on the Interpretation of the Supreme People's Court of the Civil Procedure Law of People's Republic of China' (Master Thesis, Southwest University of Political Science and Law 2015)
Ministry of Justice of the People's Republic of China, 'Civil and Commercial Judicial Assistance Treaties' <www.moj.gov.cn/Department/node_358.html > accessed 16 June 2021
Ms Kun Liu (Deputy Director of the Hong Kong and Macau Judicial Affairs-Office of the SPC), 'Practical Implementation of the Arrangement Concerning Mutual Assistance Court-Ordered Interim Measures in Aid of Arbitral Proceedings by the Courts of the Mainland and of the Hong Kong Special Administrative Region' (Online Conference of Practical Implementation of the Arrangement Concerning Mutual Assistance Court-Ordered Interim Measures in Aid of Arbitral Proceedings by the Courts of the Mainland and of the Hong Kong Special Administrative Region, Hong Kong, 17 August 2021)

National Enterprise Credit Information Publicity System, <http://www.gsxt.gov.cn/index.html> accessed 15 July 2021

Oleck Howard L, 'Historical Nature of Equity Jurisprudence' (1951) 20 (1) Fordham L Rev 23, 24, <http://ir.lawnet.fordham.edu/flr/vol20/iss1/2> accessed on 15 October 2019

Oscar G Chase, 'Some Observations on the Cultural Dimension in Civil Procedure Reform' (1997) 45 (4) Am J Comp Law 861

Pan Mingmin, 'Study on Legislation Perfection of the Property Preservation: Comments on The Interpretation of The Supreme People's Court of the Civil Procedure Law of People's Republic of China' (Master Thesis, Southwest University of Political Science and Law 2015)

Pengchao Ding, 'A Study on the System of Civil Pretrial Evidence Preservation' (2015) 6 Journal of Henan University of Economics and Law 113

'Press Conference on Intellectual Property Division of the Supreme Court' (China.com, 29 December 2018) <www.gov.cn/xinwen/2018-12/29/content_5353373.htm#allContent> accessed on 15 July 2021

Project Team of Shanghai Xujiahui Notary Public Office, 'Change and Development of Notary Institutions on Evidence Preservations in the Context of the Internet and Big Data' (2019) 5 China Notary Journal 40

Qi Zhao, Hui Zhan and Huihua Wang, 'Improvement of Property Preservation Mechanism in Commercial Arbitration' (2019) 1 (107) Beijing Arbitration Quarterly 34

Qiang Zhou, 'Report on the Work of the Supreme People's Court' (Supreme People's Court, 12 March 2019) <http://gongbao.court.gov.cn/Details/a5a0efa5a6041f6dfec0863c84d538.html> accessed 30 July 2021

Qibo Jiang, Jiahai Zhou, Yanli Si and Kun Liu, 'Understanding and Application of Arrangement Concerning Mutual Assistance in Court-*O*rdered Interim Measures in Aid of Arbitral Proceedings by the Courts of the Mainland and of the Hong Kong Special Administrative Region Mainland and Hong Kong Arrangement in Court-*O*rdered Interim Measures' People's Court Daily (Beijing, 26 September 2019)

Qibo Jiang, Jiahai Zhou, Yanli Si and Kun Liu, 'Understanding and Application of Provisions of the Supreme People's Court on Arrangement on Mutual Recognition and Enforcement of Judgments in Civil and Commercial Cases by the Courts of the Mainland and the Hong Kong Special Administrative Region 2019' (2019) 7 The People's Judicature 30

Qiuju Jiang, 'A Brief Introduction to the BAC Arbitration Rules 2019 and Annexes Concerning Schedules of Fees' <www.bjac.org.cn/english/news/view?id=3535> accessed 15 June 2021

Qunpei Xia and Enwei Lin, 'Deposits for Discharging a Preservation not Belonging to Security in Security Law'(2014) 8 The People's Judicature (Case) 71

Raack David W, 'A History of Injunctions in England Before 1700' (1986) 61 (4) Ind L J 539, <www.repository.law.indiana.edu/ilj/vol61/iss4/1> accessed on 16 September 2016

Raphael T, *The Anti-Suit Injunction* (2nd edn, Oxford University Press 2019)

Rendleman Doug, 'The Triumph of Equity Revisited: The Stages of Equitable Discretion' Nevada L Journal 2015 15 (3) 1397

Reply of the Supreme People's Court to No. 7882 Proposal of The First Session of the 13th National People's Congress (8 August 2018)

Reply of the Supreme People's Court to No. 7974 Proposal of The Second Session of the 13th National People's Congress (30 July 2019)

Research Group of the First Civil Division of the Ningxia High People's Court, 'Research on Examination of Pre-action Property Preservation and Credit Guarantee' (17 August 2018) <www.nxfxh.com.cn/njfh/njfhdej/881.htm> accessed15 July 2021

R Finkelstein, 'The Adversarial System and the Search for the Truth' (2011) 37 (1) Monash U L Rev 135

Roderick O'Brien, 'Survival of Traditional Chinese Law in the People's Republic of China (2010) 40 (1) Hong Kong LJ 165

Ronald A Brand, 'Working Paper No. 2020-32: Provisional Measures in Aid of Arbitration' Social Science Research Network Electronic Paper Collection <https://papers.ssrn.com/sol3/papers.cfm?abstract_id=3708453> accessed 16 June 2021

Samuel L Bray, 'The System of Equitable Remedies' (2016) 63 (3) UCLA L Rev 532

Shamita Etienne-Cummings and Kevin Trainer, 'Apple v. Qualcomm: Is Public Interest Apple's Best Defense in the ITC?' (White&Case, 18 October 2018) <www.whitecase.com/publications/alert/apple-v-qualcomm-public-interest-apples-best-defense-itc> accessed 30 July 2021

Shangang Zhan, 'Question on Evidence Preservation with Reference to Preservation Procedure: Examination of Article 81 of CPL' (2015) 6 Journal in Law and Business 121

Shaoping Zhang, Jiangming Li and Tufeng Zhu, 'Understanding and Judicial Application of the Behaviour Preservation System: Judges Forum No 73' (*Trial Research*, 16 July 2014) <https://mp.weixin.qq.com/s/JPq1XyjDnyNEkjIBr6Ankg> accessed 30 July 2021

Shengli Wu, 'The Restriction of the Preservation of Non-maritime Claim of Overseas Arbitration' (2015) 3 Chinese Journal of Maritime Law 68

Sheridan L A, *Keeton & Sheridan on the Law of Trusts* (12th edn, Barry Rose 1993)

Shichun Li, *Research on the Civil Preservation Procedure* (China Legal Publishing House 2005)

Shichun Li, 'Research on General Issues of Civil Preservation Procedure' (2005) 17 (1) Peking University Law Journal 43

Shichun Li, 'Studies on the Civil Securing Judgement Procedure' (PhD Thesis, China University of Political Science and Law 2002)

Song Xiaoming, Wang Chuang, Xia Junli and Lang Guimei, 'Understanding and Application of *Provisions of the Supreme People's Court on Several Issues Concerning the Application of Law in Cases Involving the Review of Behaviour Preservation in Intellectual Property Disputes*' (2019) 7 The People's Judicature 19

Songyou Huang, 'Answers of Vice-President of the Supreme People's Court to Questions on *Arrangement of Mainland and Macau Special Administrative Region on Mutual Recognition and Execution of Civil and Commercial Judgments*' in The First Civil Division of the Supreme People's Court (ed.), *Reference and Guide to Civil Trial Vol. 25* (Law Press of China 2006)

Songyou Huang, 'Answers of Vice-President of the Supreme People's Court to Questions on *Arrangement of the Supreme People's Court between the Mainland and the HKSAR on Reciprocal Recognition and Enforcement of the Decisions of Civil and Commercial Cases under Consensual Jurisdiction*' *People's Court Daily* (Beijing, 7 July 2008)

Stimson F J 'The Modern Use of Injunctions' (1895) 10 (2) Political Science Quarterly 189 <www.jstor.org/stable/2139728> accessed on 2 October 2019

St John Sutton D, Gill J and Gearing M, *Russell on Arbitration* (24th edn, Sweet & Maxwell 2015)

Subrin Stephen N, 'How Equity Conquered Common Law: The Federal Rules of Civil Procedure in Historical Perspective' (1987) 135 (4) U Pa L Rev 909

Sun Jungong, *Statement Concerning Several Provisions of the Supreme People's Court on Issuing the Information on the List of Dishonest Judgment Debtors* (Press Conference of the SPC, 19 July 2013)

Terence Xu, 'Emergency Arbitrator Proceedings and the GKML Case' (China Business Law Journal, 14 November 2014) <www.vantageasia.com/emergency-arbitrator-proceedings-gkml-case> accessed 15 June 2021

Tettenborn A, *Clerk & Lindsell on Torts* (23rd edn, Sweet & Maxwell 2020)

The First Civil Division of the Supreme People's Court (ed.), *Reference and Guide to Civil Trial Vol. 25* (Law Press of China 2006)

The First Civil Division of the Supreme People's Court (ed.), *Reference and Guide to Civil Trial* (Law Press of China 2008)

The First Civil Division of the Supreme People's Court (ed.), *Understanding and Application of New Provisions of the Supreme People's Court on Evidence in Civil Procedures, Volume I* (People's Court Press 2020)

The Leading Group of the Implementation of the Civil Code of the Supreme People's Court (ed.), *Understanding and Application of Part 'Contract Law' of the Civil Code of the People's Republic of China (Volume II)* (People's Court Press 2020)

The Leading Group of the Implementation of the Civil Code of the Supreme People's Court (ed.), *Understanding and Application of Part 'Personal Rights' of the Civil Code of the People's Republic of China* (People's Court Press 2020)

The Leading Group of the Implementation of the Civil Code of the Supreme People's Court (ed.), *Understanding and Application of Part 'Property Right' of the Civil Code of the People's Republic of China (Volume II)* (People's Court Press 2020)

The Supreme People's Court, 'Annual Report on International Commercial in China 2019' <http://www.court.gov.cn/zixun-xiangqing-281031.html> accessed 9 June 2021

The Supreme People's Court, 'Understanding and Application of Arrangement Concerning Mutual Assistance in Court-Ordered Interim Measures in Aid of Arbitral Proceedings by the Courts of the Mainland and of the Hong Kong Special Administrative Region Mainland and Hong Kong Arrangement in Court-Ordered Interim Measures' (SPC Official Weibo, 26 September 2019) <www.weibo.com/ttarticle/p/show?id=2309404420695114252467> accessed 15 June 2021

Thomas W Merrill and Henry E Smith, 'The Morality of Property' (2007) 48 William & Mary Law Review 1849

Tianjin Xiqing District People's Court, 'Investigation and Research on Property Preservation' (Tianjin Xiqing District People's Court, 8 October 2014) <http://xqqfy.chinacourt.gov.cn/public/detail.php?id=6467>accessed 15 July 2021

Tianming Lan, 'Blockchain to Facilitate Property Preservation in Shanghai No.2 Intermediate People's Court' (*Xinhua News*, 18 December 2019) <http://www.xinhuanet.com/2019-12/18/c_1125359869.htm> accessed 15 July 2021

Tijana Kojovic, 'Court Enforcement of Arbitral Decisions on Provisional Relief: How Final is Provisional' (2001) 18 (5) Journal of International Arbitration 511

Tucker L, Le Poidevin N and Brightwell J, *Lewin on Trusts* (20th edn, Sweet & Maxwell 2020)

Vivek Jain, *Insight into China through Comparative Analysis of Invisible Factors and Contexts – Common Law v. Chinese Law* (1st edn, Notion Press 2019)

Vivian Grosswald Curran, 'Cultural Immersion, Difference and Categories in U.S. Comparative Law' (1998) 46 (1) Am J Comp L 43 <www.jstor.org/stable/841076> accessed in 24 October 2016.

V V Palmer, 'From Lerotholi to Lando: Some Examples of Comparative Law Methodology' (2004) 4 (2) Global Jurist Frontiers 1, 1–29

Wang Fuhua, 'Research on Civil Preservation System' (PhD Thesis, China University of Political Science and Law 2005).

Weifeng Hu, 'Collection of Evidence by Maritime Evidence Preservation Prior to Maritime Arbitration' (Xiamen Maritime Court, 6 July 2017) <https://wemp.app/posts/0af7efcb-9e50-4b41-be5c-1c25a918d533> accessed 30 July 2021

Weiwei Yang, 'On Legitimacy of the Rule of Maritime Claim Security' (2013) 4 Journal of Henan University of Economics and Law 183,190

Wejen Chang, 'Classical Chinese Jurisprudence and Development of Chinese Legal System' (2010) 2 (2) Tsinghua China L Rev 207

Wenliang Zhang, 'Third Parties in Interim Remedies: From Chinese Civil and Commercial Interim Remedies Perspective' (2016) 38 (1) Modern Law Science 164

Wenshan Xue, 'Salute to Chinese Judge and Chinese Legal System: Port on Arrest of M/V NERISSA' *People's Court Daily* (Beijing, 19 September 2019)

Westberg Peter, 'Interim Measures and Civil Litigation' (2007) 51 Scand Stud L 538

Xiao Cheng, *Research on Secured Property Rights* (2nd edn, Renmin University of China Publishing House 2019)

Xiaofeng Li and Ping Guo, 'Comment on the Breakthrough and Deficiency of the Behaviour Preservation System under CPL' (2015) 6 Journal of Law Application 71

Xiaohong Fang, 'The First Case "Converse Behaviour Preservation": The Wrong Nature Made by Court' (*Kuaibao*, 14 July 2019) <https://kuaibao.qq.com/s/20190714AZO09T00?refer=spider> accessed 30 July 2021

Xiaoli Bai and Sheng Lv, 'Analysis on Blockchain Evidence Preservation in Legal Practice' (Zhichanli, 14 December 2018) < http://news.zhichanli.cn/article/7624.html> accessed 30 July 2021

Xiaoming Song, Chuang Wang, Junli Xia and Guimei Lang, 'Understanding and Application of *Provisions of the Supreme People's Court on Several Issues Concerning the Application of Law in Cases Involving the Review of Behaviour*

Preservation in Intellectual Property Disputes' (2019) 7 The People's Judicature (Applied) 19

Xiaoru Zhang, 'Improvement of China's Maritime Injunction System' (2006) 4 The People's Judicature 79

Xiling Chen, 'No Right for Outsider to Apply for the Litigation of Objection During the Post-Action Property Preservation: (2017) Chuan No.15 Civil Chu No.63' (2018) 20 The People's Judicature (Case) 71

Xin Cheng and Lina Chen, 'The Trend, Reflection and Prospects of Liability Insurance of Preservation in Maritime Litigation'(2016) 27 (3) Chinese Journal of Maritime Law 83

Xiuwen Zhao, 'Development of Modernization and Internationalization of Chinese International Arbitration System in 21st Century' (2001) 3 Journal of Henan Administrative Institute of Politics and Law 31

Xixiang Song, 'Mutual Recognition and Execution of Civil and Commercial Judgment Between Mainland and Macau' (2012) 4 (14) Academic Journal of One Country Two Systems 88

Xuan Li, 'The Revision of the Civil Procedure Law: From a Practitioner Perspective' (2011) 5 Journal of National Procecutors College 51

Xuehua Wang, Jing Liu and Yuan Xing, 'Annual Review on Commercial Arbitration in China (2019)' in Beijing Arbitration Commission and Beijing International Arbitration Centre (ed.), *Commercial Dispute Resolution in China: An Annual Review and Preview 2019* (China Legal Publishing House 2019)

Xun Yang, 'Development of "Interim Injunction" in IPR Cases in China' (17 January 2019) <https://wemp.app/posts/abbd7327-2d61-4546-8b23-a71f2b2b38e4?utm_source=latest-posts> accessed 30 July 2021

Yang Li, 'What Rules on Intellectual Property Behaviour Preservations Should Be Demanded in China' (2019) 5 Intellectual Property 3

Yin INT'LIP Firm, 'Different Comment on a Ruling to Recover Link' (*Yin INT'LIP Firm*, 23 July 2019) <www.suncrt.com/English/Newsen/NR5.asp?ID=909> accessed 30 July 2021

Yiqiang Fan, 'Civil Preservation Procedure' (PhD Dissertation, Southwest University of Political and Science 2008)

Yiwei Pu, Xuemian Wang and Xiaodong Guo, *Course of Civil Procedure Law* (Peking University Press 2016)

Yong Zhu (ed), *The Chinese Legal History Vol. IX* (Law Press of China 1999) 302 and 312

Yongcan Chen, 'Data Report of Applications for Maritime Injunction' (Maritime Research Centre, 7 May 2019) <https://wemp.app/posts/095556d9-8e94-49cb-bfcd-8ec847bca332> accessed 30 July 2021

Yun Gu, 'Research on Preservation Procedure of Civil Litigation' (Master Thesis, Wuhan University 2005)

Yuqian Bi, *Essentials of Evidence Law* (Law Press of China 2003)

Zhang Wenliang, 'Third Parties in Interim Remedies: From Chinese Civil and Commercial Interim Remedies Perspective' (2016) 38 (1) Modern Law Science 164.

Zhaoxiang Wu, 'Understanding and Application of *Provisions of the Supreme People's Court on Citation of Such Normative Legal Documents as Laws and Regulations in the Judgments*' (2009) 23 The People's Judicature (Applied) 29

Zheng Tang and Changli Lv, 'The Application of a Behaviour Preservation in an Infringement of Know-how' (2013) 22 The People's Judicature (Case) 48

Zhengzhou Intermediate People's Court of Henan Province, 'Opinions on Improvement of 'Total-to-Total' Online Monitoring System' *People's Court Daily* (Beijing, 11 July 2019)

Zhiwei Lin, 'A Brief Introduction of Beijing Arbitration Commission Arbitration Rules 2015' <www.bjac.org.cn/english/page/ckzl/gzsm2015.html> accessed 2 January 2020

Zhixian Shen (ed.) *Essentials of Maritime Justice* (Law Press of China 2011)

Zhu Yong (ed), *The Chinese Legal History, Vol IX* (Law Press China 1999)

Zuckerman A A S, 'Quality and Economy in Civil Procedure: The Case for Commuting Correct Judgments for Timely Judgments' (1994) 14 (3) OJLS 353

INDEX